THE FOURTH
Garfield
Fat Cat 3-Pack

BY: JIM DAVIS

Ballantine Books • New York

GARFIELD MAKES IT BIG copyright © 1985 by United Feature Syndicate, Inc.
GARFIELD ROLLS ON copyright © 1984, 1985 by United Feature Syndicate, Inc.
GARFIELD OUT TO LUNCH copyright © 1986 by United Feature Syndicate, Inc.
GARFIELD Comic Strips copyright 1983, 1984, 1985 by United Feature Syndicate, Inc.

All rights reserved under International and Pan-American Copyright
Conventions. Published in the United States by Ballantine Books, a
division of Random House, Inc., New York, and simultaneously in
Canada by Random House of Canada Limited, Toronto.

Library of Congress Catalog Card Number: 95-94612

ISBN: 0-345-40238-3

Manufactured in the United States of America

First Edition: September 1995

10 9 8 7 6 5 4 3 2 1

Garfield makes it big

BY: JIM DAVIS

NEWS FLASH!
Jim Davis a Fraud!

The Big Cheese, The Head Honcho, The Chief Muckamuck...

Teddy bear Pooky recently revealed that Jim Davis did not create the Garfield comic strip. Garfield himself writes and draws the world–famous cartoon. Garfield has been sitting at a drawing board for the last six years as Davis has gained notoriety through national television and print. Davis was not available for comment, but Garfield was. "The way I figured it, who would ever believe a cat could do a comic strip. So, I hired this down–and–out, hack cartoonist to take the credit for it. Sure ... he looked good and said all the right things, but it's time the truth was known."

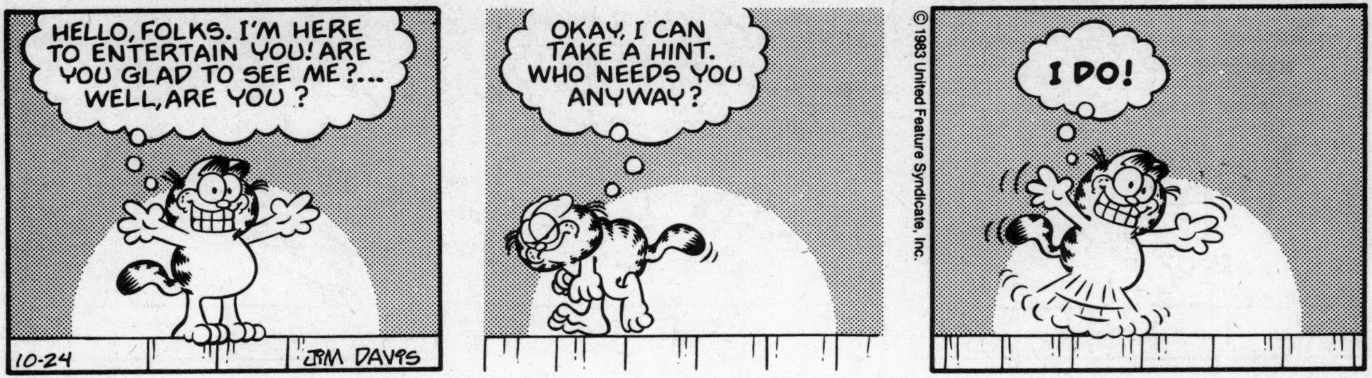
HELLO, FOLKS. I'M HERE TO ENTERTAIN YOU! ARE YOU GLAD TO SEE ME?... WELL, ARE YOU ?
10-24
JIM DAVIS
OKAY, I CAN TAKE A HINT. WHO NEEDS YOU ANYWAY?
© 1983 United Feature Syndicate, Inc.
I DO!

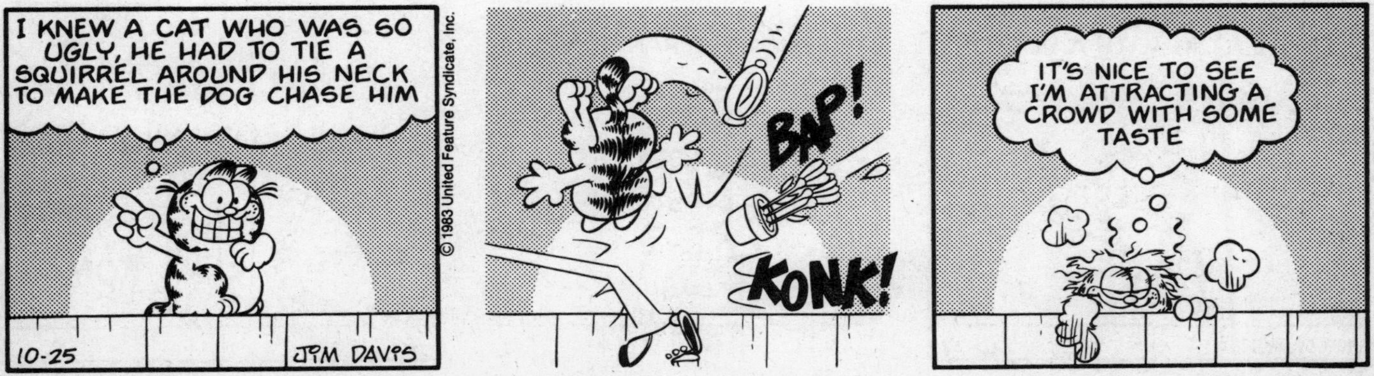
I KNEW A CAT WHO WAS SO UGLY, HE HAD TO TIE A SQUIRREL AROUND HIS NECK TO MAKE THE DOG CHASE HIM
10-25
JIM DAVIS
© 1983 United Feature Syndicate, Inc.
BAP!
KONK!
IT'S NICE TO SEE I'M ATTRACTING A CROWD WITH SOME TASTE

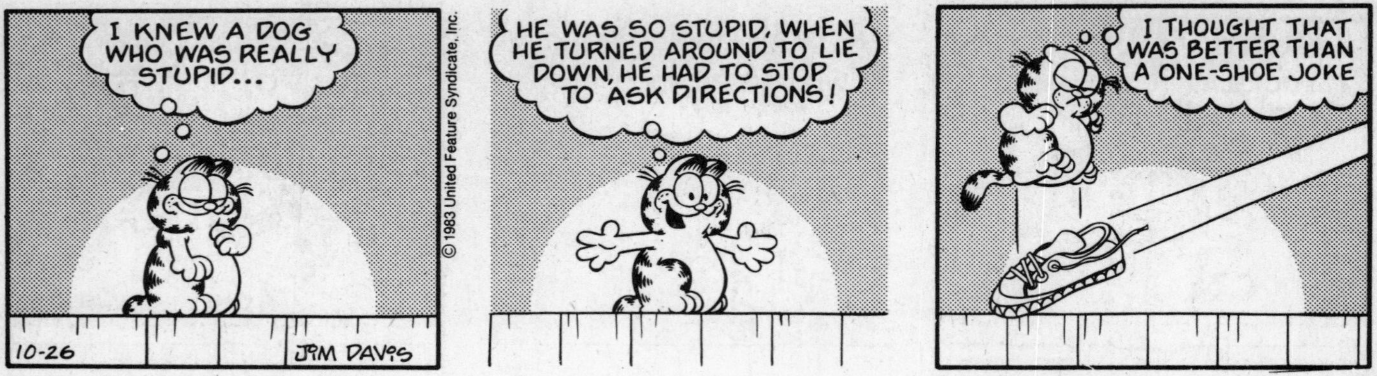
I KNEW A DOG WHO WAS REALLY STUPID...
10-26
JIM DAVIS
© 1983 United Feature Syndicate, Inc.
HE WAS SO STUPID, WHEN HE TURNED AROUND TO LIE DOWN, HE HAD TO STOP TO ASK DIRECTIONS!
I THOUGHT THAT WAS BETTER THAN A ONE-SHOE JOKE

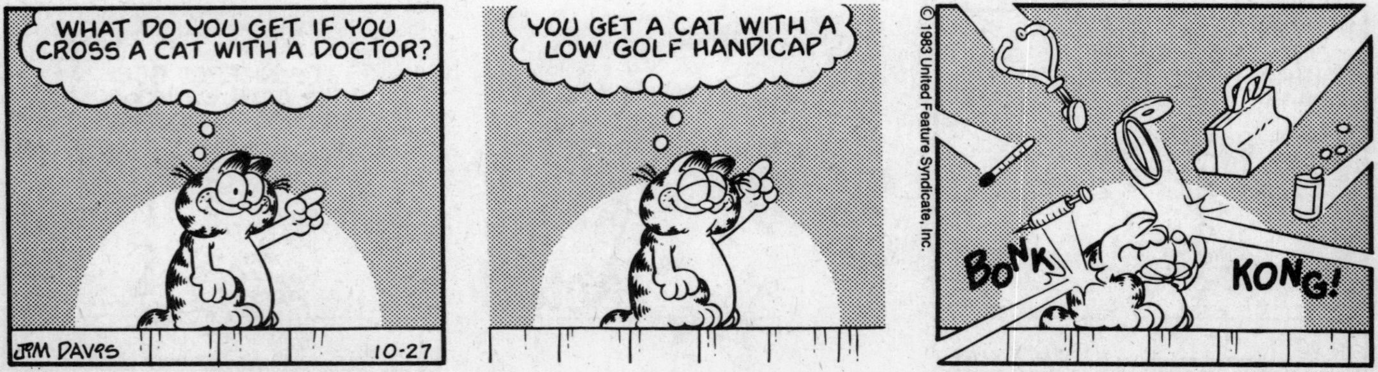
WHAT DO YOU GET IF YOU CROSS A CAT WITH A DOCTOR?
JIM DAVIS
10-27
YOU GET A CAT WITH A LOW GOLF HANDICAP
© 1983 United Feature Syndicate, Inc.
BONK
KONG!

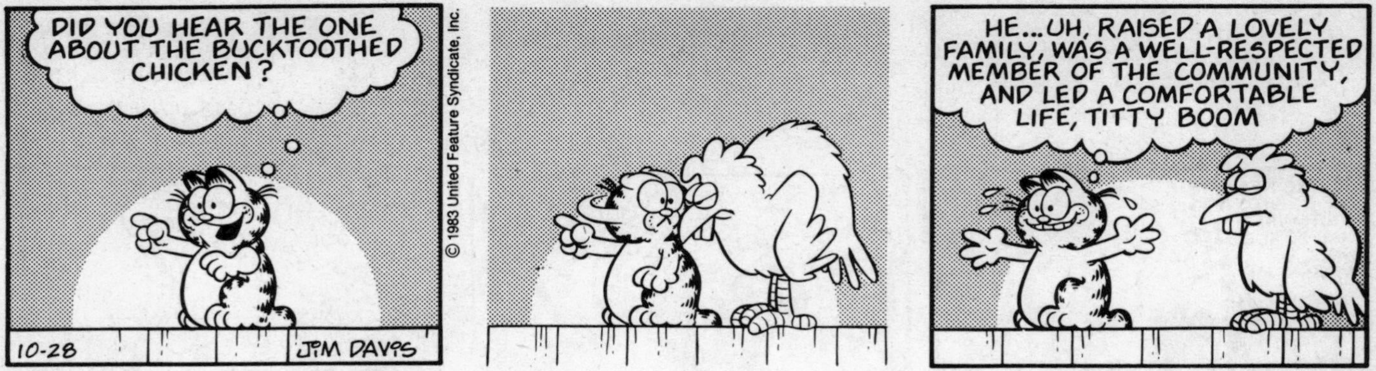
DID YOU HEAR THE ONE ABOUT THE BUCKTOOTHED CHICKEN?
10-28
JIM DAVIS
© 1983 United Feature Syndicate, Inc.
HE...UH, RAISED A LOVELY FAMILY, WAS A WELL-RESPECTED MEMBER OF THE COMMUNITY, AND LED A COMFORTABLE LIFE, TITTY BOOM

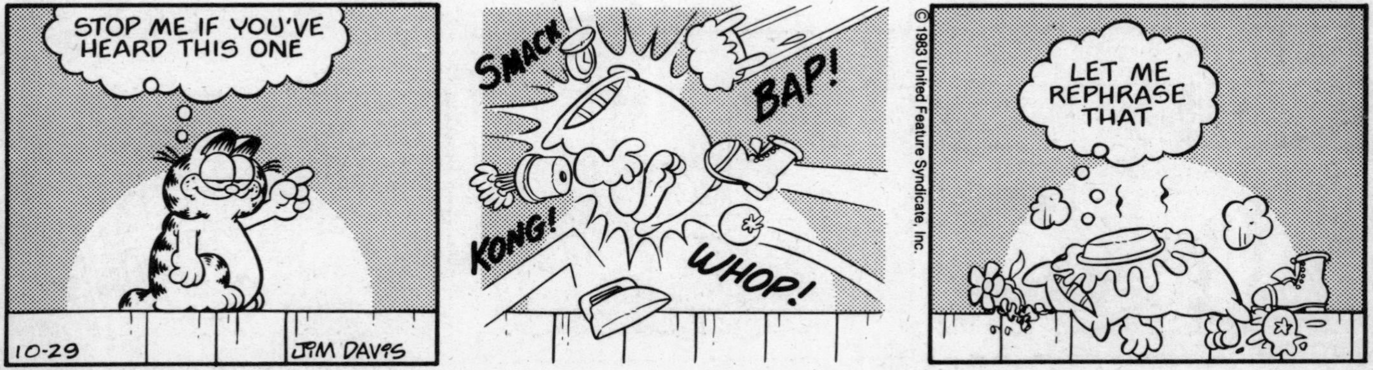
STOP ME IF YOU'VE HEARD THIS ONE
10-29
JIM DAVIS
SMACK
BAP!
KONG!
WHOP!
© 1983 United Feature Syndicate, Inc.
LET ME REPHRASE THAT

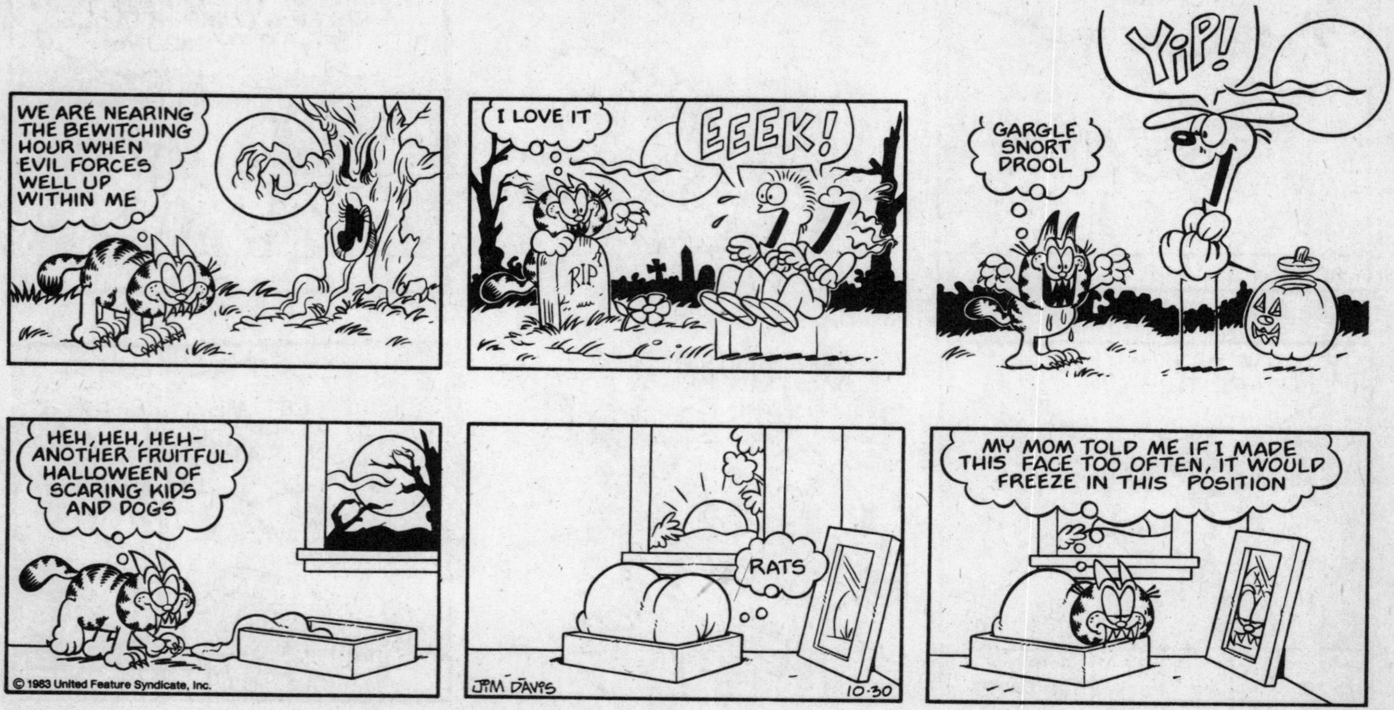
WE ARE NEARING THE BEWITCHING HOUR WHEN EVIL FORCES WELL UP WITHIN ME
I LOVE IT
EEEK!
RIP
GARGLE SNORT DROOL
YIP!
HEH, HEH, HEH- ANOTHER FRUITFUL HALLOWEEN OF SCARING KIDS AND DOGS
© 1983 United Feature Syndicate, Inc.
RATS
JIM DAVIS
10-30
MY MOM TOLD ME IF I MADE THIS FACE TOO OFTEN, IT WOULD FREEZE IN THIS POSITION

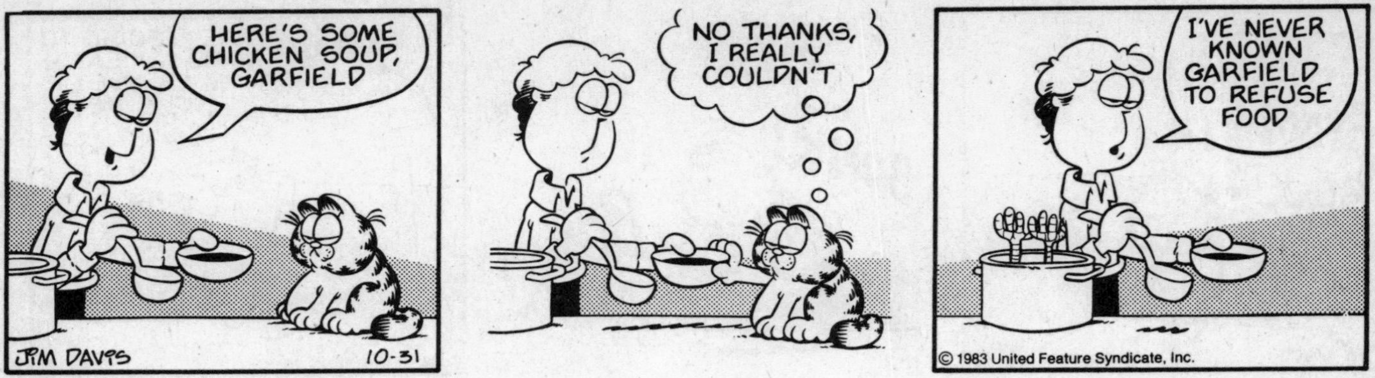
HERE'S SOME CHICKEN SOUP, GARFIELD
NO THANKS, I REALLY COULDN'T
I'VE NEVER KNOWN GARFIELD TO REFUSE FOOD
JIM DAVIS
10-31

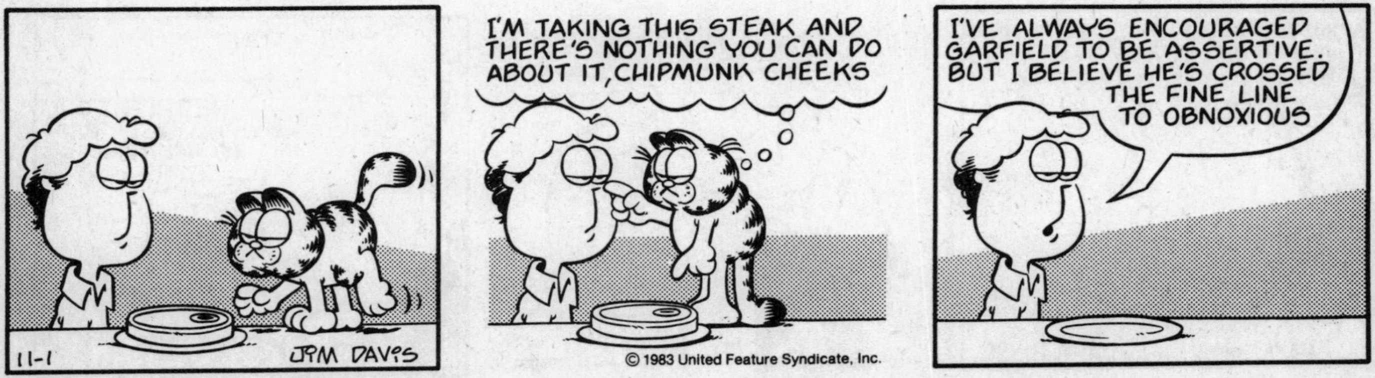
I'M TAKING THIS STEAK AND THERE'S NOTHING YOU CAN DO ABOUT IT, CHIPMUNK CHEEKS
I'VE ALWAYS ENCOURAGED GARFIELD TO BE ASSERTIVE. BUT I BELIEVE HE'S CROSSED THE FINE LINE TO OBNOXIOUS
11-1
JIM DAVIS

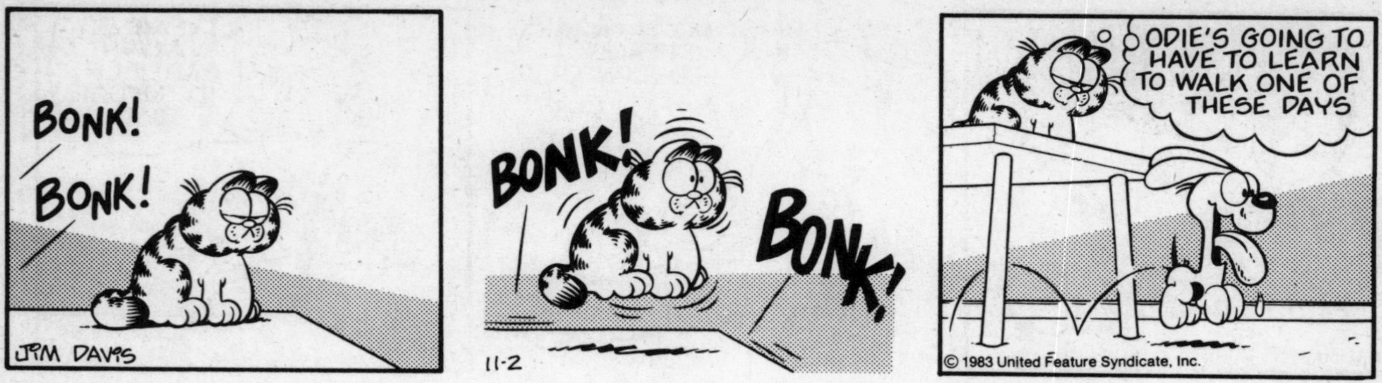
BONK!
BONK!
JIM DAVIS
BONK!
BONK!
11-2
ODIE'S GOING TO HAVE TO LEARN TO WALK ONE OF THESE DAYS
© 1983 United Feature Syndicate, Inc.

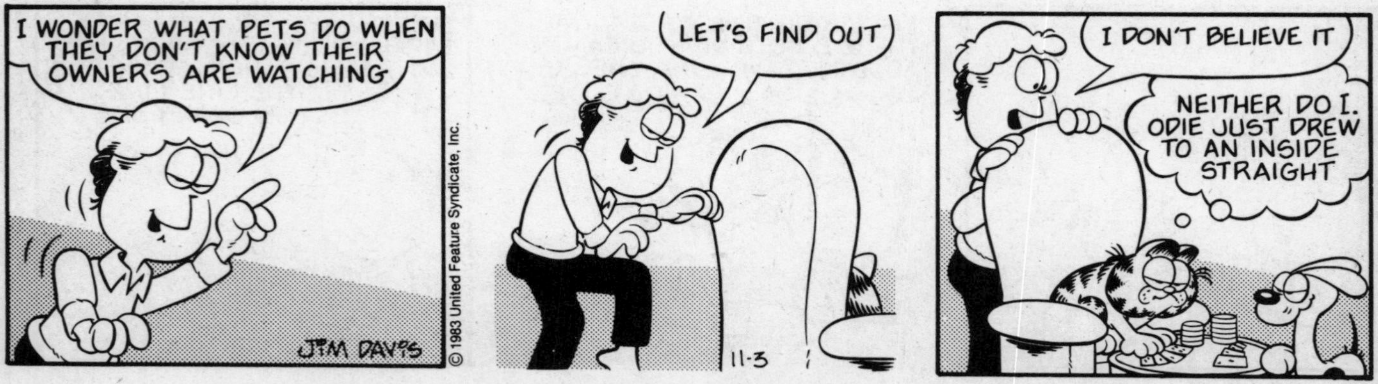
I WONDER WHAT PETS DO WHEN THEY DON'T KNOW THEIR OWNERS ARE WATCHING
JIM DAVIS
© 1983 United Feature Syndicate, Inc.
LET'S FIND OUT
11-3
I DON'T BELIEVE IT
NEITHER DO I. ODIE JUST DREW TO AN INSIDE STRAIGHT

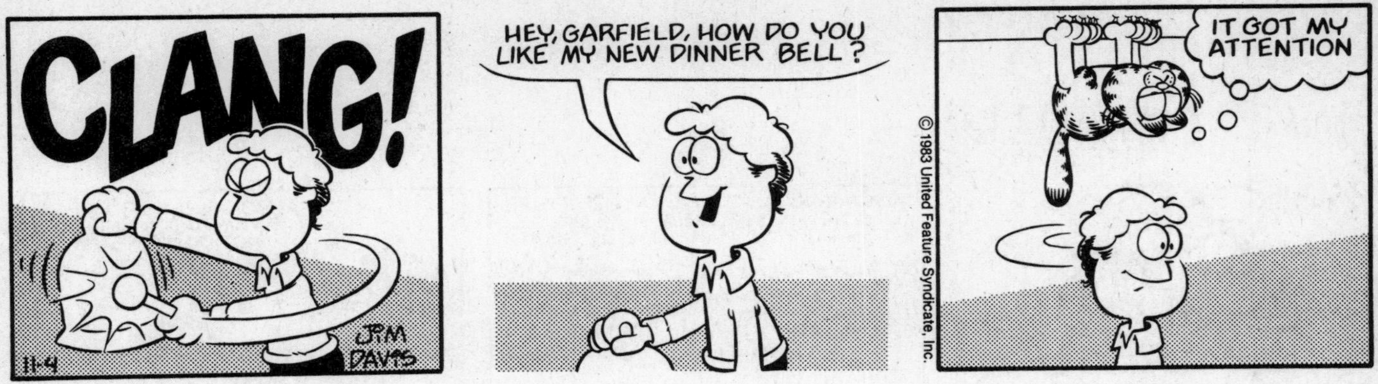
CLANG!
JIM DAVIS
11-4
HEY, GARFIELD, HOW DO YOU LIKE MY NEW DINNER BELL?
IT GOT MY ATTENTION
© 1983 United Feature Syndicate, Inc.

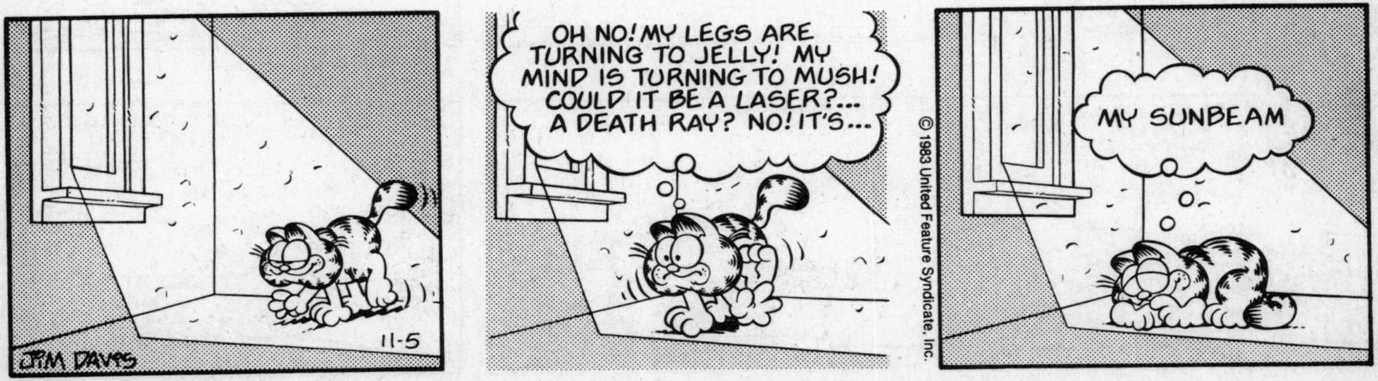
11-5
JIM DAVIS
OH NO! MY LEGS ARE TURNING TO JELLY! MY MIND IS TURNING TO MUSH! COULD IT BE A LASER?... A DEATH RAY? NO! IT'S...
MY SUNBEAM
© 1983 United Feature Syndicate, Inc.

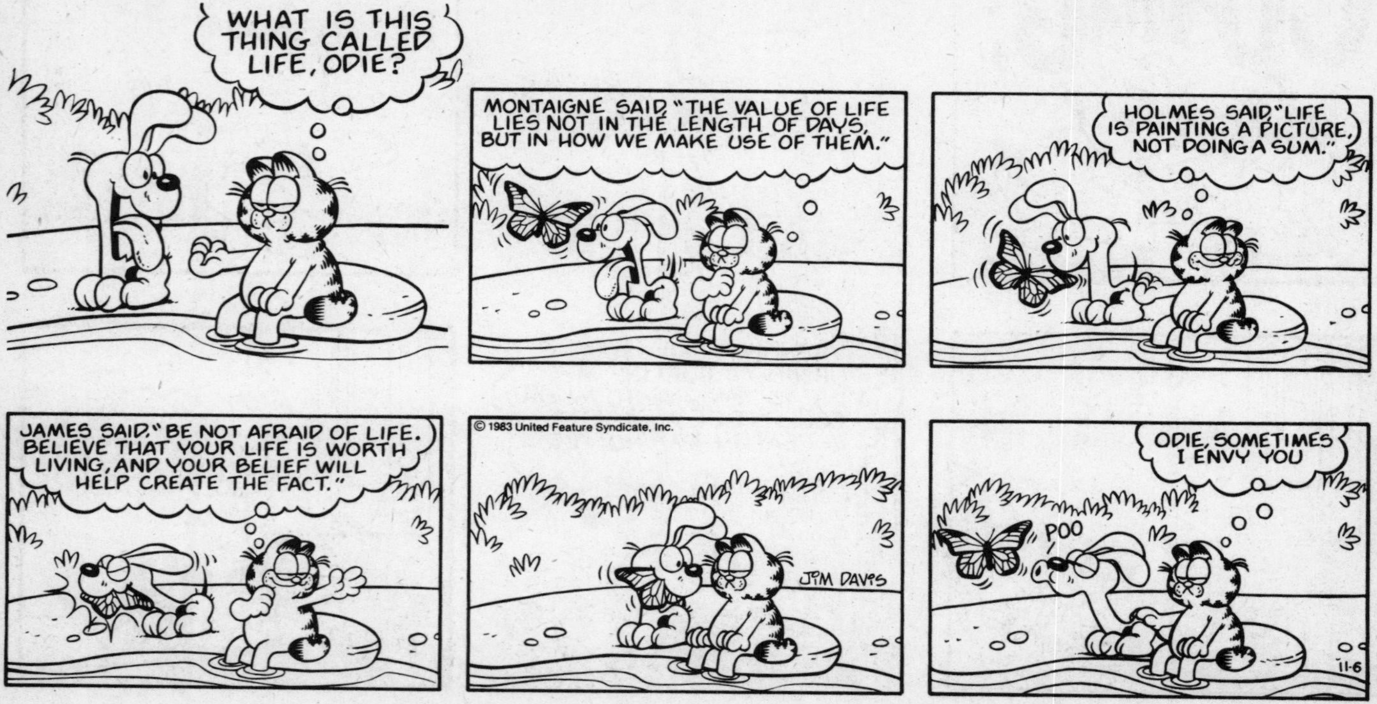
WHAT IS THIS THING CALLED LIFE, ODIE?
MONTAIGNE SAID, "THE VALUE OF LIFE LIES NOT IN THE LENGTH OF DAYS, BUT IN HOW WE MAKE USE OF THEM."
HOLMES SAID, "LIFE IS PAINTING A PICTURE, NOT DOING A SUM."
JAMES SAID, "BE NOT AFRAID OF LIFE. BELIEVE THAT YOUR LIFE IS WORTH LIVING, AND YOUR BELIEF WILL HELP CREATE THE FACT."
© 1983 United Feature Syndicate, Inc.
JIM DAVIS
POO
ODIE, SOMETIMES I ENVY YOU
11-6

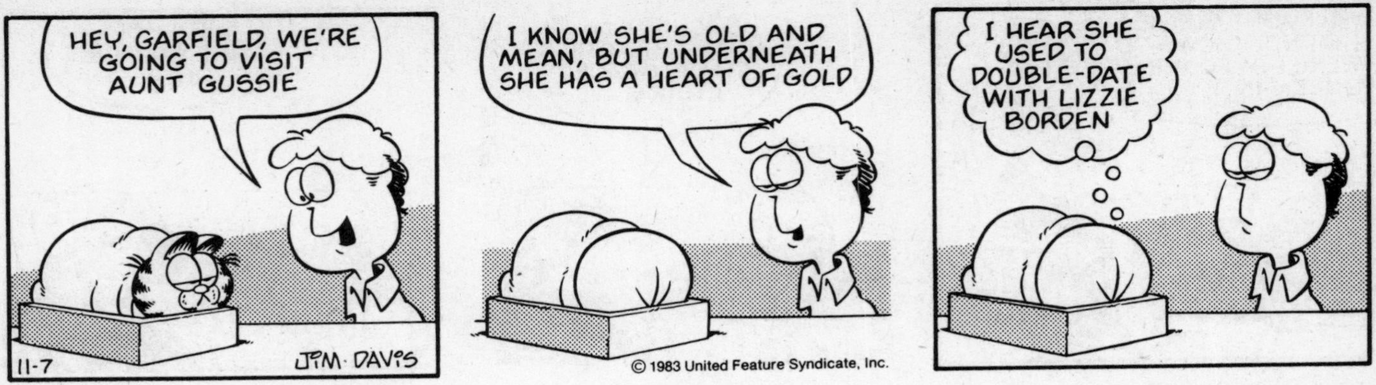
HEY, GARFIELD, WE'RE GOING TO VISIT AUNT GUSSIE
11-7
JIM DAVIS
I KNOW SHE'S OLD AND MEAN, BUT UNDERNEATH SHE HAS A HEART OF GOLD
© 1983 United Feature Syndicate, Inc.
I HEAR SHE USED TO DOUBLE-DATE WITH LIZZIE BORDEN

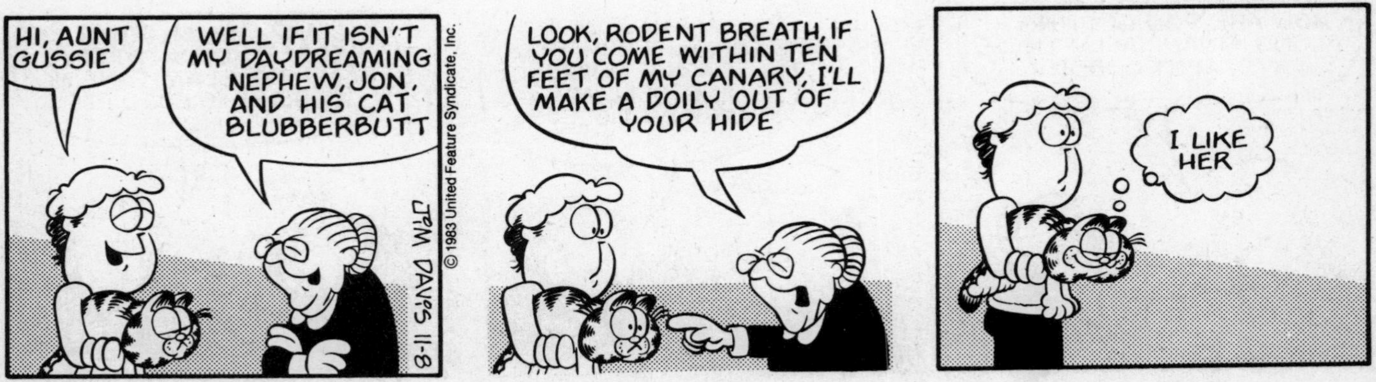
HI, AUNT GUSSIE
WELL IF IT ISN'T MY DAYDREAMING NEPHEW, JON, AND HIS CAT BLUBBERBUTT
JIM DAVIS 11-8
© 1983 United Feature Syndicate, Inc.
LOOK, RODENT BREATH, IF YOU COME WITHIN TEN FEET OF MY CANARY, I'LL MAKE A DOILY OUT OF YOUR HIDE
I LIKE HER

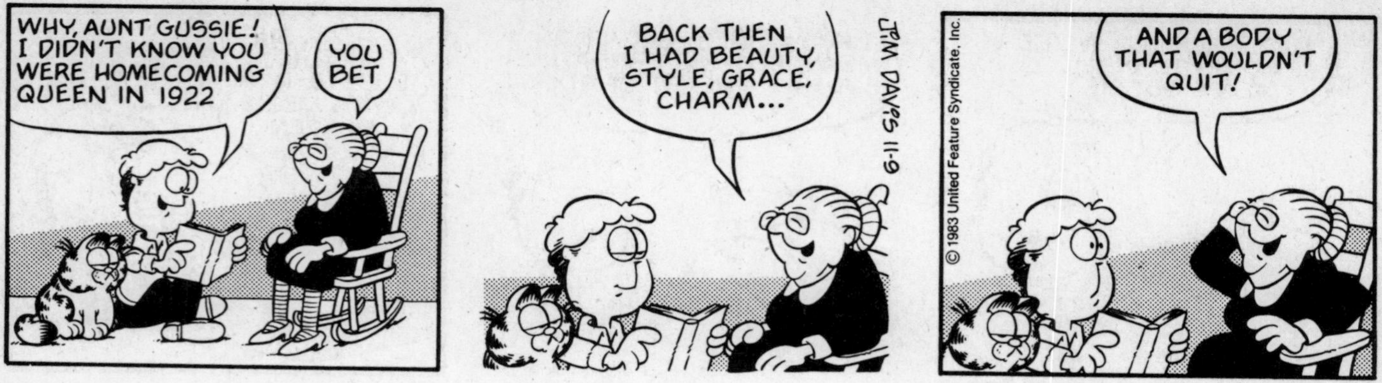
WHY, AUNT GUSSIE! I DIDN'T KNOW YOU WERE HOMECOMING QUEEN IN 1922
YOU BET
BACK THEN I HAD BEAUTY, STYLE, GRACE, CHARM...
AND A BODY THAT WOULDN'T QUIT!
JPM DAVPS 11-9
© 1983 United Feature Syndicate, Inc.

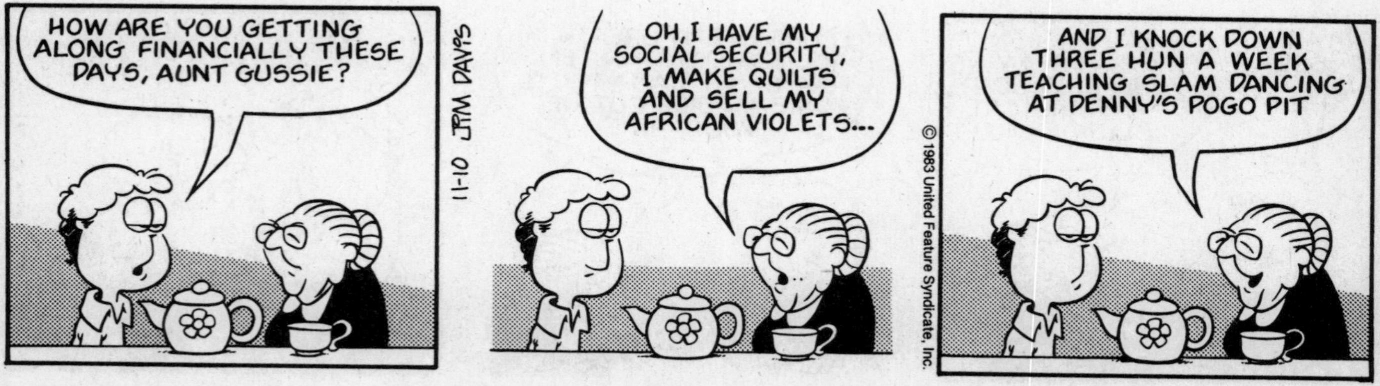
HOW ARE YOU GETTING ALONG FINANCIALLY THESE DAYS, AUNT GUSSIE?
OH, I HAVE MY SOCIAL SECURITY, I MAKE QUILTS AND SELL MY AFRICAN VIOLETS...
AND I KNOCK DOWN THREE HUN A WEEK TEACHING SLAM DANCING AT DENNY'S POGO PIT
JPM DAVPS 11-10
© 1983 United Feature Syndicate, Inc.

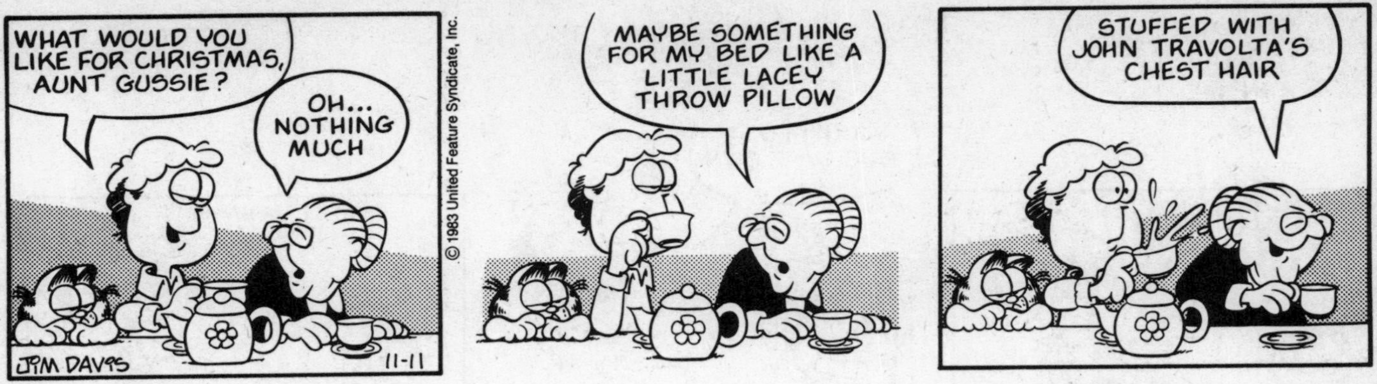
WHAT WOULD YOU LIKE FOR CHRISTMAS, AUNT GUSSIE?
OH... NOTHING MUCH
JIM DAVIS 11-11
© 1983 United Feature Syndicate, Inc.
MAYBE SOMETHING FOR MY BED LIKE A LITTLE LACEY THROW PILLOW
STUFFED WITH JOHN TRAVOLTA'S CHEST HAIR

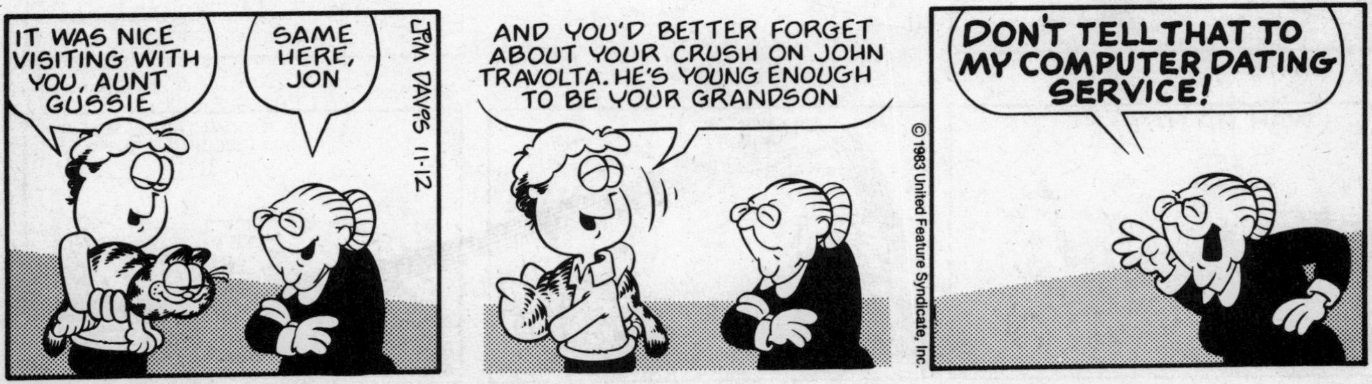
IT WAS NICE VISITING WITH YOU, AUNT GUSSIE
SAME HERE, JON
JIM DAVIS 11-12
AND YOU'D BETTER FORGET ABOUT YOUR CRUSH ON JOHN TRAVOLTA. HE'S YOUNG ENOUGH TO BE YOUR GRANDSON
© 1983 United Feature Syndicate, Inc.
DON'T TELL THAT TO MY COMPUTER DATING SERVICE!

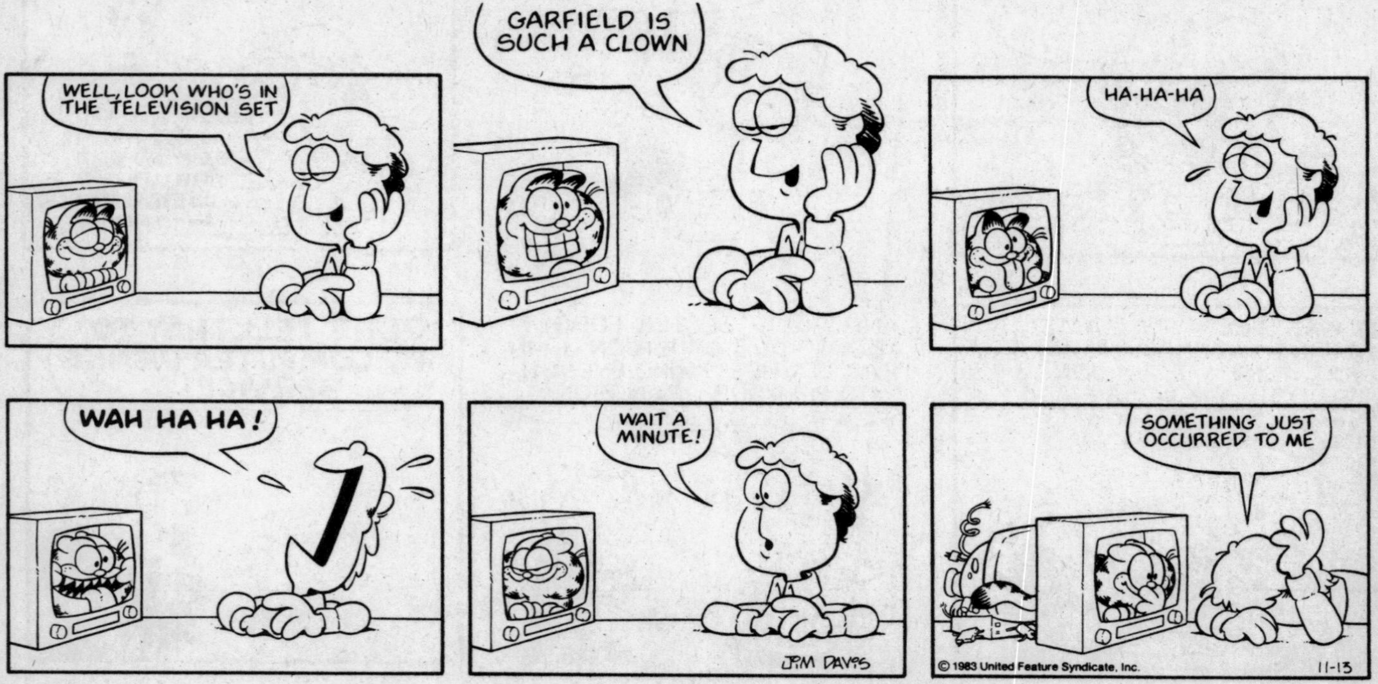
WELL, LOOK WHO'S IN THE TELEVISION SET
GARFIELD IS SUCH A CLOWN
HA-HA-HA
WAH HA HA!
WAIT A MINUTE!
SOMETHING JUST OCCURRED TO ME
JIM DAVIS
© 1983 United Feature Syndicate, Inc.
11-13

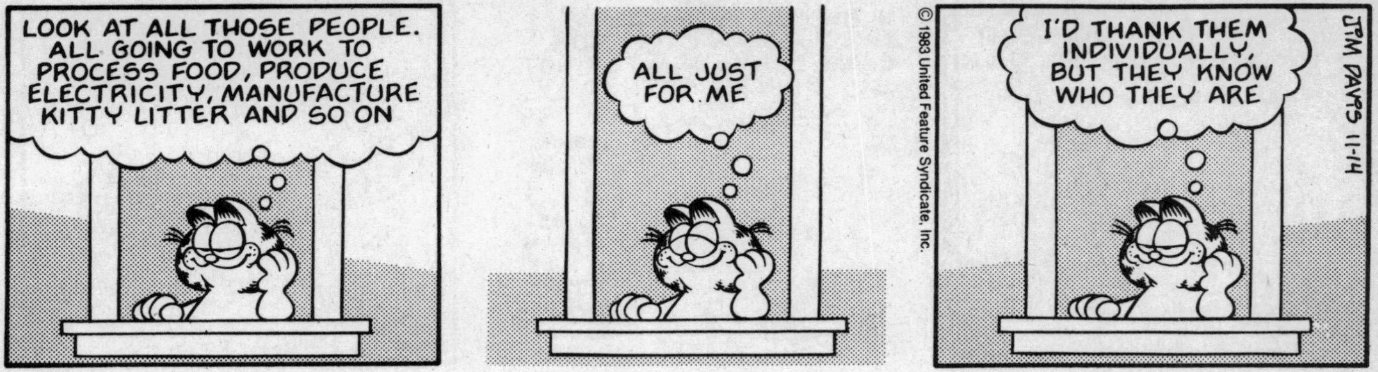
LOOK AT ALL THOSE PEOPLE. ALL GOING TO WORK TO PROCESS FOOD, PRODUCE ELECTRICITY, MANUFACTURE KITTY LITTER AND SO ON
ALL JUST FOR ME
I'D THANK THEM INDIVIDUALLY, BUT THEY KNOW WHO THEY ARE
© 1983 United Feature Syndicate, Inc.
JIM DAVIS 11-14

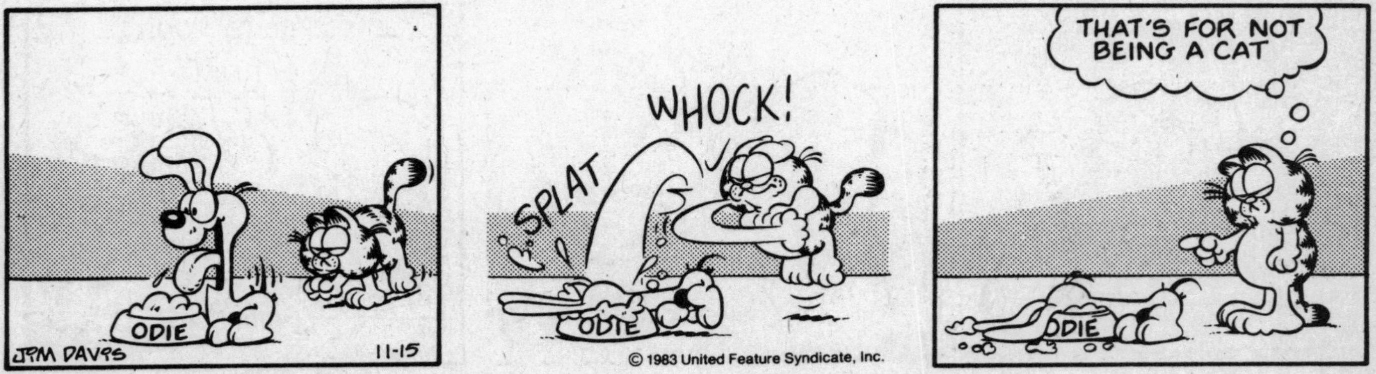
ODIE
JIM DAVIS
11-15
WHOCK!
SPLAT
ODIE
© 1983 United Feature Syndicate, Inc.
THAT'S FOR NOT BEING A CAT
ODIE

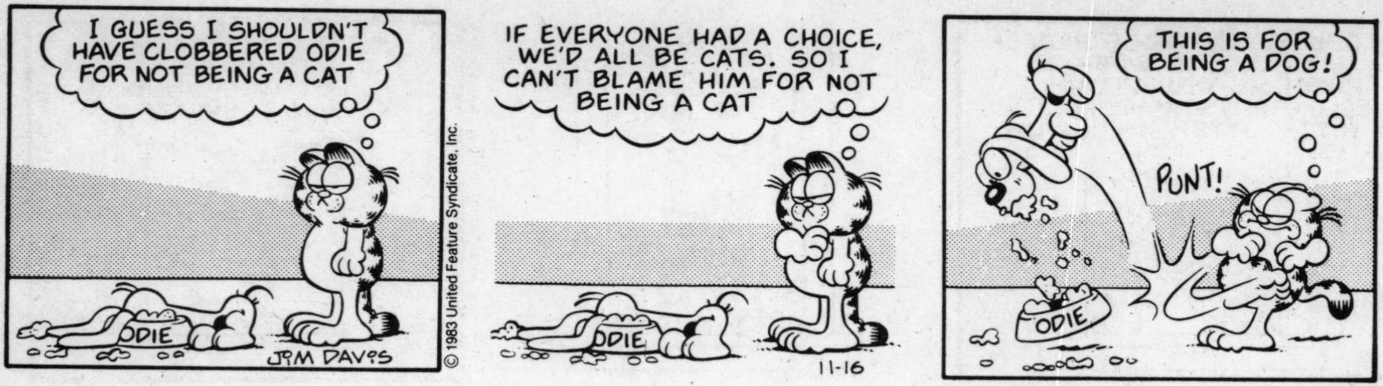
I GUESS I SHOULDN'T HAVE CLOBBERED ODIE FOR NOT BEING A CAT
ODIE
JIM DAVIS
IF EVERYONE HAD A CHOICE, WE'D ALL BE CATS. SO I CAN'T BLAME HIM FOR NOT BEING A CAT
ODIE
11-16
THIS IS FOR BEING A DOG!
PUNT!
ODIE

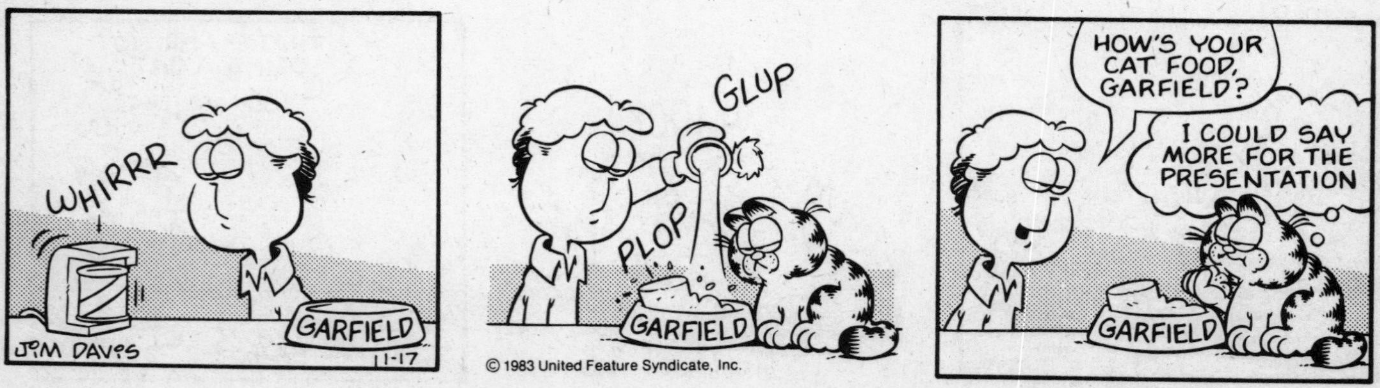
WHIRRR
GARFIELD
JIM DAVIS
11-17
GLUP
PLOP
GARFIELD
HOW'S YOUR CAT FOOD, GARFIELD?
I COULD SAY MORE FOR THE PRESENTATION
GARFIELD

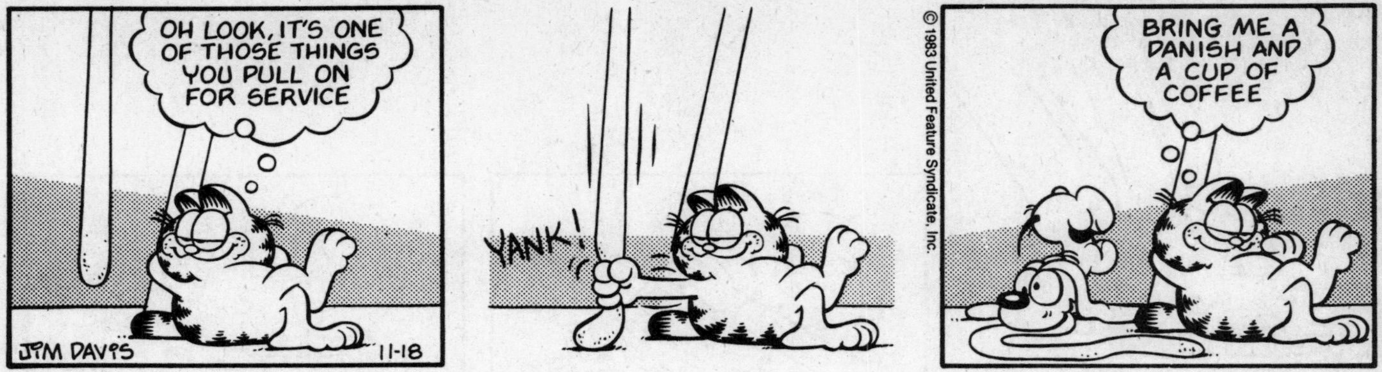
OH LOOK, IT'S ONE OF THOSE THINGS YOU PULL ON FOR SERVICE
JIM DAVIS
11-18
YANK!
BRING ME A DANISH AND A CUP OF COFFEE

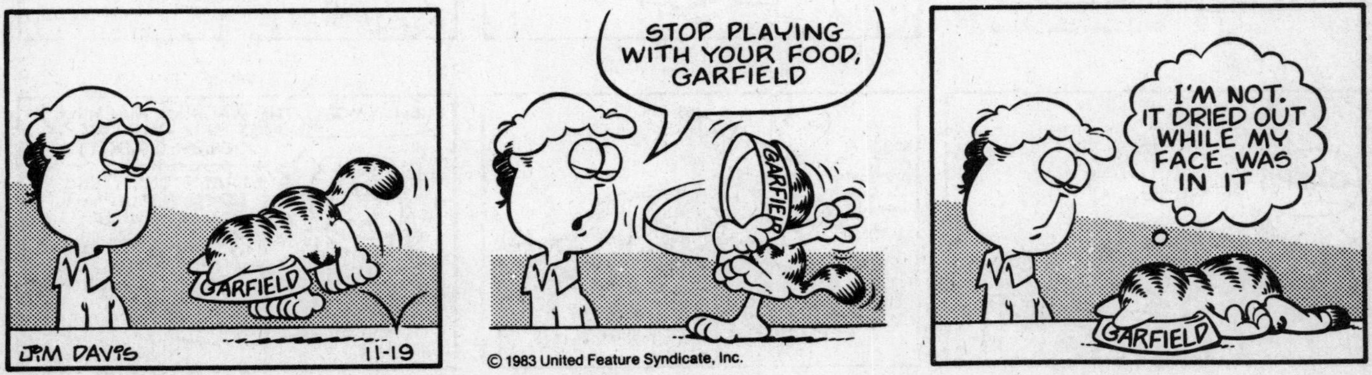
JIM DAVIS
11-19
GARFIELD
STOP PLAYING WITH YOUR FOOD, GARFIELD
GARFIELD
I'M NOT. IT DRIED OUT WHILE MY FACE WAS IN IT
GARFIELD

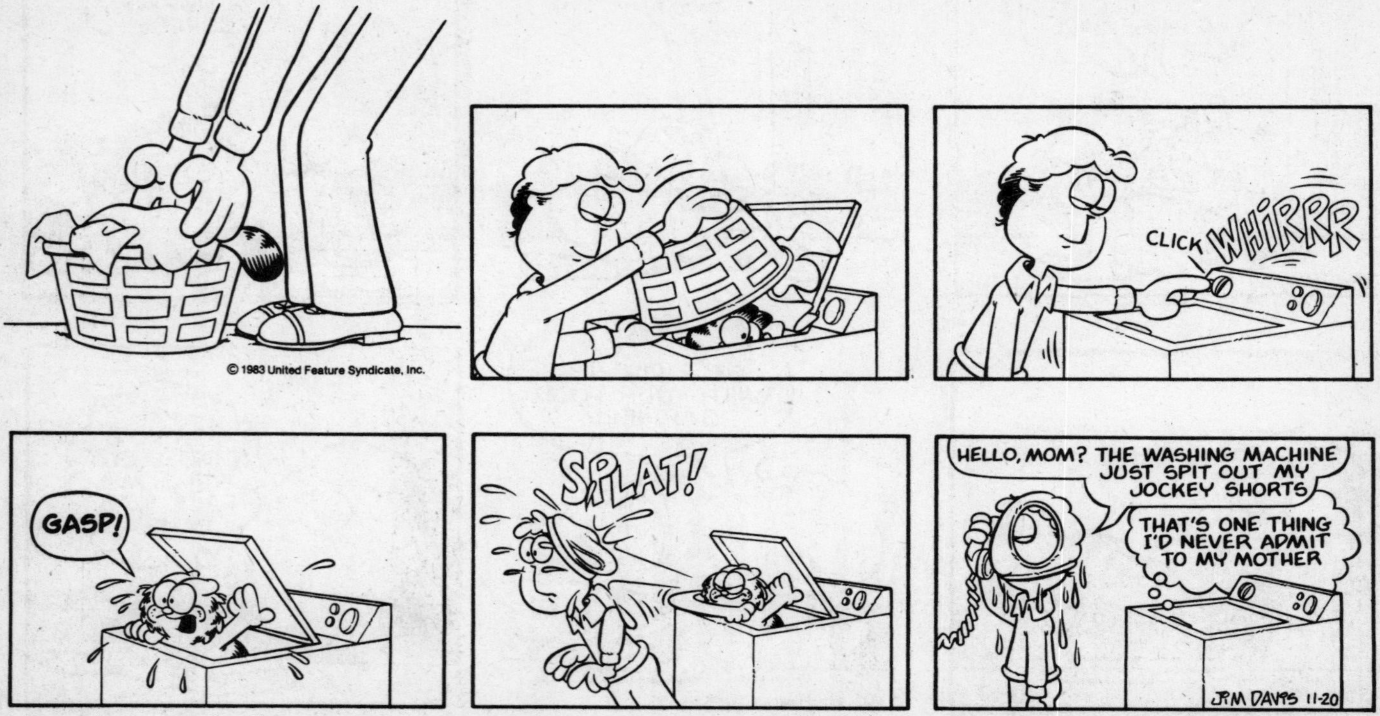
CLICK
WHIRRR
GASP!
SPLAT!
HELLO, MOM? THE WASHING MACHINE JUST SPIT OUT MY JOCKEY SHORTS
THAT'S ONE THING I'D NEVER ADMIT TO MY MOTHER
JIM DAVIS 11-20

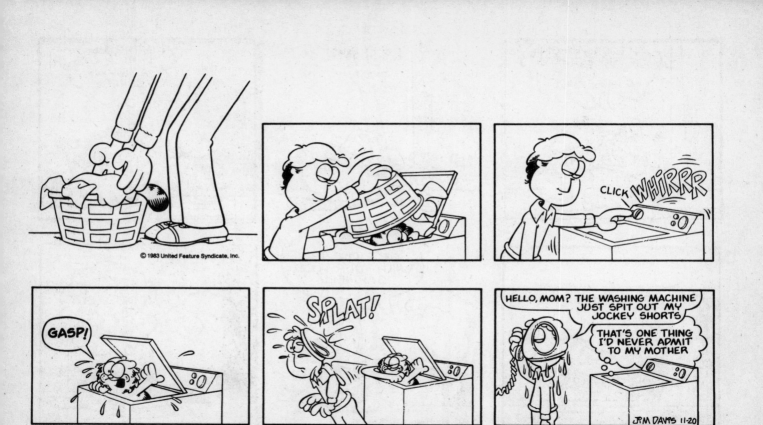

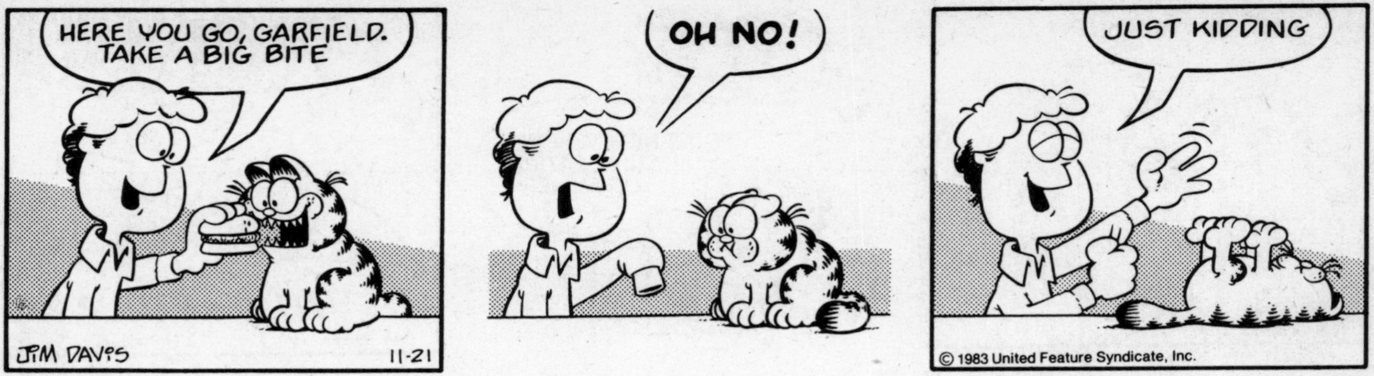
HERE YOU GO, GARFIELD. TAKE A BIG BITE
JIM DAVIS
11-21
OH NO!
JUST KIDDING
© 1983 United Feature Syndicate, Inc.

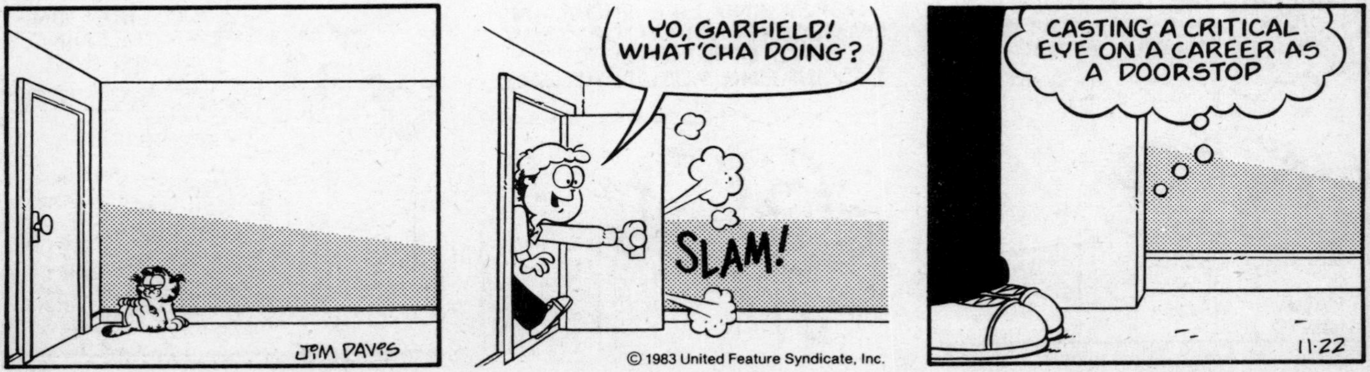
JIM DAVIS
YO, GARFIELD! WHAT'CHA DOING?
SLAM!
© 1983 United Feature Syndicate, Inc.
CASTING A CRITICAL EYE ON A CAREER AS A DOORSTOP
11·22

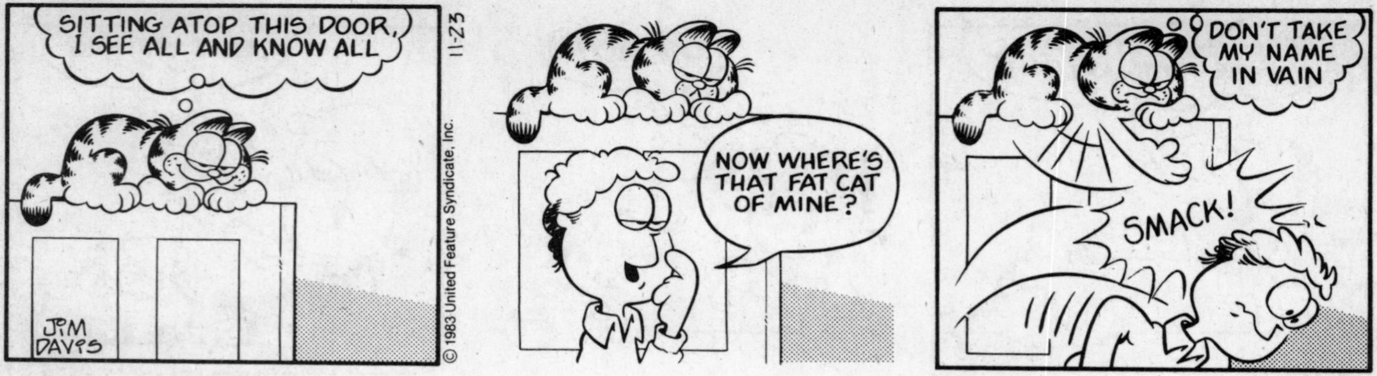
SITTING ATOP THIS DOOR, I SEE ALL AND KNOW ALL
JIM DAVIS
11-23
© 1983 United Feature Syndicate, Inc.
NOW WHERE'S THAT FAT CAT OF MINE?
DON'T TAKE MY NAME IN VAIN
SMACK!

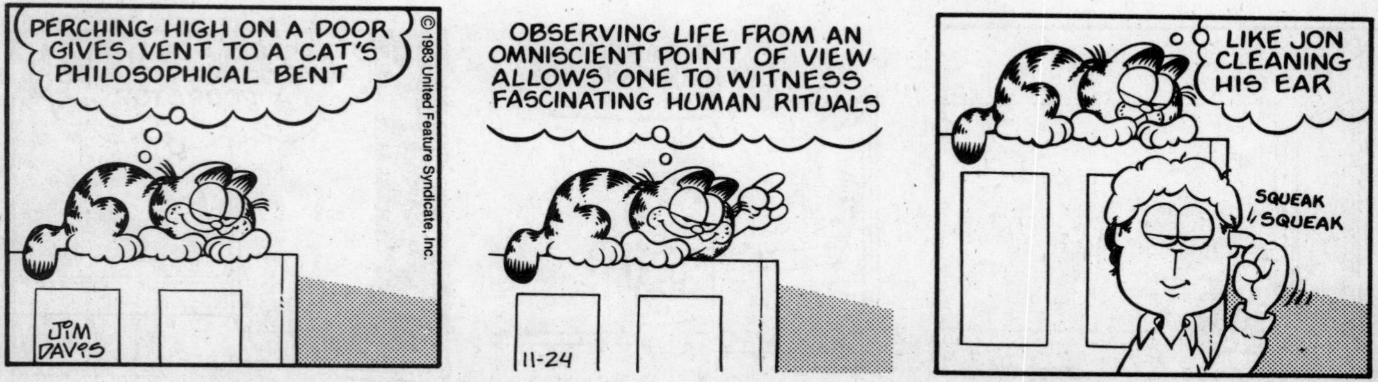
PERCHING HIGH ON A DOOR GIVES VENT TO A CAT'S PHILOSOPHICAL BENT
JIM DAVIS
© 1983 United Feature Syndicate, Inc.
OBSERVING LIFE FROM AN OMNISCIENT POINT OF VIEW ALLOWS ONE TO WITNESS FASCINATING HUMAN RITUALS
11-24
LIKE JON CLEANING HIS EAR
SQUEAK SQUEAK

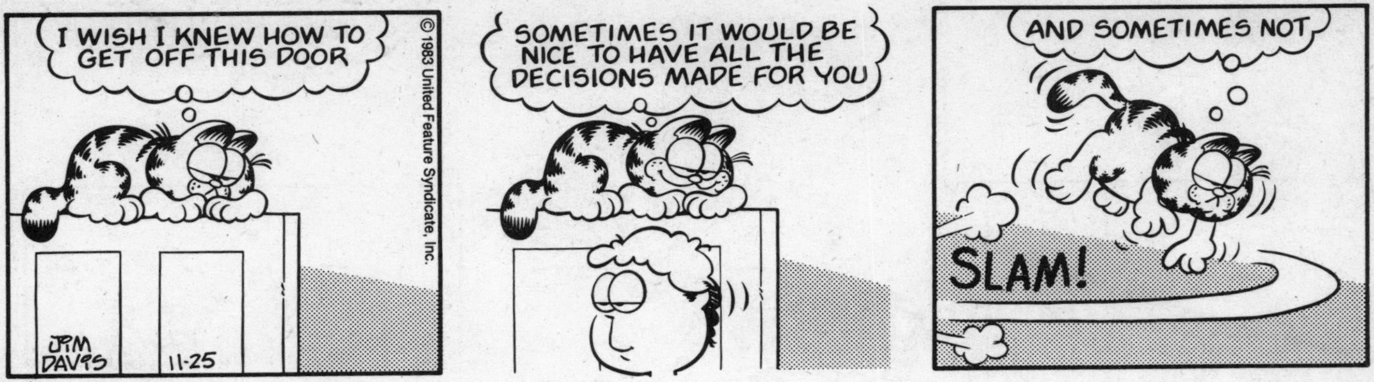
I WISH I KNEW HOW TO GET OFF THIS DOOR
JIM DAVIS 11-25
© 1983 United Feature Syndicate, Inc.
SOMETIMES IT WOULD BE NICE TO HAVE ALL THE DECISIONS MADE FOR YOU
AND SOMETIMES NOT
SLAM!

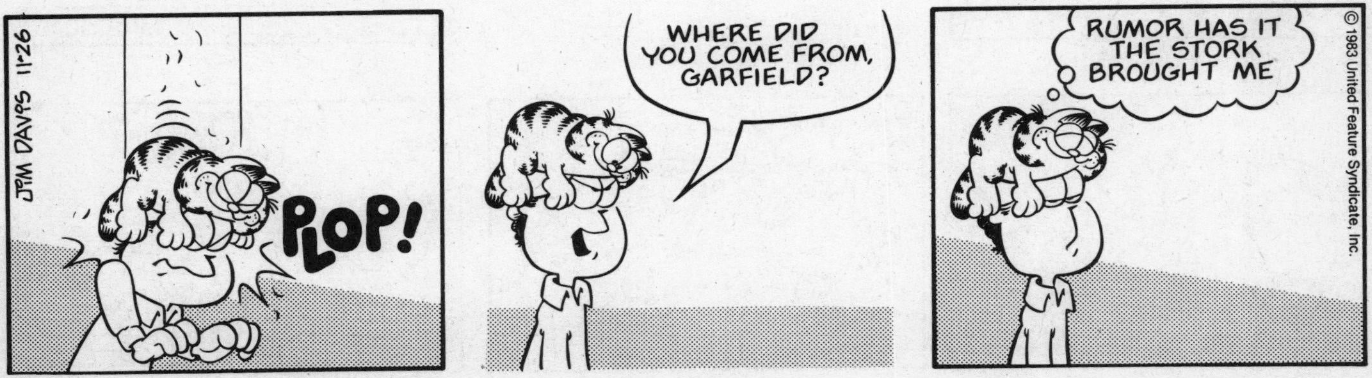
JIM DAVIS 11-26
PLOP!
WHERE DID YOU COME FROM, GARFIELD?
RUMOR HAS IT THE STORK BROUGHT ME
© 1983 United Feature Syndicate, Inc.

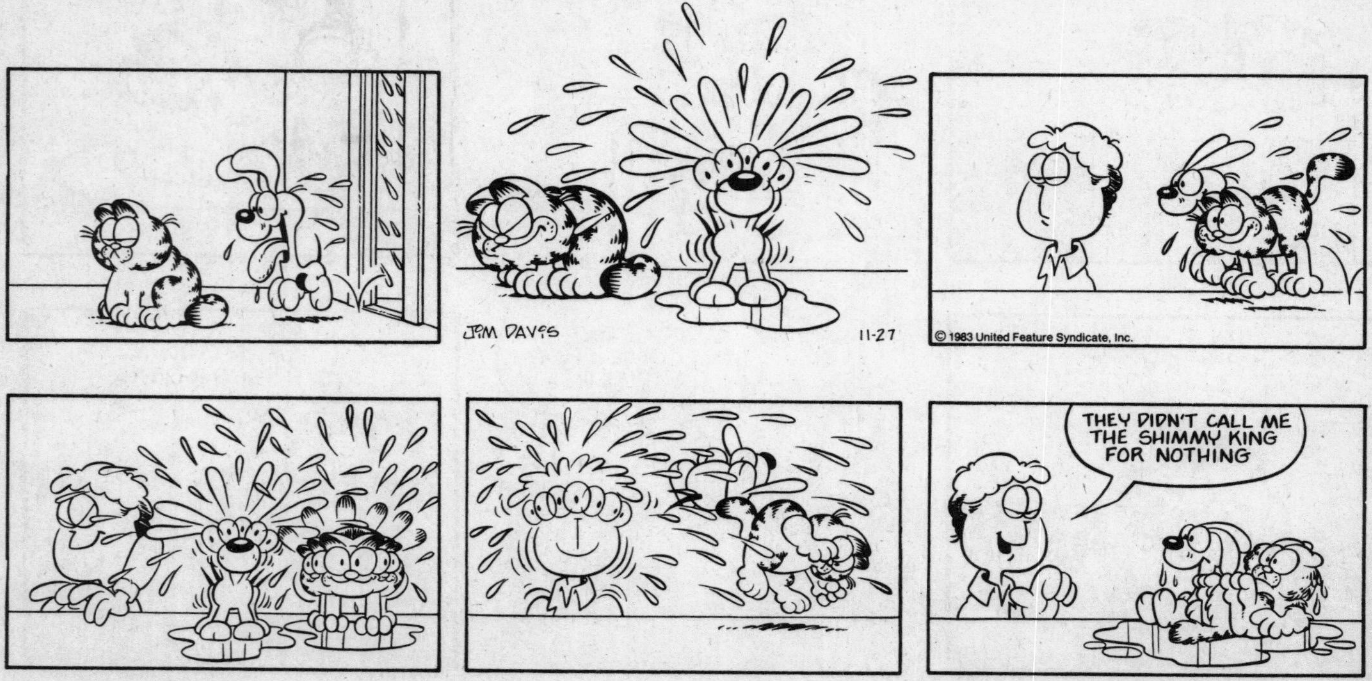
JIM DAVIS
11-27
© 1983 United Feature Syndicate, Inc.
THEY DIDN'T CALL ME THE SHIMMY KING FOR NOTHING

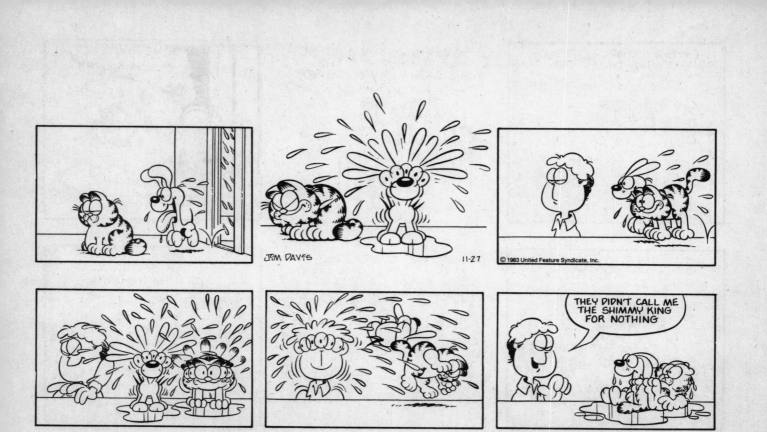

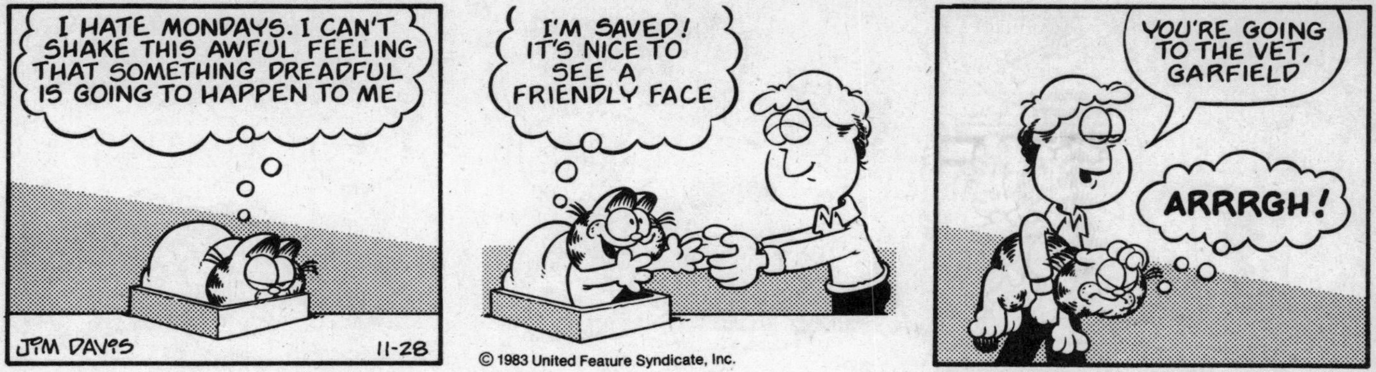
I HATE MONDAYS. I CAN'T SHAKE THIS AWFUL FEELING THAT SOMETHING DREADFUL IS GOING TO HAPPEN TO ME
JIM DAVIS
11-28
I'M SAVED! IT'S NICE TO SEE A FRIENDLY FACE
© 1983 United Feature Syndicate, Inc.
YOU'RE GOING TO THE VET, GARFIELD
ARRRGH!

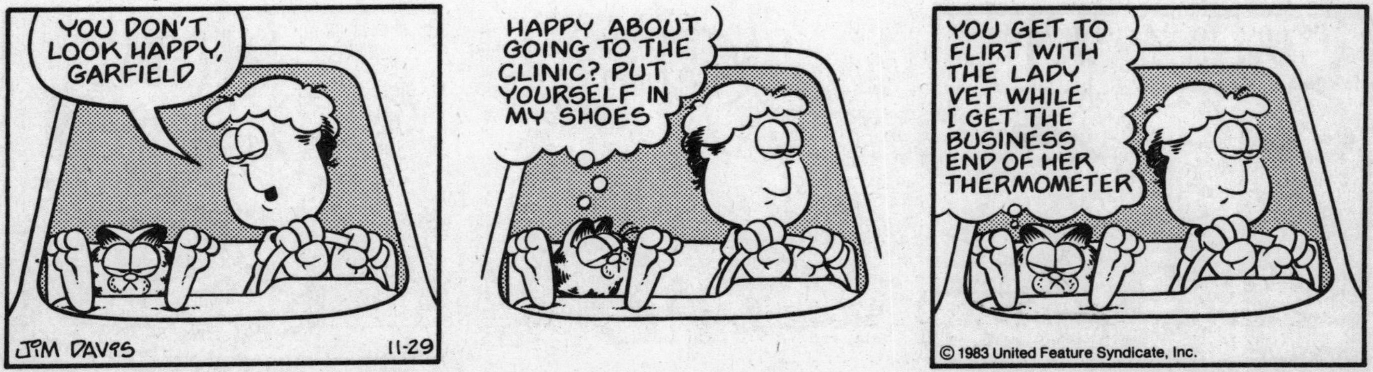
YOU DON'T LOOK HAPPY, GARFIELD
JIM DAVIS
11-29
HAPPY ABOUT GOING TO THE CLINIC? PUT YOURSELF IN MY SHOES
YOU GET TO FLIRT WITH THE LADY VET WHILE I GET THE BUSINESS END OF HER THERMOMETER
© 1983 United Feature Syndicate, Inc.

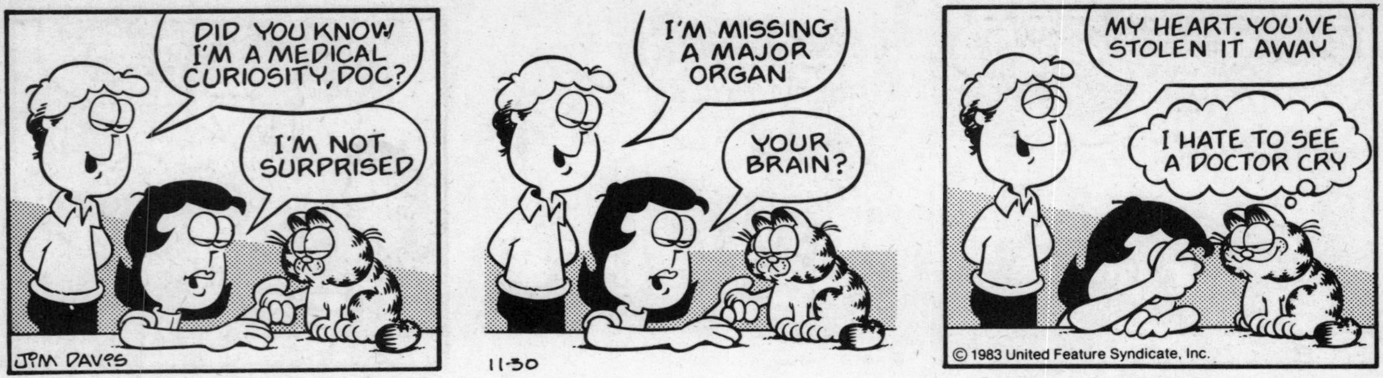
DID YOU KNOW I'M A MEDICAL CURIOSITY, DOC?
I'M NOT SURPRISED
JIM DAVIS
I'M MISSING A MAJOR ORGAN
YOUR BRAIN?
11-30
MY HEART. YOU'VE STOLEN IT AWAY
I HATE TO SEE A DOCTOR CRY
© 1983 United Feature Syndicate, Inc.

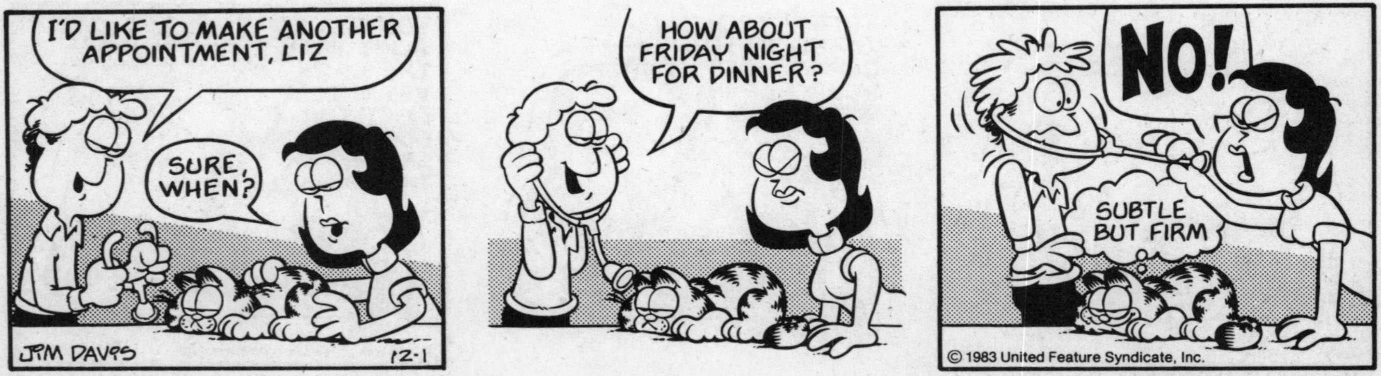
I'D LIKE TO MAKE ANOTHER APPOINTMENT, LIZ
SURE, WHEN?
JIM DAVIS
12-1
HOW ABOUT FRIDAY NIGHT FOR DINNER?
NO!
SUBTLE BUT FIRM
© 1983 United Feature Syndicate, Inc.

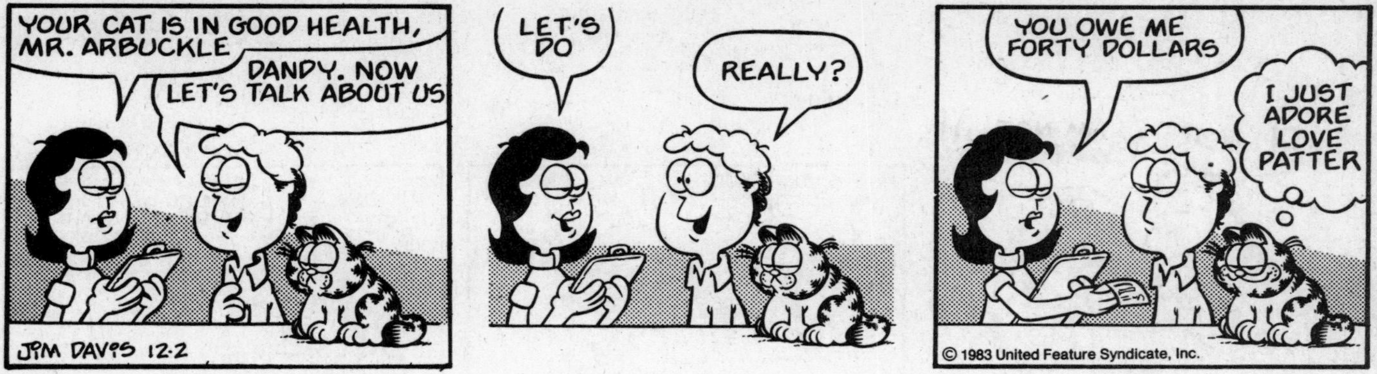
YOUR CAT IS IN GOOD HEALTH, MR. ARBUCKLE
DANDY. NOW LET'S TALK ABOUT US
JIM DAVIS 12-2
LET'S DO
REALLY?
YOU OWE ME FORTY DOLLARS
I JUST ADORE LOVE PATTER
© 1983 United Feature Syndicate, Inc.

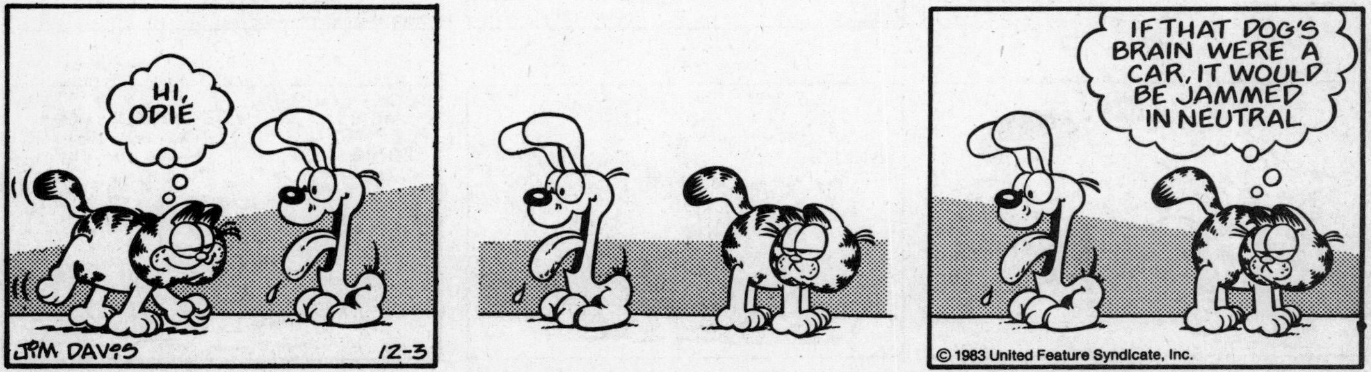
HI, ODIE
JIM DAVIS
12-3
IF THAT DOG'S BRAIN WERE A CAR, IT WOULD BE JAMMED IN NEUTRAL
© 1983 United Feature Syndicate, Inc.

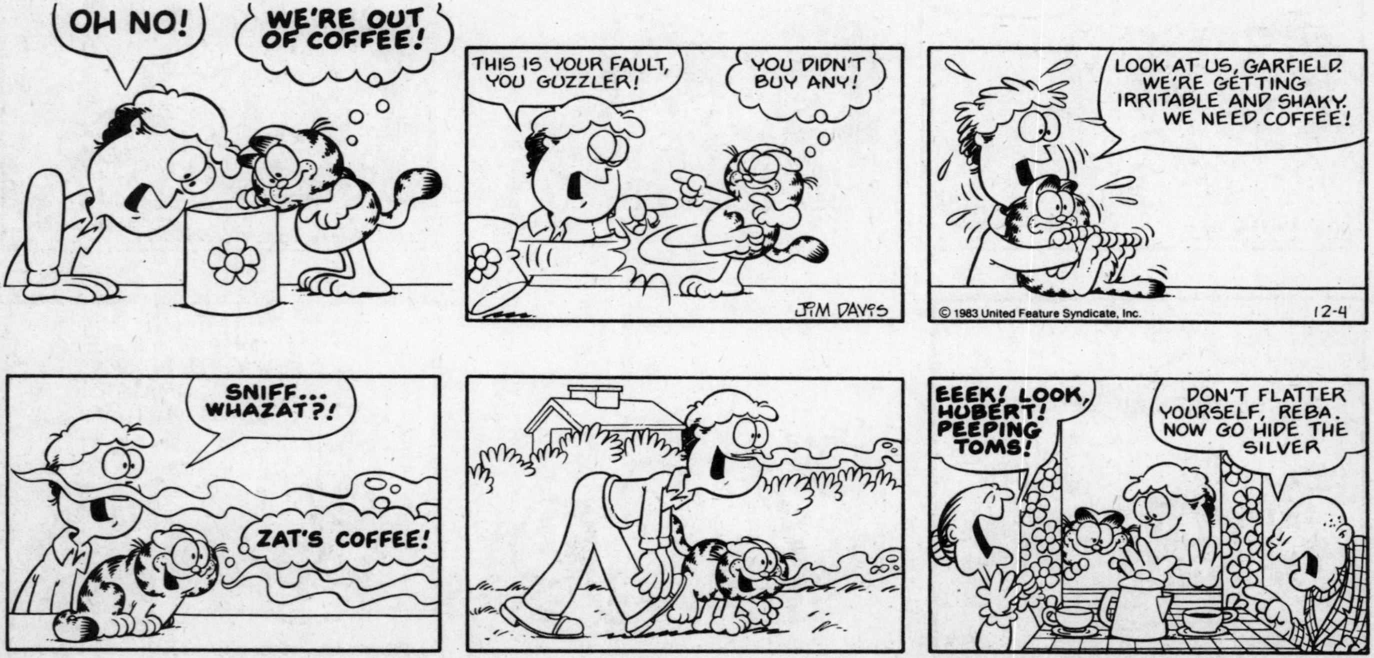
OH NO!
WE'RE OUT OF COFFEE!
THIS IS YOUR FAULT, YOU GUZZLER!
YOU DIDN'T BUY ANY!
JIM DAVIS
LOOK AT US, GARFIELD. WE'RE GETTING IRRITABLE AND SHAKY. WE NEED COFFEE!
© 1983 United Feature Syndicate, Inc.
12-4
SNIFF... WHAZAT?!
ZAT'S COFFEE!
EEEK! LOOK, HUBERT! PEEPING TOMS!
DON'T FLATTER YOURSELF, REBA. NOW GO HIDE THE SILVER

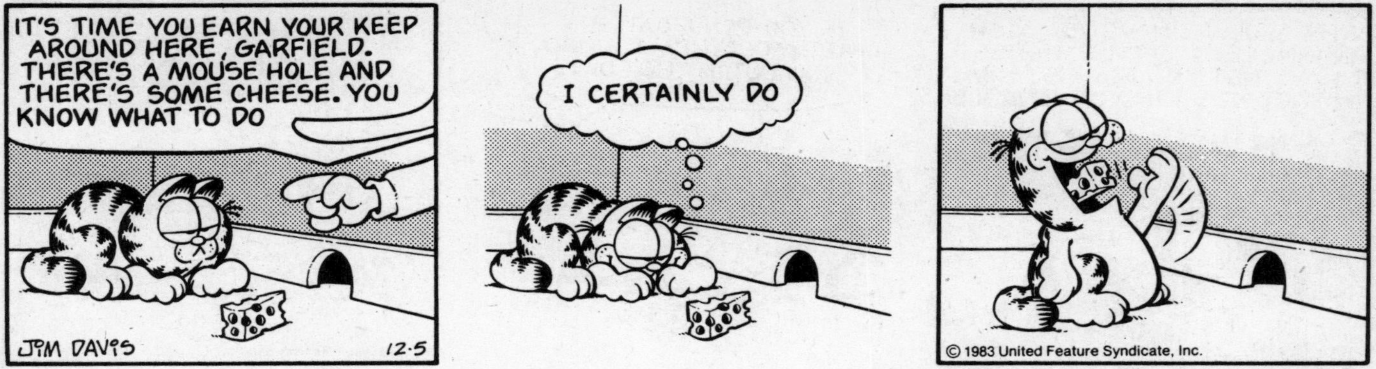
IT'S TIME YOU EARN YOUR KEEP AROUND HERE, GARFIELD. THERE'S A MOUSE HOLE AND THERE'S SOME CHEESE. YOU KNOW WHAT TO DO
JIM DAVIS
12·5
I CERTAINLY DO
© 1983 United Feature Syndicate, Inc.

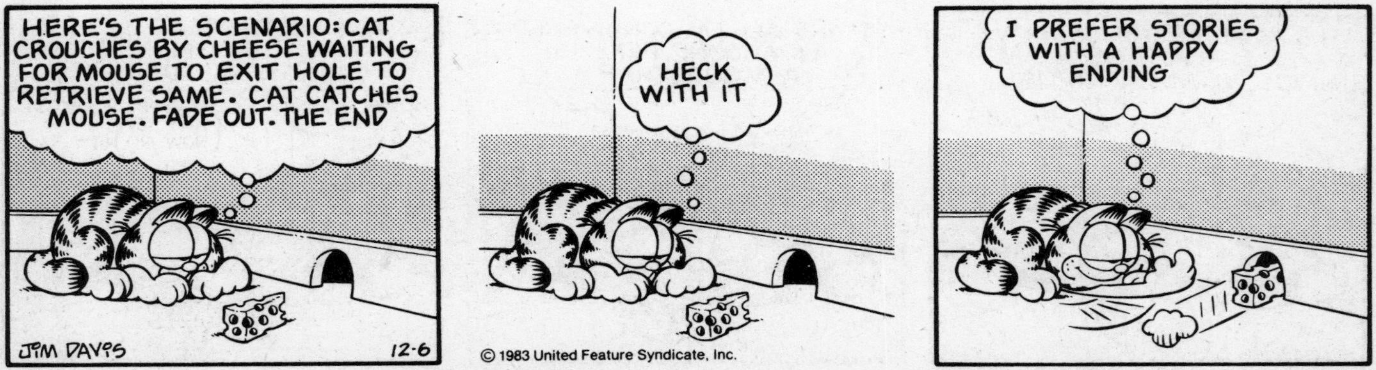
HERE'S THE SCENARIO: CAT CROUCHES BY CHEESE WAITING FOR MOUSE TO EXIT HOLE TO RETRIEVE SAME. CAT CATCHES MOUSE. FADE OUT. THE END
JIM DAVIS
12·6
HECK WITH IT
© 1983 United Feature Syndicate, Inc.
I PREFER STORIES WITH A HAPPY ENDING

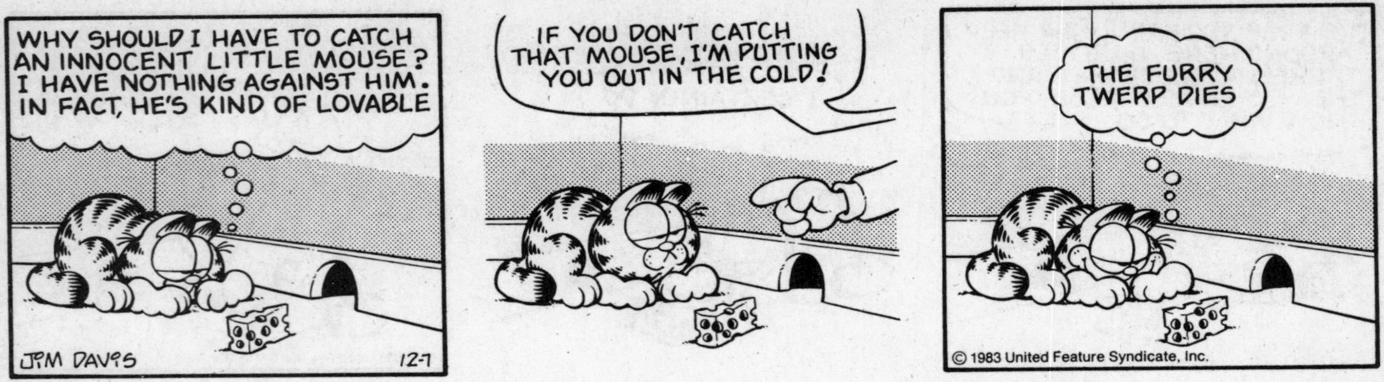
WHY SHOULD I HAVE TO CATCH AN INNOCENT LITTLE MOUSE? I HAVE NOTHING AGAINST HIM. IN FACT, HE'S KIND OF LOVABLE
JIM DAVIS 12-7
IF YOU DON'T CATCH THAT MOUSE, I'M PUTTING YOU OUT IN THE COLD!
THE FURRY TWERP DIES
© 1983 United Feature Syndicate, Inc.

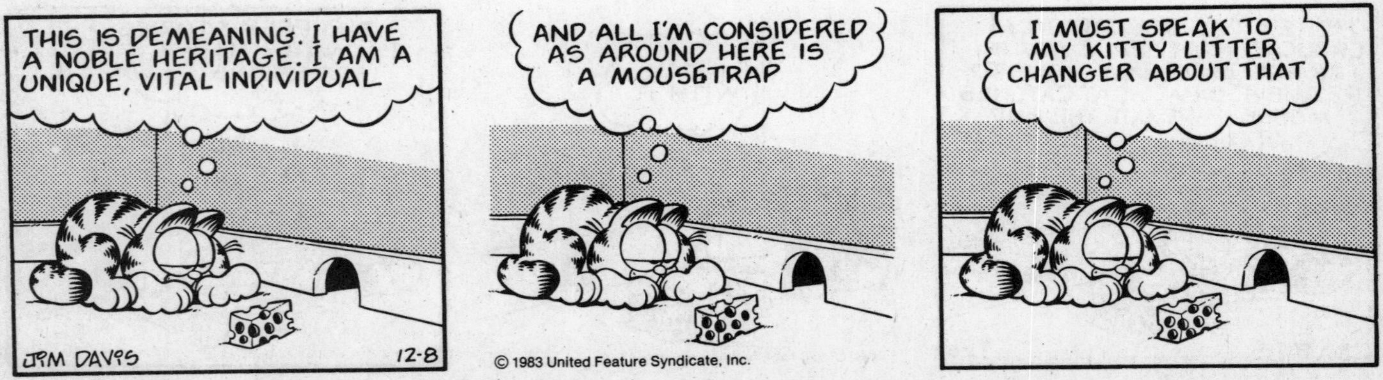
THIS IS DEMEANING. I HAVE A NOBLE HERITAGE. I AM A UNIQUE, VITAL INDIVIDUAL
JIM DAVIS 12-8
AND ALL I'M CONSIDERED AS AROUND HERE IS A MOUSETRAP
© 1983 United Feature Syndicate, Inc.
I MUST SPEAK TO MY KITTY LITTER CHANGER ABOUT THAT

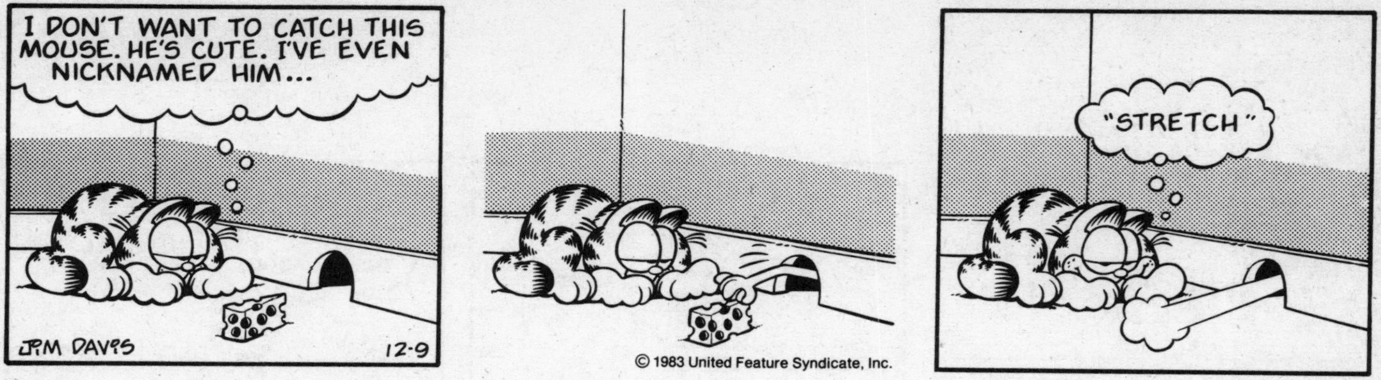
I DON'T WANT TO CATCH THIS MOUSE. HE'S CUTE. I'VE EVEN NICKNAMED HIM...
JIM DAVIS
12-9
"STRETCH"

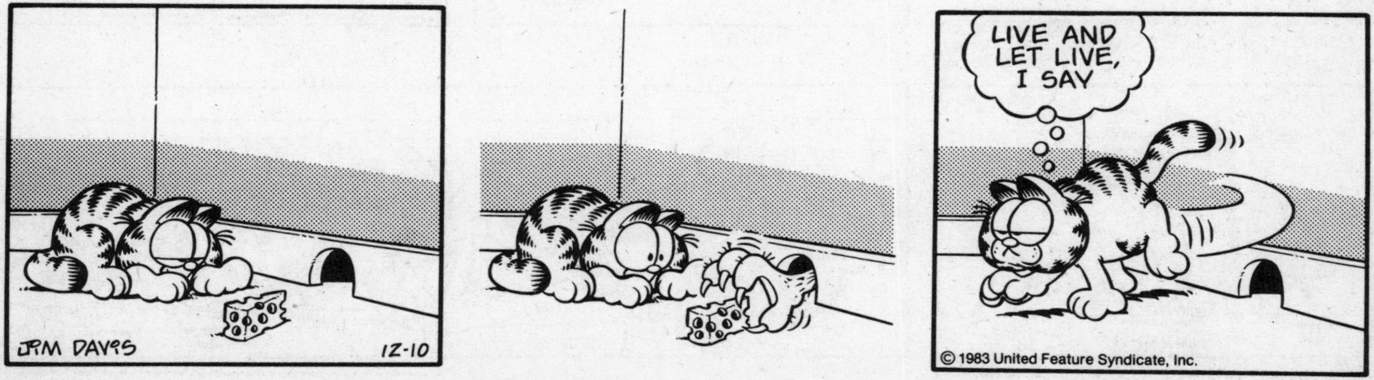
JIM DAVIS
12-10
LIVE AND LET LIVE, I SAY

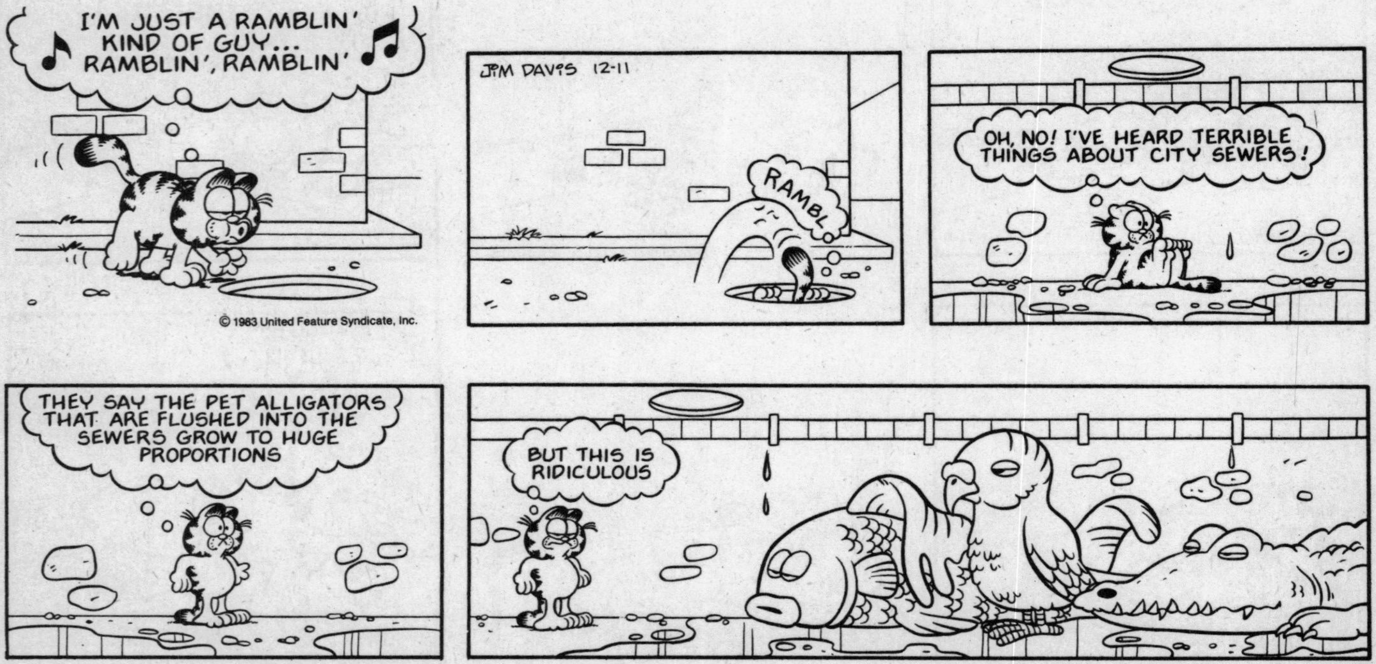
I'M JUST A RAMBLIN' KIND OF GUY... RAMBLIN', RAMBLIN'
© 1983 United Feature Syndicate, Inc.
JIM DAVIS 12-11
RAMBL
OH, NO! I'VE HEARD TERRIBLE THINGS ABOUT CITY SEWERS!
THEY SAY THE PET ALLIGATORS THAT ARE FLUSHED INTO THE SEWERS GROW TO HUGE PROPORTIONS
BUT THIS IS RIDICULOUS

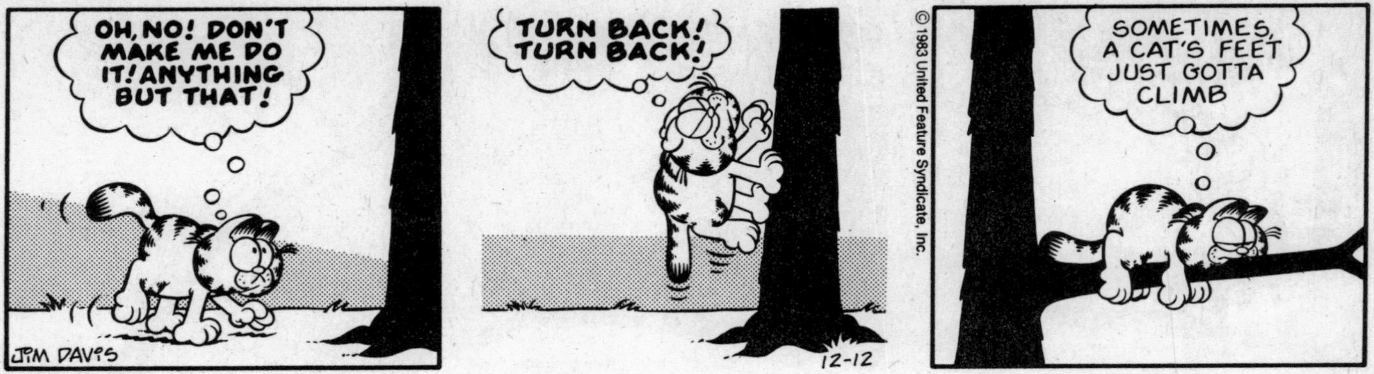
OH, NO! DON'T MAKE ME DO IT! ANYTHING BUT THAT!
JIM DAVIS
TURN BACK! TURN BACK!
12-12
© 1983 United Feature Syndicate, Inc.
SOMETIMES, A CAT'S FEET JUST GOTTA CLIMB

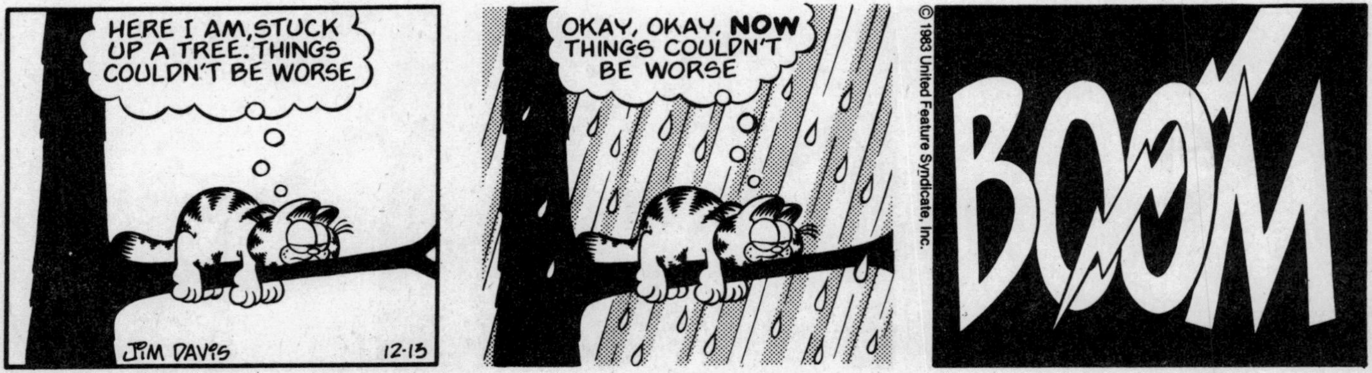
HERE I AM, STUCK UP A TREE. THINGS COULDN'T BE WORSE
JIM DAVIS
12-13
OKAY, OKAY, NOW THINGS COULDN'T BE WORSE
© 1983 United Feature Syndicate, Inc.
BOOM

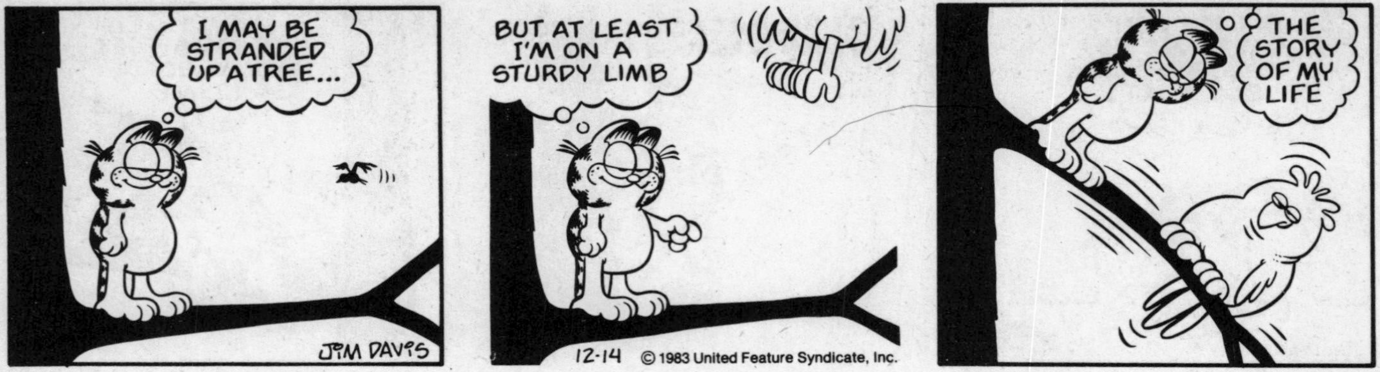
I MAY BE STRANDED UP A TREE...
JIM DAVIS
BUT AT LEAST I'M ON A STURDY LIMB
12-14
© 1983 United Feature Syndicate, Inc.
THE STORY OF MY LIFE

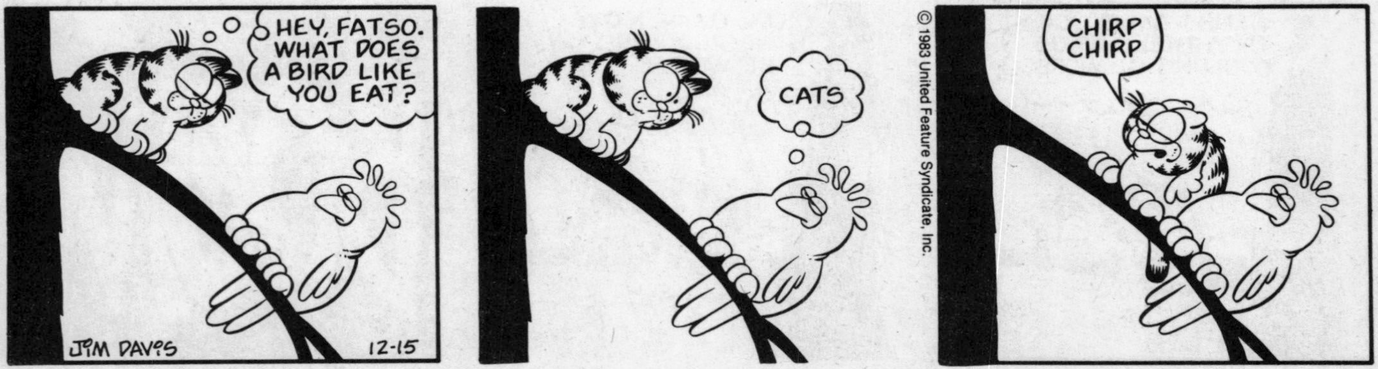
HEY, FATSO. WHAT DOES A BIRD LIKE YOU EAT?
JIM DAVIS
12-15
CATS
© 1983 United Feature Syndicate, Inc.
CHIRP CHIRP

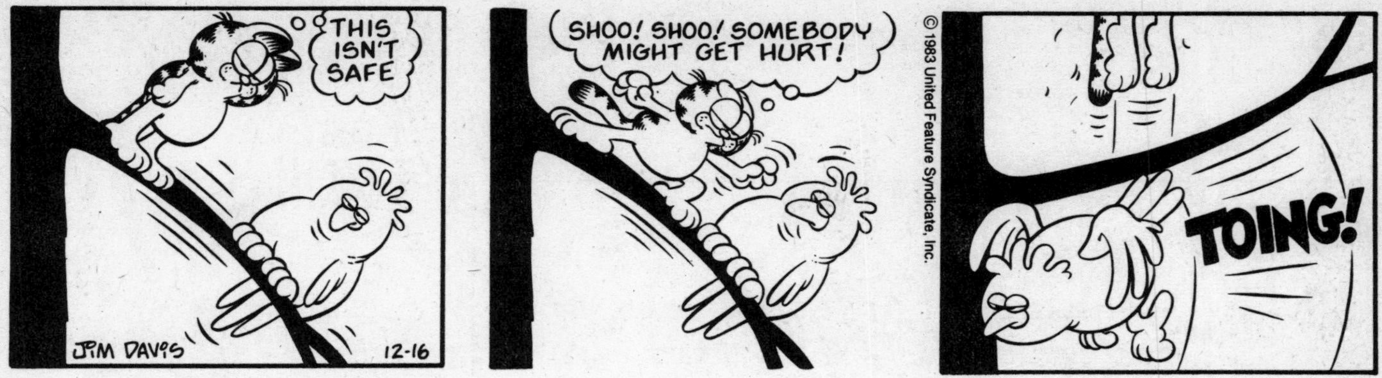
THIS ISN'T SAFE
JIM DAVIS
12-16
SHOO! SHOO! SOMEBODY MIGHT GET HURT!
© 1983 United Feature Syndicate, Inc.
TOING!

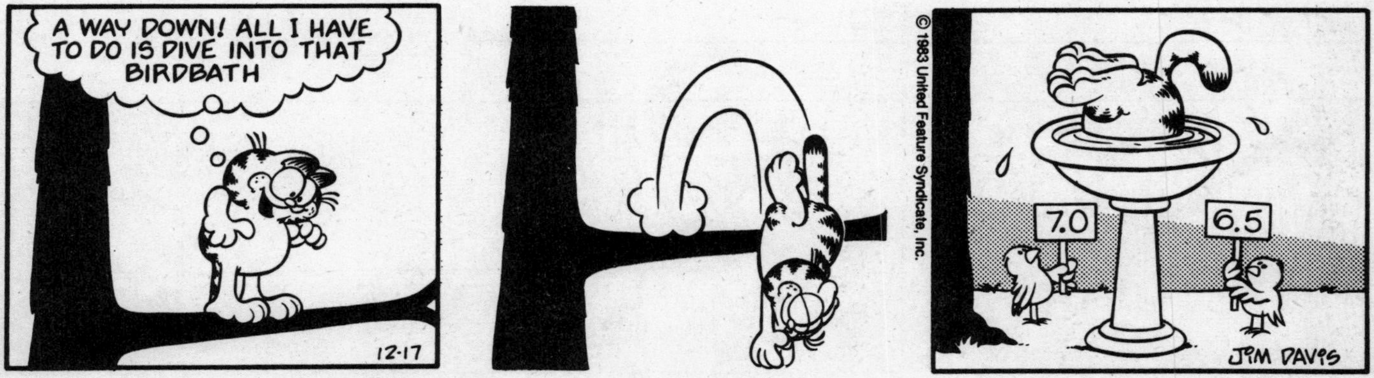
A WAY DOWN! ALL I HAVE TO DO IS DIVE INTO THAT BIRDBATH
12-17
© 1983 United Feature Syndicate, Inc.
7.0
6.5
JIM DAVIS

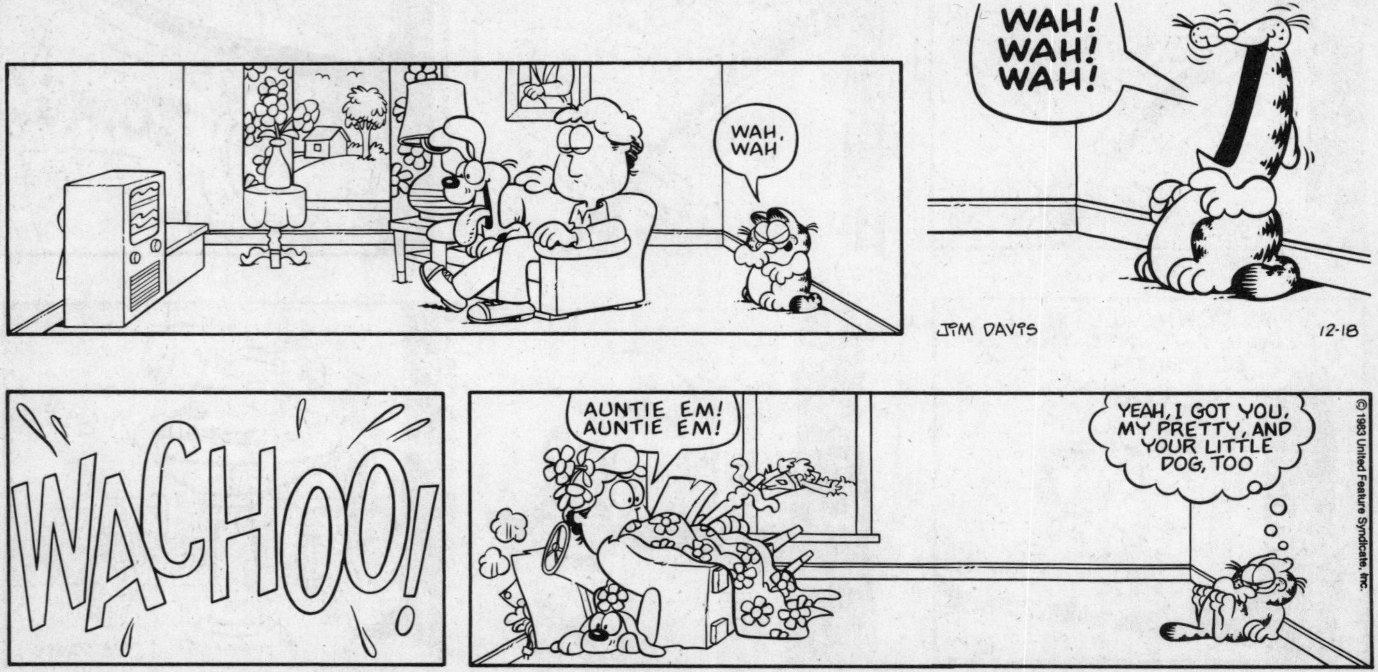
WAH, WAH
WAH! WAH! WAH!
JIM DAVIS
12-18
WACHOO!
AUNTIE EM! AUNTIE EM!
YEAH, I GOT YOU, MY PRETTY, AND YOUR LITTLE DOG, TOO
© 1983 United Feature Syndicate, Inc.

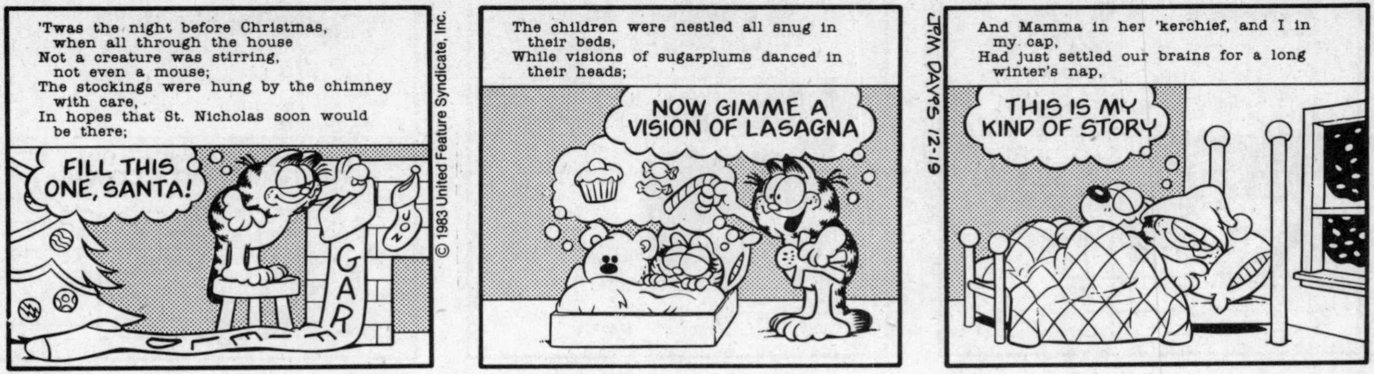
'Twas the night before Christmas, when all through the house
Not a creature was stirring, not even a mouse;
The stockings were hung by the chimney with care,
In hopes that St. Nicholas soon would be there;
FILL THIS ONE, SANTA!
© 1983 United Feature Syndicate, Inc.
The children were nestled all snug in their beds,
While visions of sugarplums danced in their heads;
NOW GIMME A VISION OF LASAGNA
JIM DAVIS 12-19
And Mamma in her 'kerchief, and I in my cap,
Had just settled our brains for a long winter's nap,
THIS IS MY KIND OF STORY

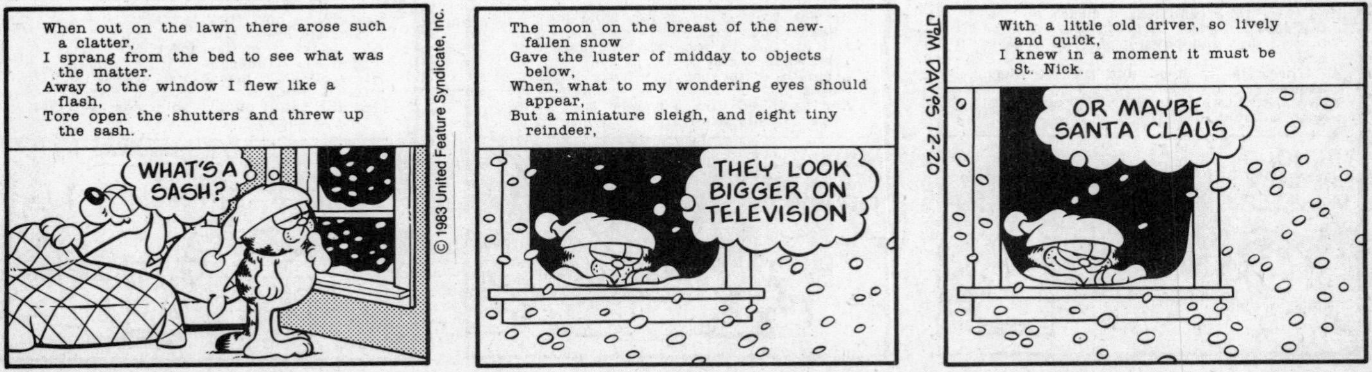
When out on the lawn there arose such a clatter,
I sprang from the bed to see what was the matter.
Away to the window I flew like a flash,
Tore open the shutters and threw up the sash.
WHAT'S A SASH?
© 1983 United Feature Syndicate, Inc.
The moon on the breast of the new-fallen snow
Gave the luster of midday to objects below,
When, what to my wondering eyes should appear,
But a miniature sleigh, and eight tiny reindeer,
THEY LOOK BIGGER ON TELEVISION
JIM DAVIS 12-20
With a little old driver, so lively and quick,
I knew in a moment it must be St. Nick.
OR MAYBE SANTA CLAUS

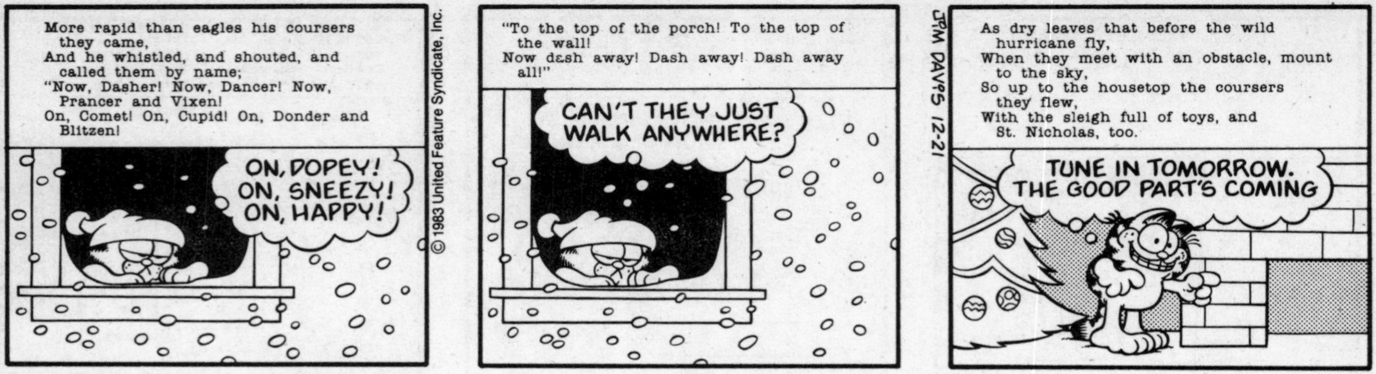
More rapid than eagles his coursers they came,
And he whistled, and shouted, and called them by name;
"Now, Dasher! Now, Dancer! Now, Prancer and Vixen!
On, Comet! On, Cupid! On, Donder and Blitzen!
ON, DOPEY! ON, SNEEZY! ON, HAPPY!
© 1983 United Feature Syndicate, Inc.
"To the top of the porch! To the top of the wall!
Now dash away! Dash away! Dash away all!"
CAN'T THEY JUST WALK ANYWHERE?
JIM DAVIS 12-21
As dry leaves that before the wild hurricane fly,
When they meet with an obstacle, mount to the sky,
So up to the housetop the coursers they flew,
With the sleigh full of toys, and St. Nicholas, too.
TUNE IN TOMORROW. THE GOOD PART'S COMING

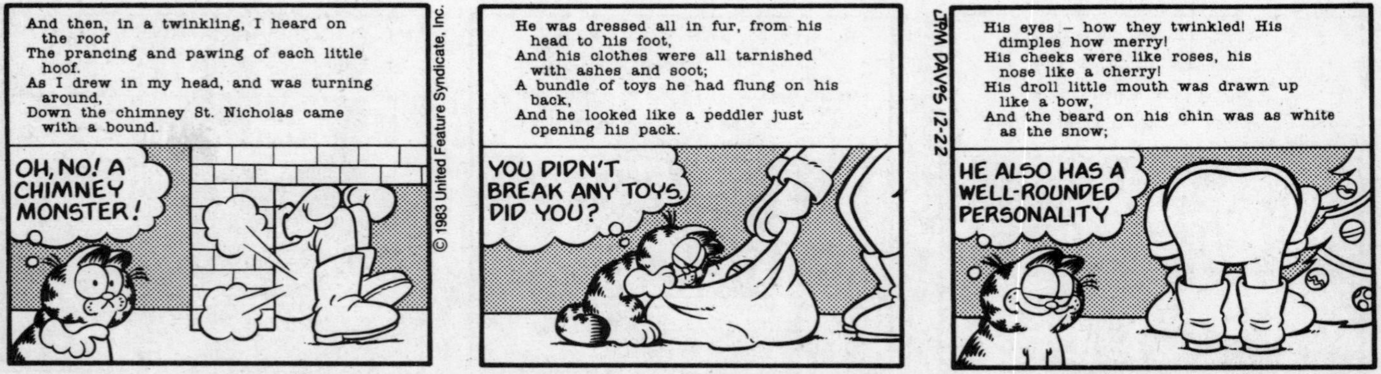
And then, in a twinkling, I heard on the roof
The prancing and pawing of each little hoof.
As I drew in my head, and was turning around,
Down the chimney St. Nicholas came with a bound.
OH, NO! A CHIMNEY MONSTER!
© 1983 United Feature Syndicate, Inc.
He was dressed all in fur, from his head to his foot,
And his clothes were all tarnished with ashes and soot;
A bundle of toys he had flung on his back,
And he looked like a peddler just opening his pack.
YOU DIDN'T BREAK ANY TOYS. DID YOU?
JIM DAVIS 12-22
His eyes – how they twinkled! His dimples how merry!
His cheeks were like roses, his nose like a cherry!
His droll little mouth was drawn up like a bow,
And the beard on his chin was as white as the snow;
HE ALSO HAS A WELL-ROUNDED PERSONALITY

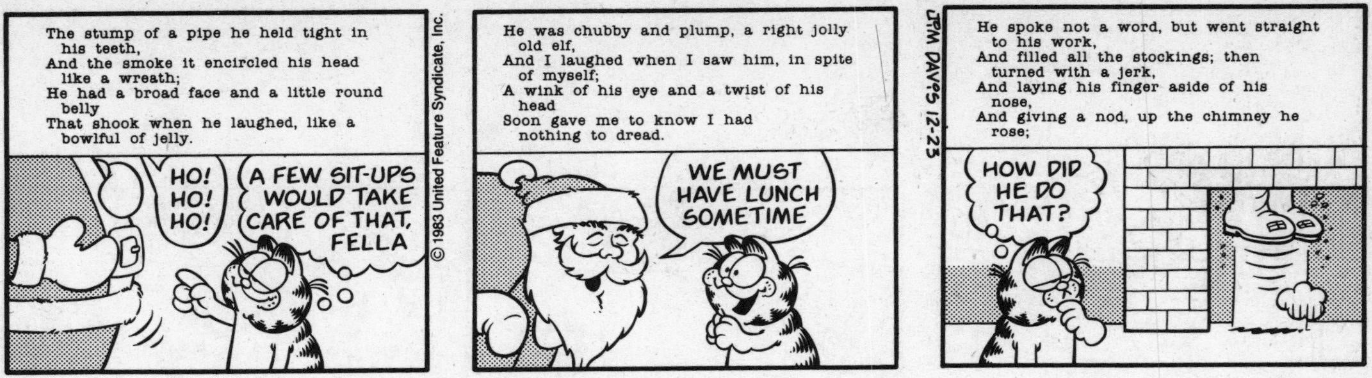
The stump of a pipe he held tight in his teeth,
And the smoke it encircled his head like a wreath;
He had a broad face and a little round belly
That shook when he laughed, like a bowlful of jelly.
HO! HO! HO!
A FEW SIT-UPS WOULD TAKE CARE OF THAT, FELLA
© 1983 United Feature Syndicate, Inc.
He was chubby and plump, a right jolly old elf,
And I laughed when I saw him, in spite of myself;
A wink of his eye and a twist of his head
Soon gave me to know I had nothing to dread.
WE MUST HAVE LUNCH SOMETIME
JPM DAVPS 12-23
He spoke not a word, but went straight to his work,
And filled all the stockings; then turned with a jerk,
And laying his finger aside of his nose,
And giving a nod, up the chimney he rose;
HOW DID HE DO THAT?

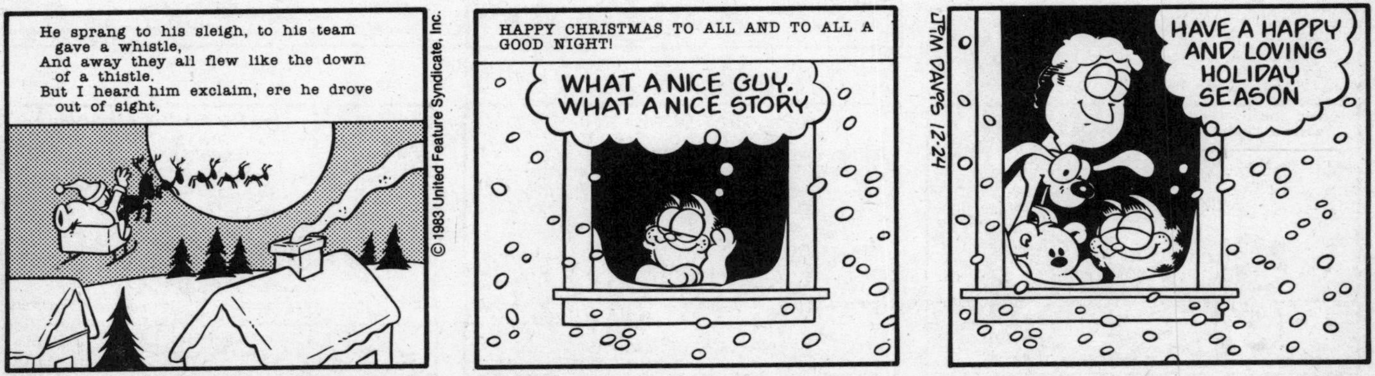
He sprang to his sleigh, to his team gave a whistle,
And away they all flew like the down of a thistle.
But I heard him exclaim, ere he drove out of sight,
© 1983 United Feature Syndicate, Inc.
HAPPY CHRISTMAS TO ALL AND TO ALL A GOOD NIGHT!
WHAT A NICE GUY. WHAT A NICE STORY
JPM DAVPS 12-24
HAVE A HAPPY AND LOVING HOLIDAY SEASON

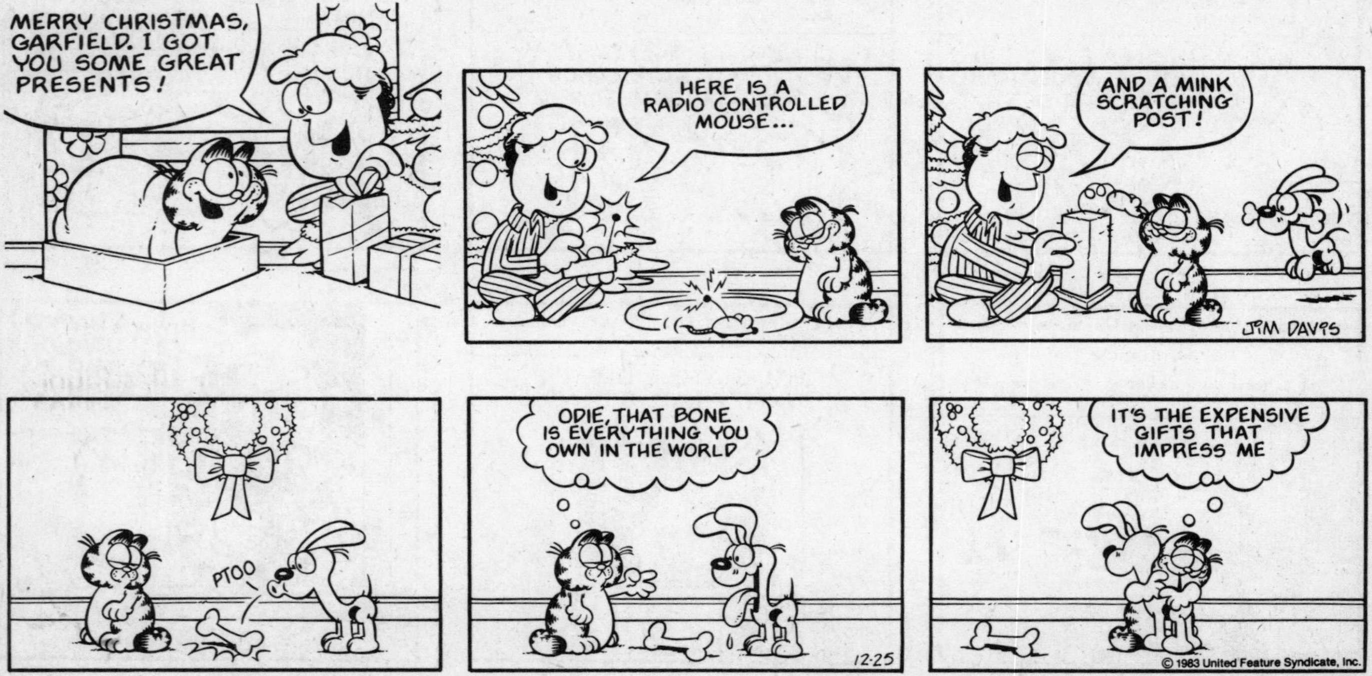
MERRY CHRISTMAS, GARFIELD. I GOT YOU SOME GREAT PRESENTS!
HERE IS A RADIO CONTROLLED MOUSE...
AND A MINK SCRATCHING POST!
JIM DAVIS
PTOO
ODIE, THAT BONE IS EVERYTHING YOU OWN IN THE WORLD
12·25
IT'S THE EXPENSIVE GIFTS THAT IMPRESS ME
© 1983 United Feature Syndicate, Inc.

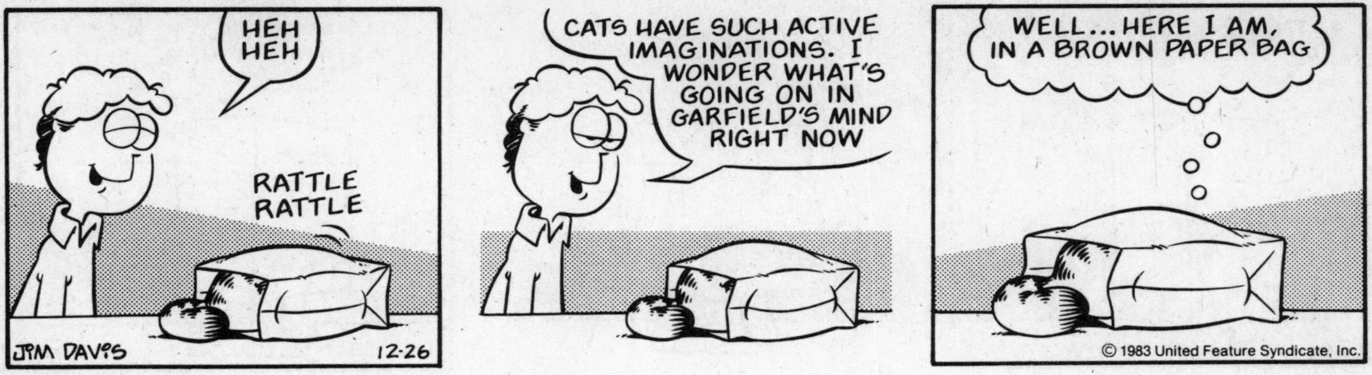
HEH HEH
RATTLE RATTLE
JIM DAVIS 12-26
CATS HAVE SUCH ACTIVE IMAGINATIONS. I WONDER WHAT'S GOING ON IN GARFIELD'S MIND RIGHT NOW
WELL... HERE I AM, IN A BROWN PAPER BAG
© 1983 United Feature Syndicate, Inc.

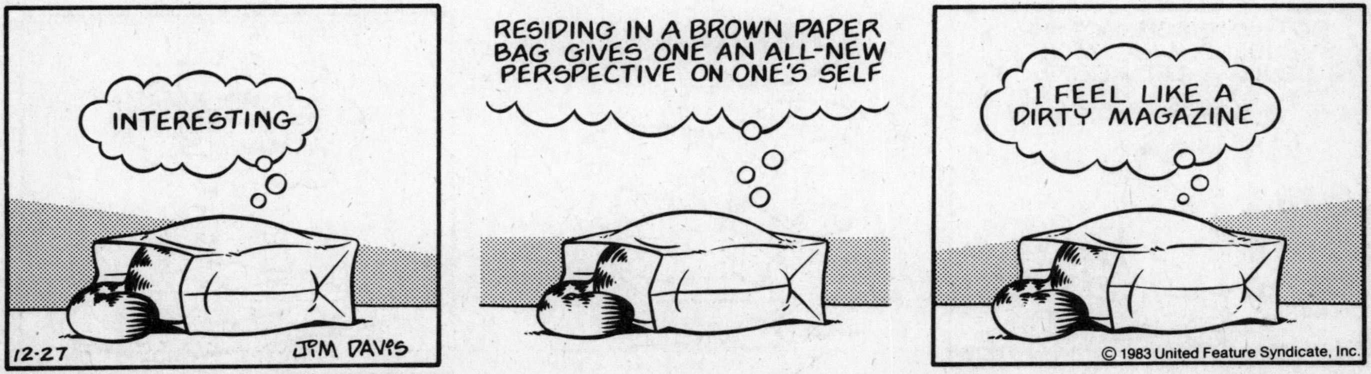
INTERESTING
12-27 JIM DAVIS
RESIDING IN A BROWN PAPER BAG GIVES ONE AN ALL-NEW PERSPECTIVE ON ONE'S SELF
I FEEL LIKE A DIRTY MAGAZINE
© 1983 United Feature Syndicate, Inc.

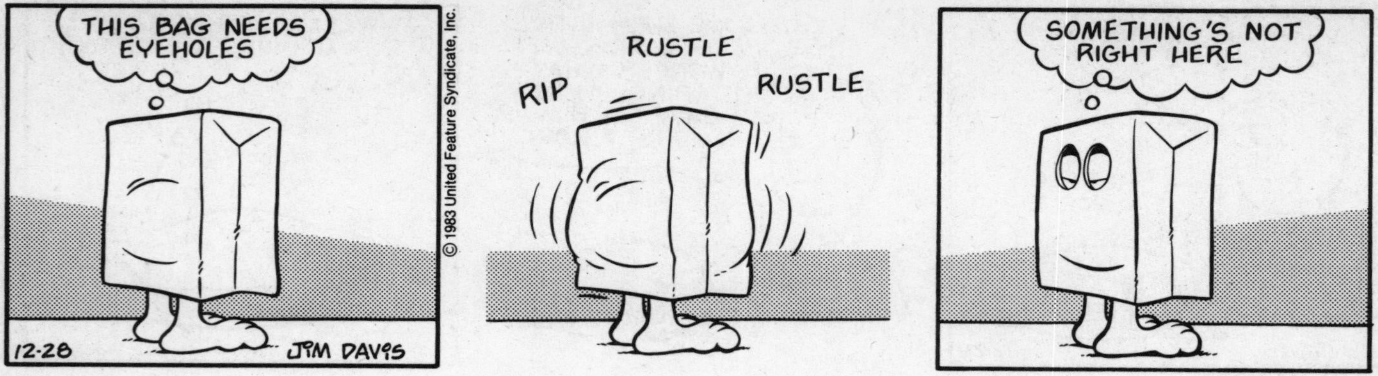
THIS BAG NEEDS EYEHOLES
12-28
JIM DAVIS
RIP
RUSTLE
RUSTLE
SOMETHING'S NOT RIGHT HERE

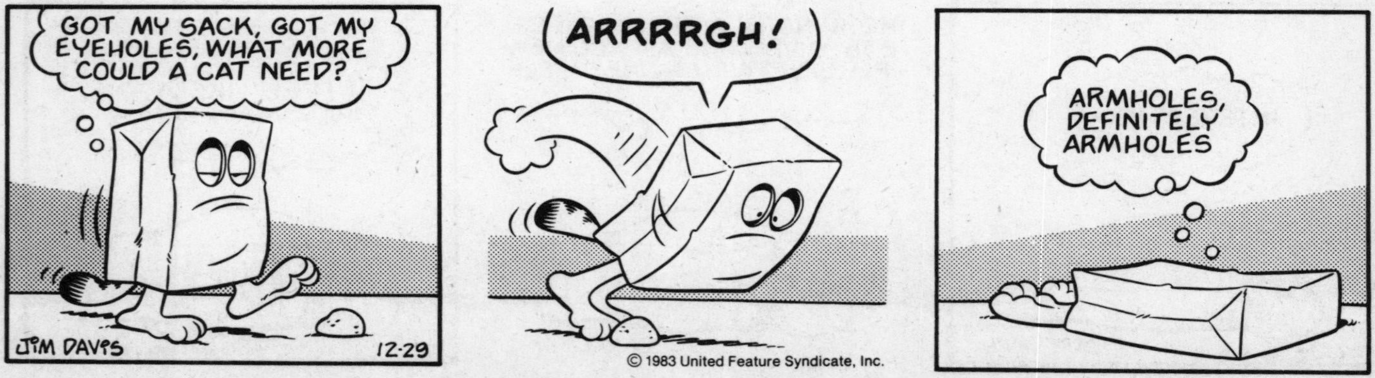
GOT MY SACK, GOT MY EYEHOLES, WHAT MORE COULD A CAT NEED?
JIM DAVIS
12-29
ARRRRGH!
ARMHOLES, DEFINITELY ARMHOLES

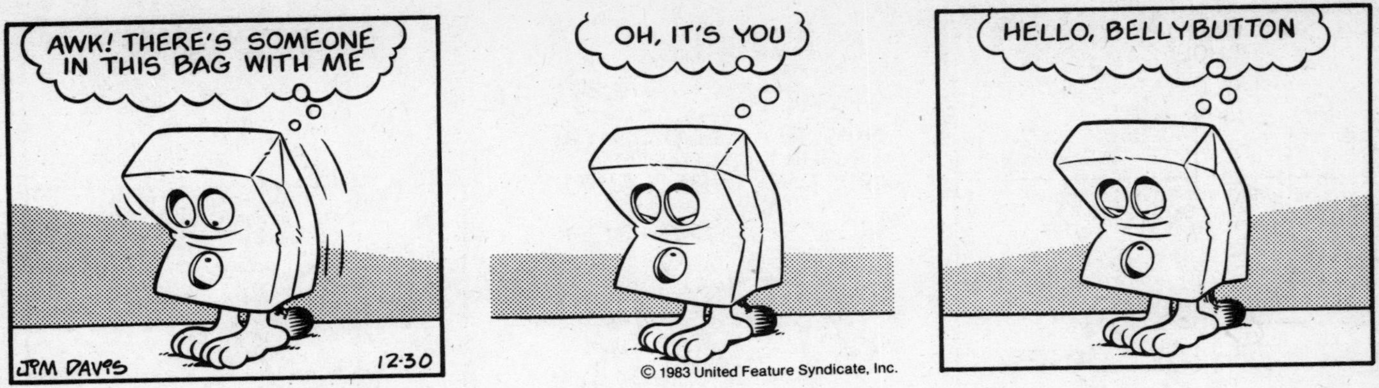
AWK! THERE'S SOMEONE IN THIS BAG WITH ME
JIM DAVIS
12-30
OH, IT'S YOU
HELLO, BELLYBUTTON

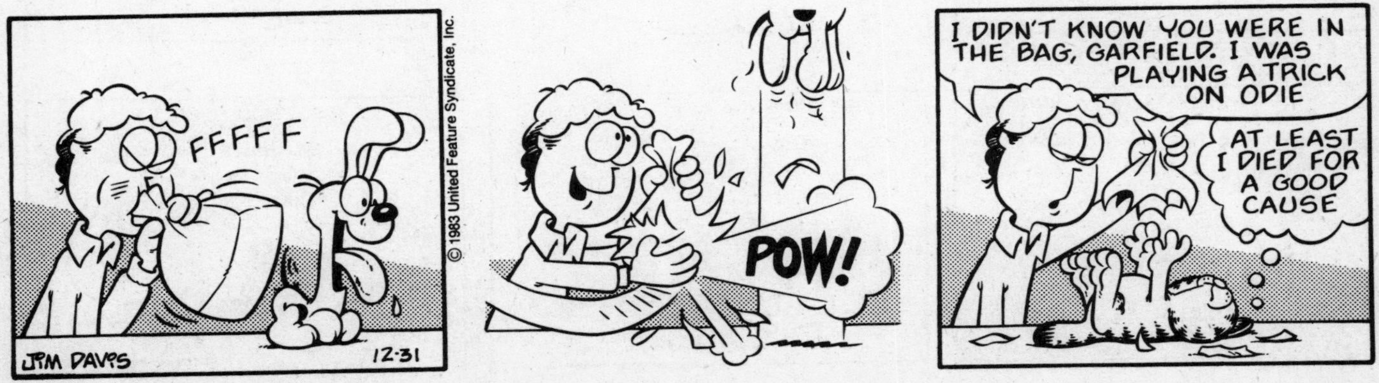
FFFFF
JIM DAVIS
12-31
POW!
I DIDN'T KNOW YOU WERE IN THE BAG, GARFIELD. I WAS PLAYING A TRICK ON ODIE
AT LEAST I DIED FOR A GOOD CAUSE

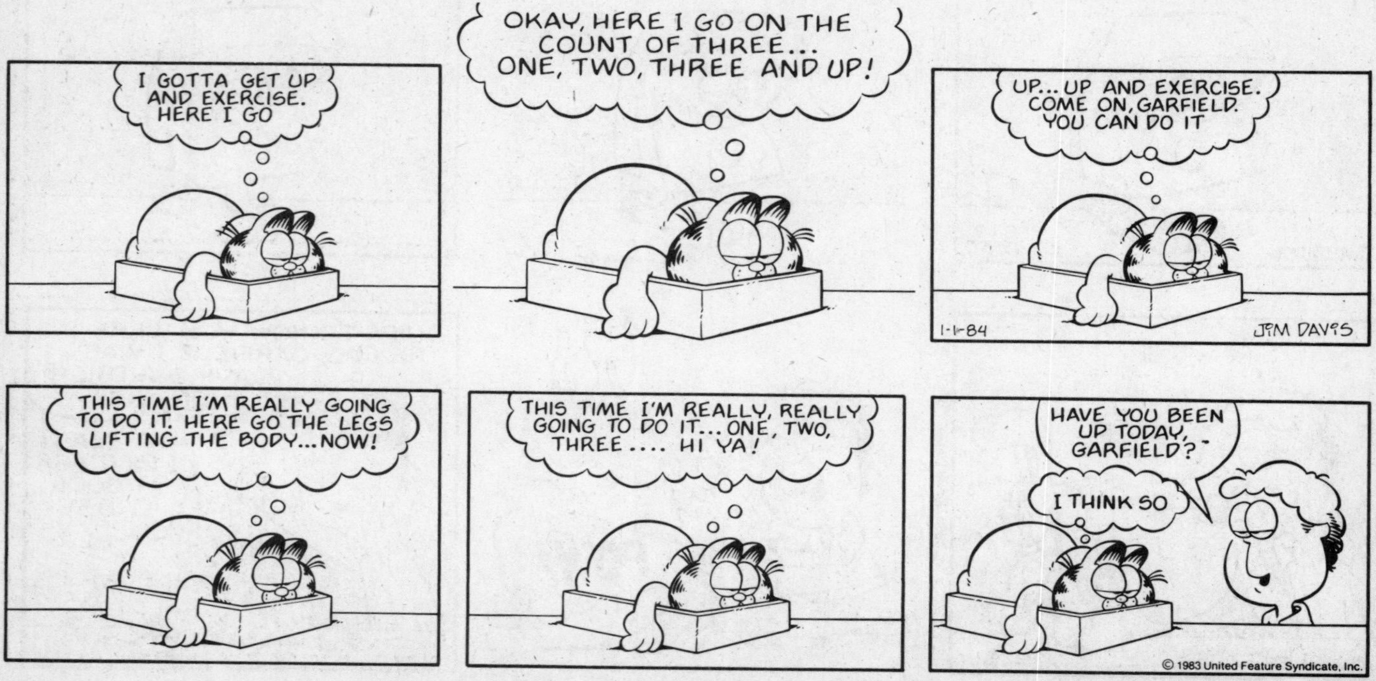
I GOTTA GET UP AND EXERCISE. HERE I GO
OKAY, HERE I GO ON THE COUNT OF THREE... ONE, TWO, THREE AND UP!
UP... UP AND EXERCISE. COME ON, GARFIELD. YOU CAN DO IT
1-1-84
JIM DAVIS
THIS TIME I'M REALLY GOING TO DO IT. HERE GO THE LEGS LIFTING THE BODY... NOW!
THIS TIME I'M REALLY, REALLY GOING TO DO IT... ONE, TWO, THREE.... HI YA!
HAVE YOU BEEN UP TODAY, GARFIELD?
I THINK SO
© 1983 United Feature Syndicate, Inc.

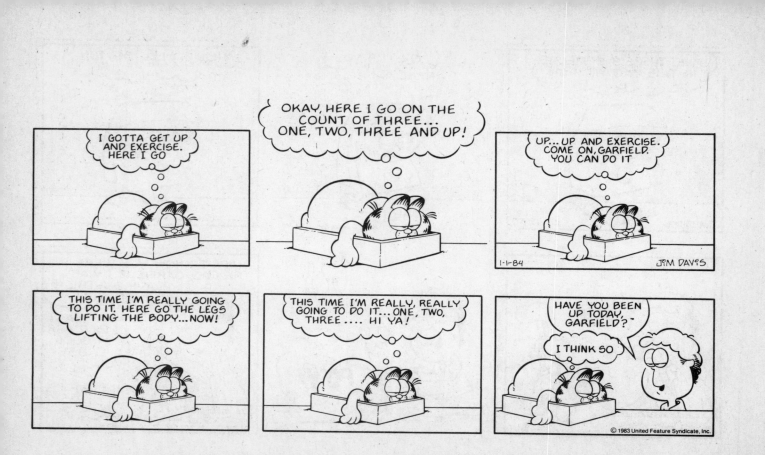

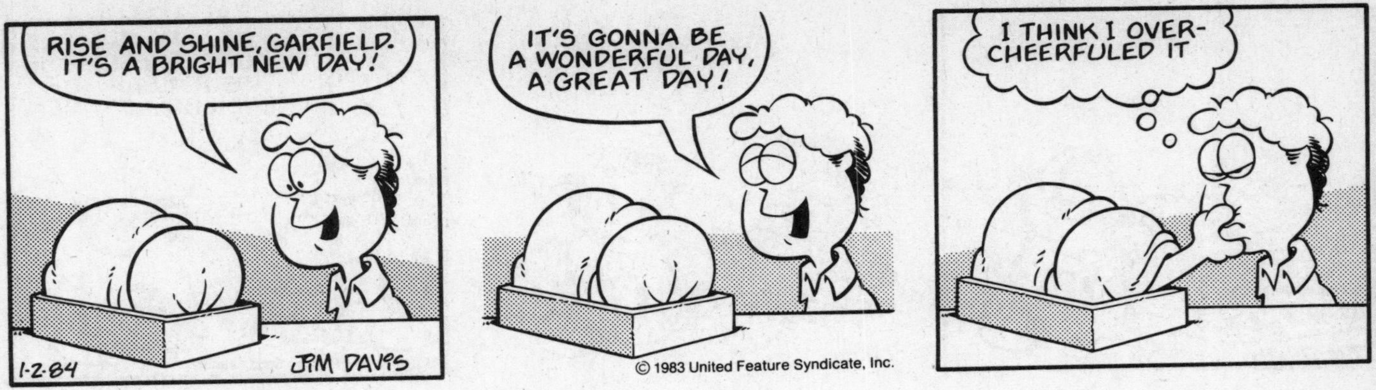
RISE AND SHINE, GARFIELD. IT'S A BRIGHT NEW DAY!
1-2-84
JIM DAVIS
IT'S GONNA BE A WONDERFUL DAY, A GREAT DAY!
I THINK I OVER-CHEERFULED IT

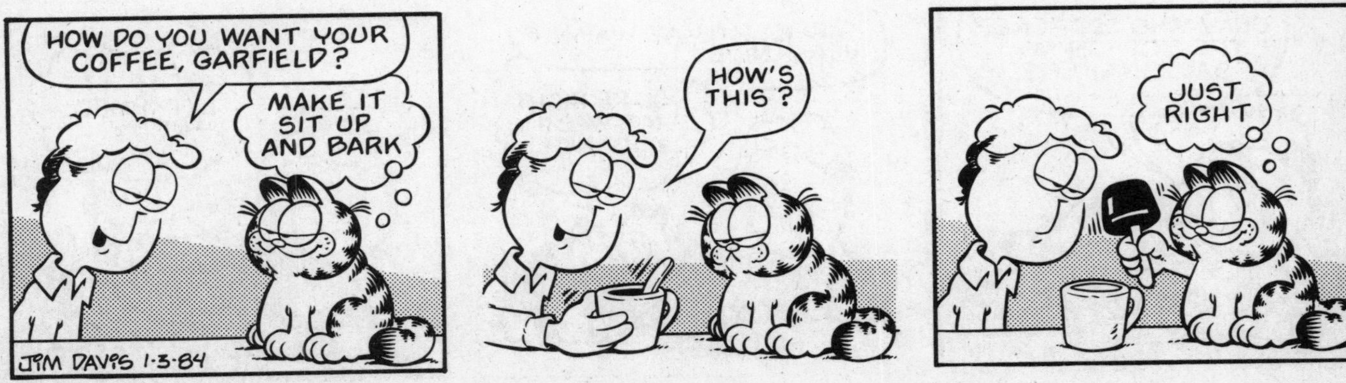
HOW DO YOU WANT YOUR COFFEE, GARFIELD?
MAKE IT SIT UP AND BARK
JIM DAVIS 1-3-84
HOW'S THIS?
JUST RIGHT

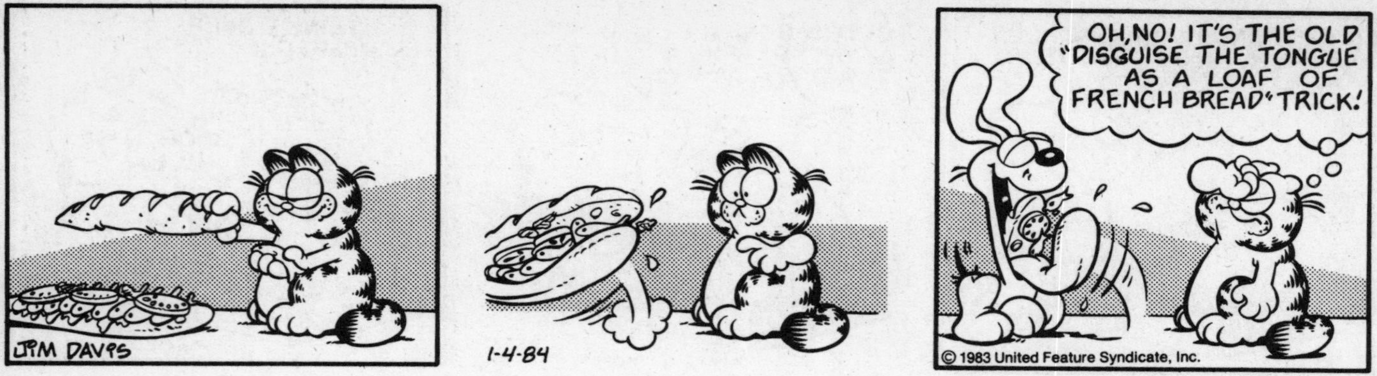
JIM DAVIS
1-4-84
OH, NO! IT'S THE OLD "DISGUISE THE TONGUE AS A LOAF OF FRENCH BREAD" TRICK!
© 1983 United Feature Syndicate, Inc.

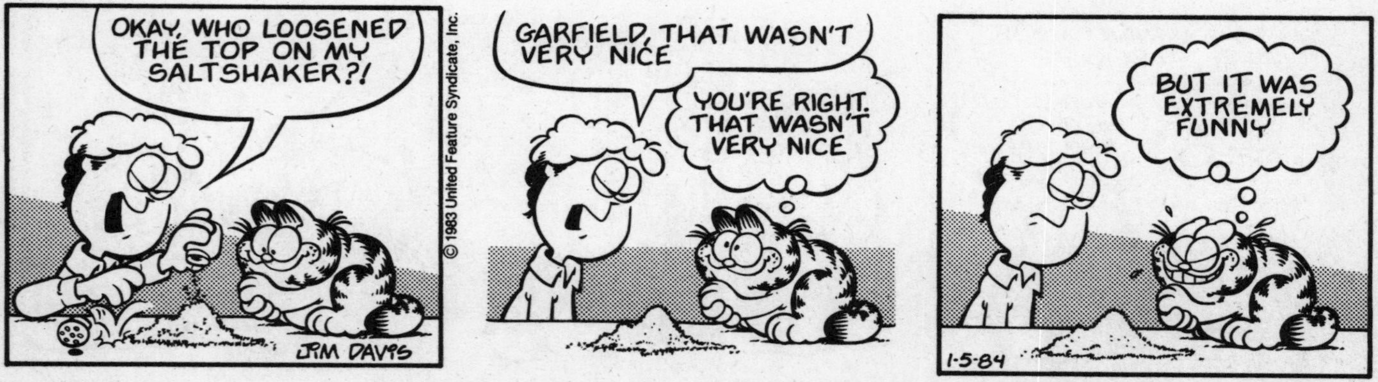
OKAY, WHO LOOSENED THE TOP ON MY SALTSHAKER?!
JIM DAVIS
© 1983 United Feature Syndicate, Inc.
GARFIELD, THAT WASN'T VERY NICE
YOU'RE RIGHT. THAT WASN'T VERY NICE
BUT IT WAS EXTREMELY FUNNY
1-5-84

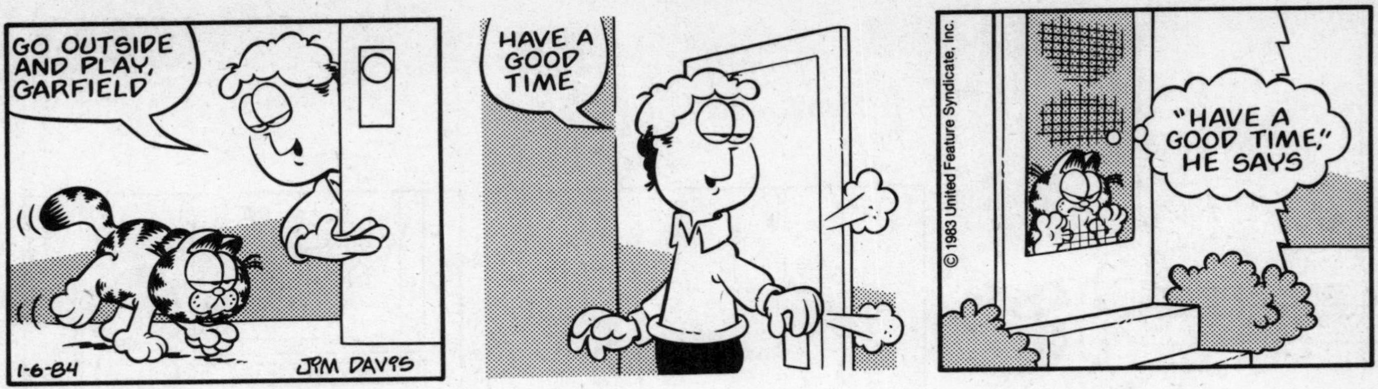
GO OUTSIDE AND PLAY, GARFIELD
1-6-84
JIM DAVIS
HAVE A GOOD TIME
© 1983 United Feature Syndicate, Inc.
"HAVE A GOOD TIME," HE SAYS

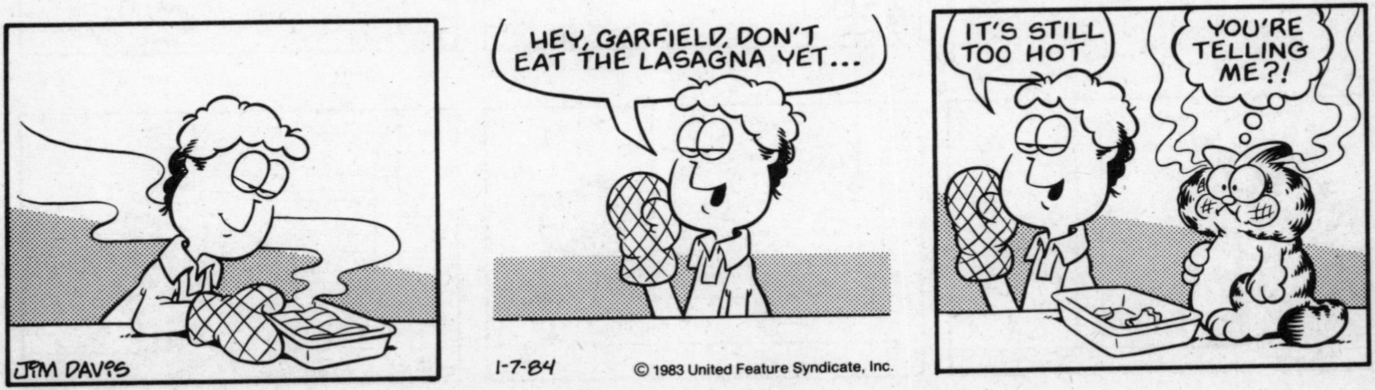
JIM DAVIS
HEY, GARFIELD, DON'T EAT THE LASAGNA YET...
1-7-84
© 1983 United Feature Syndicate, Inc.
IT'S STILL TOO HOT
YOU'RE TELLING ME?!

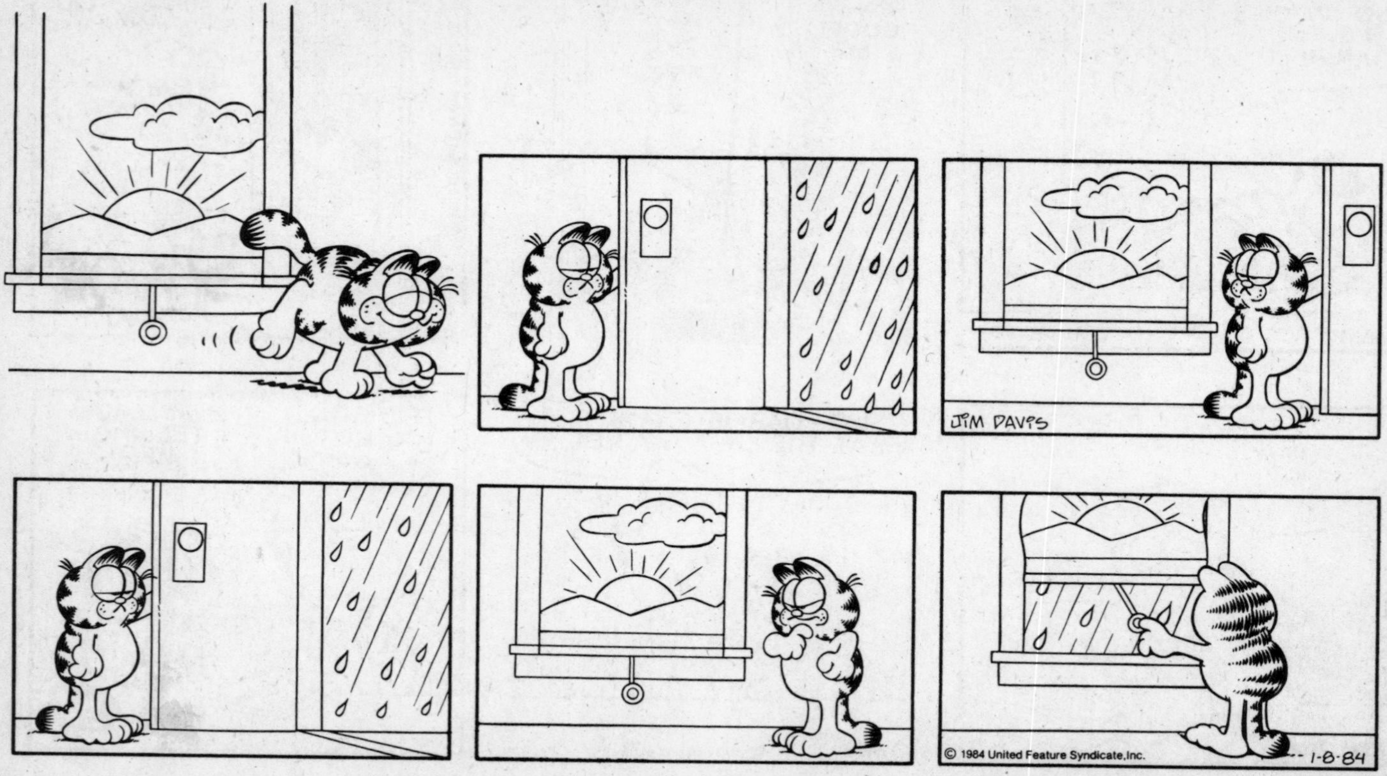
JIM DAVIS
© 1984 United Feature Syndicate, Inc.
1-8-84

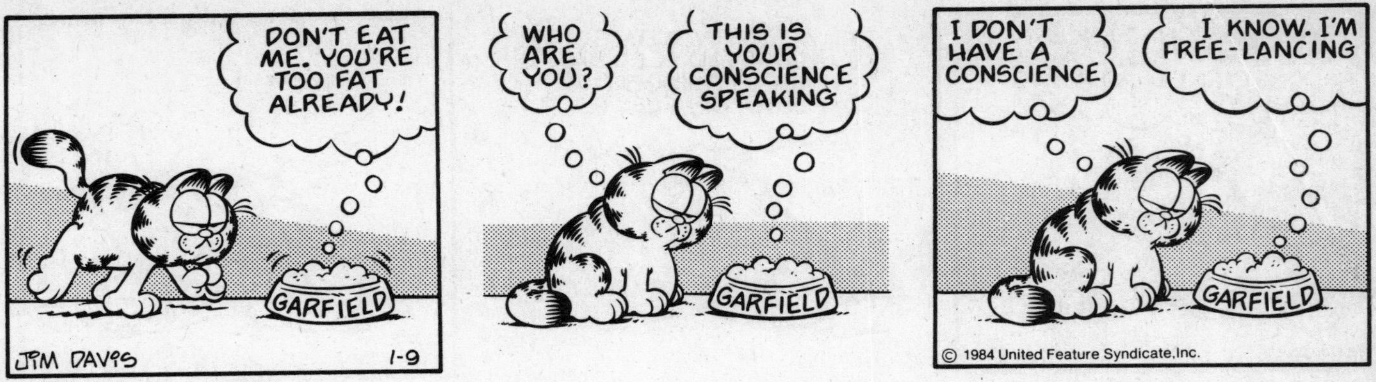
DON'T EAT ME. YOU'RE TOO FAT ALREADY!
WHO ARE YOU?
THIS IS YOUR CONSCIENCE SPEAKING
I DON'T HAVE A CONSCIENCE
I KNOW. I'M FREE-LANCING
GARFIELD
JIM DAVIS 1-9
© 1984 United Feature Syndicate, Inc.

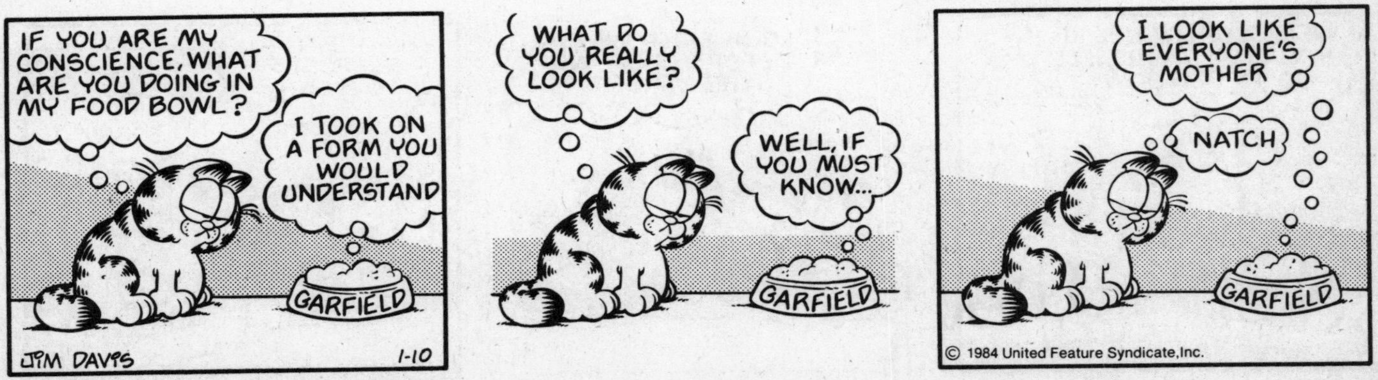
IF YOU ARE MY CONSCIENCE, WHAT ARE YOU DOING IN MY FOOD BOWL?
I TOOK ON A FORM YOU WOULD UNDERSTAND
WHAT DO YOU REALLY LOOK LIKE?
WELL, IF YOU MUST KNOW...
I LOOK LIKE EVERYONE'S MOTHER
NATCH
GARFIELD
JIM DAVIS 1-10
© 1984 United Feature Syndicate, Inc.

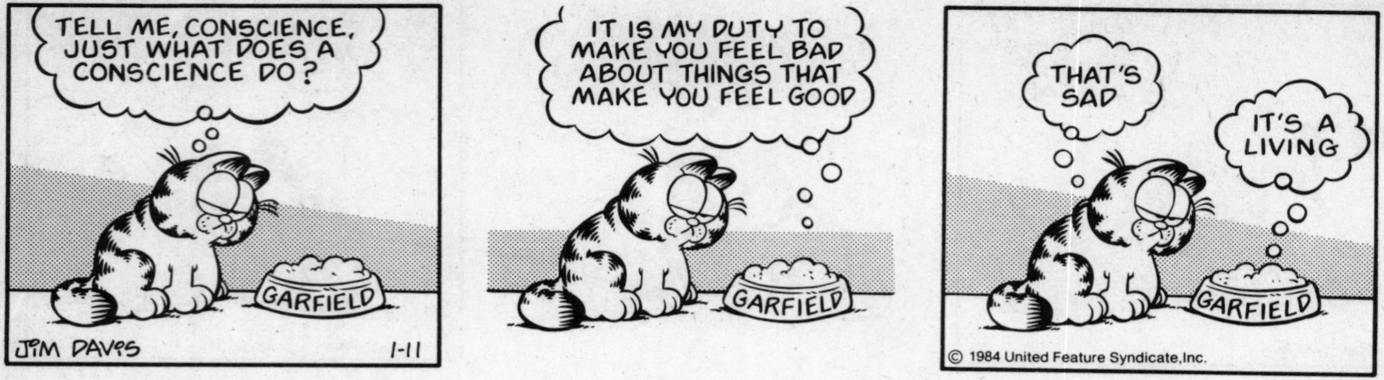
TELL ME, CONSCIENCE, JUST WHAT DOES A CONSCIENCE DO?
JIM DAVIS 1-11
IT IS MY DUTY TO MAKE YOU FEEL BAD ABOUT THINGS THAT MAKE YOU FEEL GOOD
GARFIELD
THAT'S SAD
IT'S A LIVING
© 1984 United Feature Syndicate,Inc.

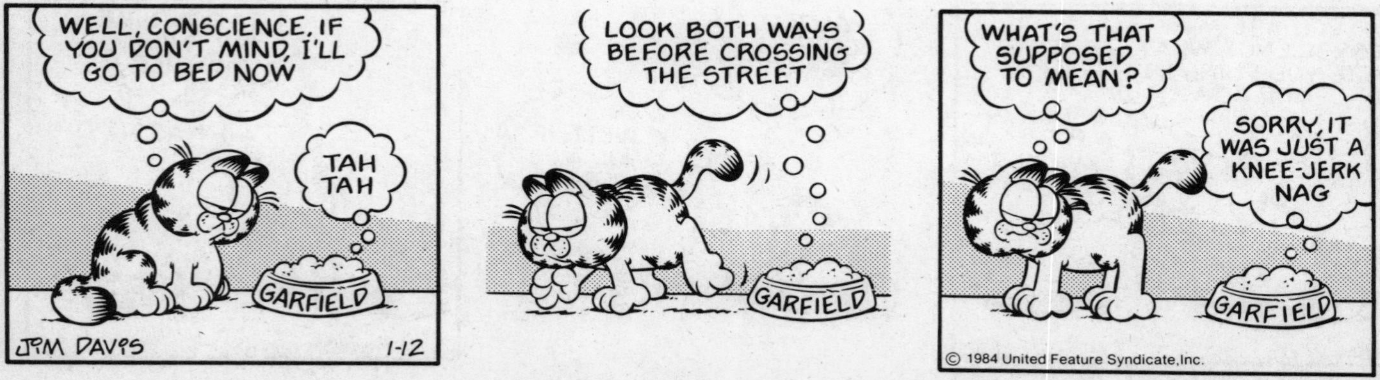
WELL, CONSCIENCE, IF YOU DON'T MIND, I'LL GO TO BED NOW
TAH TAH
JIM DAVIS 1-12
LOOK BOTH WAYS BEFORE CROSSING THE STREET
GARFIELD
WHAT'S THAT SUPPOSED TO MEAN?
SORRY, IT WAS JUST A KNEE-JERK NAG
© 1984 United Feature Syndicate,Inc.

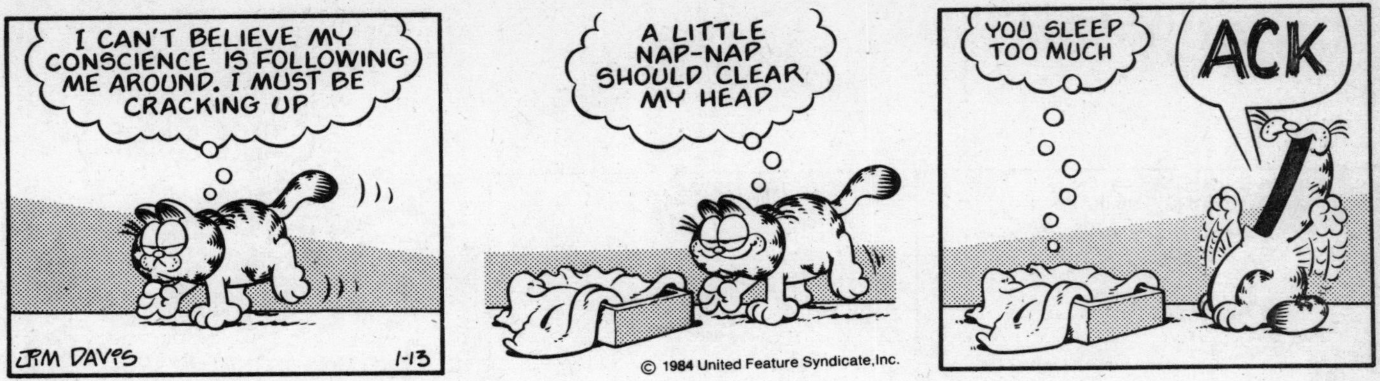
I CAN'T BELIEVE MY CONSCIENCE IS FOLLOWING ME AROUND. I MUST BE CRACKING UP
JIM DAVIS
1-13
A LITTLE NAP-NAP SHOULD CLEAR MY HEAD
© 1984 United Feature Syndicate, Inc.
YOU SLEEP TOO MUCH
ACK

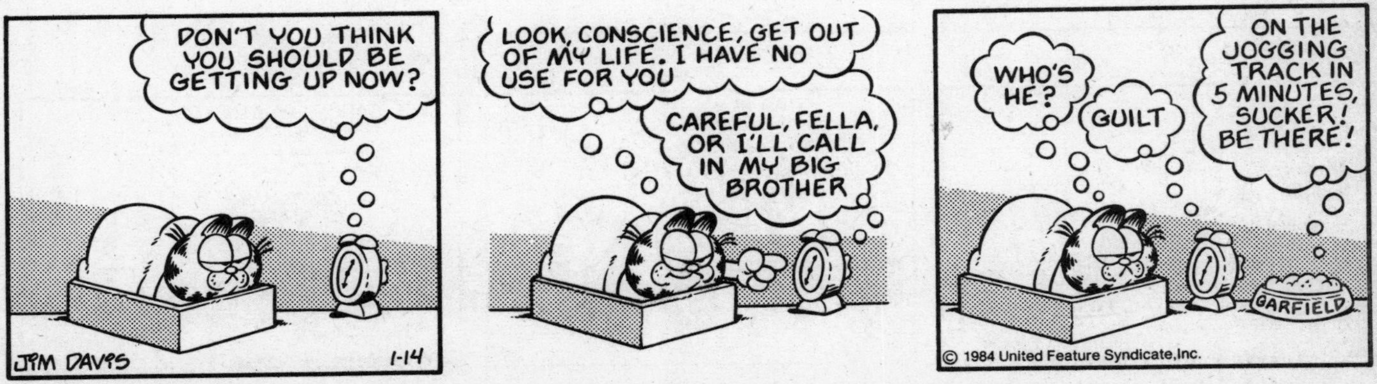
DON'T YOU THINK YOU SHOULD BE GETTING UP NOW?
JIM DAVIS
1-14
LOOK, CONSCIENCE, GET OUT OF MY LIFE. I HAVE NO USE FOR YOU
CAREFUL, FELLA, OR I'LL CALL IN MY BIG BROTHER
WHO'S HE?
GUILT
ON THE JOGGING TRACK IN 5 MINUTES, SUCKER! BE THERE!
GARFIELD
© 1984 United Feature Syndicate, Inc.

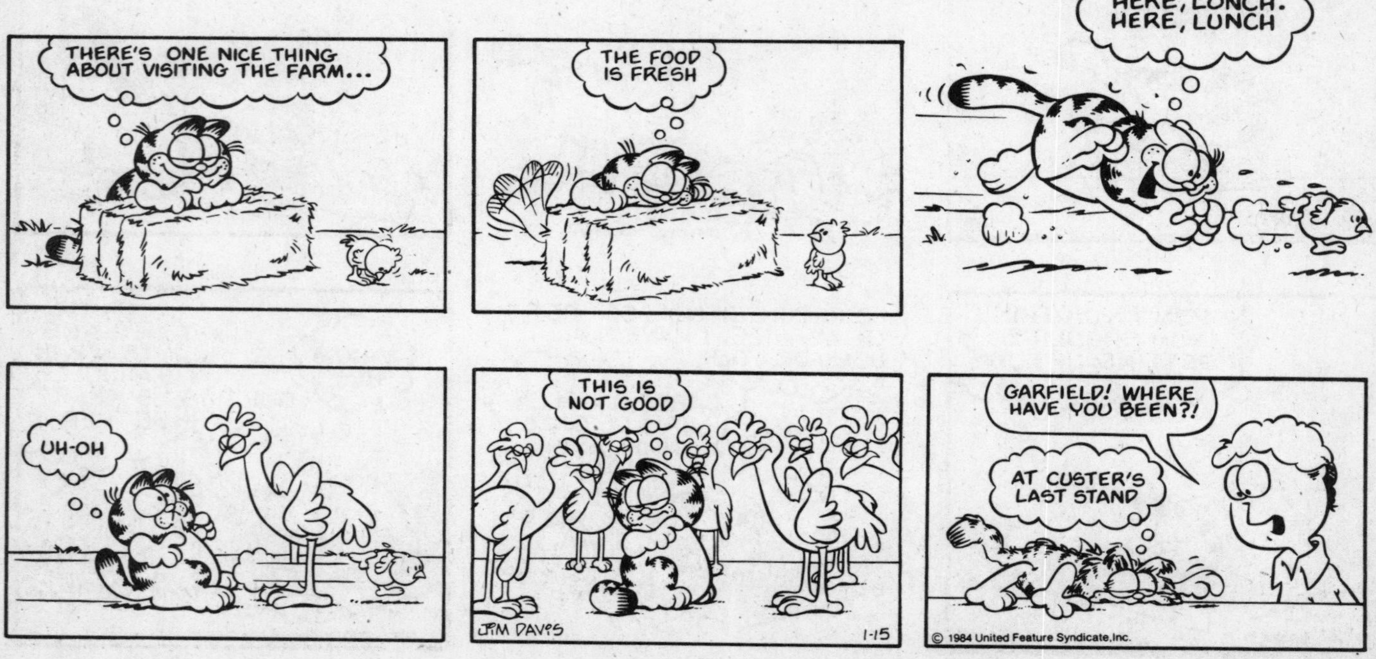
THERE'S ONE NICE THING ABOUT VISITING THE FARM...
THE FOOD IS FRESH
HERE, LUNCH. HERE, LUNCH
UH-OH
THIS IS NOT GOOD
JIM DAVIS
1-15
GARFIELD! WHERE HAVE YOU BEEN?!
AT CUSTER'S LAST STAND
© 1984 United Feature Syndicate, Inc.

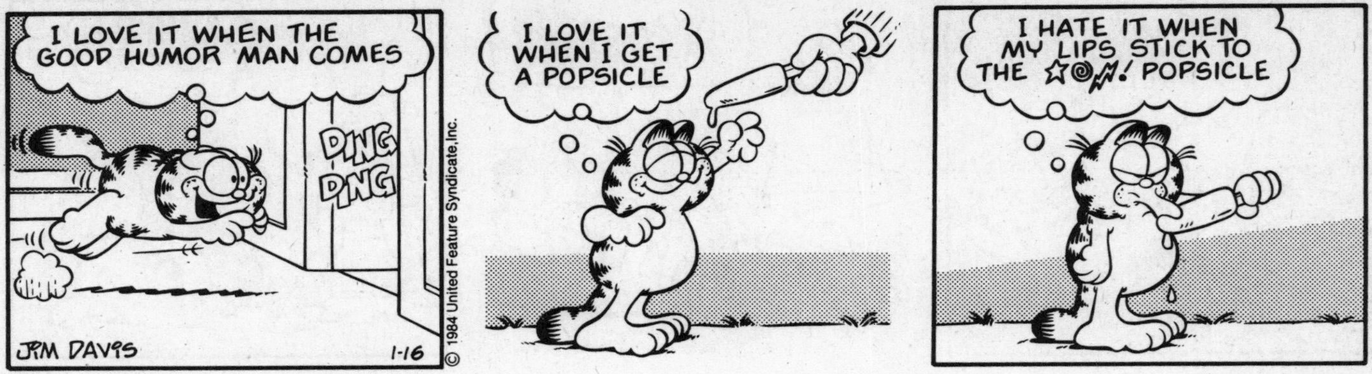
I LOVE IT WHEN THE GOOD HUMOR MAN COMES
DING DING
JIM DAVIS
1-16
© 1984 United Feature Syndicate, Inc.
I LOVE IT WHEN I GET A POPSICLE
I HATE IT WHEN MY LIPS STICK TO THE ☆@⚡! POPSICLE

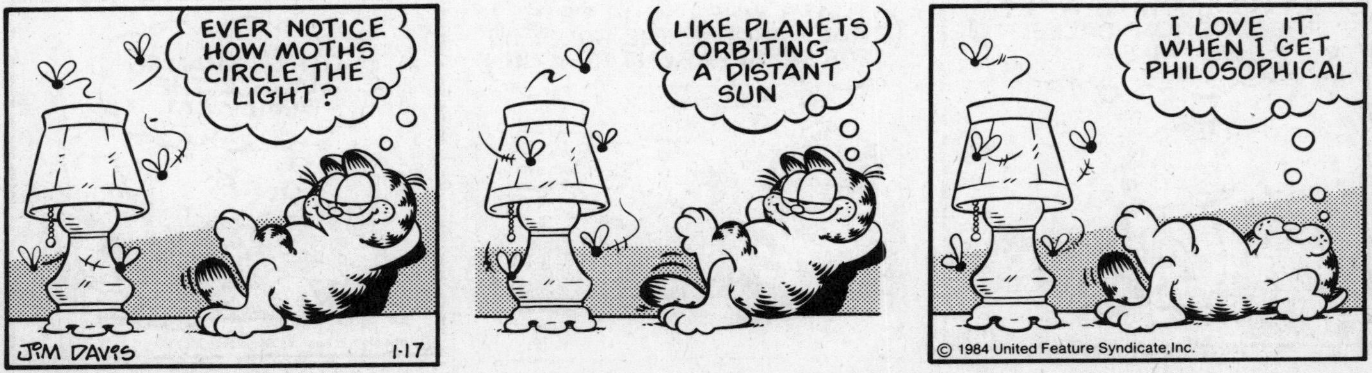
EVER NOTICE HOW MOTHS CIRCLE THE LIGHT?
JIM DAVIS
1-17
LIKE PLANETS ORBITING A DISTANT SUN
I LOVE IT WHEN I GET PHILOSOPHICAL
© 1984 United Feature Syndicate, Inc.

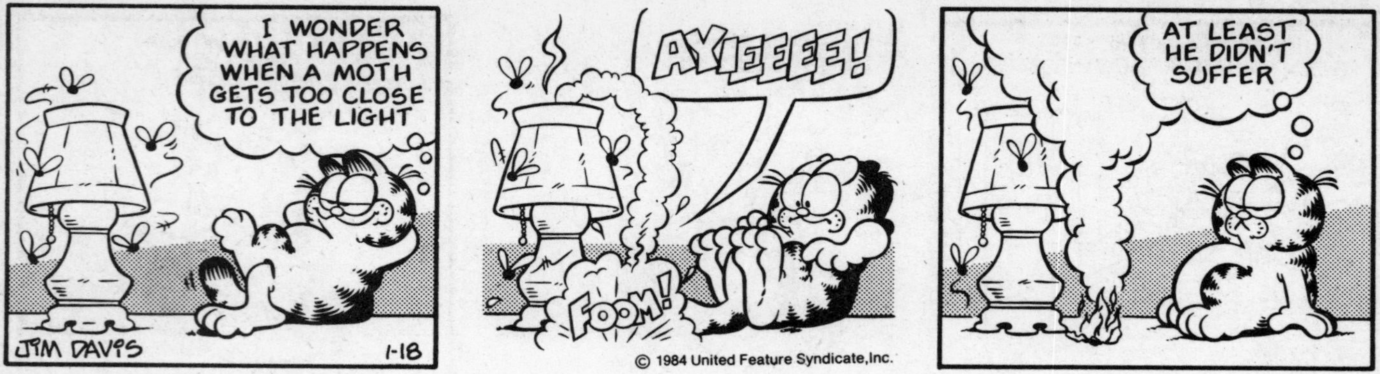
I WONDER WHAT HAPPENS WHEN A MOTH GETS TOO CLOSE TO THE LIGHT
JIM DAVIS
1-18
AYIEEEEE!
FOOM!
© 1984 United Feature Syndicate, Inc.
AT LEAST HE DIDN'T SUFFER

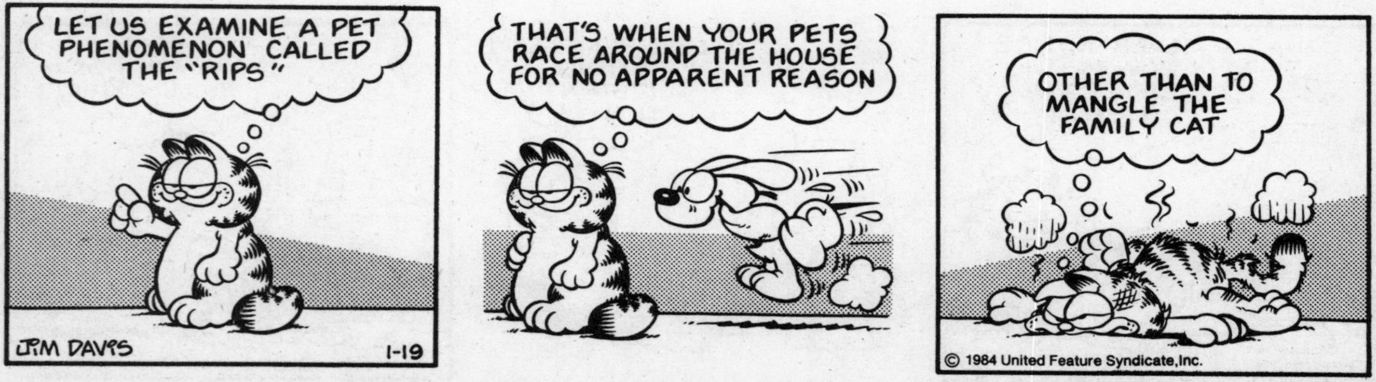
LET US EXAMINE A PET PHENOMENON CALLED THE "RIPS"
JIM DAVIS
1-19
THAT'S WHEN YOUR PETS RACE AROUND THE HOUSE FOR NO APPARENT REASON
OTHER THAN TO MANGLE THE FAMILY CAT
© 1984 United Feature Syndicate, Inc.

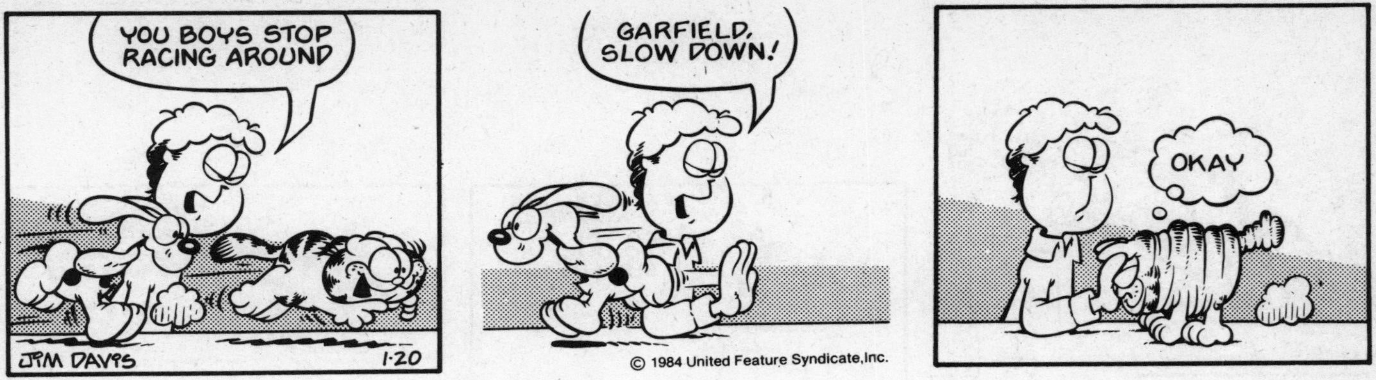
YOU BOYS STOP RACING AROUND
JIM DAVIS
1-20
GARFIELD, SLOW DOWN!
© 1984 United Feature Syndicate, Inc.
OKAY

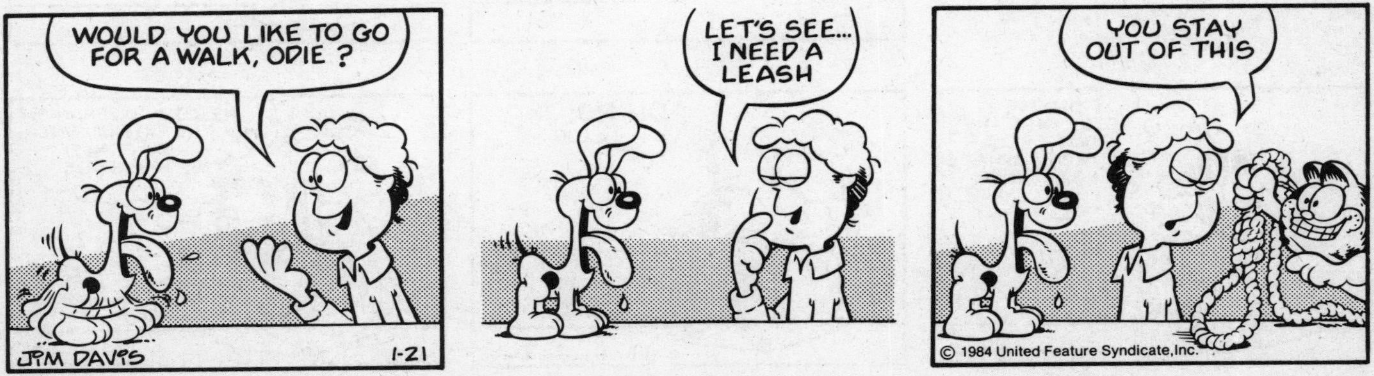
WOULD YOU LIKE TO GO FOR A WALK, ODIE ?
JIM DAVIS
1-21
LET'S SEE... I NEED A LEASH
YOU STAY OUT OF THIS
© 1984 United Feature Syndicate, Inc.

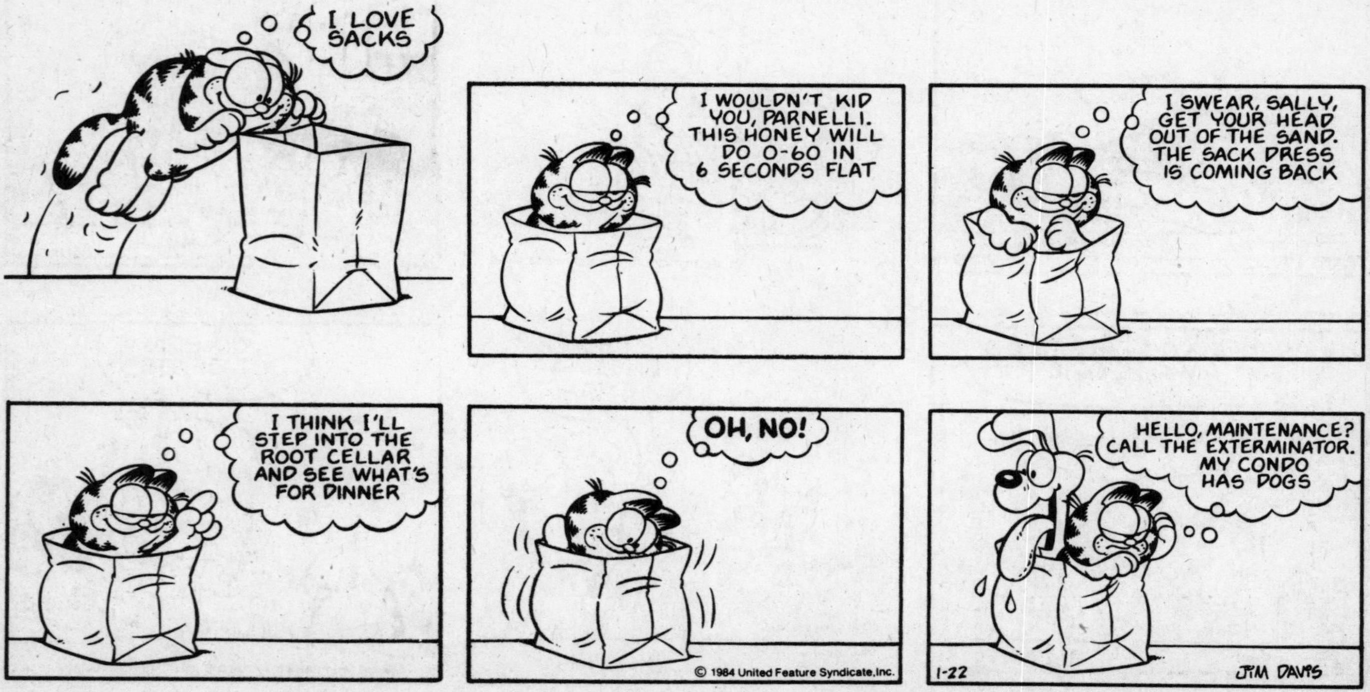
I LOVE SACKS
I WOULDN'T KID YOU, PARNELLI. THIS HONEY WILL DO 0-60 IN 6 SECONDS FLAT
I SWEAR, SALLY, GET YOUR HEAD OUT OF THE SAND. THE SACK DRESS IS COMING BACK
I THINK I'LL STEP INTO THE ROOT CELLAR AND SEE WHAT'S FOR DINNER
OH, NO!
HELLO, MAINTENANCE? CALL THE EXTERMINATOR. MY CONDO HAS DOGS
© 1984 United Feature Syndicate, Inc.
1-22
JIM DAVIS

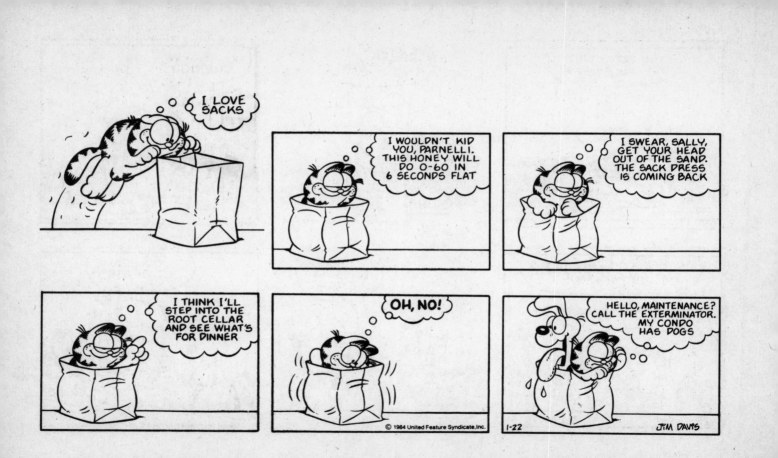

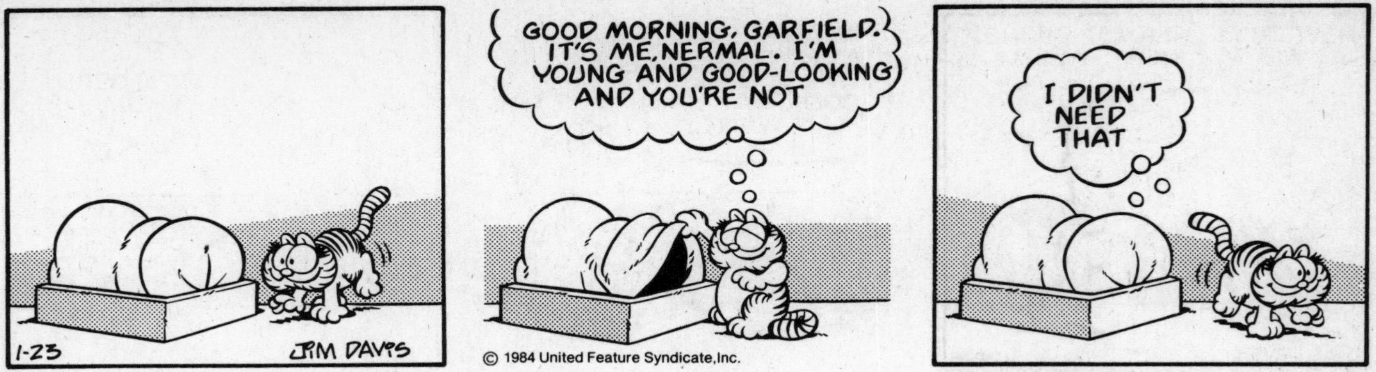
GOOD MORNING, GARFIELD. IT'S ME, NERMAL. I'M YOUNG AND GOOD-LOOKING AND YOU'RE NOT
I DIDN'T NEED THAT
1-23
JIM DAVIS
© 1984 United Feature Syndicate, Inc.

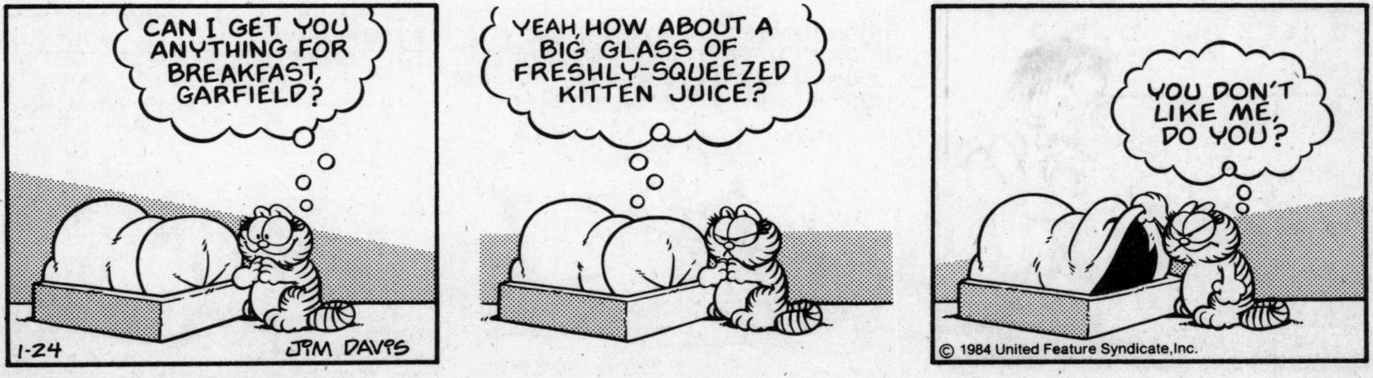
CAN I GET YOU ANYTHING FOR BREAKFAST, GARFIELD?
YEAH, HOW ABOUT A BIG GLASS OF FRESHLY-SQUEEZED KITTEN JUICE?
YOU DON'T LIKE ME, DO YOU?
1-24
JIM DAVIS
© 1984 United Feature Syndicate, Inc.

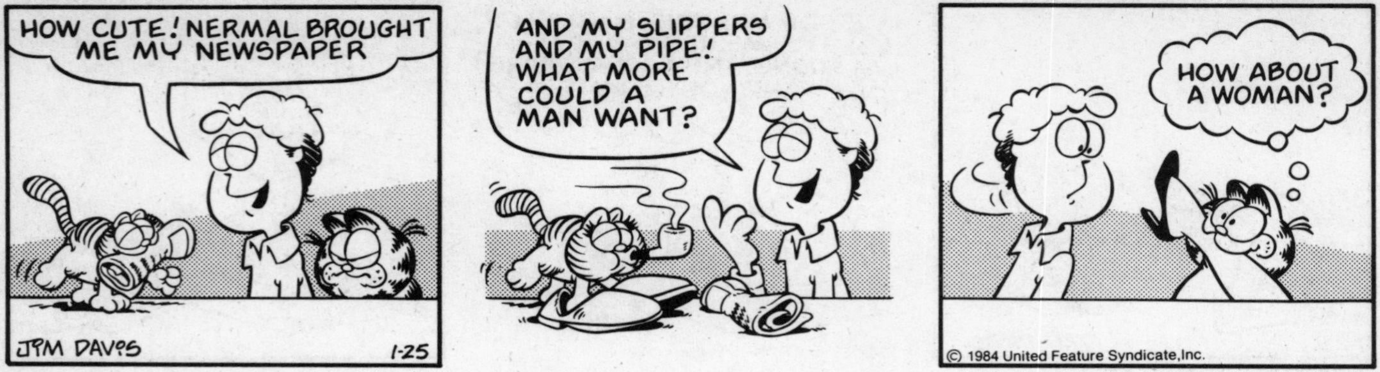
HOW CUTE! NERMAL BROUGHT ME MY NEWSPAPER
JIM DAVIS
1-25
AND MY SLIPPERS AND MY PIPE! WHAT MORE COULD A MAN WANT?
HOW ABOUT A WOMAN?
© 1984 United Feature Syndicate, Inc.

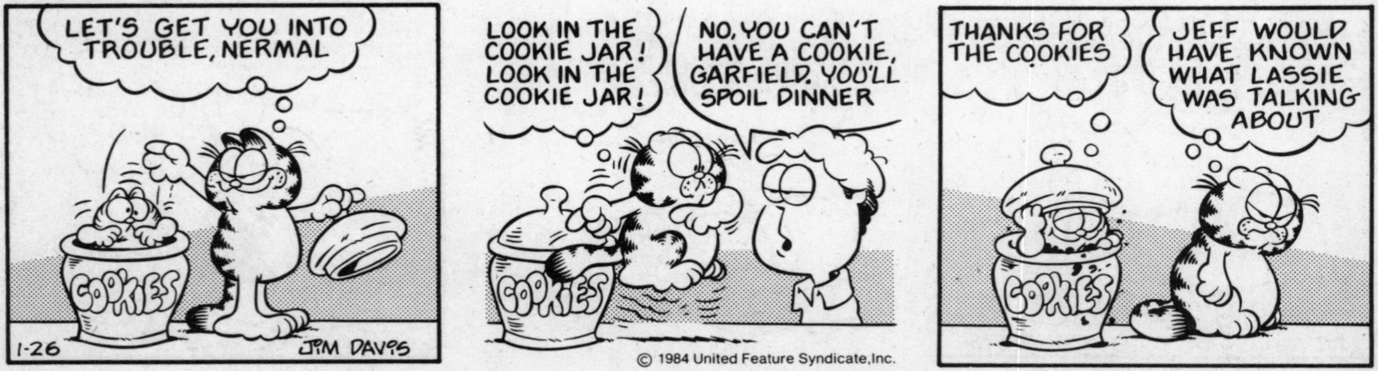
LET'S GET YOU INTO TROUBLE, NERMAL
COOKIES
1-26
JIM DAVIS
LOOK IN THE COOKIE JAR! LOOK IN THE COOKIE JAR!
NO, YOU CAN'T HAVE A COOKIE, GARFIELD. YOU'LL SPOIL DINNER
COOKIES
© 1984 United Feature Syndicate, Inc.
THANKS FOR THE COOKIES
JEFF WOULD HAVE KNOWN WHAT LASSIE WAS TALKING ABOUT
COOKIES

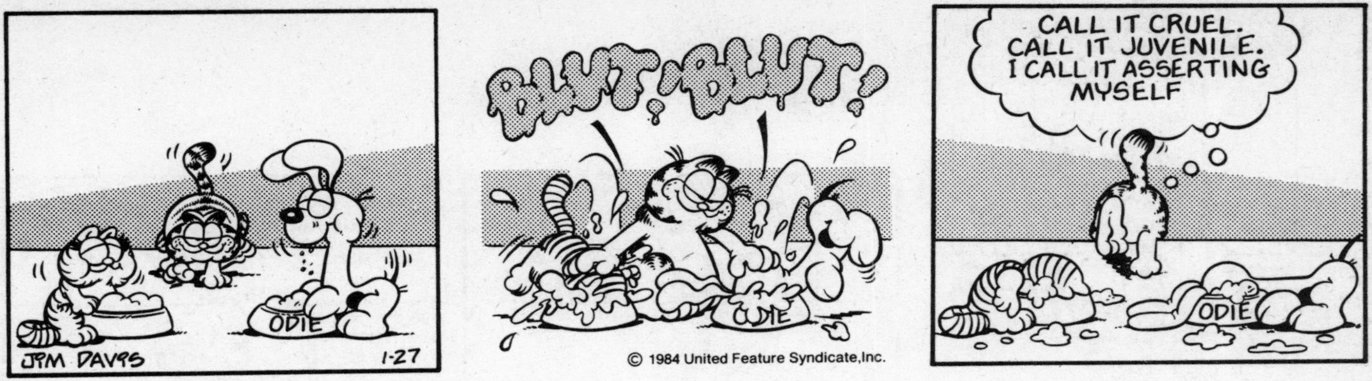
JIM DAVIS
1-27
BLUT! BLUT!
CALL IT CRUEL. CALL IT JUVENILE. I CALL IT ASSERTING MYSELF
ODIE

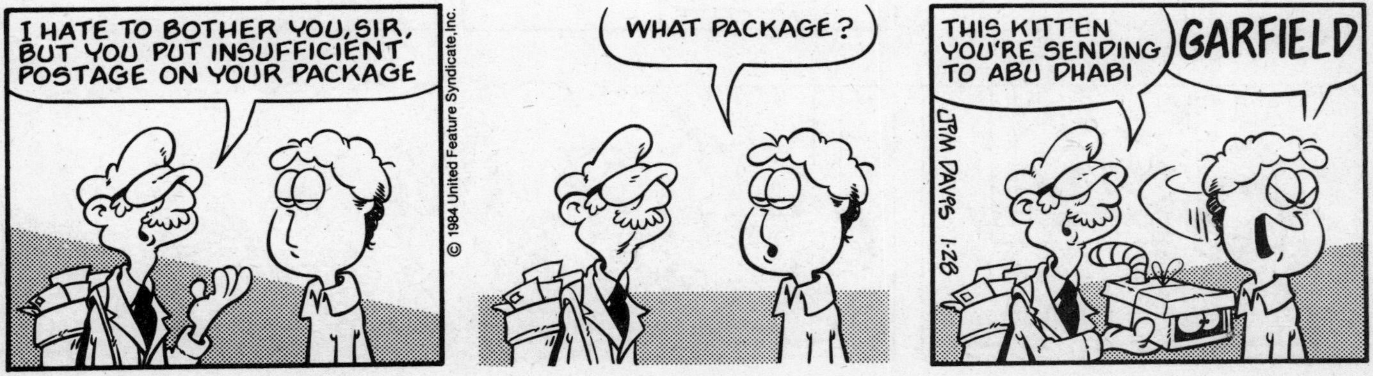
I HATE TO BOTHER YOU, SIR, BUT YOU PUT INSUFFICIENT POSTAGE ON YOUR PACKAGE
WHAT PACKAGE?
THIS KITTEN YOU'RE SENDING TO ABU DHABI
GARFIELD
JIM DAVIS
1-28

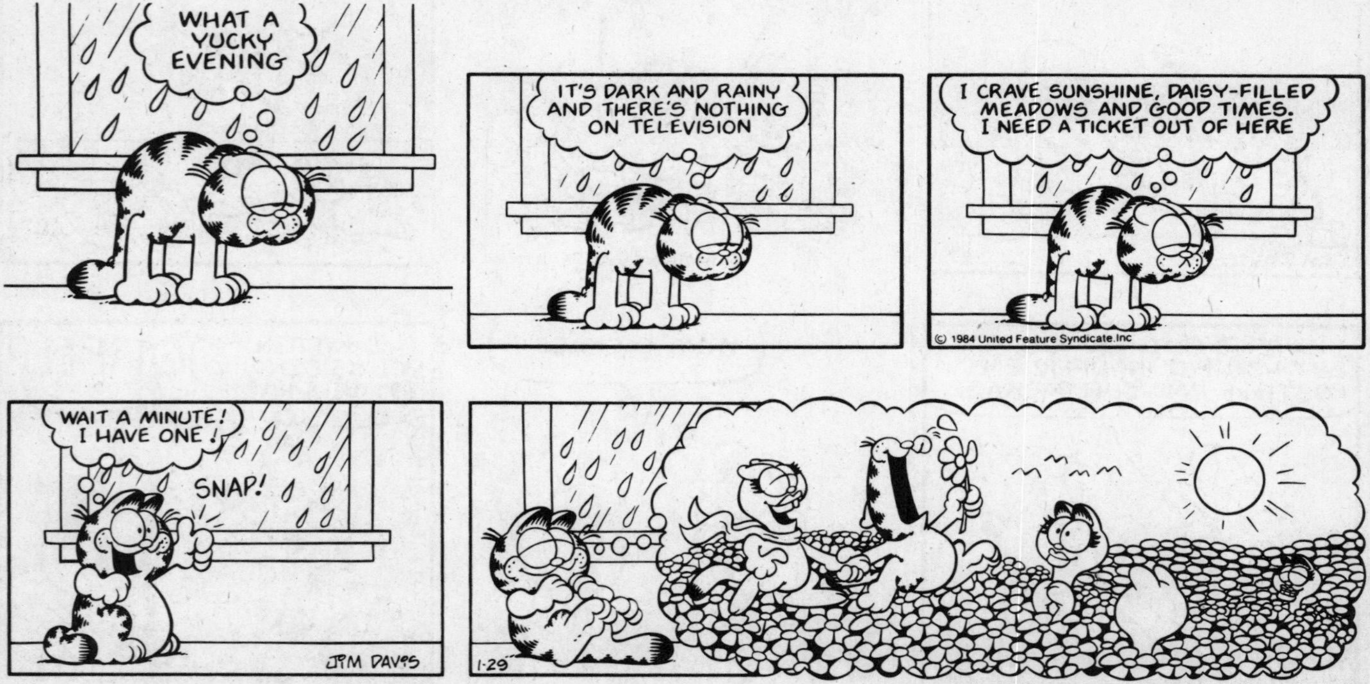

WHAT A YUCKY EVENING
IT'S DARK AND RAINY AND THERE'S NOTHING ON TELEVISION
I CRAVE SUNSHINE, DAISY-FILLED MEADOWS AND GOOD TIMES. I NEED A TICKET OUT OF HERE
© 1984 United Feature Syndicate, Inc
WAIT A MINUTE! I HAVE ONE!
SNAP!
JIM DAVIS
1-29

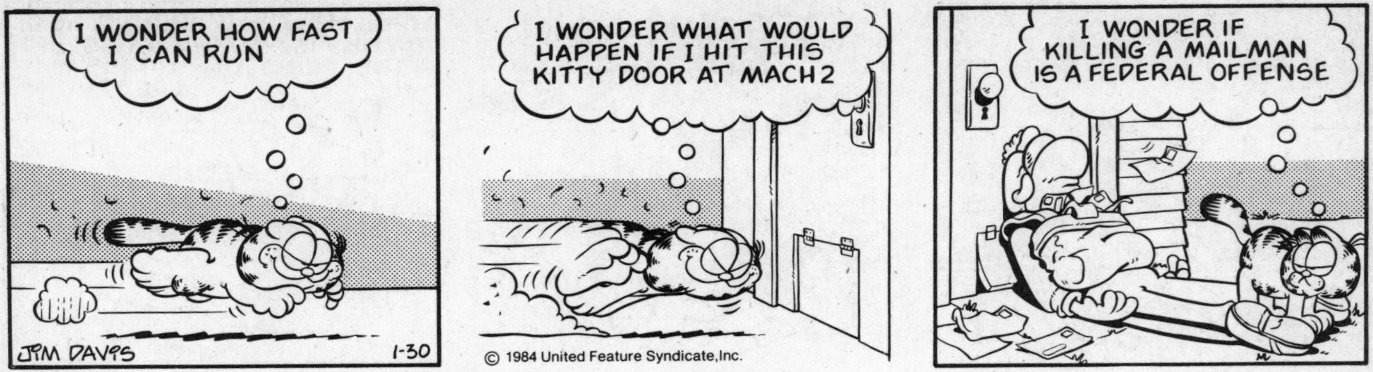
I WONDER HOW FAST I CAN RUN
I WONDER WHAT WOULD HAPPEN IF I HIT THIS KITTY DOOR AT MACH 2
I WONDER IF KILLING A MAILMAN IS A FEDERAL OFFENSE
JIM DAVIS
1-30
© 1984 United Feature Syndicate, Inc.

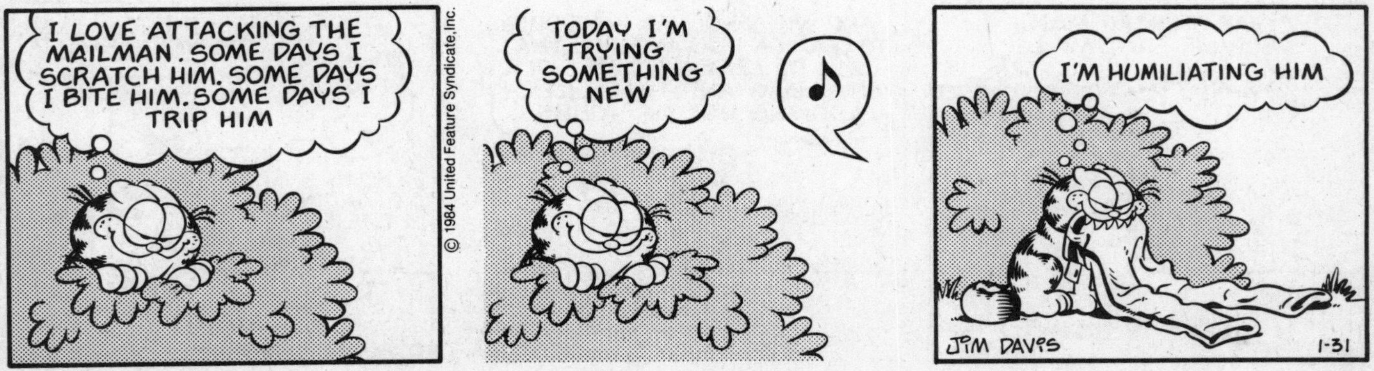
I LOVE ATTACKING THE MAILMAN. SOME DAYS I SCRATCH HIM. SOME DAYS I BITE HIM. SOME DAYS I TRIP HIM
© 1984 United Feature Syndicate, Inc.
TODAY I'M TRYING SOMETHING NEW
♪
I'M HUMILIATING HIM
JIM DAVIS
1-31

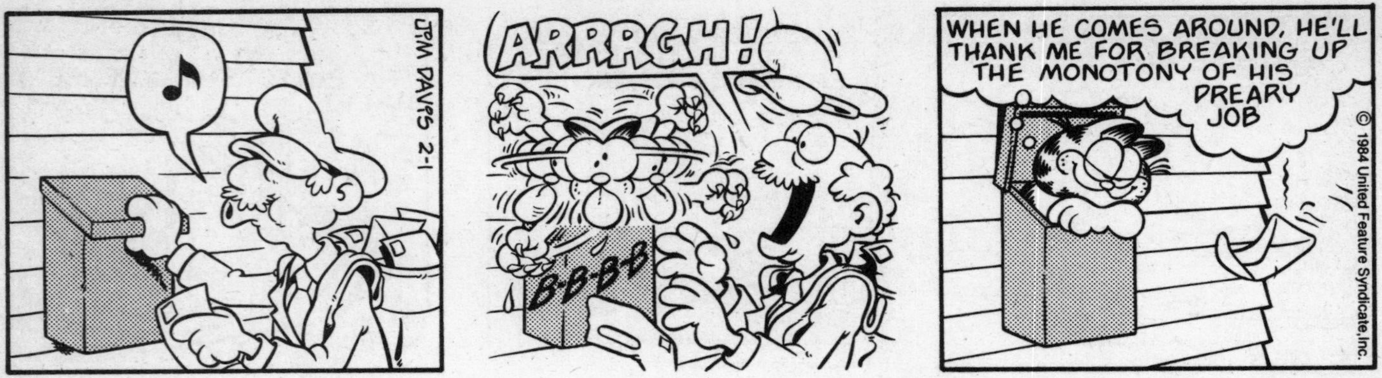
JIM DAVIS 2-1
♪
ARRRGH!
B-B-B-B
WHEN HE COMES AROUND, HE'LL THANK ME FOR BREAKING UP THE MONOTONY OF HIS DREARY JOB
© 1984 United Feature Syndicate,Inc.

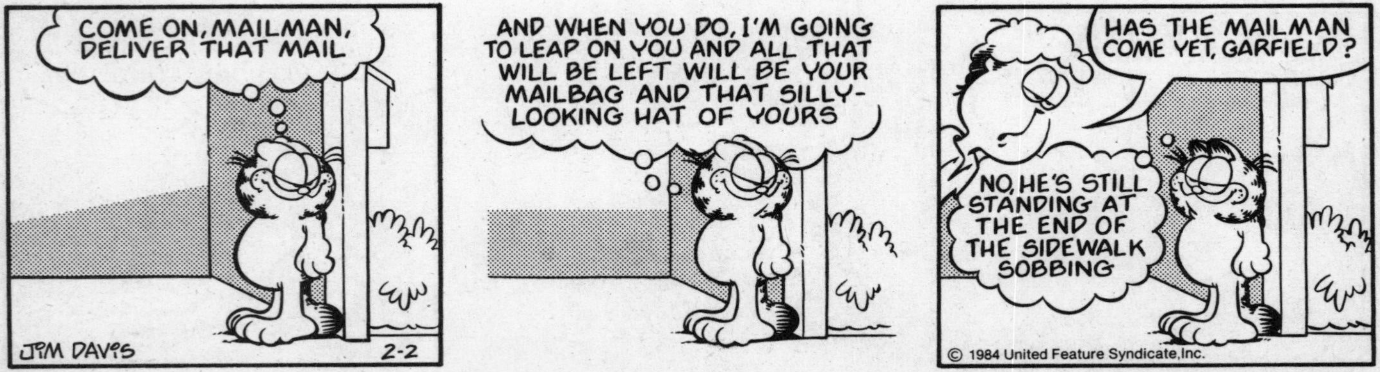
COME ON, MAILMAN, DELIVER THAT MAIL
JIM DAVIS 2-2
AND WHEN YOU DO, I'M GOING TO LEAP ON YOU AND ALL THAT WILL BE LEFT WILL BE YOUR MAILBAG AND THAT SILLY-LOOKING HAT OF YOURS
HAS THE MAILMAN COME YET, GARFIELD?
NO, HE'S STILL STANDING AT THE END OF THE SIDEWALK SOBBING
© 1984 United Feature Syndicate,Inc.

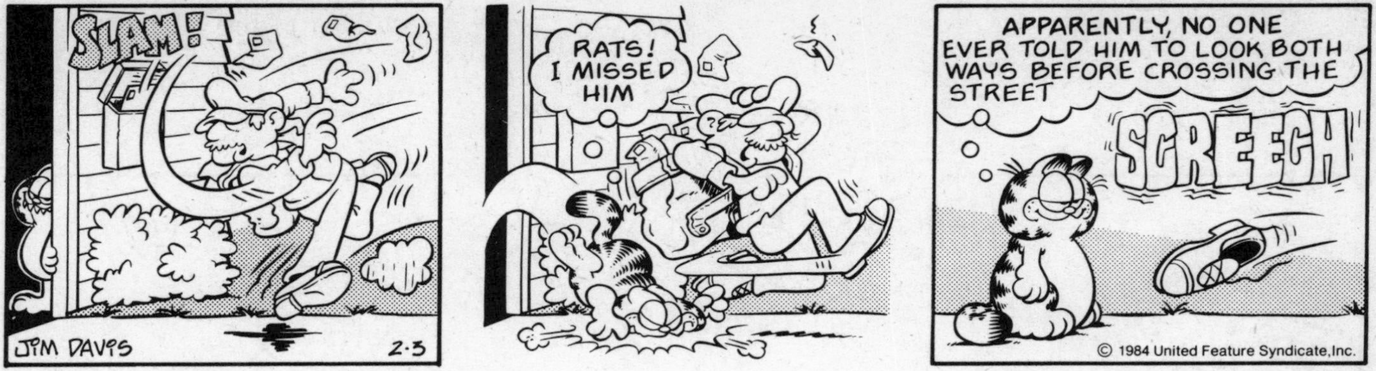
SLAM!
JIM DAVIS
2-3
RATS! I MISSED HIM
APPARENTLY, NO ONE EVER TOLD HIM TO LOOK BOTH WAYS BEFORE CROSSING THE STREET
SCREECH
© 1984 United Feature Syndicate,Inc.

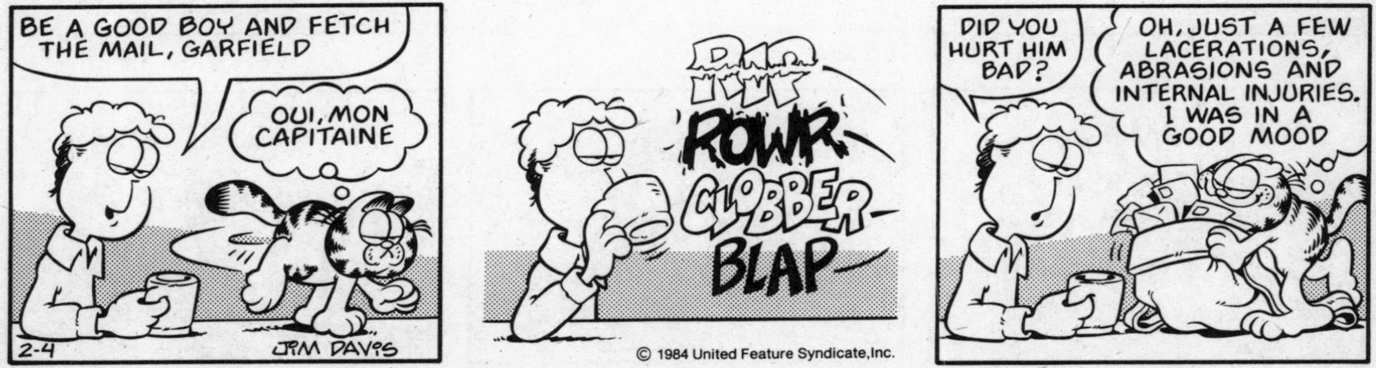
BE A GOOD BOY AND FETCH THE MAIL, GARFIELD
OUI, MON CAPITAINE
2-4
JIM DAVIS
RIP
ROWR
CLOBBER
BLAP
© 1984 United Feature Syndicate,Inc.
DID YOU HURT HIM BAD?
OH, JUST A FEW LACERATIONS, ABRASIONS AND INTERNAL INJURIES. I WAS IN A GOOD MOOD

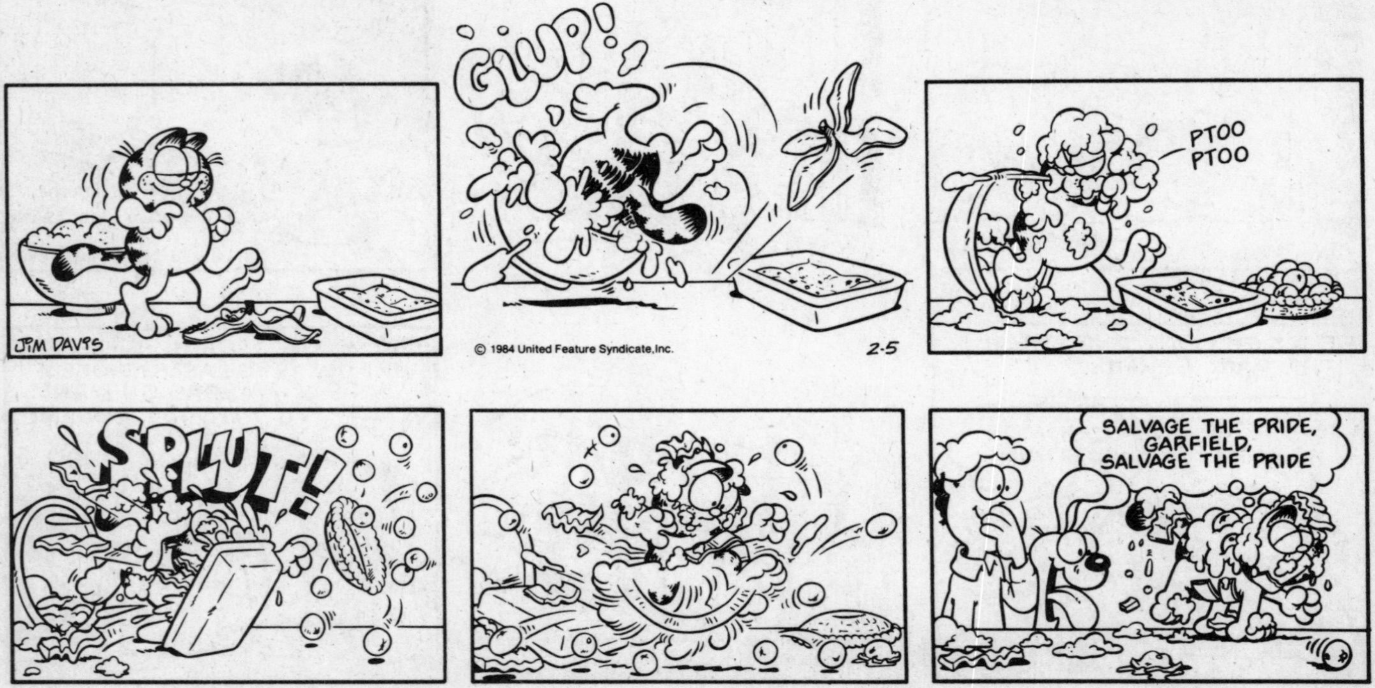

JIM DAVIS
GLUP!
© 1984 United Feature Syndicate, Inc.
2-5
PTOO PTOO
SPLUT!
SALVAGE THE PRIDE, GARFIELD, SALVAGE THE PRIDE

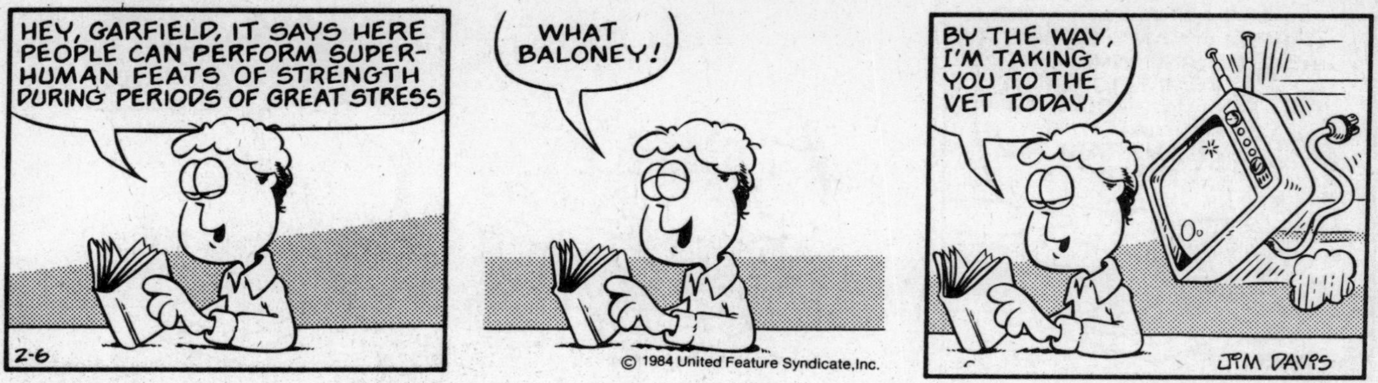
HEY, GARFIELD, IT SAYS HERE PEOPLE CAN PERFORM SUPER-HUMAN FEATS OF STRENGTH DURING PERIODS OF GREAT STRESS
WHAT BALONEY!
BY THE WAY, I'M TAKING YOU TO THE VET TODAY
2-6
© 1984 United Feature Syndicate, Inc.
JIM DAVIS

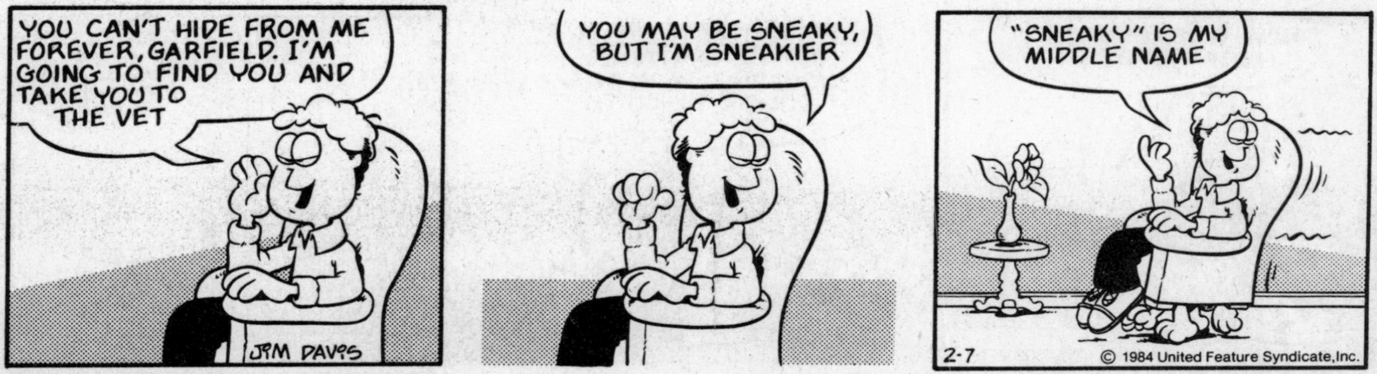
YOU CAN'T HIDE FROM ME FOREVER, GARFIELD. I'M GOING TO FIND YOU AND TAKE YOU TO THE VET
JIM DAVIS
YOU MAY BE SNEAKY, BUT I'M SNEAKIER
"SNEAKY" IS MY MIDDLE NAME
2-7
© 1984 United Feature Syndicate, Inc.

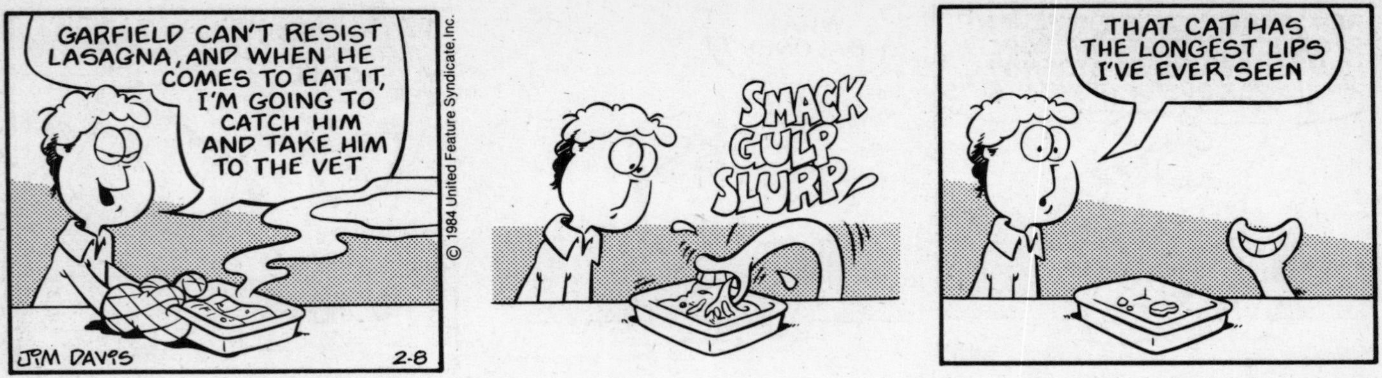
GARFIELD CAN'T RESIST LASAGNA, AND WHEN HE COMES TO EAT IT, I'M GOING TO CATCH HIM AND TAKE HIM TO THE VET
JIM DAVIS
2-8
© 1984 United Feature Syndicate, Inc.
SMACK
GULP
SLURP
THAT CAT HAS THE LONGEST LIPS I'VE EVER SEEN

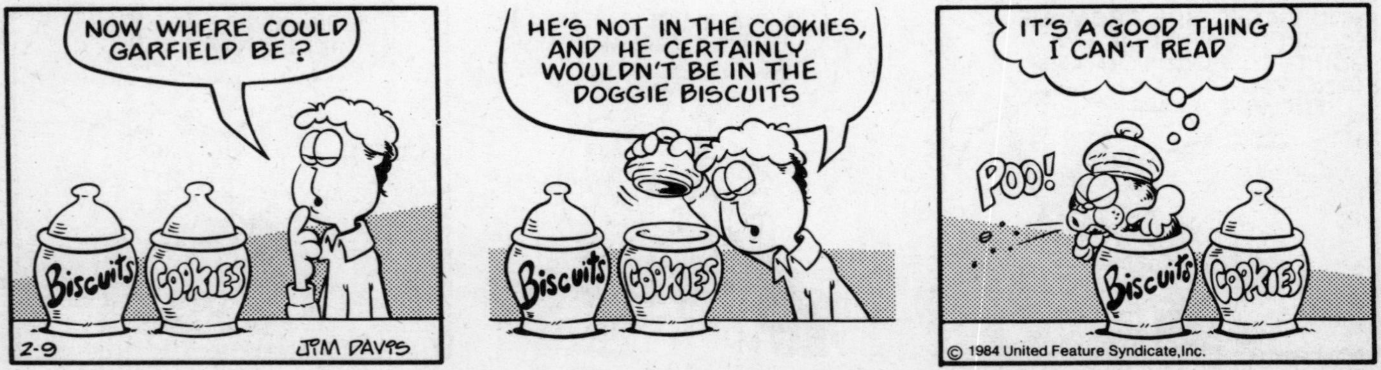
NOW WHERE COULD GARFIELD BE?
Biscuits
COOKIES
2-9
JIM DAVIS
HE'S NOT IN THE COOKIES, AND HE CERTAINLY WOULDN'T BE IN THE DOGGIE BISCUITS
IT'S A GOOD THING I CAN'T READ
POO!
© 1984 United Feature Syndicate, Inc.

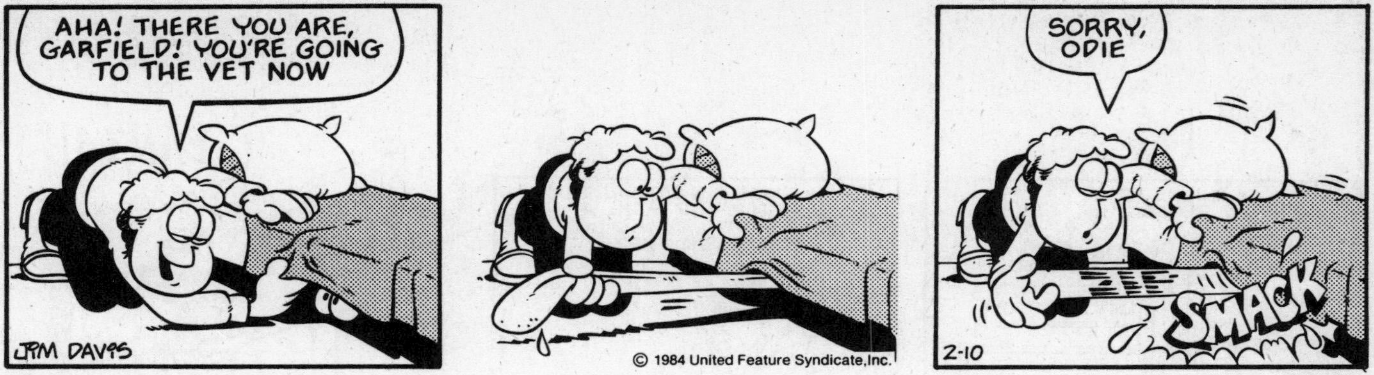
AHA! THERE YOU ARE, GARFIELD! YOU'RE GOING TO THE VET NOW
JIM DAVIS
© 1984 United Feature Syndicate,Inc.
SORRY, ODIE
SMACK
2-10

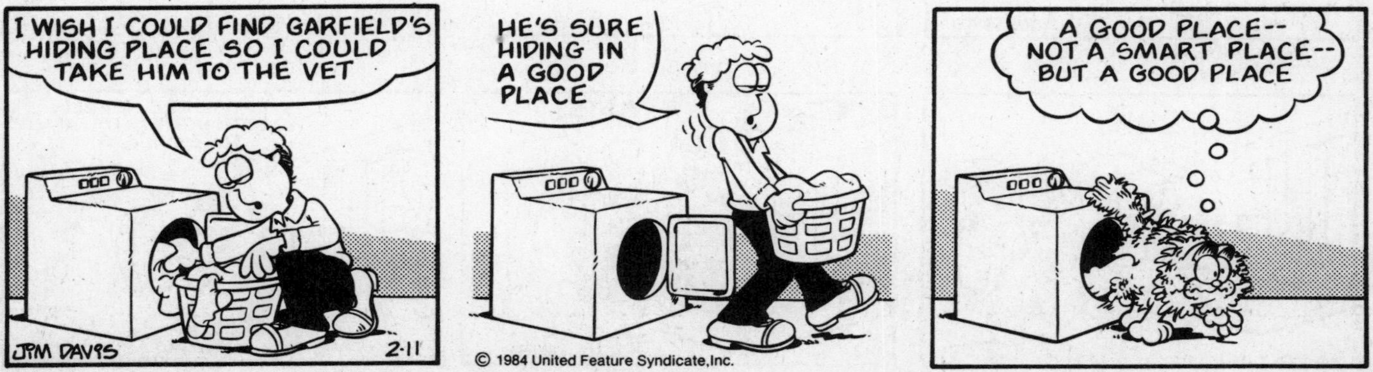
I WISH I COULD FIND GARFIELD'S HIDING PLACE SO I COULD TAKE HIM TO THE VET
JIM DAVIS
2-11
HE'S SURE HIDING IN A GOOD PLACE
© 1984 United Feature Syndicate,Inc.
A GOOD PLACE-- NOT A SMART PLACE-- BUT A GOOD PLACE

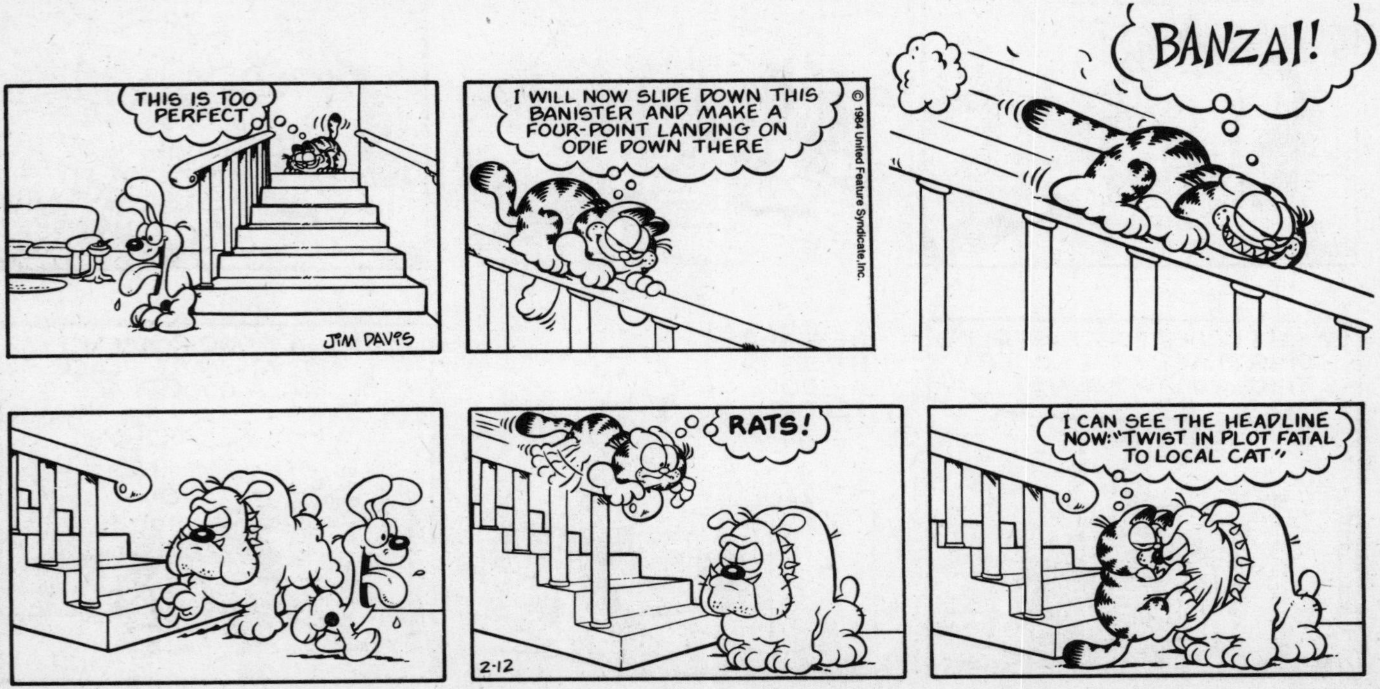
THIS IS TOO PERFECT
JIM DAVIS
I WILL NOW SLIDE DOWN THIS BANISTER AND MAKE A FOUR-POINT LANDING ON ODIE DOWN THERE
© 1984 United Feature Syndicate, Inc.
BANZAI!
RATS!
2-12
I CAN SEE THE HEADLINE NOW: "TWIST IN PLOT FATAL TO LOCAL CAT"

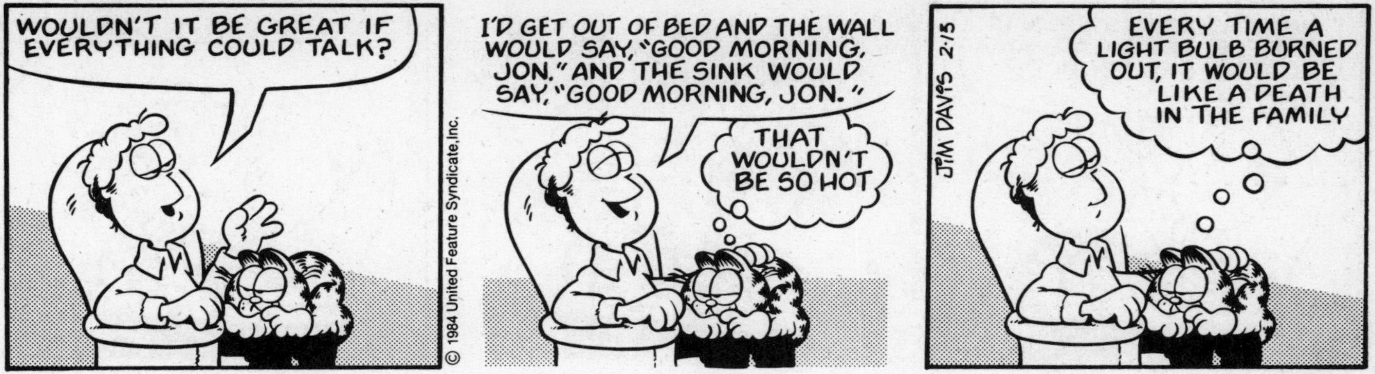
WOULDN'T IT BE GREAT IF EVERYTHING COULD TALK?
I'D GET OUT OF BED AND THE WALL WOULD SAY, "GOOD MORNING, JON." AND THE SINK WOULD SAY, "GOOD MORNING, JON."
THAT WOULDN'T BE SO HOT
EVERY TIME A LIGHT BULB BURNED OUT, IT WOULD BE LIKE A DEATH IN THE FAMILY
JIM DAVIS 2-13

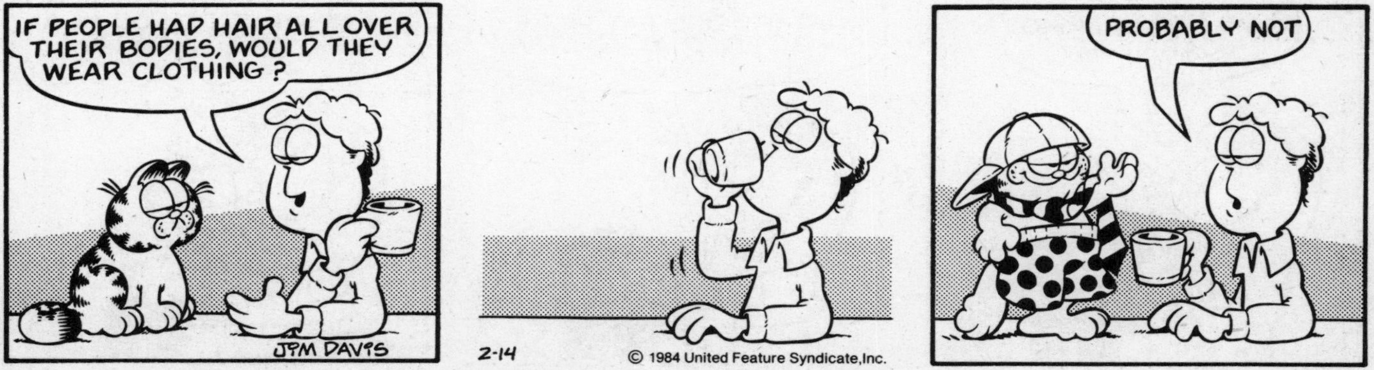
IF PEOPLE HAD HAIR ALL OVER THEIR BODIES, WOULD THEY WEAR CLOTHING?
JIM DAVIS
2-14
PROBABLY NOT

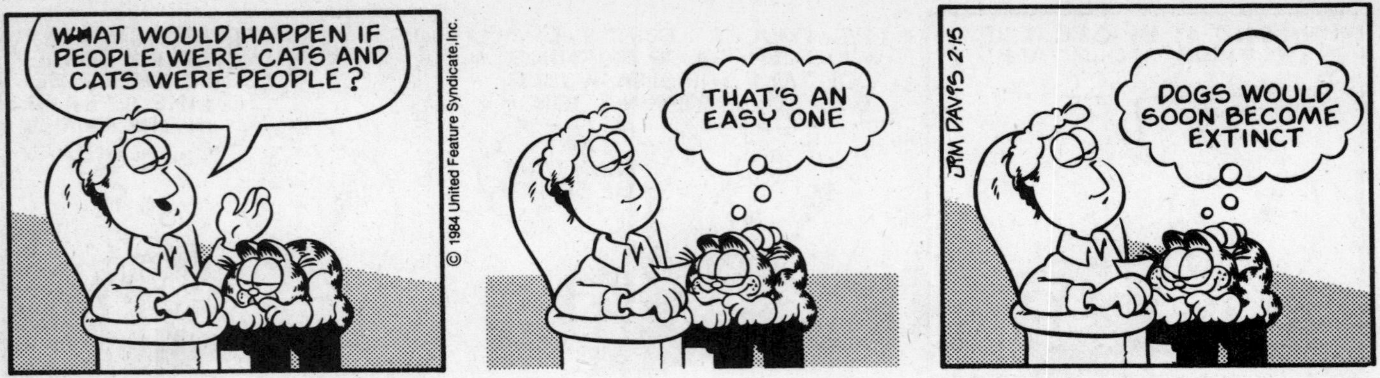
WHAT WOULD HAPPEN IF PEOPLE WERE CATS AND CATS WERE PEOPLE?
© 1984 United Feature Syndicate, Inc.
THAT'S AN EASY ONE
JIM DAVIS 2-15
DOGS WOULD SOON BECOME EXTINCT

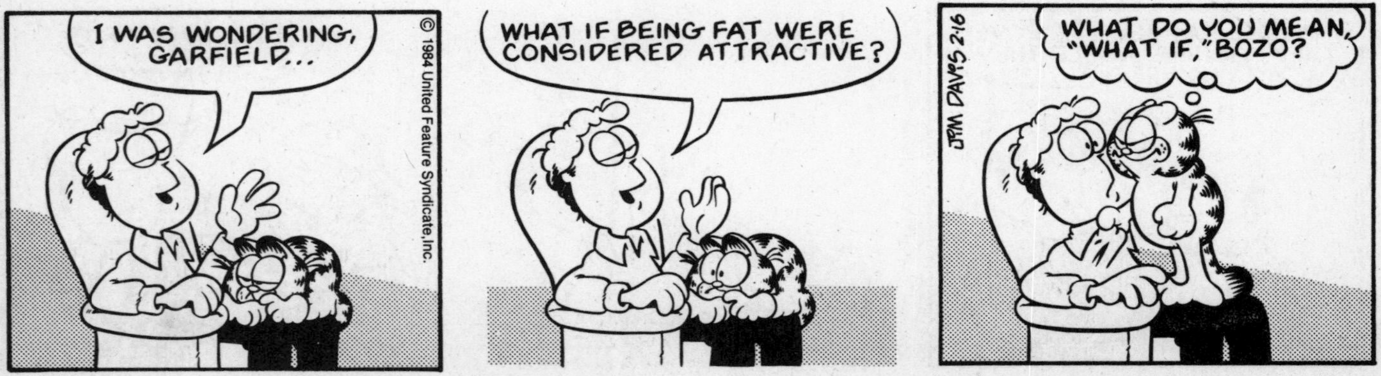
I WAS WONDERING, GARFIELD...
© 1984 United Feature Syndicate, Inc.
WHAT IF BEING FAT WERE CONSIDERED ATTRACTIVE?
JIM DAVIS 2-16
WHAT DO YOU MEAN, "WHAT IF," BOZO?

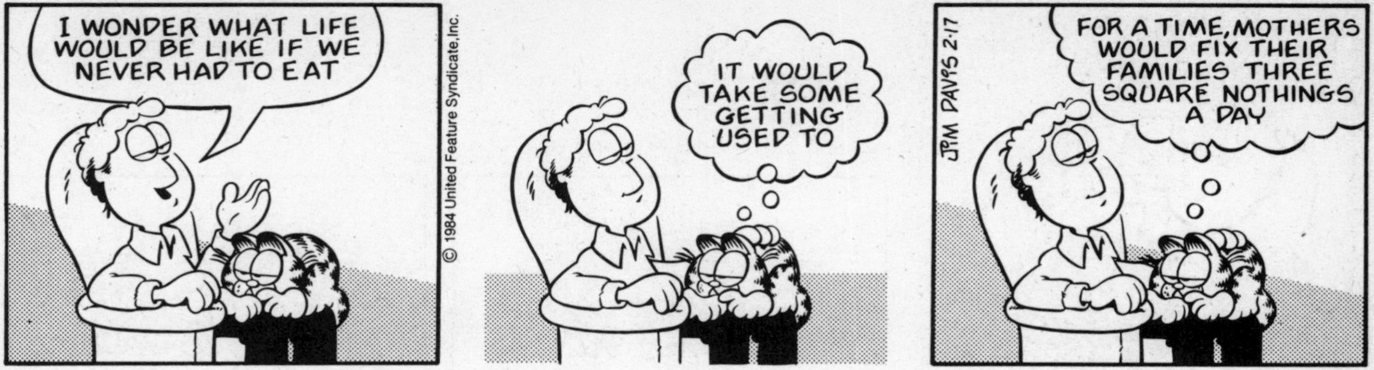
I WONDER WHAT LIFE WOULD BE LIKE IF WE NEVER HAD TO EAT
© 1984 United Feature Syndicate, Inc.
IT WOULD TAKE SOME GETTING USED TO
JIM DAVIS 2·17
FOR A TIME, MOTHERS WOULD FIX THEIR FAMILIES THREE SQUARE NOTHINGS A DAY

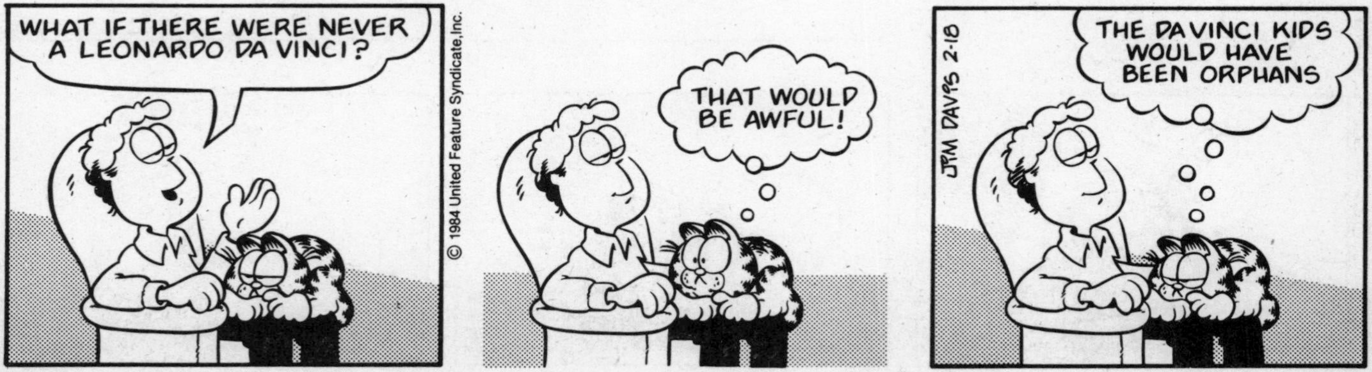
WHAT IF THERE WERE NEVER A LEONARDO DA VINCI?
© 1984 United Feature Syndicate, Inc.
THAT WOULD BE AWFUL!
JIM DAVIS 2·18
THE DA VINCI KIDS WOULD HAVE BEEN ORPHANS

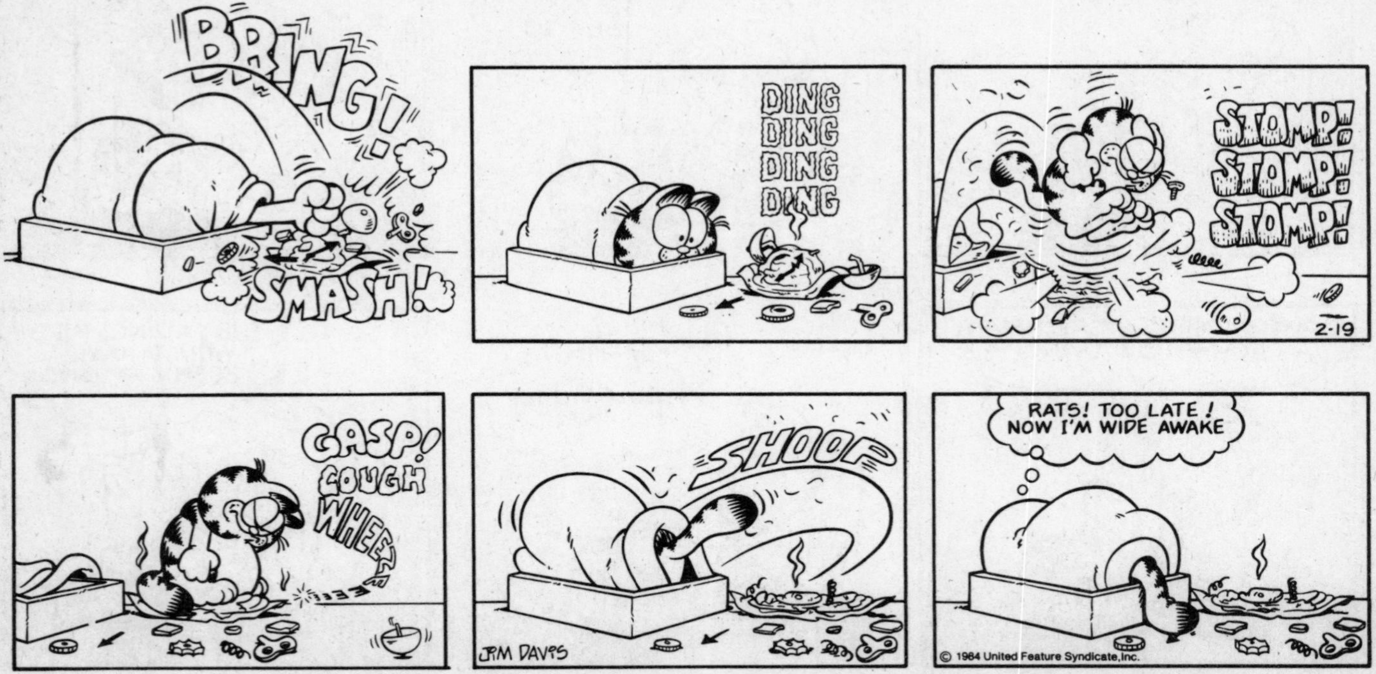
BRING!
SMASH!
DING
DING
DING
DING
STOMP!
STOMP!
STOMP!
2-19
GASP!
COUGH
WHEEZE
SHOOP
JIM DAVIS
RATS! TOO LATE !
NOW I'M WIDE AWAKE
© 1984 United Feature Syndicate, Inc.

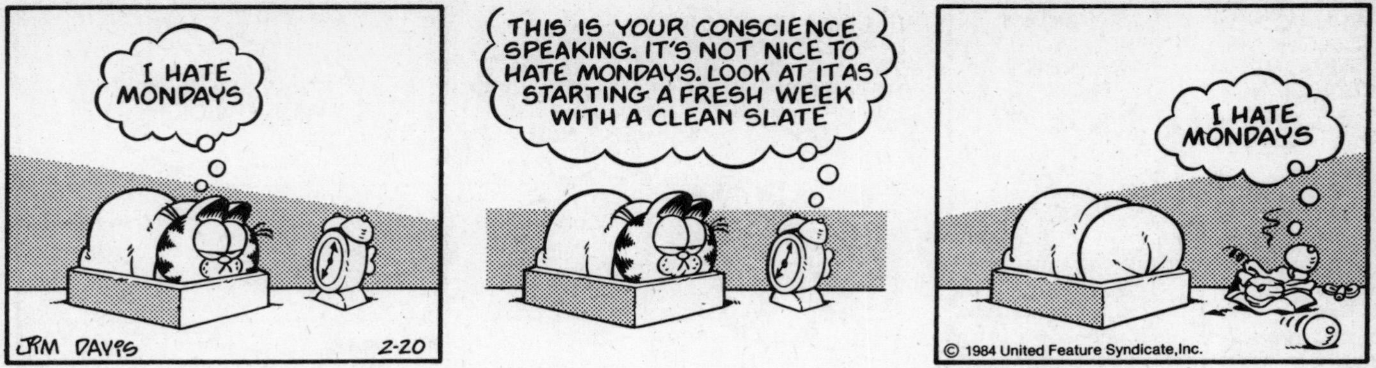
I HATE MONDAYS
JIM DAVIS
2-20
THIS IS YOUR CONSCIENCE SPEAKING. IT'S NOT NICE TO HATE MONDAYS. LOOK AT IT AS STARTING A FRESH WEEK WITH A CLEAN SLATE
I HATE MONDAYS
© 1984 United Feature Syndicate, Inc.

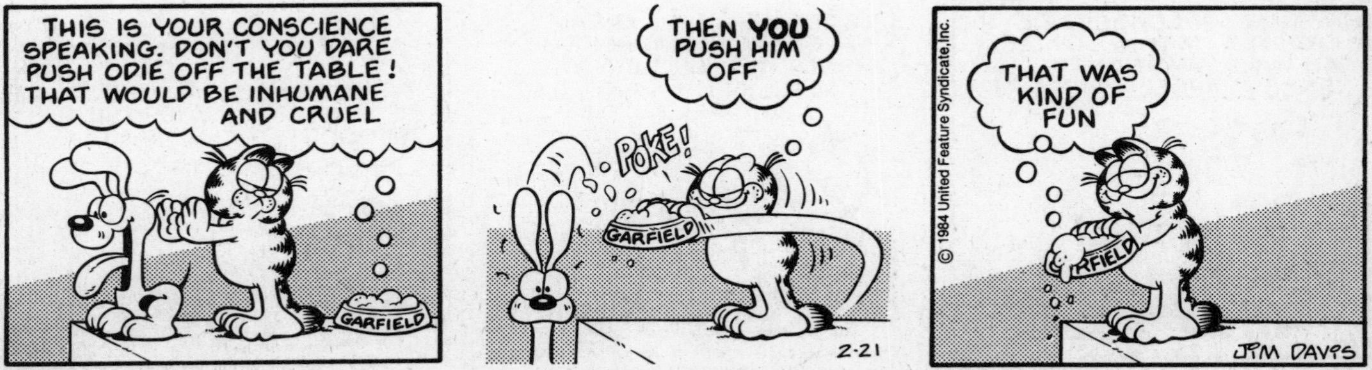
THIS IS YOUR CONSCIENCE SPEAKING. DON'T YOU DARE PUSH ODIE OFF THE TABLE! THAT WOULD BE INHUMANE AND CRUEL
GARFIELD
THEN **YOU** PUSH HIM OFF
POKE!
GARFIELD
2-21
© 1984 United Feature Syndicate, Inc.
THAT WAS KIND OF FUN
RFIELD
JIM DAVIS

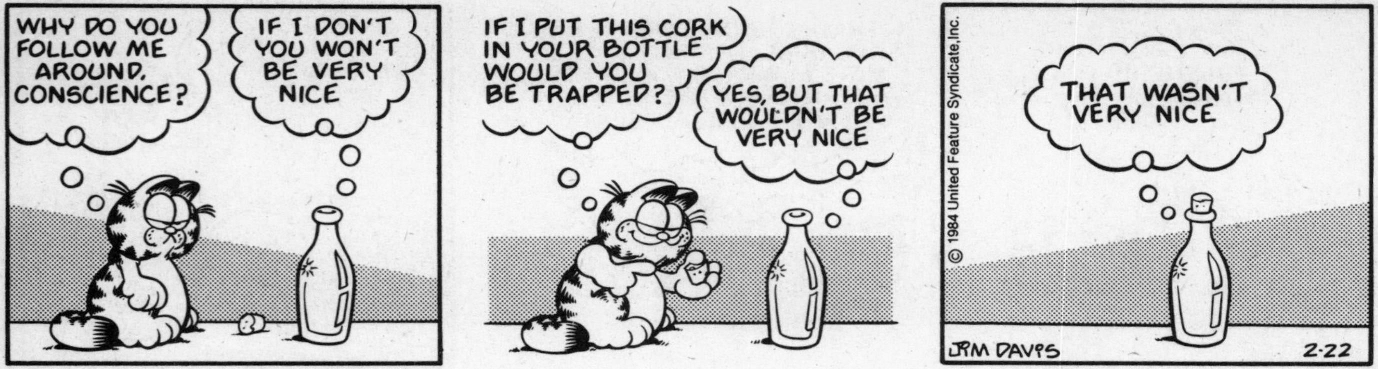
WHY DO YOU FOLLOW ME AROUND, CONSCIENCE?
IF I DON'T YOU WON'T BE VERY NICE
IF I PUT THIS CORK IN YOUR BOTTLE WOULD YOU BE TRAPPED?
YES, BUT THAT WOULDN'T BE VERY NICE
THAT WASN'T VERY NICE
© 1984 United Feature Syndicate, Inc.
JIM DAVIS
2-22

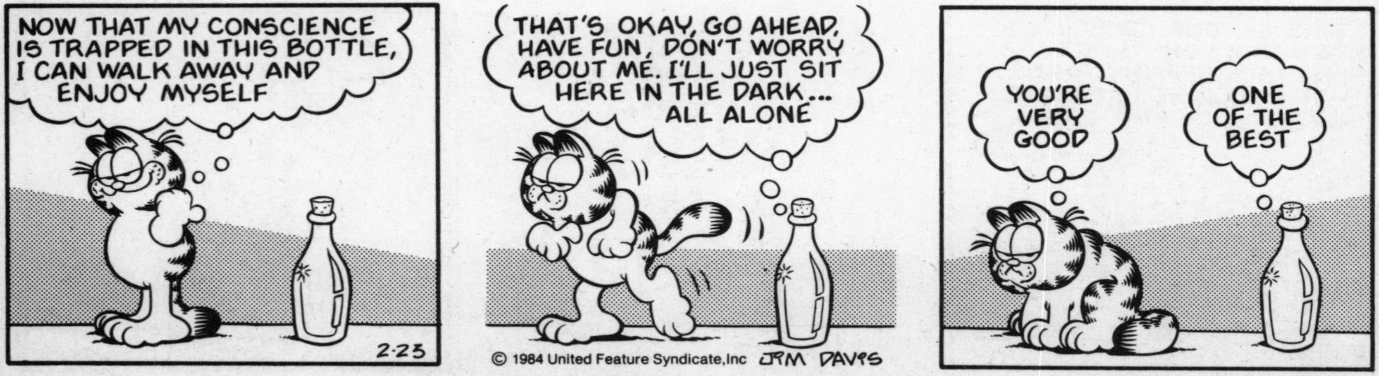
NOW THAT MY CONSCIENCE IS TRAPPED IN THIS BOTTLE, I CAN WALK AWAY AND ENJOY MYSELF
2-23
THAT'S OKAY, GO AHEAD, HAVE FUN, DON'T WORRY ABOUT ME. I'LL JUST SIT HERE IN THE DARK... ALL ALONE
YOU'RE VERY GOOD
ONE OF THE BEST

 JIM DAVIS

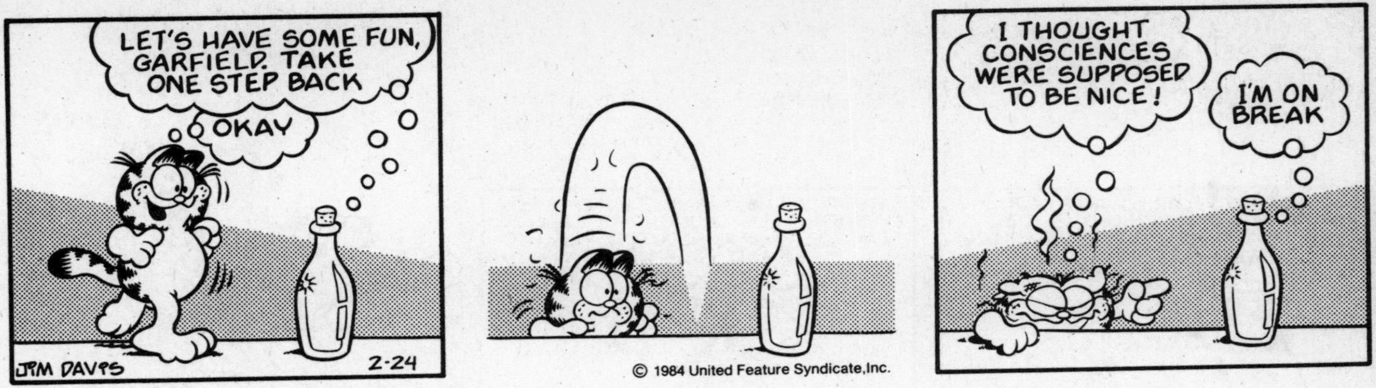
LET'S HAVE SOME FUN, GARFIELD. TAKE ONE STEP BACK
OKAY
JIM DAVIS
2-24
I THOUGHT CONSCIENCES WERE SUPPOSED TO BE NICE!
I'M ON BREAK

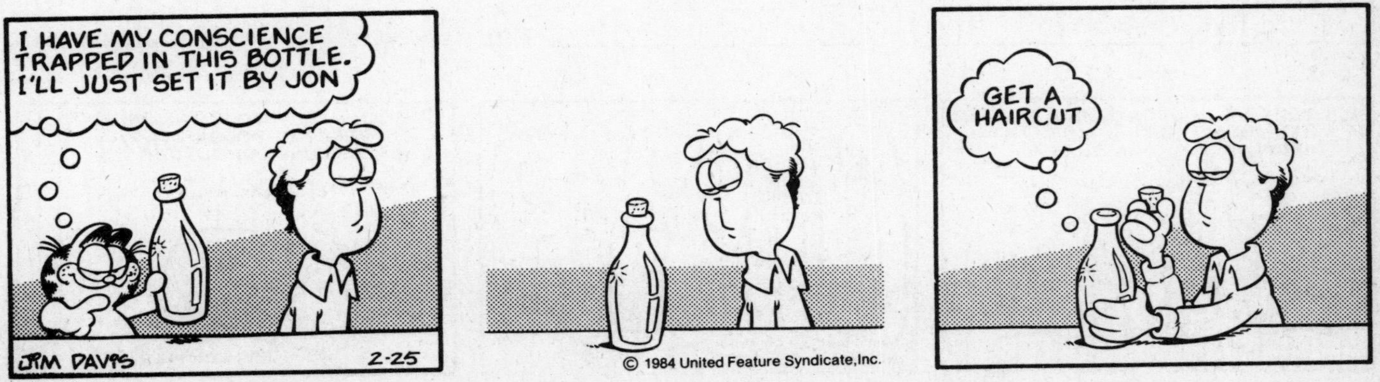
I HAVE MY CONSCIENCE TRAPPED IN THIS BOTTLE. I'LL JUST SET IT BY JON
JIM DAVIS
2-25
GET A HAIRCUT

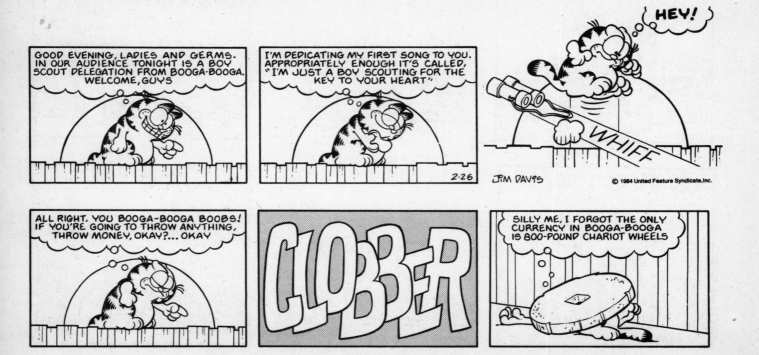

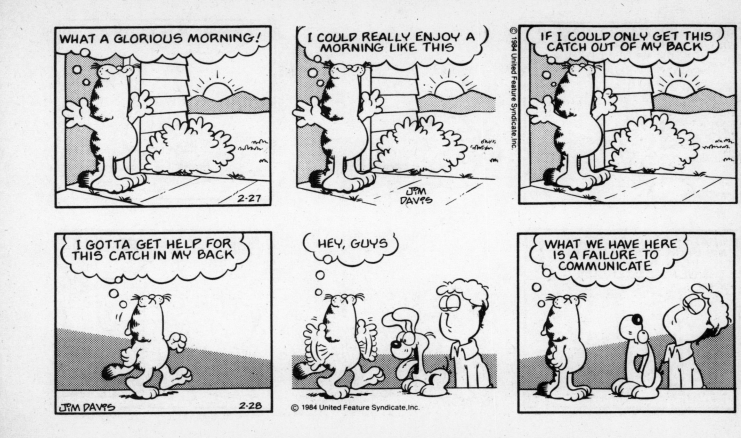

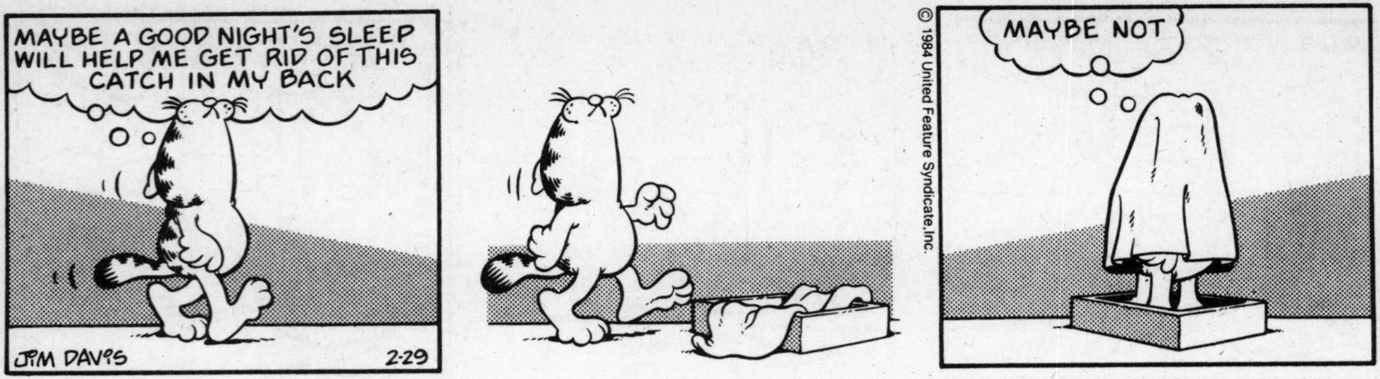
MAYBE A GOOD NIGHT'S SLEEP WILL HELP ME GET RID OF THIS CATCH IN MY BACK
JIM DAVIS
2-29
MAYBE NOT
© 1984 United Feature Syndicate,Inc.

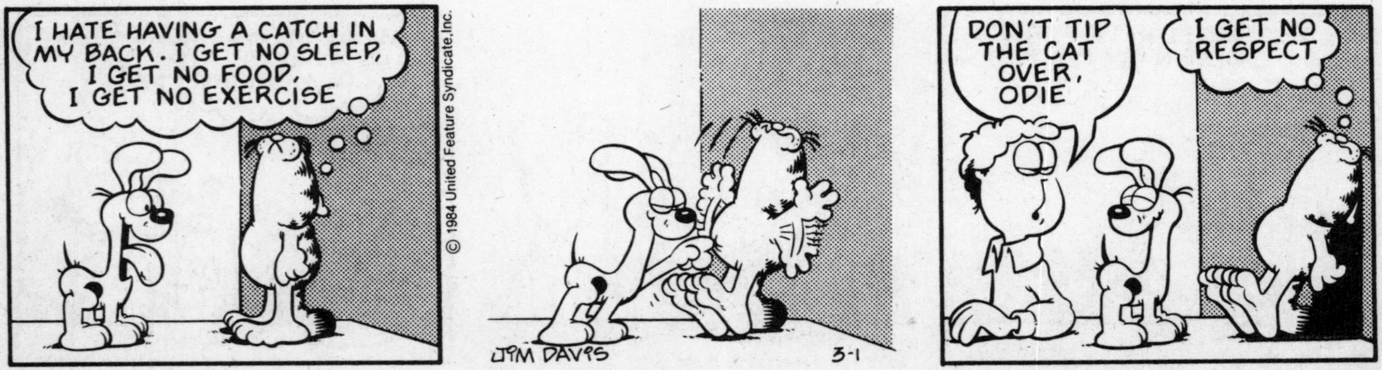
I HATE HAVING A CATCH IN MY BACK. I GET NO SLEEP, I GET NO FOOD, I GET NO EXERCISE
© 1984 United Feature Syndicate,Inc.
JIM DAVIS
3-1
DON'T TIP THE CAT OVER, ODIE
I GET NO RESPECT

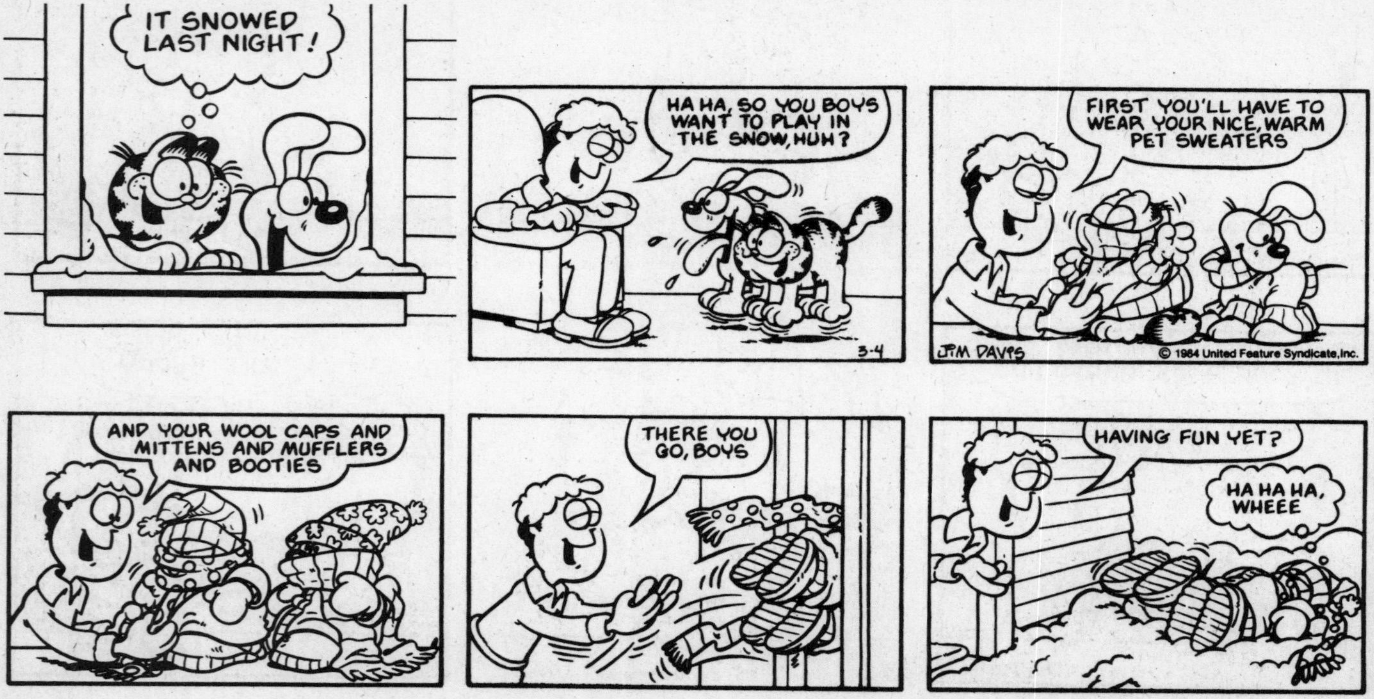
IT SNOWED LAST NIGHT!
HA HA, SO YOU BOYS WANT TO PLAY IN THE SNOW, HUH?
3-4
FIRST YOU'LL HAVE TO WEAR YOUR NICE, WARM PET SWEATERS
JIM DAVIS
© 1984 United Feature Syndicate, Inc.
AND YOUR WOOL CAPS AND MITTENS AND MUFFLERS AND BOOTIES
THERE YOU GO, BOYS
HAVING FUN YET?
HA HA HA, WHEEE

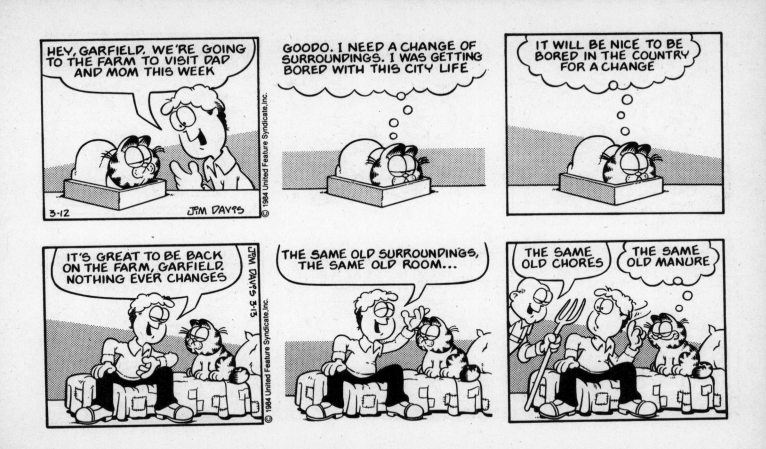

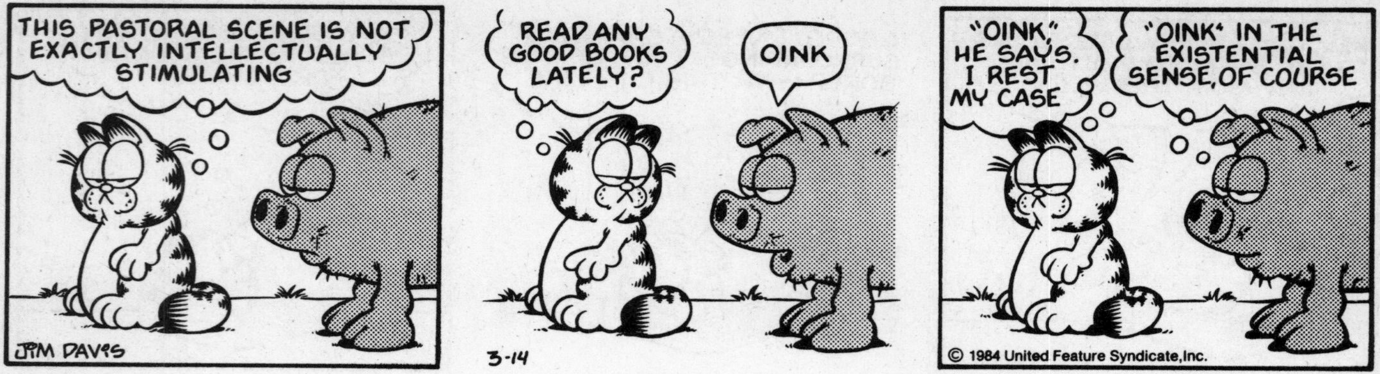
THIS PASTORAL SCENE IS NOT EXACTLY INTELLECTUALLY STIMULATING
JIM DAVIS
READ ANY GOOD BOOKS LATELY?
OINK
3-14
"OINK," HE SAYS. I REST MY CASE
"OINK" IN THE EXISTENTIAL SENSE, OF COURSE
© 1984 United Feature Syndicate, Inc.

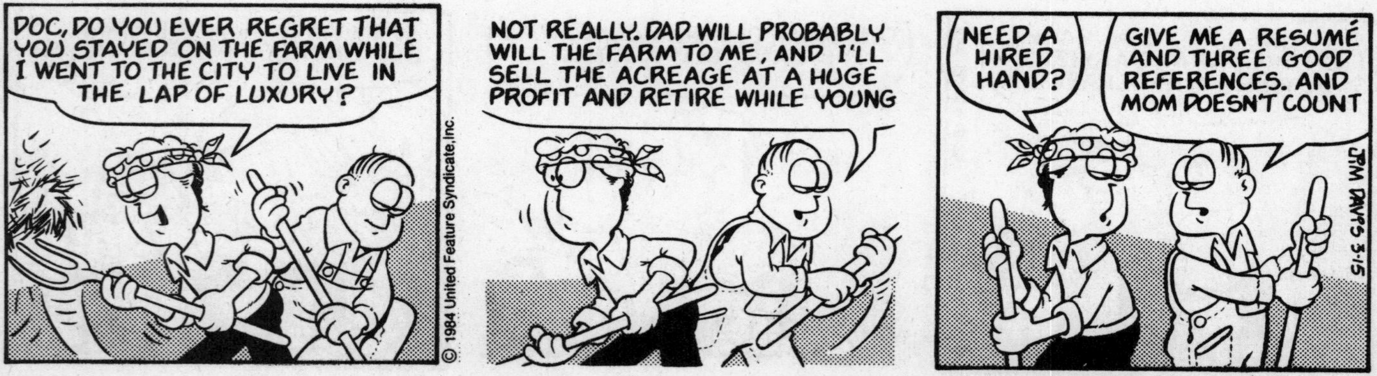
DOC, DO YOU EVER REGRET THAT YOU STAYED ON THE FARM WHILE I WENT TO THE CITY TO LIVE IN THE LAP OF LUXURY?
© 1984 United Feature Syndicate, Inc.
NOT REALLY. DAD WILL PROBABLY WILL THE FARM TO ME, AND I'LL SELL THE ACREAGE AT A HUGE PROFIT AND RETIRE WHILE YOUNG
NEED A HIRED HAND?
GIVE ME A RESUMÉ AND THREE GOOD REFERENCES. AND MOM DOESN'T COUNT
JIM DAVIS 3-15

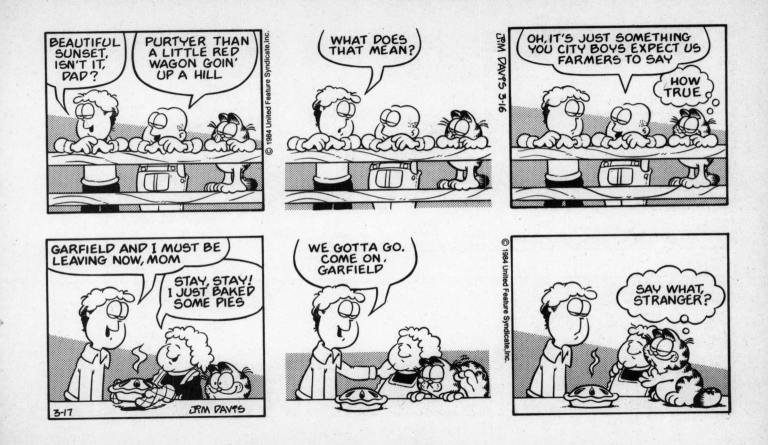

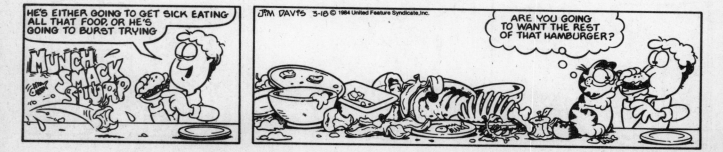

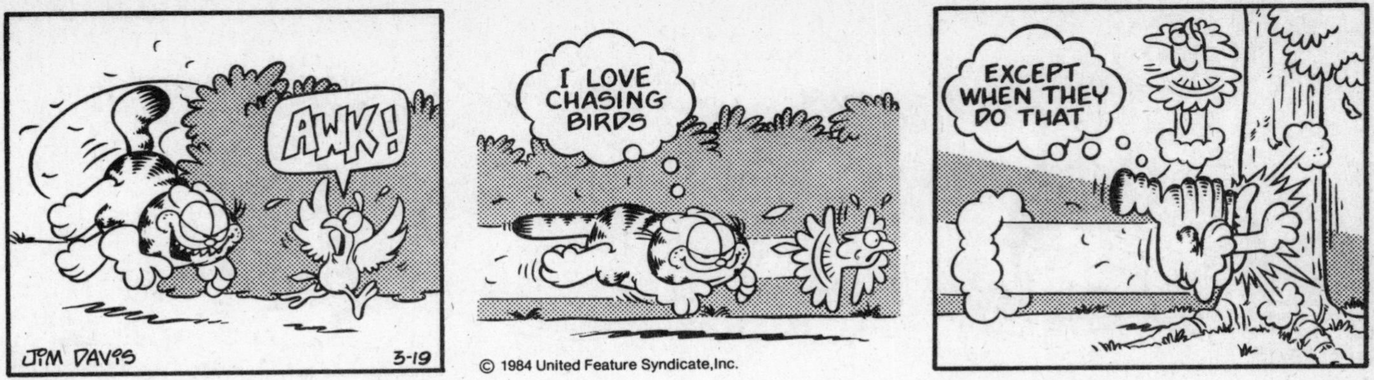
AWK!
I LOVE CHASING BIRDS
EXCEPT WHEN THEY DO THAT
JIM DAVIS
3-19

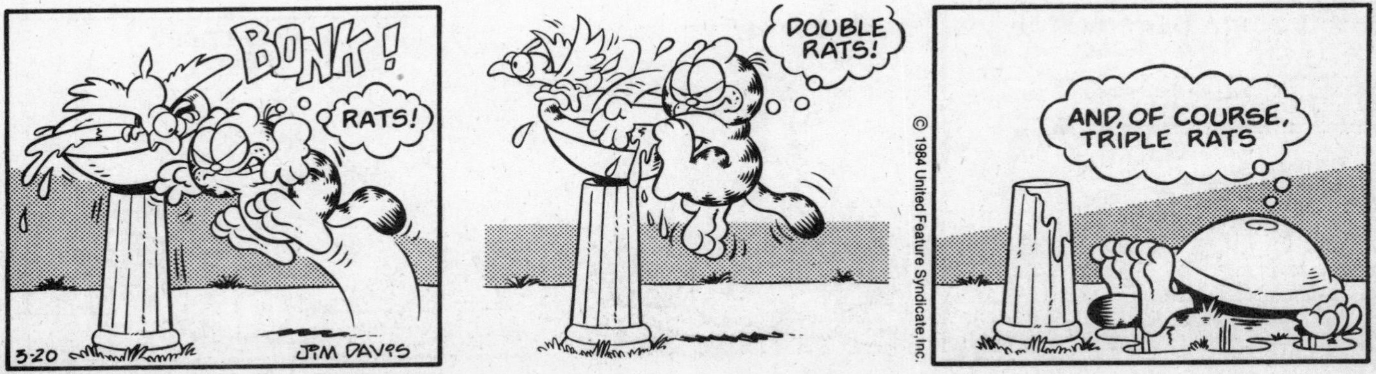
BONK!
RATS!
3-20
JIM DAVIS
DOUBLE RATS!
AND, OF COURSE, TRIPLE RATS

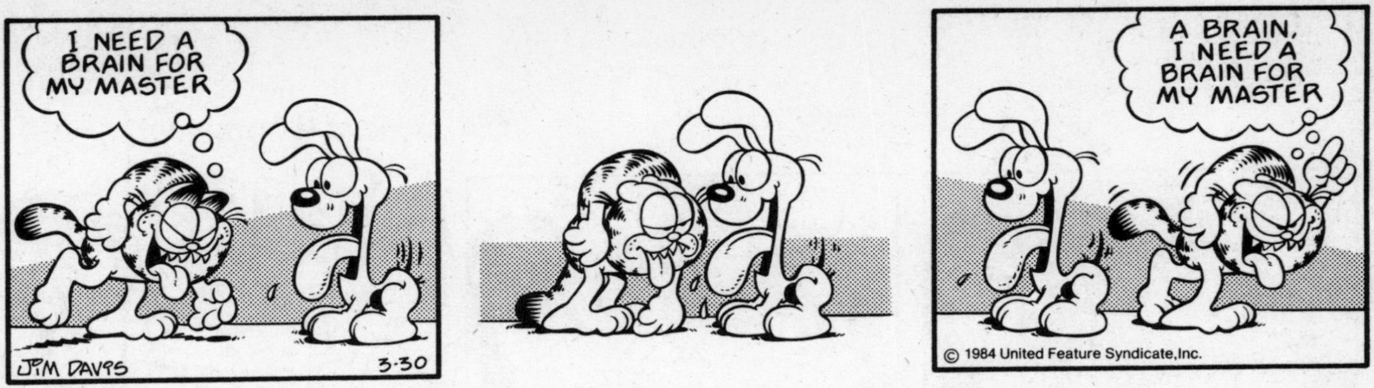
I NEED A BRAIN FOR MY MASTER
JIM DAVIS
3-30
A BRAIN, I NEED A BRAIN FOR MY MASTER
© 1984 United Feature Syndicate, Inc.

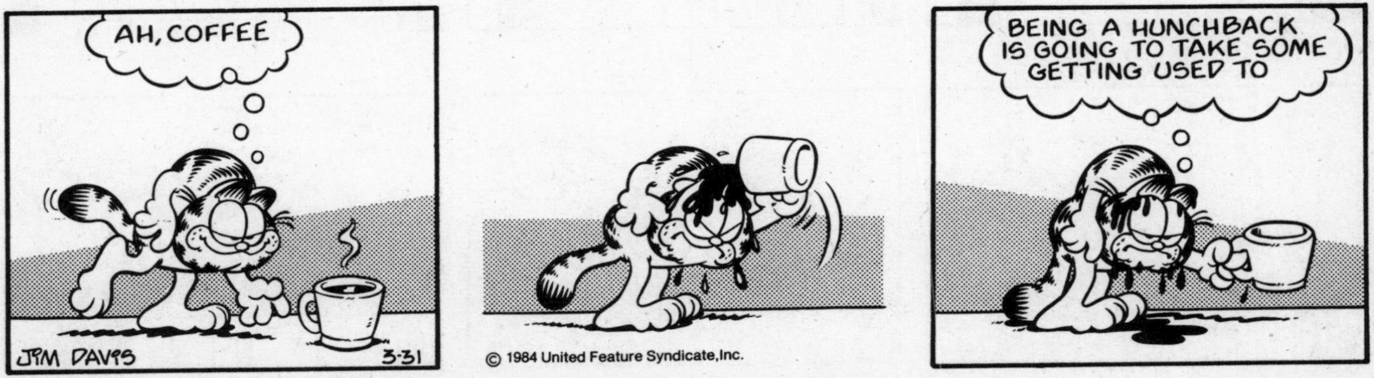
AH, COFFEE
JIM DAVIS
3-31
© 1984 United Feature Syndicate, Inc.
BEING A HUNCHBACK IS GOING TO TAKE SOME GETTING USED TO

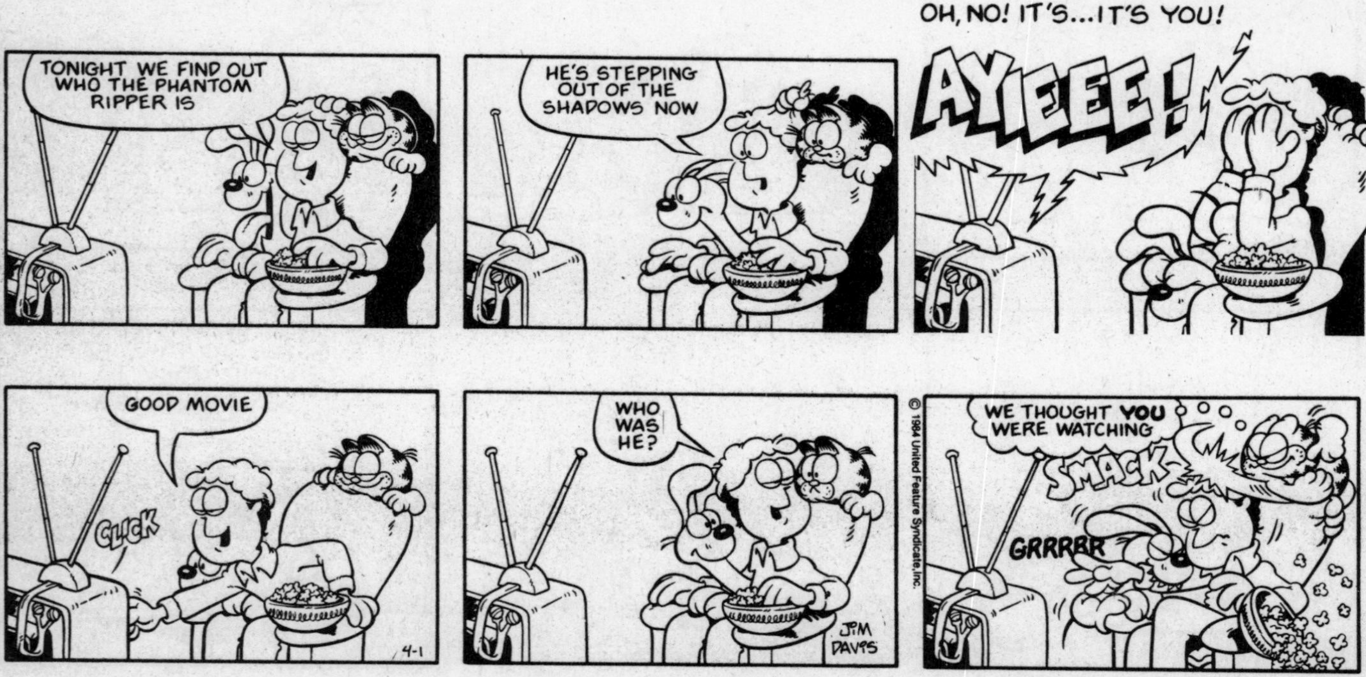
TONIGHT WE FIND OUT WHO THE PHANTOM RIPPER IS
HE'S STEPPING OUT OF THE SHADOWS NOW
OH, NO! IT'S...IT'S YOU!
AYIEEE!
GOOD MOVIE
CLICK
4-1
WHO WAS HE?
JIM DAVIS
© 1984 United Feature Syndicate, Inc.
WE THOUGHT YOU WERE WATCHING
SMACK
GRRRRR

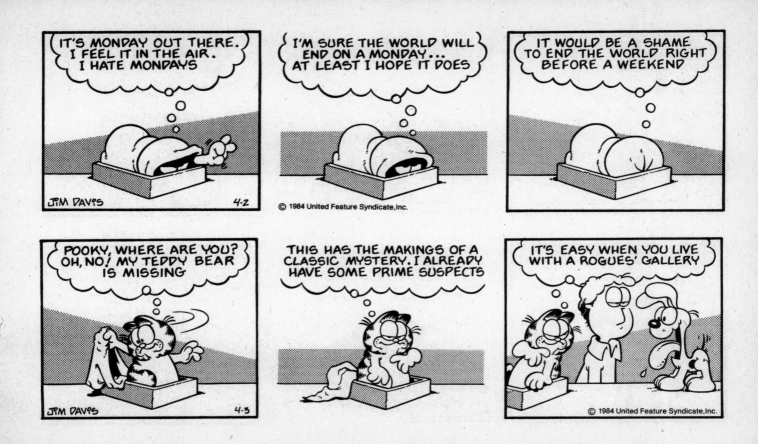

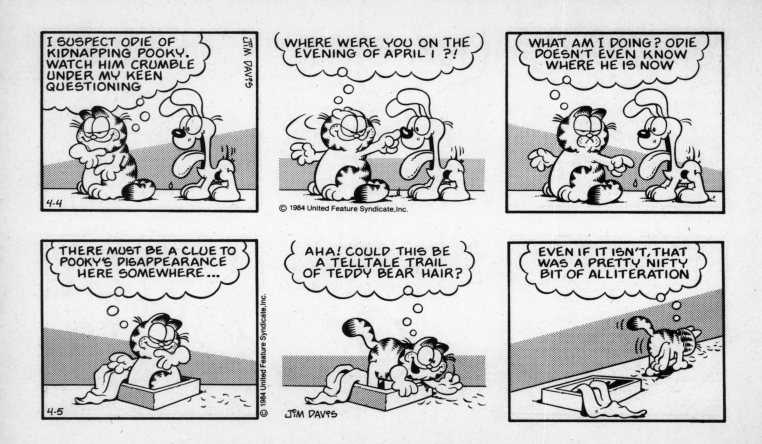

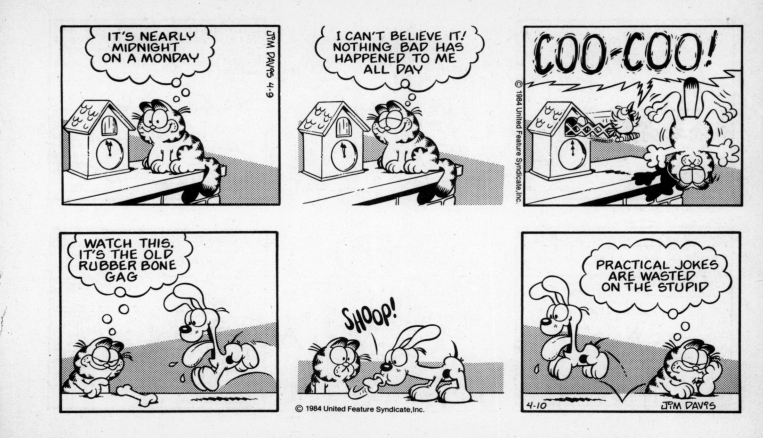

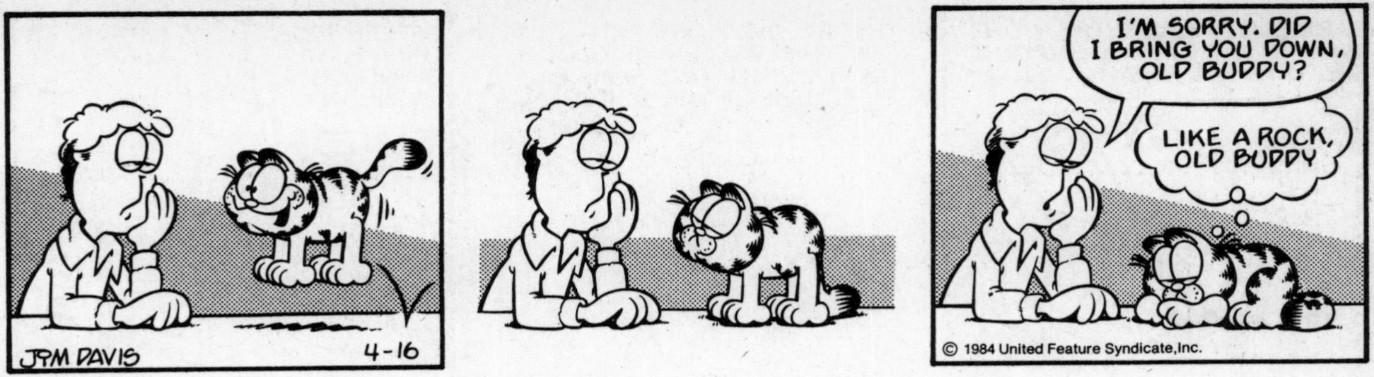
JIM DAVIS
4-16
I'M SORRY. DID I BRING YOU DOWN, OLD BUDDY?
LIKE A ROCK, OLD BUDDY
© 1984 United Feature Syndicate, Inc.

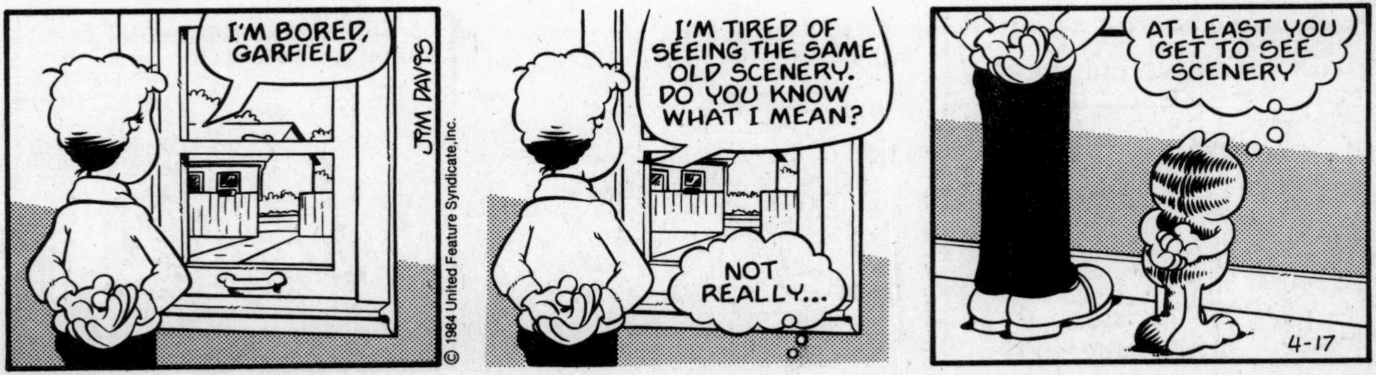
I'M BORED, GARFIELD
JIM DAVIS
© 1984 United Feature Syndicate, Inc.
I'M TIRED OF SEEING THE SAME OLD SCENERY. DO YOU KNOW WHAT I MEAN?
NOT REALLY...
AT LEAST YOU GET TO SEE SCENERY
4-17

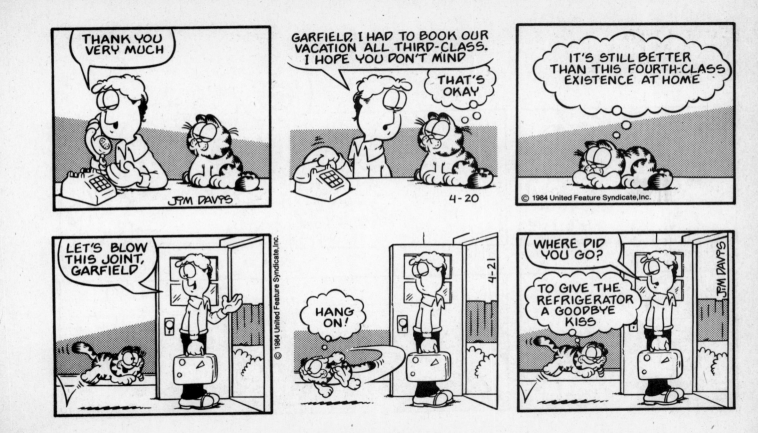

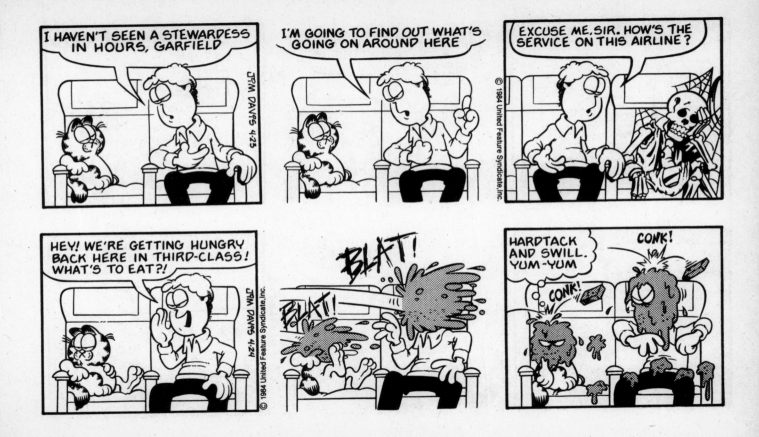

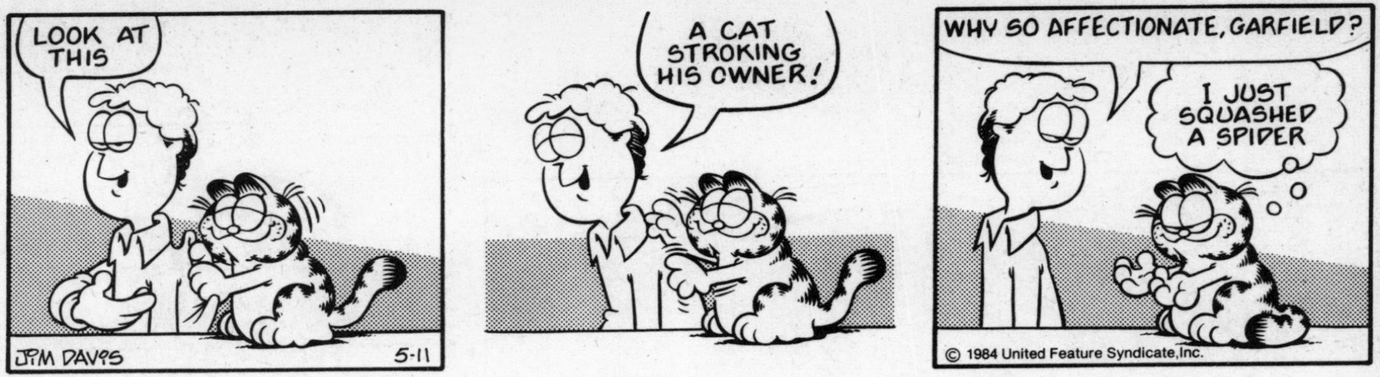
LOOK AT THIS
A CAT STROKING HIS OWNER!
WHY SO AFFECTIONATE, GARFIELD?
I JUST SQUASHED A SPIDER
JIM DAVIS
5-11
© 1984 United Feature Syndicate,Inc.

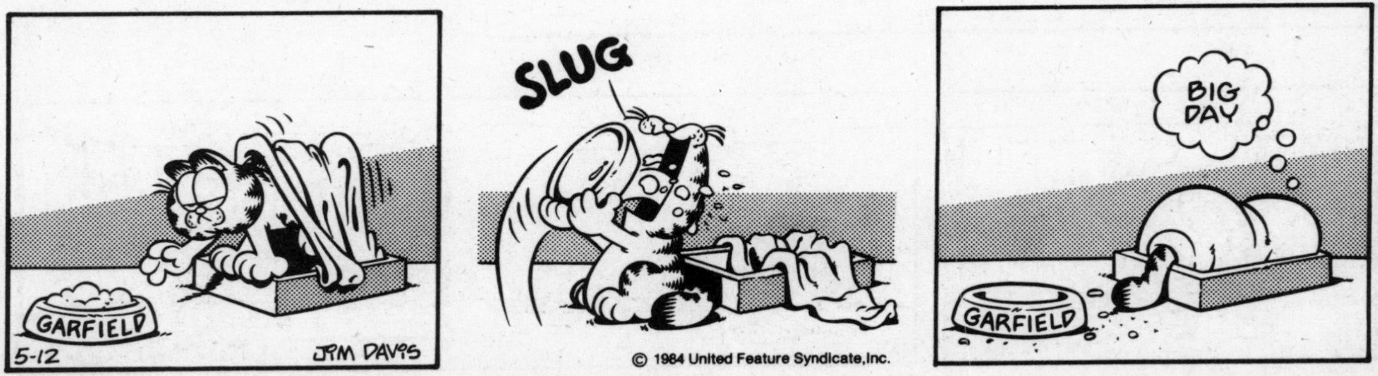
GARFIELD
5-12
JIM DAVIS
SLUG
BIG DAY
GARFIELD
© 1984 United Feature Syndicate,Inc.

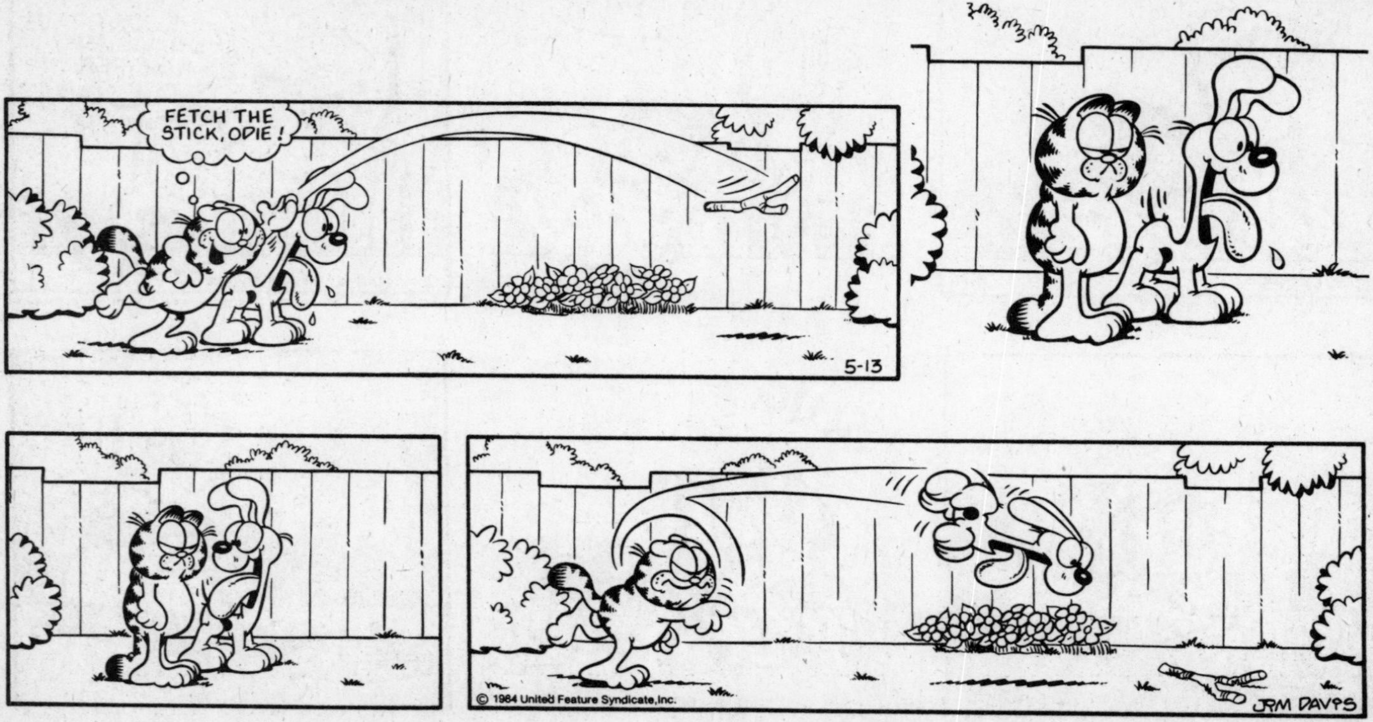
FETCH THE STICK, ODIE!
5-13
© 1984 United Feature Syndicate, Inc.
JIM DAVIS

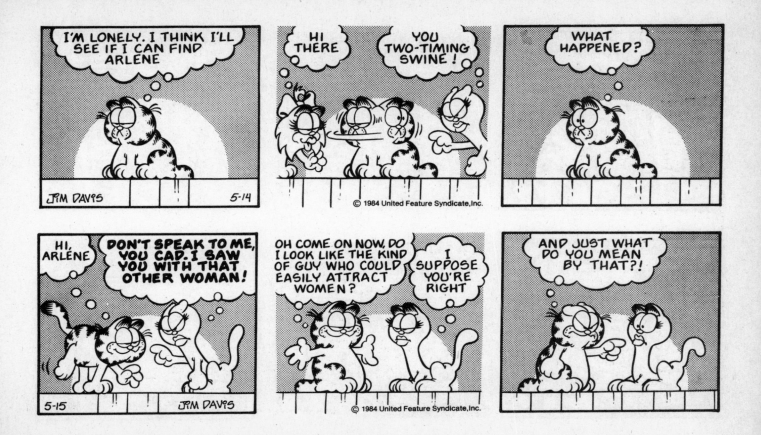

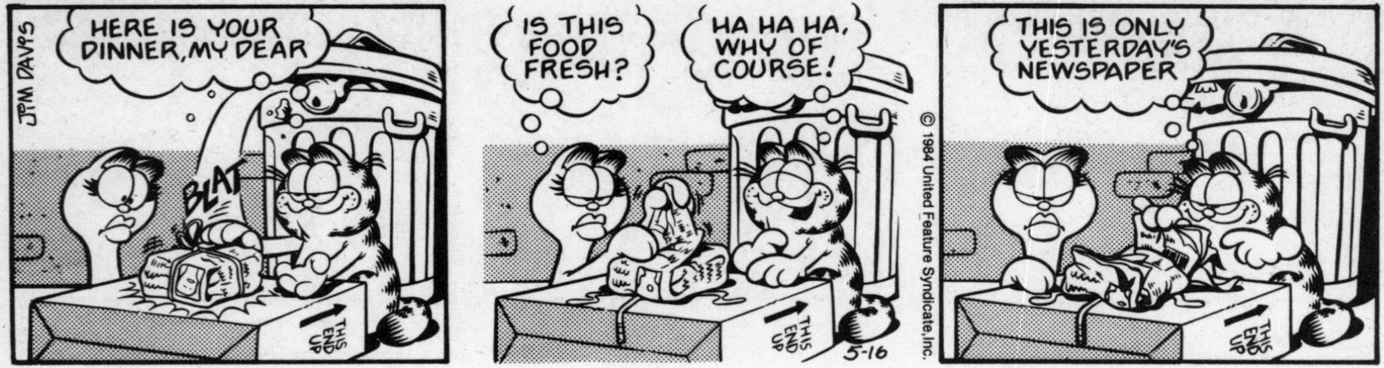
JIM DAVIS
HERE IS YOUR DINNER, MY DEAR
BLAT
THIS END UP
IS THIS FOOD FRESH?
HA HA HA, WHY OF COURSE!
THIS END UP
5-16
© 1984 United Feature Syndicate, Inc.
THIS IS ONLY YESTERDAY'S NEWSPAPER
THIS END UP

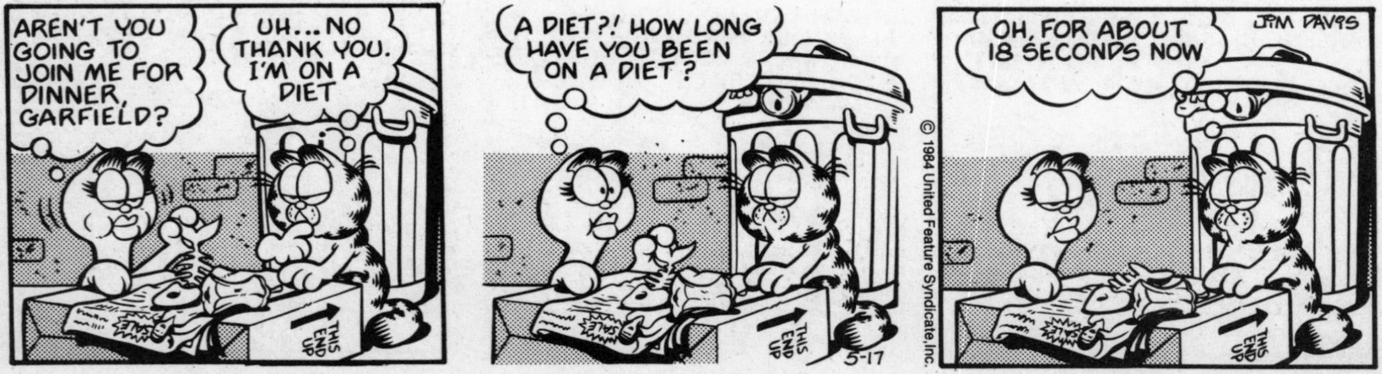
AREN'T YOU GOING TO JOIN ME FOR DINNER, GARFIELD?
UH... NO THANK YOU. I'M ON A DIET
SALE
THIS END UP
A DIET?! HOW LONG HAVE YOU BEEN ON A DIET?
SALE
THIS END UP
5-17
© 1984 United Feature Syndicate, Inc.
JIM DAVIS
OH, FOR ABOUT 18 SECONDS NOW
SALE
THIS END UP

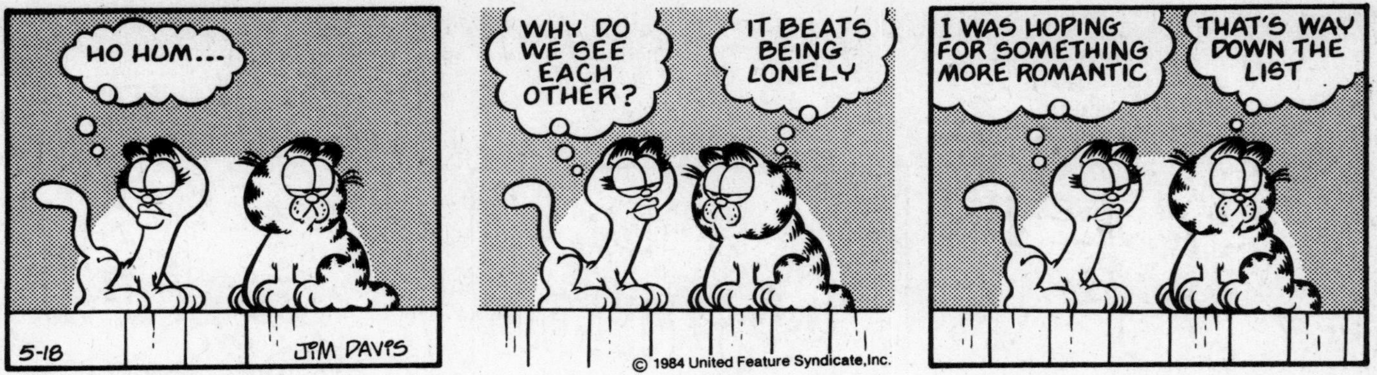
HO HUM...
5-18
JIM DAVIS
WHY DO WE SEE EACH OTHER?
IT BEATS BEING LONELY
© 1984 United Feature Syndicate, Inc.
I WAS HOPING FOR SOMETHING MORE ROMANTIC
THAT'S WAY DOWN THE LIST

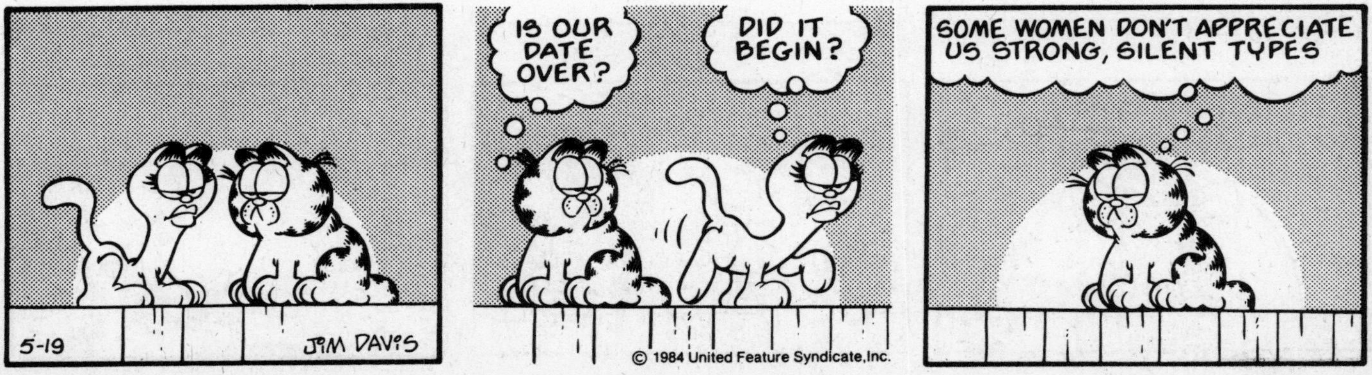
5-19
JIM DAVIS
IS OUR DATE OVER?
DID IT BEGIN?
© 1984 United Feature Syndicate, Inc.
SOME WOMEN DON'T APPRECIATE US STRONG, SILENT TYPES

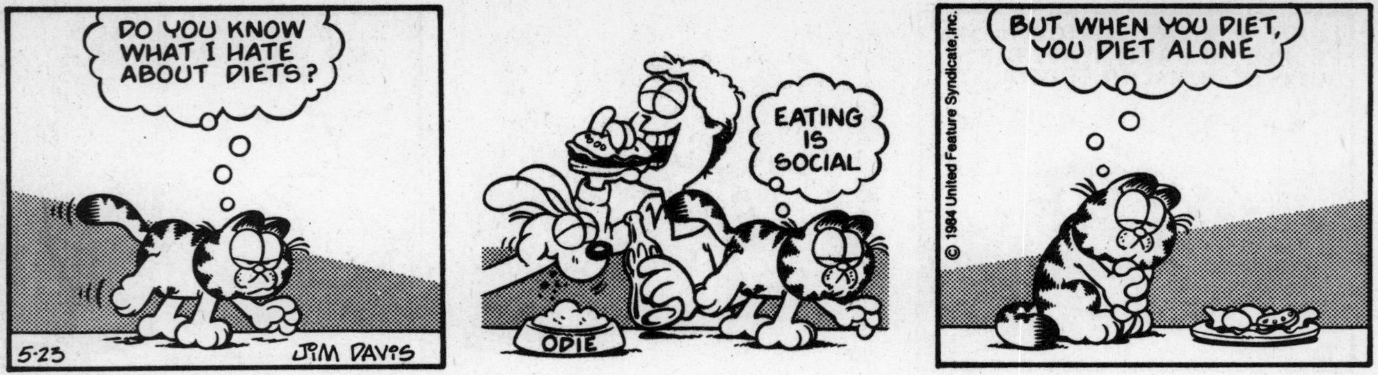
DO YOU KNOW WHAT I HATE ABOUT DIETS?
5-23
JIM DAVIS
ODIE
EATING IS SOCIAL
© 1984 United Feature Syndicate, Inc.
BUT WHEN YOU DIET, YOU DIET ALONE

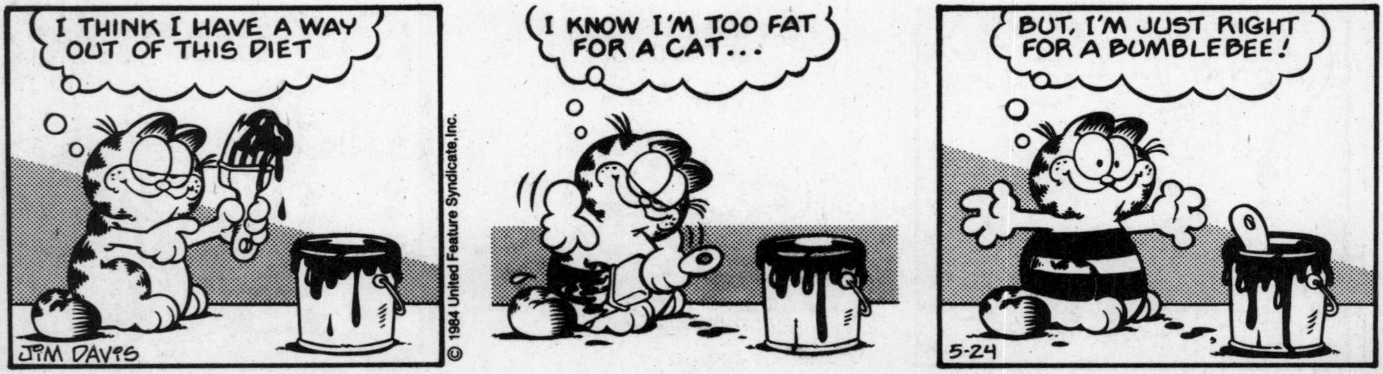
I THINK I HAVE A WAY OUT OF THIS DIET
JIM DAVIS
© 1984 United Feature Syndicate, Inc.
I KNOW I'M TOO FAT FOR A CAT...
BUT, I'M JUST RIGHT FOR A BUMBLEBEE!
5-24

Garfield's Loves & Hates

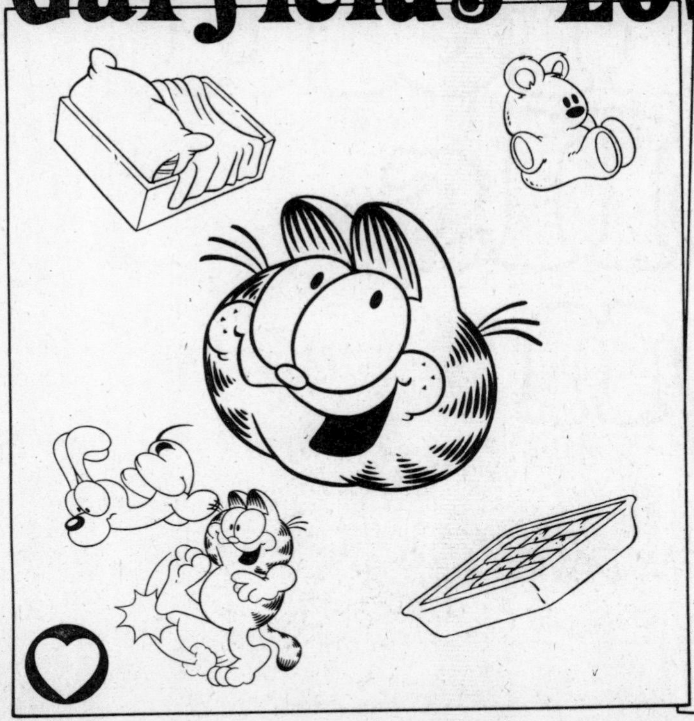

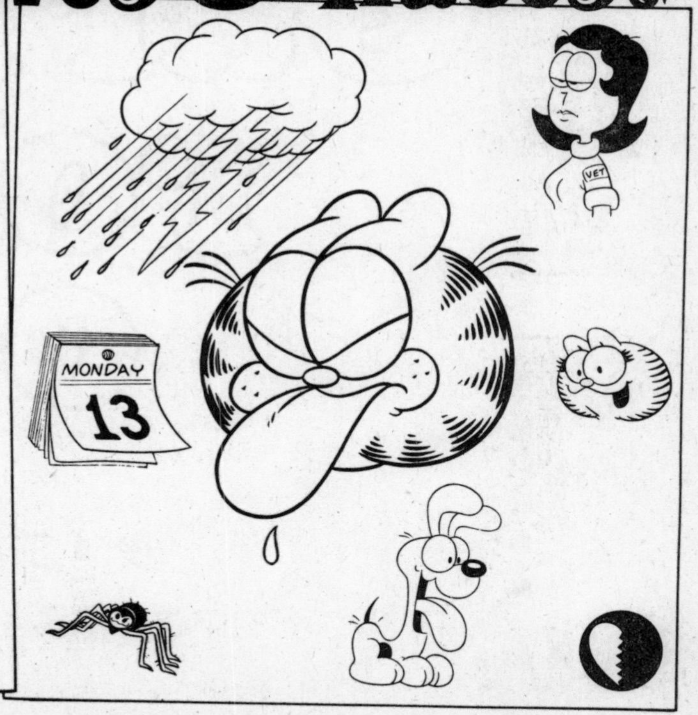
VET
MONDAY
13

Garfield rolls on

BY: JIM DAVIS

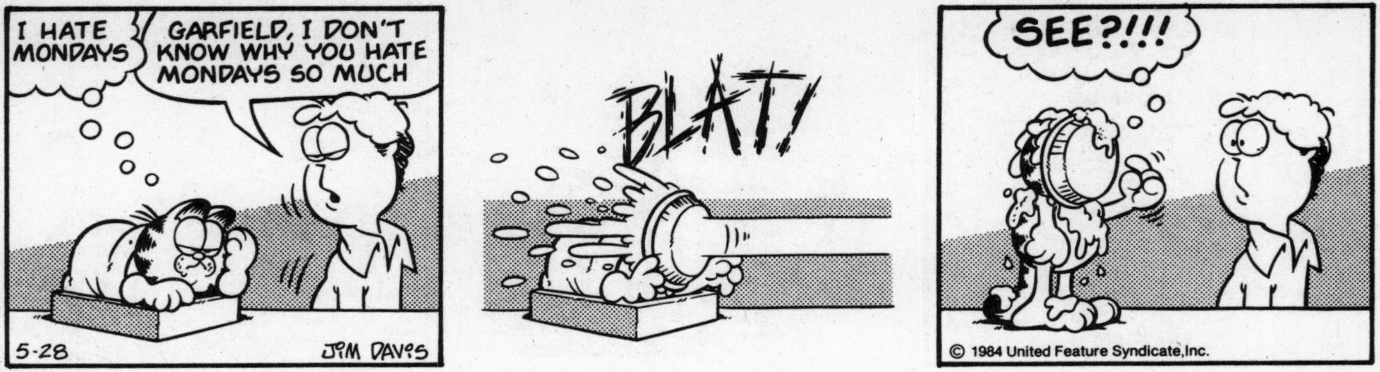
I HATE MONDAYS
GARFIELD, I DON'T KNOW WHY YOU HATE MONDAYS SO MUCH
5-28
JIM DAVIS
BLAT!
SEE?!!!
© 1984 United Feature Syndicate, Inc.

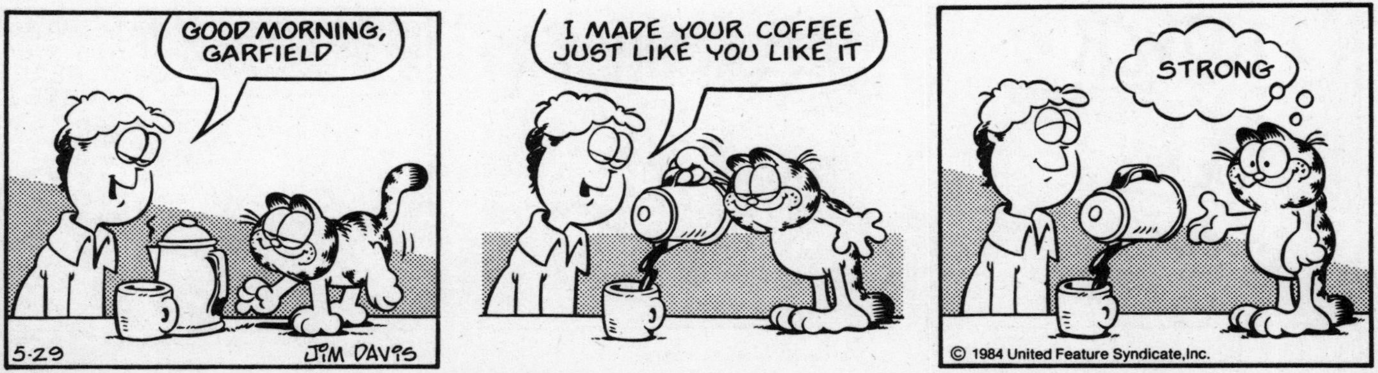
GOOD MORNING, GARFIELD
5-29
JIM DAVIS
I MADE YOUR COFFEE JUST LIKE YOU LIKE IT
STRONG
© 1984 United Feature Syndicate, Inc.

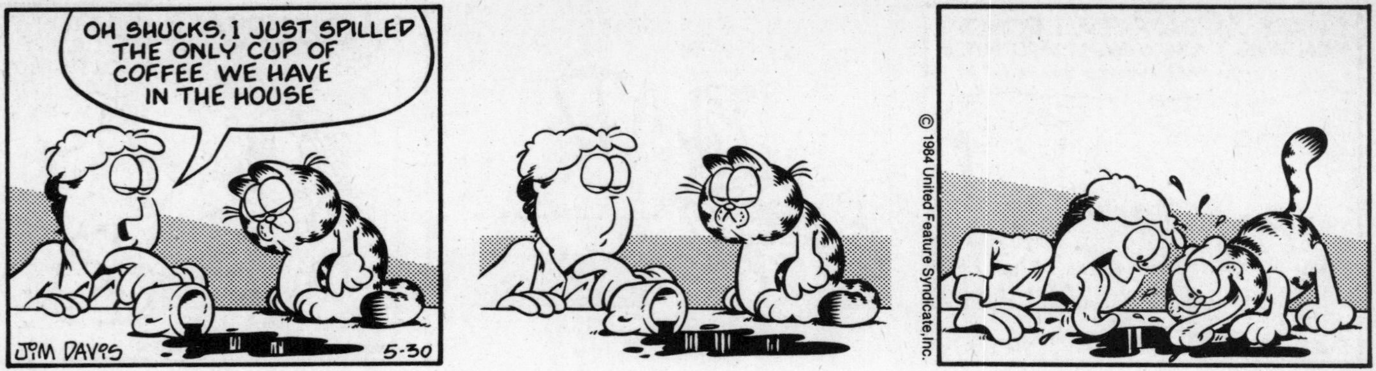
OH SHUCKS, I JUST SPILLED THE ONLY CUP OF COFFEE WE HAVE IN THE HOUSE
JIM DAVIS
5-30
© 1984 United Feature Syndicate, Inc.

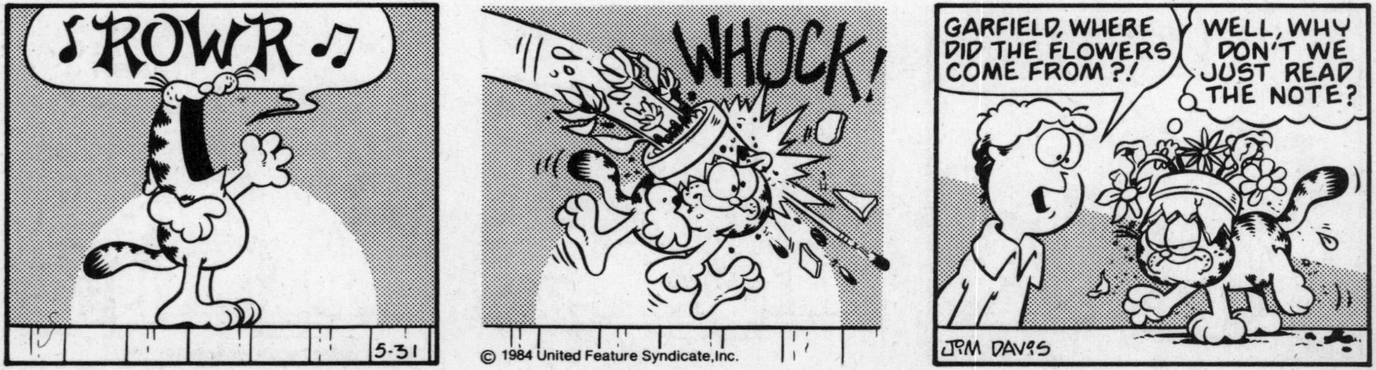
♪ ROWR ♫
5-31
WHOCK!
© 1984 United Feature Syndicate, Inc.
GARFIELD, WHERE DID THE FLOWERS COME FROM?!
WELL, WHY DON'T WE JUST READ THE NOTE?
JIM DAVIS

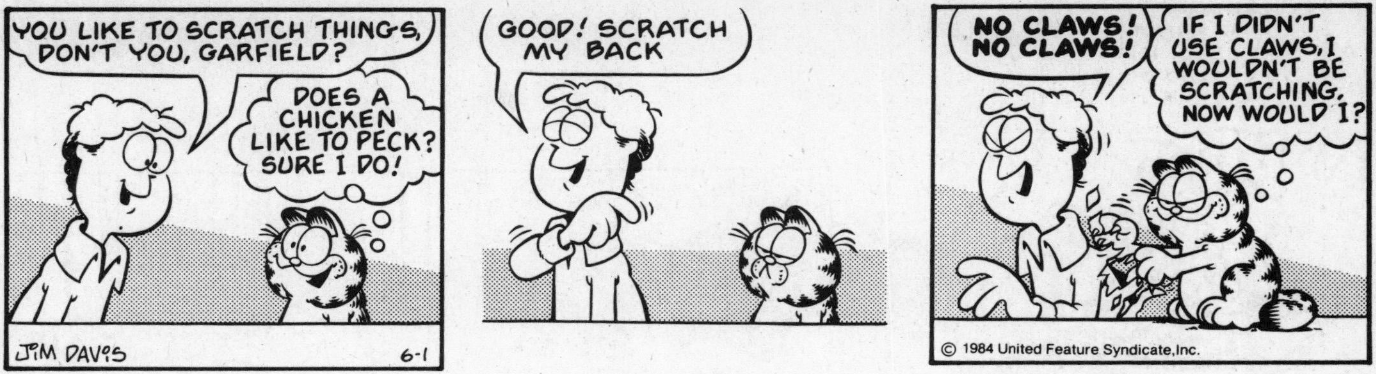
YOU LIKE TO SCRATCH THINGS, DON'T YOU, GARFIELD?
DOES A CHICKEN LIKE TO PECK? SURE I DO!
JIM DAVIS
6-1
GOOD! SCRATCH MY BACK
NO CLAWS! NO CLAWS!
IF I DIDN'T USE CLAWS, I WOULDN'T BE SCRATCHING, NOW WOULD I?
© 1984 United Feature Syndicate, Inc.

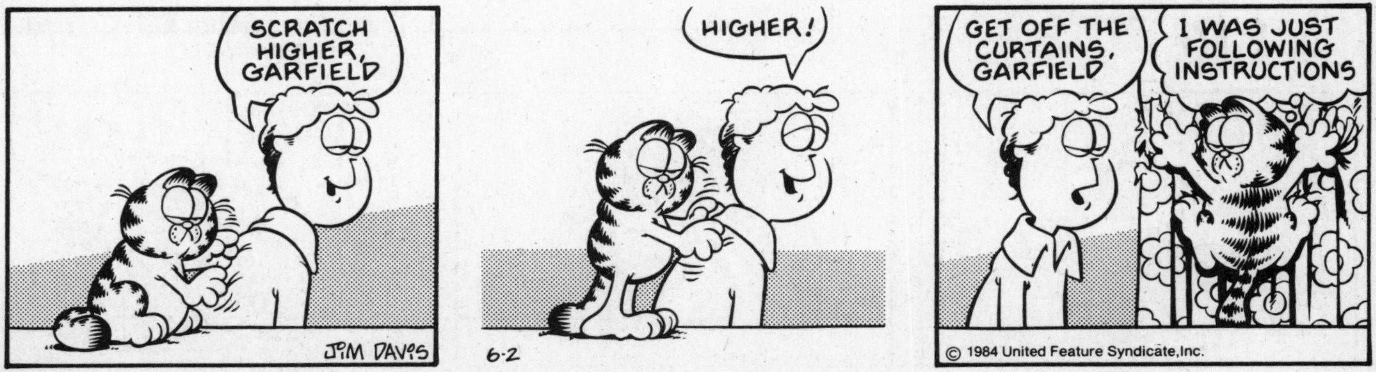
SCRATCH HIGHER, GARFIELD
JIM DAVIS
HIGHER!
6-2
GET OFF THE CURTAINS, GARFIELD
I WAS JUST FOLLOWING INSTRUCTIONS
© 1984 United Feature Syndicate, Inc.

RRRRRR

JON'S BEST SHOES!

SOMETIMES ODIE MAKES ME SO ANGRY, I COULD JUST SCREAM

ARRRRRGH!

© 1984 United Feature Syndicate, Inc.

JIM DAVIS   6-3

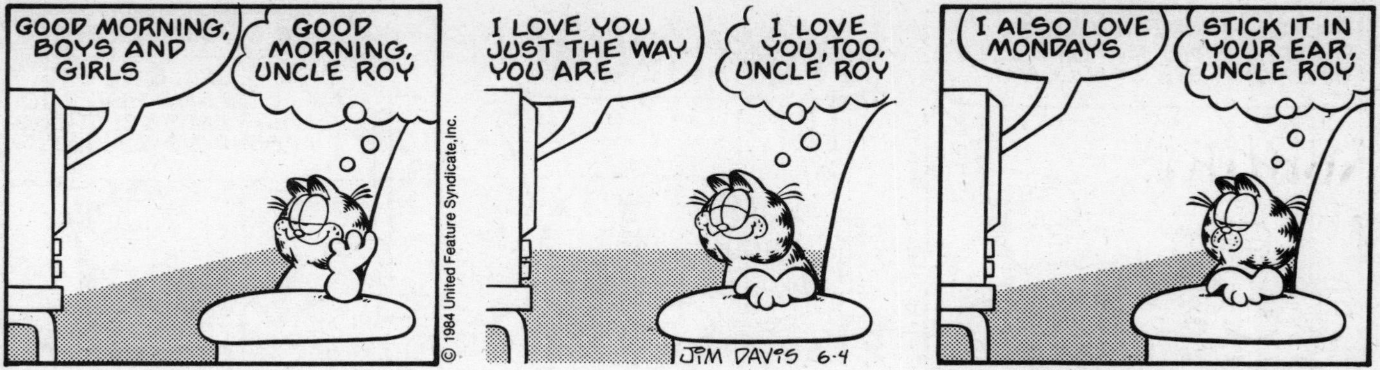
GOOD MORNING, BOYS AND GIRLS
GOOD MORNING, UNCLE ROY
I LOVE YOU JUST THE WAY YOU ARE
I LOVE YOU, TOO, UNCLE ROY
I ALSO LOVE MONDAYS
STICK IT IN YOUR EAR, UNCLE ROY
JIM DAVIS 6-4
© 1984 United Feature Syndicate, Inc.

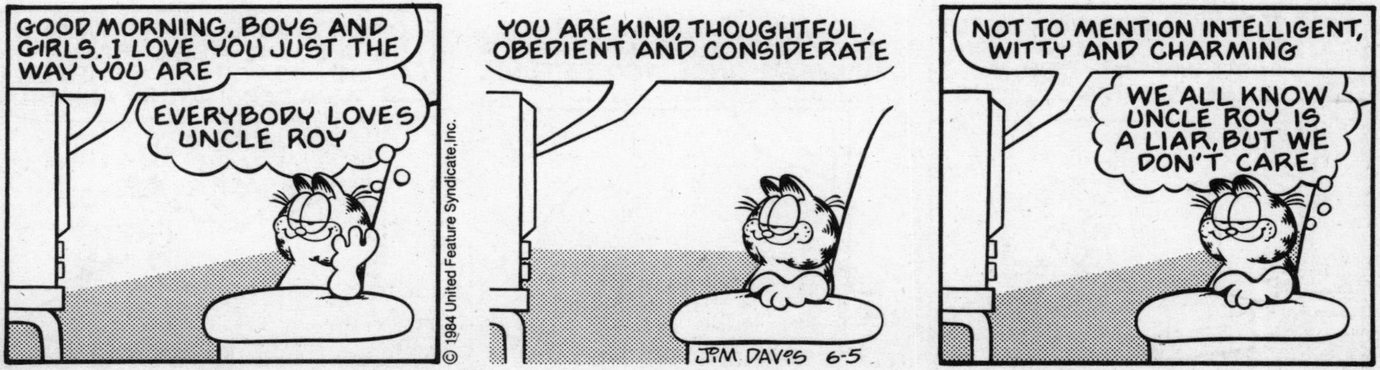
GOOD MORNING, BOYS AND GIRLS. I LOVE YOU JUST THE WAY YOU ARE
EVERYBODY LOVES UNCLE ROY
YOU ARE KIND, THOUGHTFUL, OBEDIENT AND CONSIDERATE
NOT TO MENTION INTELLIGENT, WITTY AND CHARMING
WE ALL KNOW UNCLE ROY IS A LIAR, BUT WE DON'T CARE
JIM DAVIS 6-5
© 1984 United Feature Syndicate, Inc.

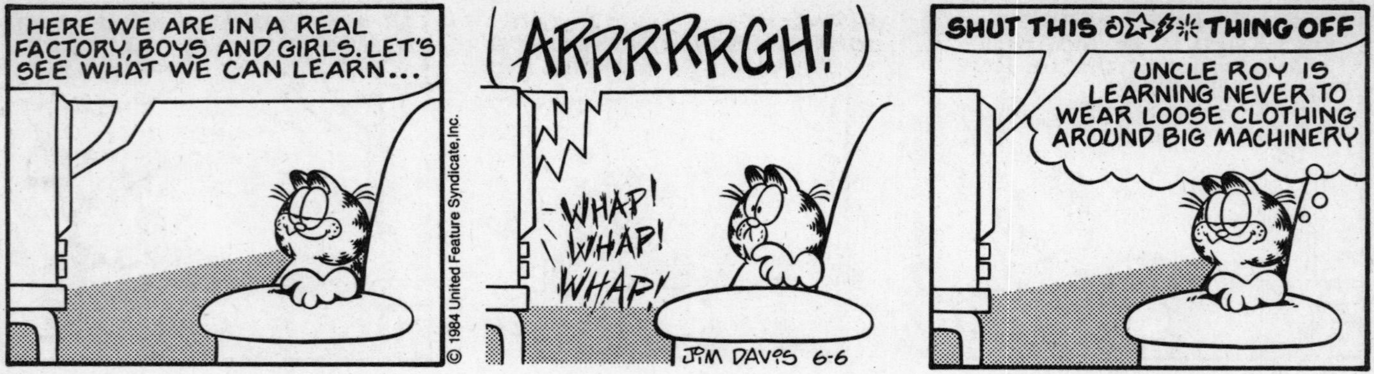
HERE WE ARE IN A REAL FACTORY, BOYS AND GIRLS. LET'S SEE WHAT WE CAN LEARN...
© 1984 United Feature Syndicate, Inc.
ARRRRRGH!
WHAP! WHAP! WHAP!
JIM DAVIS 6-6
SHUT THIS @☆⚡✳ THING OFF
UNCLE ROY IS LEARNING NEVER TO WEAR LOOSE CLOTHING AROUND BIG MACHINERY

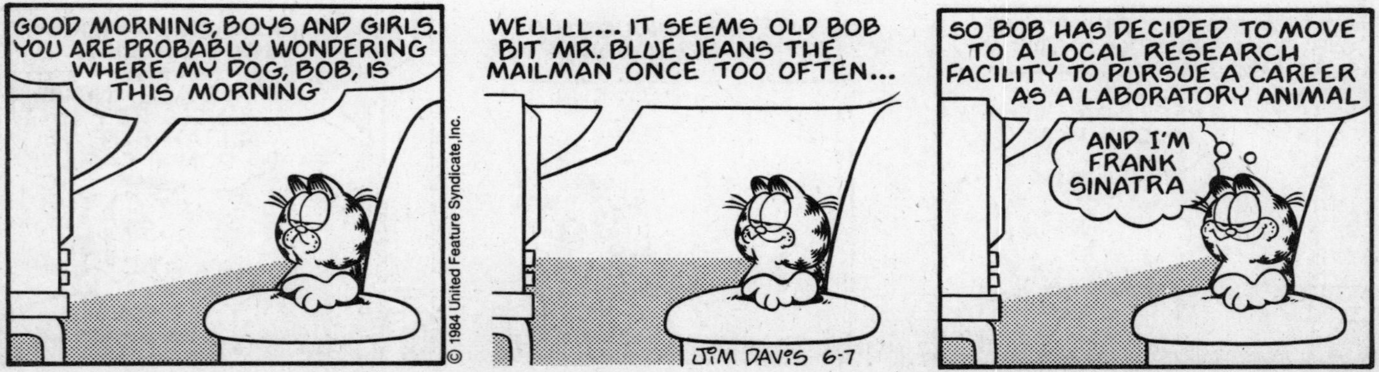
GOOD MORNING, BOYS AND GIRLS. YOU ARE PROBABLY WONDERING WHERE MY DOG, BOB, IS THIS MORNING
© 1984 United Feature Syndicate, Inc.
WELLLL... IT SEEMS OLD BOB BIT MR. BLUE JEANS THE MAILMAN ONCE TOO OFTEN...
JIM DAVIS 6-7
SO BOB HAS DECIDED TO MOVE TO A LOCAL RESEARCH FACILITY TO PURSUE A CAREER AS A LABORATORY ANIMAL
AND I'M FRANK SINATRA

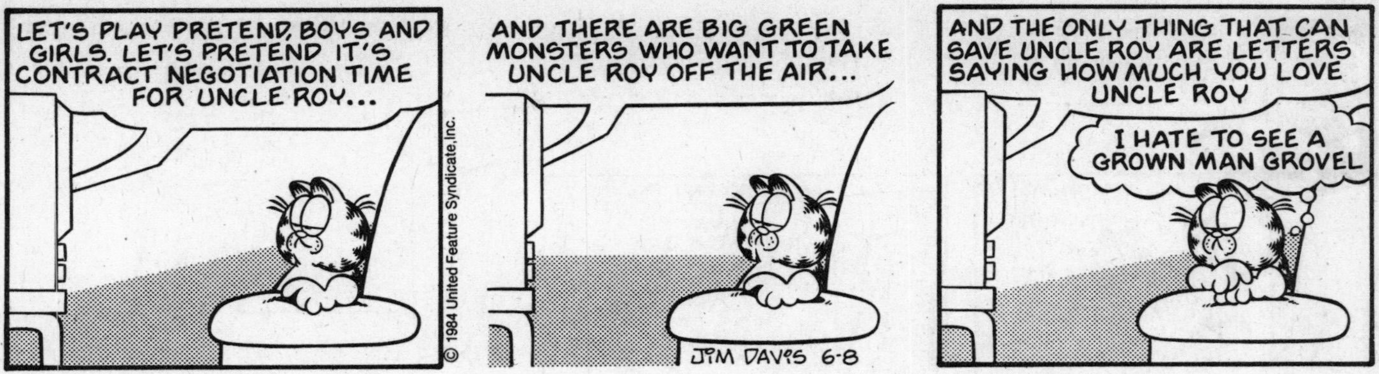
LET'S PLAY PRETEND, BOYS AND GIRLS. LET'S PRETEND IT'S CONTRACT NEGOTIATION TIME FOR UNCLE ROY...
© 1984 United Feature Syndicate, Inc.
AND THERE ARE BIG GREEN MONSTERS WHO WANT TO TAKE UNCLE ROY OFF THE AIR...
JIM DAVIS 6-8
AND THE ONLY THING THAT CAN SAVE UNCLE ROY ARE LETTERS SAYING HOW MUCH YOU LOVE UNCLE ROY
I HATE TO SEE A GROWN MAN GROVEL

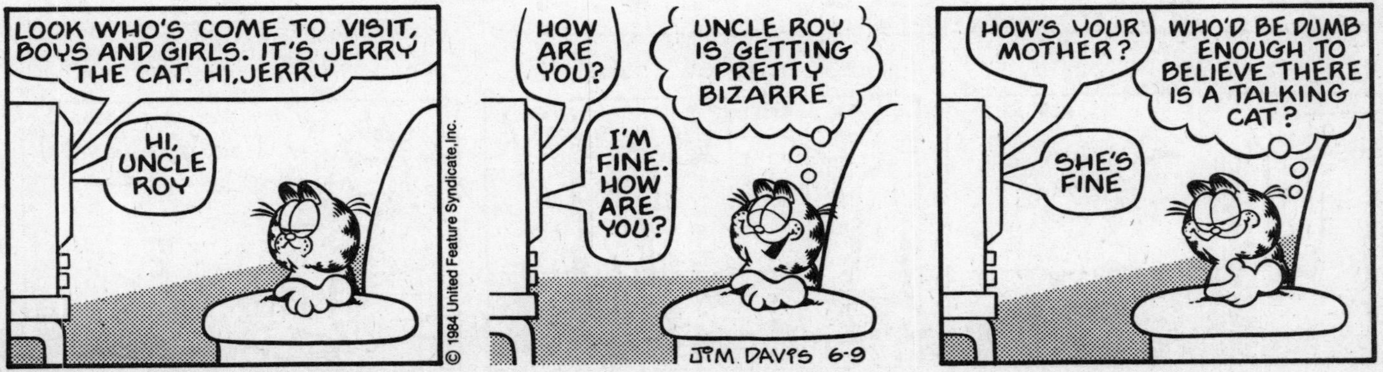
LOOK WHO'S COME TO VISIT, BOYS AND GIRLS. IT'S JERRY THE CAT. HI, JERRY
HI, UNCLE ROY
© 1984 United Feature Syndicate, Inc.
HOW ARE YOU?
I'M FINE. HOW ARE YOU?
UNCLE ROY IS GETTING PRETTY BIZARRE
JIM DAVIS 6-9
HOW'S YOUR MOTHER?
SHE'S FINE
WHO'D BE DUMB ENOUGH TO BELIEVE THERE IS A TALKING CAT?

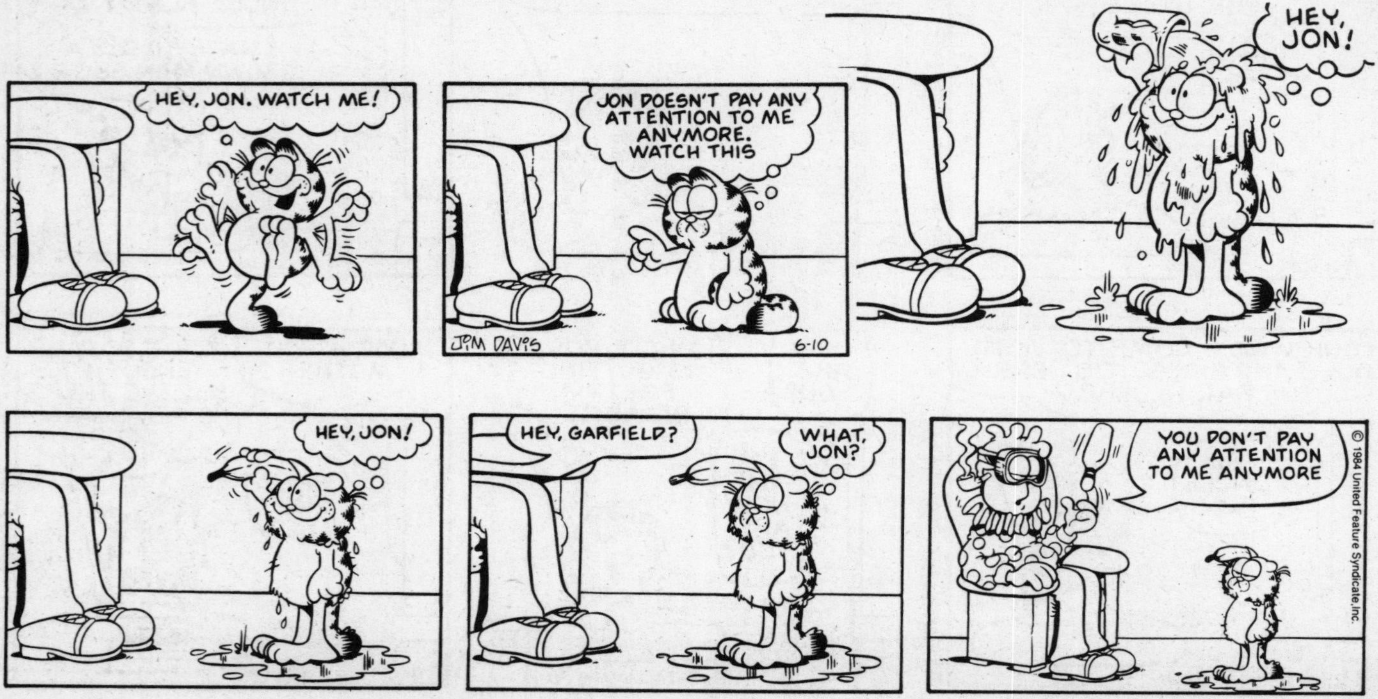

HEY, JON. WATCH ME!
JON DOESN'T PAY ANY ATTENTION TO ME ANYMORE. WATCH THIS
JIM DAVIS
6-10
HEY, JON!
HEY, JON!
HEY, GARFIELD?
WHAT, JON?
YOU DON'T PAY ANY ATTENTION TO ME ANYMORE
© 1984 United Feature Syndicate, Inc.

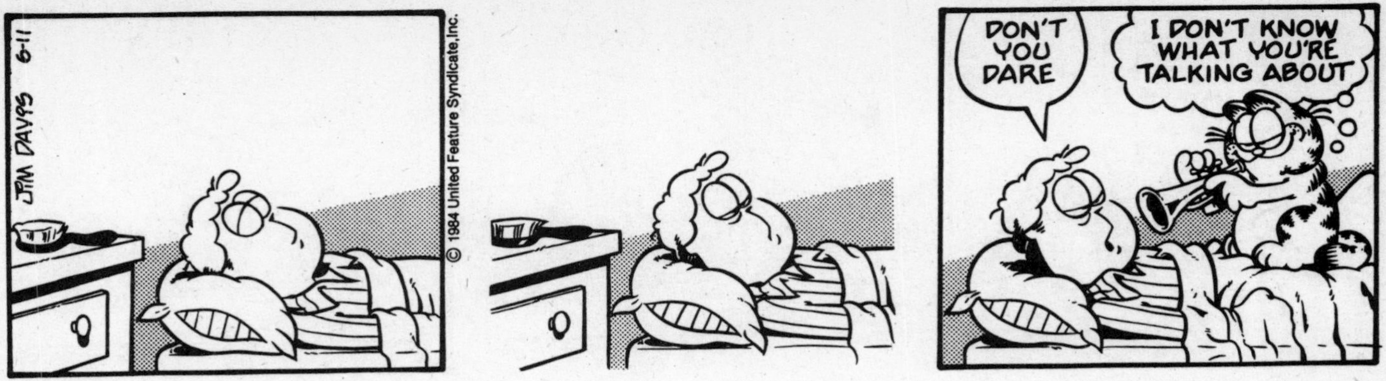
JIM DAVIS 6-11
© 1984 United Feature Syndicate, Inc.
DON'T YOU DARE
I DON'T KNOW WHAT YOU'RE TALKING ABOUT

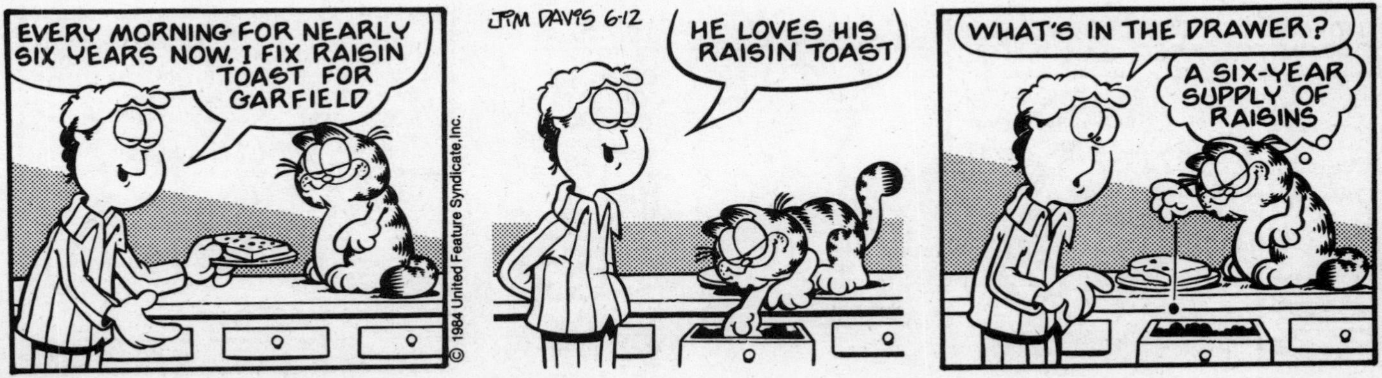
EVERY MORNING FOR NEARLY SIX YEARS NOW, I FIX RAISIN TOAST FOR GARFIELD
© 1984 United Feature Syndicate, Inc.
JIM DAVIS 6-12
HE LOVES HIS RAISIN TOAST
WHAT'S IN THE DRAWER?
A SIX-YEAR SUPPLY OF RAISINS

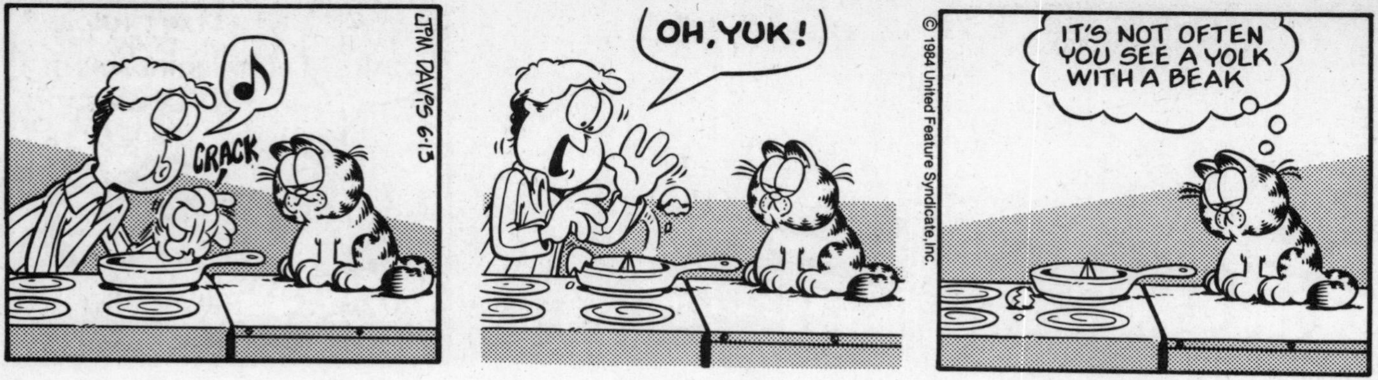

JIM DAVIS 6-13
CRACK
OH, YUK!
© 1984 United Feature Syndicate, Inc.
IT'S NOT OFTEN YOU SEE A YOLK WITH A BEAK

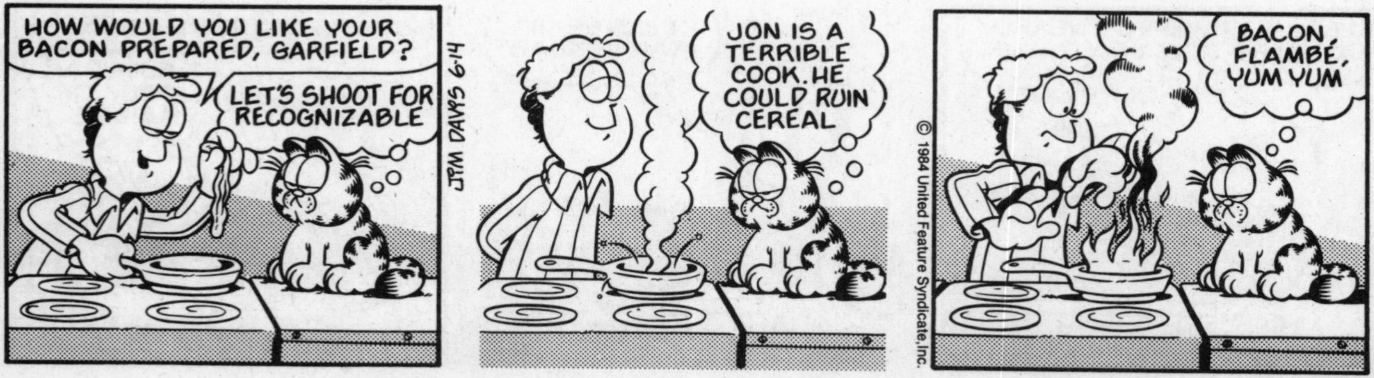

HOW WOULD YOU LIKE YOUR BACON PREPARED, GARFIELD?
LET'S SHOOT FOR RECOGNIZABLE
JIM DAVIS 6-14
JON IS A TERRIBLE COOK. HE COULD RUIN CEREAL
© 1984 United Feature Syndicate, Inc.
BACON FLAMBÉ, YUM YUM

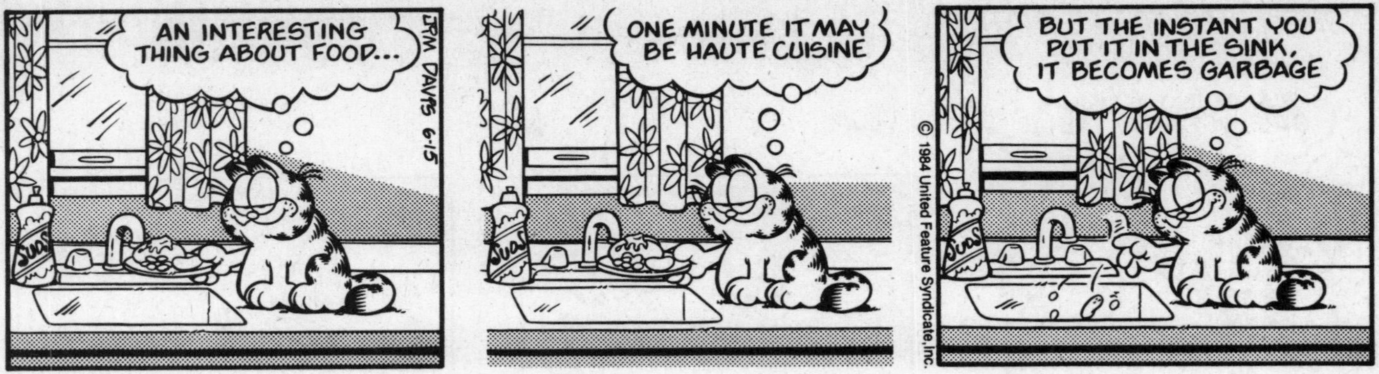
AN INTERESTING THING ABOUT FOOD...
JIM DAVIS 6-15
ONE MINUTE IT MAY BE HAUTE CUISINE
BUT THE INSTANT YOU PUT IT IN THE SINK, IT BECOMES GARBAGE

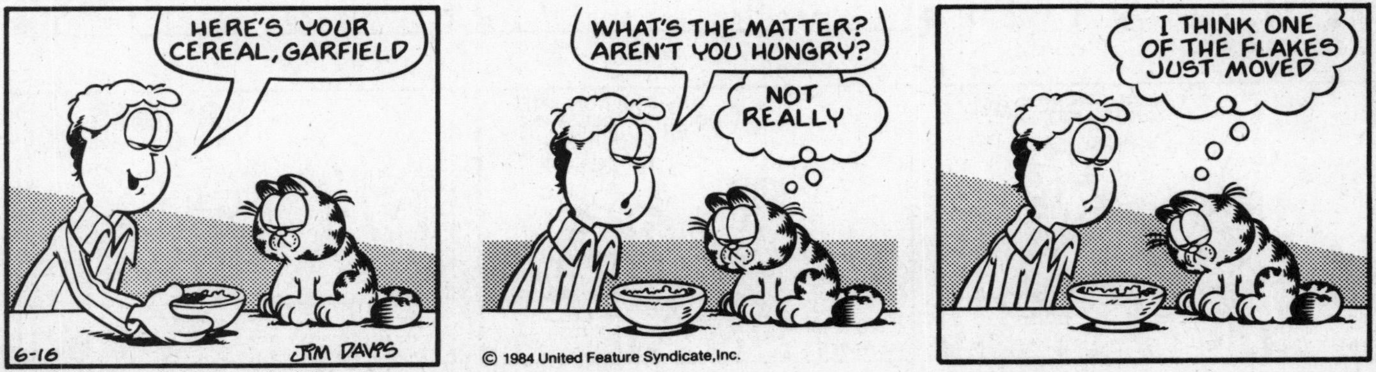
HERE'S YOUR CEREAL, GARFIELD
6-16
JIM DAVIS
WHAT'S THE MATTER? AREN'T YOU HUNGRY?
NOT REALLY
I THINK ONE OF THE FLAKES JUST MOVED

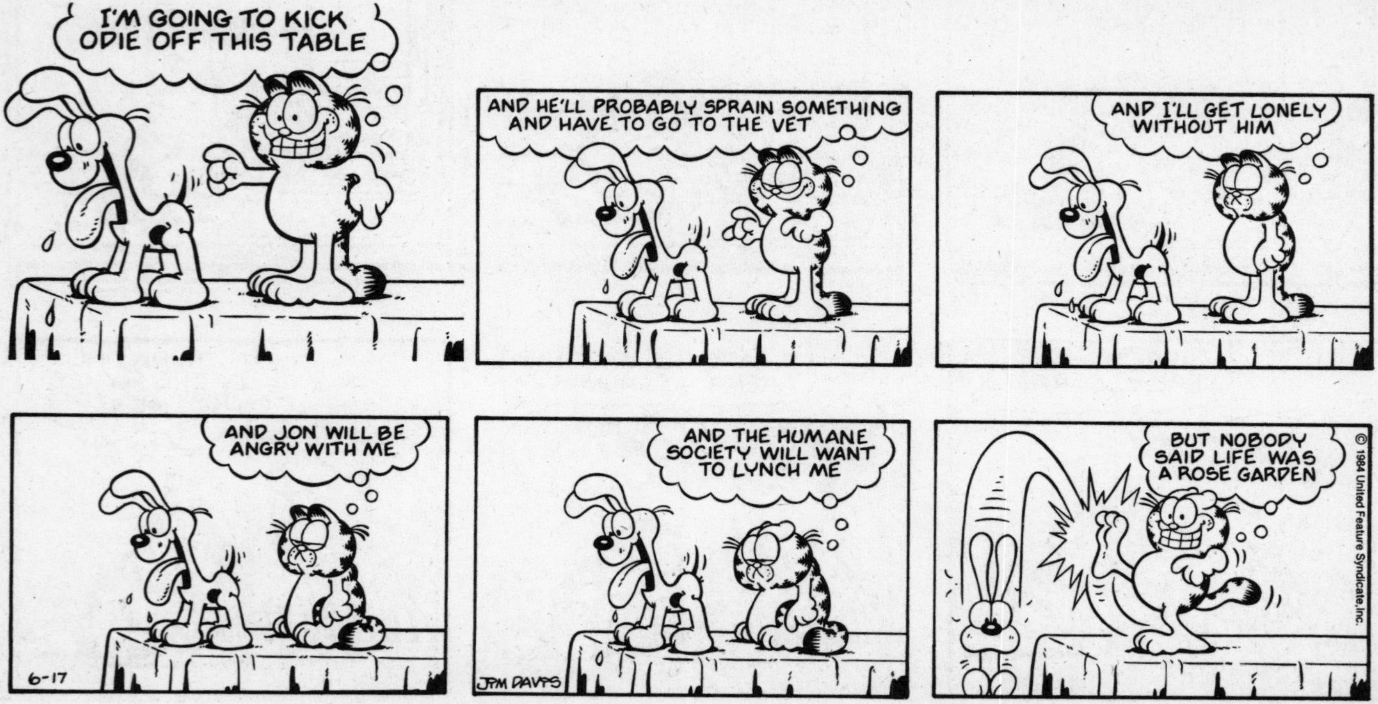
I'M GOING TO KICK ODIE OFF THIS TABLE
AND HE'LL PROBABLY SPRAIN SOMETHING AND HAVE TO GO TO THE VET
AND I'LL GET LONELY WITHOUT HIM
AND JON WILL BE ANGRY WITH ME
AND THE HUMANE SOCIETY WILL WANT TO LYNCH ME
BUT NOBODY SAID LIFE WAS A ROSE GARDEN
6-17
JPM DAVPS
© 1984 United Feature Syndicate, Inc.

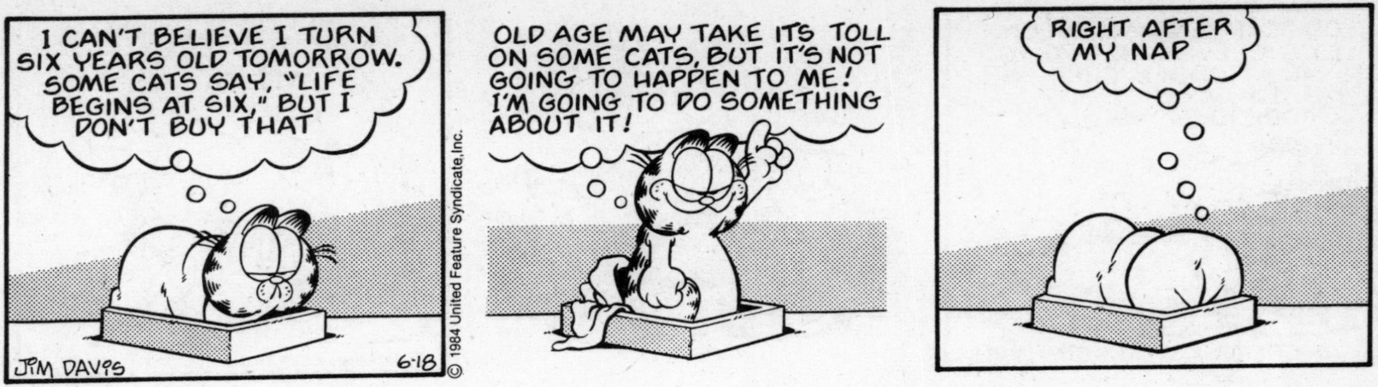
I CAN'T BELIEVE I TURN SIX YEARS OLD TOMORROW. SOME CATS SAY, "LIFE BEGINS AT SIX," BUT I DON'T BUY THAT
JIM DAVIS
6-18
OLD AGE MAY TAKE ITS TOLL ON SOME CATS, BUT IT'S NOT GOING TO HAPPEN TO ME! I'M GOING TO DO SOMETHING ABOUT IT!
RIGHT AFTER MY NAP

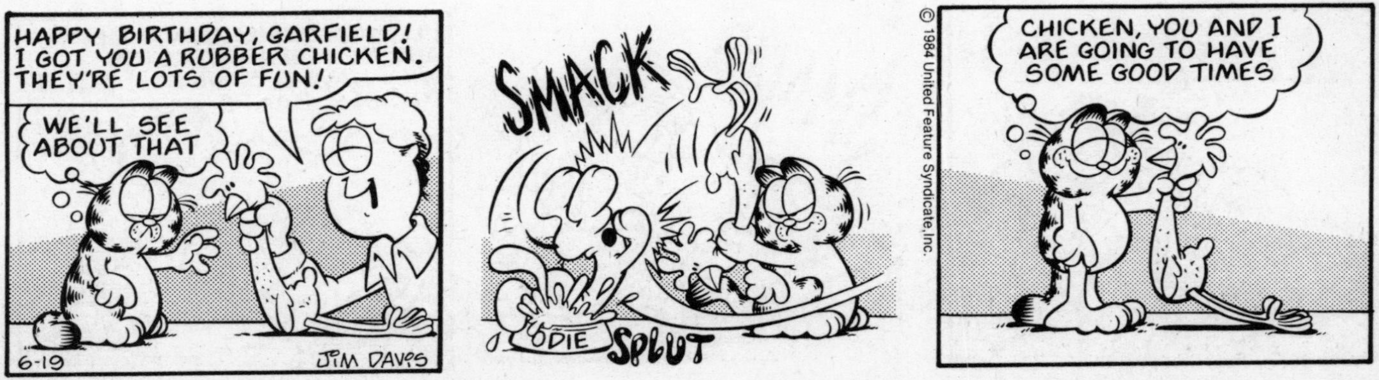
HAPPY BIRTHDAY, GARFIELD! I GOT YOU A RUBBER CHICKEN. THEY'RE LOTS OF FUN!
WE'LL SEE ABOUT THAT
6-19
JIM DAVIS
SMACK
ODIE
SPLUT
CHICKEN, YOU AND I ARE GOING TO HAVE SOME GOOD TIMES

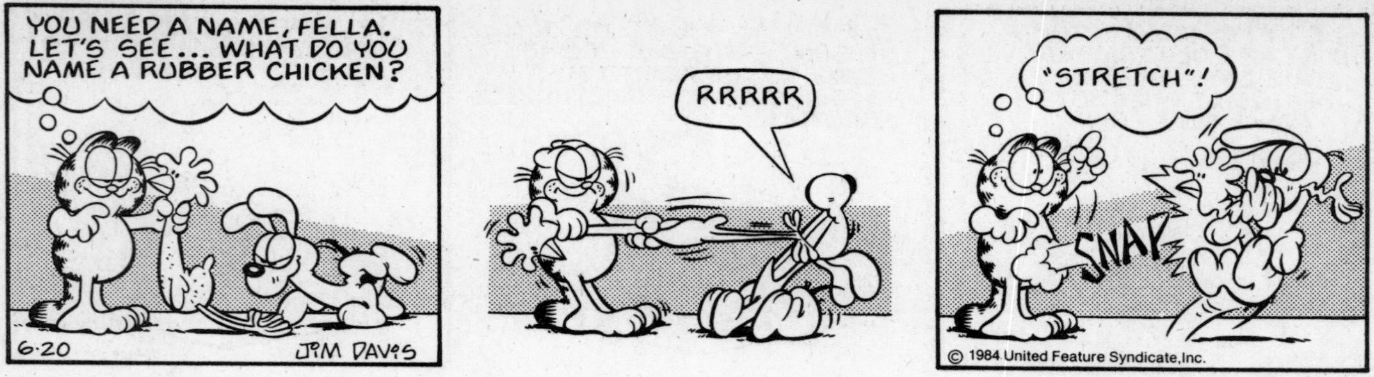
YOU NEED A NAME, FELLA. LET'S SEE... WHAT DO YOU NAME A RUBBER CHICKEN?
6·20
JIM DAVIS
RRRRR
"STRETCH"!
SNAP
© 1984 United Feature Syndicate,Inc.

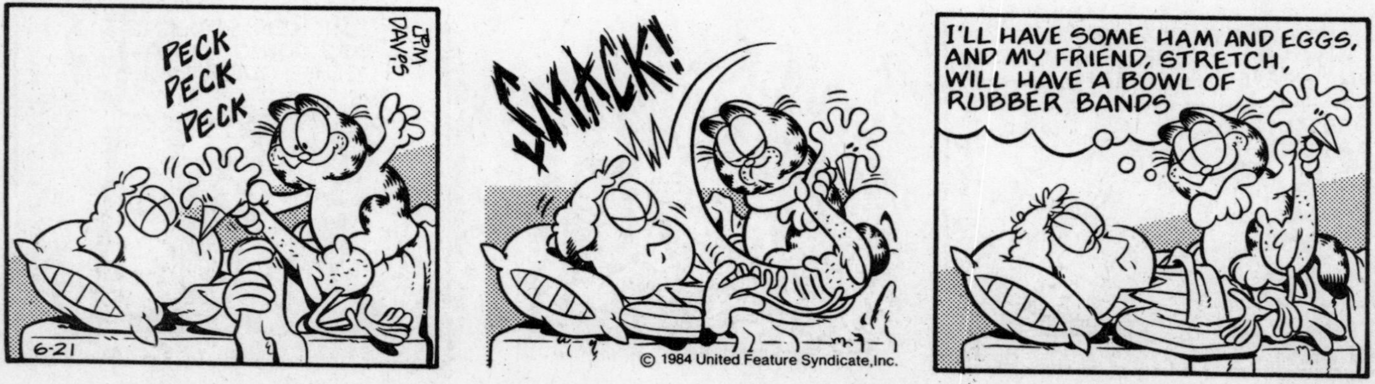
PECK
PECK
PECK
JIM DAVIS
6·21
SMACK!
© 1984 United Feature Syndicate,Inc.
I'LL HAVE SOME HAM AND EGGS, AND MY FRIEND, STRETCH, WILL HAVE A BOWL OF RUBBER BANDS

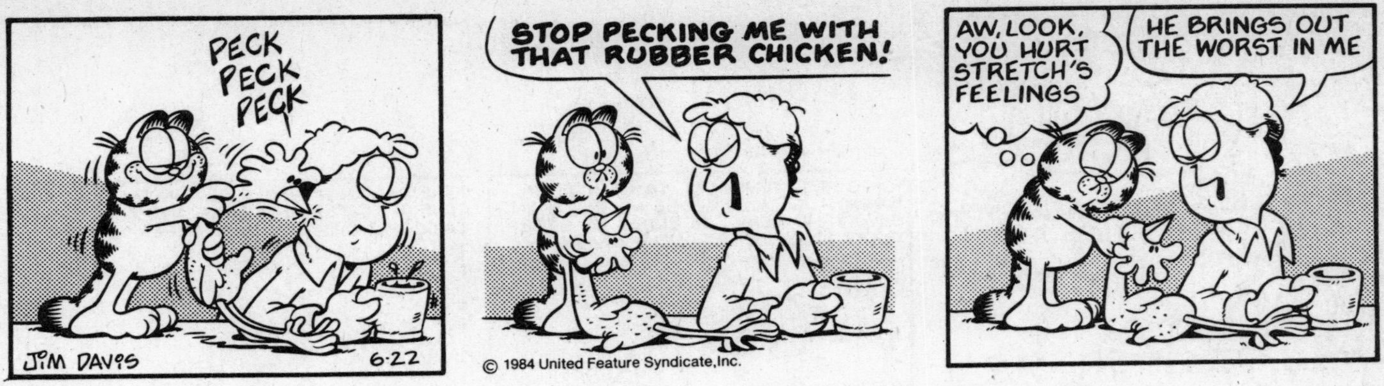
PECK
PECK
PECK
JIM DAVIS
6-22
STOP PECKING ME WITH THAT RUBBER CHICKEN!
AW, LOOK, YOU HURT STRETCH'S FEELINGS
HE BRINGS OUT THE WORST IN ME

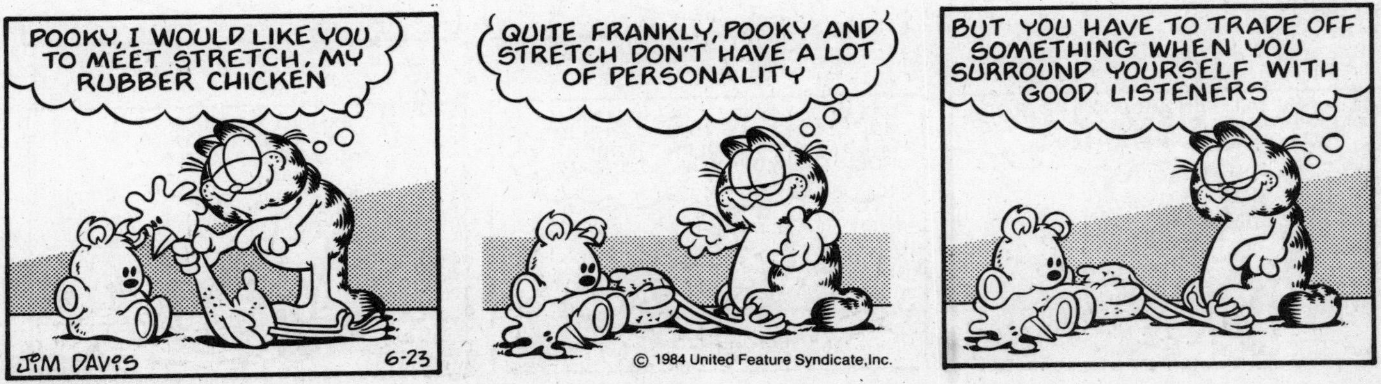
POOKY, I WOULD LIKE YOU TO MEET STRETCH, MY RUBBER CHICKEN
JIM DAVIS
6-23
QUITE FRANKLY, POOKY AND STRETCH DON'T HAVE A LOT OF PERSONALITY
BUT YOU HAVE TO TRADE OFF SOMETHING WHEN YOU SURROUND YOURSELF WITH GOOD LISTENERS

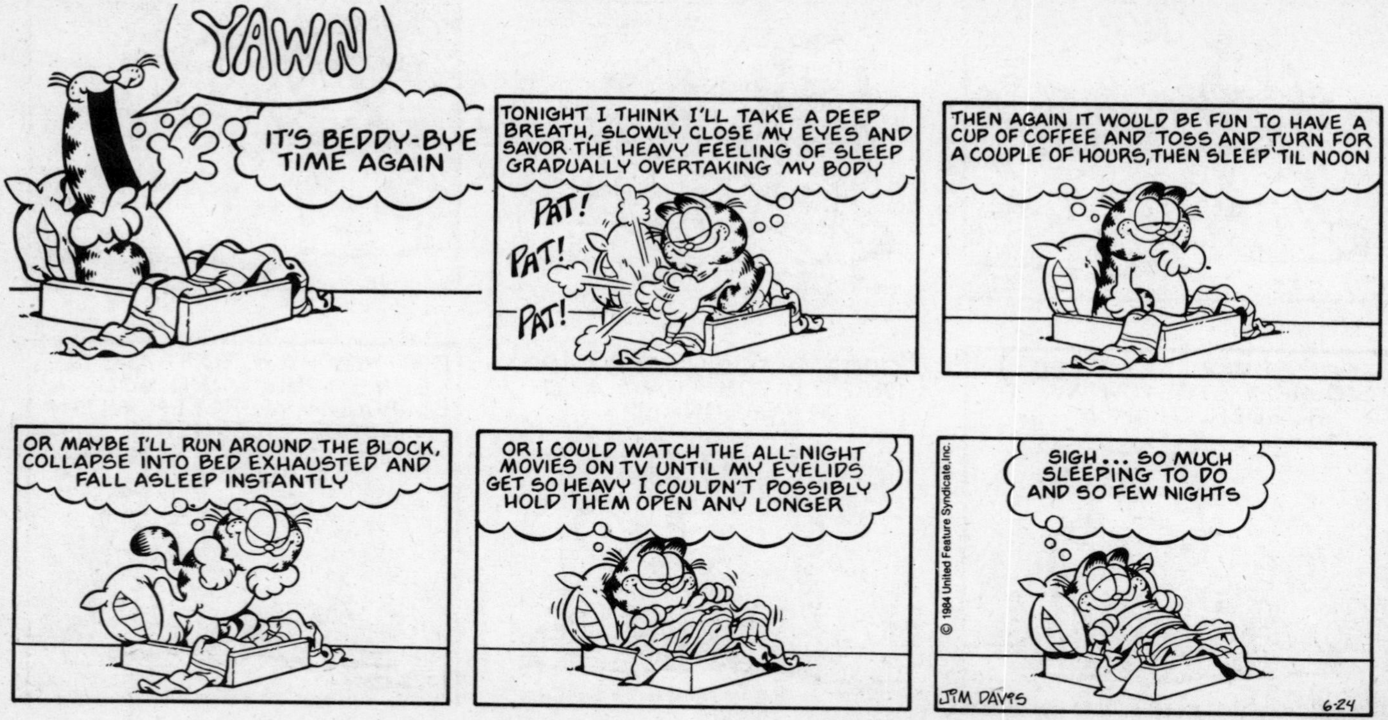
YAWN
IT'S BEDDY-BYE TIME AGAIN
TONIGHT I THINK I'LL TAKE A DEEP BREATH, SLOWLY CLOSE MY EYES AND SAVOR THE HEAVY FEELING OF SLEEP GRADUALLY OVERTAKING MY BODY
PAT! PAT! PAT!
THEN AGAIN IT WOULD BE FUN TO HAVE A CUP OF COFFEE AND TOSS AND TURN FOR A COUPLE OF HOURS, THEN SLEEP 'TIL NOON
OR MAYBE I'LL RUN AROUND THE BLOCK, COLLAPSE INTO BED EXHAUSTED AND FALL ASLEEP INSTANTLY
OR I COULD WATCH THE ALL-NIGHT MOVIES ON TV UNTIL MY EYELIDS GET SO HEAVY I COULDN'T POSSIBLY HOLD THEM OPEN ANY LONGER
SIGH... SO MUCH SLEEPING TO DO AND SO FEW NIGHTS
© 1984 United Feature Syndicate, Inc.
JIM DAVIS
6-24

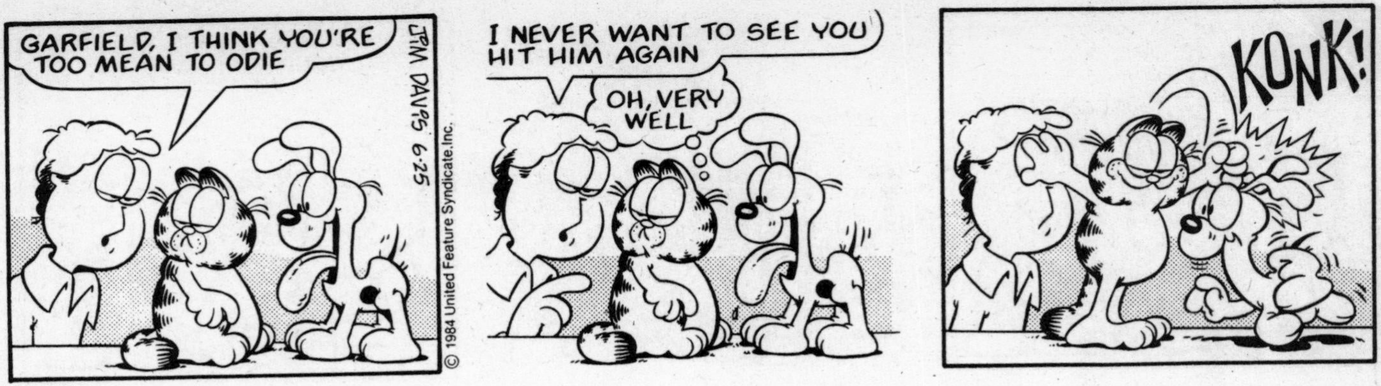
GARFIELD, I THINK YOU'RE TOO MEAN TO ODIE
JIM DAVIS 6·25
I NEVER WANT TO SEE YOU HIT HIM AGAIN
OH, VERY WELL
KONK!
© 1984 United Feature Syndicate, Inc.

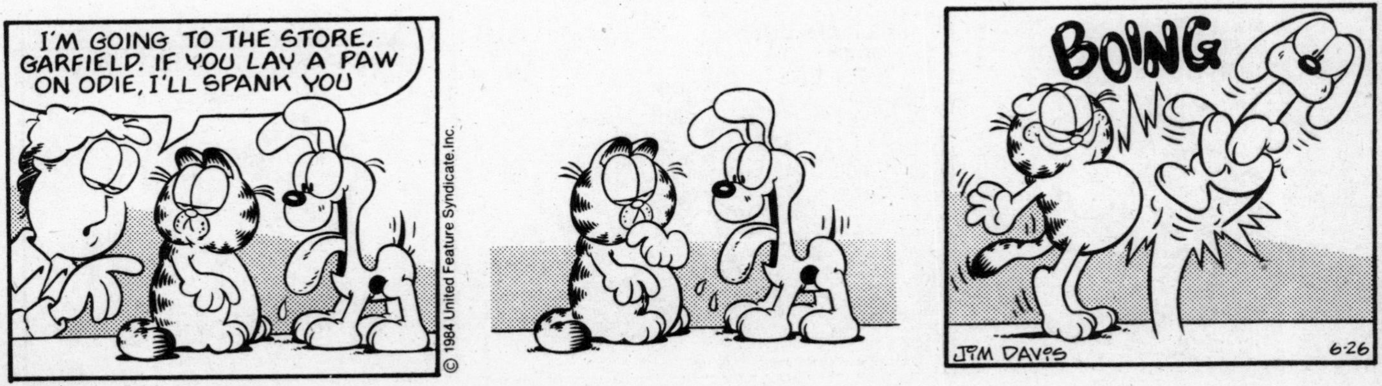
I'M GOING TO THE STORE, GARFIELD. IF YOU LAY A PAW ON ODIE, I'LL SPANK YOU
© 1984 United Feature Syndicate, Inc.
BOING
JIM DAVIS
6·26

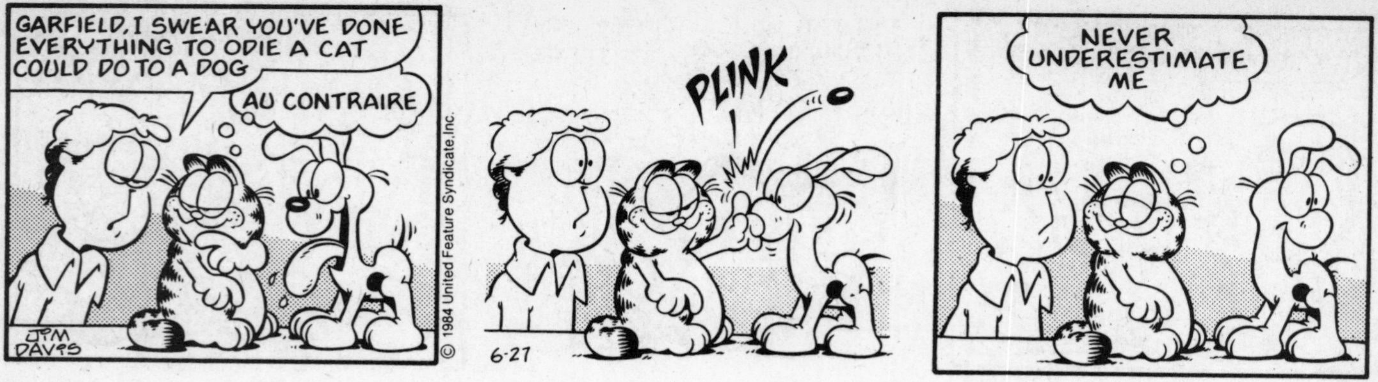

GARFIELD, I SWEAR YOU'VE DONE EVERYTHING TO ODIE A CAT COULD DO TO A DOG
AU CONTRAIRE
JIM DAVIS
© 1984 United Feature Syndicate, Inc.
PLINK
6-27
NEVER UNDERESTIMATE ME

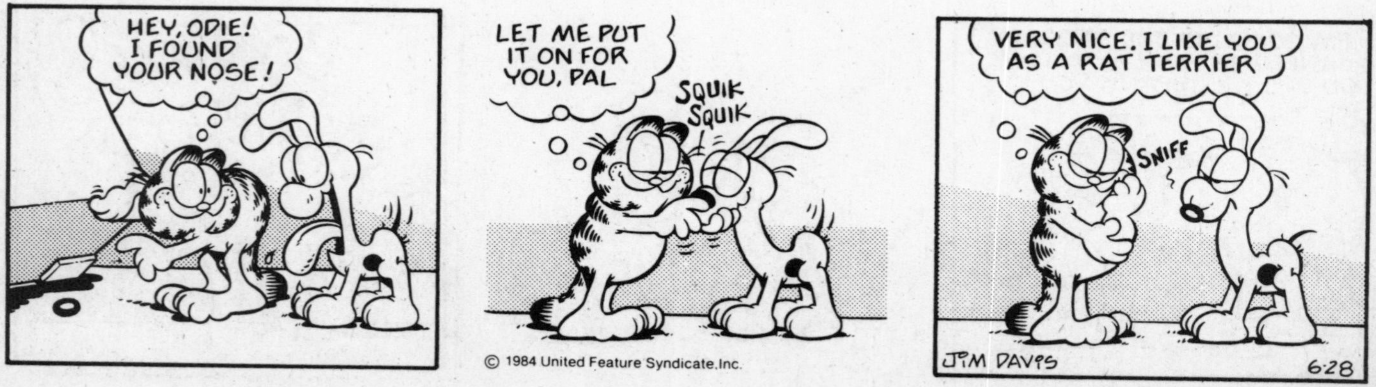

HEY, ODIE! I FOUND YOUR NOSE!
LET ME PUT IT ON FOR YOU, PAL
SQUIK SQUIK
VERY NICE. I LIKE YOU AS A RAT TERRIER
SNIFF
© 1984 United Feature Syndicate, Inc.
JIM DAVIS
6-28

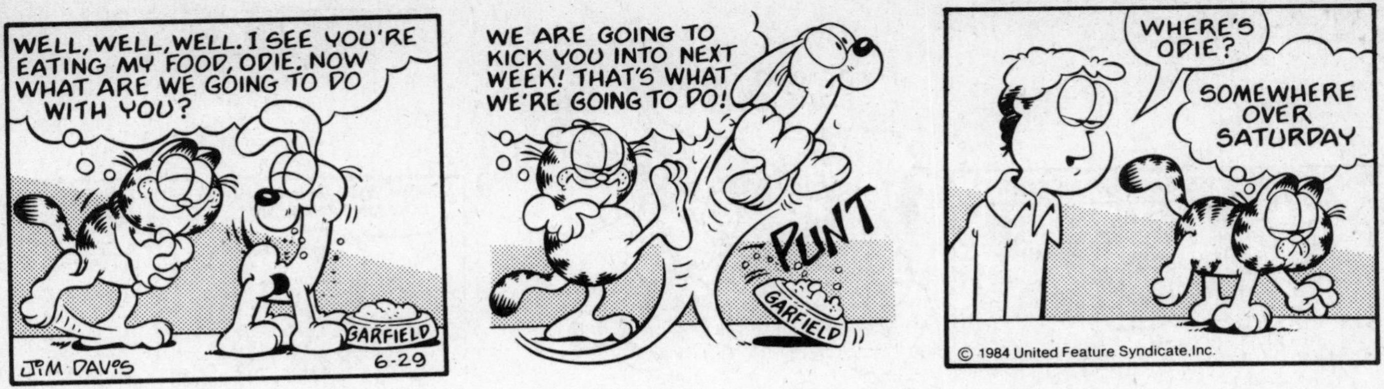
WELL, WELL, WELL. I SEE YOU'RE EATING MY FOOD, ODIE. NOW WHAT ARE WE GOING TO DO WITH YOU?
GARFIELD
JIM DAVIS
6-29
WE ARE GOING TO KICK YOU INTO NEXT WEEK! THAT'S WHAT WE'RE GOING TO DO!
PUNT
GARFIELD
WHERE'S ODIE?
SOMEWHERE OVER SATURDAY
© 1984 United Feature Syndicate, Inc.

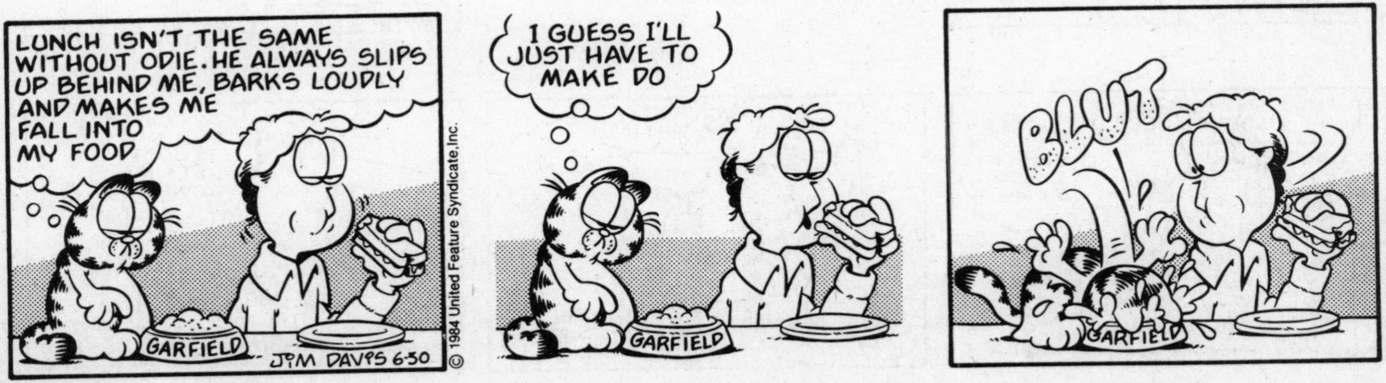
LUNCH ISN'T THE SAME WITHOUT ODIE. HE ALWAYS SLIPS UP BEHIND ME, BARKS LOUDLY AND MAKES ME FALL INTO MY FOOD
GARFIELD
JIM DAVIS 6-30
© 1984 United Feature Syndicate, Inc.
I GUESS I'LL JUST HAVE TO MAKE DO
GARFIELD
BLUT
GARFIELD

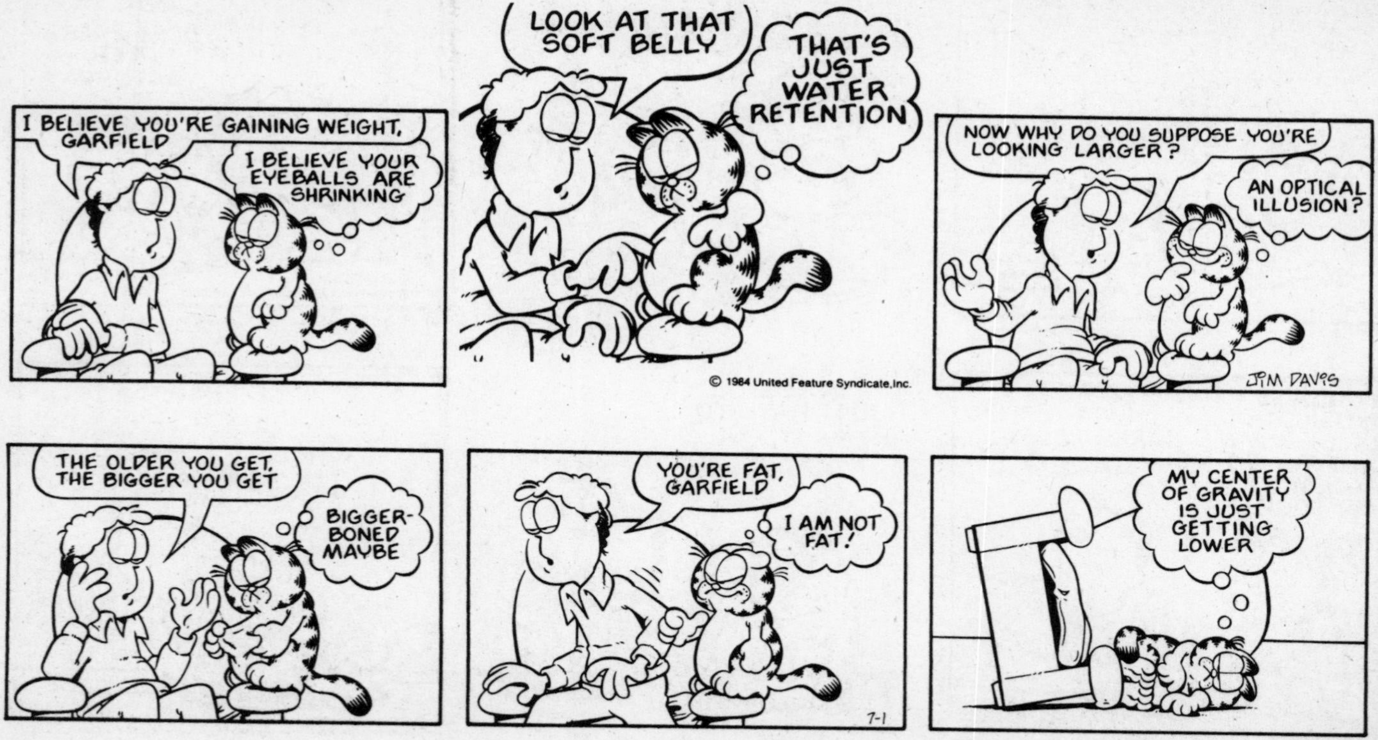
I BELIEVE YOU'RE GAINING WEIGHT, GARFIELD
I BELIEVE YOUR EYEBALLS ARE SHRINKING
LOOK AT THAT SOFT BELLY
THAT'S JUST WATER RETENTION
NOW WHY DO YOU SUPPOSE YOU'RE LOOKING LARGER?
AN OPTICAL ILLUSION?
JIM DAVIS
THE OLDER YOU GET, THE BIGGER YOU GET
BIGGER-BONED MAYBE
YOU'RE FAT, GARFIELD
I AM NOT FAT!
7-1
MY CENTER OF GRAVITY IS JUST GETTING LOWER

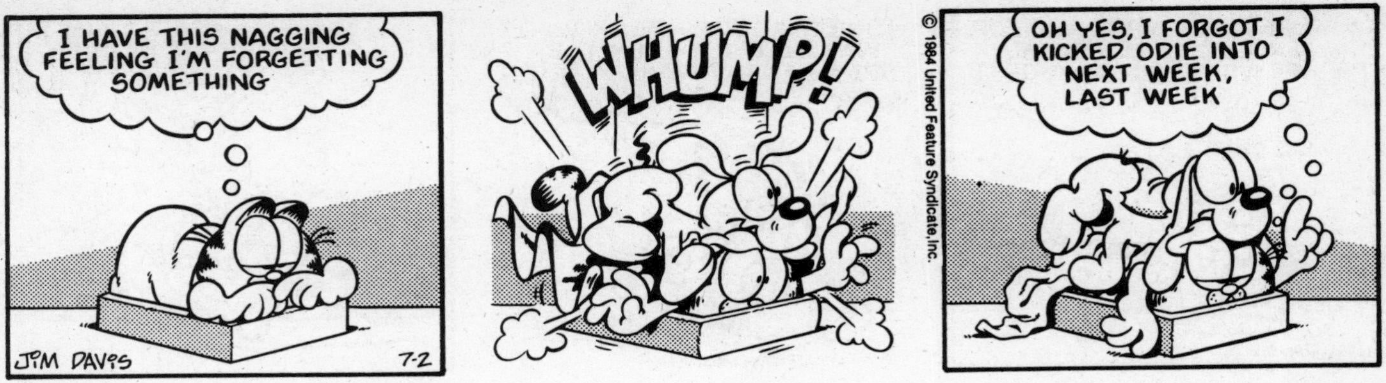
I HAVE THIS NAGGING FEELING I'M FORGETTING SOMETHING
JIM DAVIS
7-2
WHUMP!
OH YES, I FORGOT I KICKED ODIE INTO NEXT WEEK, LAST WEEK
© 1984 United Feature Syndicate, Inc.

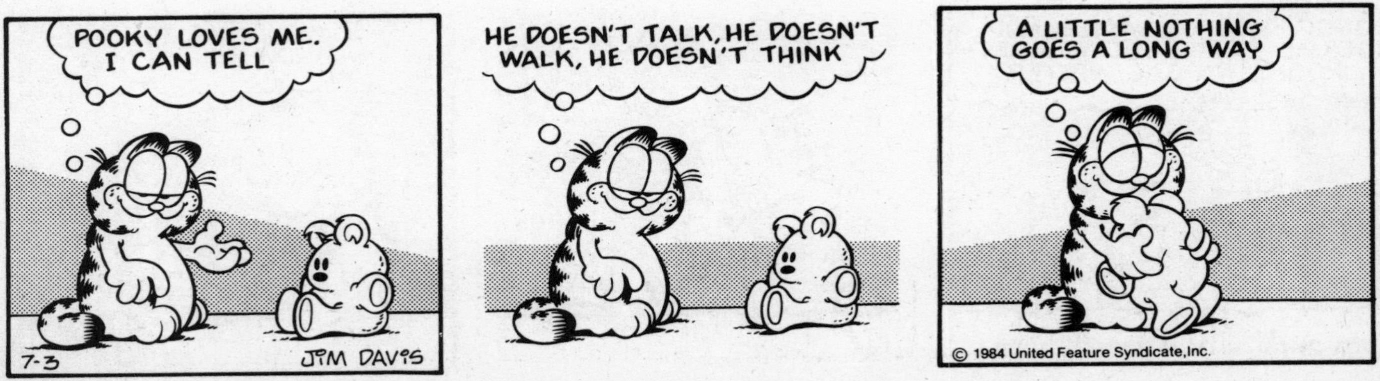
POOKY LOVES ME. I CAN TELL
7-3
JIM DAVIS
HE DOESN'T TALK, HE DOESN'T WALK, HE DOESN'T THINK
A LITTLE NOTHING GOES A LONG WAY
© 1984 United Feature Syndicate, Inc.

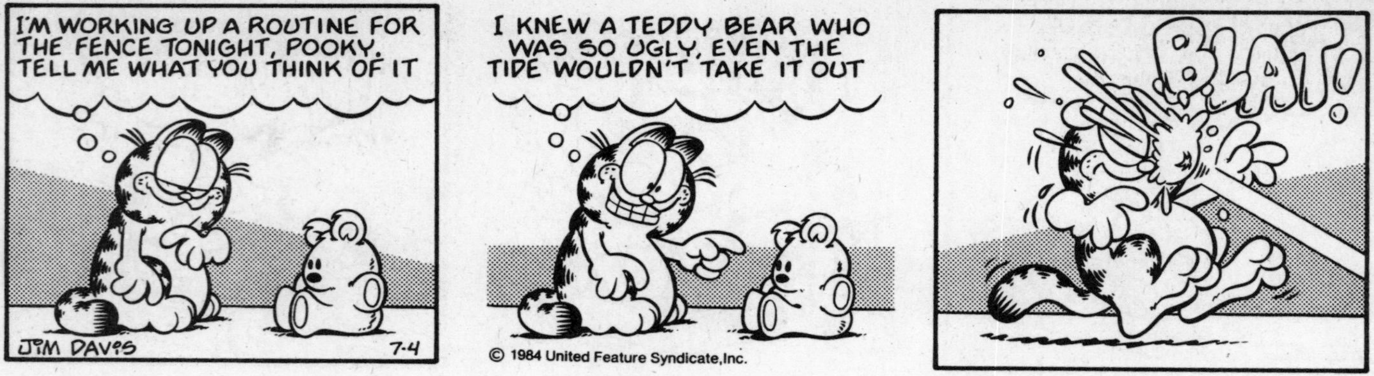
I'M WORKING UP A ROUTINE FOR THE FENCE TONIGHT, POOKY. TELL ME WHAT YOU THINK OF IT
JIM DAVIS
7-4
I KNEW A TEDDY BEAR WHO WAS SO UGLY, EVEN THE TIDE WOULDN'T TAKE IT OUT
© 1984 United Feature Syndicate,Inc.
BLAT!

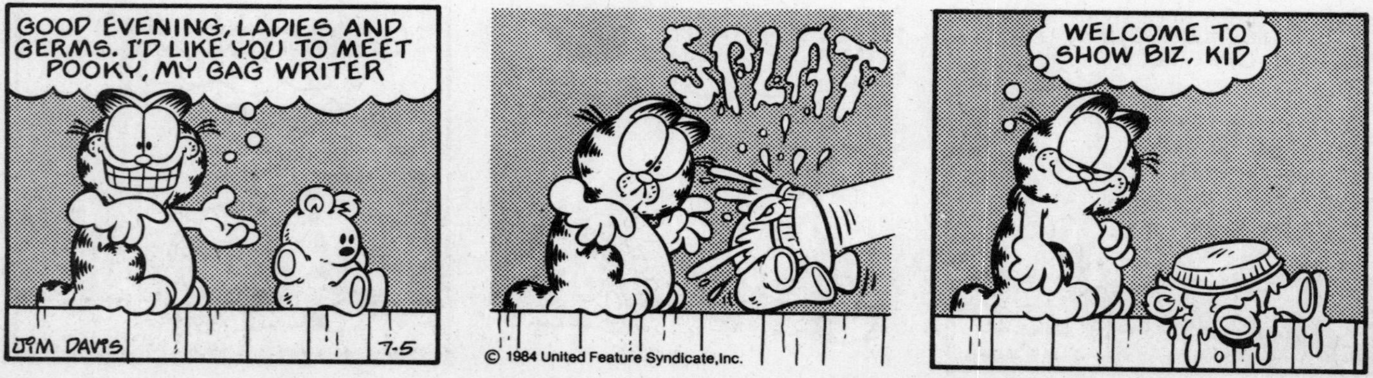
GOOD EVENING, LADIES AND GERMS. I'D LIKE YOU TO MEET POOKY, MY GAG WRITER
JIM DAVIS
7-5
SPLAT
© 1984 United Feature Syndicate,Inc.
WELCOME TO SHOW BIZ, KID

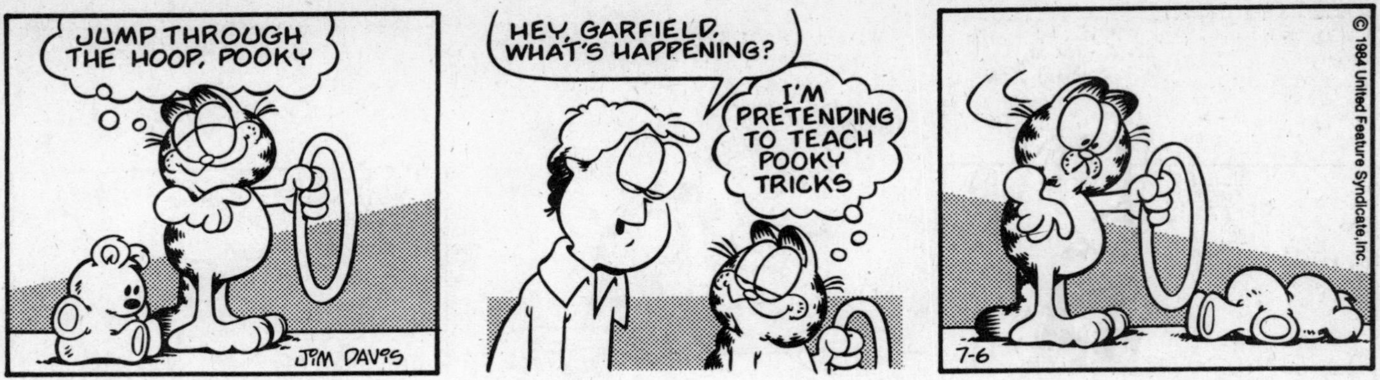
JUMP THROUGH THE HOOP, POOKY
JIM DAVIS
HEY, GARFIELD. WHAT'S HAPPENING?
I'M PRETENDING TO TEACH POOKY TRICKS
© 1984 United Feature Syndicate, Inc.
7-6

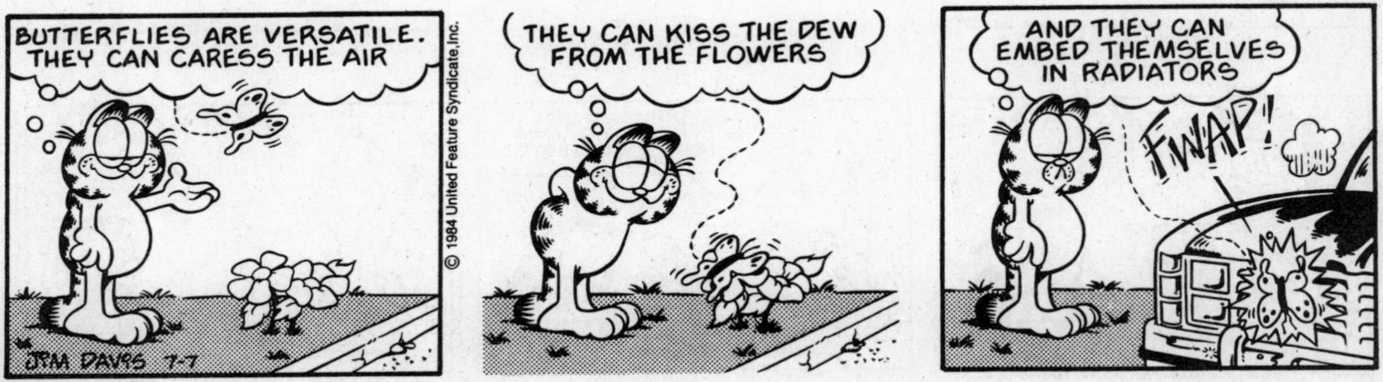
BUTTERFLIES ARE VERSATILE. THEY CAN CARESS THE AIR
JIM DAVIS 7-7
© 1984 United Feature Syndicate, Inc.
THEY CAN KISS THE DEW FROM THE FLOWERS
AND THEY CAN EMBED THEMSELVES IN RADIATORS
FWAP!

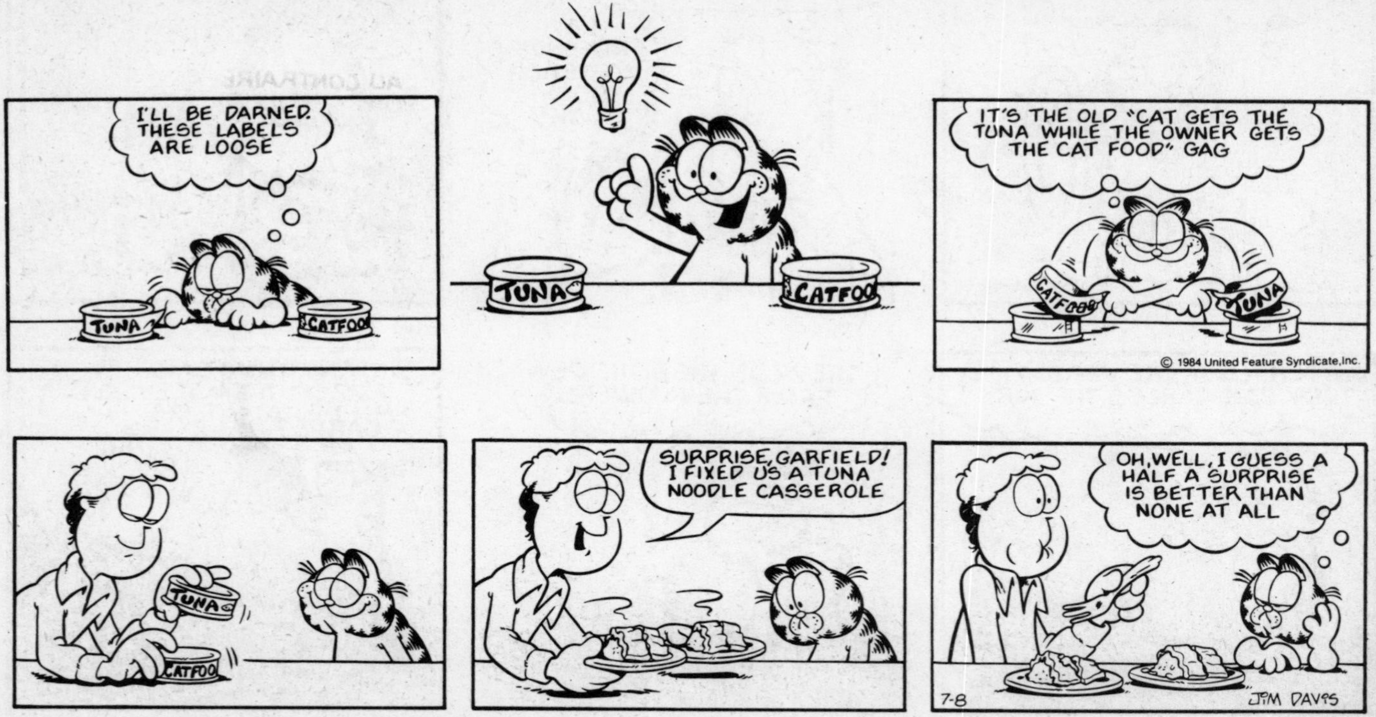
I'LL BE DARNED. THESE LABELS ARE LOOSE
TUNA
CATFOO
TUNA
CATFOO
IT'S THE OLD "CAT GETS THE TUNA WHILE THE OWNER GETS THE CAT FOOD" GAG
CATFOOD
TUNA
© 1984 United Feature Syndicate, Inc.
TUNA
CATFOO
SURPRISE, GARFIELD! I FIXED US A TUNA NOODLE CASSEROLE
OH, WELL, I GUESS A HALF A SURPRISE IS BETTER THAN NONE AT ALL
7-8
JIM DAVIS

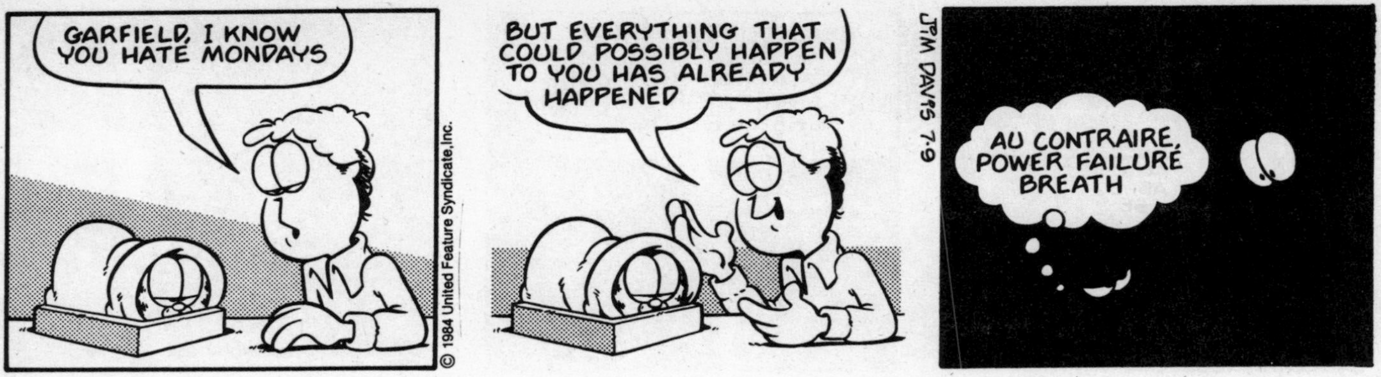
GARFIELD, I KNOW YOU HATE MONDAYS
© 1984 United Feature Syndicate,Inc.
BUT EVERYTHING THAT COULD POSSIBLY HAPPEN TO YOU HAS ALREADY HAPPENED
JIM DAVIS 7-9
AU CONTRAIRE, POWER FAILURE BREATH

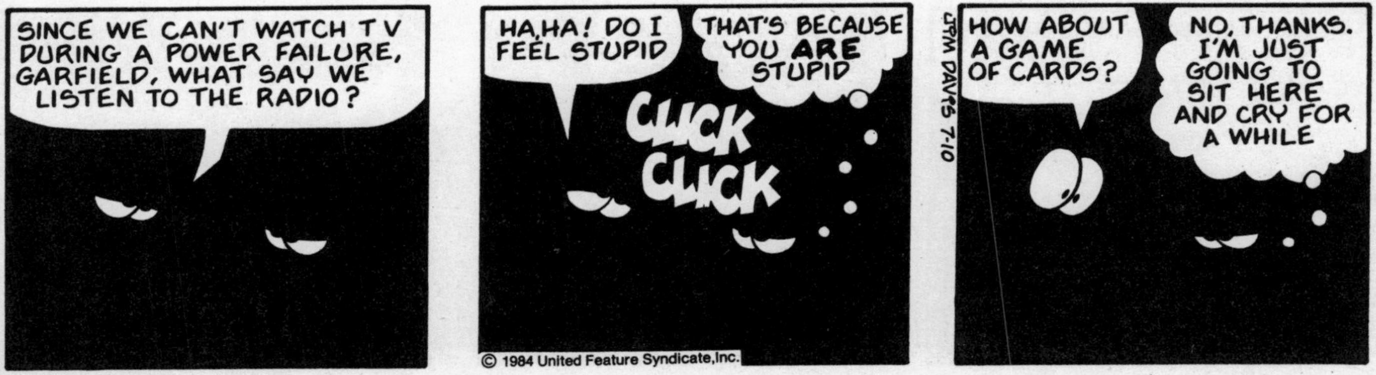
SINCE WE CAN'T WATCH T V DURING A POWER FAILURE, GARFIELD, WHAT SAY WE LISTEN TO THE RADIO?
HA,HA! DO I FEEL STUPID
THAT'S BECAUSE YOU **ARE** STUPID
CLICK CLICK
© 1984 United Feature Syndicate,Inc.
JIM DAVIS 7-10
HOW ABOUT A GAME OF CARDS?
NO, THANKS. I'M JUST GOING TO SIT HERE AND CRY FOR A WHILE

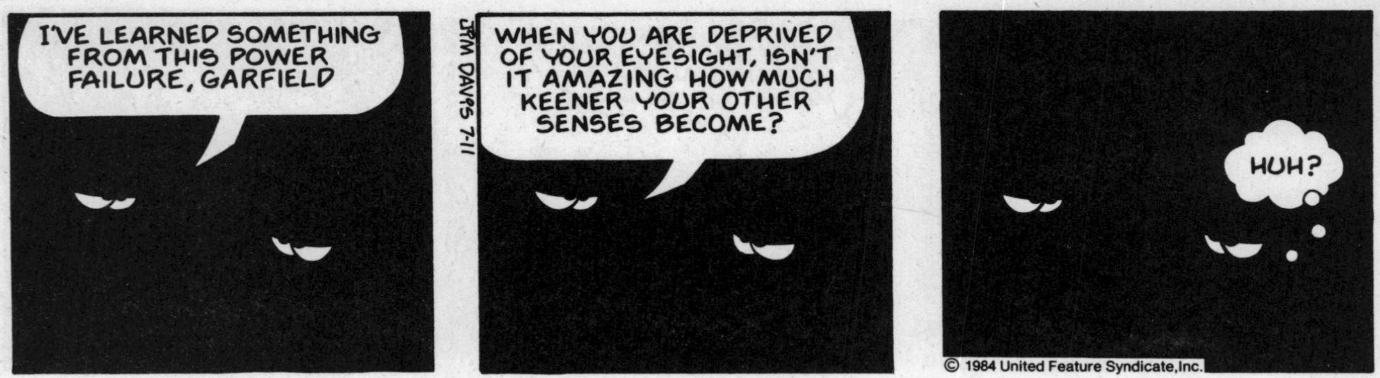
I'VE LEARNED SOMETHING FROM THIS POWER FAILURE, GARFIELD
JIM DAVIS 7-11
WHEN YOU ARE DEPRIVED OF YOUR EYESIGHT, ISN'T IT AMAZING HOW MUCH KEENER YOUR OTHER SENSES BECOME?
HUH?
© 1984 United Feature Syndicate, Inc.

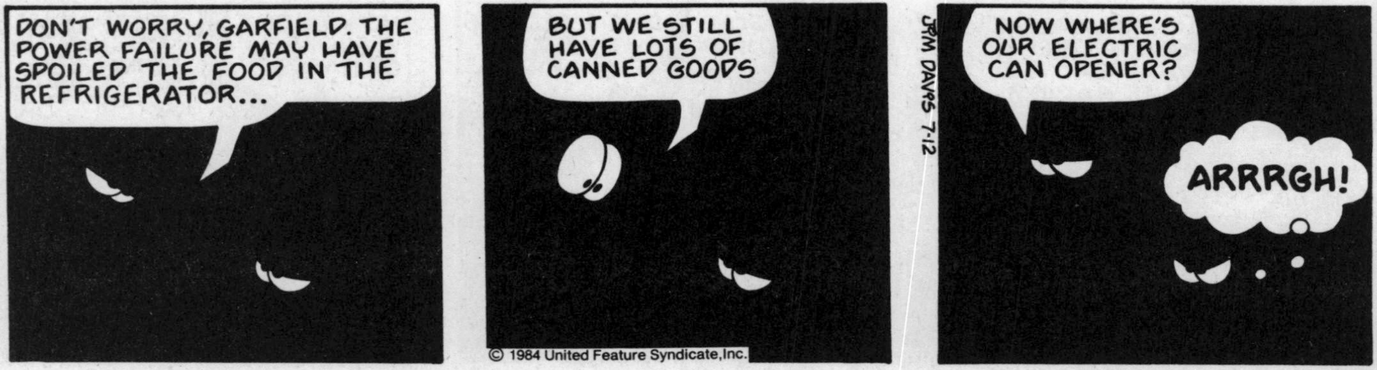
DON'T WORRY, GARFIELD. THE POWER FAILURE MAY HAVE SPOILED THE FOOD IN THE REFRIGERATOR...
BUT WE STILL HAVE LOTS OF CANNED GOODS
© 1984 United Feature Syndicate, Inc.
JIM DAVIS 7-12
NOW WHERE'S OUR ELECTRIC CAN OPENER?
ARRRGH!

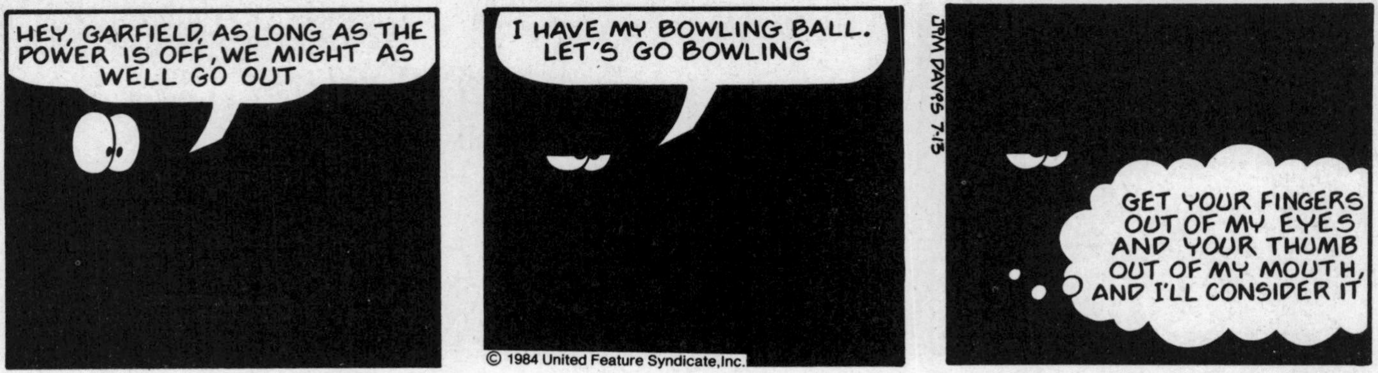
HEY, GARFIELD, AS LONG AS THE POWER IS OFF, WE MIGHT AS WELL GO OUT
I HAVE MY BOWLING BALL. LET'S GO BOWLING
JIM DAVIS 7-13
GET YOUR FINGERS OUT OF MY EYES AND YOUR THUMB OUT OF MY MOUTH, AND I'LL CONSIDER IT

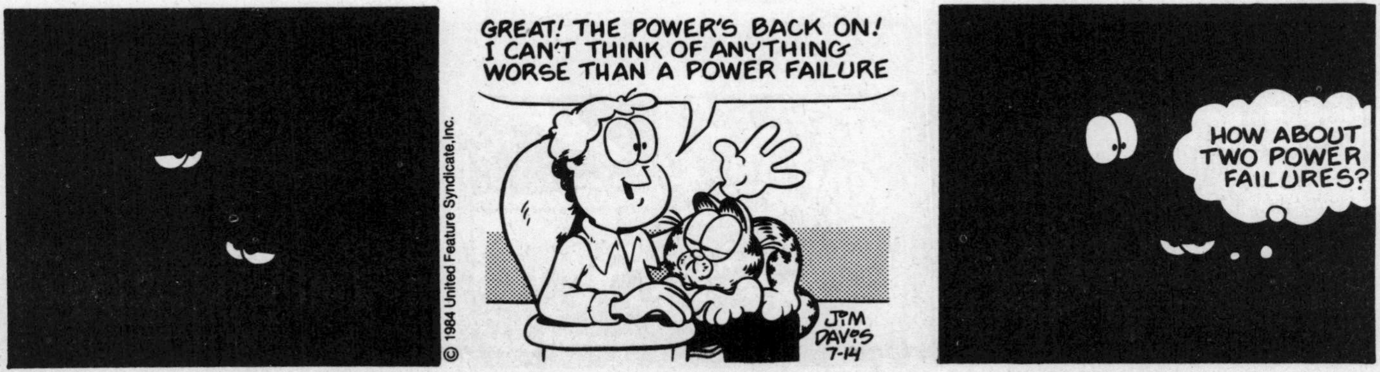
GREAT! THE POWER'S BACK ON! I CAN'T THINK OF ANYTHING WORSE THAN A POWER FAILURE
JIM DAVIS 7-14
HOW ABOUT TWO POWER FAILURES?

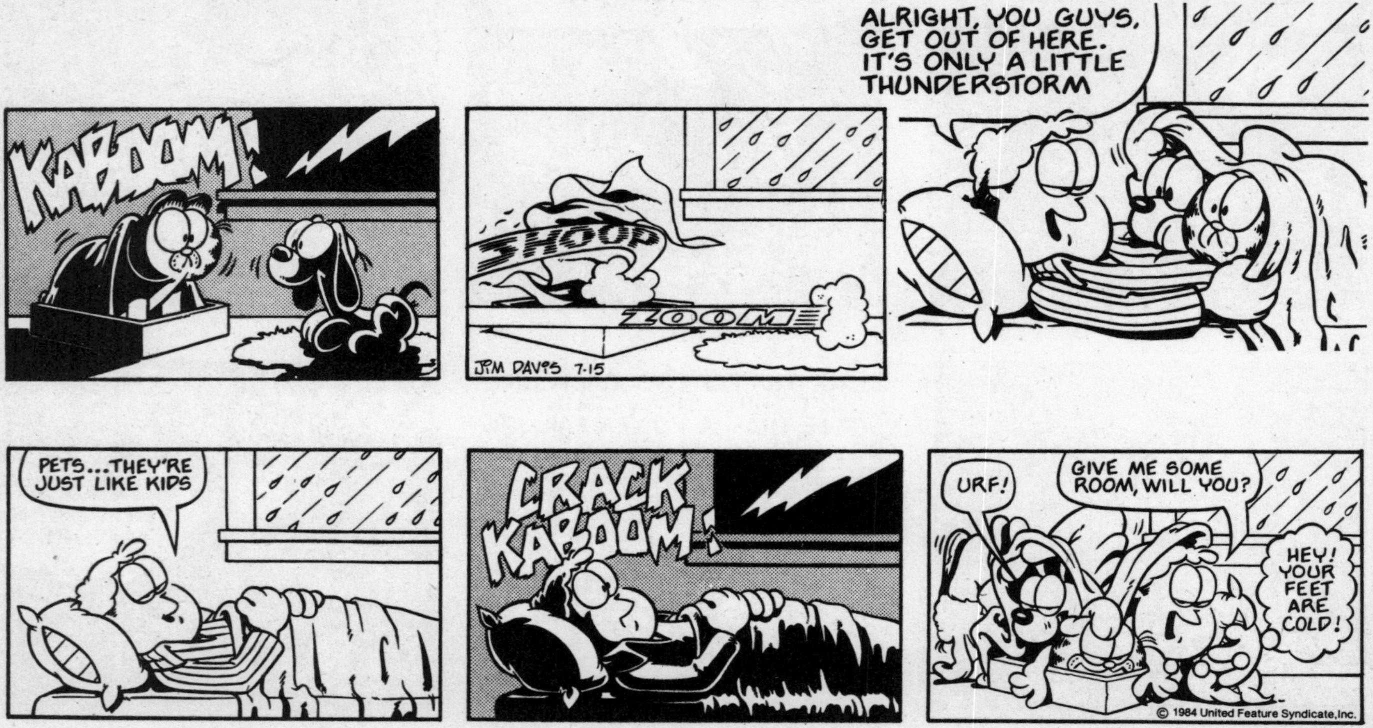
KABOOM!
SHOOP
ZOOM
JIM DAVIS 7-15
ALRIGHT, YOU GUYS, GET OUT OF HERE. IT'S ONLY A LITTLE THUNDERSTORM
PETS...THEY'RE JUST LIKE KIDS
CRACK KABOOM!
URF!
GIVE ME SOME ROOM, WILL YOU?
HEY! YOUR FEET ARE COLD!
© 1984 United Feature Syndicate, Inc.

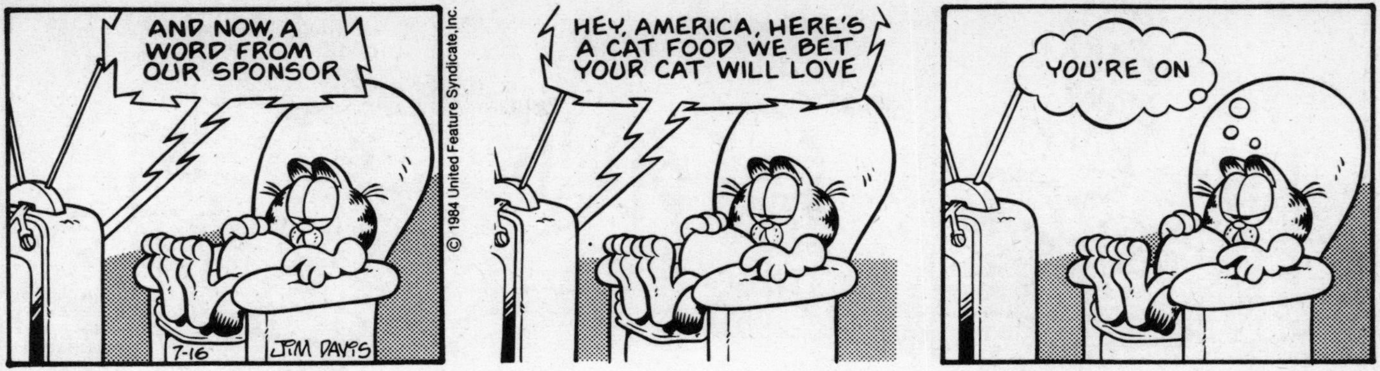
AND NOW, A WORD FROM OUR SPONSOR
7-16
JIM DAVIS
© 1984 United Feature Syndicate, Inc.
HEY, AMERICA, HERE'S A CAT FOOD WE BET YOUR CAT WILL LOVE
YOU'RE ON

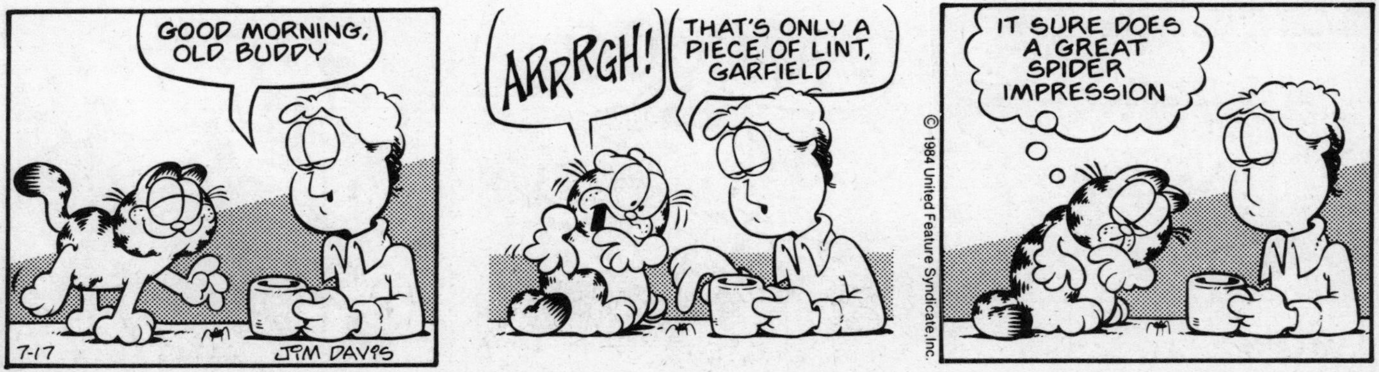
GOOD MORNING, OLD BUDDY
7-17
JIM DAVIS
ARRRGH!
THAT'S ONLY A PIECE OF LINT, GARFIELD
© 1984 United Feature Syndicate, Inc.
IT SURE DOES A GREAT SPIDER IMPRESSION

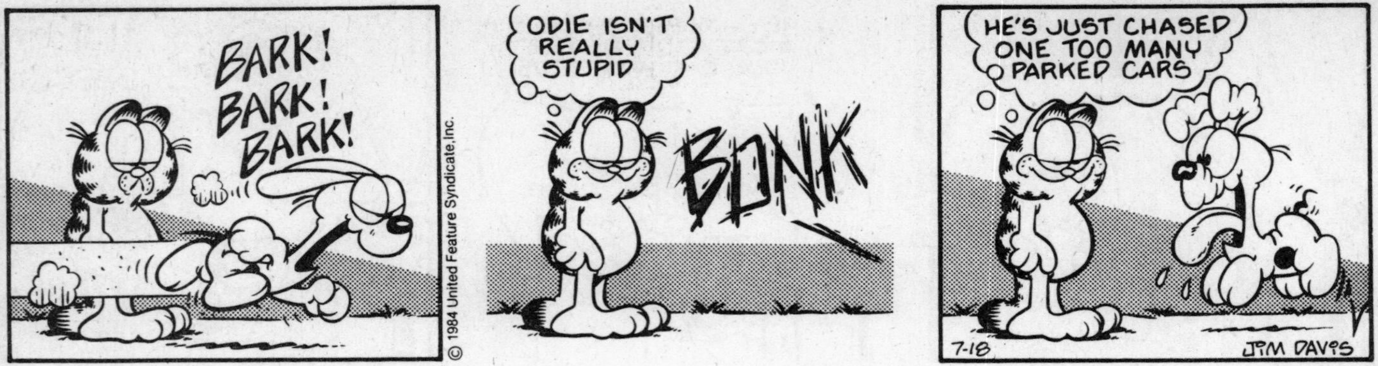
BARK!
BARK!
BARK!
ODIE ISN'T REALLY STUPID
BONK
HE'S JUST CHASED ONE TOO MANY PARKED CARS
7-18
JIM DAVIS

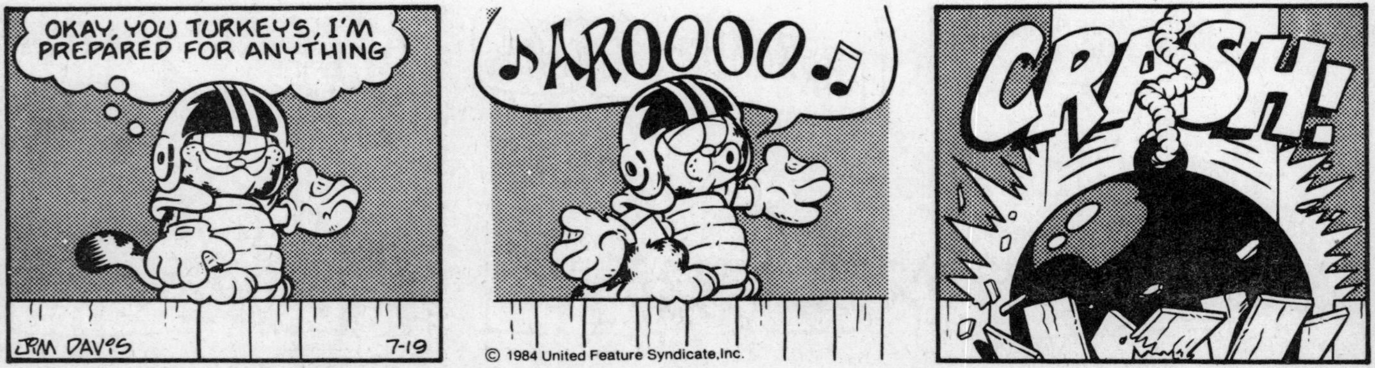
OKAY, YOU TURKEYS, I'M PREPARED FOR ANYTHING
JIM DAVIS
7-19
♪AROOOO♪
CRASH!

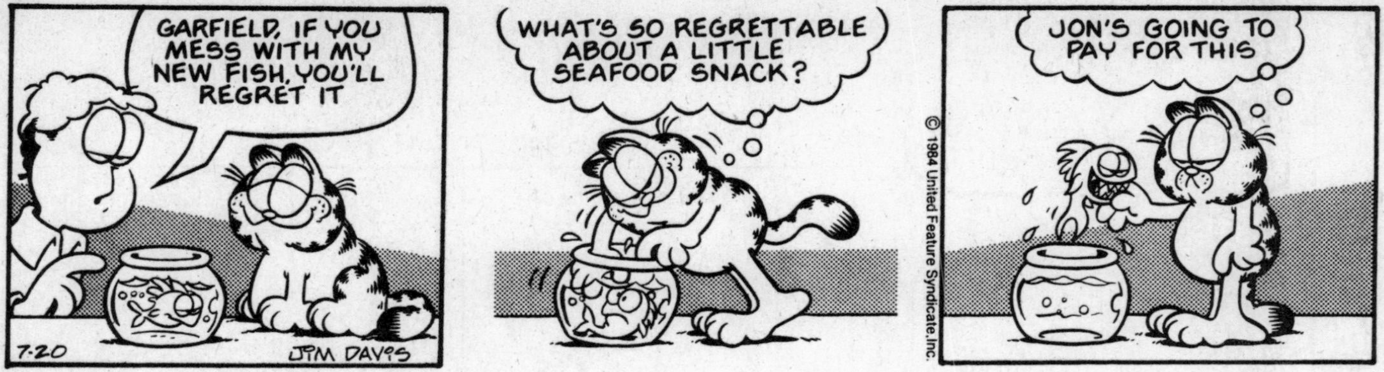
GARFIELD, IF YOU MESS WITH MY NEW FISH, YOU'LL REGRET IT
7-20
JIM DAVIS
WHAT'S SO REGRETTABLE ABOUT A LITTLE SEAFOOD SNACK?
© 1984 United Feature Syndicate, Inc.
JON'S GOING TO PAY FOR THIS

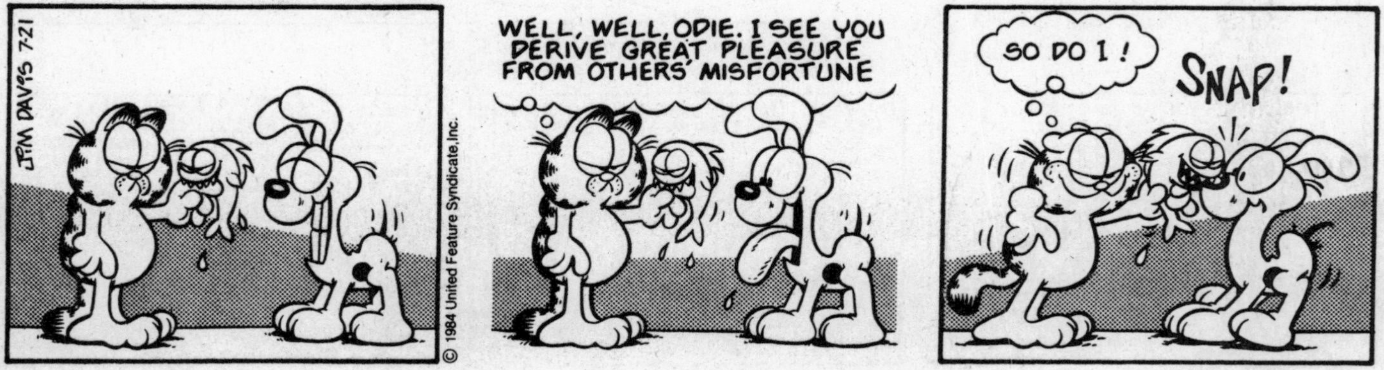
JIM DAVIS 7-21
© 1984 United Feature Syndicate, Inc.
WELL, WELL, ODIE. I SEE YOU DERIVE GREAT PLEASURE FROM OTHERS' MISFORTUNE
SO DO I!
SNAP!

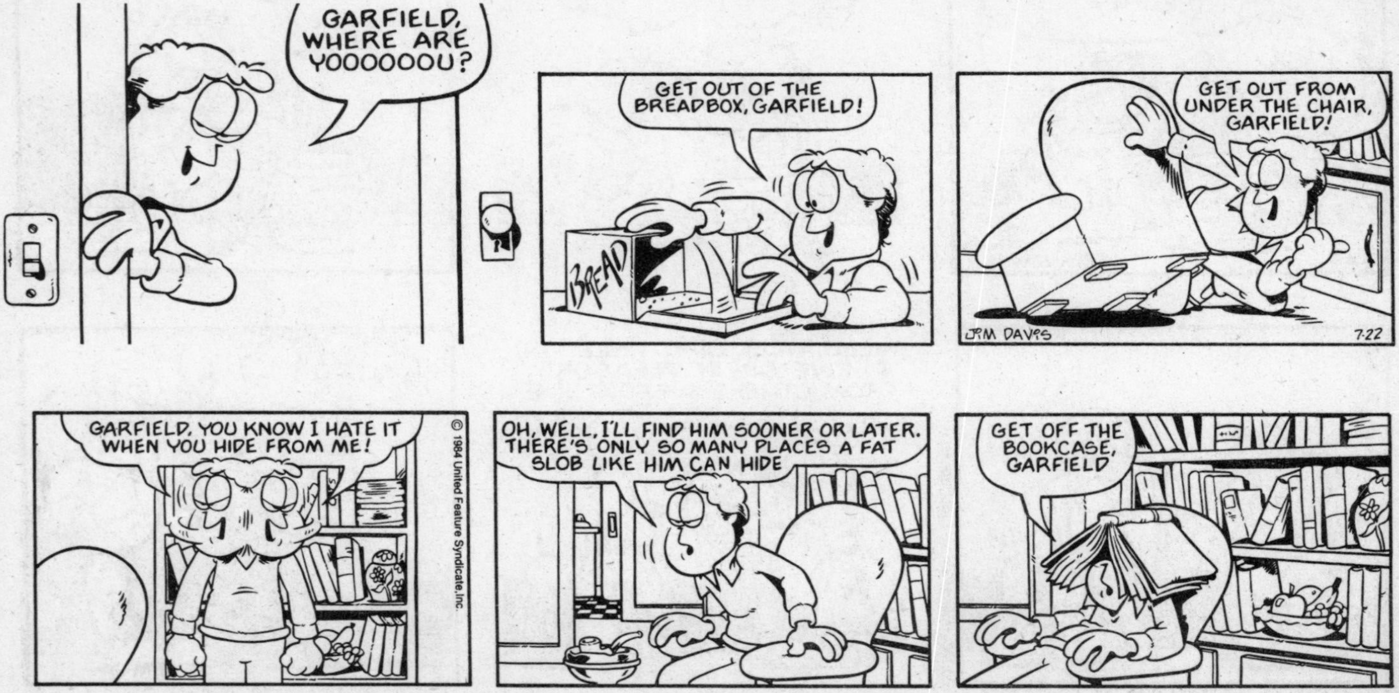
GARFIELD, WHERE ARE YOOOOOOU?
GET OUT OF THE BREADBOX, GARFIELD!
BREAD
GET OUT FROM UNDER THE CHAIR, GARFIELD!
JIM DAVIS
7-22
GARFIELD, YOU KNOW I HATE IT WHEN YOU HIDE FROM ME!
© 1984 United Feature Syndicate, Inc.
OH, WELL, I'LL FIND HIM SOONER OR LATER. THERE'S ONLY SO MANY PLACES A FAT SLOB LIKE HIM CAN HIDE
GET OFF THE BOOKCASE, GARFIELD

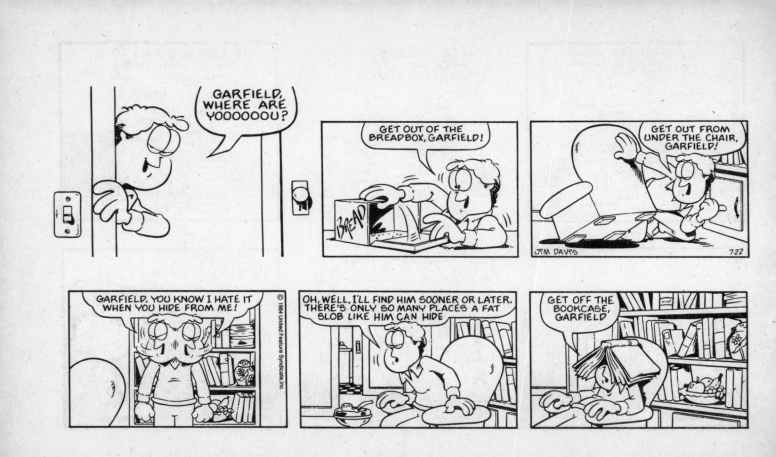

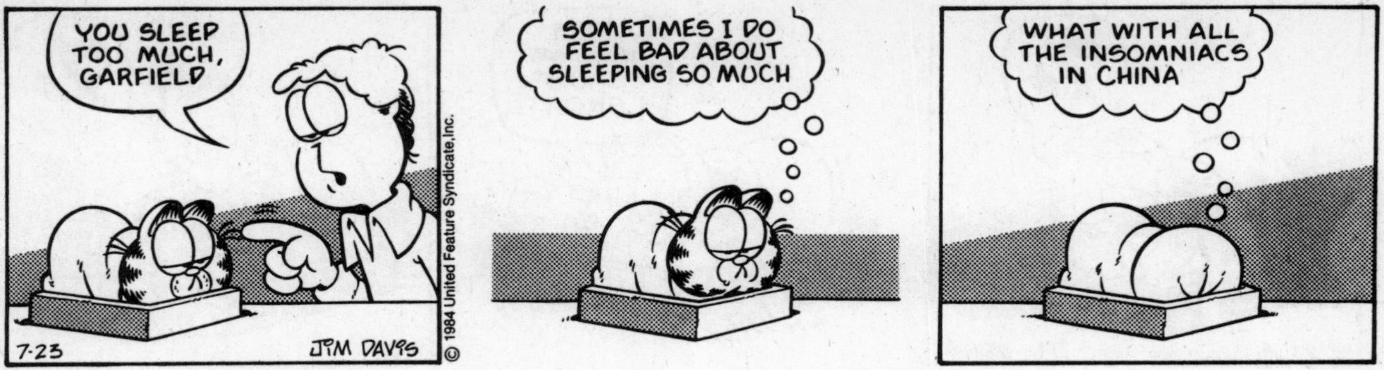
YOU SLEEP TOO MUCH, GARFIELD
7-23
JIM DAVIS
© 1984 United Feature Syndicate,Inc.
SOMETIMES I DO FEEL BAD ABOUT SLEEPING SO MUCH
WHAT WITH ALL THE INSOMNIACS IN CHINA

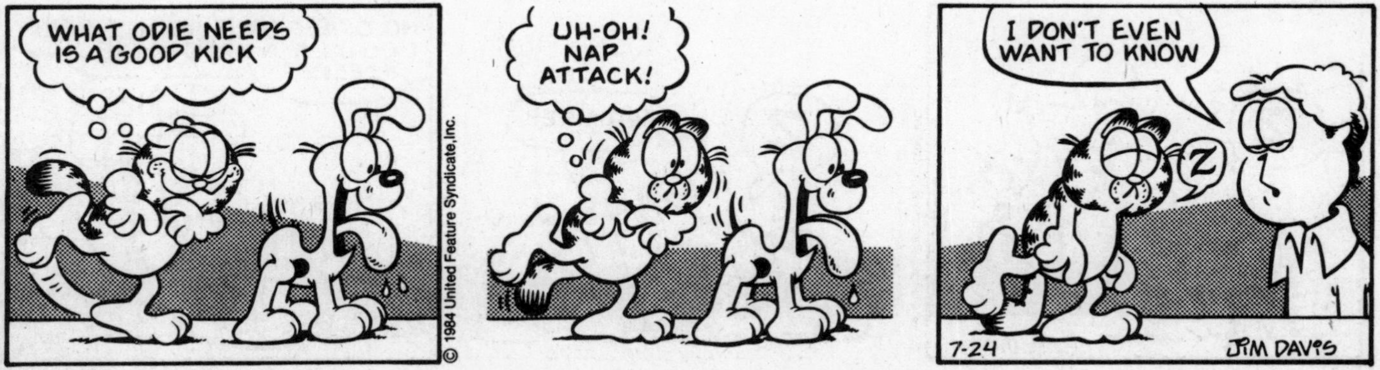
WHAT ODIE NEEDS IS A GOOD KICK
© 1984 United Feature Syndicate,Inc.
UH-OH! NAP ATTACK!
I DON'T EVEN WANT TO KNOW
Z
7-24
JIM DAVIS

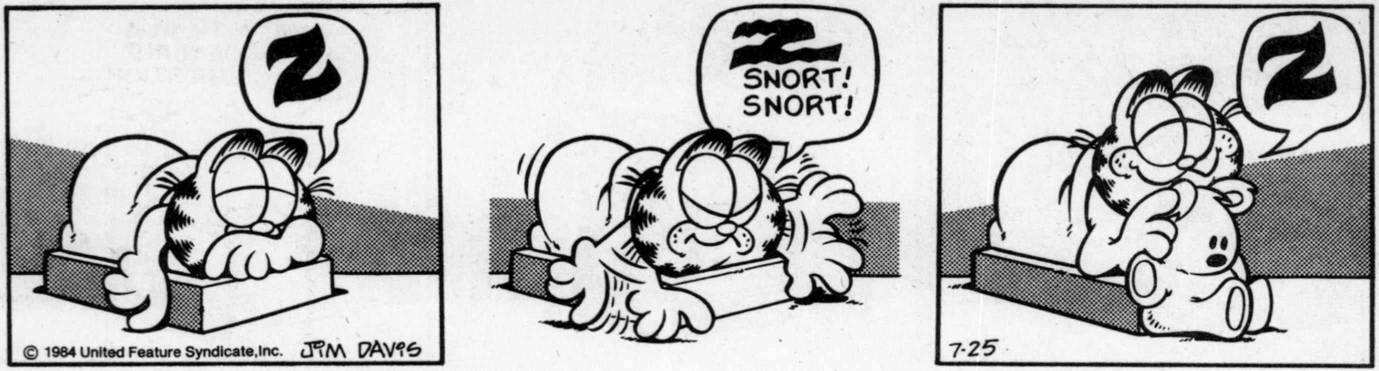
Z
© 1984 United Feature Syndicate,Inc.
JIM DAVIS
Z
SNORT!
SNORT!
Z
7-25

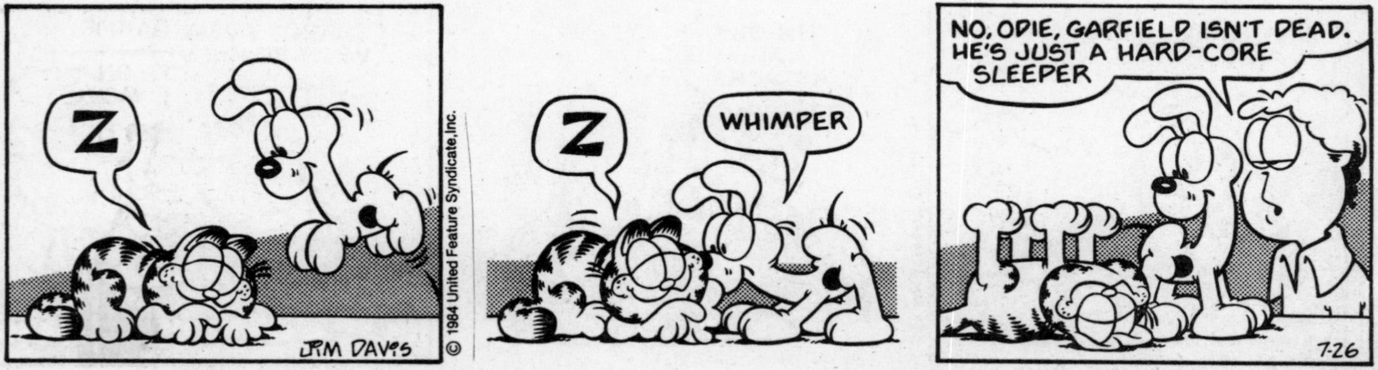
Z
JIM DAVIS
© 1984 United Feature Syndicate,Inc.
Z
WHIMPER
NO, ODIE, GARFIELD ISN'T DEAD.
HE'S JUST A HARD-CORE
SLEEPER
7-26

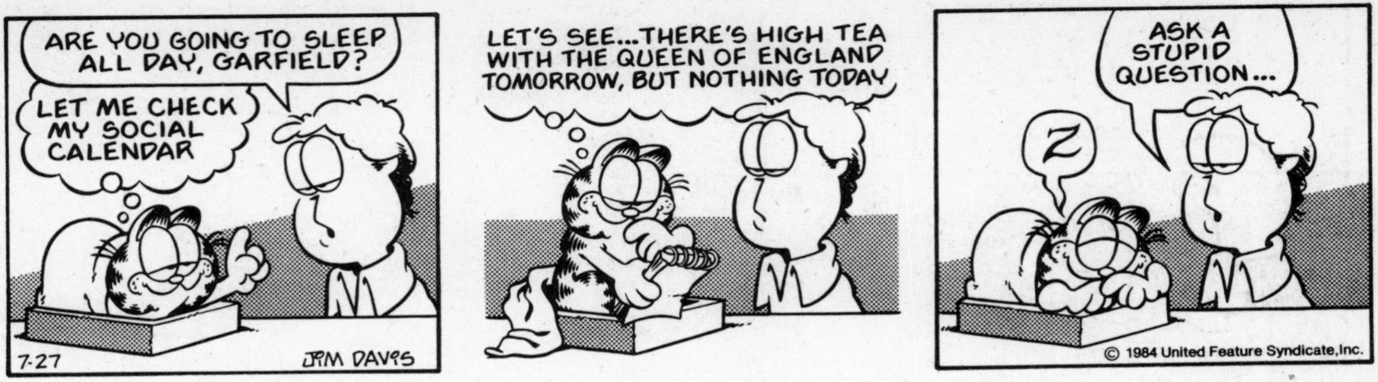
ARE YOU GOING TO SLEEP ALL DAY, GARFIELD?
LET ME CHECK MY SOCIAL CALENDAR
7-27
JIM DAVIS
LET'S SEE...THERE'S HIGH TEA WITH THE QUEEN OF ENGLAND TOMORROW, BUT NOTHING TODAY
Z
ASK A STUPID QUESTION...
© 1984 United Feature Syndicate,Inc.

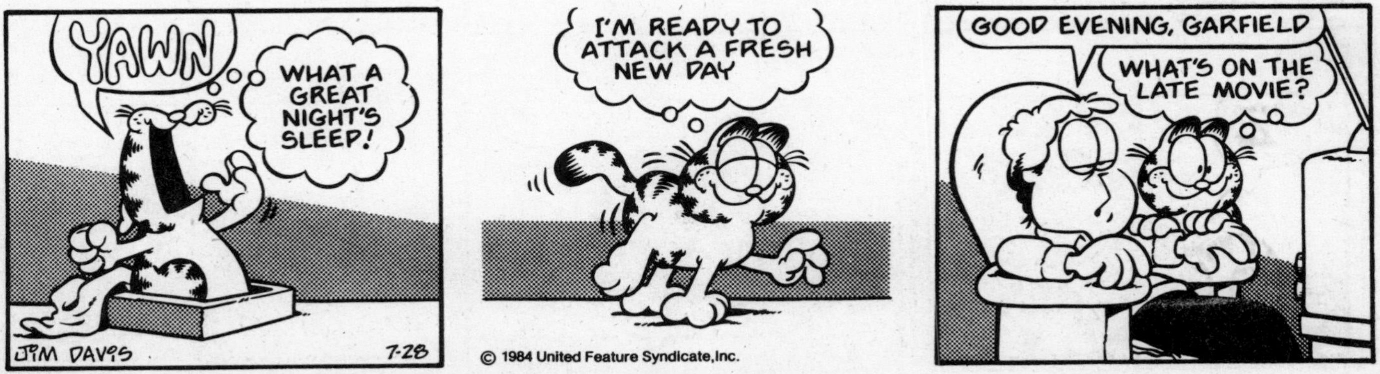
YAWN
WHAT A GREAT NIGHT'S SLEEP!
JIM DAVIS
7-28
I'M READY TO ATTACK A FRESH NEW DAY
© 1984 United Feature Syndicate,Inc.
GOOD EVENING, GARFIELD
WHAT'S ON THE LATE MOVIE?

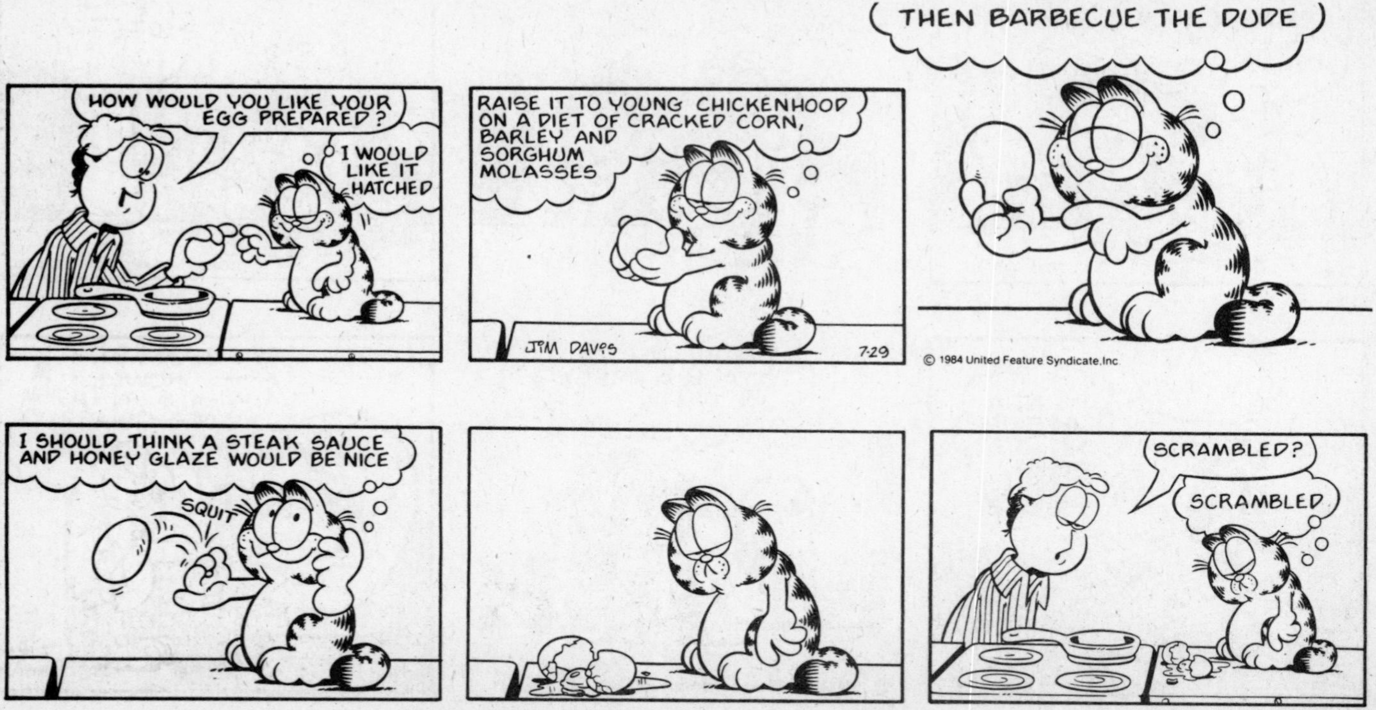
HOW WOULD YOU LIKE YOUR EGG PREPARED?
I WOULD LIKE IT HATCHED
RAISE IT TO YOUNG CHICKENHOOD ON A DIET OF CRACKED CORN, BARLEY AND SORGHUM MOLASSES
JIM DAVIS
7-29
THEN BARBECUE THE DUDE
I SHOULD THINK A STEAK SAUCE AND HONEY GLAZE WOULD BE NICE
SQUIT
SCRAMBLED?
SCRAMBLED

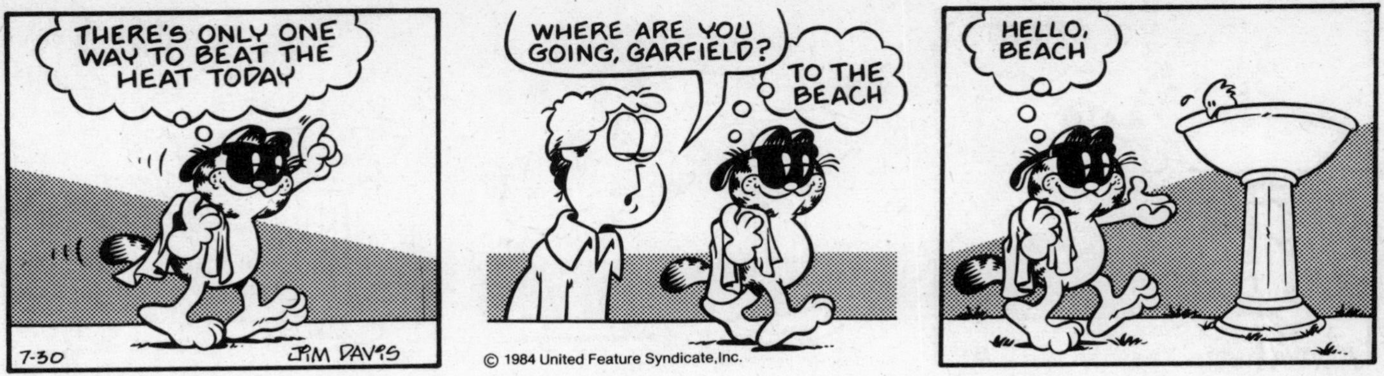
THERE'S ONLY ONE WAY TO BEAT THE HEAT TODAY
7-30
JIM DAVIS
WHERE ARE YOU GOING, GARFIELD?
TO THE BEACH
© 1984 United Feature Syndicate, Inc.
HELLO, BEACH

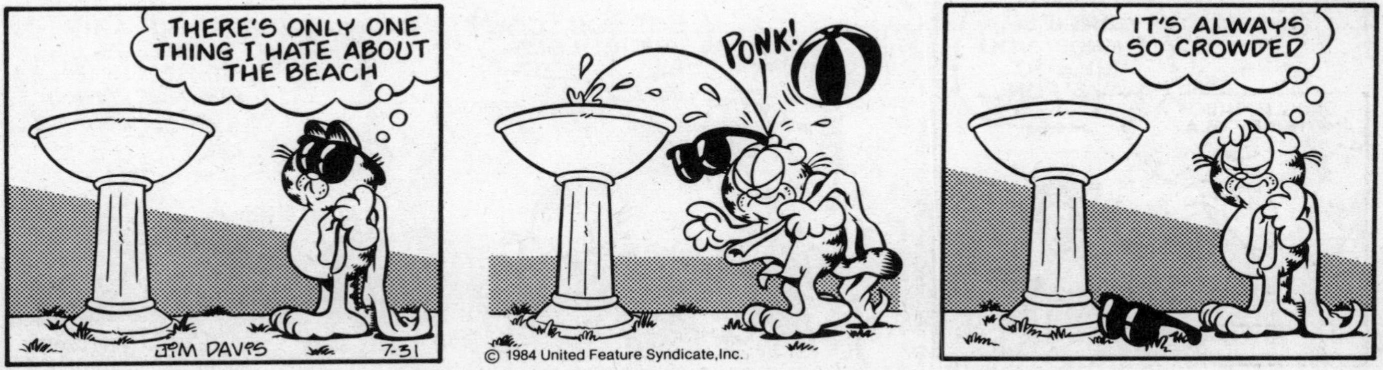
THERE'S ONLY ONE THING I HATE ABOUT THE BEACH
JIM DAVIS
7-31
PONK!
© 1984 United Feature Syndicate, Inc.
IT'S ALWAYS SO CROWDED

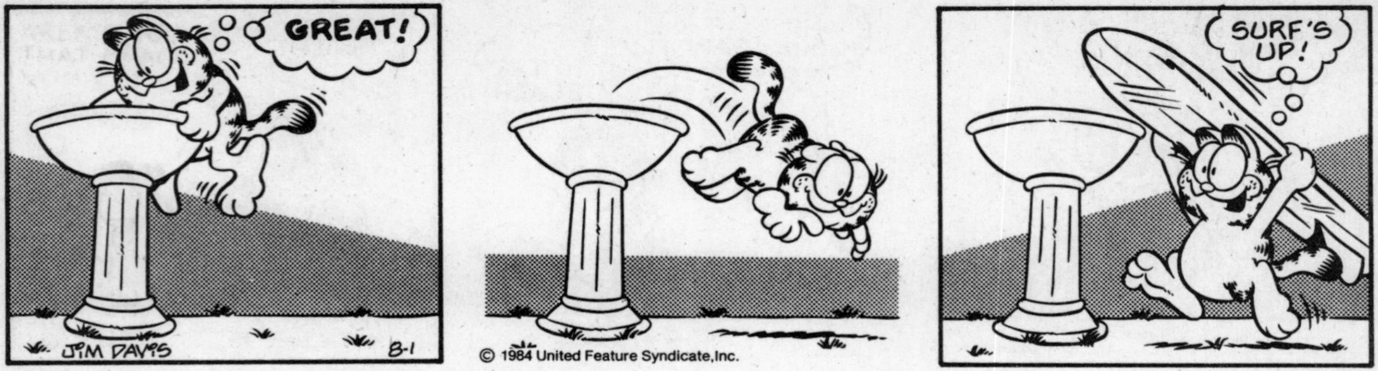
GREAT!
SURF'S UP!
JIM DAVIS
8-1
© 1984 United Feature Syndicate,Inc.

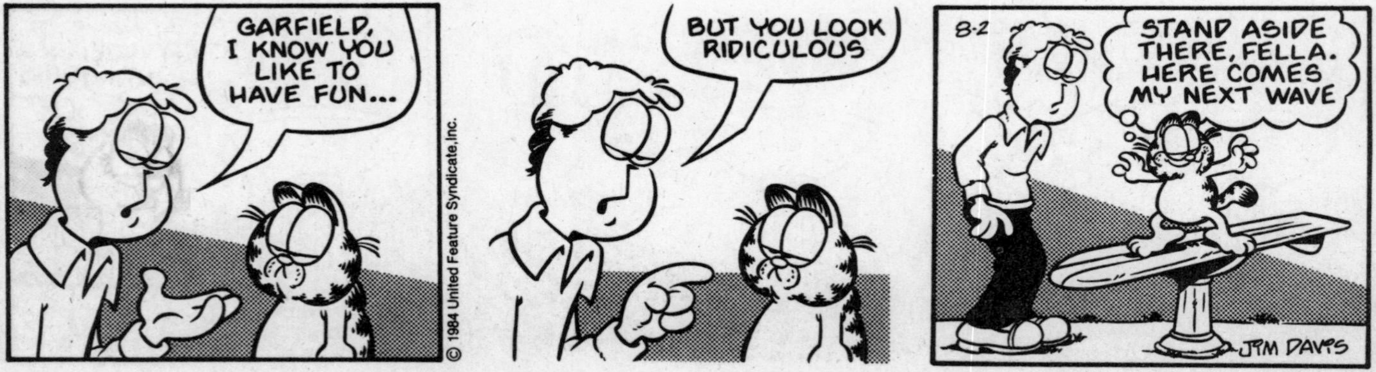
GARFIELD, I KNOW YOU LIKE TO HAVE FUN...
BUT YOU LOOK RIDICULOUS
STAND ASIDE THERE, FELLA. HERE COMES MY NEXT WAVE
8-2
JIM DAVIS
© 1984 United Feature Syndicate,Inc.

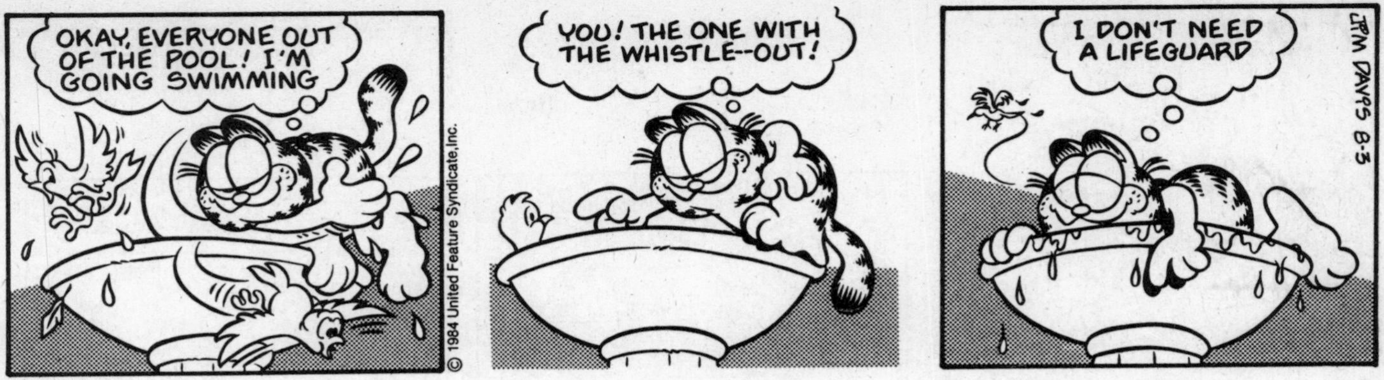
OKAY, EVERYONE OUT OF THE POOL! I'M GOING SWIMMING
© 1984 United Feature Syndicate, Inc.
YOU! THE ONE WITH THE WHISTLE--OUT!
I DON'T NEED A LIFEGUARD
JIM DAVIS 8-3

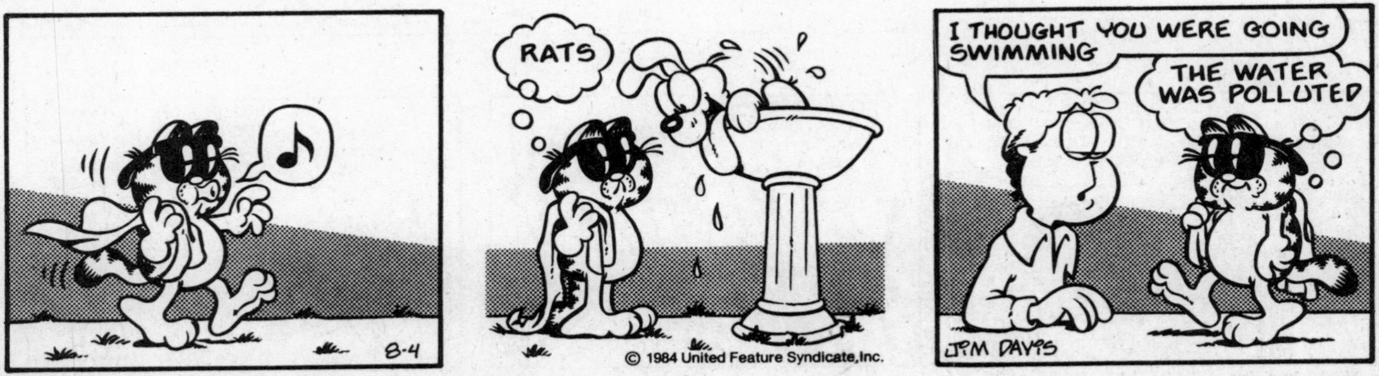
♪
8-4
RATS
© 1984 United Feature Syndicate, Inc.
I THOUGHT YOU WERE GOING SWIMMING
THE WATER WAS POLLUTED
JIM DAVIS

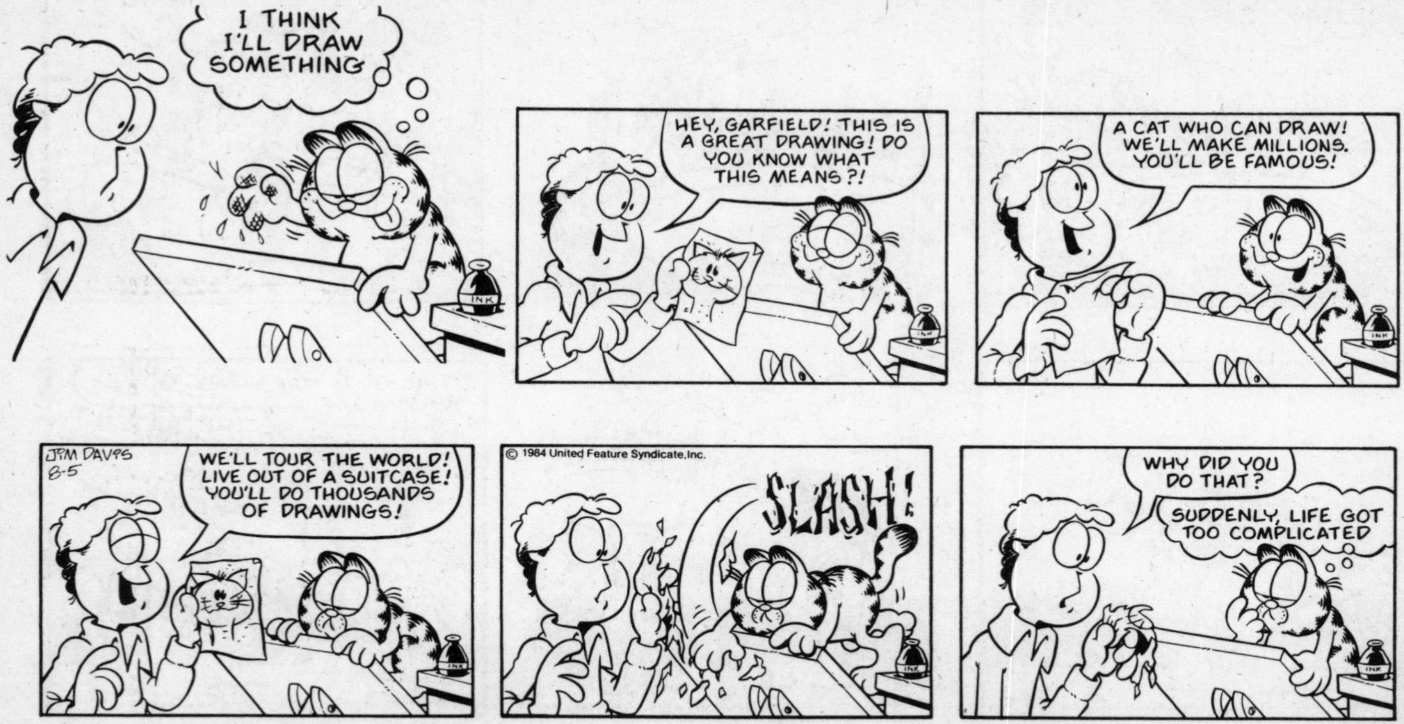
I THINK I'LL DRAW SOMETHING
INK
HEY, GARFIELD! THIS IS A GREAT DRAWING! DO YOU KNOW WHAT THIS MEANS?!
A CAT WHO CAN DRAW! WE'LL MAKE MILLIONS. YOU'LL BE FAMOUS!
JIM DAVIS 8-5
WE'LL TOUR THE WORLD! LIVE OUT OF A SUITCASE! YOU'LL DO THOUSANDS OF DRAWINGS!
© 1984 United Feature Syndicate, Inc.
SLASH!
WHY DID YOU DO THAT?
SUDDENLY, LIFE GOT TOO COMPLICATED

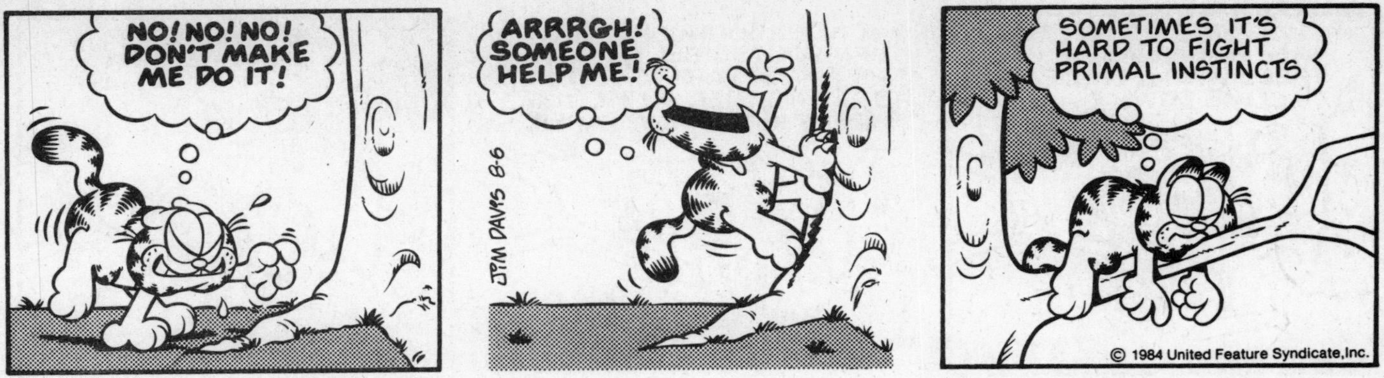
NO! NO! NO! DON'T MAKE ME DO IT!
ARRRGH! SOMEONE HELP ME!
JIM DAVIS 8-6
SOMETIMES IT'S HARD TO FIGHT PRIMAL INSTINCTS
© 1984 United Feature Syndicate, Inc.

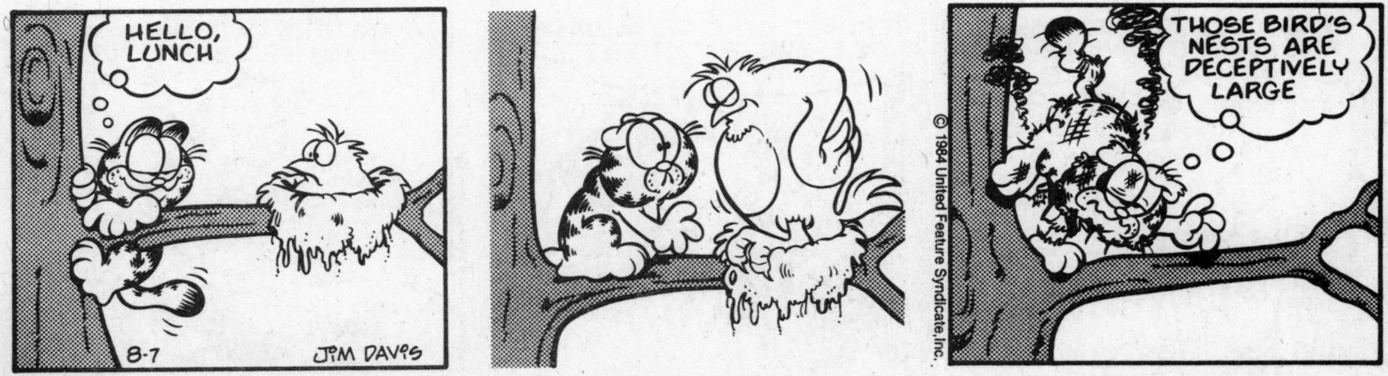
HELLO, LUNCH
8-7
JIM DAVIS
© 1984 United Feature Syndicate, Inc.
THOSE BIRD'S NESTS ARE DECEPTIVELY LARGE

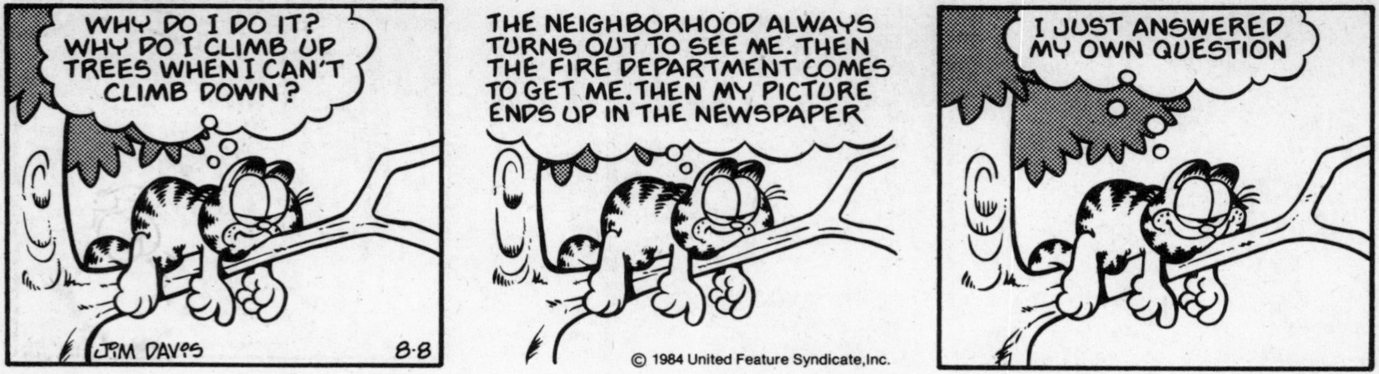
WHY DO I DO IT? WHY DO I CLIMB UP TREES WHEN I CAN'T CLIMB DOWN?
JIM DAVIS 8-8
THE NEIGHBORHOOD ALWAYS TURNS OUT TO SEE ME. THEN THE FIRE DEPARTMENT COMES TO GET ME. THEN MY PICTURE ENDS UP IN THE NEWSPAPER
I JUST ANSWERED MY OWN QUESTION

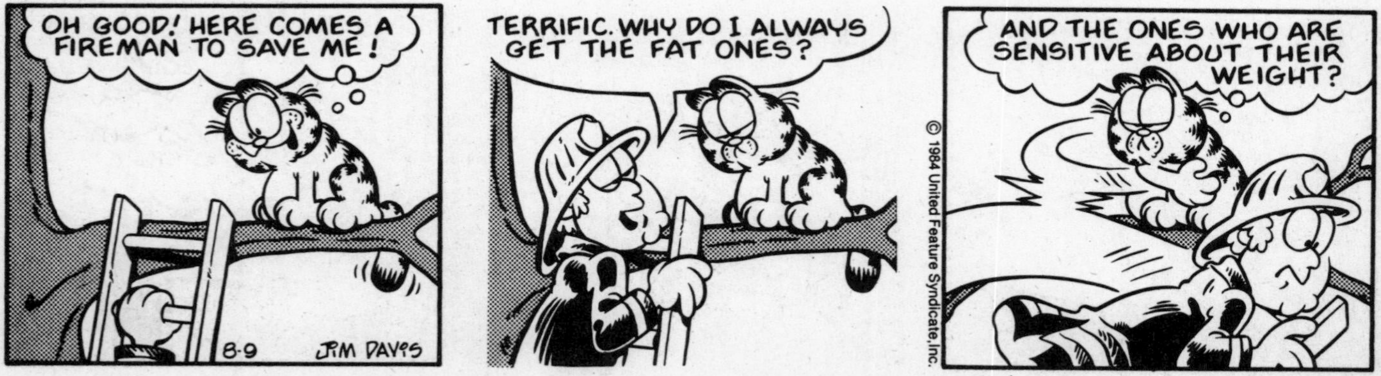
OH GOOD! HERE COMES A FIREMAN TO SAVE ME!
8-9 JIM DAVIS
TERRIFIC. WHY DO I ALWAYS GET THE FAT ONES?
AND THE ONES WHO ARE SENSITIVE ABOUT THEIR WEIGHT?

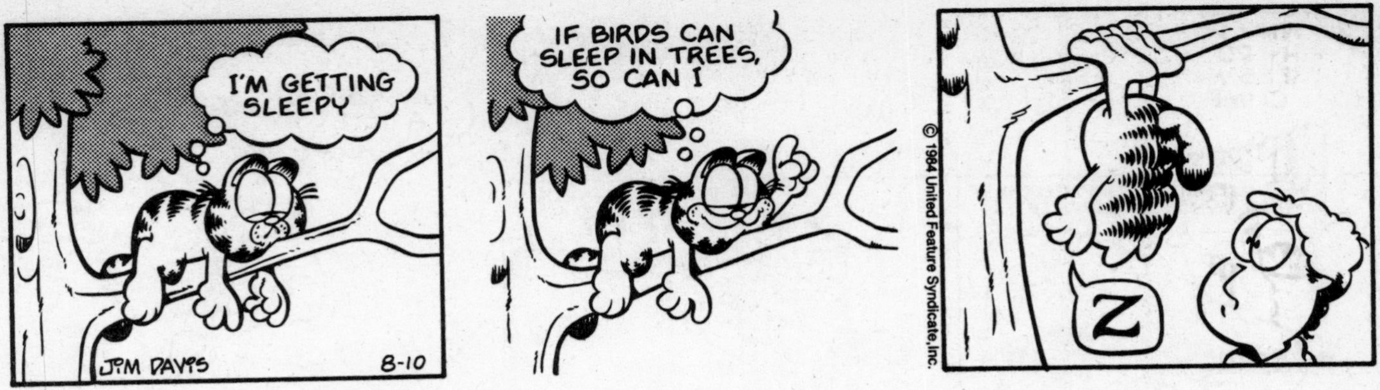
I'M GETTING SLEEPY
JIM DAVIS
8-10
IF BIRDS CAN SLEEP IN TREES, SO CAN I
© 1984 United Feature Syndicate, Inc.
Z

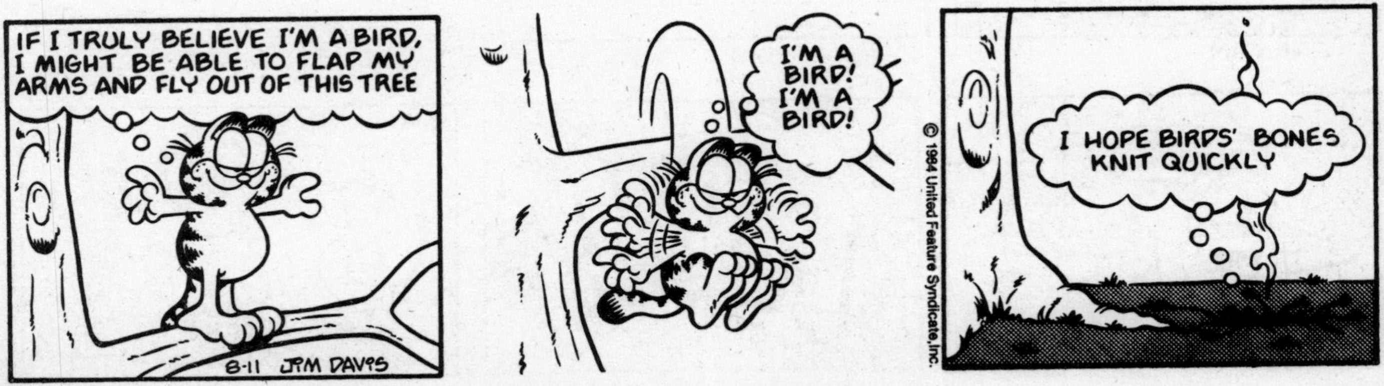
IF I TRULY BELIEVE I'M A BIRD, I MIGHT BE ABLE TO FLAP MY ARMS AND FLY OUT OF THIS TREE
8-11
JIM DAVIS
I'M A BIRD! I'M A BIRD!
© 1984 United Feature Syndicate, Inc.
I HOPE BIRDS' BONES KNIT QUICKLY

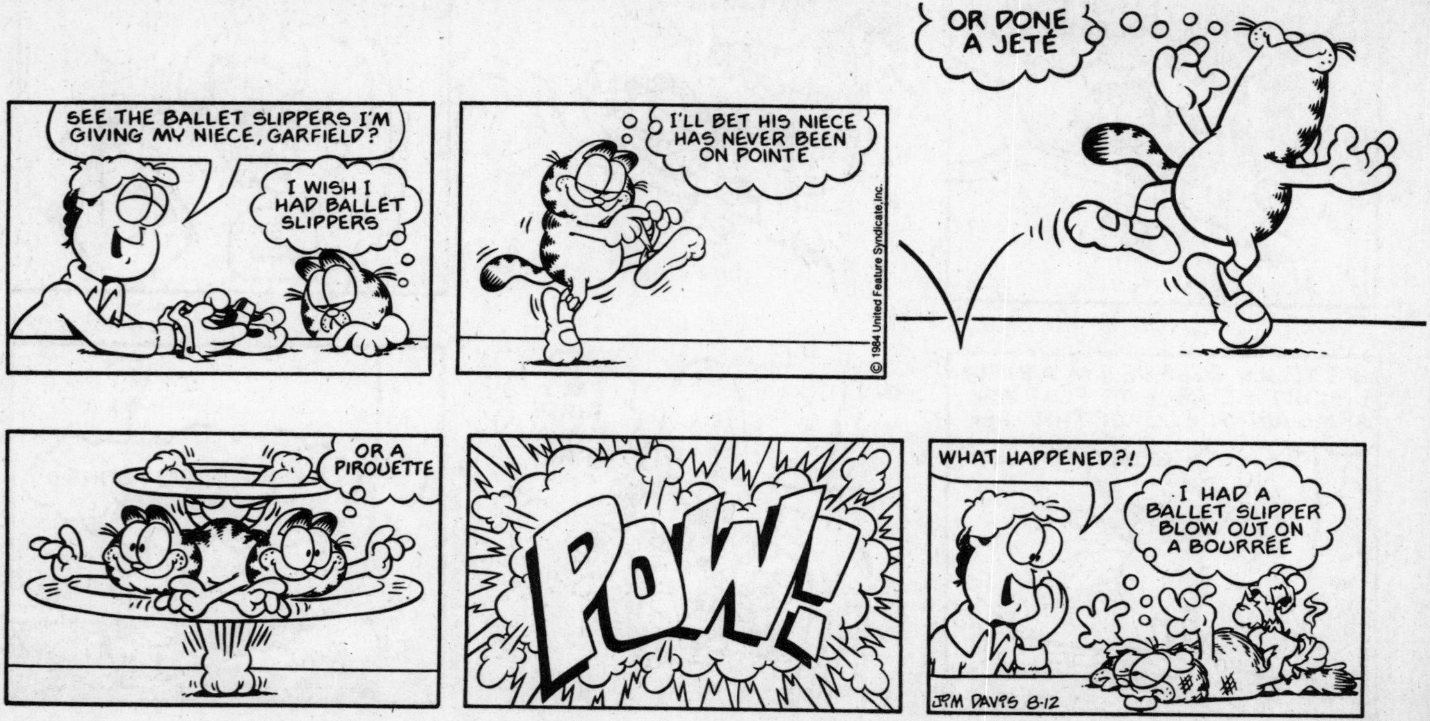
SEE THE BALLET SLIPPERS I'M GIVING MY NIECE, GARFIELD?
I WISH I HAD BALLET SLIPPERS
I'LL BET HIS NIECE HAS NEVER BEEN ON POINTE
© 1984 United Feature Syndicate, Inc.
OR DONE A JETÉ
OR A PIROUETTE
POW!
WHAT HAPPENED?!
I HAD A BALLET SLIPPER BLOW OUT ON A BOURRÉE
JIM DAVIS 8-12

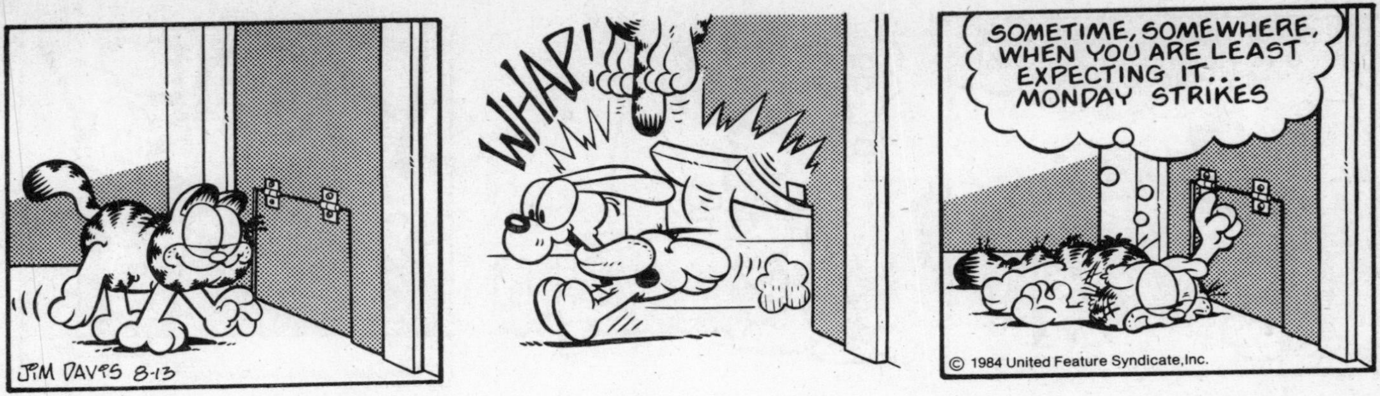
JIM DAVIS 8-13
WHAP!
SOMETIME, SOMEWHERE, WHEN YOU ARE LEAST EXPECTING IT... MONDAY STRIKES
© 1984 United Feature Syndicate, Inc.

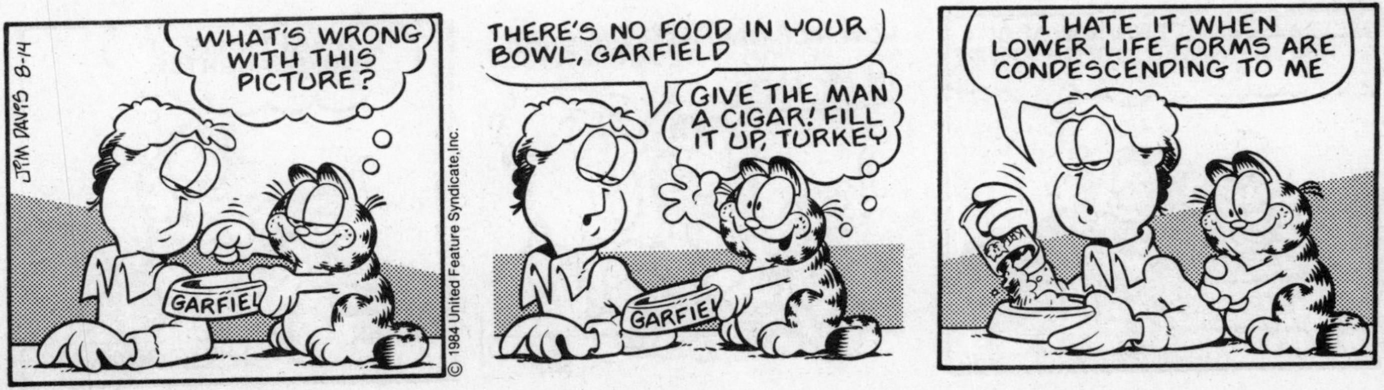
JIM DAVIS 8-14
WHAT'S WRONG WITH THIS PICTURE?
GARFIEL
© 1984 United Feature Syndicate, Inc.
THERE'S NO FOOD IN YOUR BOWL, GARFIELD
GIVE THE MAN A CIGAR! FILL IT UP, TURKEY
GARFIEL
I HATE IT WHEN LOWER LIFE FORMS ARE CONDESCENDING TO ME

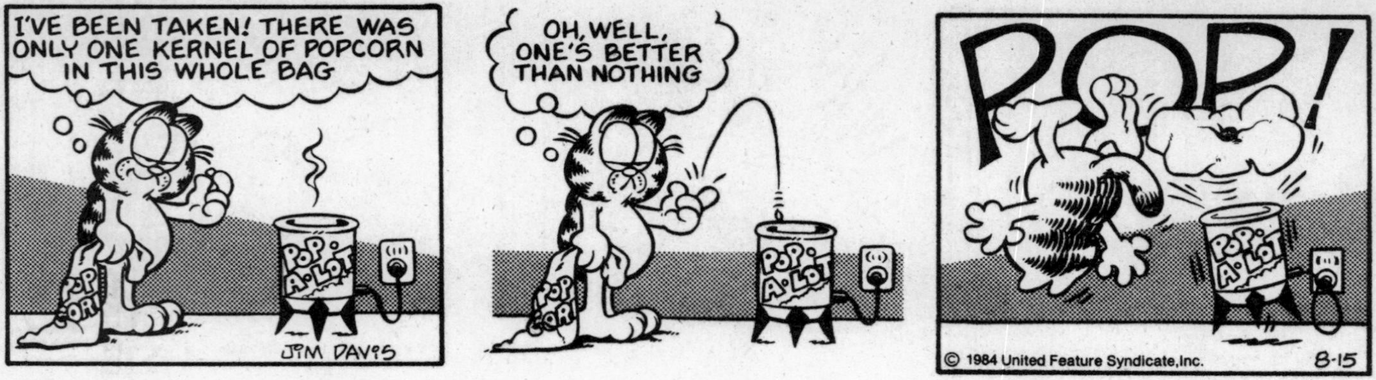
I'VE BEEN TAKEN! THERE WAS ONLY ONE KERNEL OF POPCORN IN THIS WHOLE BAG
POP-A-LOT
JIM DAVIS
OH, WELL, ONE'S BETTER THAN NOTHING
POP-A-LOT
POP!
POP-A-LOT
© 1984 United Feature Syndicate,Inc.
8-15

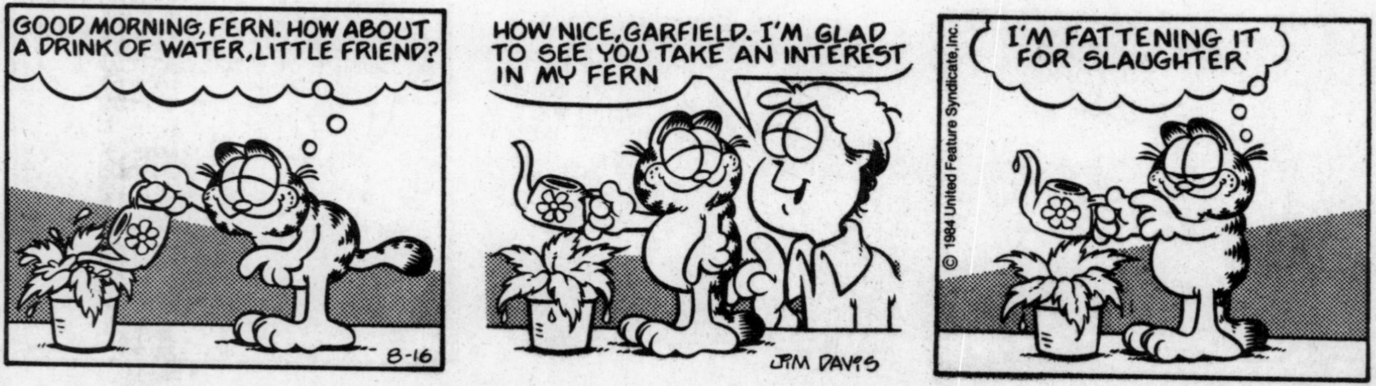
GOOD MORNING, FERN. HOW ABOUT A DRINK OF WATER, LITTLE FRIEND?
8-16
HOW NICE, GARFIELD. I'M GLAD TO SEE YOU TAKE AN INTEREST IN MY FERN
JIM DAVIS
© 1984 United Feature Syndicate,Inc.
I'M FATTENING IT FOR SLAUGHTER

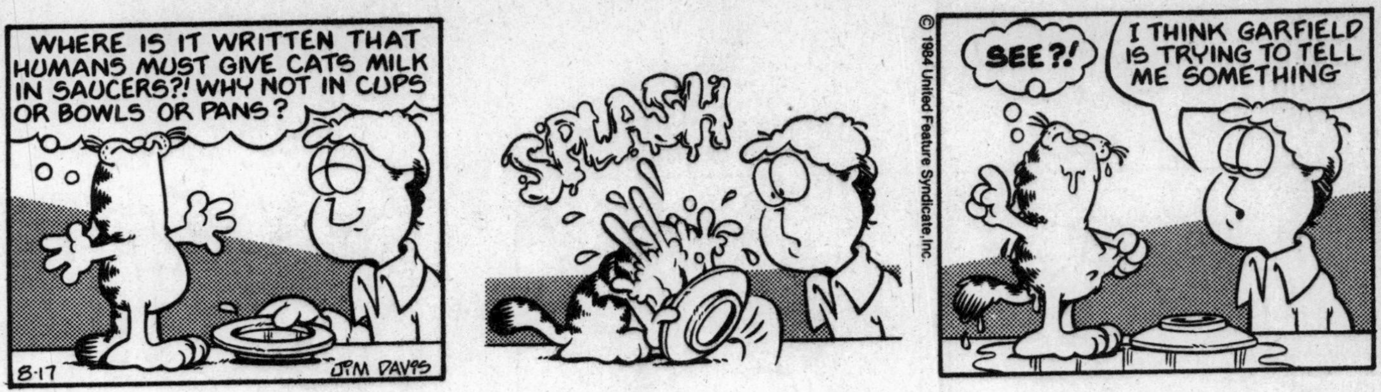
WHERE IS IT WRITTEN THAT HUMANS MUST GIVE CATS MILK IN SAUCERS?! WHY NOT IN CUPS OR BOWLS OR PANS?
8·17
JIM DAVIS
SPLASH
© 1984 United Feature Syndicate,Inc.
SEE?!
I THINK GARFIELD IS TRYING TO TELL ME SOMETHING

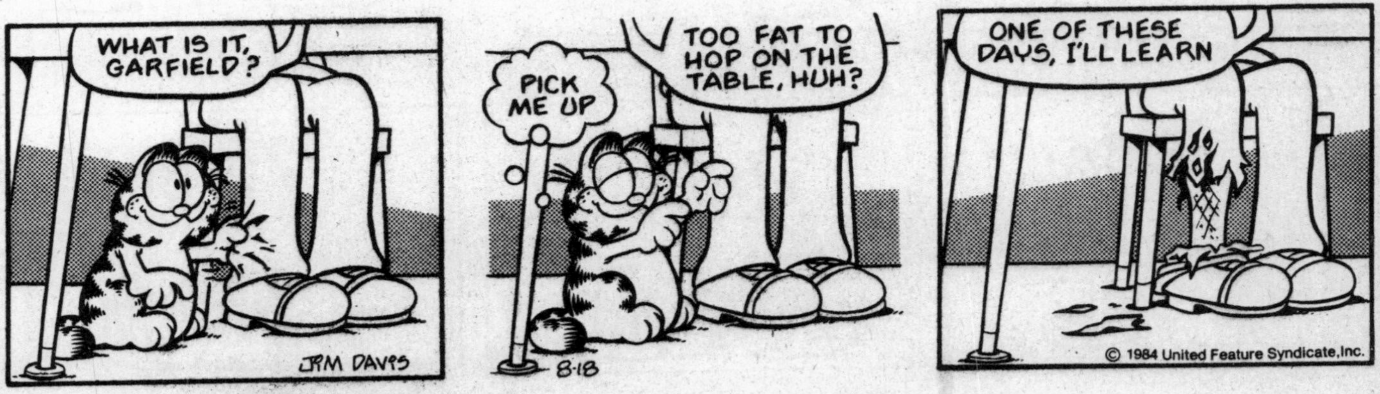
WHAT IS IT, GARFIELD?
JIM DAVIS
PICK ME UP
TOO FAT TO HOP ON THE TABLE, HUH?
8·18
ONE OF THESE DAYS, I'LL LEARN
© 1984 United Feature Syndicate,Inc.

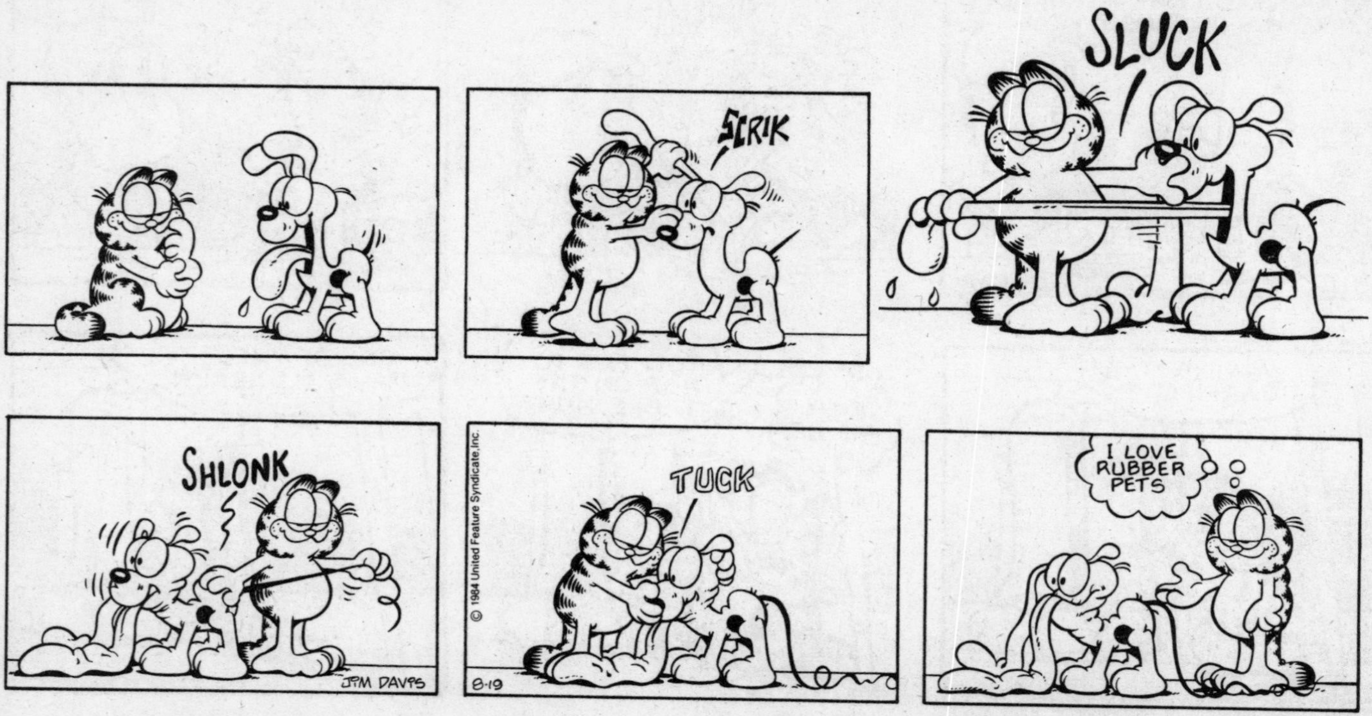
SCRIK
SLUCK
SHLONK
JIM DAVIS
© 1984 United Feature Syndicate, Inc.
8-19
TUCK
I LOVE RUBBER PETS

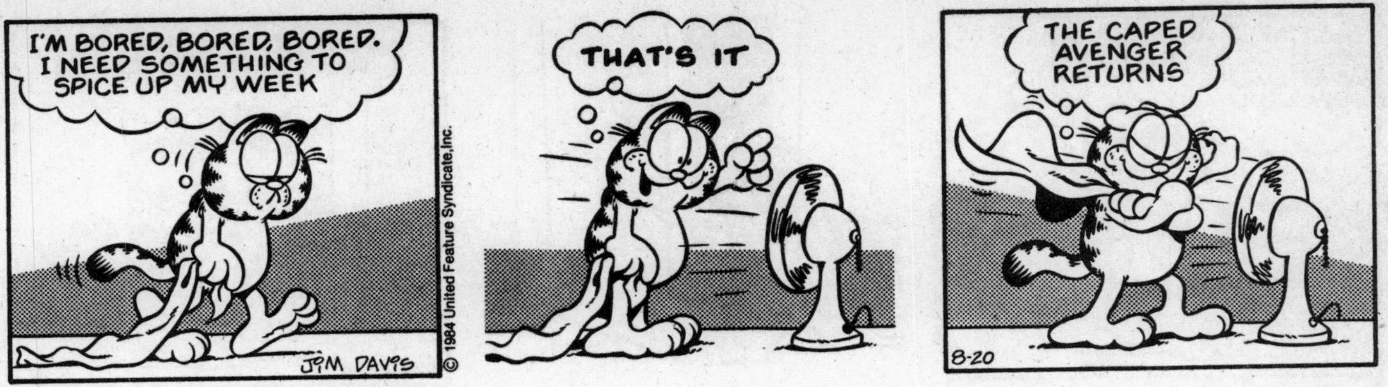

I'M BORED, BORED, BORED. I NEED SOMETHING TO SPICE UP MY WEEK
JIM DAVIS
© 1984 United Feature Syndicate,Inc.
THAT'S IT
THE CAPED AVENGER RETURNS
8-20

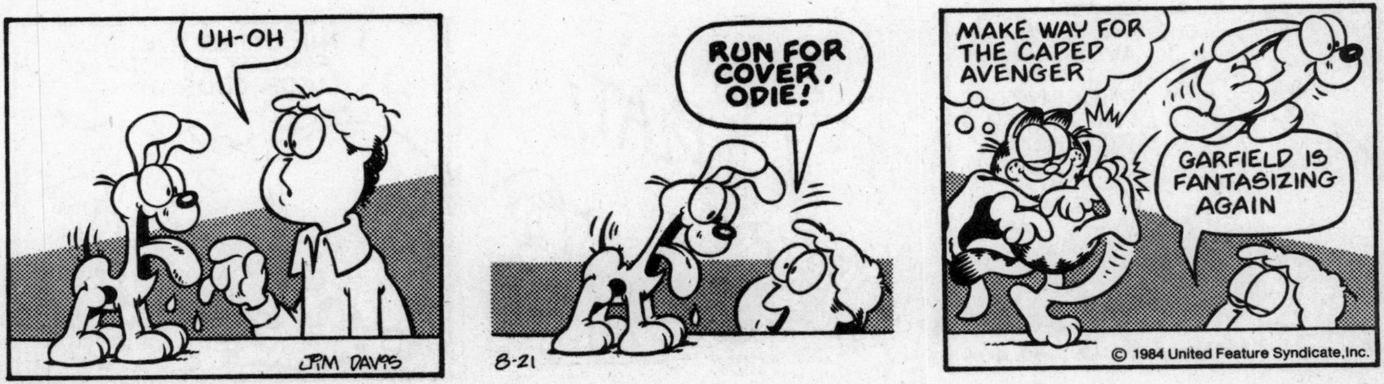

UH-OH
JIM DAVIS
RUN FOR COVER, ODIE!
8-21
MAKE WAY FOR THE CAPED AVENGER
GARFIELD IS FANTASIZING AGAIN
© 1984 United Feature Syndicate,Inc.

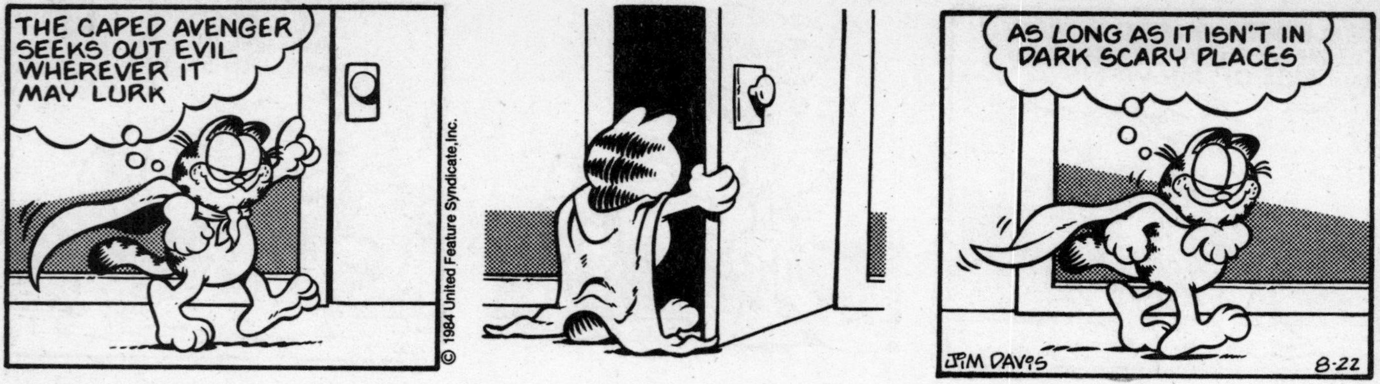
THE CAPED AVENGER SEEKS OUT EVIL WHEREVER IT MAY LURK
© 1984 United Feature Syndicate,Inc.
AS LONG AS IT ISN'T IN DARK SCARY PLACES
JIM DAVIS
8-22

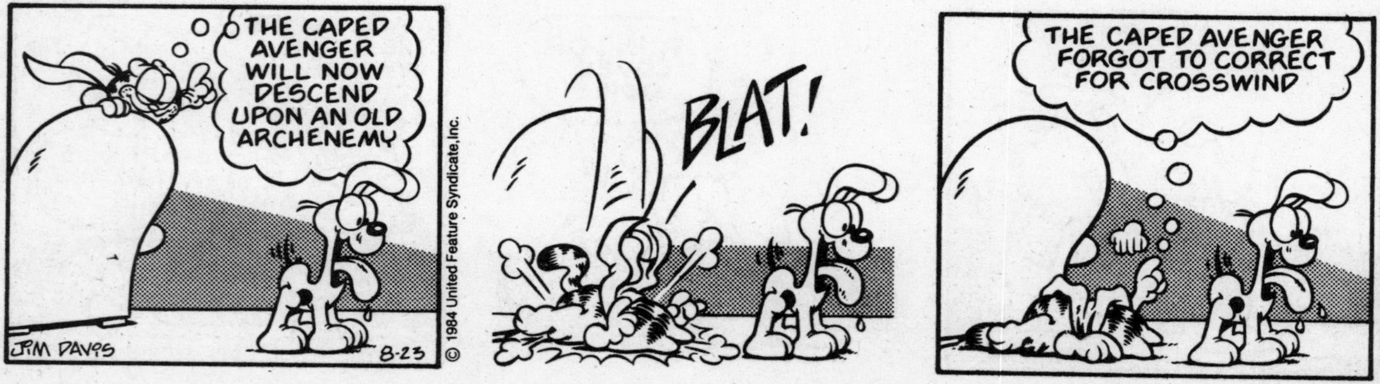
THE CAPED AVENGER WILL NOW DESCEND UPON AN OLD ARCHENEMY
JIM DAVIS
8-23
© 1984 United Feature Syndicate,Inc.
BLAT!
THE CAPED AVENGER FORGOT TO CORRECT FOR CROSSWIND

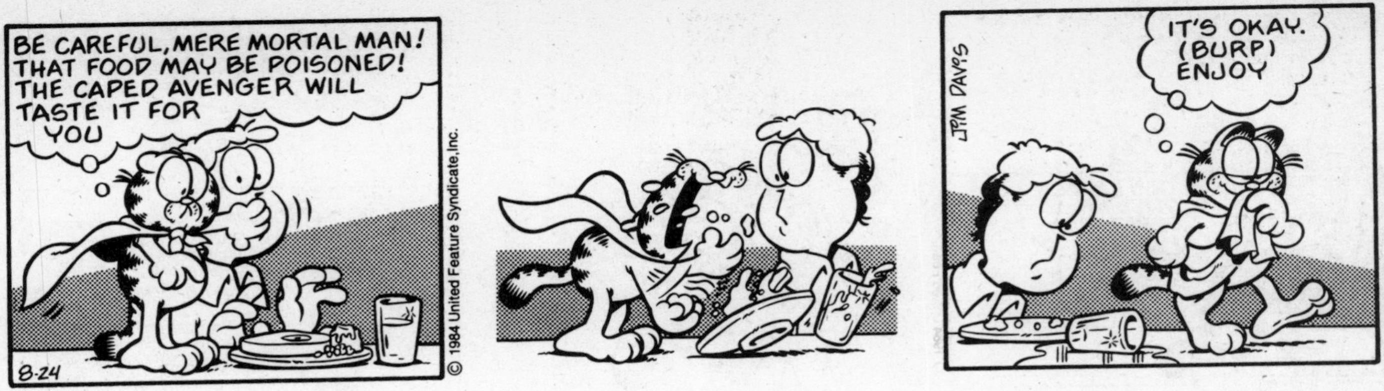
BE CAREFUL, MERE MORTAL MAN! THAT FOOD MAY BE POISONED! THE CAPED AVENGER WILL TASTE IT FOR YOU
8·24
© 1984 United Feature Syndicate, Inc.
JPM DAV9S
IT'S OKAY. (BURP) ENJOY

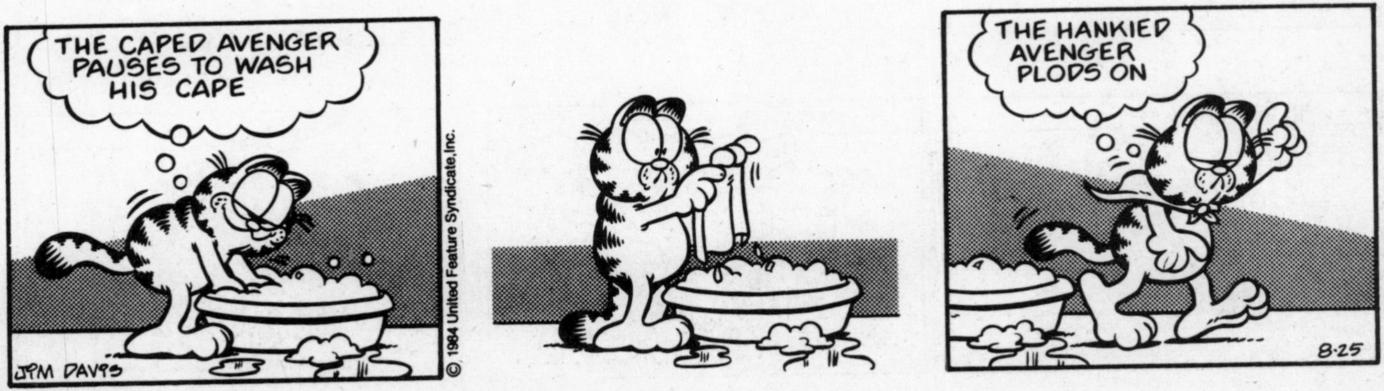
THE CAPED AVENGER PAUSES TO WASH HIS CAPE
JPM DAV9S
© 1984 United Feature Syndicate, Inc.
THE HANKIED AVENGER PLODS ON
8·25

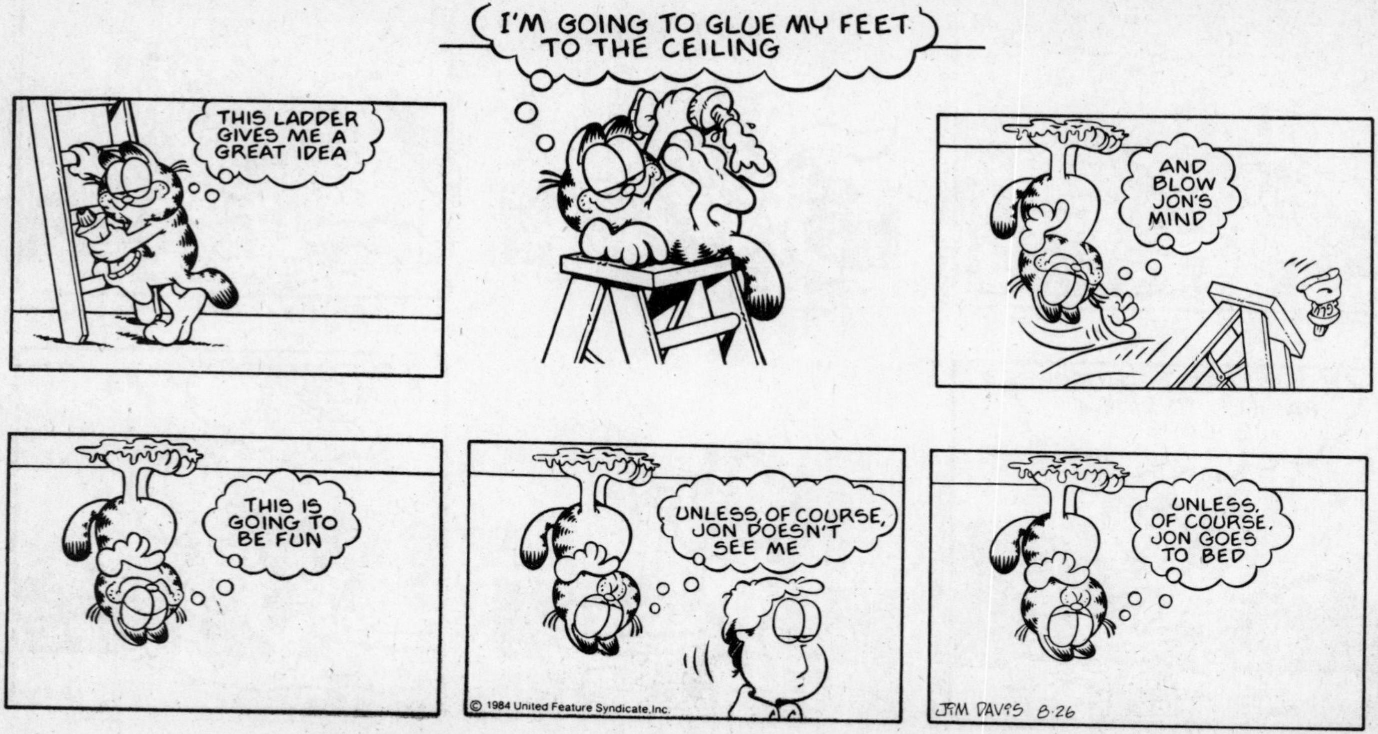
I'M GOING TO GLUE MY FEET TO THE CEILING
THIS LADDER GIVES ME A GREAT IDEA
AND BLOW JON'S MIND
GLUE
THIS IS GOING TO BE FUN
UNLESS, OF COURSE, JON DOESN'T SEE ME
UNLESS, OF COURSE, JON GOES TO BED
© 1984 United Feature Syndicate, Inc.
JIM DAVIS 8-26

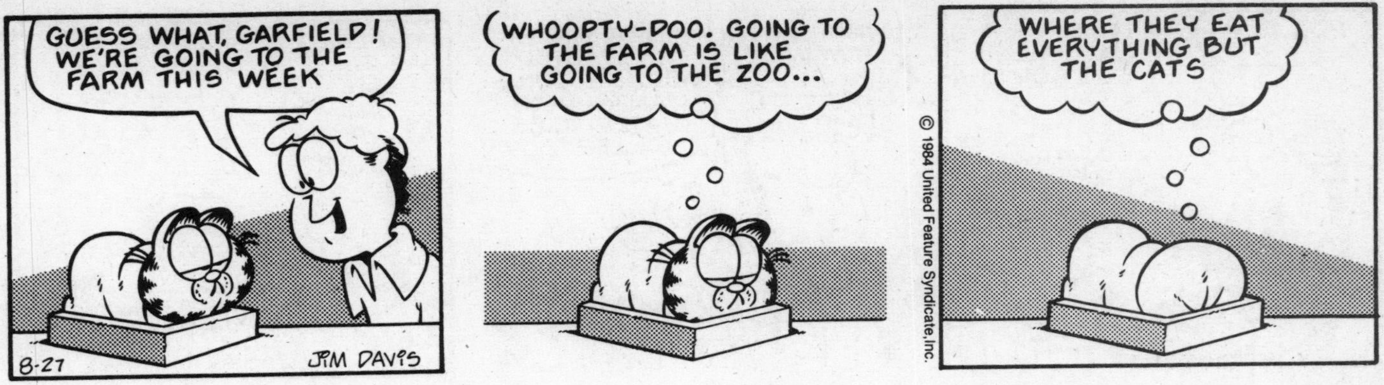
GUESS WHAT, GARFIELD! WE'RE GOING TO THE FARM THIS WEEK
8-27
JIM DAVIS
WHOOPTY-DOO. GOING TO THE FARM IS LIKE GOING TO THE ZOO...
WHERE THEY EAT EVERYTHING BUT THE CATS
© 1984 United Feature Syndicate, Inc.

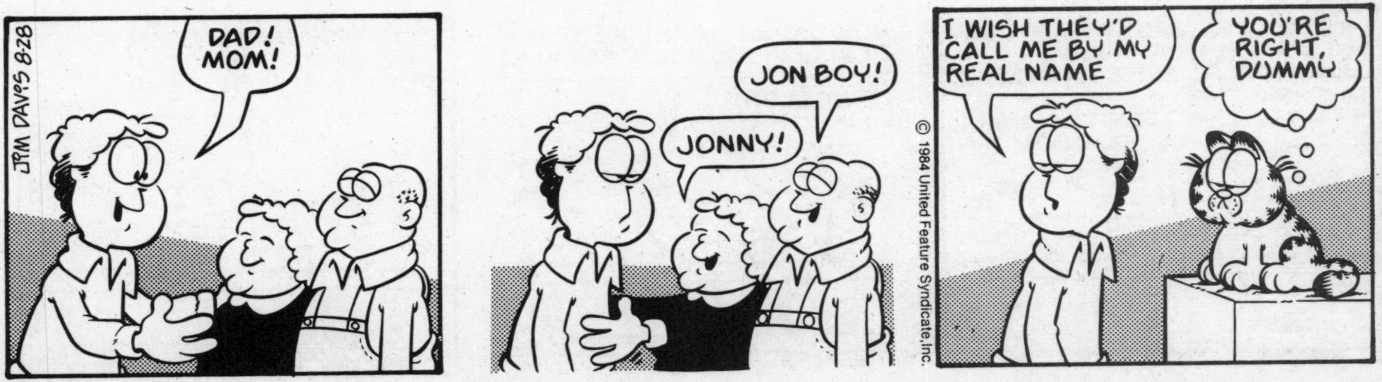
JIM DAVIS 8-28
DAD! MOM!
JONNY!
JON BOY!
I WISH THEY'D CALL ME BY MY REAL NAME
YOU'RE RIGHT, DUMMY
© 1984 United Feature Syndicate, Inc.

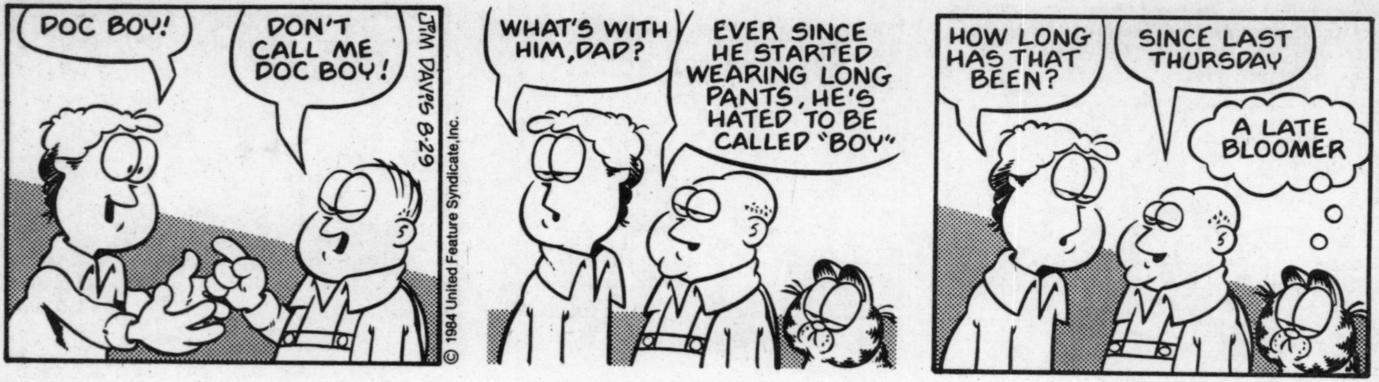
DOC BOY!
DON'T CALL ME DOC BOY!
JIM DAVIS 8-29
© 1984 United Feature Syndicate, Inc.
WHAT'S WITH HIM, DAD?
EVER SINCE HE STARTED WEARING LONG PANTS, HE'S HATED TO BE CALLED "BOY"
HOW LONG HAS THAT BEEN?
SINCE LAST THURSDAY
A LATE BLOOMER

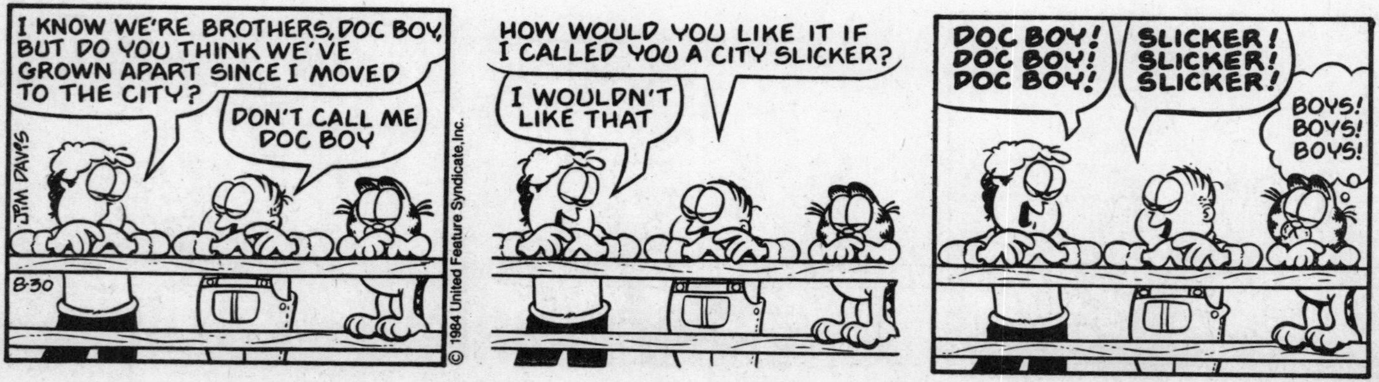
I KNOW WE'RE BROTHERS, DOC BOY, BUT DO YOU THINK WE'VE GROWN APART SINCE I MOVED TO THE CITY?
DON'T CALL ME DOC BOY
JIM DAVIS
8-30
© 1984 United Feature Syndicate, Inc.
HOW WOULD YOU LIKE IT IF I CALLED YOU A CITY SLICKER?
I WOULDN'T LIKE THAT
DOC BOY! DOC BOY! DOC BOY!
SLICKER! SLICKER! SLICKER!
BOYS! BOYS! BOYS!

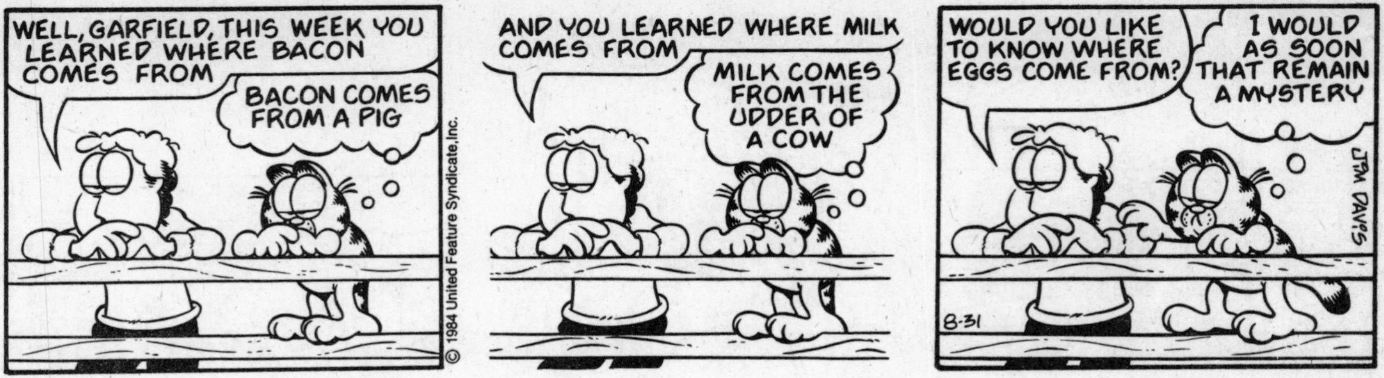
WELL, GARFIELD, THIS WEEK YOU LEARNED WHERE BACON COMES FROM
BACON COMES FROM A PIG
© 1984 United Feature Syndicate, Inc.
AND YOU LEARNED WHERE MILK COMES FROM
MILK COMES FROM THE UDDER OF A COW
WOULD YOU LIKE TO KNOW WHERE EGGS COME FROM?
I WOULD AS SOON THAT REMAIN A MYSTERY
JIM DAVIS
8-31

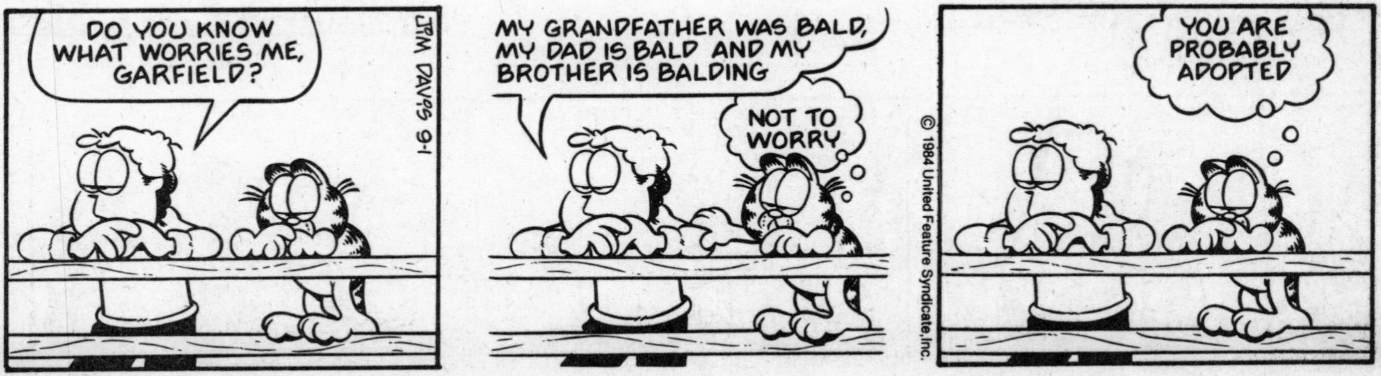
DO YOU KNOW WHAT WORRIES ME, GARFIELD?
JIM DAVIS 9-1
MY GRANDFATHER WAS BALD, MY DAD IS BALD AND MY BROTHER IS BALDING
NOT TO WORRY
© 1984 United Feature Syndicate, Inc.
YOU ARE PROBABLY ADOPTED

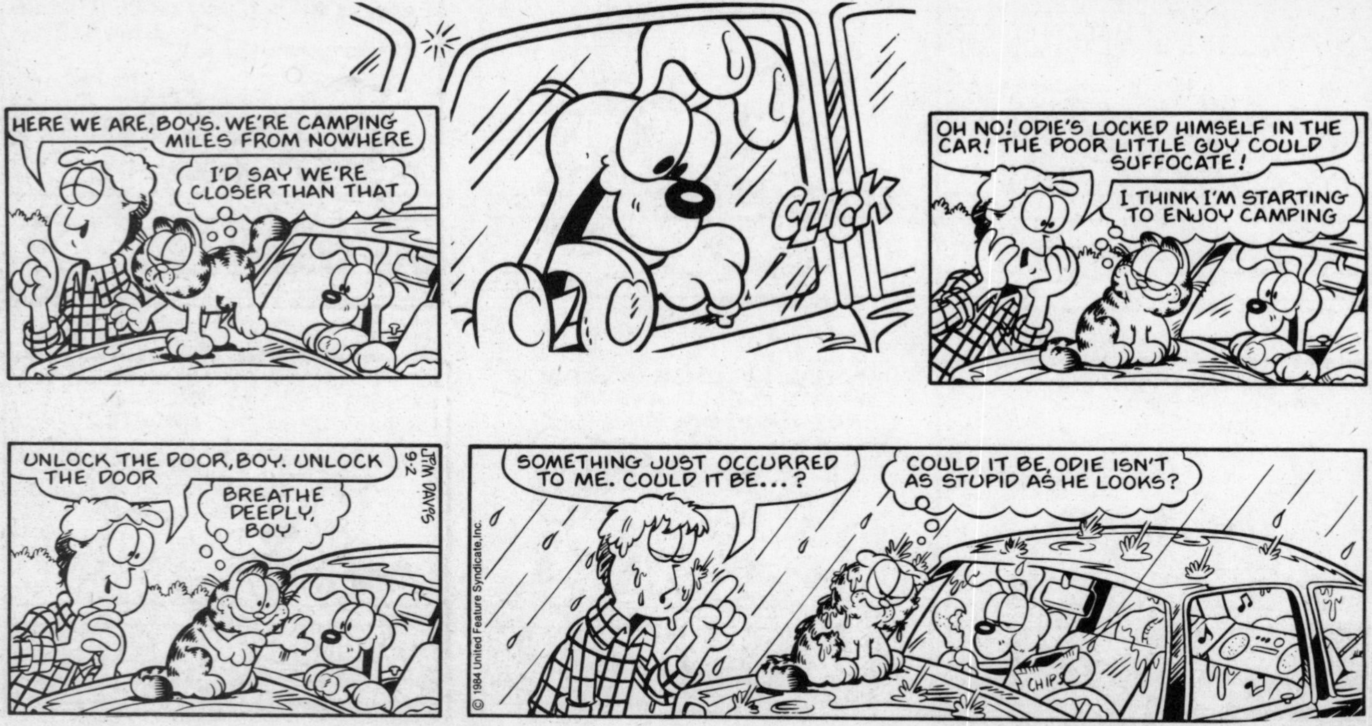
HERE WE ARE, BOYS. WE'RE CAMPING MILES FROM NOWHERE
I'D SAY WE'RE CLOSER THAN THAT
CLICK
OH NO! ODIE'S LOCKED HIMSELF IN THE CAR! THE POOR LITTLE GUY COULD SUFFOCATE!
I THINK I'M STARTING TO ENJOY CAMPING
UNLOCK THE DOOR, BOY. UNLOCK THE DOOR
BREATHE DEEPLY, BOY
JPM DAVIS 9-2
© 1984 United Feature Syndicate, Inc.
SOMETHING JUST OCCURRED TO ME. COULD IT BE...?
COULD IT BE, ODIE ISN'T AS STUPID AS HE LOOKS?
CHIPS

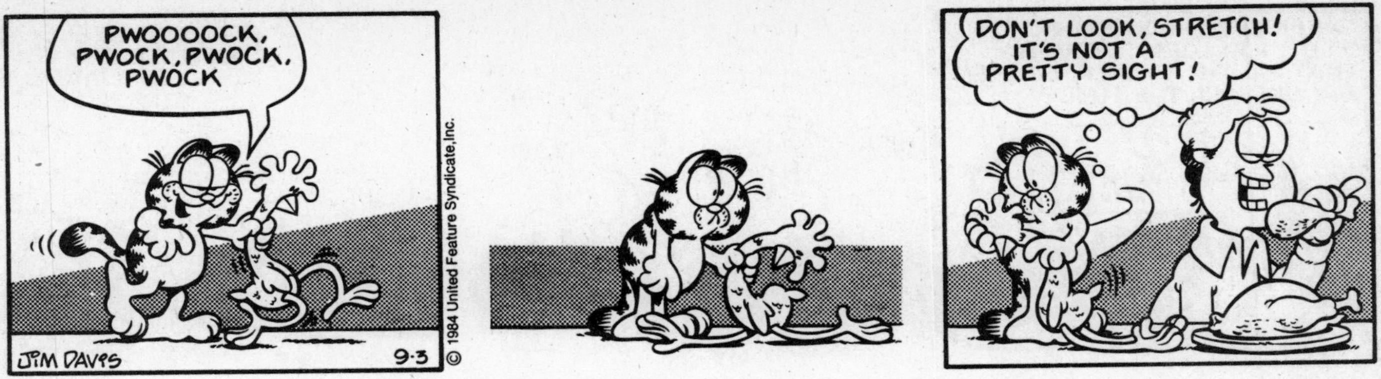
PWOOOOCK, PWOCK, PWOCK, PWOCK
JIM DAVIS
9-3
© 1984 United Feature Syndicate, Inc.
DON'T LOOK, STRETCH! IT'S NOT A PRETTY SIGHT!

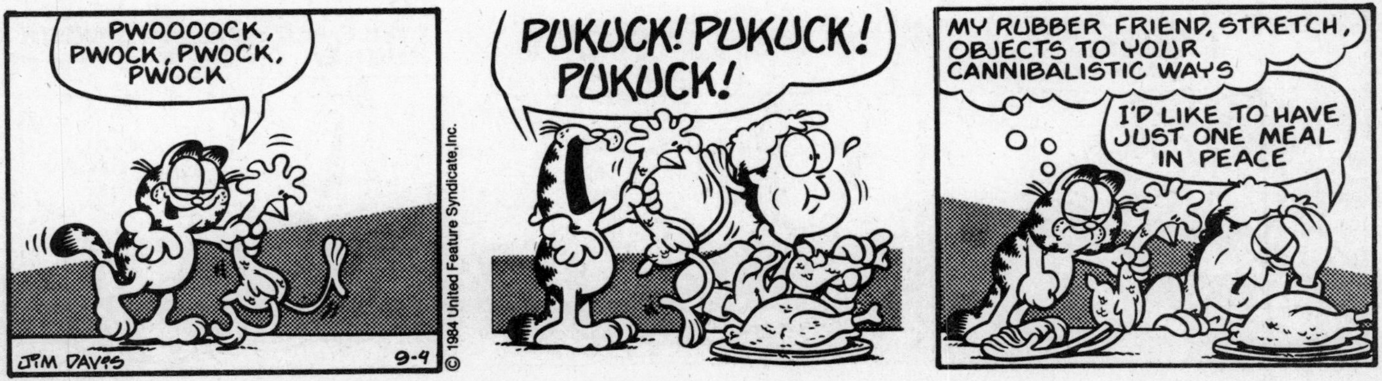
PWOOOOCK, PWOCK, PWOCK, PWOCK
JIM DAVIS
9-4
© 1984 United Feature Syndicate, Inc.
PUKUCK! PUKUCK! PUKUCK!
MY RUBBER FRIEND, STRETCH, OBJECTS TO YOUR CANNIBALISTIC WAYS
I'D LIKE TO HAVE JUST ONE MEAL IN PEACE

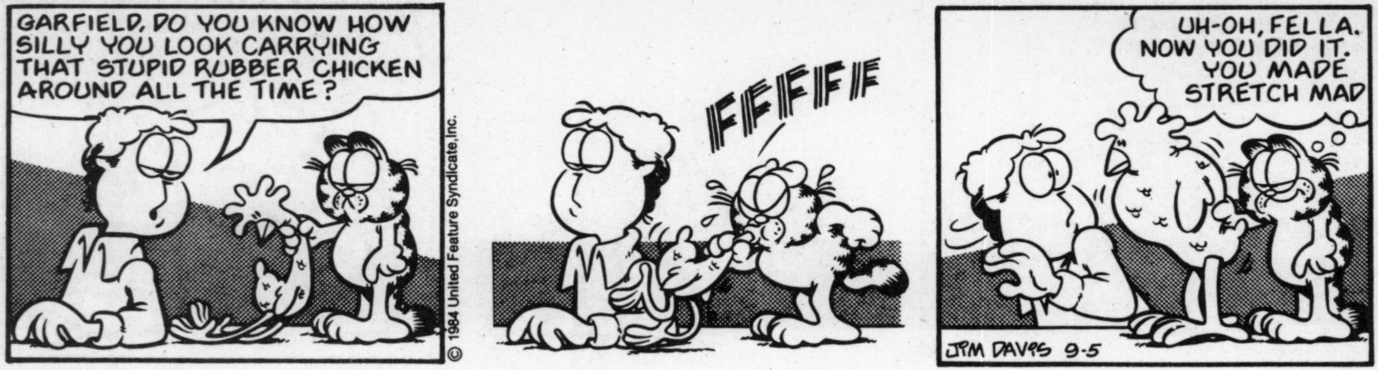
GARFIELD, DO YOU KNOW HOW SILLY YOU LOOK CARRYING THAT STUPID RUBBER CHICKEN AROUND ALL THE TIME?
© 1984 United Feature Syndicate, Inc.
FFFFFF
UH-OH, FELLA. NOW YOU DID IT. YOU MADE STRETCH MAD
JIM DAVIS 9-5

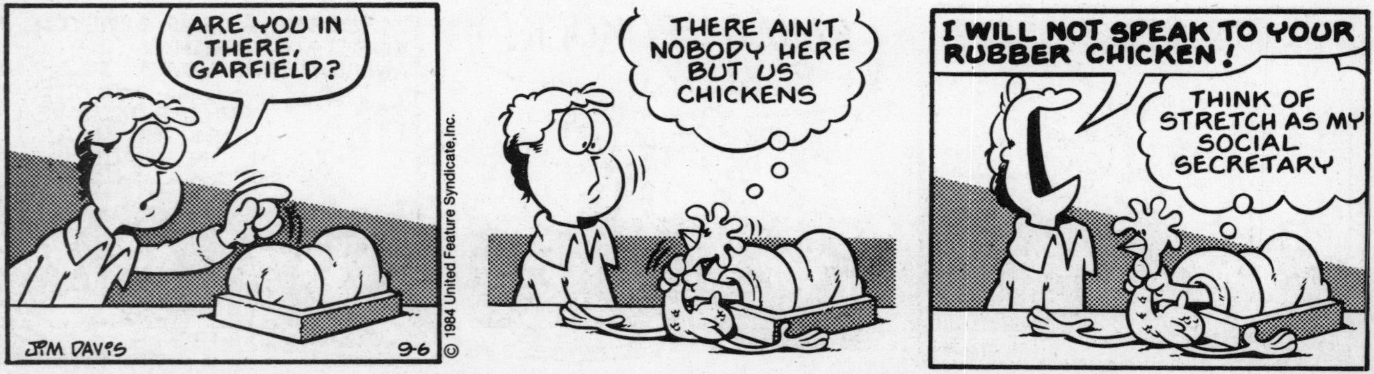
ARE YOU IN THERE, GARFIELD?
JIM DAVIS 9-6
© 1984 United Feature Syndicate, Inc.
THERE AIN'T NOBODY HERE BUT US CHICKENS
I WILL NOT SPEAK TO YOUR RUBBER CHICKEN!
THINK OF STRETCH AS MY SOCIAL SECRETARY

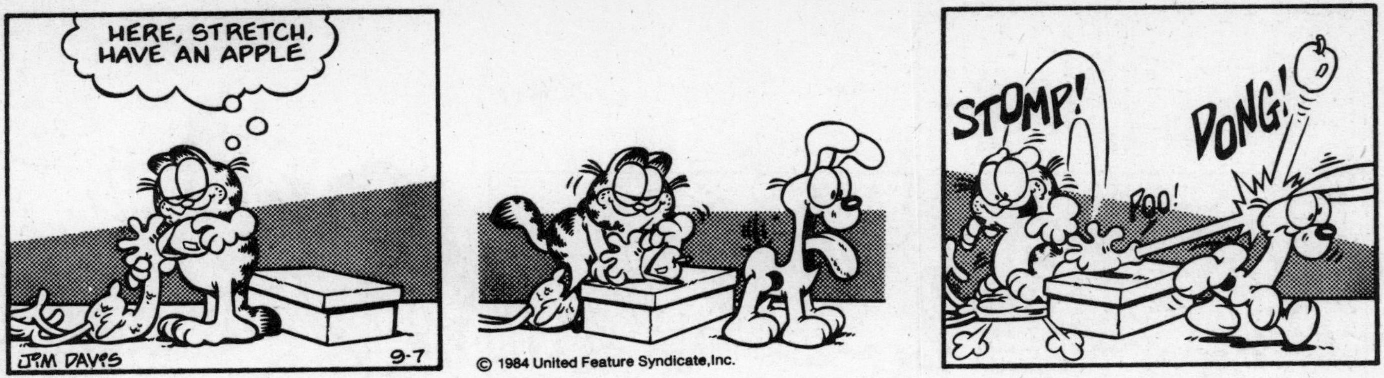
HERE, STRETCH, HAVE AN APPLE
STOMP!
POO!
DONG!
JIM DAVIS
9-7
© 1984 United Feature Syndicate, Inc.

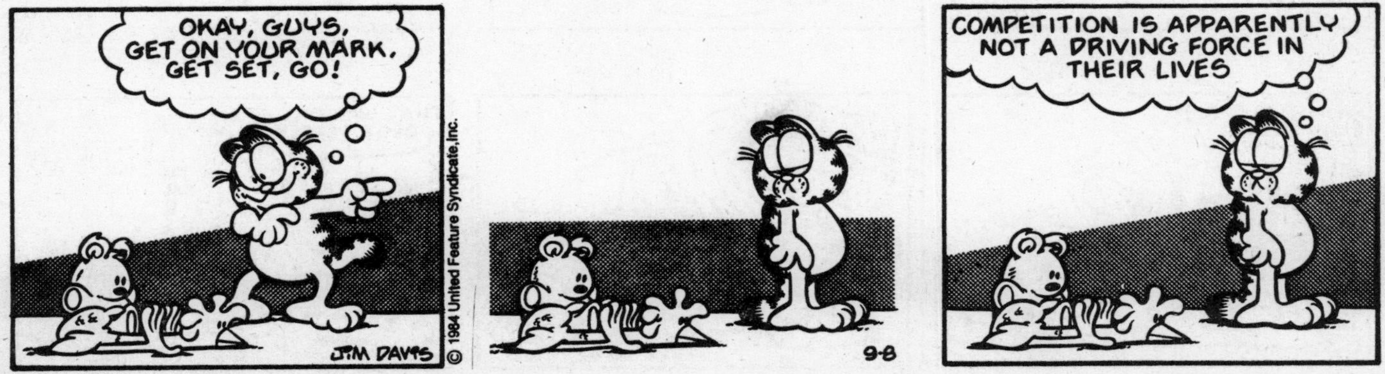
OKAY, GUYS, GET ON YOUR MARK, GET SET, GO!
COMPETITION IS APPARENTLY NOT A DRIVING FORCE IN THEIR LIVES
JIM DAVIS
© 1984 United Feature Syndicate, Inc.
9-8

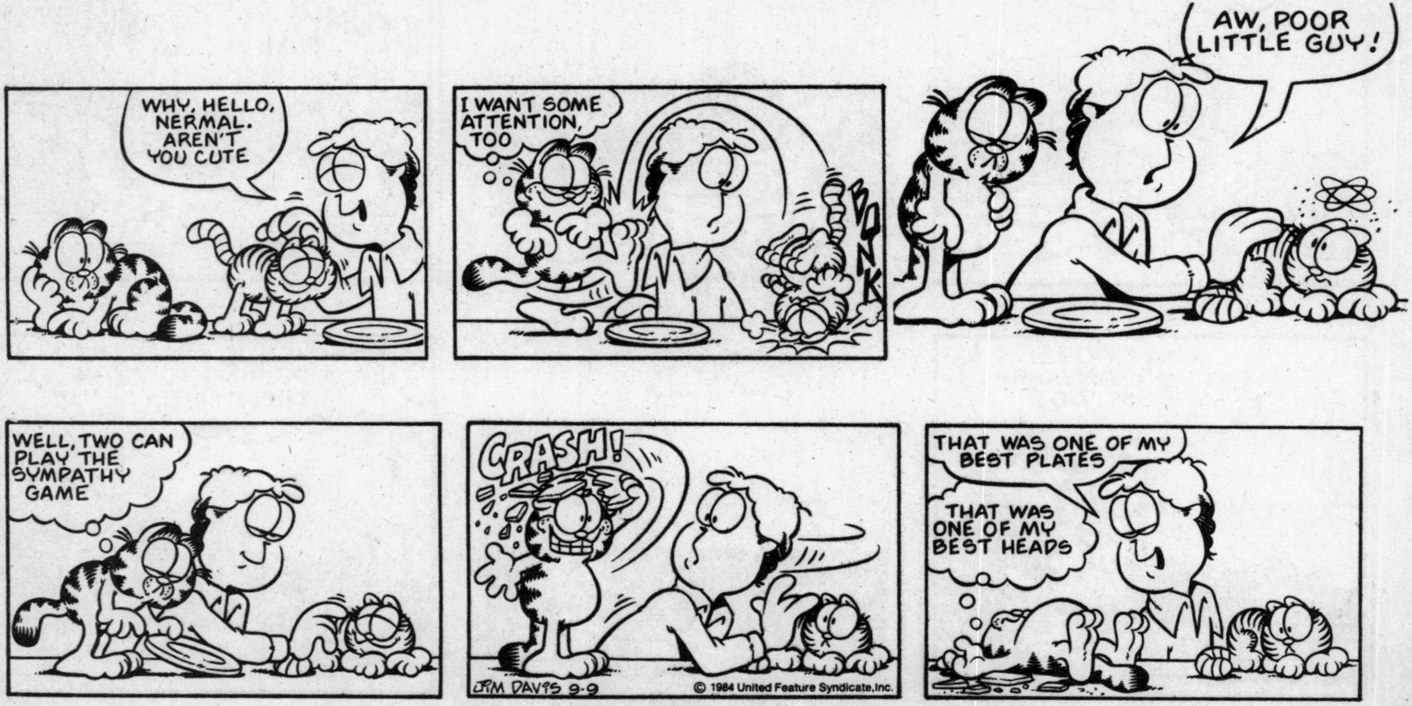
WHY, HELLO, NERMAL. AREN'T YOU CUTE
I WANT SOME ATTENTION, TOO
BONK
AW, POOR LITTLE GUY!
WELL, TWO CAN PLAY THE SYMPATHY GAME
CRASH!
JIM DAVIS 9-9
© 1984 United Feature Syndicate, Inc.
THAT WAS ONE OF MY BEST PLATES
THAT WAS ONE OF MY BEST HEADS

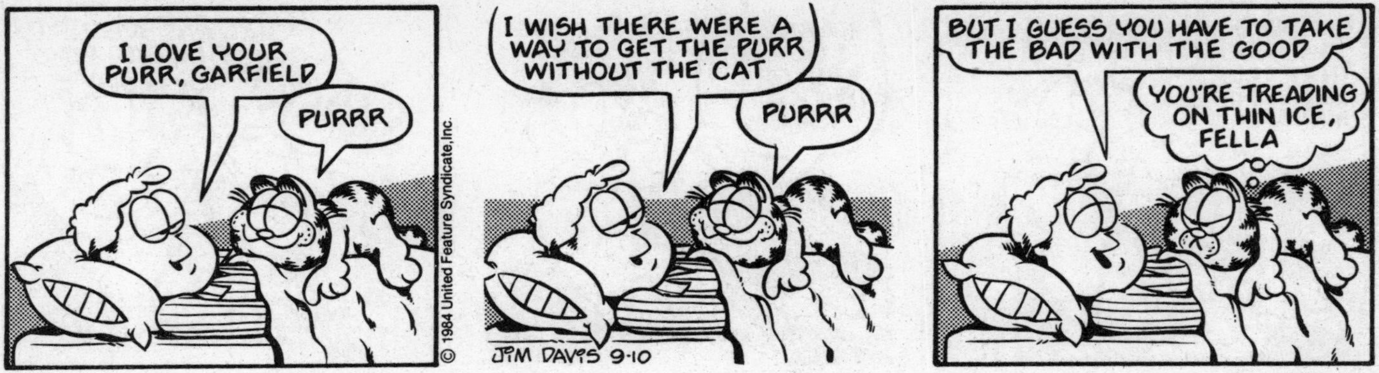
I LOVE YOUR PURR, GARFIELD
PURRR
I WISH THERE WERE A WAY TO GET THE PURR WITHOUT THE CAT
PURRR
BUT I GUESS YOU HAVE TO TAKE THE BAD WITH THE GOOD
YOU'RE TREADING ON THIN ICE, FELLA
JIM DAVIS 9-10
© 1984 United Feature Syndicate, Inc.

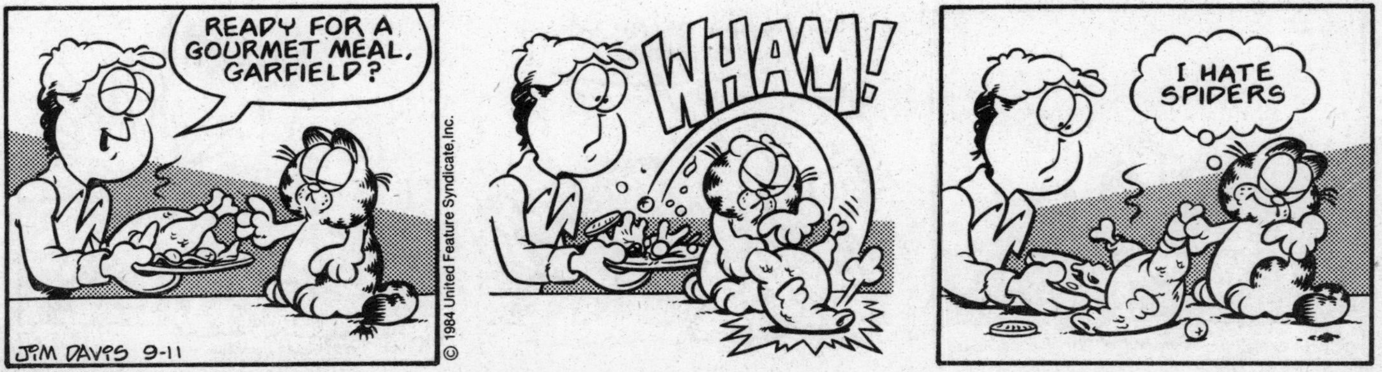
READY FOR A GOURMET MEAL, GARFIELD?
WHAM!
I HATE SPIDERS
JIM DAVIS 9-11
© 1984 United Feature Syndicate, Inc.

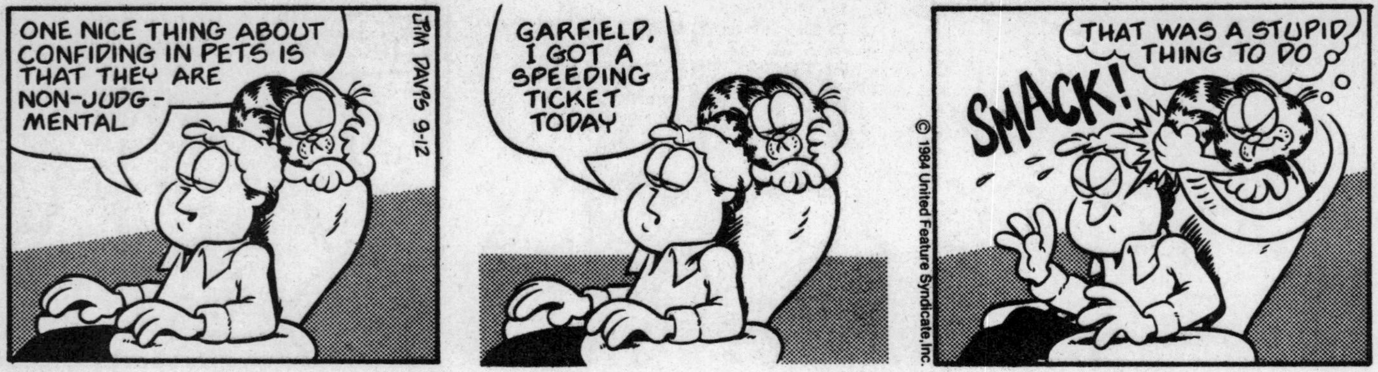
ONE NICE THING ABOUT CONFIDING IN PETS IS THAT THEY ARE NON-JUDG-MENTAL
JIM DAVIS 9-12
GARFIELD, I GOT A SPEEDING TICKET TODAY
SMACK!
THAT WAS A STUPID THING TO DO
© 1984 United Feature Syndicate, Inc.

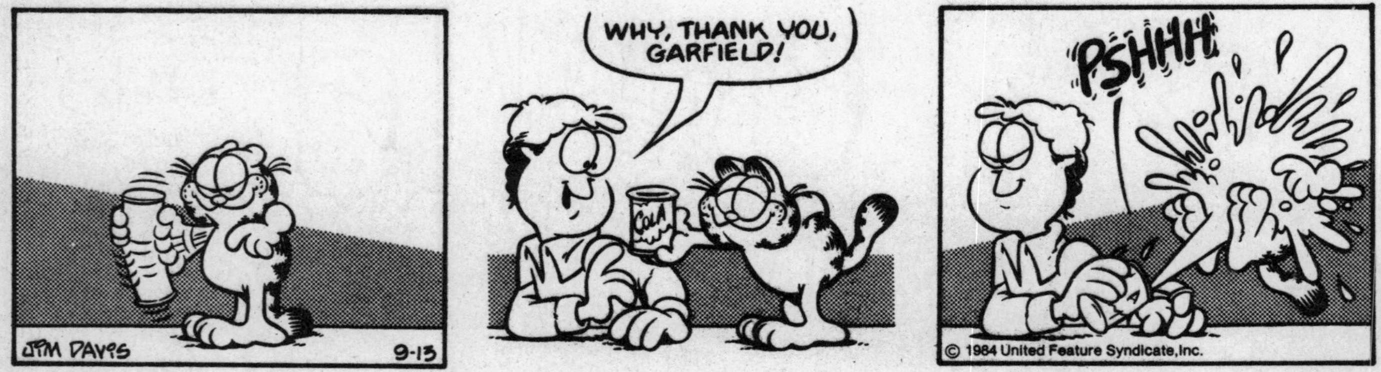
JIM DAVIS
9-13
WHY, THANK YOU, GARFIELD!
PSHHH
© 1984 United Feature Syndicate, Inc.

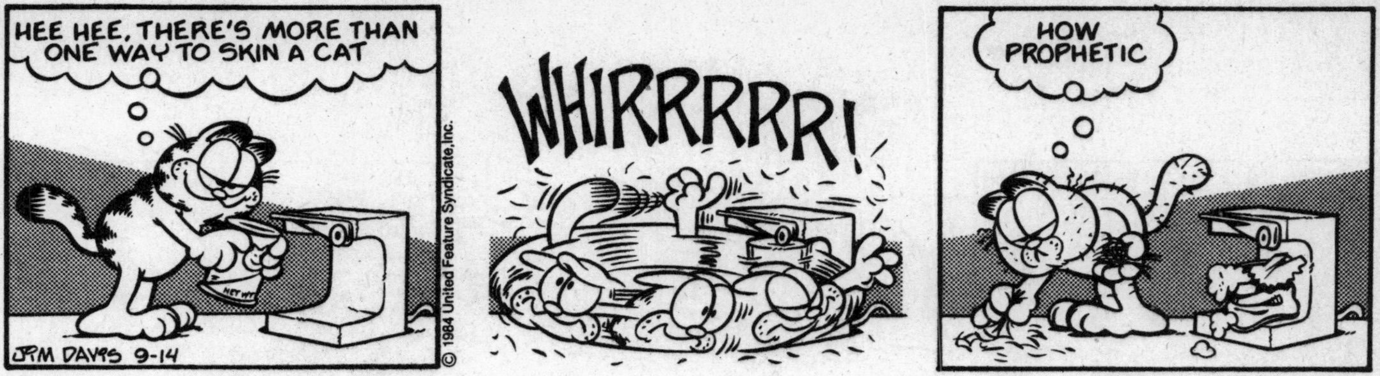
HEE HEE, THERE'S MORE THAN ONE WAY TO SKIN A CAT
JIM DAVIS 9-14
© 1984 United Feature Syndicate,Inc.
WHIRRRRRR!
HOW PROPHETIC

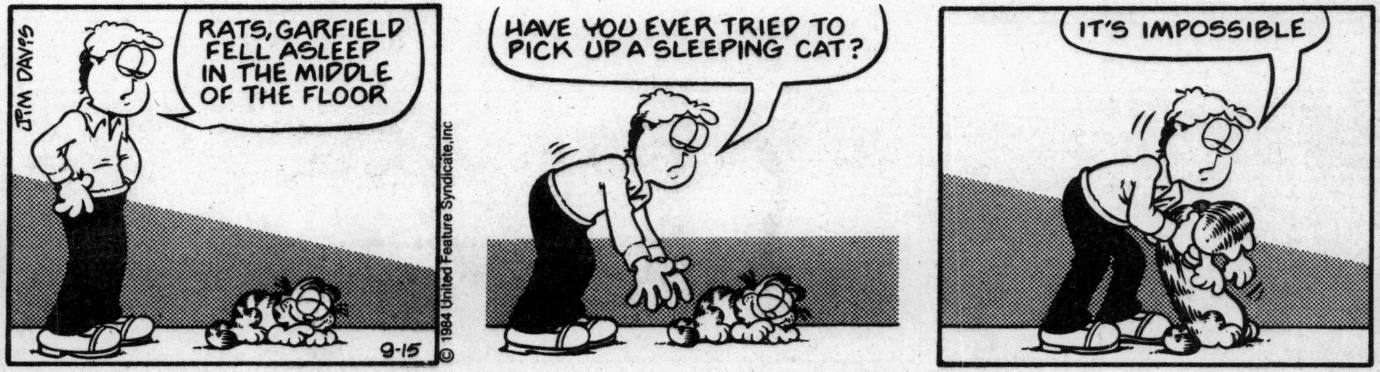
JIM DAVIS
RATS, GARFIELD FELL ASLEEP IN THE MIDDLE OF THE FLOOR
9-15
© 1984 United Feature Syndicate,Inc
HAVE YOU EVER TRIED TO PICK UP A SLEEPING CAT?
IT'S IMPOSSIBLE

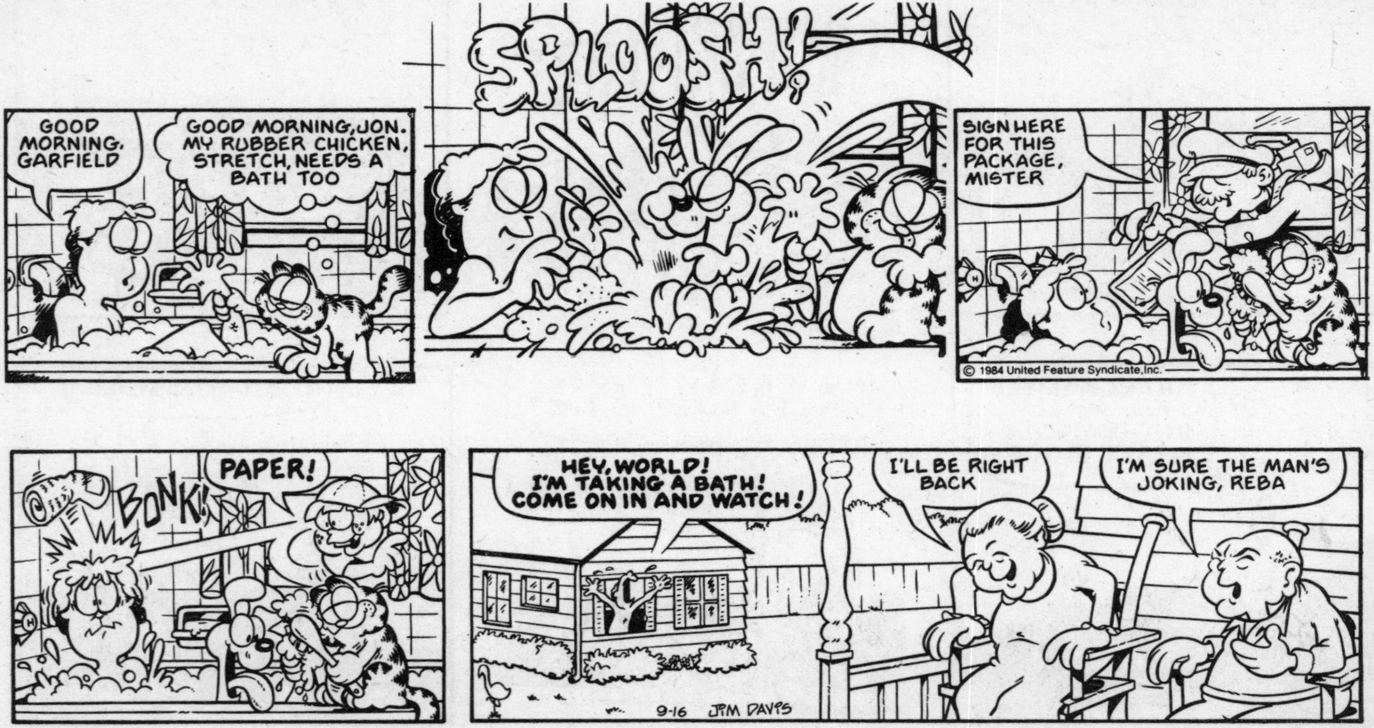
GOOD MORNING, GARFIELD
GOOD MORNING, JON. MY RUBBER CHICKEN, STRETCH, NEEDS A BATH TOO
SPLOOSH!
SIGN HERE FOR THIS PACKAGE, MISTER
© 1984 United Feature Syndicate, Inc.
BONK!
PAPER!
HEY, WORLD! I'M TAKING A BATH! COME ON IN AND WATCH!
I'LL BE RIGHT BACK
I'M SURE THE MAN'S JOKING, REBA
9-16 JIM DAVIS

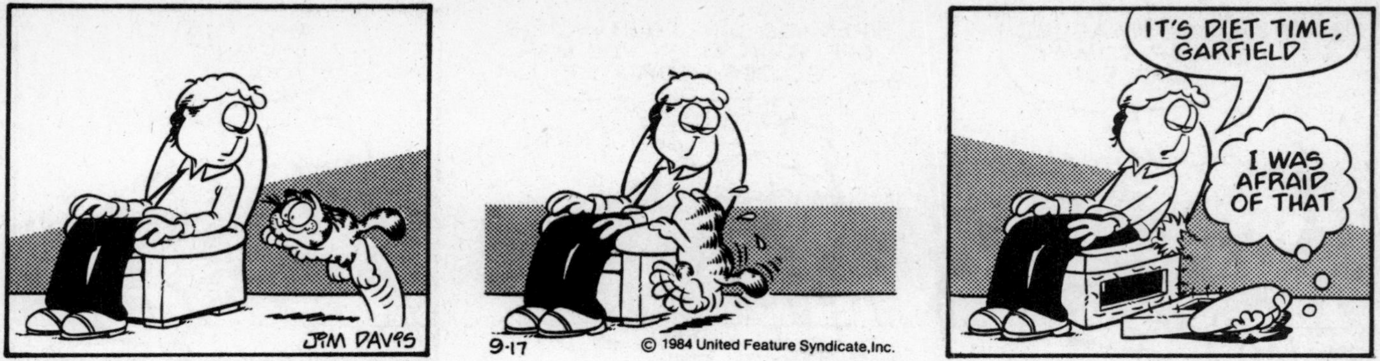
JIM DAVIS
9-17
© 1984 United Feature Syndicate, Inc.
IT'S DIET TIME, GARFIELD
I WAS AFRAID OF THAT

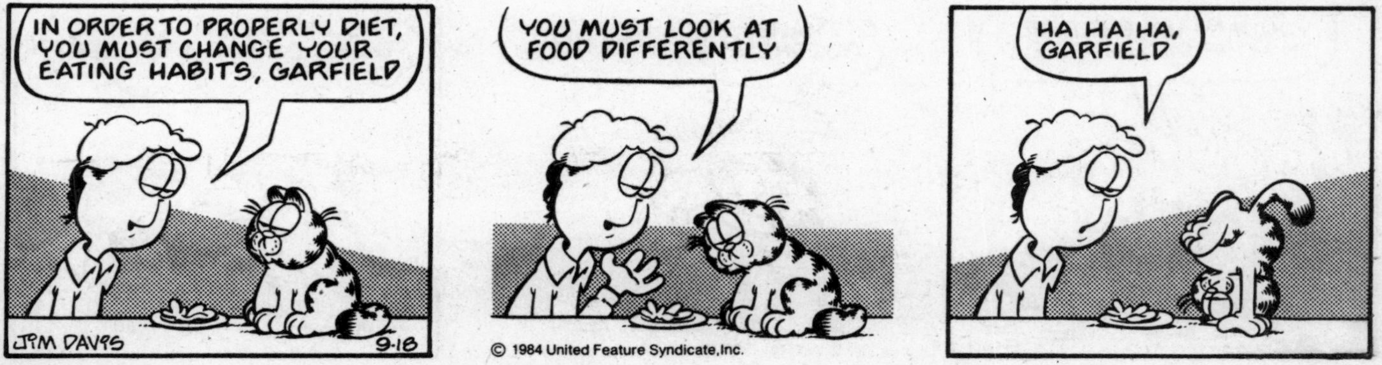
IN ORDER TO PROPERLY DIET, YOU MUST CHANGE YOUR EATING HABITS, GARFIELD
JIM DAVIS
9-18
YOU MUST LOOK AT FOOD DIFFERENTLY
© 1984 United Feature Syndicate, Inc.
HA HA HA, GARFIELD

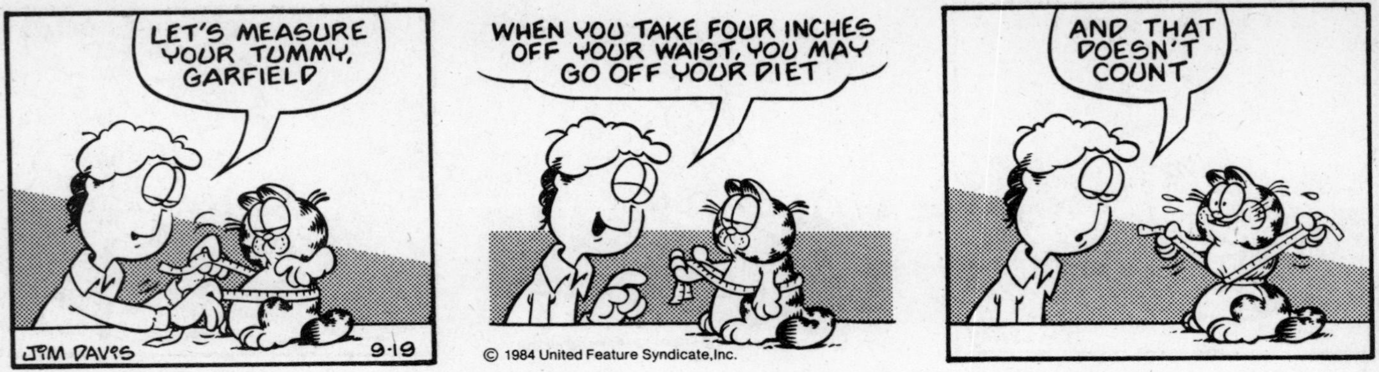
LET'S MEASURE YOUR TUMMY, GARFIELD
JIM DAVIS
9-19
WHEN YOU TAKE FOUR INCHES OFF YOUR WAIST, YOU MAY GO OFF YOUR DIET
AND THAT DOESN'T COUNT

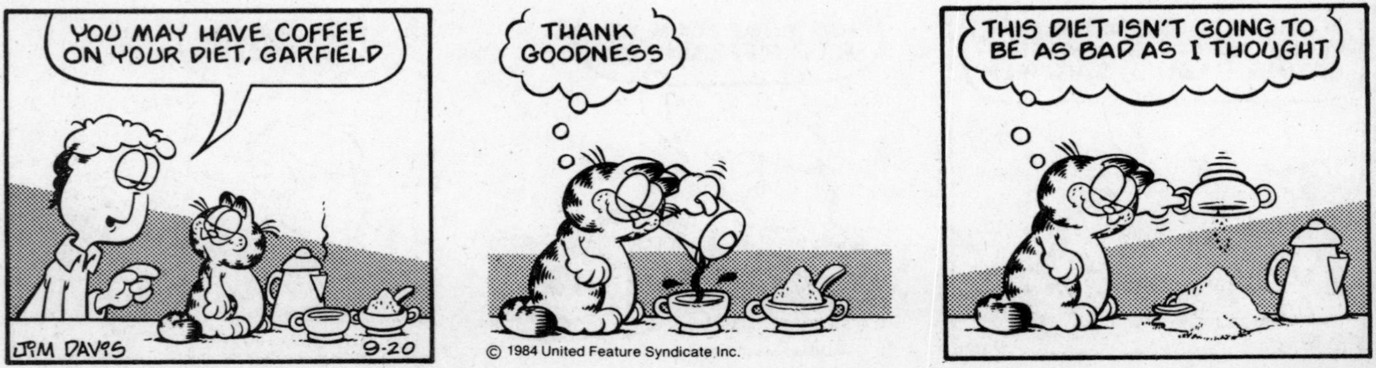
YOU MAY HAVE COFFEE ON YOUR DIET, GARFIELD
JIM DAVIS
9-20
THANK GOODNESS
THIS DIET ISN'T GOING TO BE AS BAD AS I THOUGHT

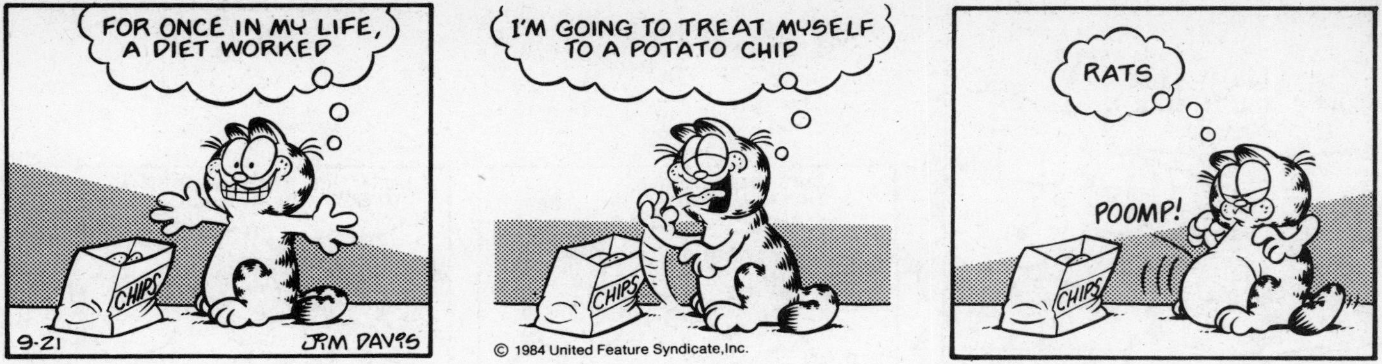
FOR ONCE IN MY LIFE, A DIET WORKED
CHIPS
9-21
JIM DAVIS
I'M GOING TO TREAT MYSELF TO A POTATO CHIP
CHIPS
© 1984 United Feature Syndicate, Inc.
RATS
POOMP!
CHIPS

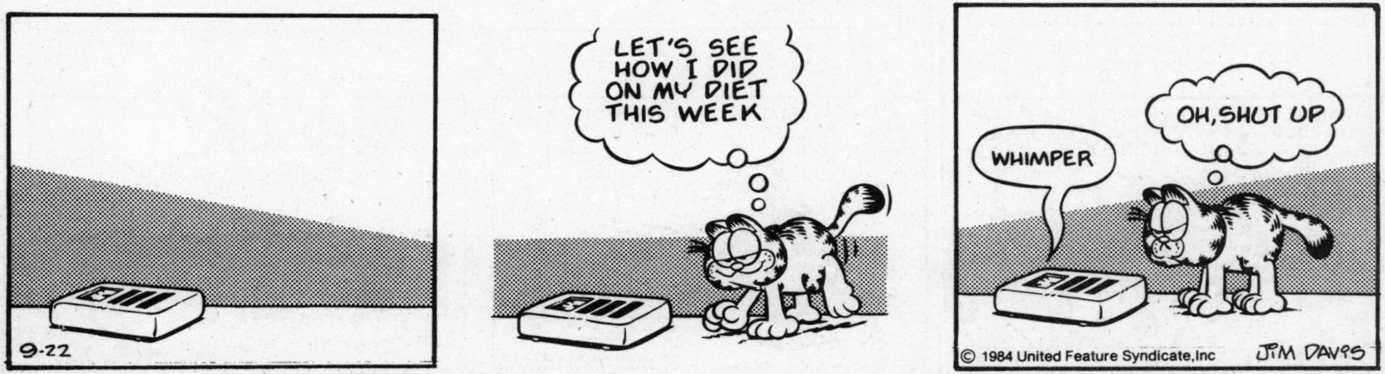
9-22
LET'S SEE HOW I DID ON MY DIET THIS WEEK
WHIMPER
OH, SHUT UP
© 1984 United Feature Syndicate, Inc
JIM DAVIS

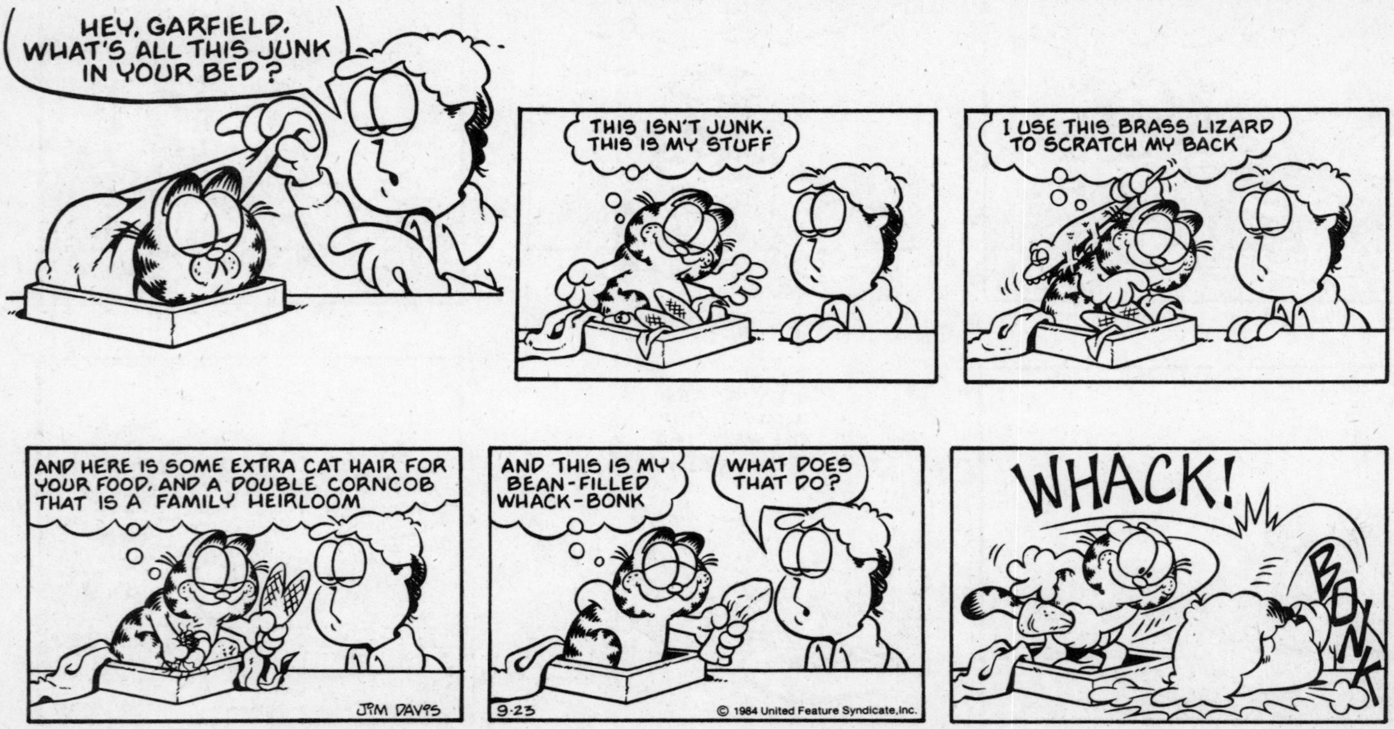
HEY, GARFIELD, WHAT'S ALL THIS JUNK IN YOUR BED?
THIS ISN'T JUNK. THIS IS MY STUFF
I USE THIS BRASS LIZARD TO SCRATCH MY BACK
AND HERE IS SOME EXTRA CAT HAIR FOR YOUR FOOD, AND A DOUBLE CORNCOB THAT IS A FAMILY HEIRLOOM
JIM DAVIS
AND THIS IS MY BEAN-FILLED WHACK-BONK
WHAT DOES THAT DO?
9-23
© 1984 United Feature Syndicate, Inc.
WHACK!
BONK

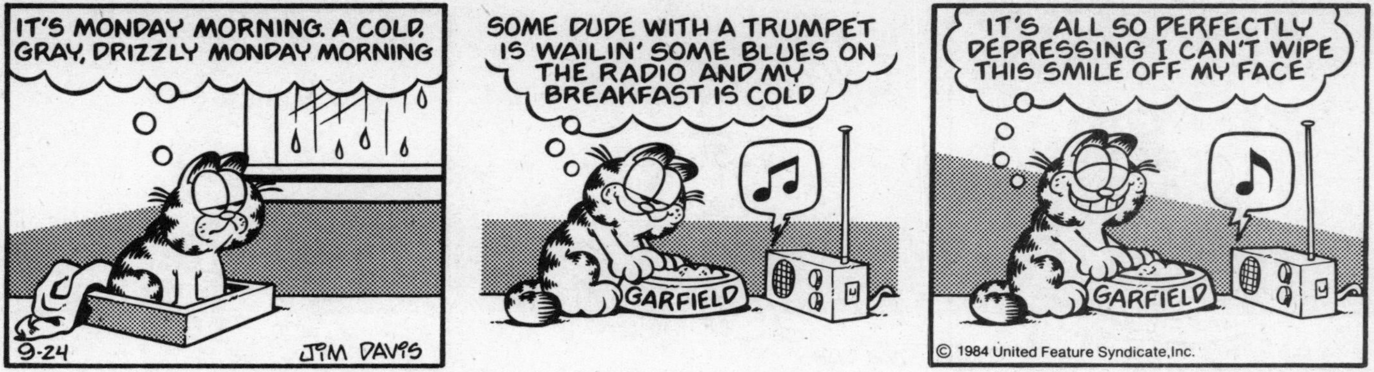
IT'S MONDAY MORNING. A COLD, GRAY, DRIZZLY MONDAY MORNING
9-24
JIM DAVIS
SOME DUDE WITH A TRUMPET IS WAILIN' SOME BLUES ON THE RADIO AND MY BREAKFAST IS COLD
GARFIELD
IT'S ALL SO PERFECTLY DEPRESSING I CAN'T WIPE THIS SMILE OFF MY FACE
GARFIELD
© 1984 United Feature Syndicate, Inc.

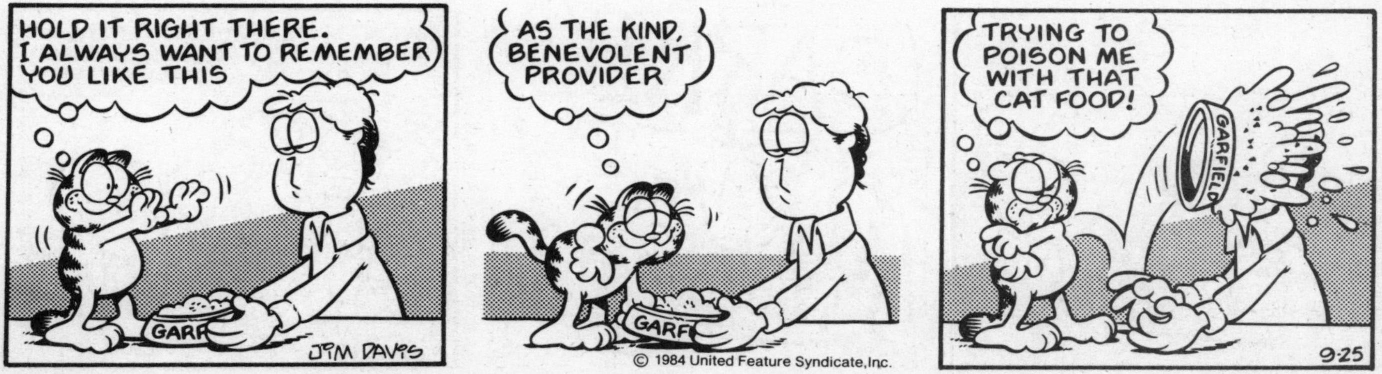
HOLD IT RIGHT THERE. I ALWAYS WANT TO REMEMBER YOU LIKE THIS
GARF
JIM DAVIS
AS THE KIND, BENEVOLENT PROVIDER
GARF
© 1984 United Feature Syndicate, Inc.
TRYING TO POISON ME WITH THAT CAT FOOD!
GARFIELD
9-25

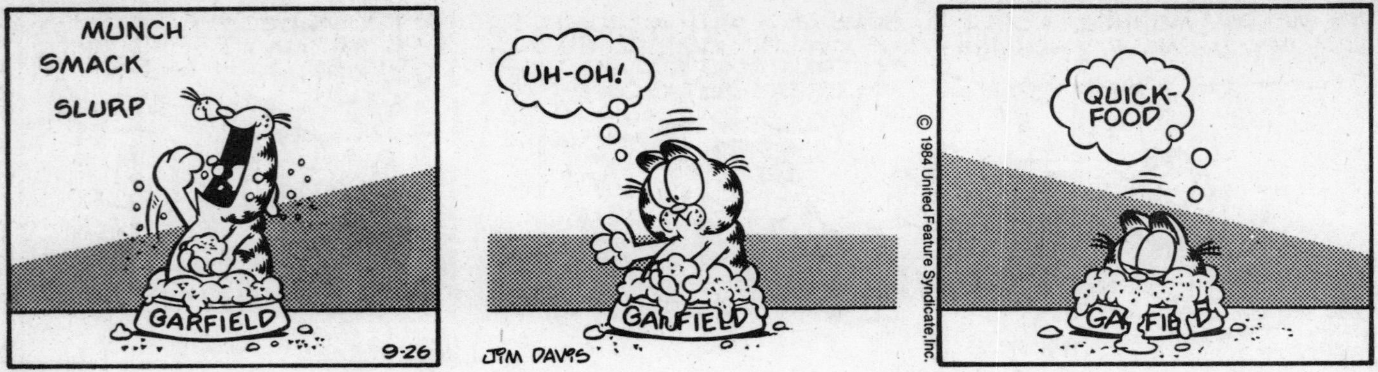
MUNCH
SMACK
SLURP
GARFIELD
9-26
UH-OH!
GARFIELD
JIM DAVIS
© 1984 United Feature Syndicate,Inc.
QUICK-FOOD
GA FI D

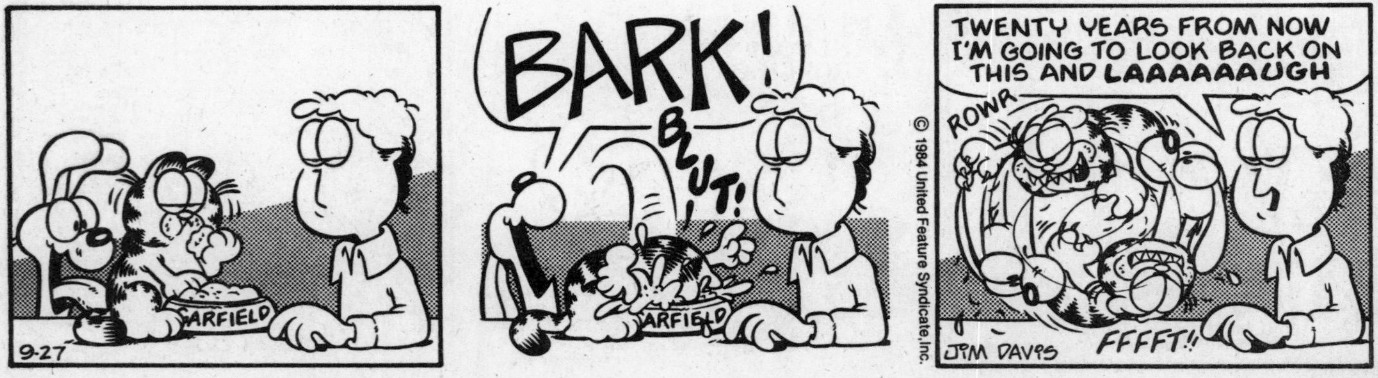
GARFIELD
9-27
BARK!
BLUT!
ARFIELD
© 1984 United Feature Syndicate,Inc.
TWENTY YEARS FROM NOW I'M GOING TO LOOK BACK ON THIS AND LAAAAAAUGH
ROWR
FFFFT!!
JIM DAVIS

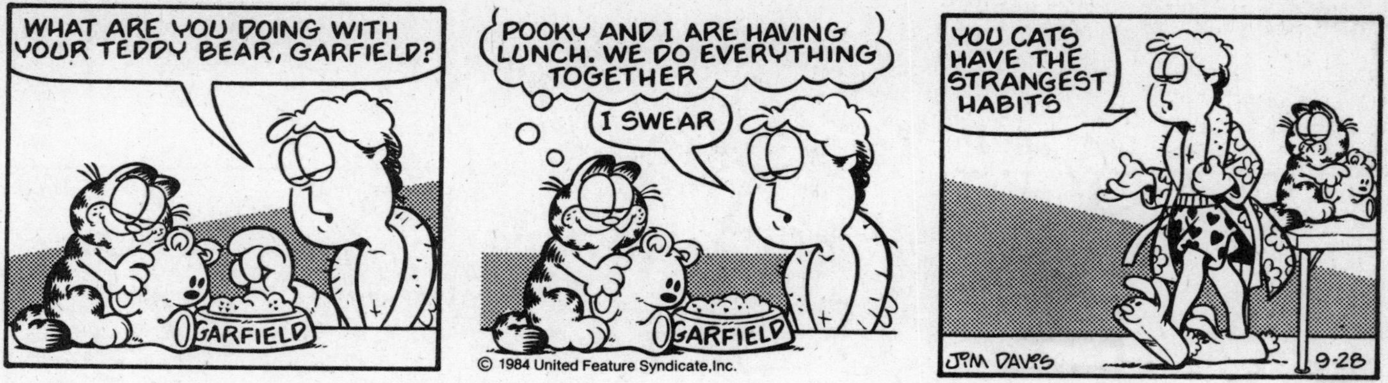
WHAT ARE YOU DOING WITH YOUR TEDDY BEAR, GARFIELD?
POOKY AND I ARE HAVING LUNCH. WE DO EVERYTHING TOGETHER
I SWEAR
YOU CATS HAVE THE STRANGEST HABITS
GARFIELD
GARFIELD
JIM DAVIS
9-28

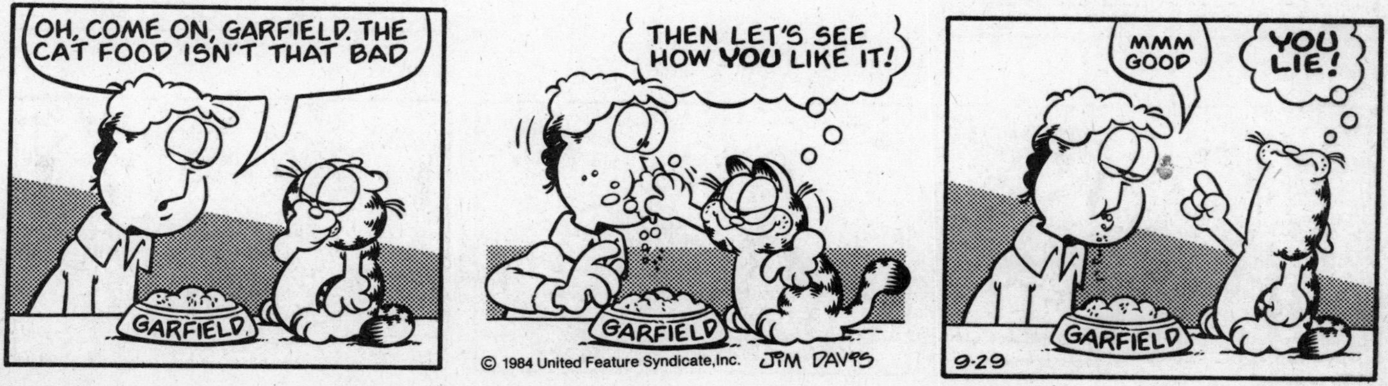
OH, COME ON, GARFIELD. THE CAT FOOD ISN'T THAT BAD
THEN LET'S SEE HOW **YOU** LIKE IT!
MMM GOOD
YOU LIE!
GARFIELD
GARFIELD
GARFIELD
JIM DAVIS
9-29

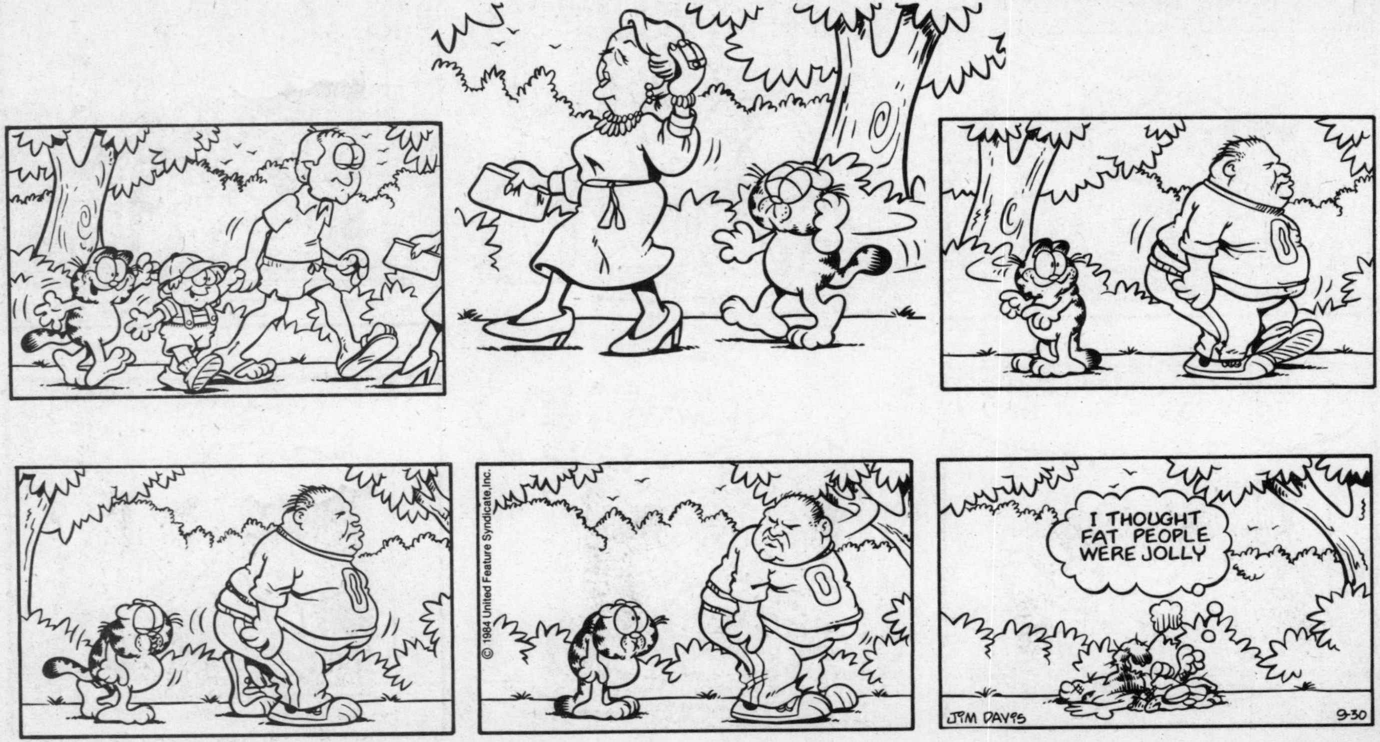
© 1984 United Feature Syndicate, Inc.
I THOUGHT FAT PEOPLE WERE JOLLY
JIM DAVIS
9-30

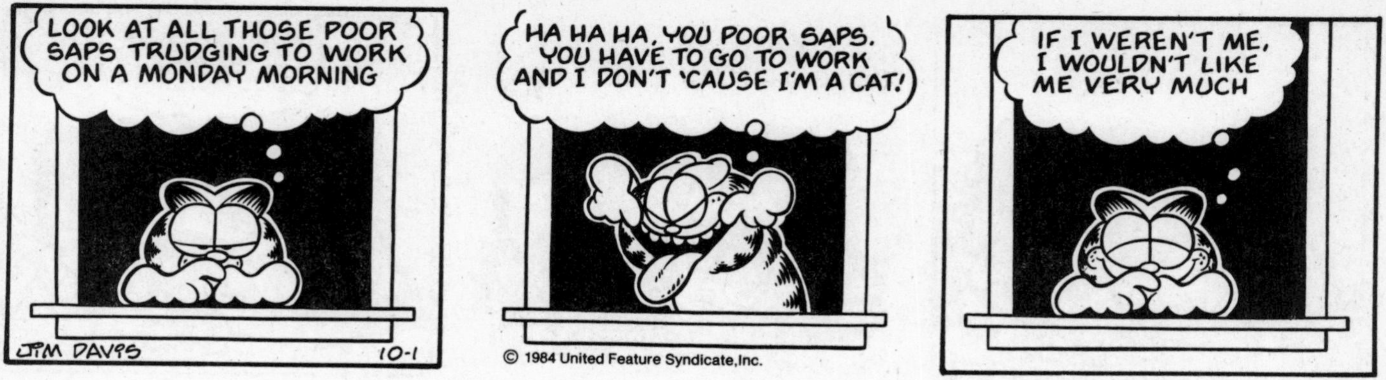
LOOK AT ALL THOSE POOR SAPS TRUDGING TO WORK ON A MONDAY MORNING
JIM DAVIS
10-1
HA HA HA, YOU POOR SAPS. YOU HAVE TO GO TO WORK AND I DON'T 'CAUSE I'M A CAT!
© 1984 United Feature Syndicate,Inc.
IF I WEREN'T ME, I WOULDN'T LIKE ME VERY MUCH

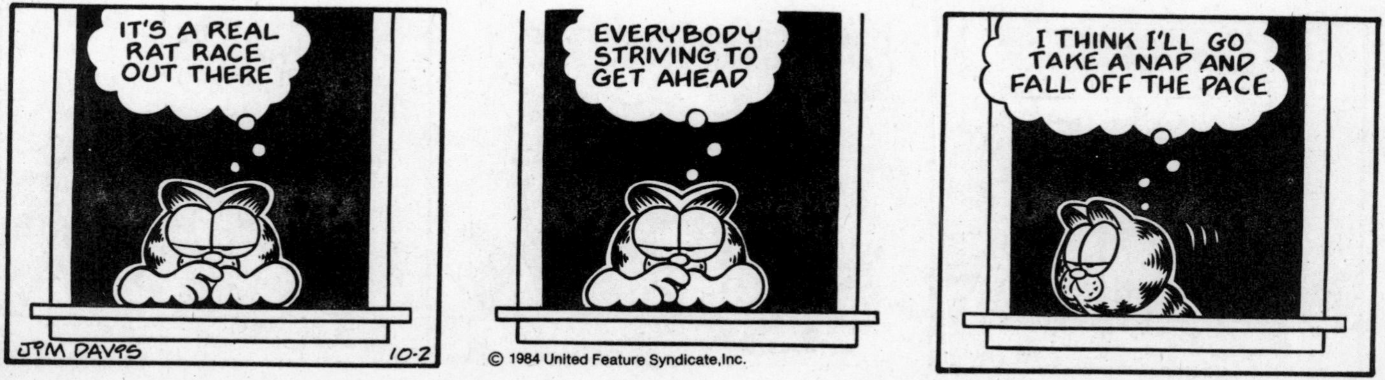
IT'S A REAL RAT RACE OUT THERE
JIM DAVIS
10-2
EVERYBODY STRIVING TO GET AHEAD
© 1984 United Feature Syndicate,Inc.
I THINK I'LL GO TAKE A NAP AND FALL OFF THE PACE

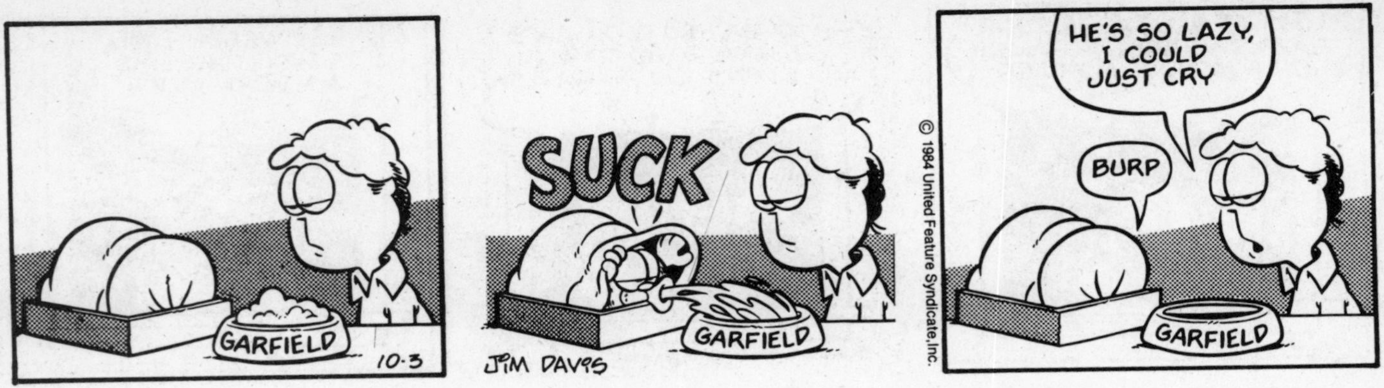
10-3
SUCK
JIM DAVIS
GARFIELD
GARFIELD
BURP
HE'S SO LAZY, I COULD JUST CRY
GARFIELD

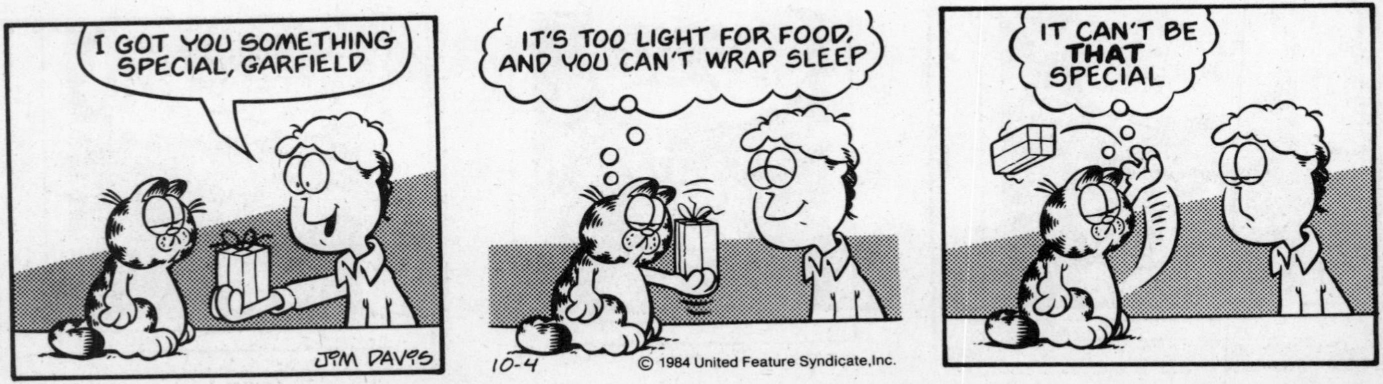
I GOT YOU SOMETHING SPECIAL, GARFIELD
JIM DAVIS
IT'S TOO LIGHT FOR FOOD, AND YOU CAN'T WRAP SLEEP
10-4
IT CAN'T BE **THAT** SPECIAL

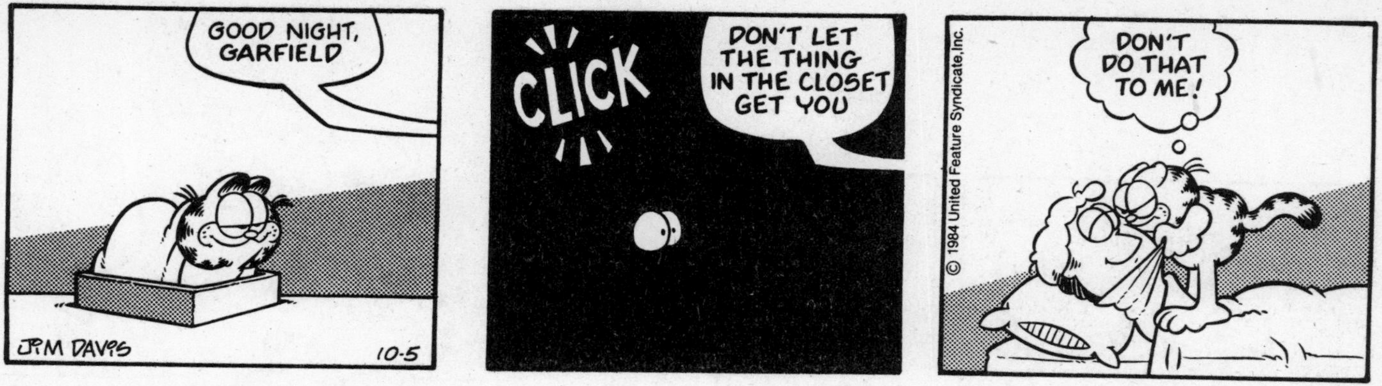
GOOD NIGHT, GARFIELD
JIM DAVIS
10-5
CLICK
DON'T LET THE THING IN THE CLOSET GET YOU
© 1984 United Feature Syndicate, Inc.
DON'T DO THAT TO ME!

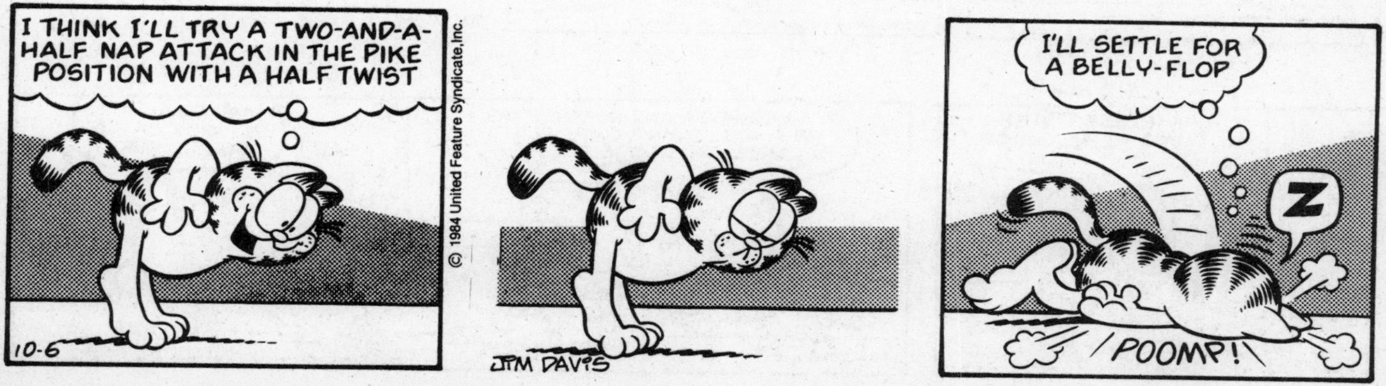
I THINK I'LL TRY A TWO-AND-A-HALF NAP ATTACK IN THE PIKE POSITION WITH A HALF TWIST
10-6
© 1984 United Feature Syndicate, Inc.
JIM DAVIS
I'LL SETTLE FOR A BELLY-FLOP
Z
POOMP!

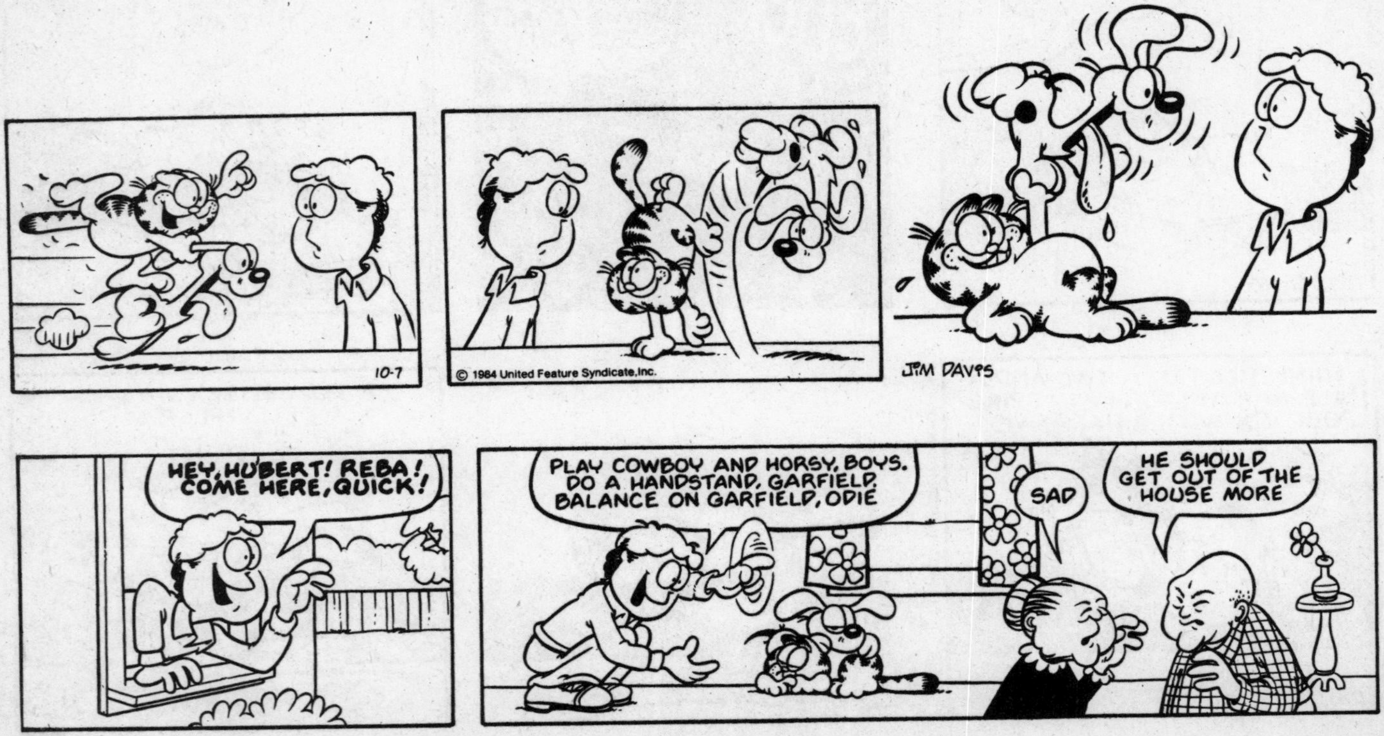
10-7
© 1984 United Feature Syndicate, Inc.
JIM DAVIS
HEY, HUBERT! REBA! COME HERE, QUICK!
PLAY COWBOY AND HORSY, BOYS. DO A HANDSTAND, GARFIELD. BALANCE ON GARFIELD, ODIE
SAD
HE SHOULD GET OUT OF THE HOUSE MORE

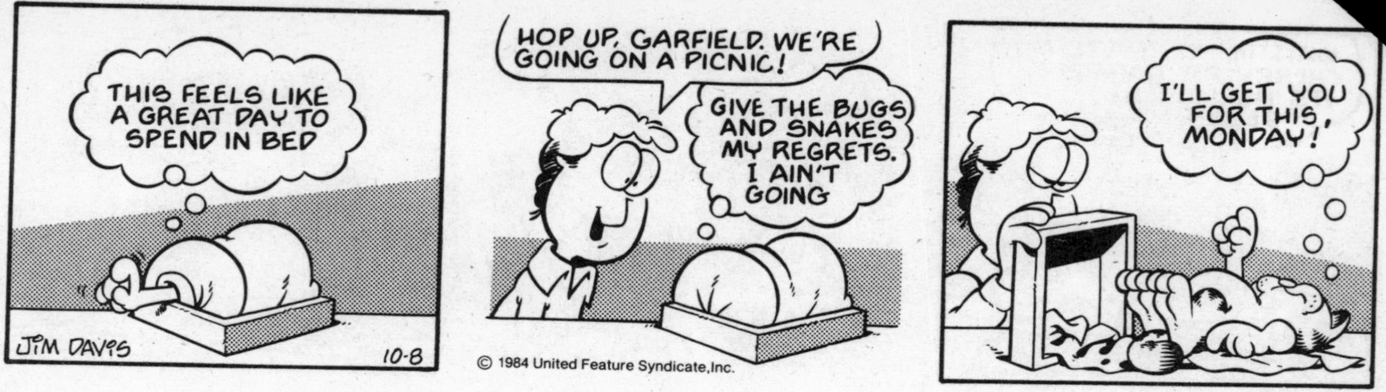
THIS FEELS LIKE A GREAT DAY TO SPEND IN BED
JIM DAVIS
10-8
HOP UP, GARFIELD. WE'RE GOING ON A PICNIC!
GIVE THE BUGS AND SNAKES MY REGRETS. I AIN'T GOING
I'LL GET YOU FOR THIS, MONDAY!

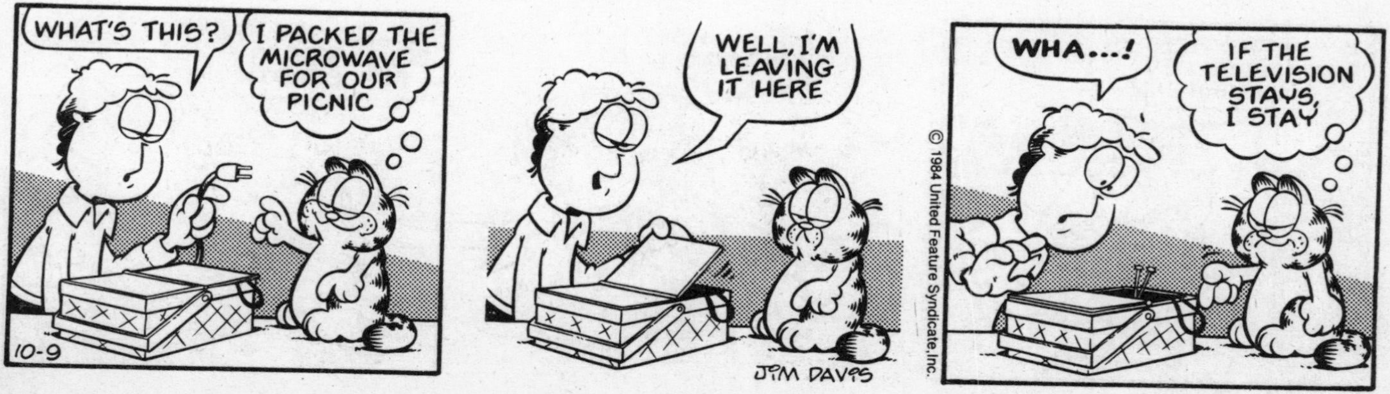
WHAT'S THIS?
I PACKED THE MICROWAVE FOR OUR PICNIC
10-9
WELL, I'M LEAVING IT HERE
JIM DAVIS
WHA...!
IF THE TELEVISION STAYS, I STAY

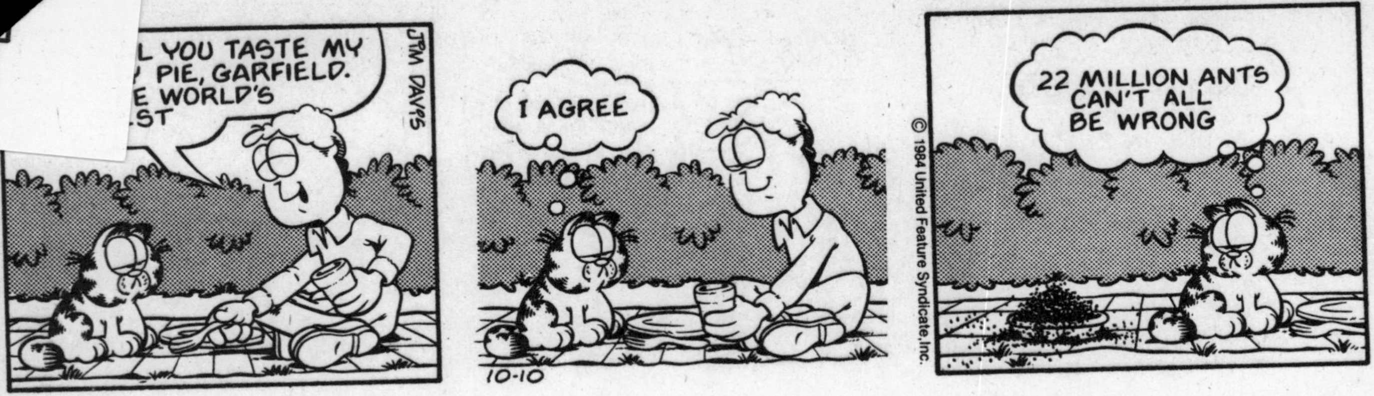
L YOU TASTE MY
PIE, GARFIELD.
E WORLD'S
ST
JIM DAVIS
I AGREE
10-10
© 1984 United Feature Syndicate, Inc.
22 MILLION ANTS CAN'T ALL BE WRONG

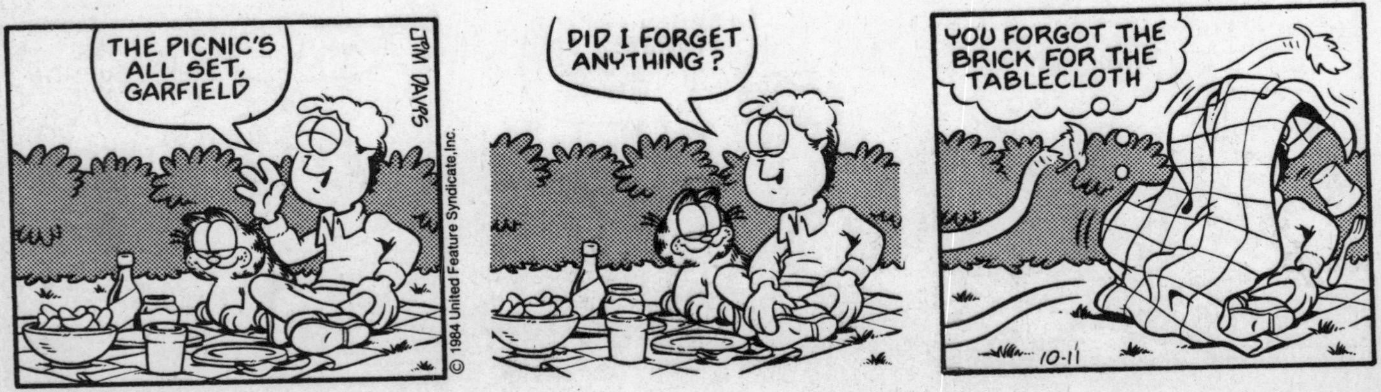
THE PICNIC'S ALL SET, GARFIELD
JIM DAVIS
© 1984 United Feature Syndicate, Inc.
DID I FORGET ANYTHING?
YOU FORGOT THE BRICK FOR THE TABLECLOTH
10-11

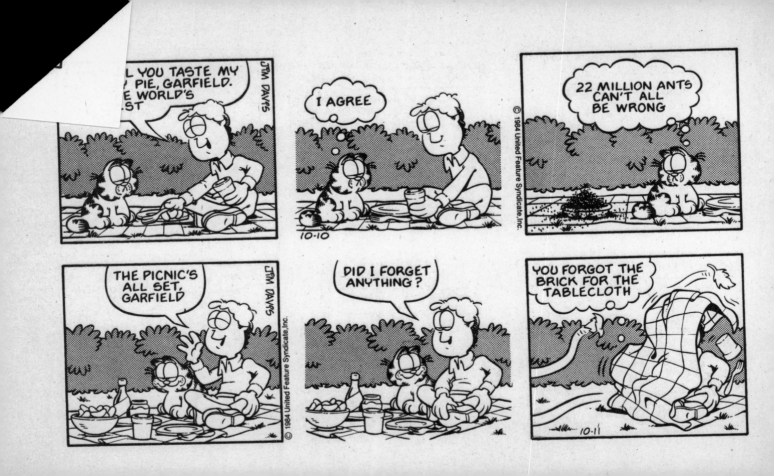

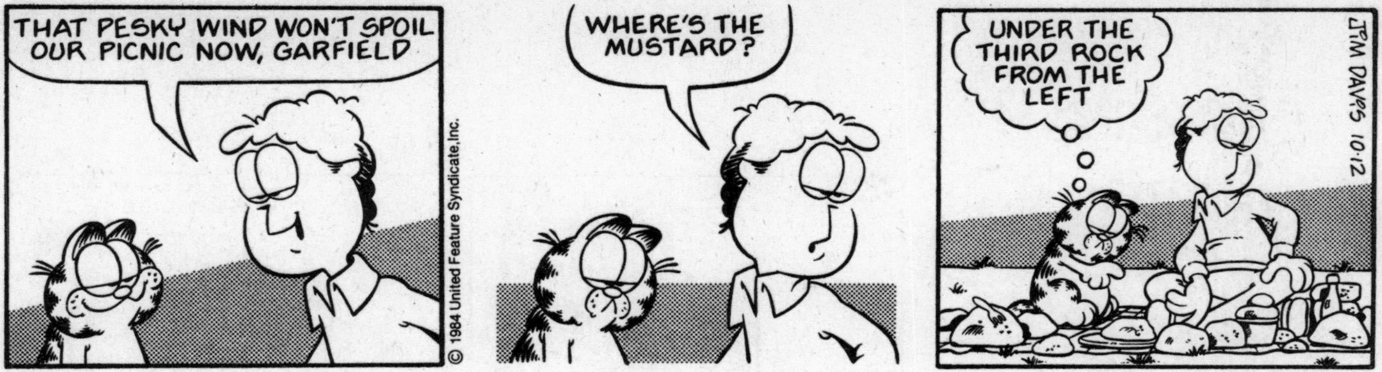
THAT PESKY WIND WON'T SPOIL OUR PICNIC NOW, GARFIELD
© 1984 United Feature Syndicate, Inc.
WHERE'S THE MUSTARD?
UNDER THE THIRD ROCK FROM THE LEFT
JIM DAVIS 10·12

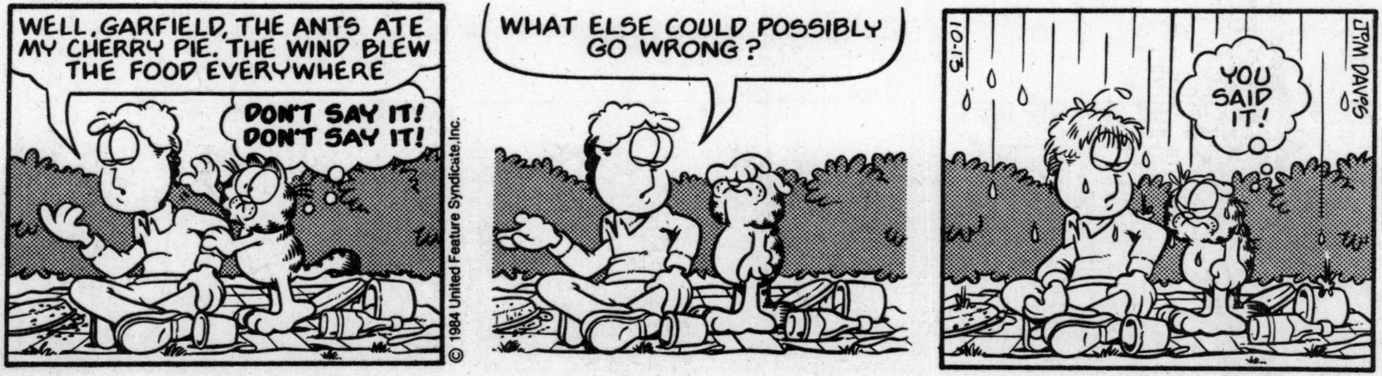
WELL, GARFIELD, THE ANTS ATE MY CHERRY PIE. THE WIND BLEW THE FOOD EVERYWHERE
DON'T SAY IT! DON'T SAY IT!
© 1984 United Feature Syndicate, Inc.
WHAT ELSE COULD POSSIBLY GO WRONG?
10·13
JIM DAVIS
YOU SAID IT!

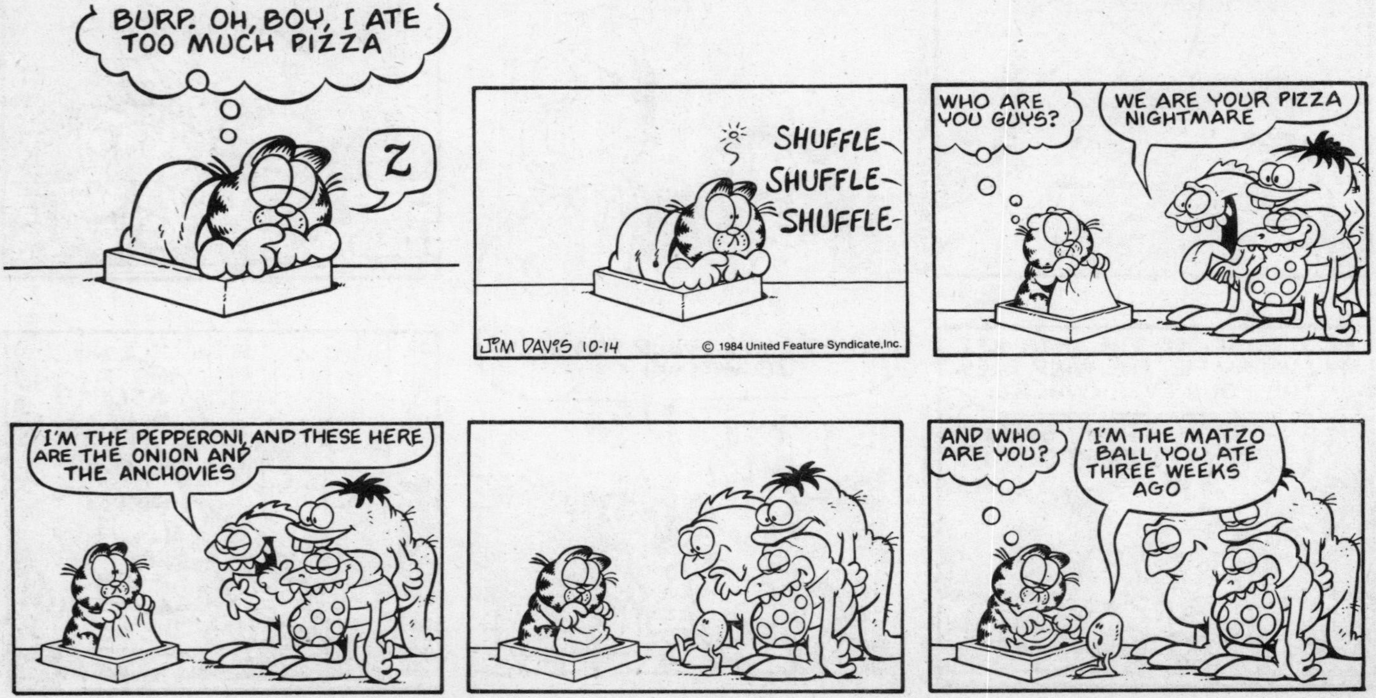
BURP. OH, BOY, I ATE TOO MUCH PIZZA
Z
SHUFFLE
SHUFFLE
SHUFFLE
JIM DAVIS 10-14
© 1984 United Feature Syndicate, Inc.
WHO ARE YOU GUYS?
WE ARE YOUR PIZZA NIGHTMARE
I'M THE PEPPERONI, AND THESE HERE ARE THE ONION AND THE ANCHOVIES
AND WHO ARE YOU?
I'M THE MATZO BALL YOU ATE THREE WEEKS AGO

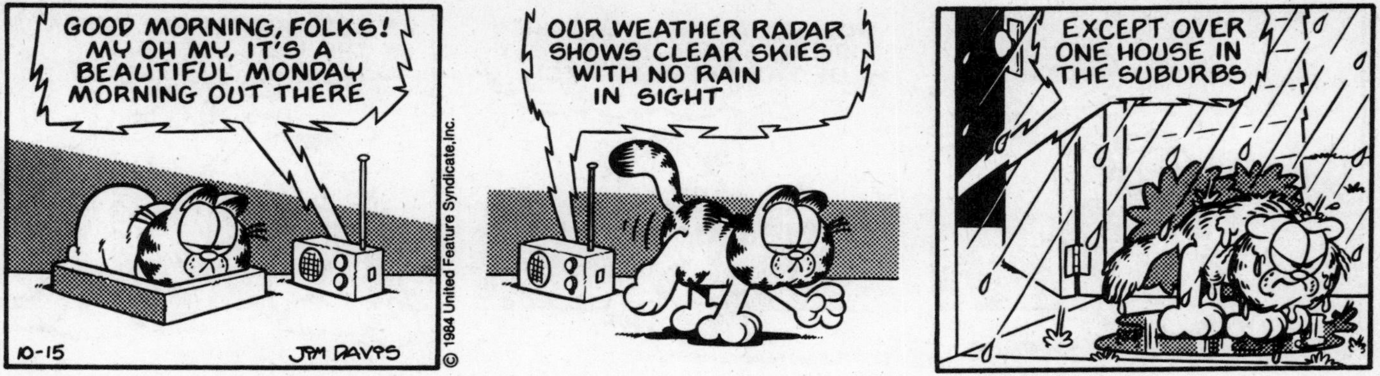
GOOD MORNING, FOLKS! MY OH MY, IT'S A BEAUTIFUL MONDAY MORNING OUT THERE
10-15
JIM DAVIS
© 1984 United Feature Syndicate, Inc.
OUR WEATHER RADAR SHOWS CLEAR SKIES WITH NO RAIN IN SIGHT
EXCEPT OVER ONE HOUSE IN THE SUBURBS

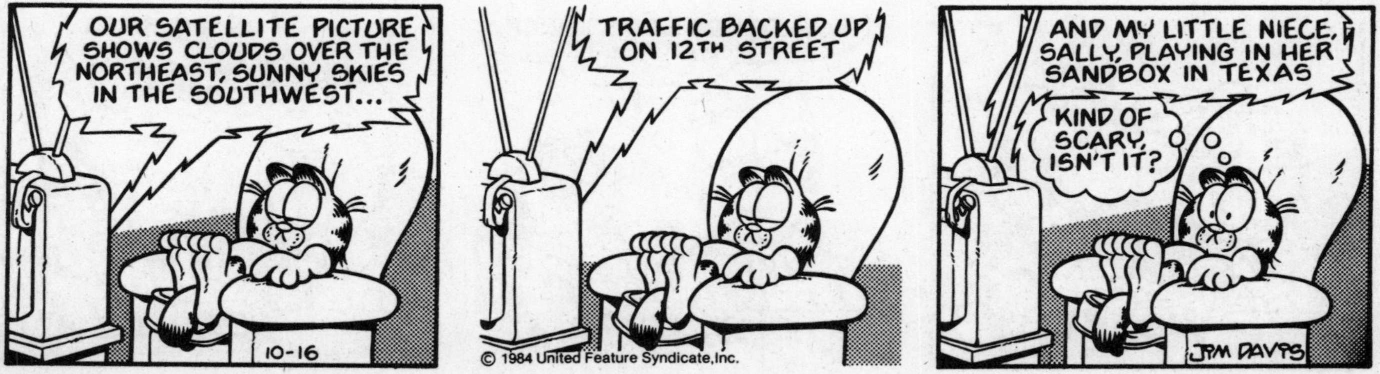
OUR SATELLITE PICTURE SHOWS CLOUDS OVER THE NORTHEAST, SUNNY SKIES IN THE SOUTHWEST...
10-16
TRAFFIC BACKED UP ON 12TH STREET
© 1984 United Feature Syndicate, Inc.
AND MY LITTLE NIECE, SALLY, PLAYING IN HER SANDBOX IN TEXAS
KIND OF SCARY, ISN'T IT?
JIM DAVIS

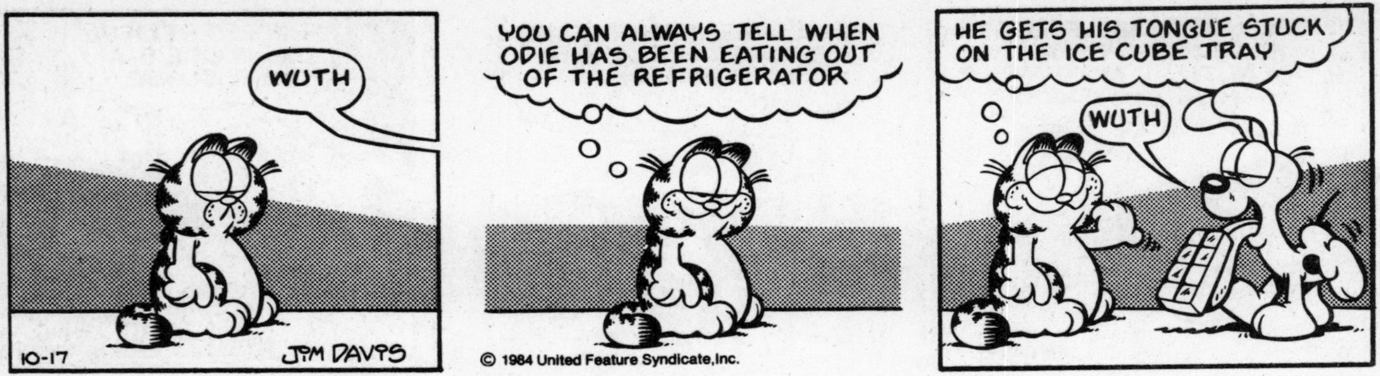
WUTH
10-17
JIM DAVIS
YOU CAN ALWAYS TELL WHEN ODIE HAS BEEN EATING OUT OF THE REFRIGERATOR
© 1984 United Feature Syndicate, Inc.
HE GETS HIS TONGUE STUCK ON THE ICE CUBE TRAY
WUTH

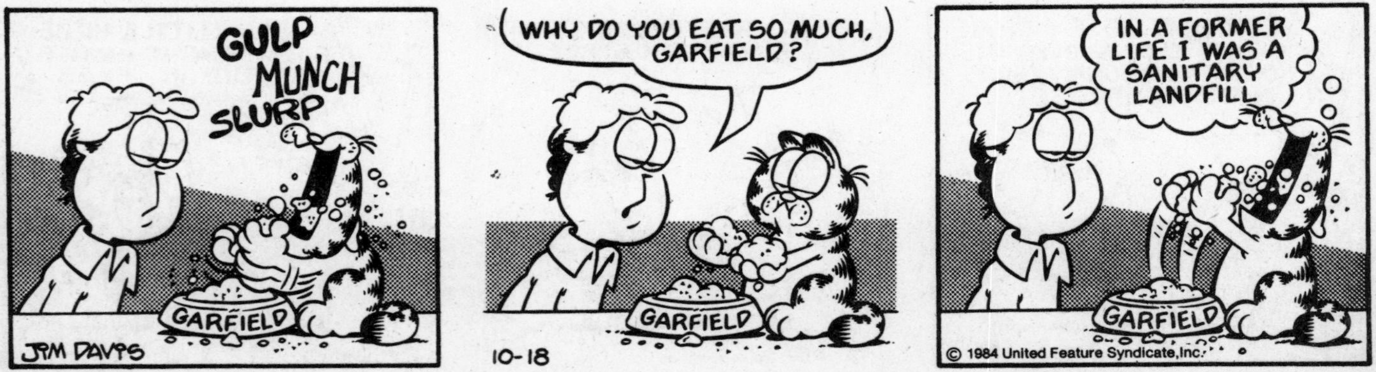
GULP
MUNCH
SLURP
GARFIELD
JIM DAVIS
WHY DO YOU EAT SO MUCH, GARFIELD?
GARFIELD
10-18
IN A FORMER LIFE I WAS A SANITARY LANDFILL
GARFIELD
© 1984 United Feature Syndicate, Inc.

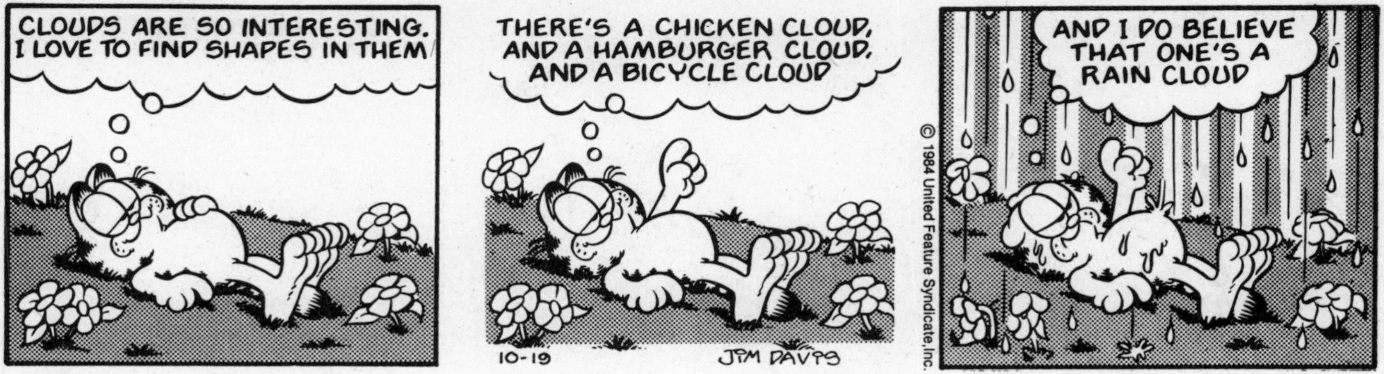
CLOUDS ARE SO INTERESTING. I LOVE TO FIND SHAPES IN THEM
THERE'S A CHICKEN CLOUD, AND A HAMBURGER CLOUD, AND A BICYCLE CLOUD
AND I DO BELIEVE THAT ONE'S A RAIN CLOUD
10-19
JIM DAVIS
© 1984 United Feature Syndicate,Inc.

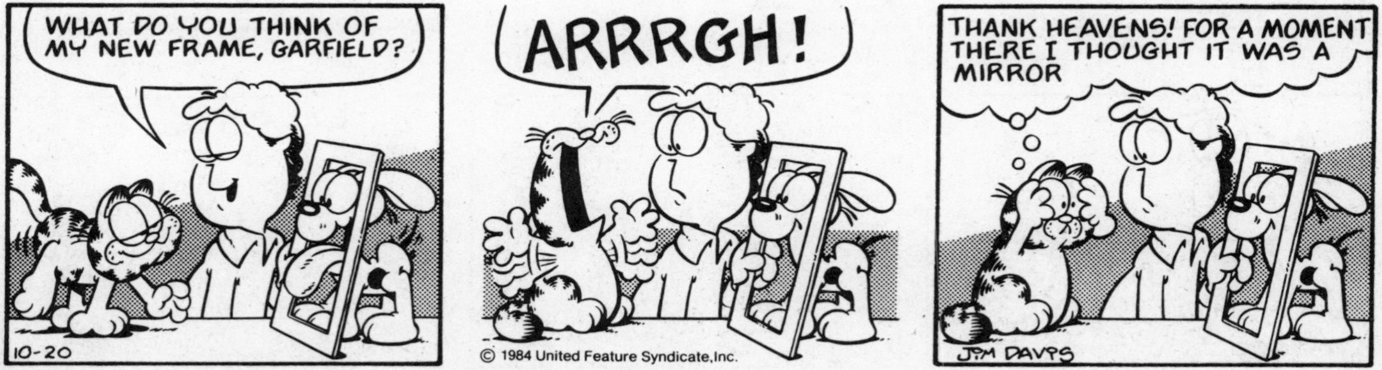
WHAT DO YOU THINK OF MY NEW FRAME, GARFIELD?
ARRRGH!
THANK HEAVENS! FOR A MOMENT THERE I THOUGHT IT WAS A MIRROR
10-20
© 1984 United Feature Syndicate,Inc.
JIM DAVIS

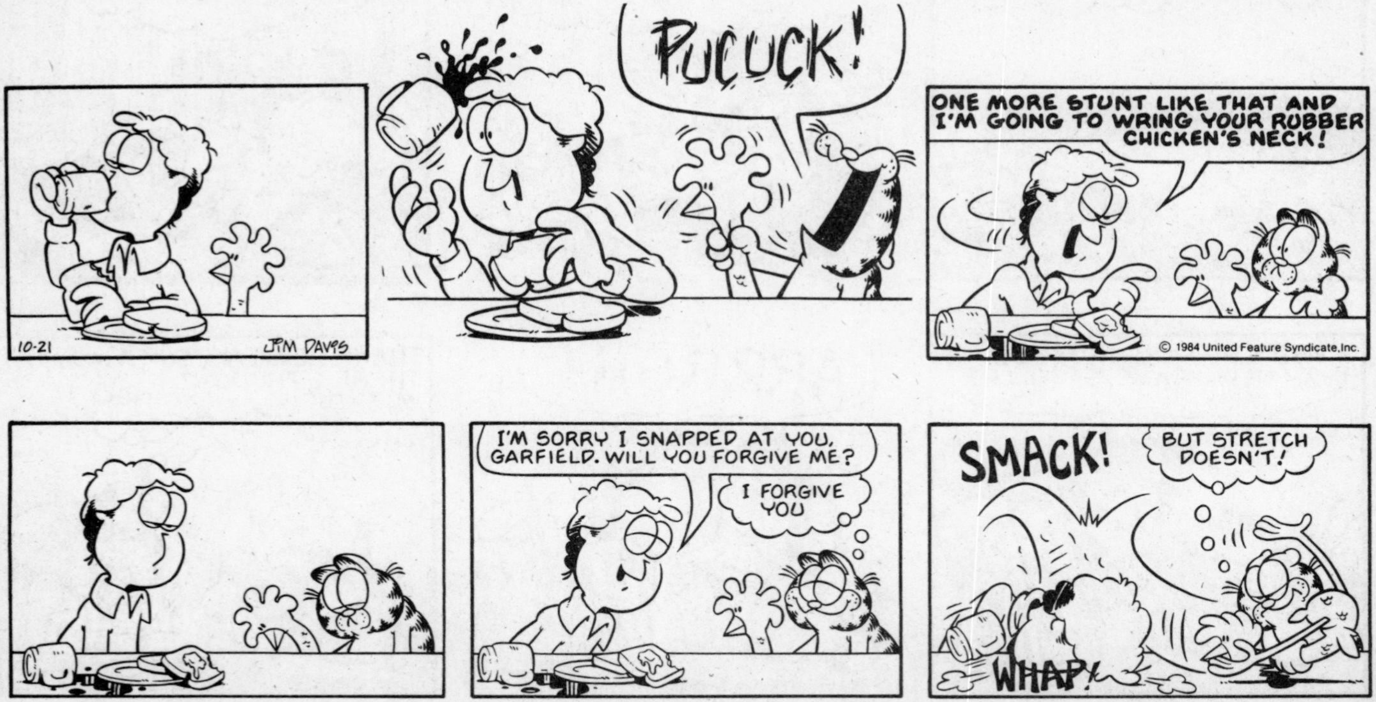

10-21
JIM DAVIS
PUCUCK!
ONE MORE STUNT LIKE THAT AND I'M GOING TO WRING YOUR RUBBER CHICKEN'S NECK!
© 1984 United Feature Syndicate, Inc.
I'M SORRY I SNAPPED AT YOU, GARFIELD. WILL YOU FORGIVE ME?
I FORGIVE YOU
SMACK!
BUT STRETCH DOESN'T!
WHAP!

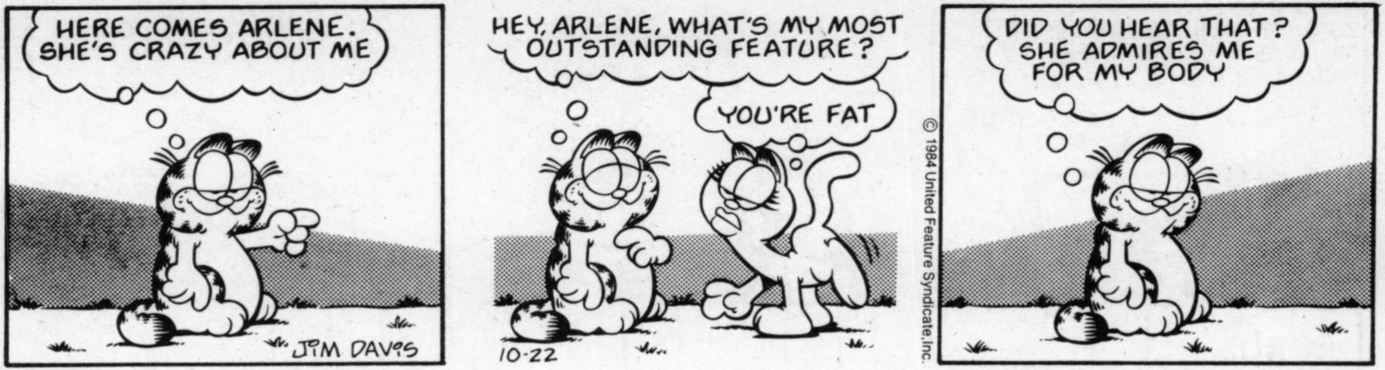
HERE COMES ARLENE. SHE'S CRAZY ABOUT ME
JIM DAVIS
HEY, ARLENE, WHAT'S MY MOST OUTSTANDING FEATURE?
YOU'RE FAT
10-22
© 1984 United Feature Syndicate, Inc.
DID YOU HEAR THAT? SHE ADMIRES ME FOR MY BODY

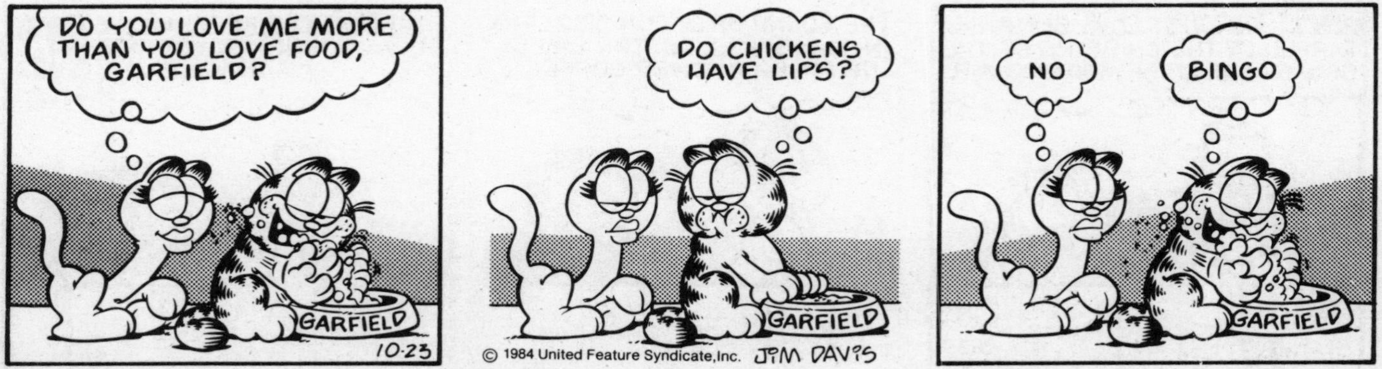
DO YOU LOVE ME MORE THAN YOU LOVE FOOD, GARFIELD?
GARFIELD
10-23
DO CHICKENS HAVE LIPS?
GARFIELD
© 1984 United Feature Syndicate, Inc.
JIM DAVIS
NO
BINGO
GARFIELD

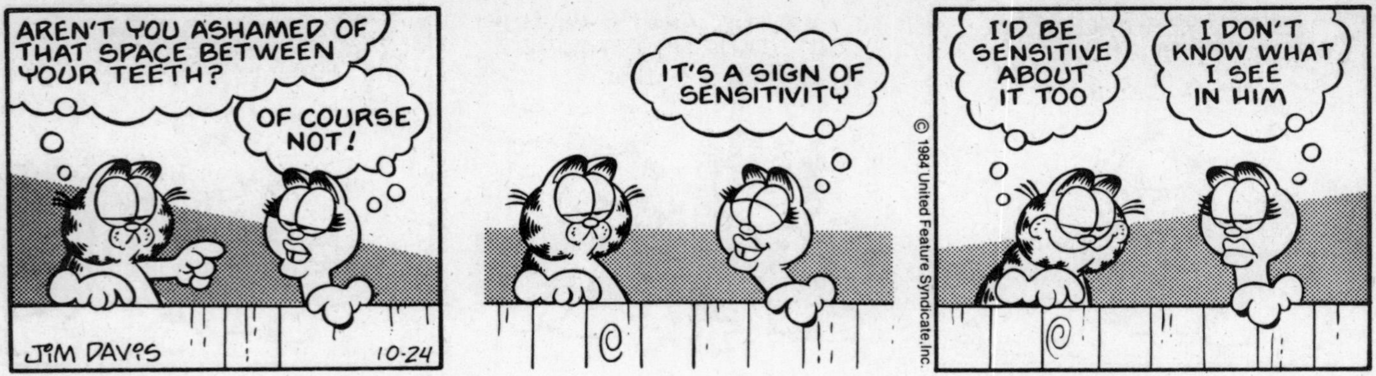
ARE'NT YOU ASHAMED OF THAT SPACE BETWEEN YOUR TEETH?
OF COURSE NOT!
JIM DAVIS
10-24
IT'S A SIGN OF SENSITIVITY
© 1984 United Feature Syndicate, Inc.
I'D BE SENSITIVE ABOUT IT TOO
I DON'T KNOW WHAT I SEE IN HIM

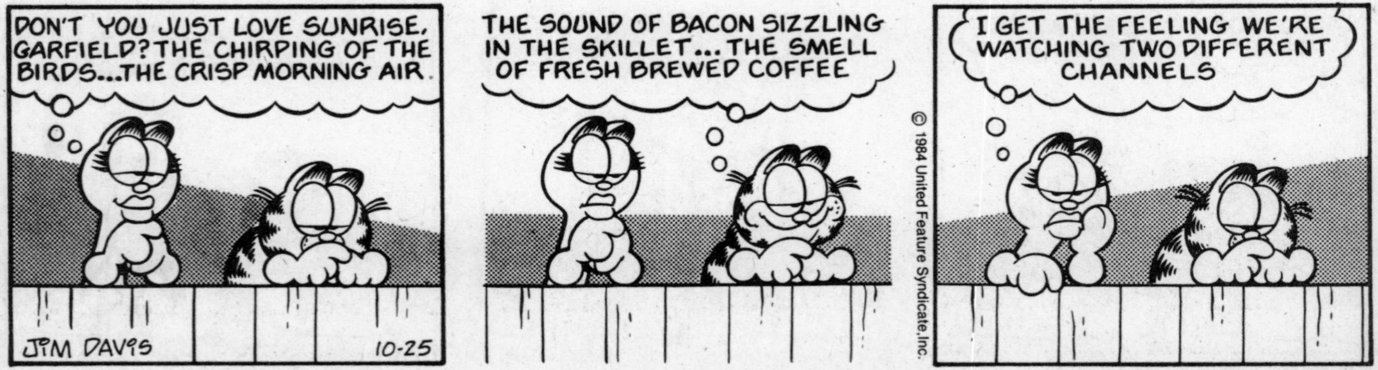
DON'T YOU JUST LOVE SUNRISE, GARFIELD? THE CHIRPING OF THE BIRDS...THE CRISP MORNING AIR
JIM DAVIS
10-25
THE SOUND OF BACON SIZZLING IN THE SKILLET... THE SMELL OF FRESH BREWED COFFEE
© 1984 United Feature Syndicate, Inc.
I GET THE FEELING WE'RE WATCHING TWO DIFFERENT CHANNELS

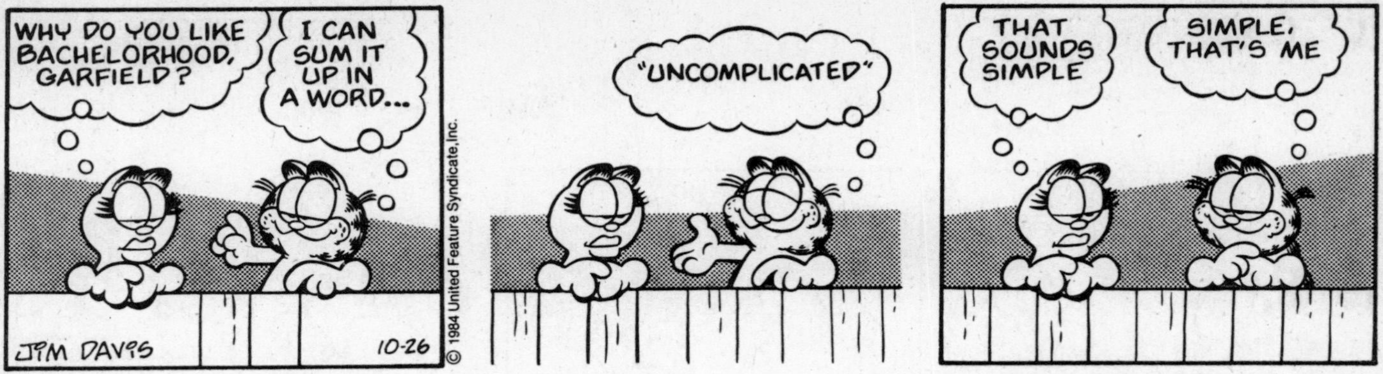
WHY DO YOU LIKE BACHELORHOOD, GARFIELD?
I CAN SUM IT UP IN A WORD...
"UNCOMPLICATED"
THAT SOUNDS SIMPLE
SIMPLE, THAT'S ME
JIM DAVIS
10-26
© 1984 United Feature Syndicate, Inc.

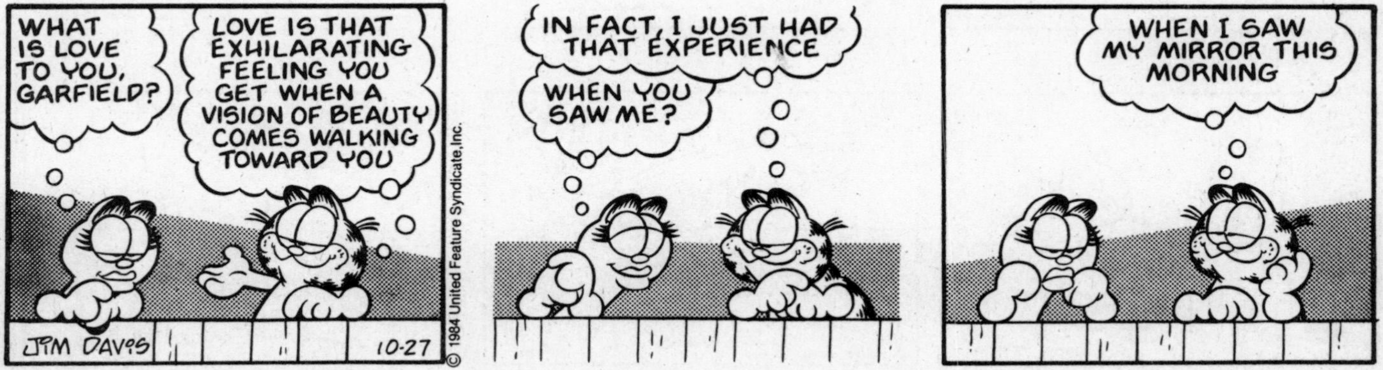
WHAT IS LOVE TO YOU, GARFIELD?
LOVE IS THAT EXHILARATING FEELING YOU GET WHEN A VISION OF BEAUTY COMES WALKING TOWARD YOU
IN FACT, I JUST HAD THAT EXPERIENCE
WHEN YOU SAW ME?
WHEN I SAW MY MIRROR THIS MORNING
JIM DAVIS
10-27
© 1984 United Feature Syndicate, Inc.

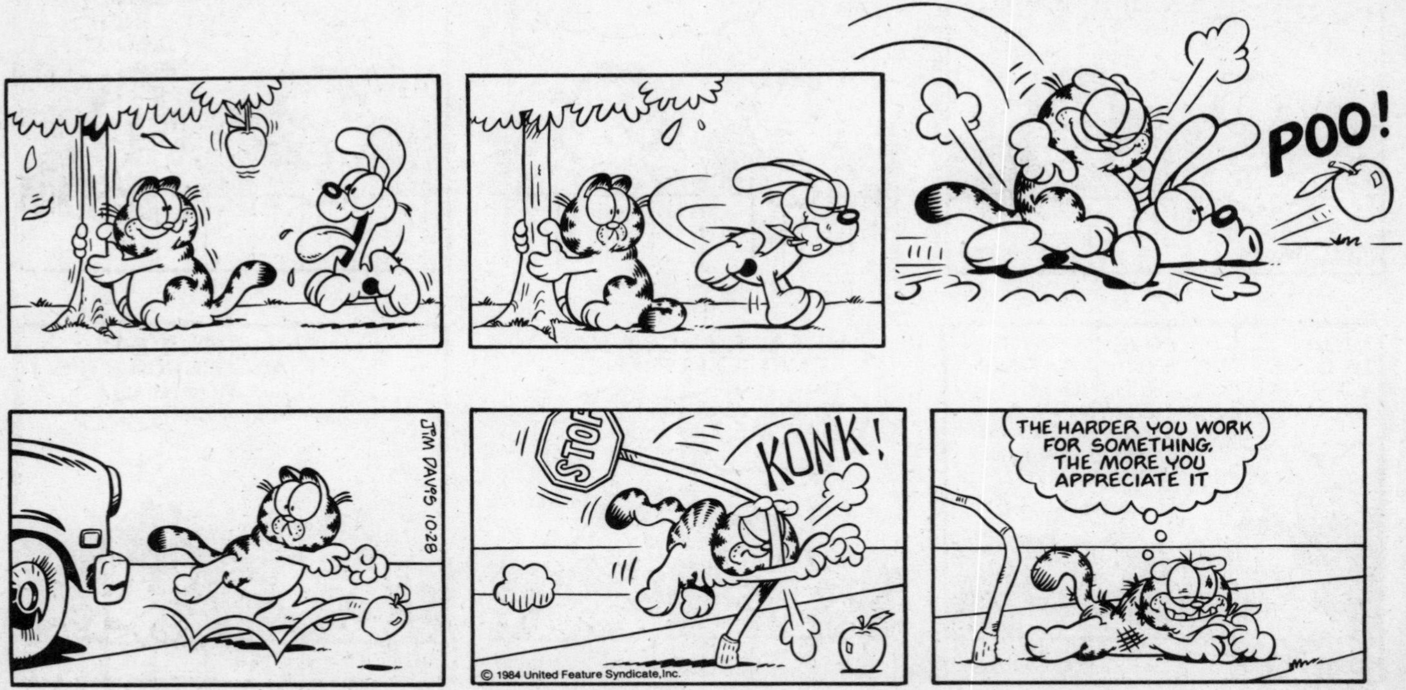
POO!
JIM DAVIS 10-28
STOP
KONK!
© 1984 United Feature Syndicate, Inc.
THE HARDER YOU WORK FOR SOMETHING, THE MORE YOU APPRECIATE IT

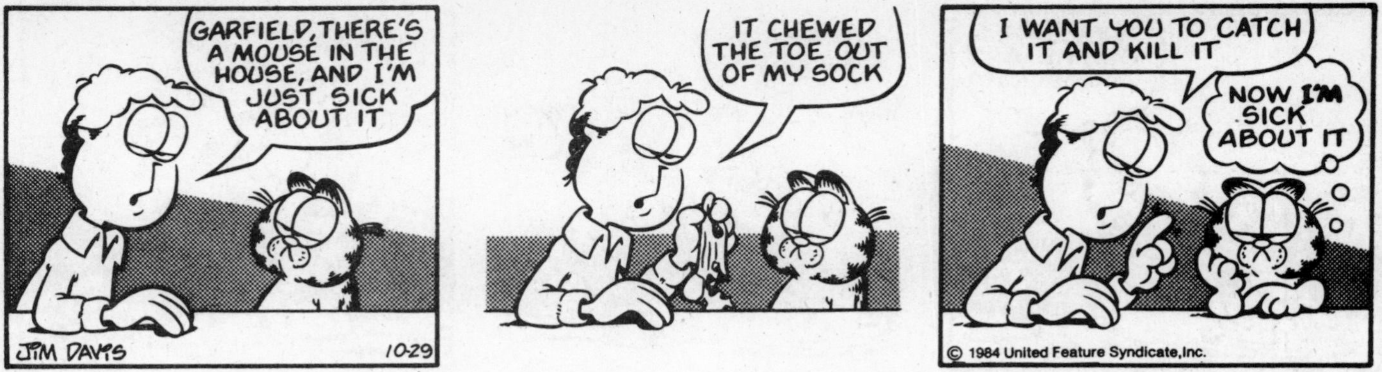
GARFIELD, THERE'S A MOUSE IN THE HOUSE, AND I'M JUST SICK ABOUT IT
JIM DAVIS
10-29
IT CHEWED THE TOE OUT OF MY SOCK
I WANT YOU TO CATCH IT AND KILL IT
NOW I'M SICK ABOUT IT
© 1984 United Feature Syndicate, Inc.

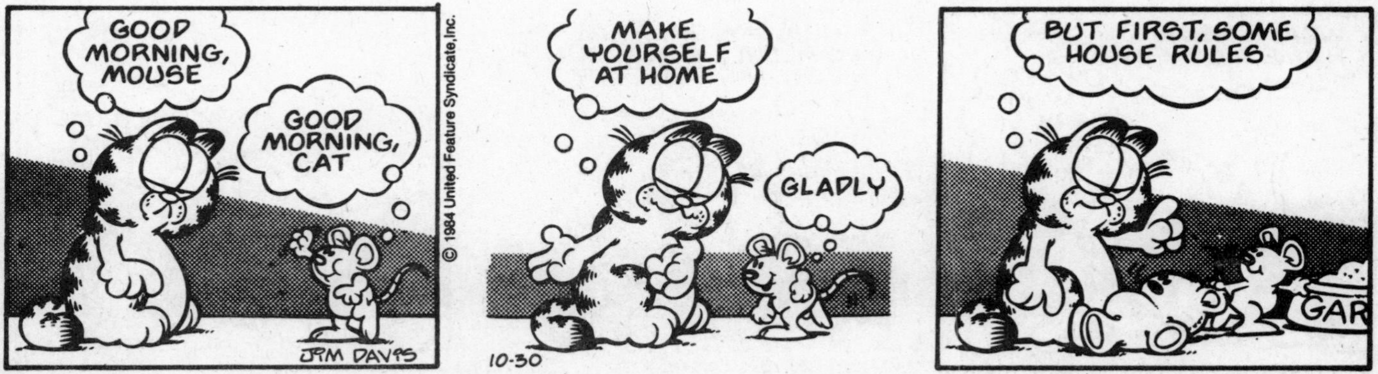
GOOD MORNING, MOUSE
GOOD MORNING, CAT
JIM DAVIS
© 1984 United Feature Syndicate, Inc.
MAKE YOURSELF AT HOME
GLADLY
10-30
BUT FIRST, SOME HOUSE RULES
GAR

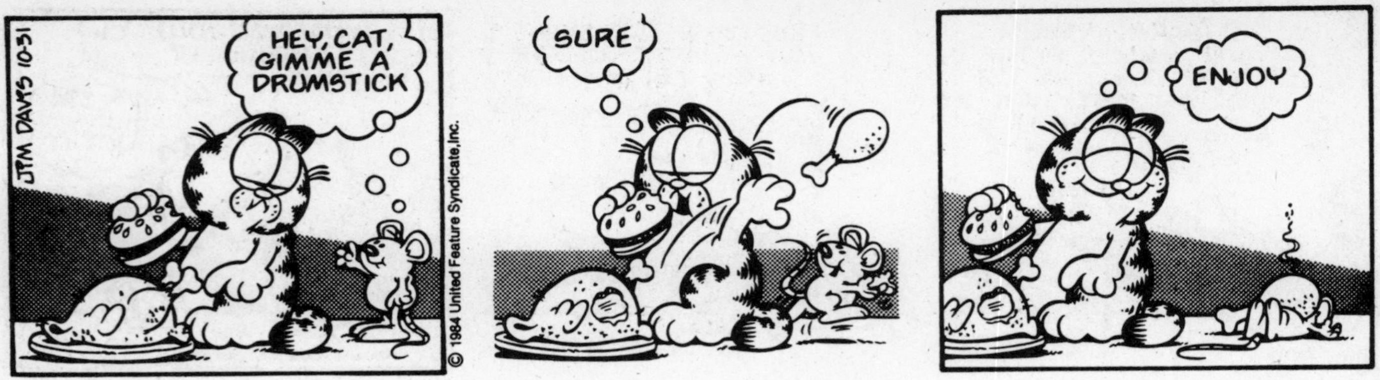
JIM DAVIS 10-31
HEY, CAT, GIMME A DRUMSTICK
SURE
ENJOY
© 1984 United Feature Syndicate, Inc.

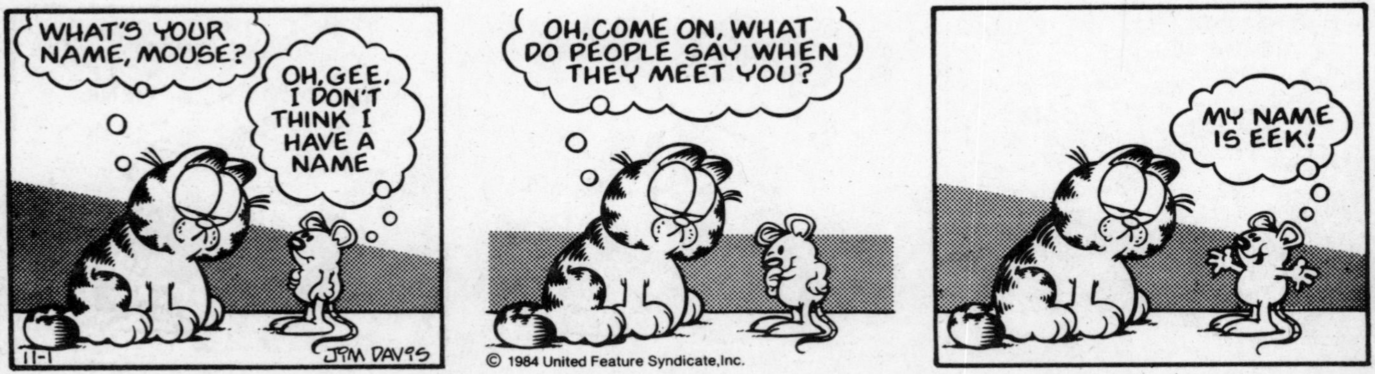
WHAT'S YOUR NAME, MOUSE?
OH, GEE, I DON'T THINK I HAVE A NAME
11-1
JIM DAVIS
OH, COME ON, WHAT DO PEOPLE SAY WHEN THEY MEET YOU?
MY NAME IS EEK!

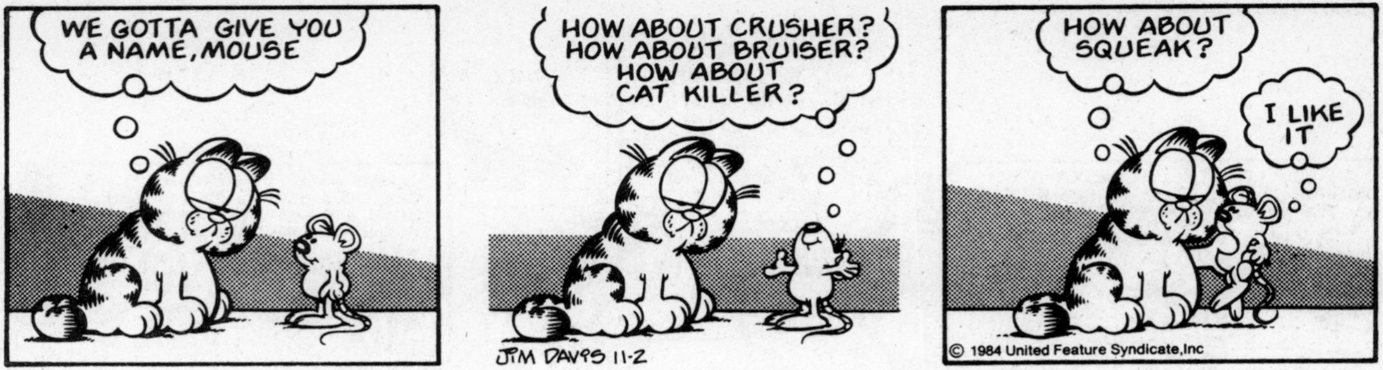
WE GOTTA GIVE YOU A NAME, MOUSE
HOW ABOUT CRUSHER? HOW ABOUT BRUISER? HOW ABOUT CAT KILLER?
JIM DAVIS 11-2
HOW ABOUT SQUEAK?
I LIKE IT

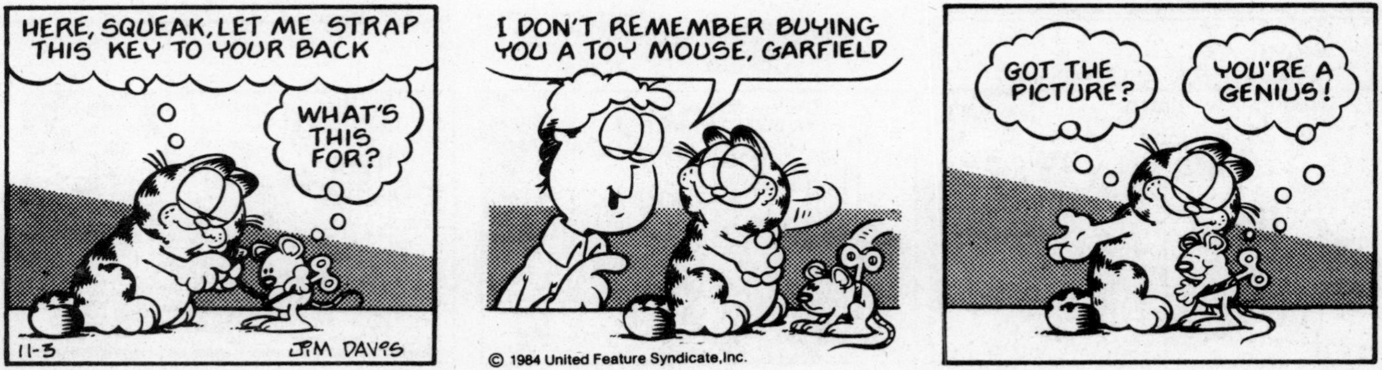
HERE, SQUEAK, LET ME STRAP THIS KEY TO YOUR BACK
WHAT'S THIS FOR?
11-3
JIM DAVIS
I DON'T REMEMBER BUYING YOU A TOY MOUSE, GARFIELD
GOT THE PICTURE?
YOU'RE A GENIUS!

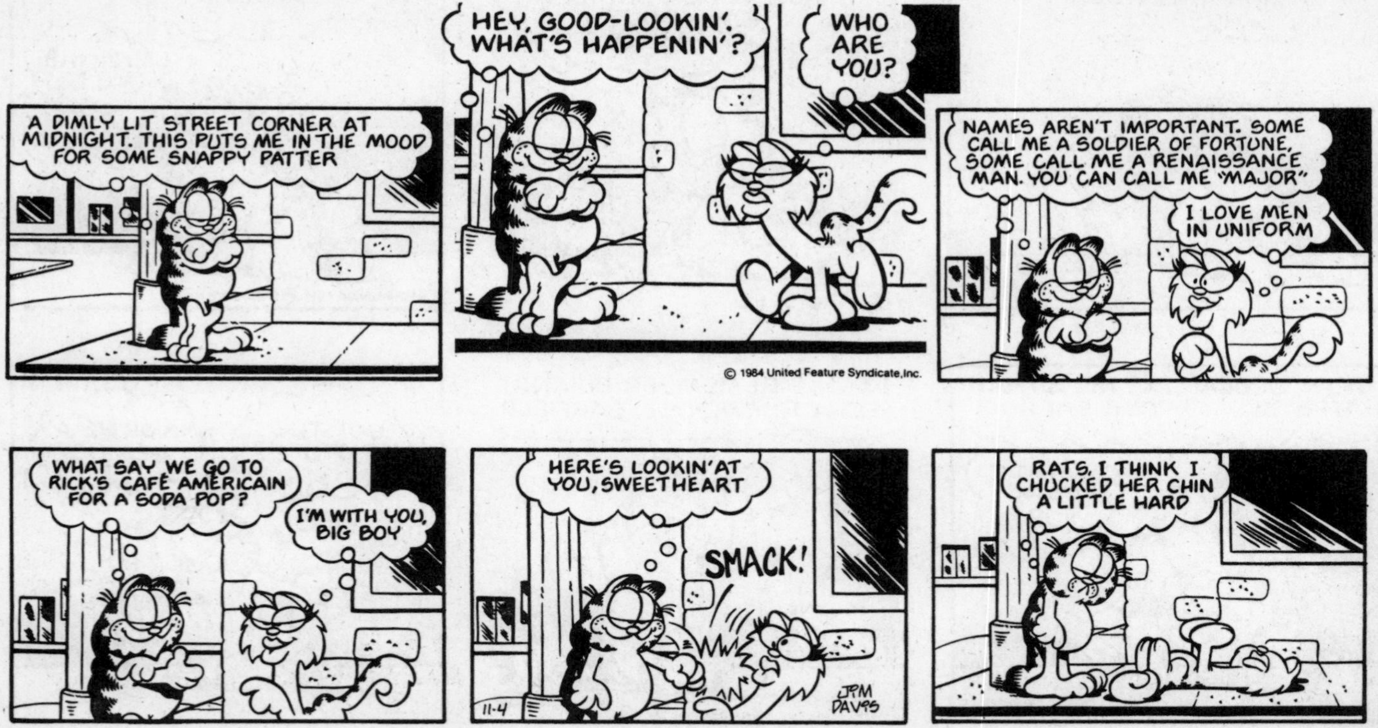
A DIMLY LIT STREET CORNER AT MIDNIGHT. THIS PUTS ME IN THE MOOD FOR SOME SNAPPY PATTER
HEY, GOOD-LOOKIN'. WHAT'S HAPPENIN'?
WHO ARE YOU?
NAMES AREN'T IMPORTANT. SOME CALL ME A SOLDIER OF FORTUNE, SOME CALL ME A RENAISSANCE MAN. YOU CAN CALL ME "MAJOR"
I LOVE MEN IN UNIFORM
WHAT SAY WE GO TO RICK'S CAFÉ AMÉRICAIN FOR A SODA POP?
I'M WITH YOU, BIG BOY
HERE'S LOOKIN' AT YOU, SWEETHEART
SMACK!
11-4
JIM DAVIS
RATS, I THINK I CHUCKED HER CHIN A LITTLE HARD

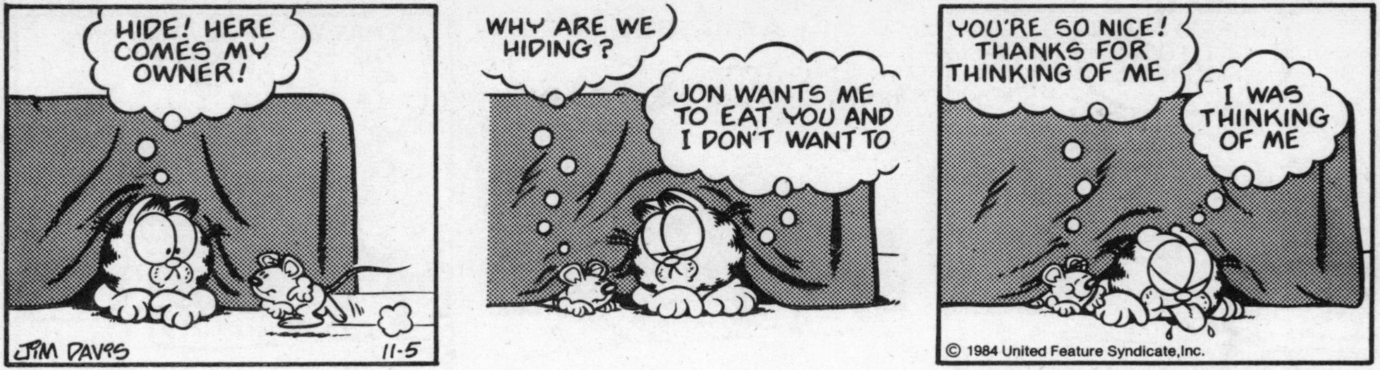
HIDE! HERE COMES MY OWNER!
JIM DAVIS
11-5
WHY ARE WE HIDING?
JON WANTS ME TO EAT YOU AND I DON'T WANT TO
YOU'RE SO NICE! THANKS FOR THINKING OF ME
I WAS THINKING OF ME
© 1984 United Feature Syndicate, Inc.

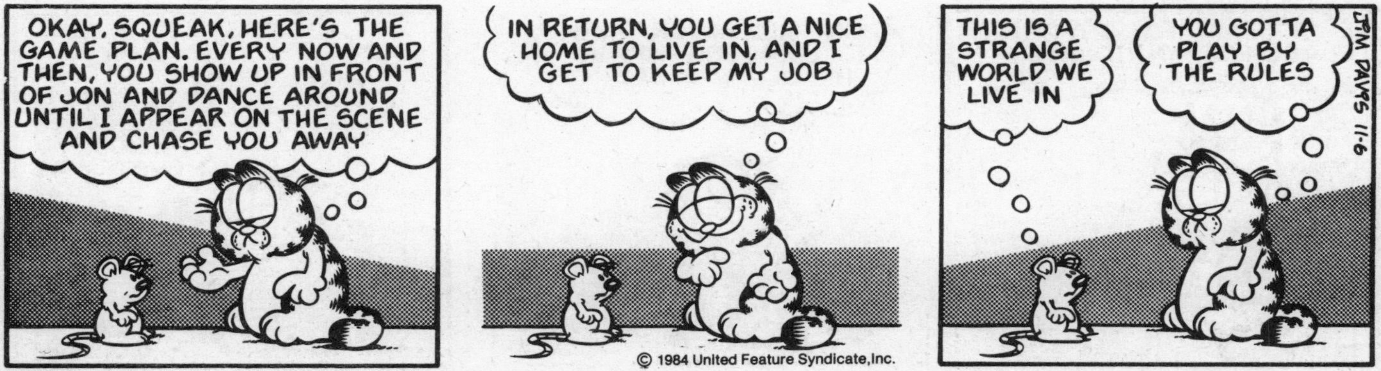
OKAY, SQUEAK, HERE'S THE GAME PLAN. EVERY NOW AND THEN, YOU SHOW UP IN FRONT OF JON AND DANCE AROUND UNTIL I APPEAR ON THE SCENE AND CHASE YOU AWAY
IN RETURN, YOU GET A NICE HOME TO LIVE IN, AND I GET TO KEEP MY JOB
© 1984 United Feature Syndicate, Inc.
THIS IS A STRANGE WORLD WE LIVE IN
YOU GOTTA PLAY BY THE RULES
JIM DAVIS 11-6

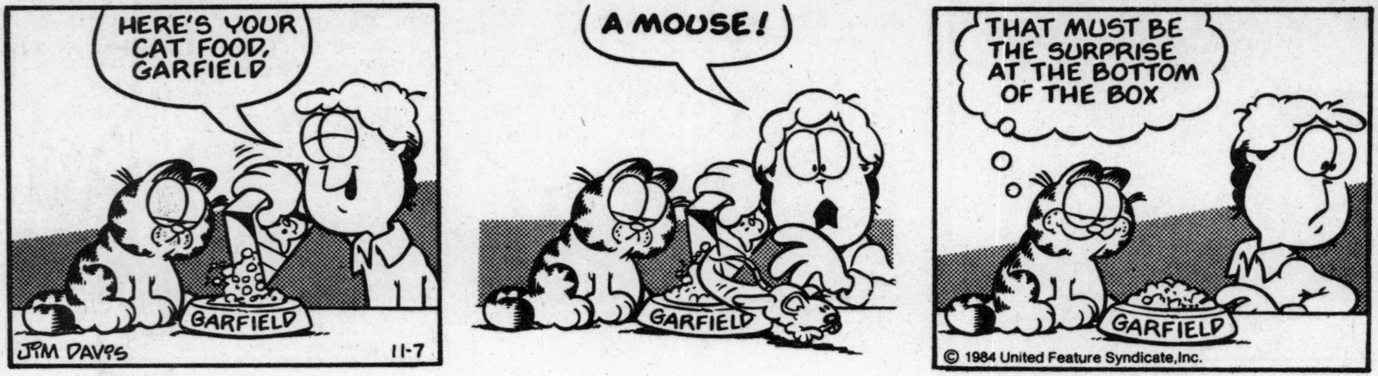
HERE'S YOUR CAT FOOD, GARFIELD
GARFIELD
JIM DAVIS
11-7
A MOUSE!
GARFIELD
THAT MUST BE THE SURPRISE AT THE BOTTOM OF THE BOX
GARFIELD
© 1984 United Feature Syndicate, Inc.

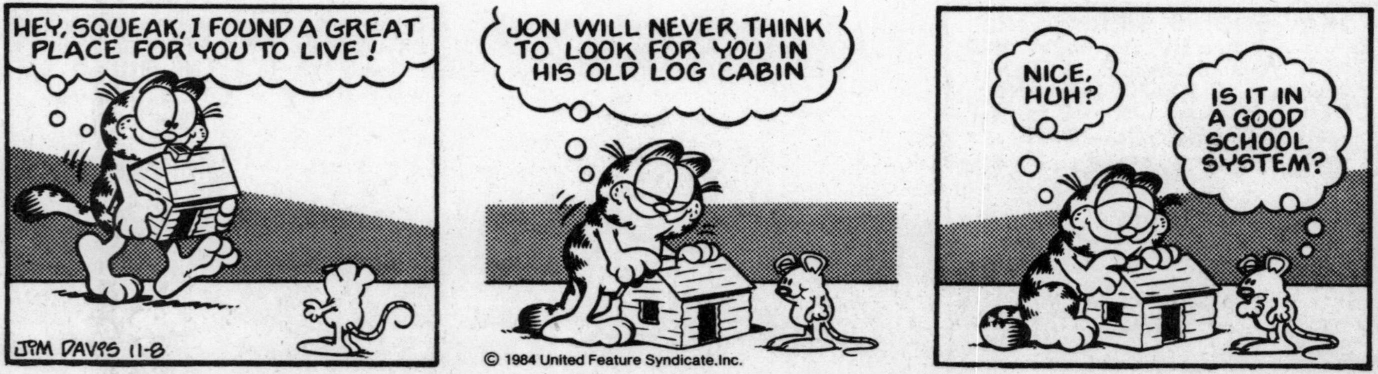
HEY, SQUEAK, I FOUND A GREAT PLACE FOR YOU TO LIVE!
JIM DAVIS 11-8
JON WILL NEVER THINK TO LOOK FOR YOU IN HIS OLD LOG CABIN
© 1984 United Feature Syndicate, Inc.
NICE, HUH?
IS IT IN A GOOD SCHOOL SYSTEM?

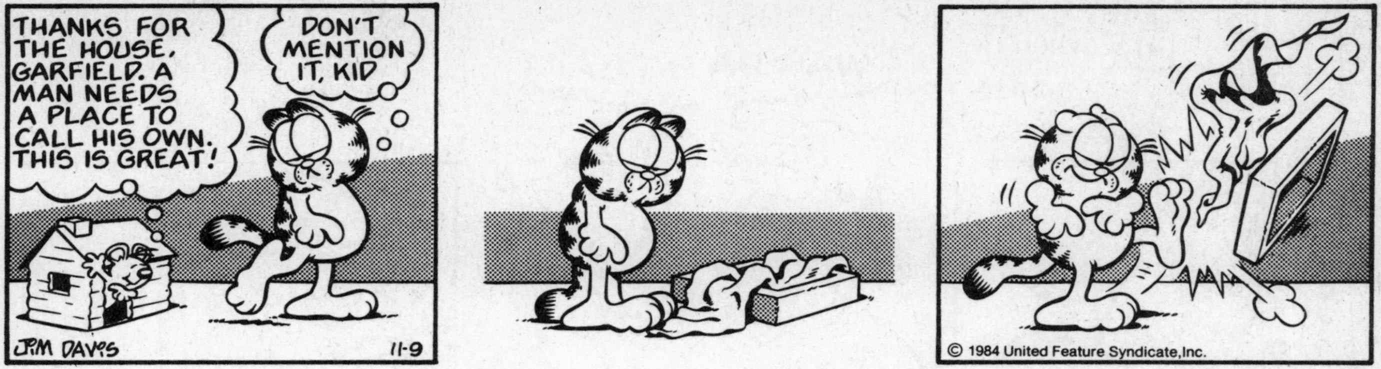
THANKS FOR THE HOUSE, GARFIELD. A MAN NEEDS A PLACE TO CALL HIS OWN. THIS IS GREAT!
DON'T MENTION IT, KID
JIM DAVIS
11-9
© 1984 United Feature Syndicate, Inc.

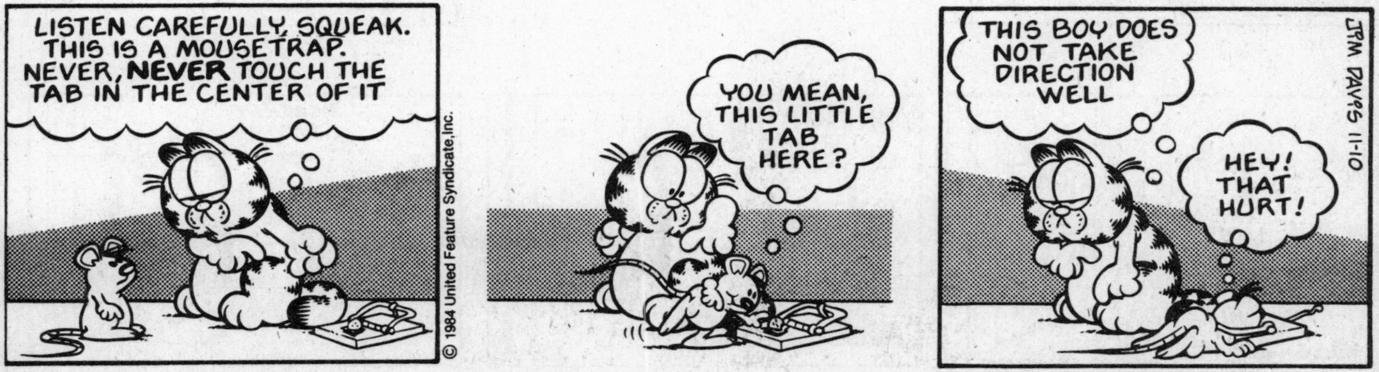
LISTEN CAREFULLY, SQUEAK. THIS IS A MOUSETRAP. NEVER, NEVER TOUCH THE TAB IN THE CENTER OF IT
© 1984 United Feature Syndicate, Inc.
YOU MEAN, THIS LITTLE TAB HERE?
THIS BOY DOES NOT TAKE DIRECTION WELL
HEY! THAT HURT!
JIM DAVIS 11-10

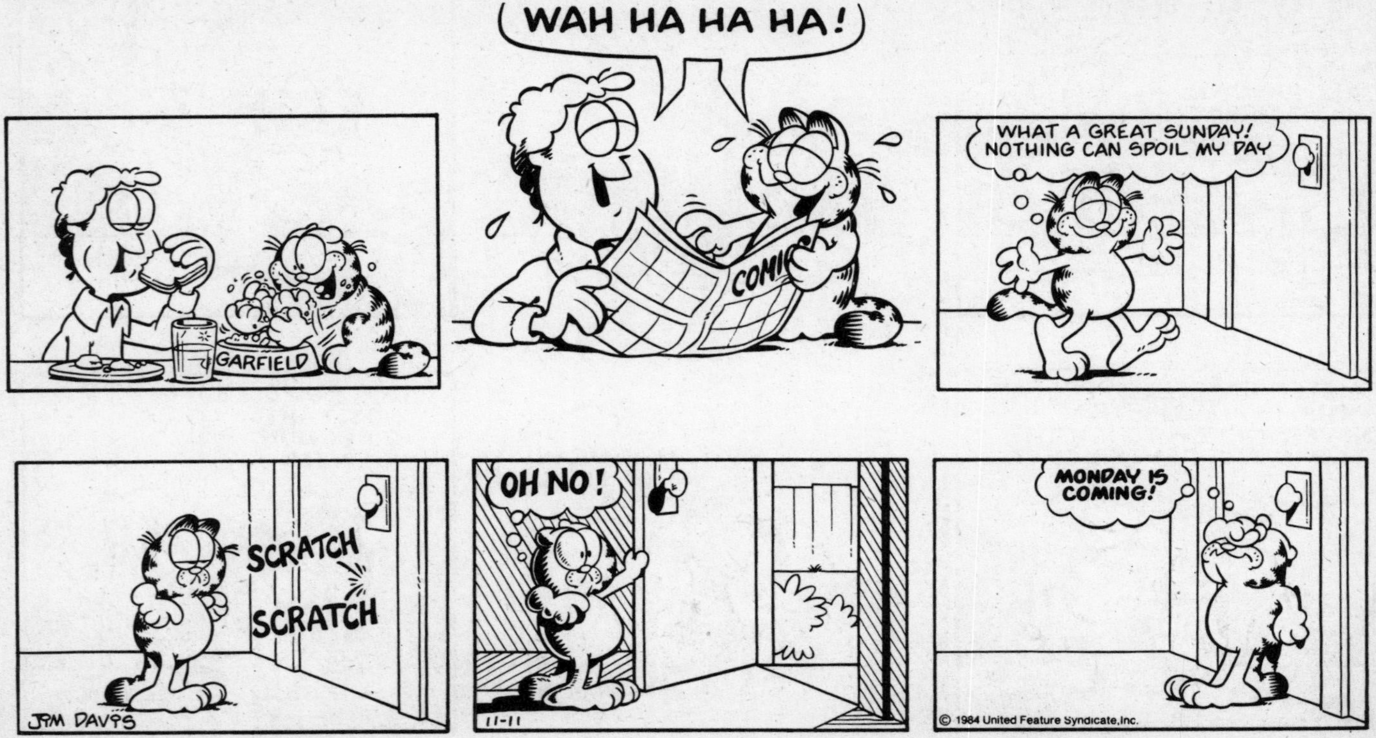
GARFIELD
WAH HA HA HA!
COMI
WHAT A GREAT SUNDAY! NOTHING CAN SPOIL MY DAY
SCRATCH
SCRATCH
JIM DAVIS
OH NO!
11-11
MONDAY IS COMING!
© 1984 United Feature Syndicate, Inc.

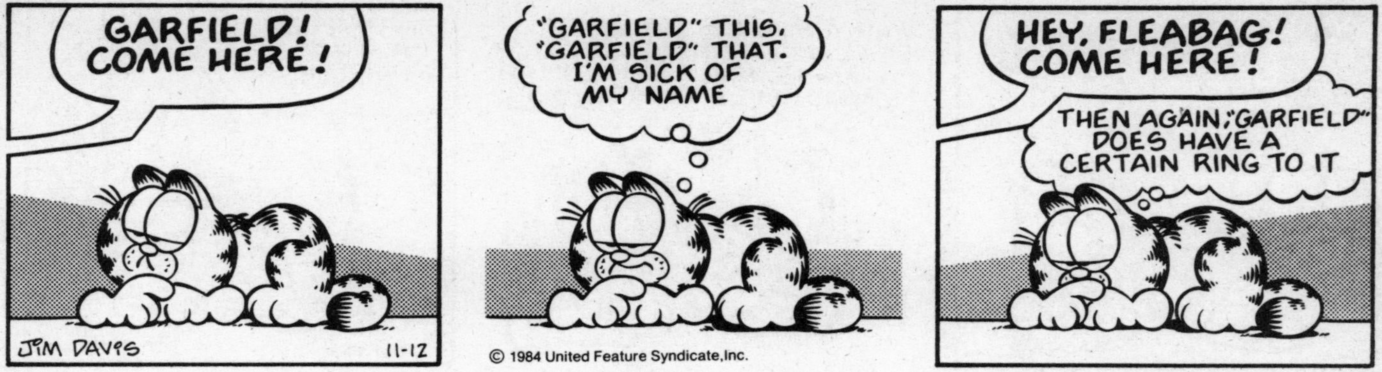
GARFIELD! COME HERE!
JIM DAVIS
11-12
"GARFIELD" THIS, "GARFIELD" THAT. I'M SICK OF MY NAME
© 1984 United Feature Syndicate,Inc.
HEY, FLEABAG! COME HERE!
THEN AGAIN, "GARFIELD" DOES HAVE A CERTAIN RING TO IT

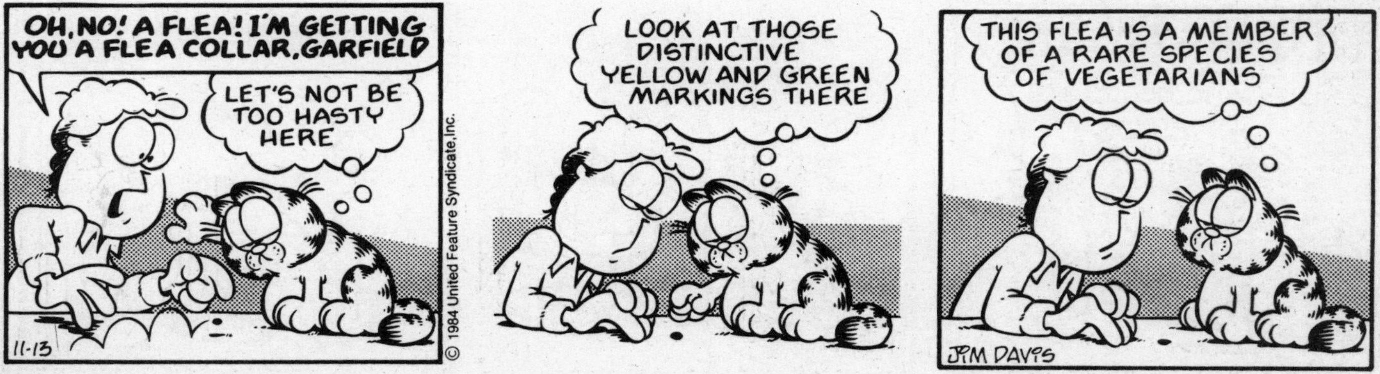
OH, NO! A FLEA! I'M GETTING YOU A FLEA COLLAR, GARFIELD
LET'S NOT BE TOO HASTY HERE
11-13
© 1984 United Feature Syndicate,Inc.
LOOK AT THOSE DISTINCTIVE YELLOW AND GREEN MARKINGS THERE
THIS FLEA IS A MEMBER OF A RARE SPECIES OF VEGETARIANS
JIM DAVIS

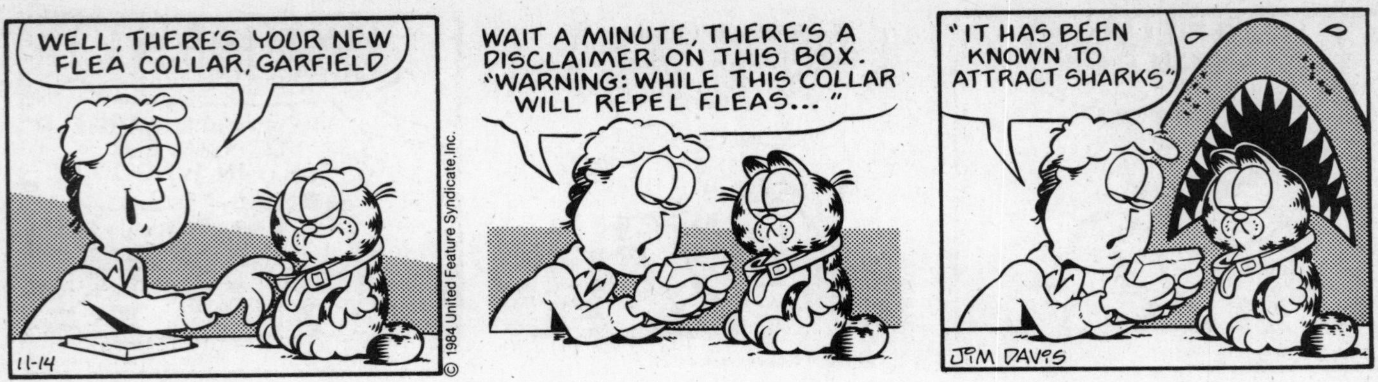
WELL, THERE'S YOUR NEW FLEA COLLAR, GARFIELD
11-14
© 1984 United Feature Syndicate, Inc.
WAIT A MINUTE, THERE'S A DISCLAIMER ON THIS BOX. "WARNING: WHILE THIS COLLAR WILL REPEL FLEAS..."
"IT HAS BEEN KNOWN TO ATTRACT SHARKS"
JIM DAVIS

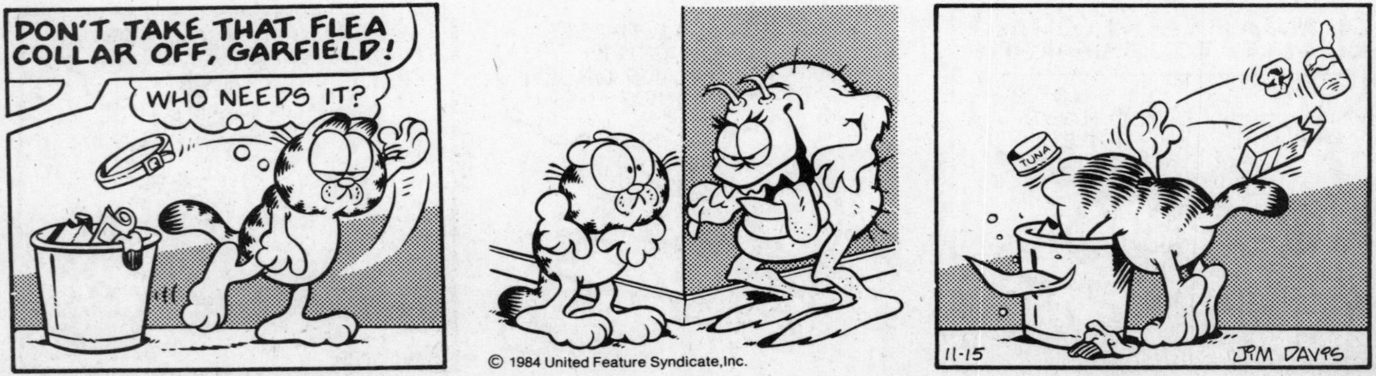
DON'T TAKE THAT FLEA COLLAR OFF, GARFIELD!
WHO NEEDS IT?
© 1984 United Feature Syndicate, Inc.
TUNA
11-15
JIM DAVIS

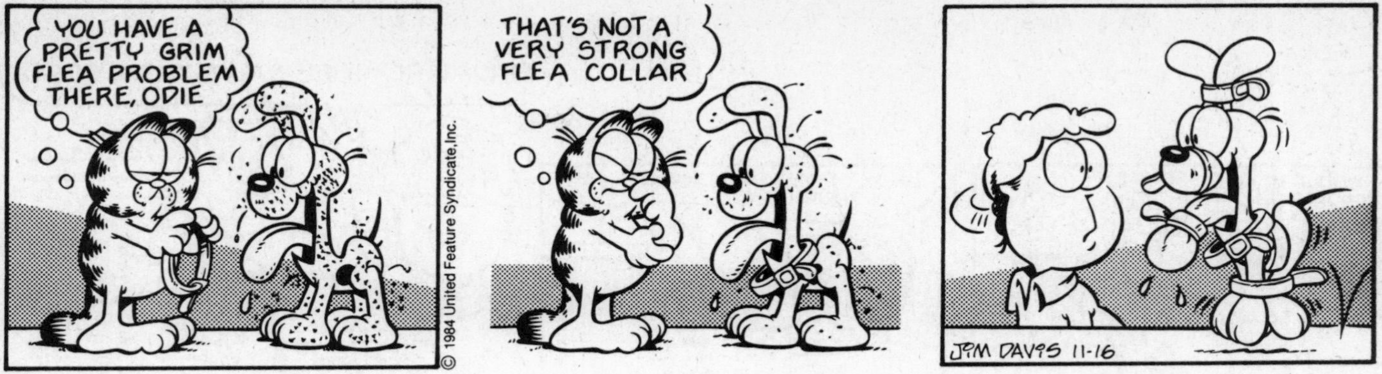
YOU HAVE A PRETTY GRIM FLEA PROBLEM THERE, ODIE
© 1984 United Feature Syndicate, Inc.
THAT'S NOT A VERY STRONG FLEA COLLAR
JIM DAVIS 11-16

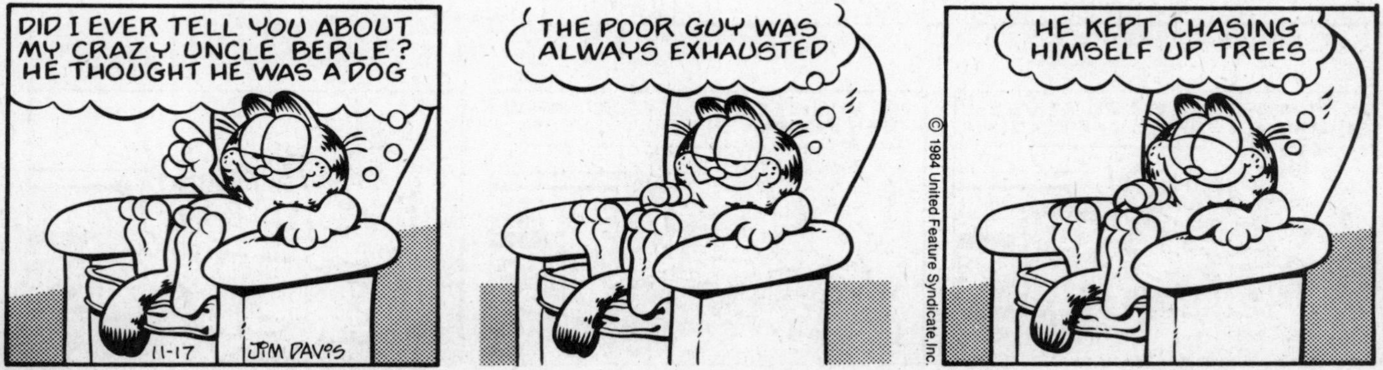
DID I EVER TELL YOU ABOUT MY CRAZY UNCLE BERLE? HE THOUGHT HE WAS A DOG
11-17
JIM DAVIS
THE POOR GUY WAS ALWAYS EXHAUSTED
© 1984 United Feature Syndicate, Inc.
HE KEPT CHASING HIMSELF UP TREES

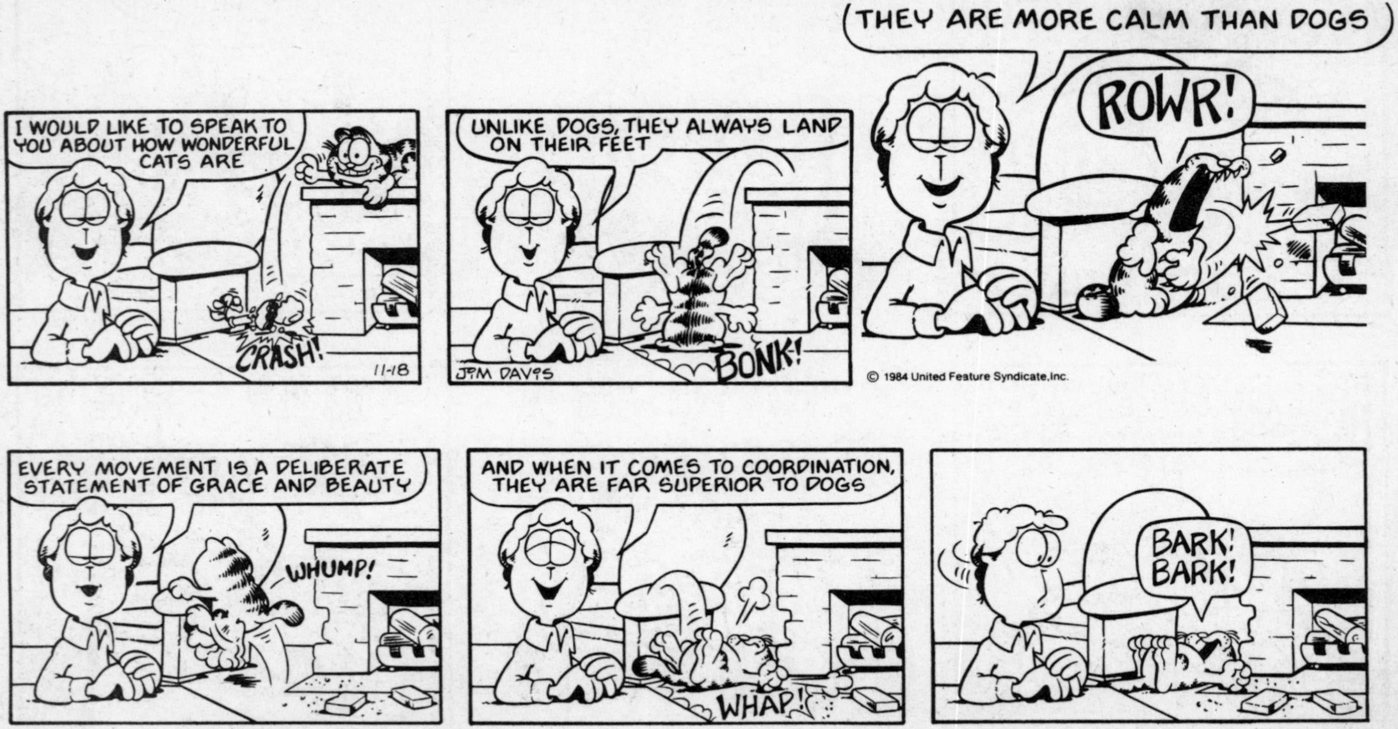

I WOULD LIKE TO SPEAK TO YOU ABOUT HOW WONDERFUL CATS ARE
CRASH!
11-18
UNLIKE DOGS, THEY ALWAYS LAND ON THEIR FEET
BONK!
JIM DAVIS
THEY ARE MORE CALM THAN DOGS
ROWR!
© 1984 United Feature Syndicate, Inc.
EVERY MOVEMENT IS A DELIBERATE STATEMENT OF GRACE AND BEAUTY
WHUMP!
AND WHEN IT COMES TO COORDINATION, THEY ARE FAR SUPERIOR TO DOGS
WHAP!
BARK! BARK!

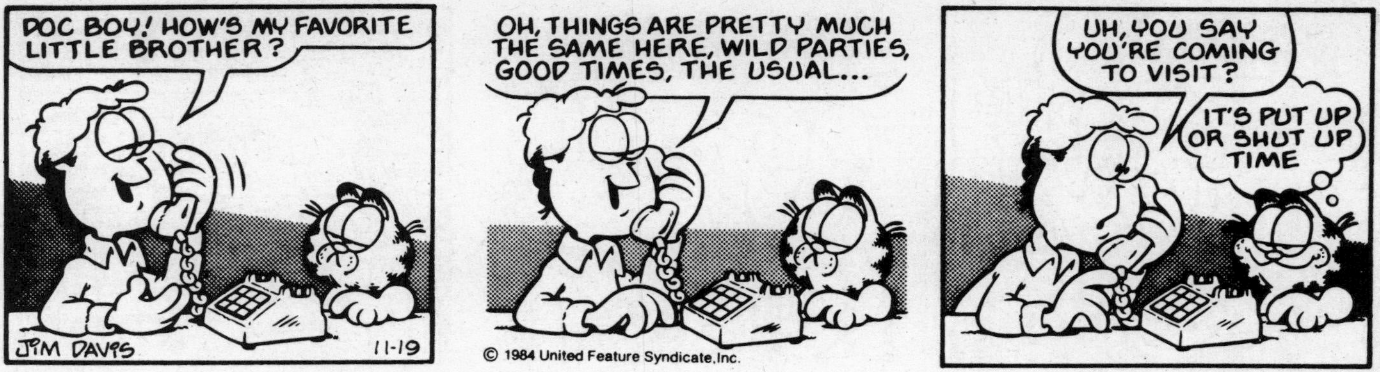
DOC BOY! HOW'S MY FAVORITE LITTLE BROTHER?
JIM DAVIS
11-19
OH, THINGS ARE PRETTY MUCH THE SAME HERE, WILD PARTIES, GOOD TIMES, THE USUAL...
© 1984 United Feature Syndicate, Inc.
UH, YOU SAY YOU'RE COMING TO VISIT?
IT'S PUT UP OR SHUT UP TIME

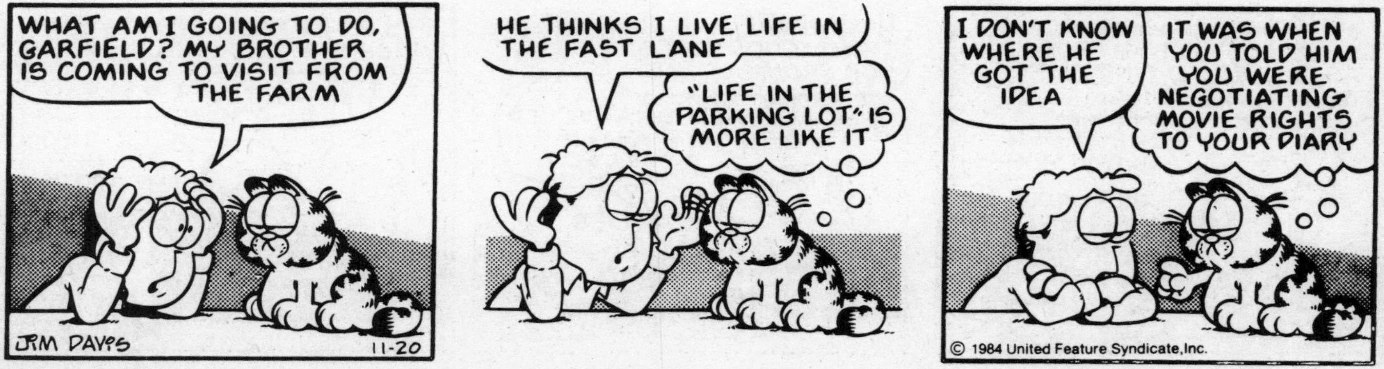
WHAT AM I GOING TO DO, GARFIELD? MY BROTHER IS COMING TO VISIT FROM THE FARM
JIM DAVIS
11-20
HE THINKS I LIVE LIFE IN THE FAST LANE
"LIFE IN THE PARKING LOT" IS MORE LIKE IT
I DON'T KNOW WHERE HE GOT THE IDEA
IT WAS WHEN YOU TOLD HIM YOU WERE NEGOTIATING MOVIE RIGHTS TO YOUR DIARY
© 1984 United Feature Syndicate, Inc.

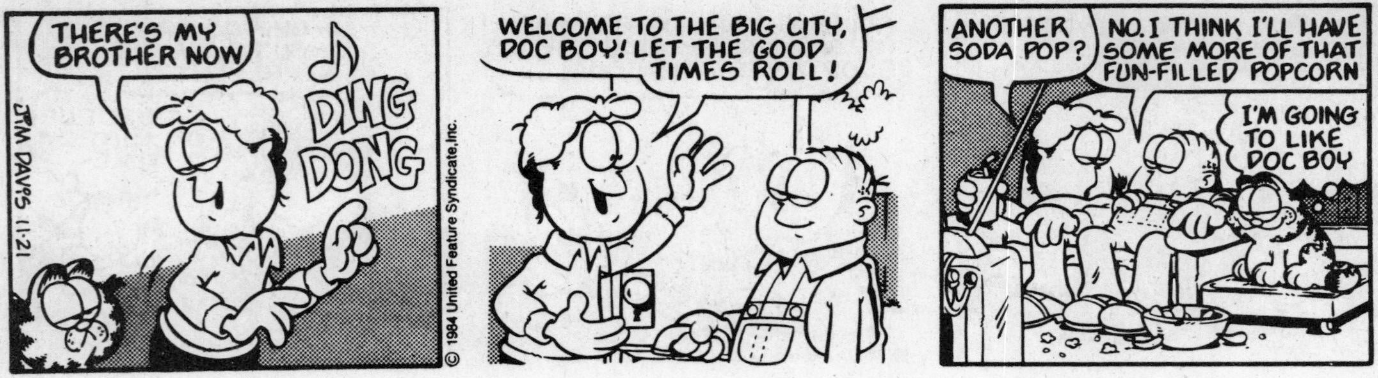
THERE'S MY BROTHER NOW
DING DONG
JIM DAVIS 11-21
© 1984 United Feature Syndicate, Inc.
WELCOME TO THE BIG CITY, DOC BOY! LET THE GOOD TIMES ROLL!
ANOTHER SODA POP?
NO. I THINK I'LL HAVE SOME MORE OF THAT FUN-FILLED POPCORN
I'M GOING TO LIKE DOC BOY

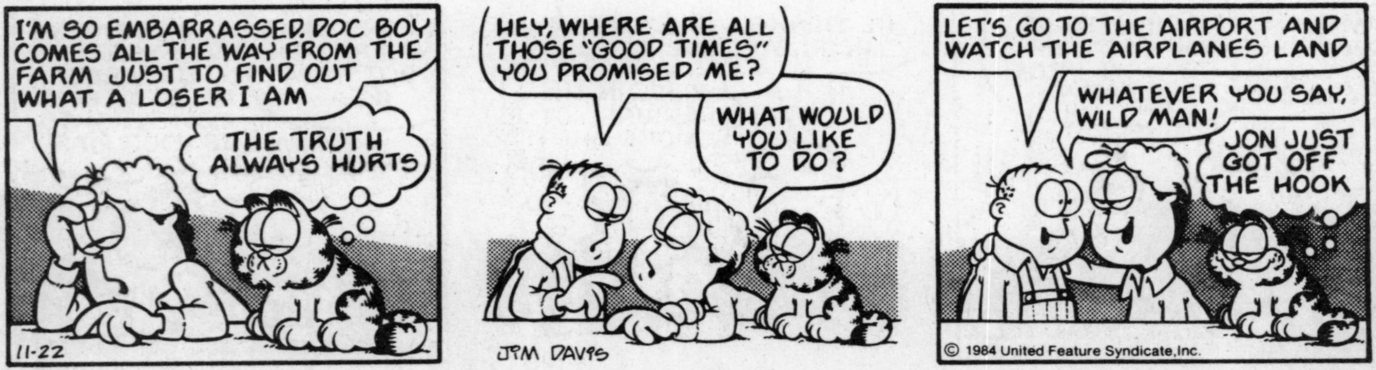
I'M SO EMBARRASSED. DOC BOY COMES ALL THE WAY FROM THE FARM JUST TO FIND OUT WHAT A LOSER I AM
THE TRUTH ALWAYS HURTS
11-22
HEY, WHERE ARE ALL THOSE "GOOD TIMES" YOU PROMISED ME?
WHAT WOULD YOU LIKE TO DO?
JIM DAVIS
LET'S GO TO THE AIRPORT AND WATCH THE AIRPLANES LAND
WHATEVER YOU SAY, WILD MAN!
JON JUST GOT OFF THE HOOK
© 1984 United Feature Syndicate, Inc.

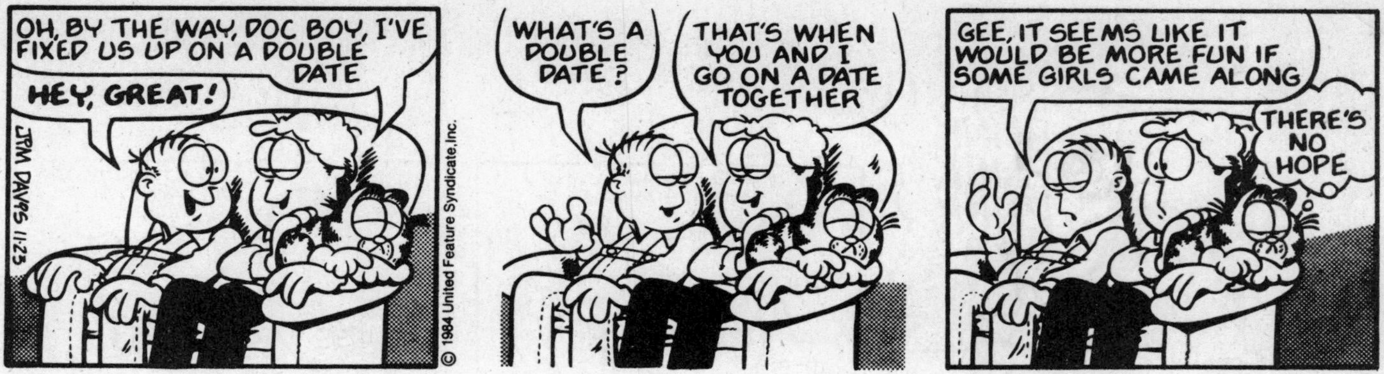
OH, BY THE WAY, DOC BOY, I'VE FIXED US UP ON A DOUBLE DATE
HEY, GREAT!
JIM DAVIS 11-23
© 1984 United Feature Syndicate, Inc.
WHAT'S A DOUBLE DATE ?
THAT'S WHEN YOU AND I GO ON A DATE TOGETHER
GEE, IT SEEMS LIKE IT WOULD BE MORE FUN IF SOME GIRLS CAME ALONG
THERE'S NO HOPE

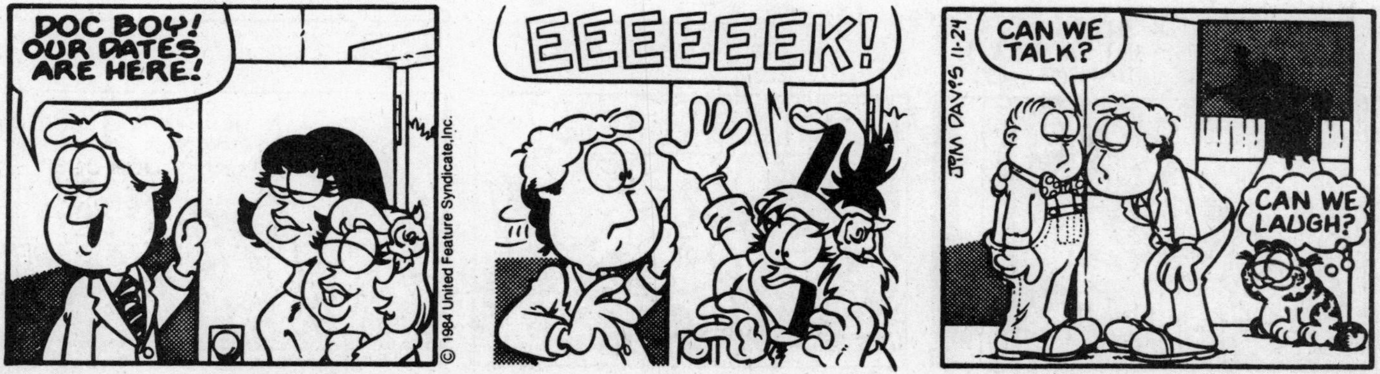
DOC BOY! OUR DATES ARE HERE!
© 1984 United Feature Syndicate, Inc.
EEEEEEK!
JIM DAVIS 11-24
CAN WE TALK?
CAN WE LAUGH?

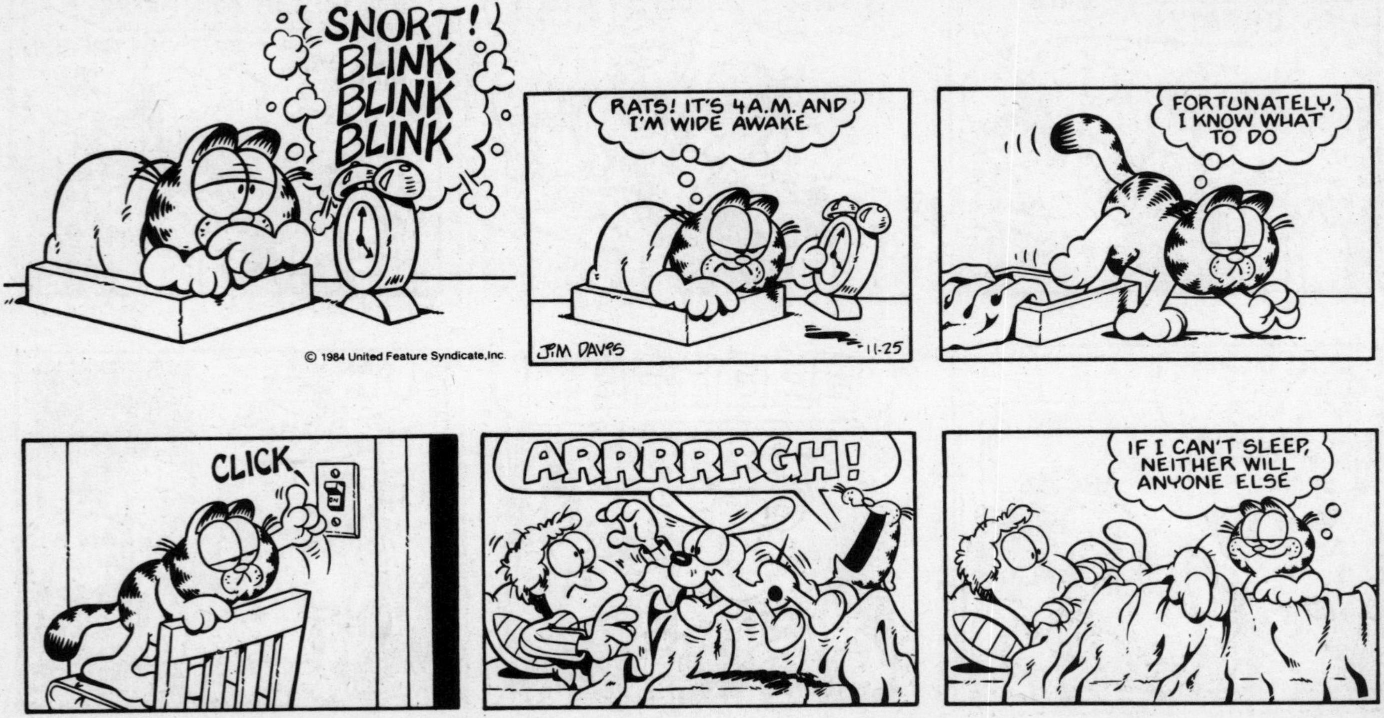
SNORT!
BLINK
BLINK
BLINK
RATS! IT'S 4 A.M. AND I'M WIDE AWAKE
JIM DAVIS
11-25
FORTUNATELY, I KNOW WHAT TO DO
CLICK
ON
ARRRRRRGH!
IF I CAN'T SLEEP, NEITHER WILL ANYONE ELSE

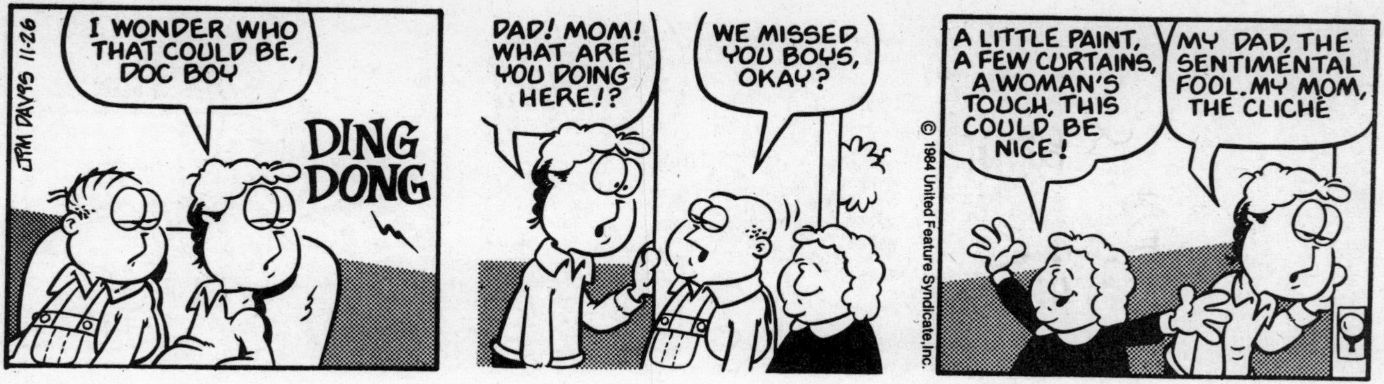

JIM DAVIS 11-26
I WONDER WHO THAT COULD BE, DOC BOY
DING DONG
DAD! MOM! WHAT ARE YOU DOING HERE!?
WE MISSED YOU BOYS, OKAY?
A LITTLE PAINT, A FEW CURTAINS, A WOMAN'S TOUCH, THIS COULD BE NICE!
MY DAD, THE SENTIMENTAL FOOL. MY MOM, THE CLICHÉ

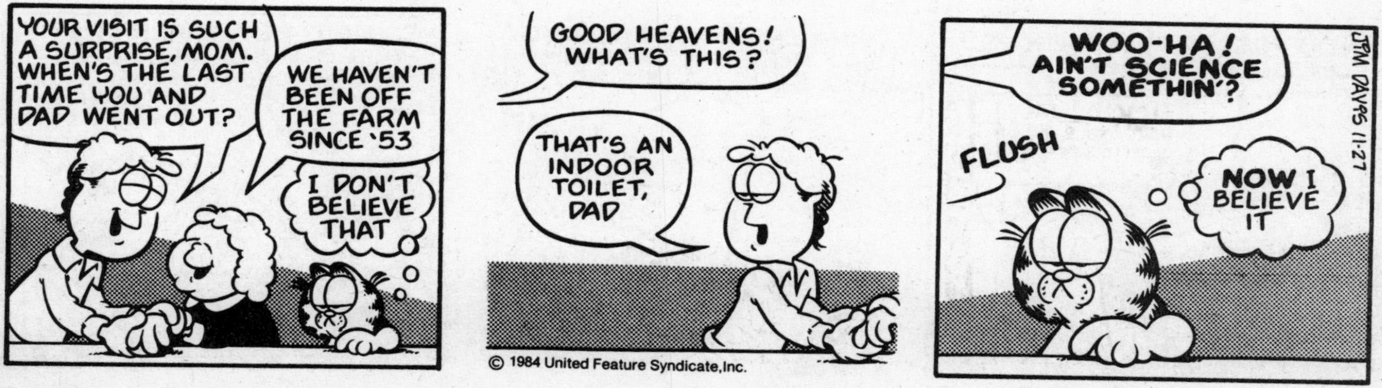

YOUR VISIT IS SUCH A SURPRISE, MOM. WHEN'S THE LAST TIME YOU AND DAD WENT OUT?
WE HAVEN'T BEEN OFF THE FARM SINCE '53
I DON'T BELIEVE THAT
GOOD HEAVENS! WHAT'S THIS?
THAT'S AN INDOOR TOILET, DAD
JIM DAVIS 11-27
WOO-HA! AIN'T SCIENCE SOMETHIN'?
FLUSH
NOW I BELIEVE IT

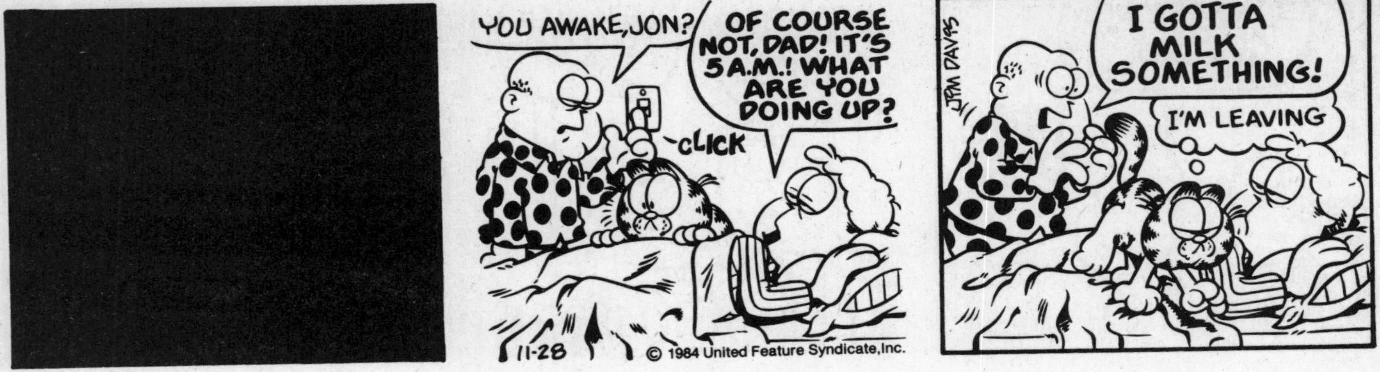
YOU AWAKE, JON?
OF COURSE NOT, DAD! IT'S 5 A.M.! WHAT ARE YOU DOING UP?
CLICK
I GOTTA MILK SOMETHING!
I'M LEAVING
JIM DAVIS
11-28
© 1984 United Feature Syndicate, Inc.

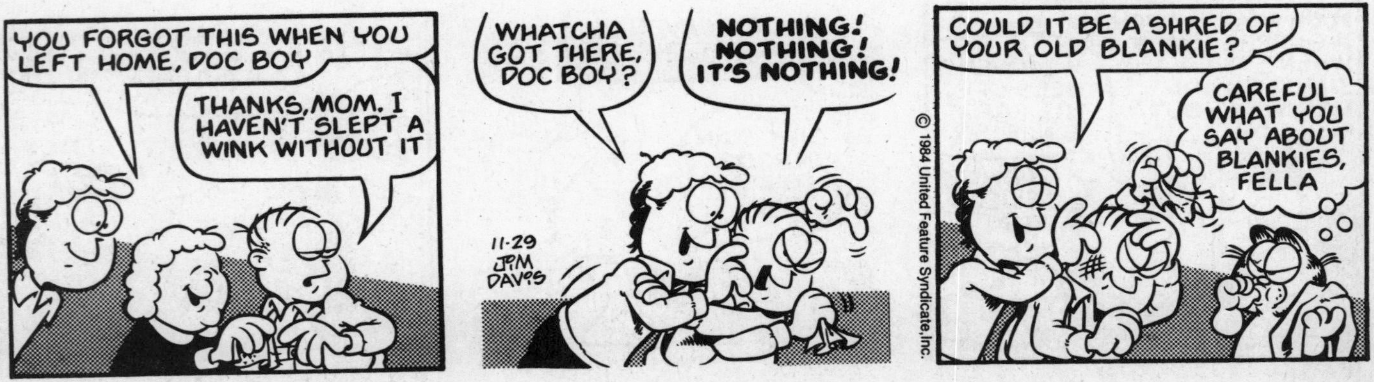
YOU FORGOT THIS WHEN YOU LEFT HOME, DOC BOY
THANKS, MOM. I HAVEN'T SLEPT A WINK WITHOUT IT
WHATCHA GOT THERE, DOC BOY?
NOTHING! NOTHING! IT'S NOTHING!
11-29
JIM DAVIS
COULD IT BE A SHRED OF YOUR OLD BLANKIE?
CAREFUL WHAT YOU SAY ABOUT BLANKIES, FELLA
© 1984 United Feature Syndicate, Inc.

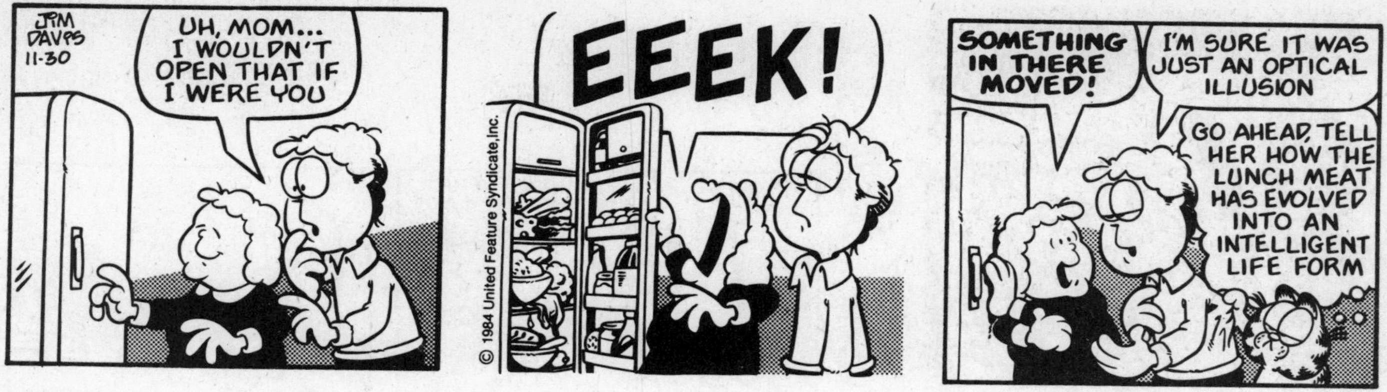
JIM DAVIS 11-30
UH, MOM... I WOULDN'T OPEN THAT IF I WERE YOU
EEEK!
© 1984 United Feature Syndicate, Inc.
SOMETHING IN THERE MOVED!
I'M SURE IT WAS JUST AN OPTICAL ILLUSION
GO AHEAD, TELL HER HOW THE LUNCH MEAT HAS EVOLVED INTO AN INTELLIGENT LIFE FORM

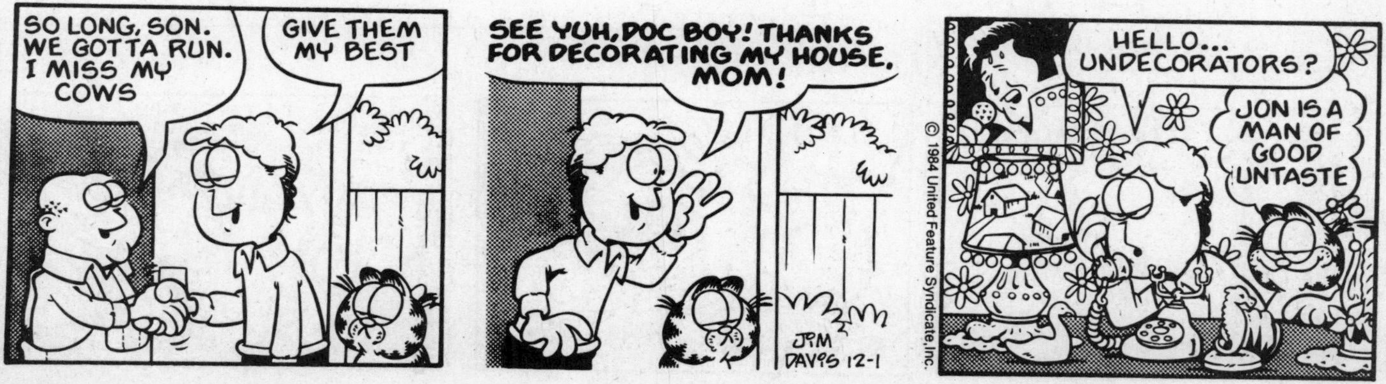
SO LONG, SON. WE GOTTA RUN. I MISS MY COWS
GIVE THEM MY BEST
SEE YUH, DOC BOY! THANKS FOR DECORATING MY HOUSE, MOM!
JIM DAVIS 12-1
© 1984 United Feature Syndicate, Inc.
HELLO... UNDECORATORS?
JON IS A MAN OF GOOD UNTASTE

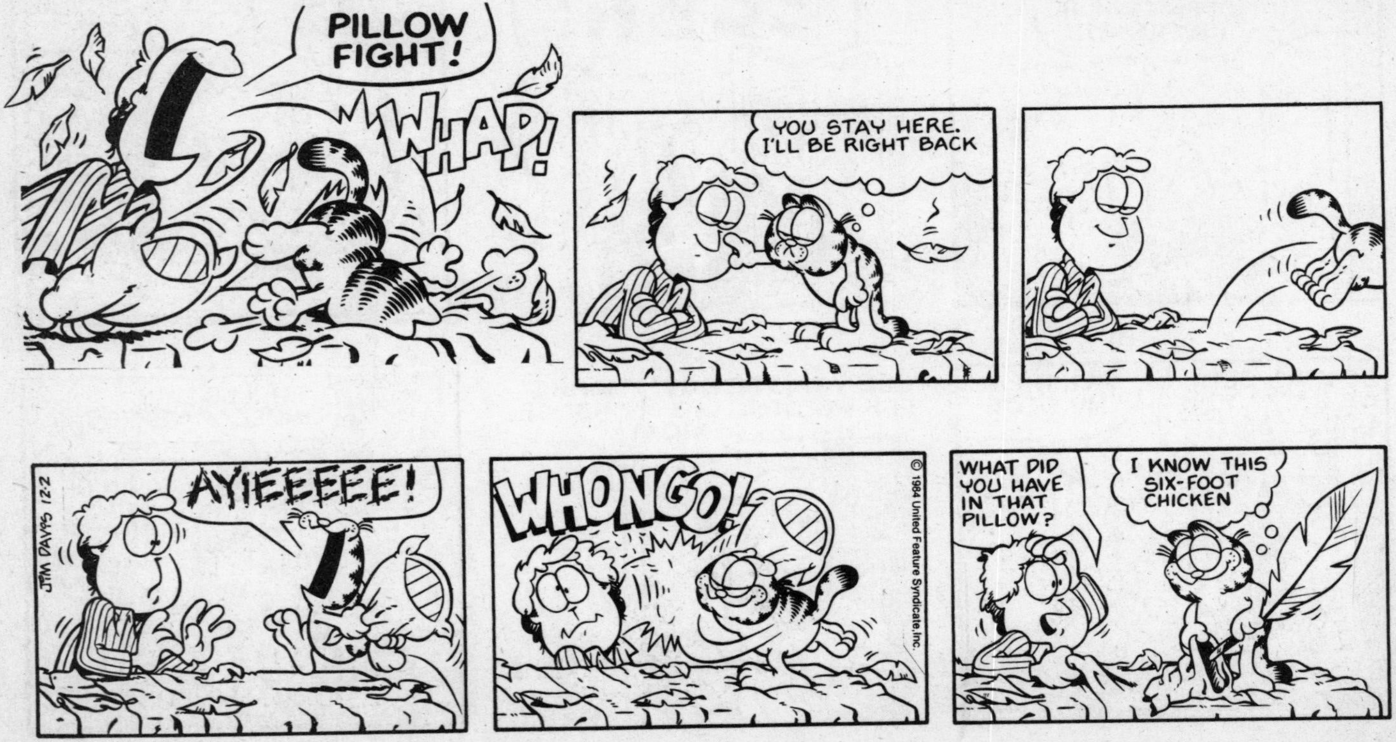
PILLOW FIGHT!
WHAP!
YOU STAY HERE. I'LL BE RIGHT BACK
JIM DAVIS 12-2
AYIEEEEEE!
WHONGO!
© 1984 United Feature Syndicate, Inc.
WHAT DID YOU HAVE IN THAT PILLOW?
I KNOW THIS SIX-FOOT CHICKEN

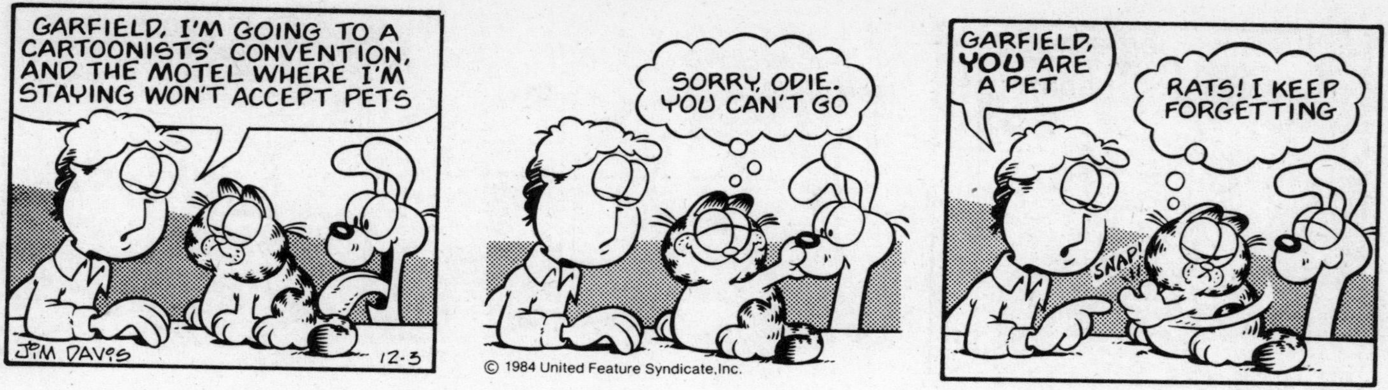
GARFIELD, I'M GOING TO A CARTOONISTS' CONVENTION, AND THE MOTEL WHERE I'M STAYING WON'T ACCEPT PETS
JIM DAVIS
12-3
SORRY, ODIE. YOU CAN'T GO
GARFIELD, YOU ARE A PET
RATS! I KEEP FORGETTING
SNAP!

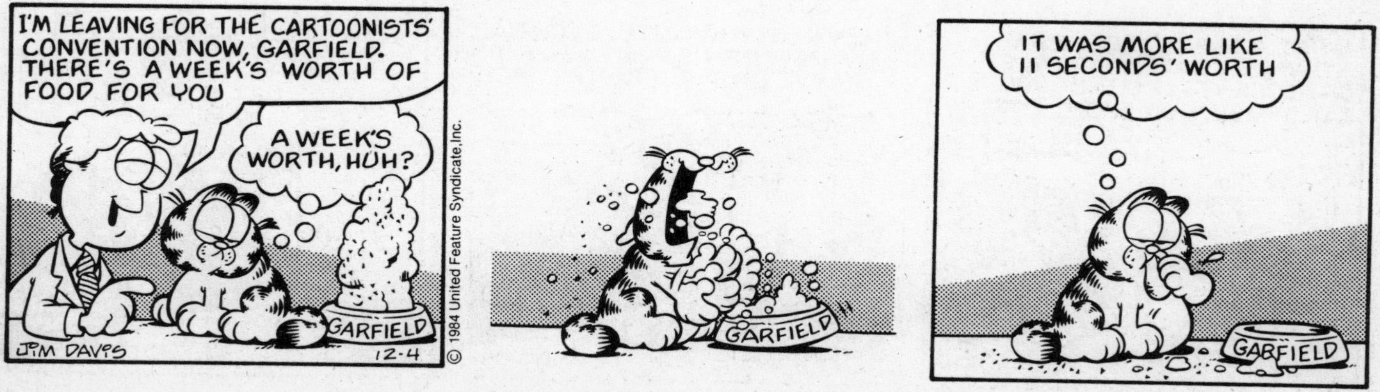
I'M LEAVING FOR THE CARTOONISTS' CONVENTION NOW, GARFIELD. THERE'S A WEEK'S WORTH OF FOOD FOR YOU
A WEEK'S WORTH, HUH?
GARFIELD
JIM DAVIS
12-4
GARFIELD
IT WAS MORE LIKE 11 SECONDS' WORTH
GARFIELD

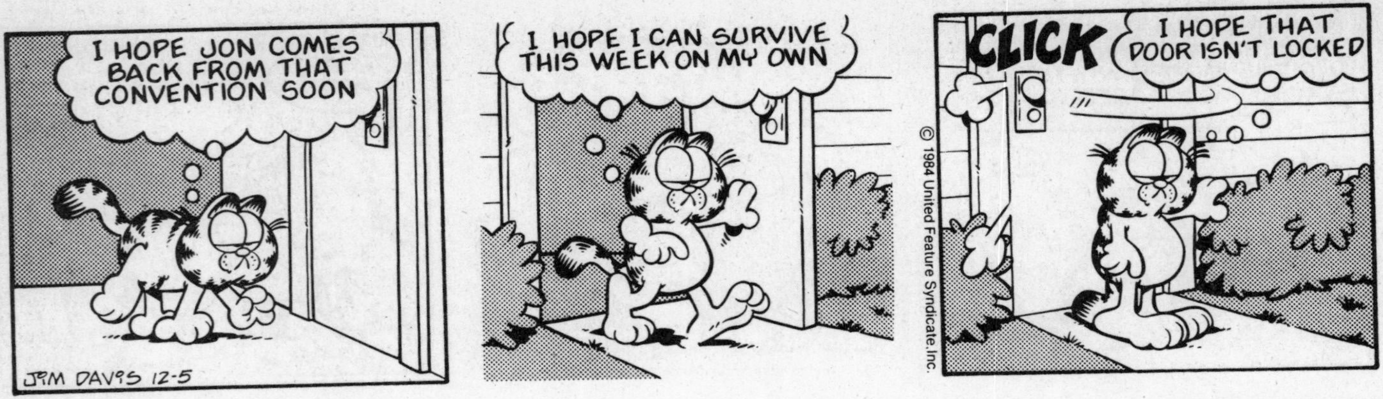
I HOPE JON COMES BACK FROM THAT CONVENTION SOON
JIM DAVIS 12-5
I HOPE I CAN SURVIVE THIS WEEK ON MY OWN
CLICK
I HOPE THAT DOOR ISN'T LOCKED
© 1984 United Feature Syndicate, Inc.

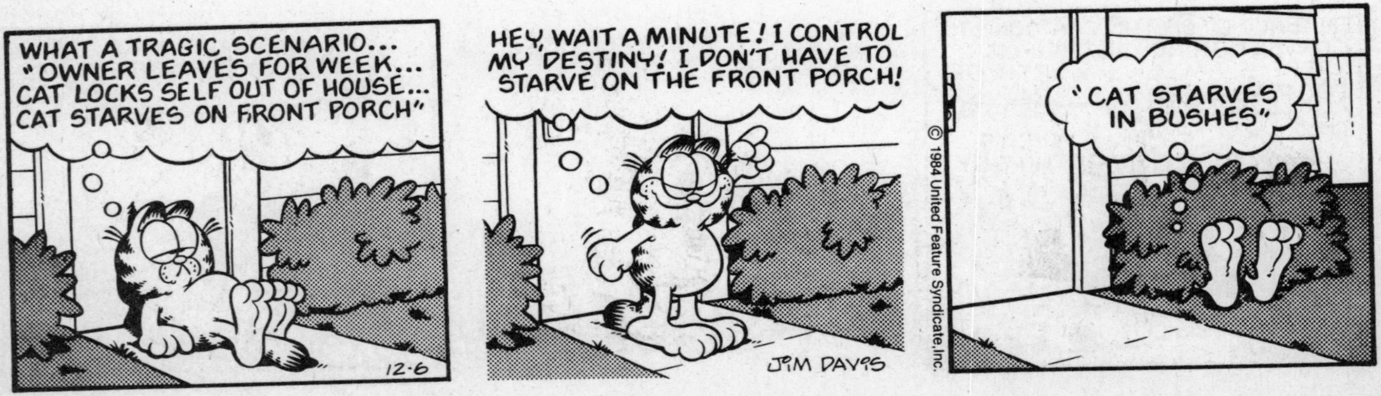
WHAT A TRAGIC SCENARIO... "OWNER LEAVES FOR WEEK... CAT LOCKS SELF OUT OF HOUSE... CAT STARVES ON FRONT PORCH"
12-6
HEY, WAIT A MINUTE! I CONTROL MY DESTINY! I DON'T HAVE TO STARVE ON THE FRONT PORCH!
JIM DAVIS
"CAT STARVES IN BUSHES"
© 1984 United Feature Syndicate, Inc.

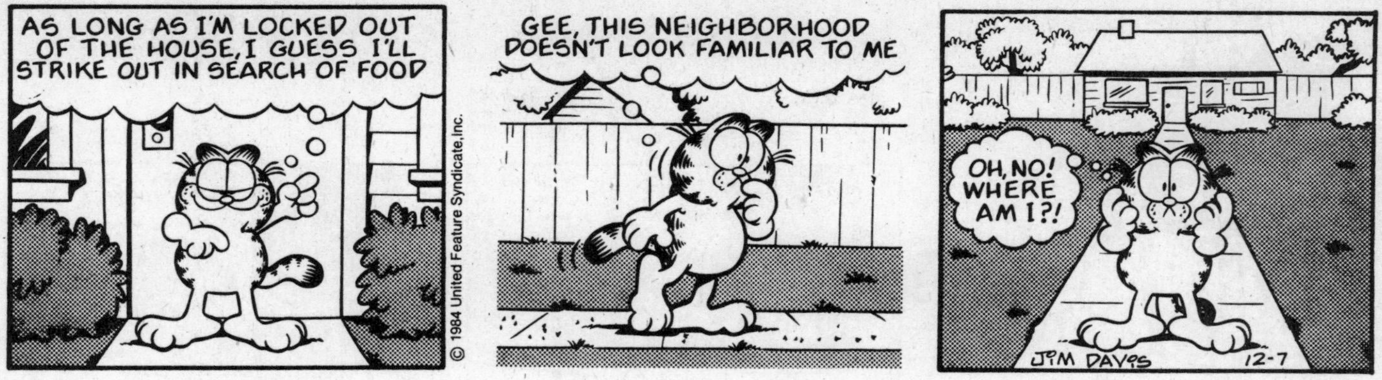
AS LONG AS I'M LOCKED OUT OF THE HOUSE, I GUESS I'LL STRIKE OUT IN SEARCH OF FOOD
GEE, THIS NEIGHBORHOOD DOESN'T LOOK FAMILIAR TO ME
OH, NO! WHERE AM I?!
JIM DAVIS 12-7

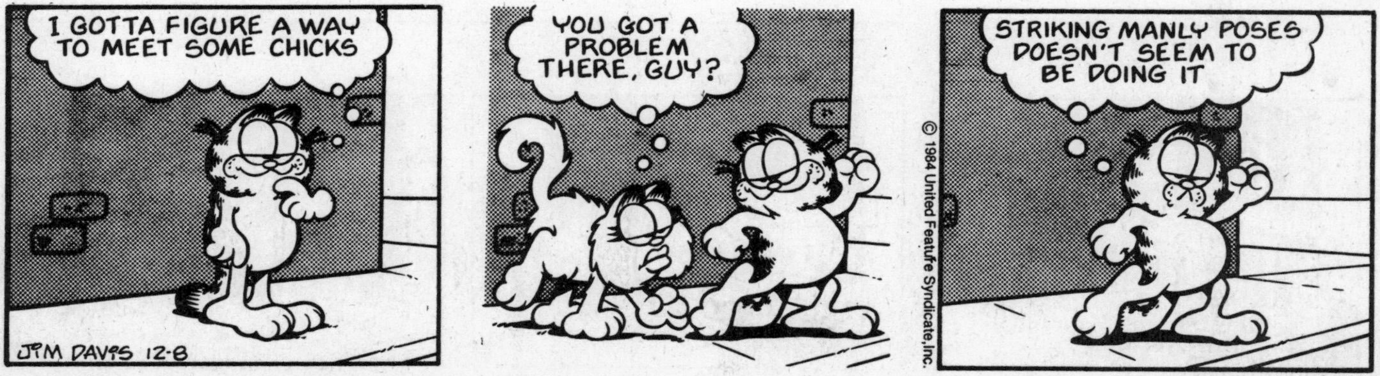
I GOTTA FIGURE A WAY TO MEET SOME CHICKS
JIM DAVIS 12-8
YOU GOT A PROBLEM THERE, GUY?
STRIKING MANLY POSES DOESN'T SEEM TO BE DOING IT

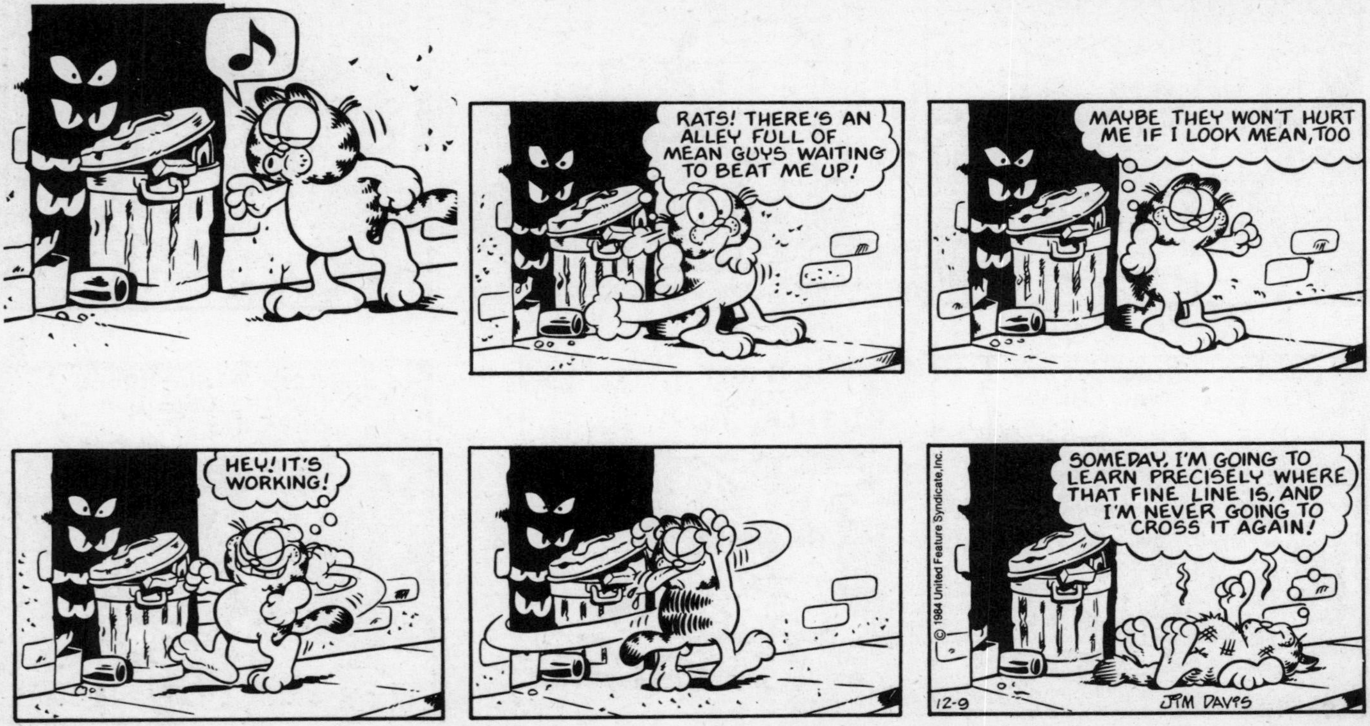

♪
RATS! THERE'S AN ALLEY FULL OF MEAN GUYS WAITING TO BEAT ME UP!
MAYBE THEY WON'T HURT ME IF I LOOK MEAN, TOO
HEY! IT'S WORKING!
SOMEDAY, I'M GOING TO LEARN PRECISELY WHERE THAT FINE LINE IS, AND I'M NEVER GOING TO CROSS IT AGAIN!
© 1984 United Feature Syndicate, Inc.
12-9
JIM DAVIS

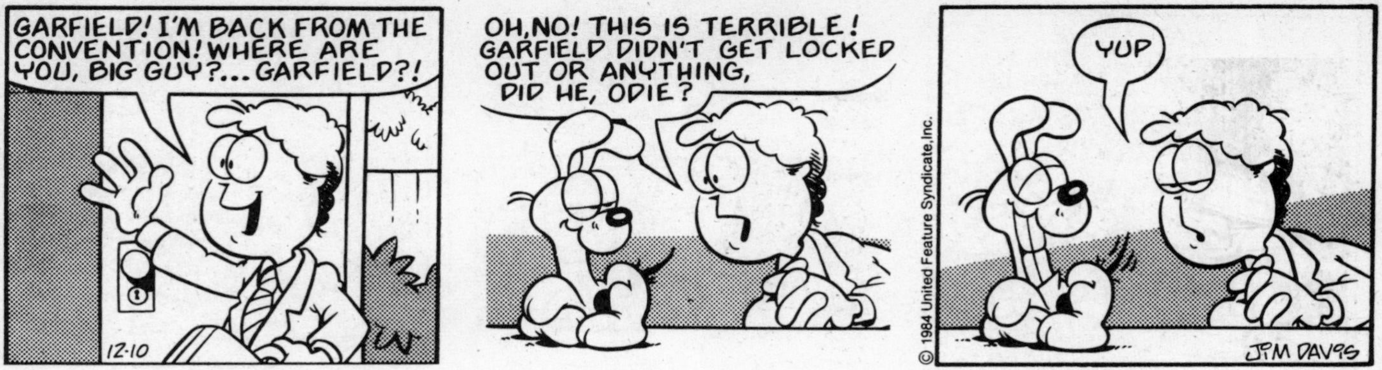
GARFIELD! I'M BACK FROM THE CONVENTION! WHERE ARE YOU, BIG GUY?... GARFIELD?!
12·10
OH, NO! THIS IS TERRIBLE! GARFIELD DIDN'T GET LOCKED OUT OR ANYTHING, DID HE, ODIE?
YUP
© 1984 United Feature Syndicate, Inc.
JIM DAVIS

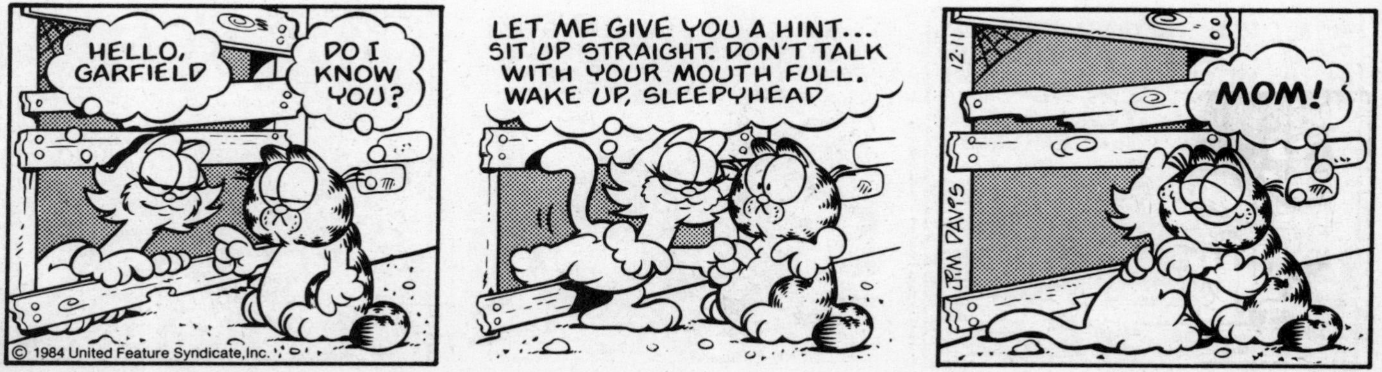
HELLO, GARFIELD
DO I KNOW YOU?
© 1984 United Feature Syndicate, Inc.
LET ME GIVE YOU A HINT... SIT UP STRAIGHT. DON'T TALK WITH YOUR MOUTH FULL. WAKE UP, SLEEPYHEAD
12·11
JIM DAVIS
MOM!

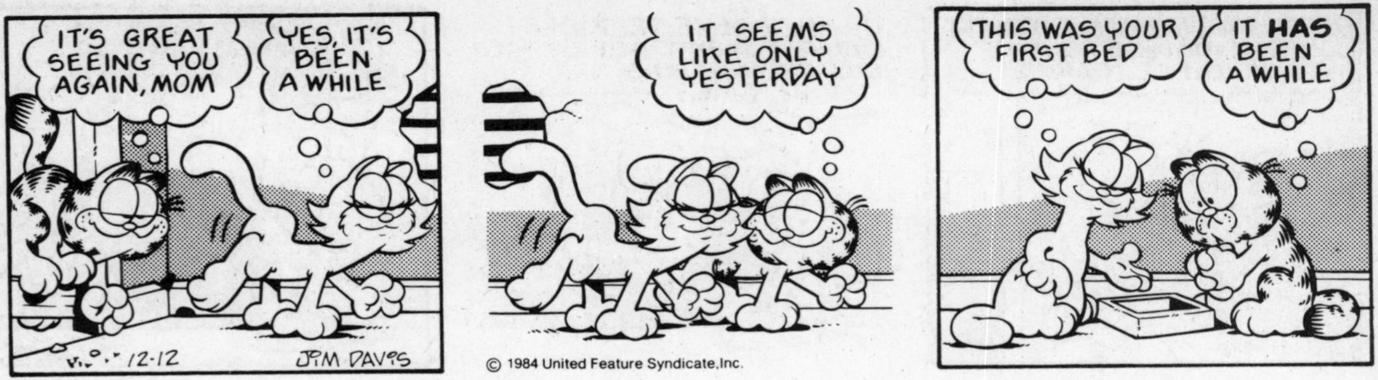
IT'S GREAT SEEING YOU AGAIN, MOM
YES, IT'S BEEN A WHILE
12-12
JIM DAVIS
IT SEEMS LIKE ONLY YESTERDAY
THIS WAS YOUR FIRST BED
IT **HAS** BEEN A WHILE

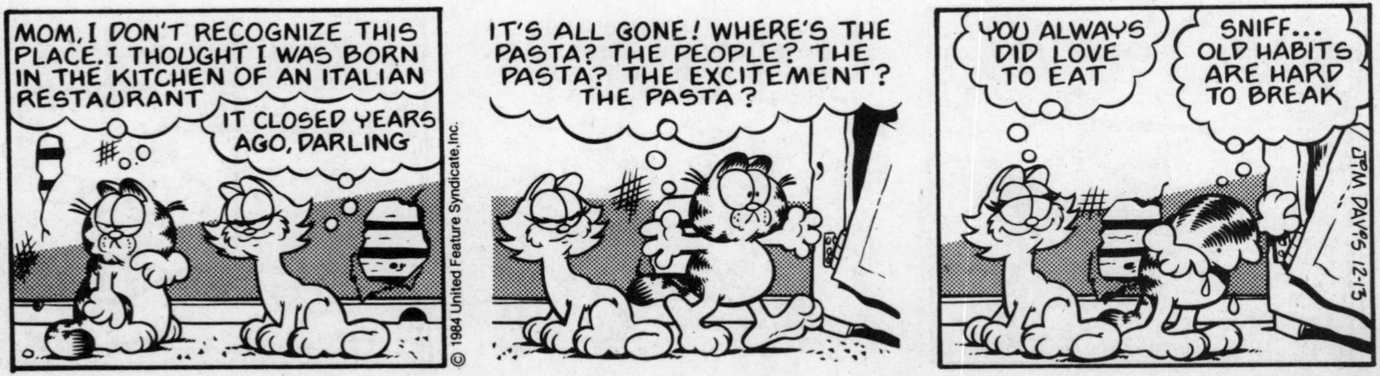
MOM, I DON'T RECOGNIZE THIS PLACE. I THOUGHT I WAS BORN IN THE KITCHEN OF AN ITALIAN RESTAURANT
IT CLOSED YEARS AGO, DARLING
IT'S ALL GONE! WHERE'S THE PASTA? THE PEOPLE? THE PASTA? THE EXCITEMENT? THE PASTA?
YOU ALWAYS DID LOVE TO EAT
SNIFF... OLD HABITS ARE HARD TO BREAK
JIM DAVIS 12-13

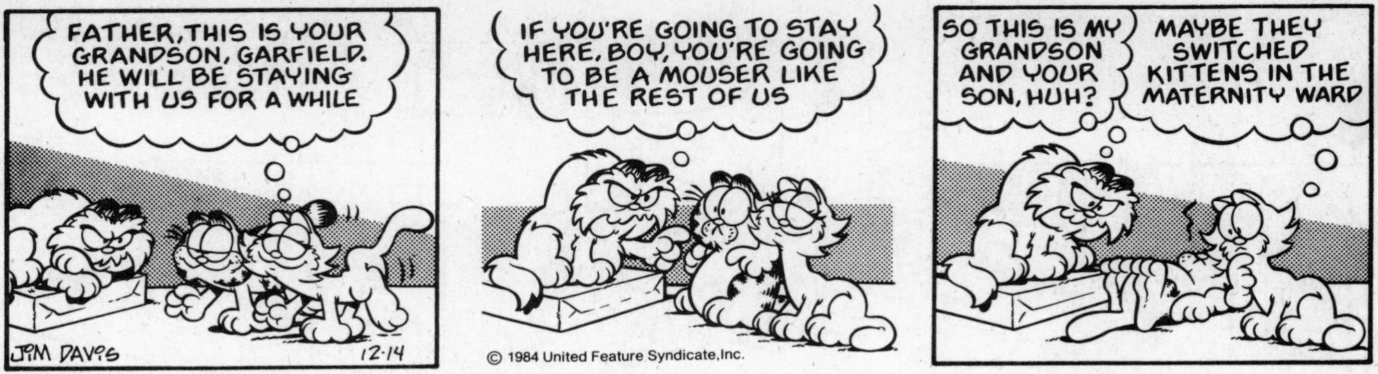
FATHER, THIS IS YOUR GRANDSON, GARFIELD. HE WILL BE STAYING WITH US FOR A WHILE
JIM DAVIS
12-14
IF YOU'RE GOING TO STAY HERE, BOY, YOU'RE GOING TO BE A MOUSER LIKE THE REST OF US
© 1984 United Feature Syndicate, Inc.
SO THIS IS MY GRANDSON AND YOUR SON, HUH?
MAYBE THEY SWITCHED KITTENS IN THE MATERNITY WARD

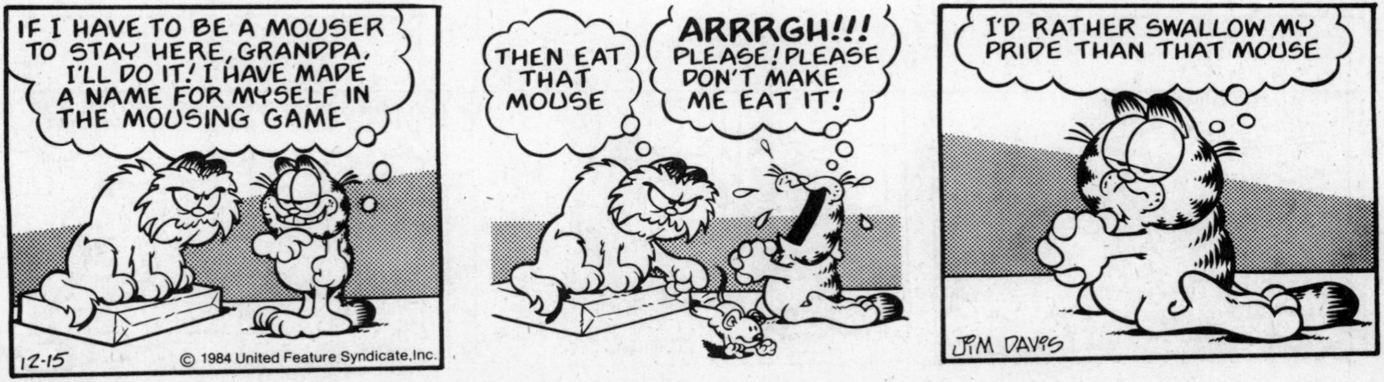
IF I HAVE TO BE A MOUSER TO STAY HERE, GRANDPA, I'LL DO IT! I HAVE MADE A NAME FOR MYSELF IN THE MOUSING GAME
12-15
© 1984 United Feature Syndicate, Inc.
THEN EAT THAT MOUSE
ARRRGH!!! PLEASE! PLEASE DON'T MAKE ME EAT IT!
I'D RATHER SWALLOW MY PRIDE THAN THAT MOUSE
JIM DAVIS

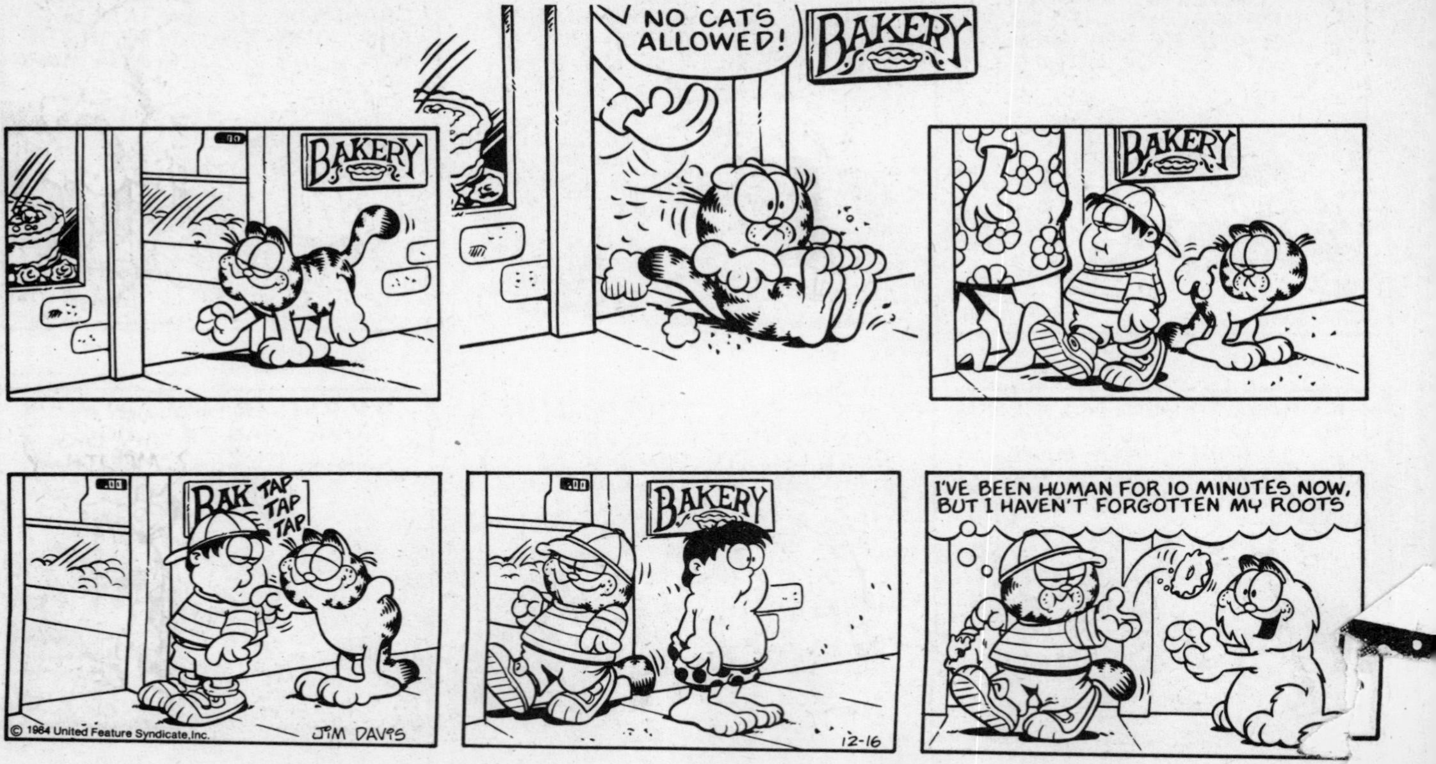
BAKERY
NO CATS ALLOWED!
BAKERY
BAKERY
TAP TAP TAP
BAKERY
I'VE BEEN HUMAN FOR 10 MINUTES NOW, BUT I HAVEN'T FORGOTTEN MY ROOTS
© 1984 United Feature Syndicate, Inc.
JIM DAVIS
12-16

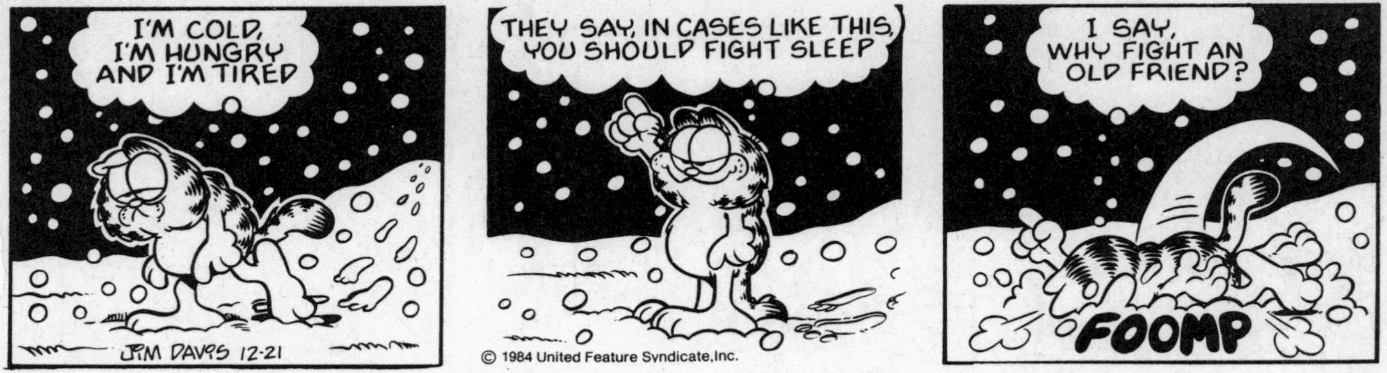
I'M COLD, I'M HUNGRY AND I'M TIRED
JIM DAVIS 12-21
THEY SAY, IN CASES LIKE THIS, YOU SHOULD FIGHT SLEEP
I SAY, WHY FIGHT AN OLD FRIEND?
FOOMP

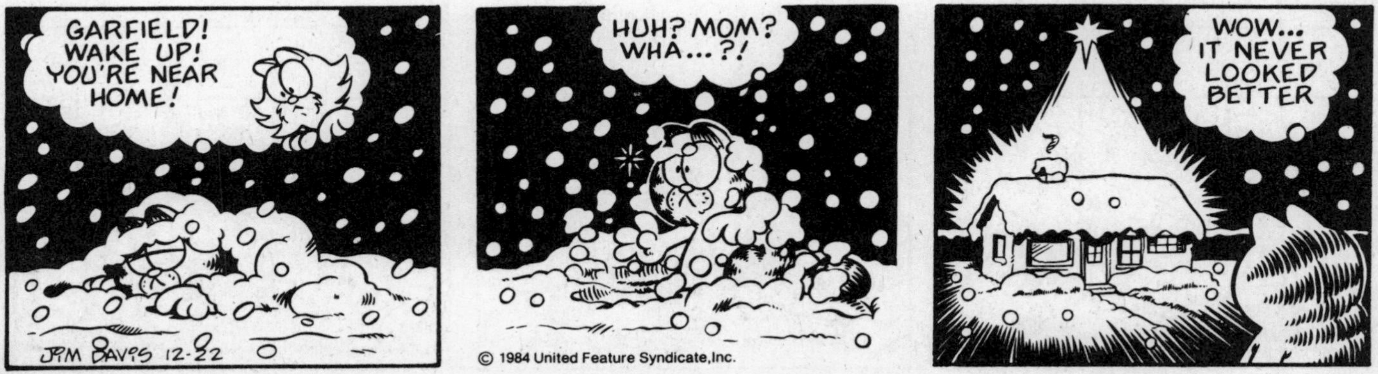
GARFIELD! WAKE UP! YOU'RE NEAR HOME!
JIM DAVIS 12-22
HUH? MOM? WHA...?!
WOW... IT NEVER LOOKED BETTER

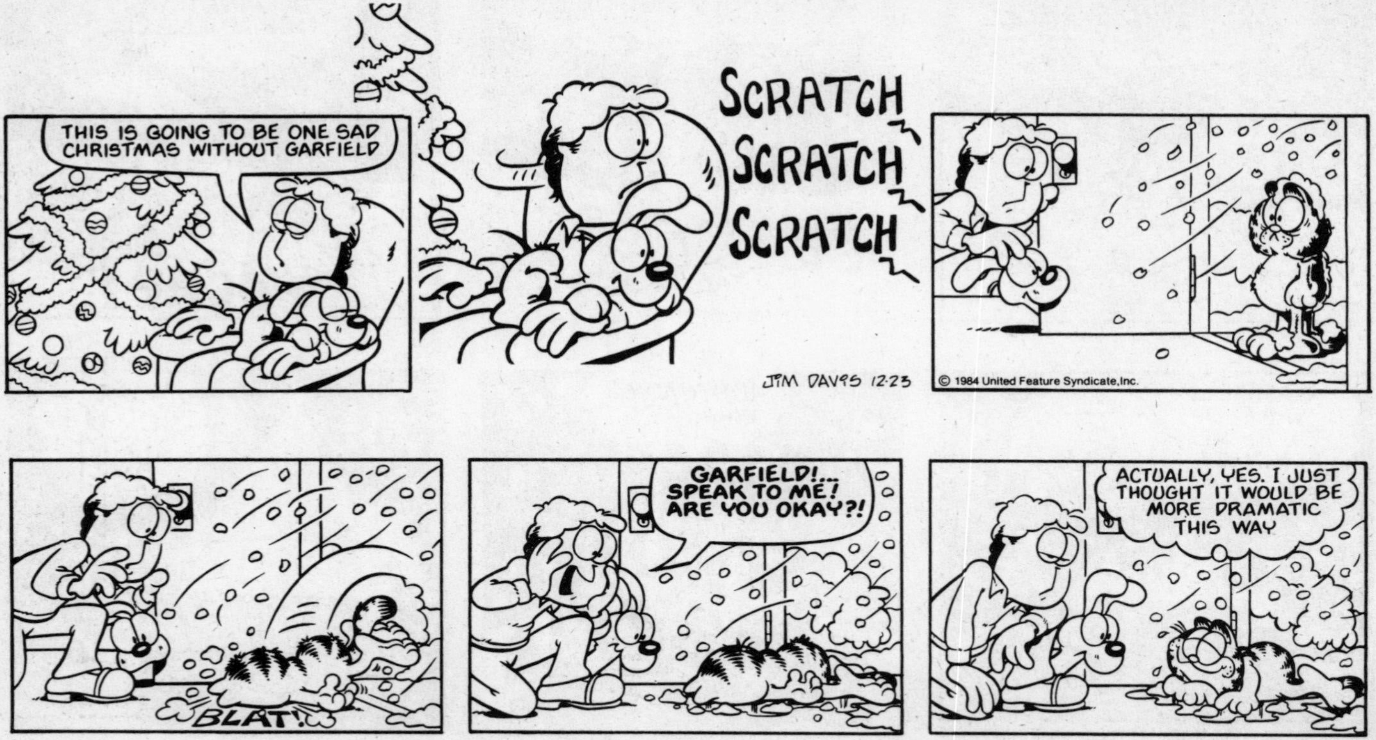
THIS IS GOING TO BE ONE SAD CHRISTMAS WITHOUT GARFIELD
SCRATCH
SCRATCH
SCRATCH
JIM DAVIS 12-23
© 1984 United Feature Syndicate, Inc.
BLAT!
GARFIELD!... SPEAK TO ME! ARE YOU OKAY?!
ACTUALLY, YES. I JUST THOUGHT IT WOULD BE MORE DRAMATIC THIS WAY

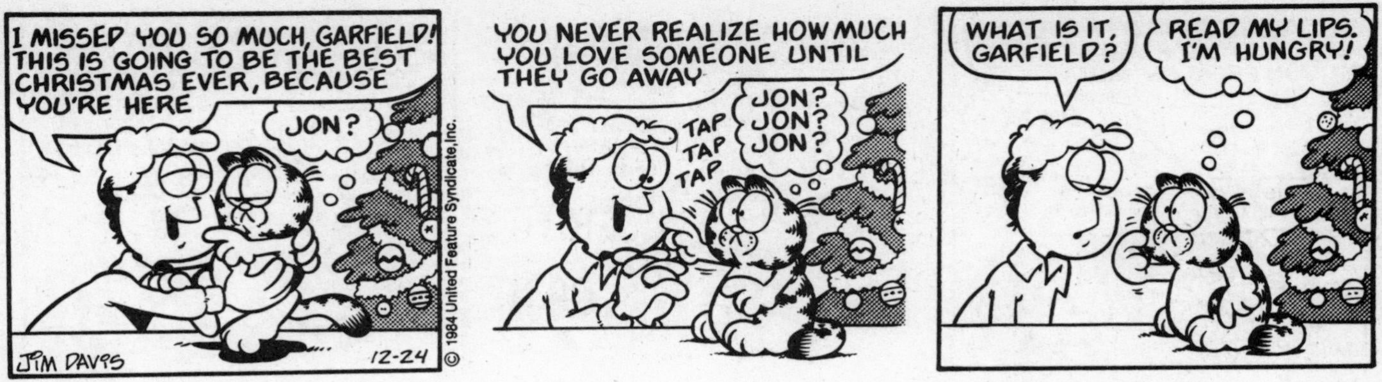
I MISSED YOU SO MUCH, GARFIELD! THIS IS GOING TO BE THE BEST CHRISTMAS EVER, BECAUSE YOU'RE HERE
JON?
JIM DAVIS
12-24
© 1984 United Feature Syndicate,Inc.
YOU NEVER REALIZE HOW MUCH YOU LOVE SOMEONE UNTIL THEY GO AWAY
TAP TAP TAP
JON? JON? JON?
WHAT IS IT, GARFIELD?
READ MY LIPS. I'M HUNGRY!

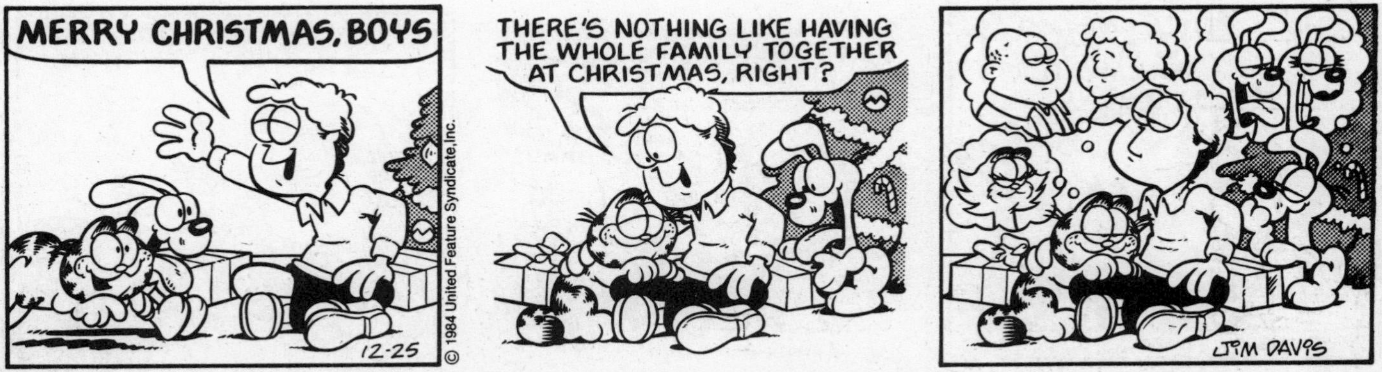
MERRY CHRISTMAS, BOYS
12-25
© 1984 United Feature Syndicate,Inc.
THERE'S NOTHING LIKE HAVING THE WHOLE FAMILY TOGETHER AT CHRISTMAS, RIGHT?
JIM DAVIS

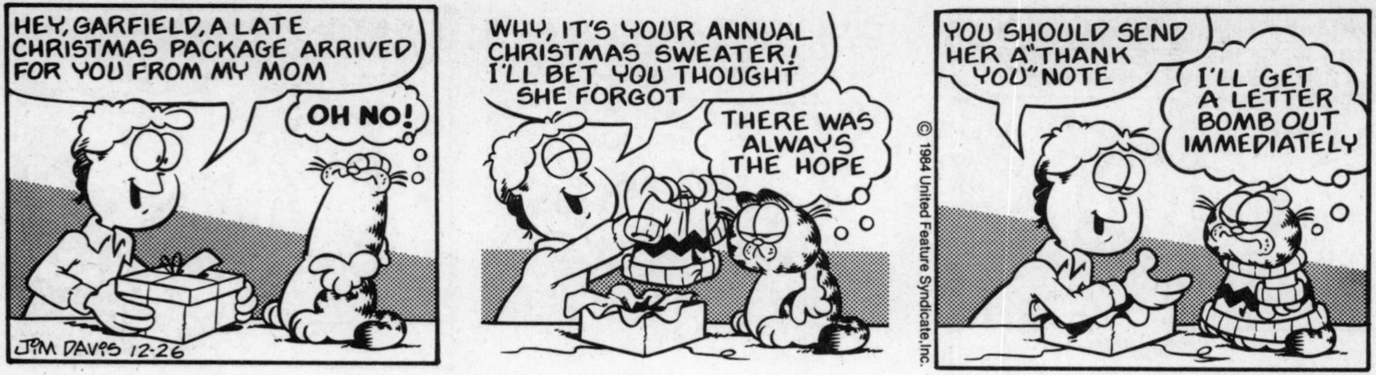
HEY, GARFIELD, A LATE CHRISTMAS PACKAGE ARRIVED FOR YOU FROM MY MOM
OH NO!
JIM DAVIS 12-26
WHY, IT'S YOUR ANNUAL CHRISTMAS SWEATER! I'LL BET YOU THOUGHT SHE FORGOT
THERE WAS ALWAYS THE HOPE
© 1984 United Feature Syndicate, Inc.
YOU SHOULD SEND HER A "THANK YOU" NOTE
I'LL GET A LETTER BOMB OUT IMMEDIATELY

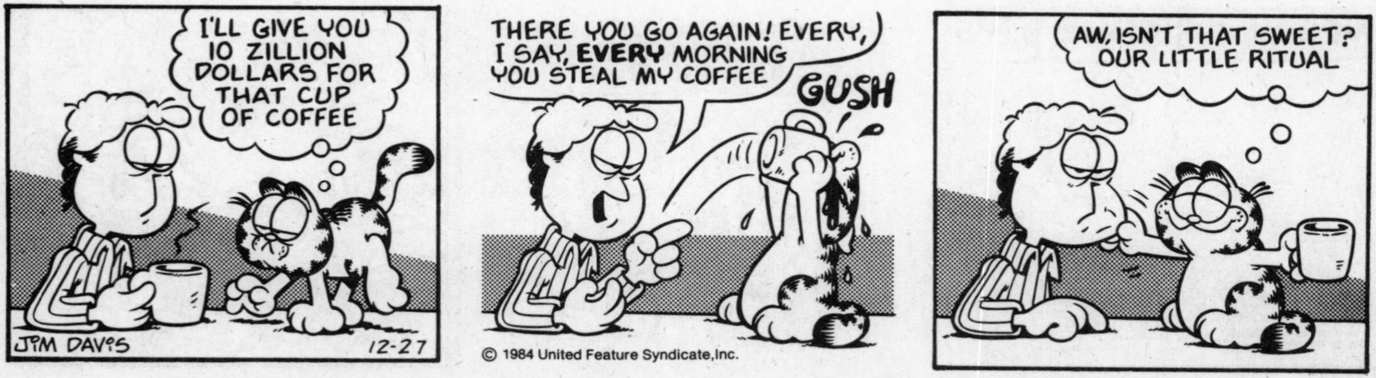
I'LL GIVE YOU 10 ZILLION DOLLARS FOR THAT CUP OF COFFEE
JIM DAVIS
12-27
THERE YOU GO AGAIN! EVERY, I SAY, **EVERY** MORNING YOU STEAL MY COFFEE
GUSH
© 1984 United Feature Syndicate, Inc.
AW, ISN'T THAT SWEET? OUR LITTLE RITUAL

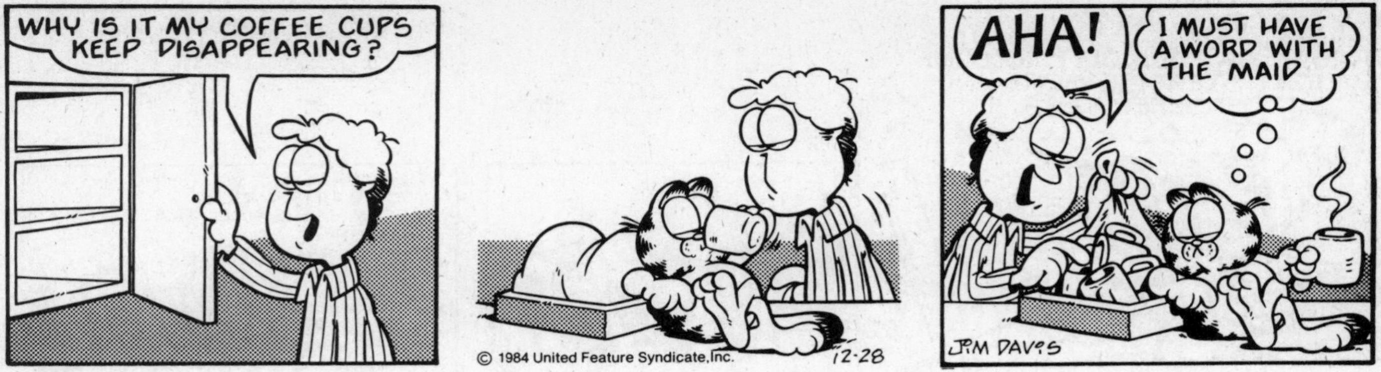
WHY IS IT MY COFFEE CUPS KEEP DISAPPEARING?
AHA!
I MUST HAVE A WORD WITH THE MAID
12-28
JIM DAVIS

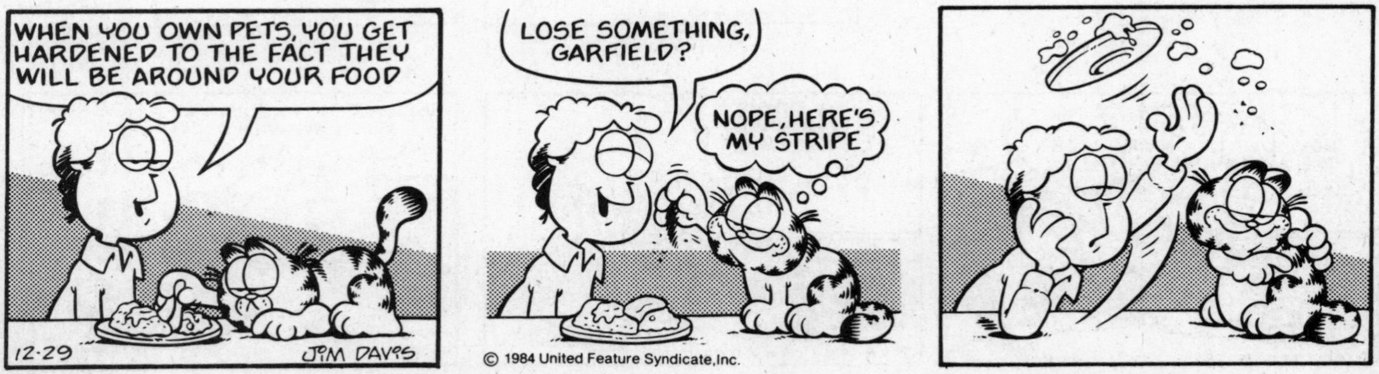
WHEN YOU OWN PETS, YOU GET HARDENED TO THE FACT THEY WILL BE AROUND YOUR FOOD
12-29
JIM DAVIS
LOSE SOMETHING, GARFIELD?
NOPE, HERE'S MY STRIPE

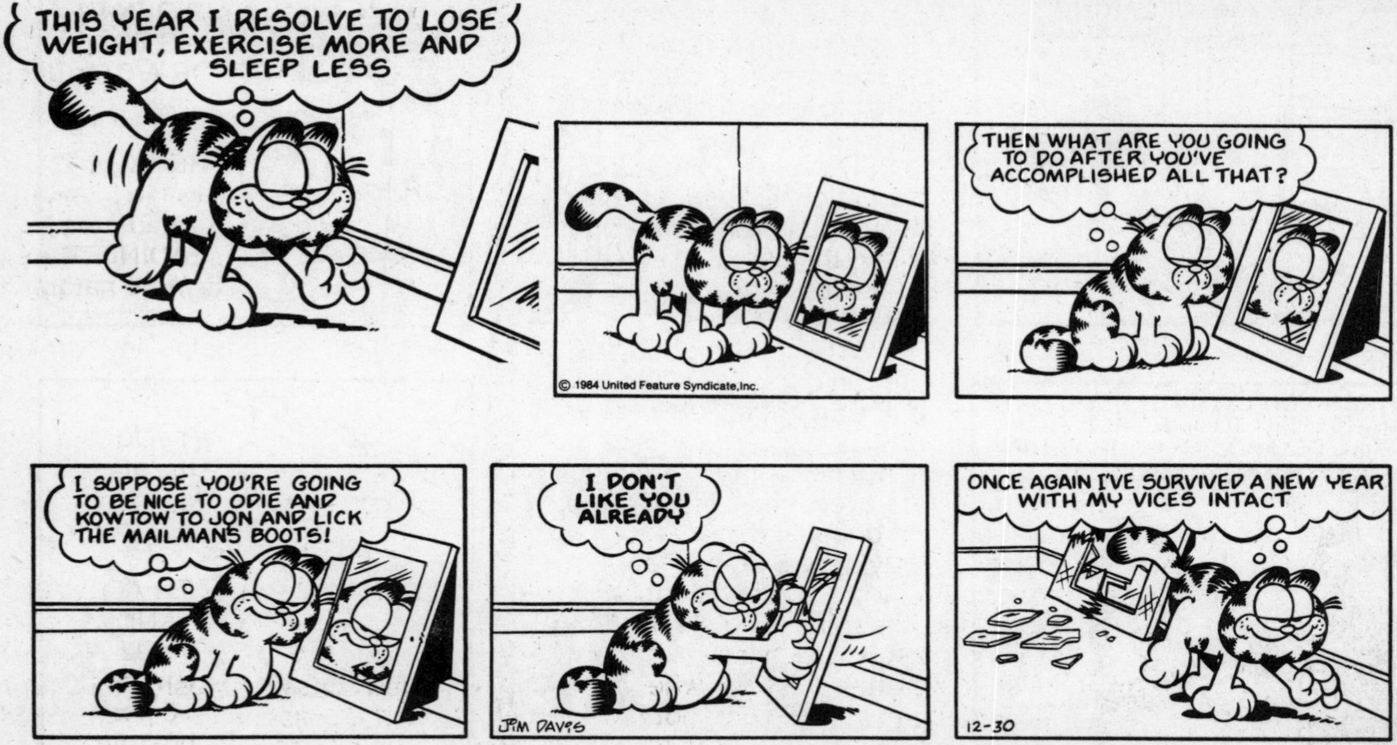
THIS YEAR I RESOLVE TO LOSE WEIGHT, EXERCISE MORE AND SLEEP LESS
© 1984 United Feature Syndicate,Inc.
THEN WHAT ARE YOU GOING TO DO AFTER YOU'VE ACCOMPLISHED ALL THAT?
I SUPPOSE YOU'RE GOING TO BE NICE TO ODIE AND KOWTOW TO JON AND LICK THE MAILMAN'S BOOTS!
I DON'T LIKE YOU ALREADY
JIM DAVIS
ONCE AGAIN I'VE SURVIVED A NEW YEAR WITH MY VICES INTACT
12-30

TO THE PROSPECTIVE CARTOONIST

Al Capp once said, "You must have two qualities to be a successful cartoonist. First, it helps to have been dropped on your head as a small child. Second, you must have no desire, talent, or ability to do anything useful in life."

While his may seem a somewhat flippant observation, it nevertheless reflects how seriously cartoonists take themselves and their art. If I had only one piece of advice to give a prospective cartoonist, it would be:

HAVE FUN WITH YOUR FEATURE!

If you have fun doing it, people have fun reading it. Your enthusiasm comes through.

Most hopeful cartoonists labor their creations. An overworked, heavily laden cartoon strip or panel doesn't have the charm or witty appeal of a simply drawn, simply stated sentiment. All a cartoonist has to do is hold a mirror to life and show it back with a humorous twist. More often than not, when a reader laughs at a strip, it's not because it's funny, but because it's true.

PREPARE YOURSELF...

HERE ARE SOME GENERAL RECOMMENDATIONS TO LAY THE GROUNDWORK FOR A CAREER IN CARTOONING...

1) GET A GOOD LIBERAL ARTS EDUCATION. Enroll in journalism courses, as well as art classes. DO A LOT OF READING. The better read you are, the more natural depth your writing will have. Learn to draw realistically. It helps any cartooning style.

2) SEEK AN ART OR JOURNALISM RELATED JOB. This affords you the luxury of having food to eat until you make a go of it in cartooning.

3) EXPERIMENT WITH ALL KINDS OF ART EQUIPMENT AND MATERIALS. I use India ink and a #2 Windsor-Newton sable brush. For lettering, I use a Speedball B-6 point. I work on Strathmore 3-ply bristol board, smooth surface.

4) STAY MOTIVATED. Try to get your work published in a school paper, local newspaper or local publication. Many cartoonists give up the quest a year or two before they would have become marketable.

5) PREPARE NEAT, THOUGHTFUL SUBMISSIONS TO THE SYNDICATE EDITORS. Send only your best work and be prepared to submit it many times. I could wallpaper a bedroom with *my* rejection slips.

Again, don't forget to keep it simple and have fun. Oh, yes . . . a little luck along the way never hurts.

JIM DAVIS

GOOD LUCK!

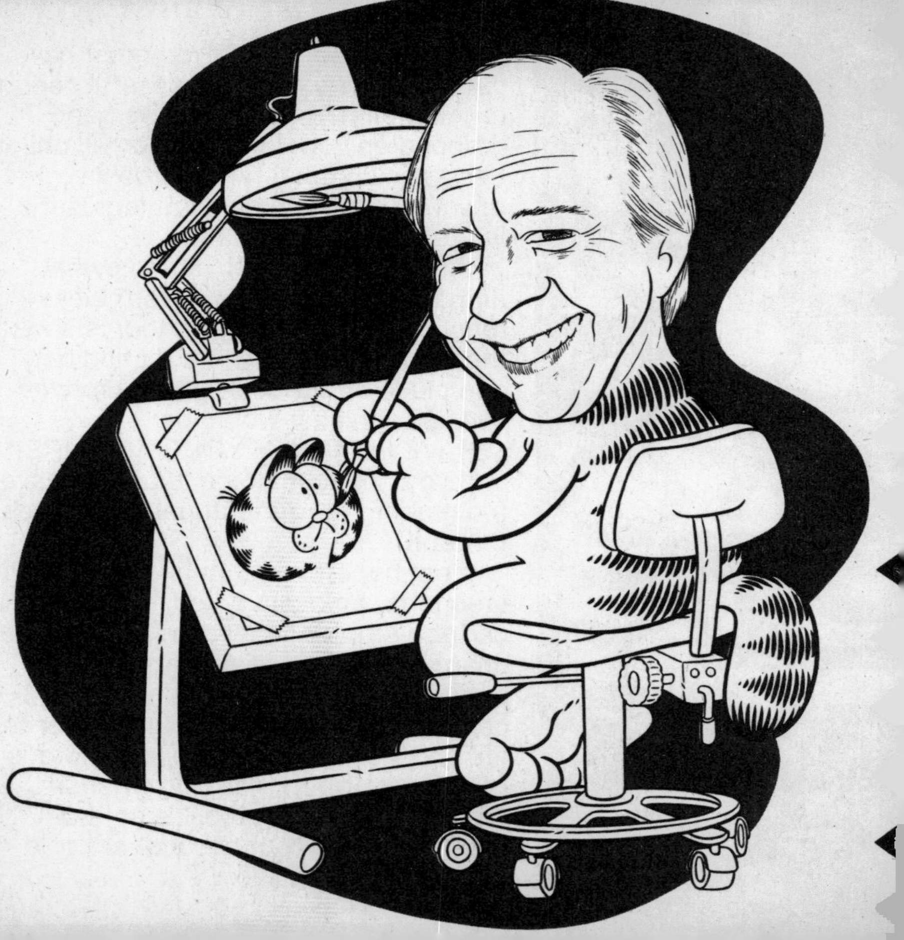

Garfield out to lunch

BY: JIM DAVIS

EARLIEST KNOWN GARFIELD!

Presented here for the first time anywhere is the earliest known Garfield strip.

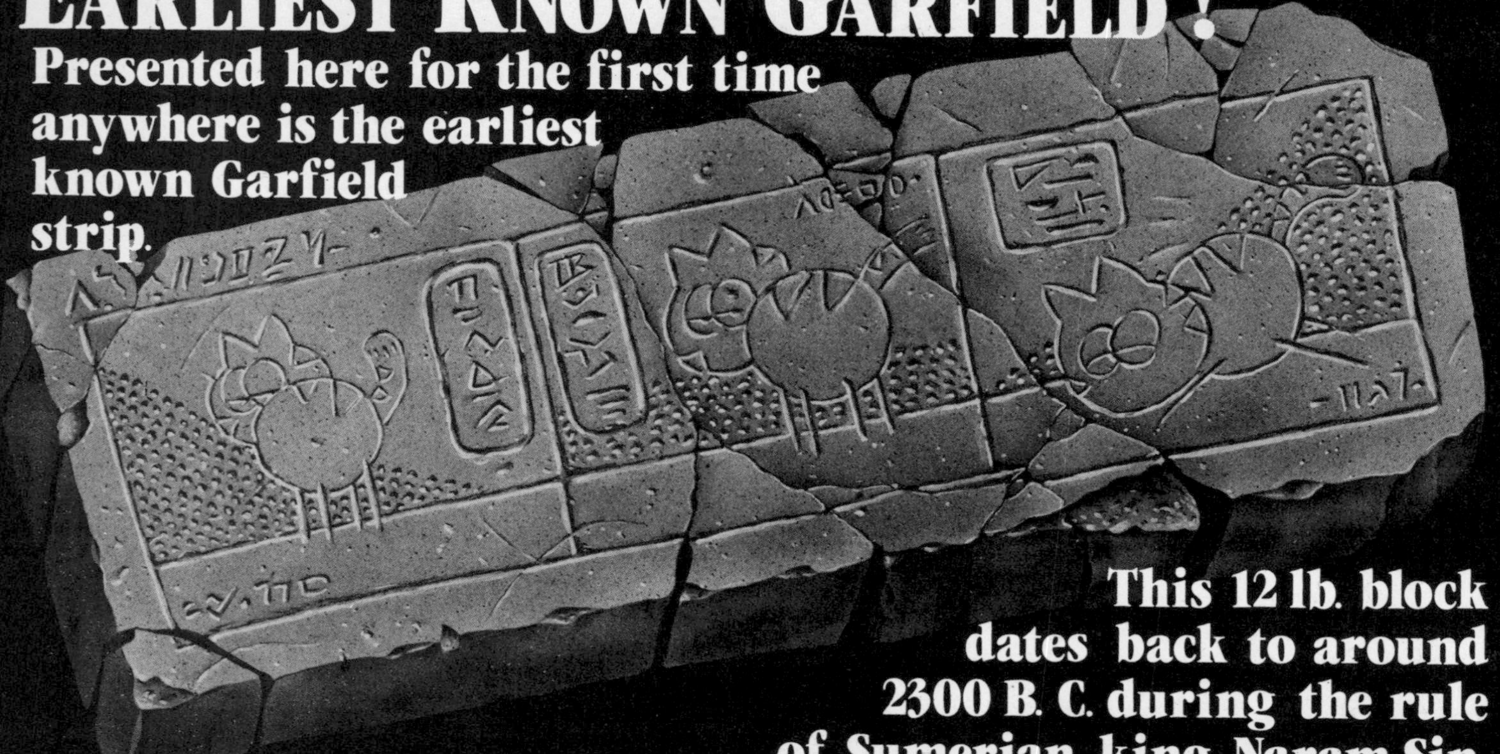

This 12 lb. block dates back to around 2300 B. C. during the rule of Sumerian king Naram-Sin. Jim Davis' name appears in lower right.

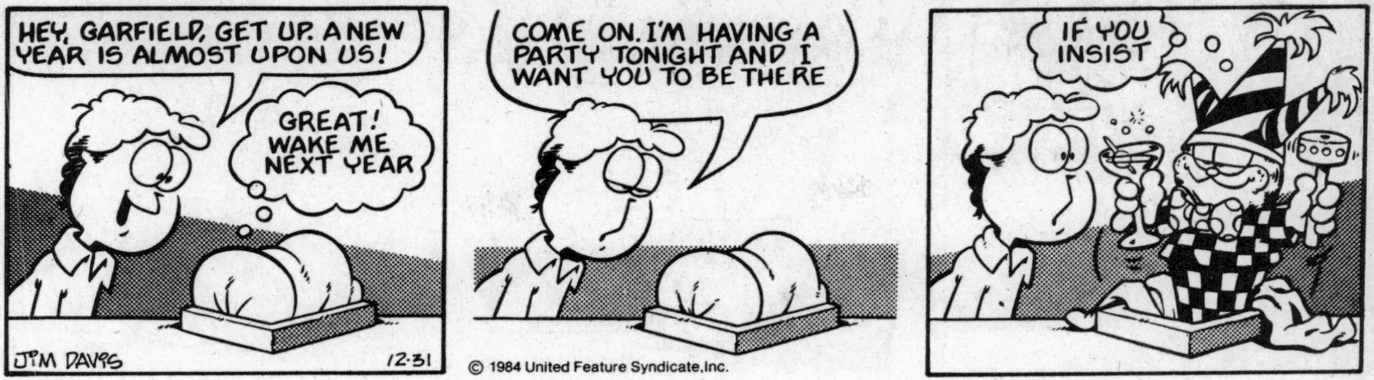
HEY, GARFIELD, GET UP. A NEW YEAR IS ALMOST UPON US!
GREAT! WAKE ME NEXT YEAR
JIM DAVIS
12-31
COME ON. I'M HAVING A PARTY TONIGHT AND I WANT YOU TO BE THERE
IF YOU INSIST

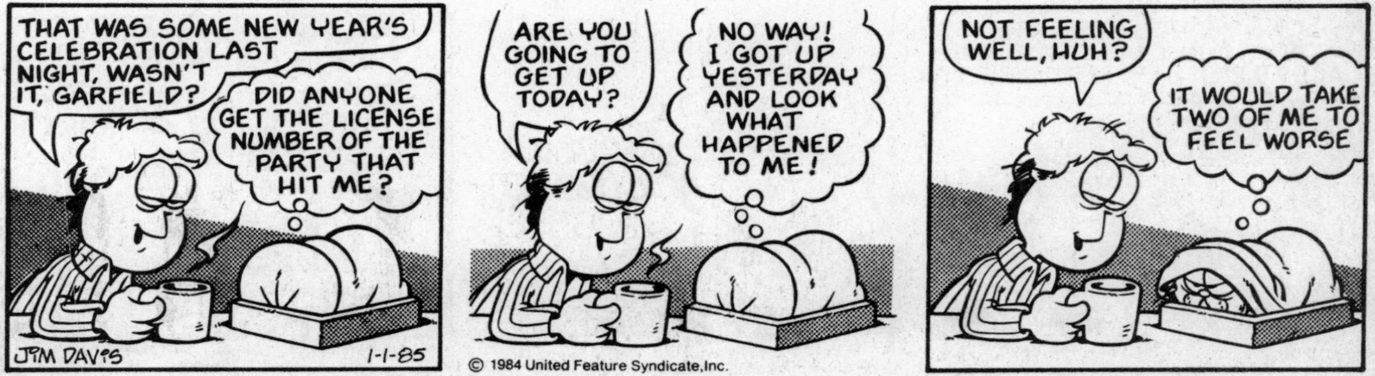
THAT WAS SOME NEW YEAR'S CELEBRATION LAST NIGHT, WASN'T IT, GARFIELD?
DID ANYONE GET THE LICENSE NUMBER OF THE PARTY THAT HIT ME?
JIM DAVIS
1-1-85
ARE YOU GOING TO GET UP TODAY?
NO WAY! I GOT UP YESTERDAY AND LOOK WHAT HAPPENED TO ME!
NOT FEELING WELL, HUH?
IT WOULD TAKE TWO OF ME TO FEEL WORSE

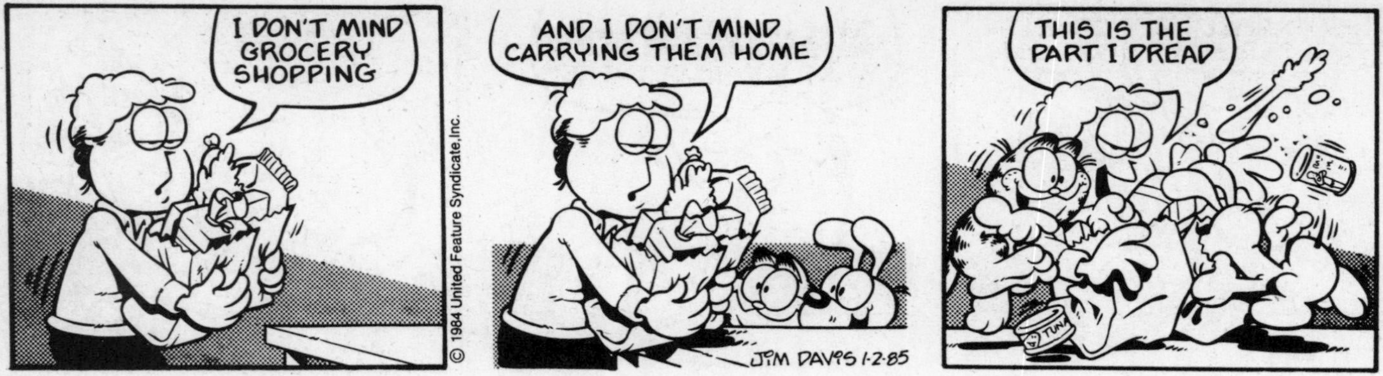
I DON'T MIND GROCERY SHOPPING
AND I DON'T MIND CARRYING THEM HOME
THIS IS THE PART I DREAD
TUNA
© 1984 United Feature Syndicate, Inc.
JIM DAVIS 1-2-85

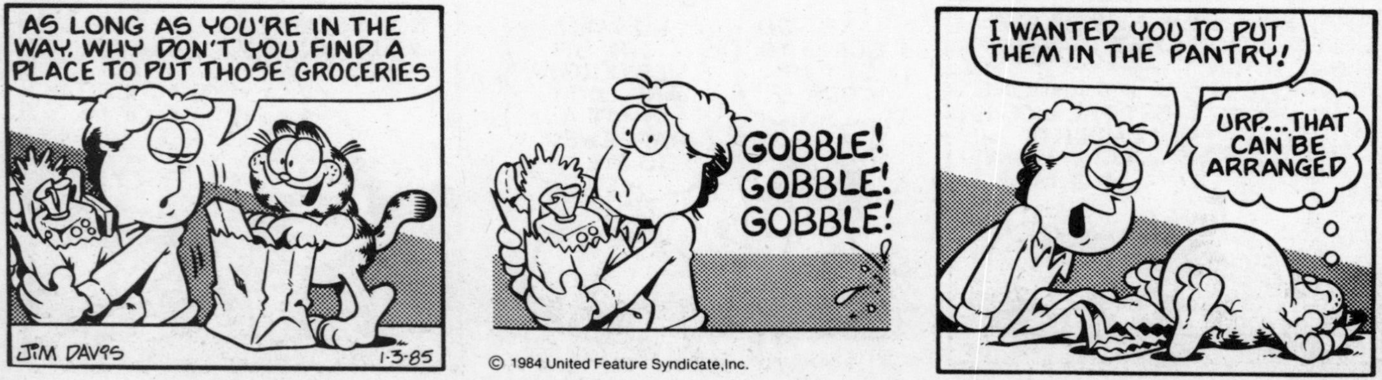
AS LONG AS YOU'RE IN THE WAY, WHY DON'T YOU FIND A PLACE TO PUT THOSE GROCERIES
JIM DAVIS
1-3-85
GOBBLE! GOBBLE! GOBBLE!
I WANTED YOU TO PUT THEM IN THE PANTRY!
URP...THAT CAN BE ARRANGED
© 1984 United Feature Syndicate, Inc.

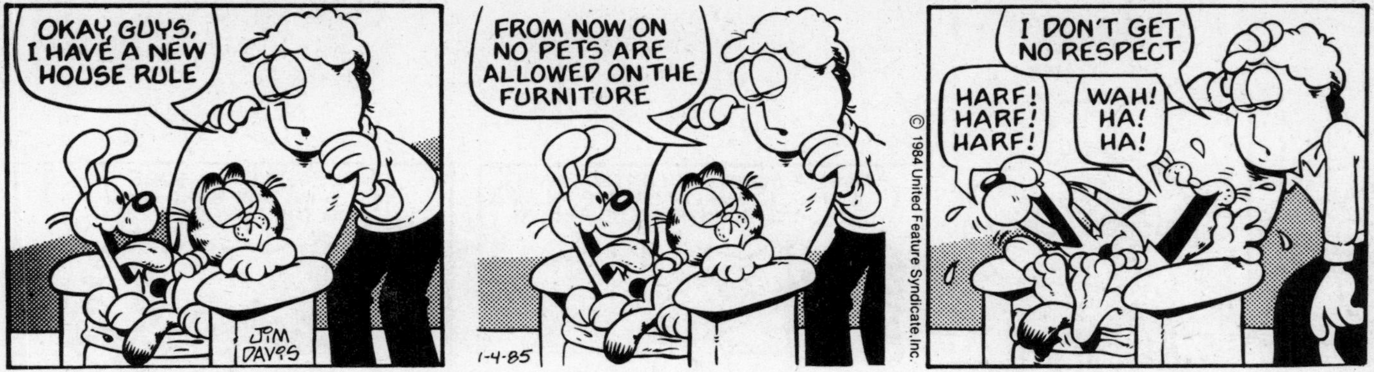
OKAY, GUYS, I HAVE A NEW HOUSE RULE
JIM DAVIS
FROM NOW ON NO PETS ARE ALLOWED ON THE FURNITURE
1-4-85
I DON'T GET NO RESPECT
HARF! HARF! HARF!
WAH! HA! HA!
© 1984 United Feature Syndicate,Inc.

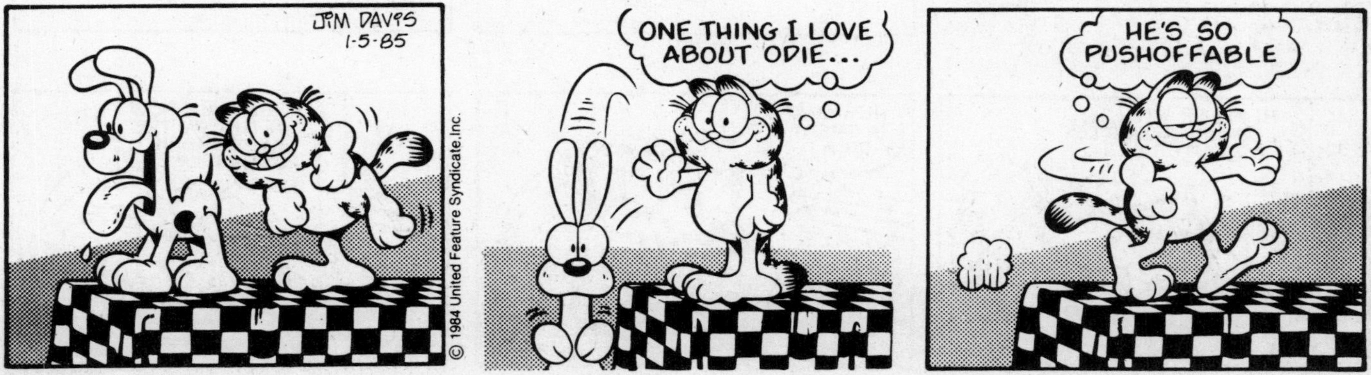
JIM DAVIS
1-5-85
© 1984 United Feature Syndicate,Inc.
ONE THING I LOVE ABOUT ODIE...
HE'S SO PUSHOFFABLE

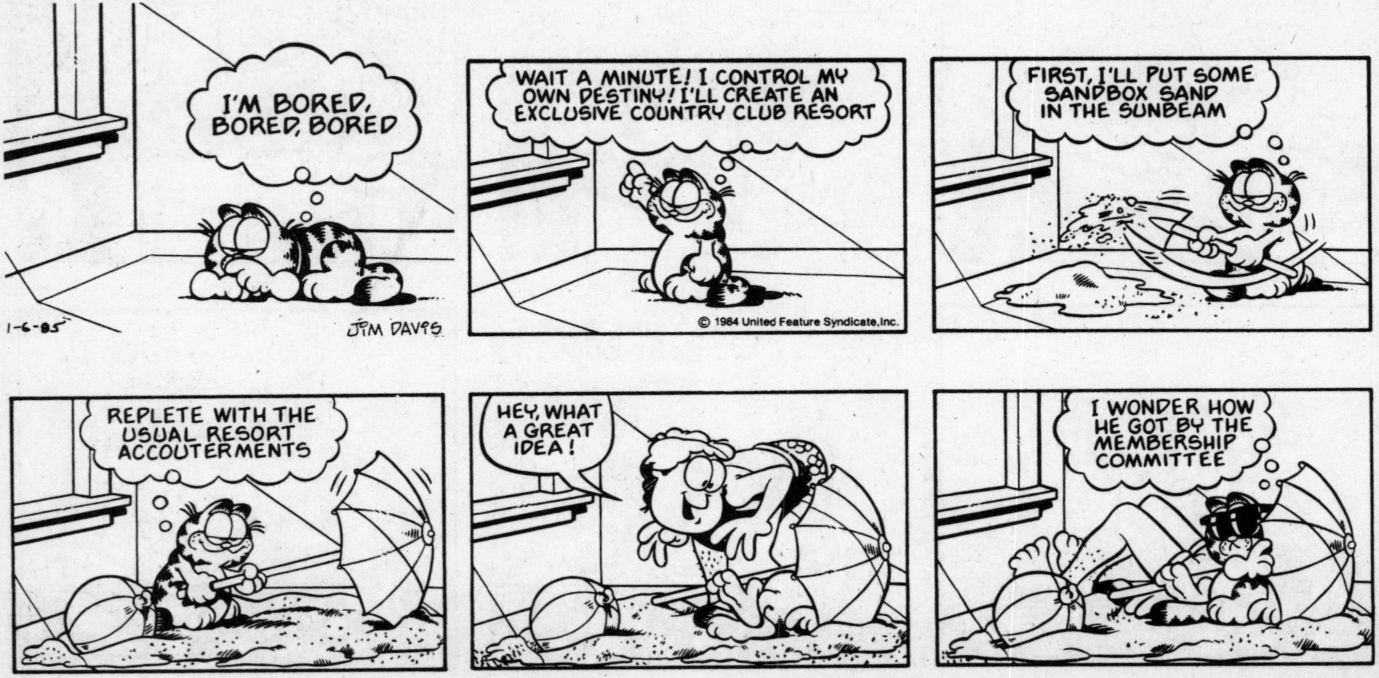
I'M BORED, BORED, BORED
1-6-85
JIM DAVIS
WAIT A MINUTE! I CONTROL MY OWN DESTINY! I'LL CREATE AN EXCLUSIVE COUNTRY CLUB RESORT
© 1984 United Feature Syndicate, Inc.
FIRST, I'LL PUT SOME SANDBOX SAND IN THE SUNBEAM
REPLETE WITH THE USUAL RESORT ACCOUTERMENTS
HEY, WHAT A GREAT IDEA!
I WONDER HOW HE GOT BY THE MEMBERSHIP COMMITTEE

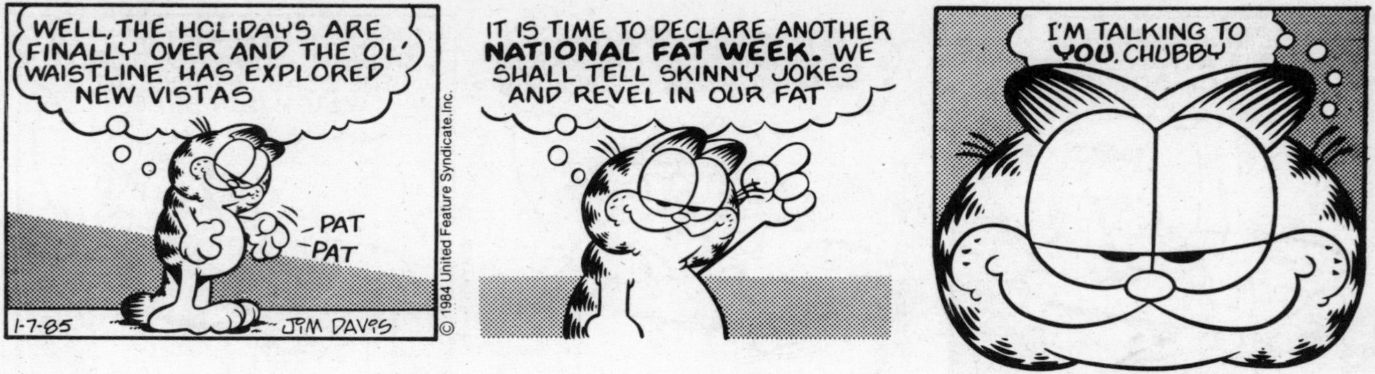
WELL, THE HOLIDAYS ARE FINALLY OVER AND THE OL' WAISTLINE HAS EXPLORED NEW VISTAS
PAT
PAT
1-7-85
JIM DAVIS
© 1984 United Feature Syndicate, Inc.
IT IS TIME TO DECLARE ANOTHER **NATIONAL FAT WEEK.** WE SHALL TELL SKINNY JOKES AND REVEL IN OUR FAT
I'M TALKING TO **YOU**, CHUBBY

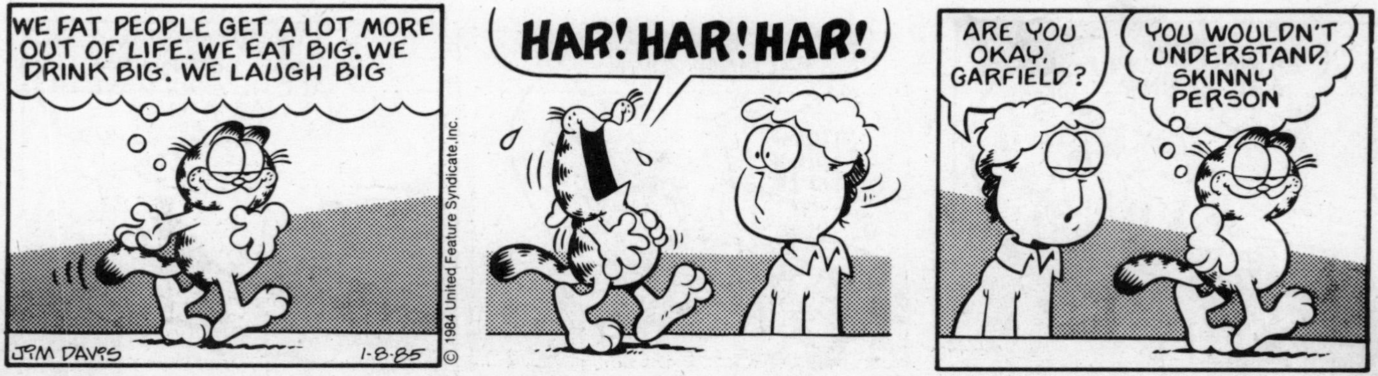
WE FAT PEOPLE GET A LOT MORE OUT OF LIFE. WE EAT BIG. WE DRINK BIG. WE LAUGH BIG
JIM DAVIS
1-8-85
© 1984 United Feature Syndicate, Inc.
HAR! HAR! HAR!
ARE YOU OKAY, GARFIELD?
YOU WOULDN'T UNDERSTAND, SKINNY PERSON

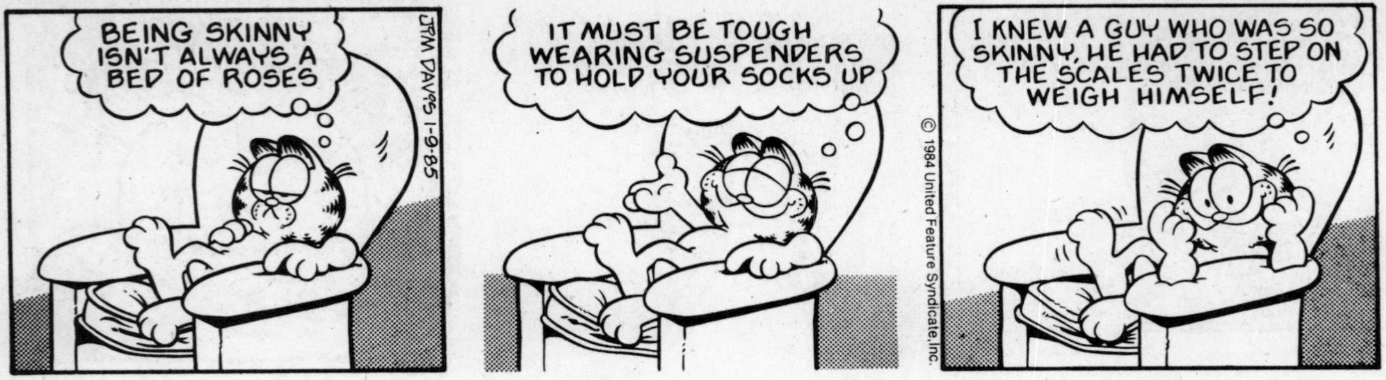
BEING SKINNY ISN'T ALWAYS A BED OF ROSES
JIM DAVIS 1-9-85
IT MUST BE TOUGH WEARING SUSPENDERS TO HOLD YOUR SOCKS UP
© 1984 United Feature Syndicate,Inc.
I KNEW A GUY WHO WAS SO SKINNY, HE HAD TO STEP ON THE SCALES TWICE TO WEIGH HIMSELF!

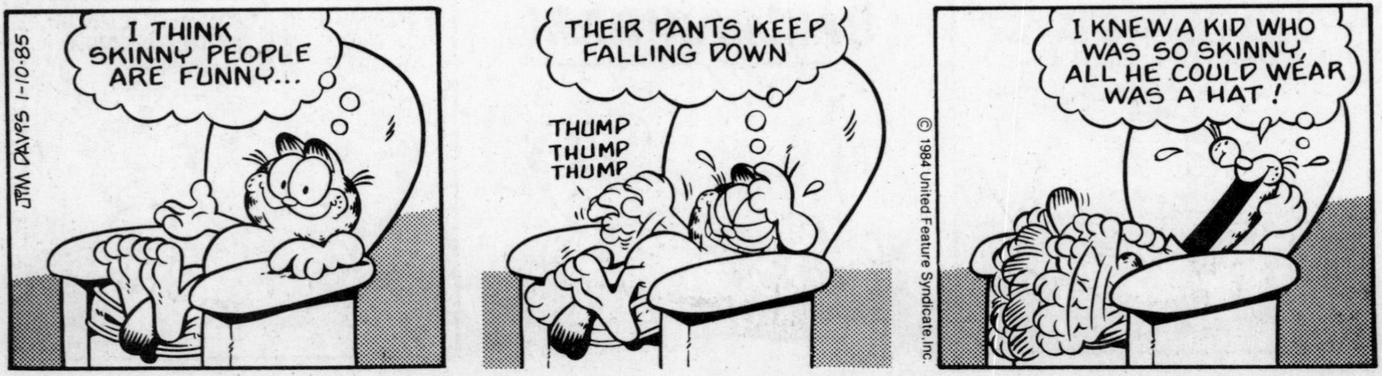
JIM DAVIS 1-10-85
I THINK SKINNY PEOPLE ARE FUNNY...
THEIR PANTS KEEP FALLING DOWN
THUMP THUMP THUMP
© 1984 United Feature Syndicate,Inc.
I KNEW A KID WHO WAS SO SKINNY, ALL HE COULD WEAR WAS A HAT!

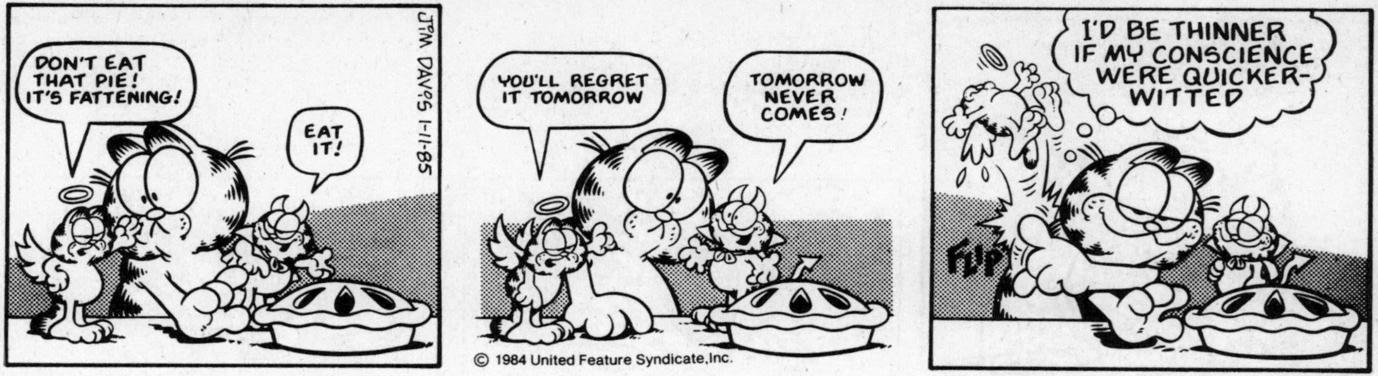
JIM DAVIS 1-11-85
DON'T EAT THAT PIE! IT'S FATTENING!
EAT IT!
YOU'LL REGRET IT TOMORROW
TOMORROW NEVER COMES!
I'D BE THINNER IF MY CONSCIENCE WERE QUICKER-WITTED
FLIP

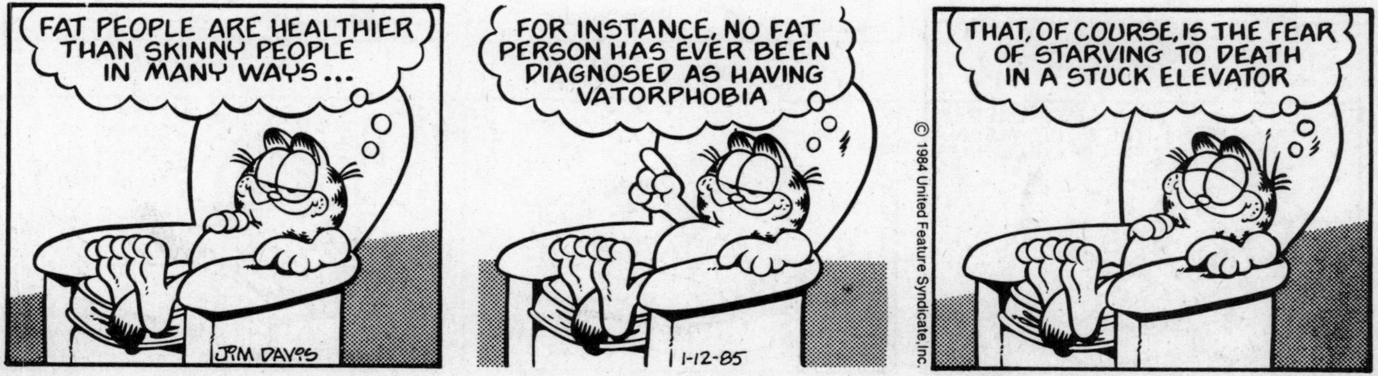
FAT PEOPLE ARE HEALTHIER THAN SKINNY PEOPLE IN MANY WAYS...
JIM DAVIS
FOR INSTANCE, NO FAT PERSON HAS EVER BEEN DIAGNOSED AS HAVING VATORPHOBIA
1-12-85
THAT, OF COURSE, IS THE FEAR OF STARVING TO DEATH IN A STUCK ELEVATOR

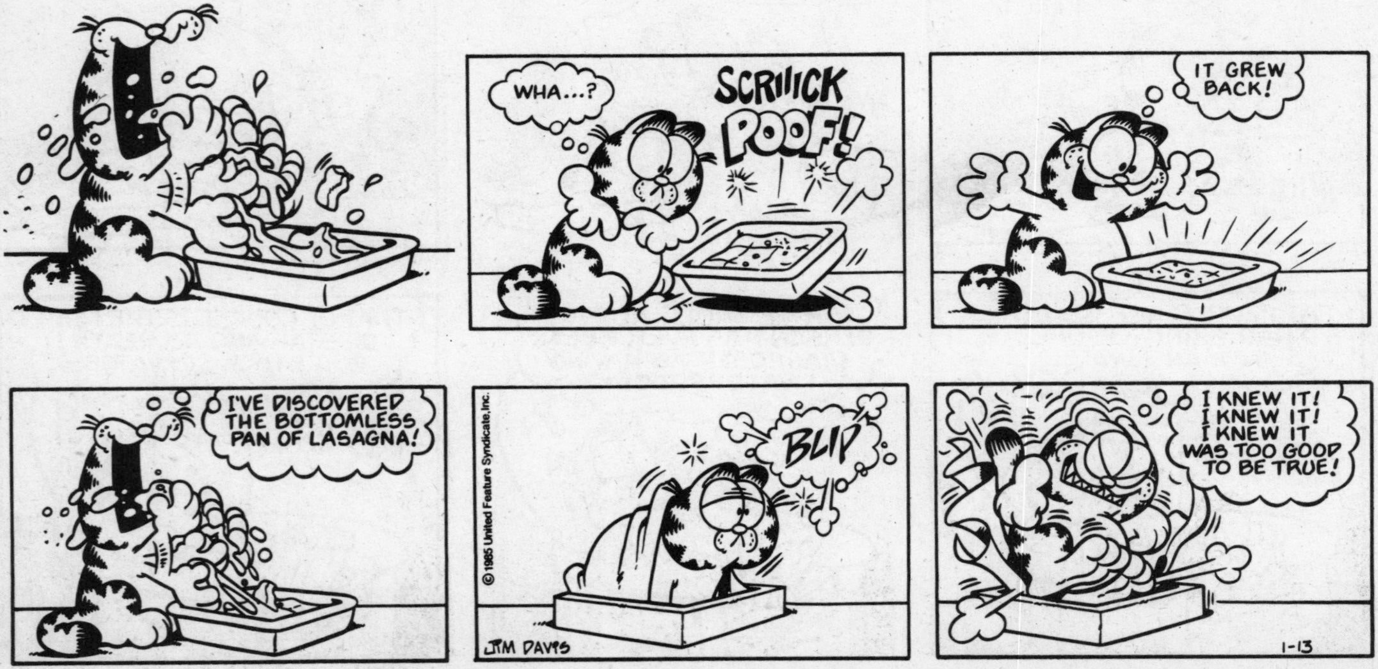
WHA...?
SCRIIICK
POOF!
IT GREW BACK!
I'VE DISCOVERED THE BOTTOMLESS PAN OF LASAGNA!
© 1985 United Feature Syndicate, Inc.
BLIP
I KNEW IT! I KNEW IT! I KNEW IT WAS TOO GOOD TO BE TRUE!
JIM DAVIS
1-13

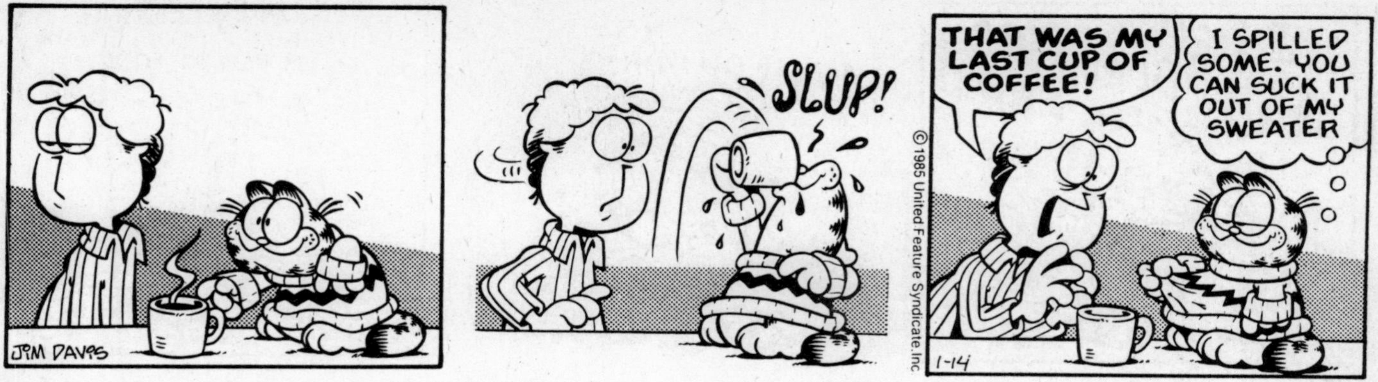
JIM DAVIS
SLUP!
© 1985 United Feature Syndicate, Inc.
THAT WAS MY LAST CUP OF COFFEE!
I SPILLED SOME. YOU CAN SUCK IT OUT OF MY SWEATER
1-14

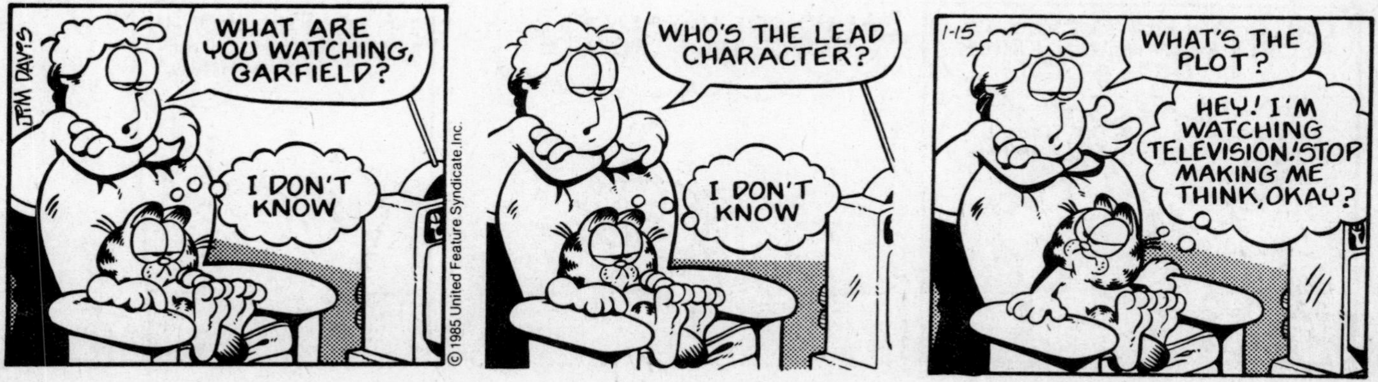
JIM DAVIS
WHAT ARE YOU WATCHING, GARFIELD?
I DON'T KNOW
© 1985 United Feature Syndicate, Inc.
WHO'S THE LEAD CHARACTER?
I DON'T KNOW
1-15
WHAT'S THE PLOT?
HEY! I'M WATCHING TELEVISION! STOP MAKING ME THINK, OKAY?

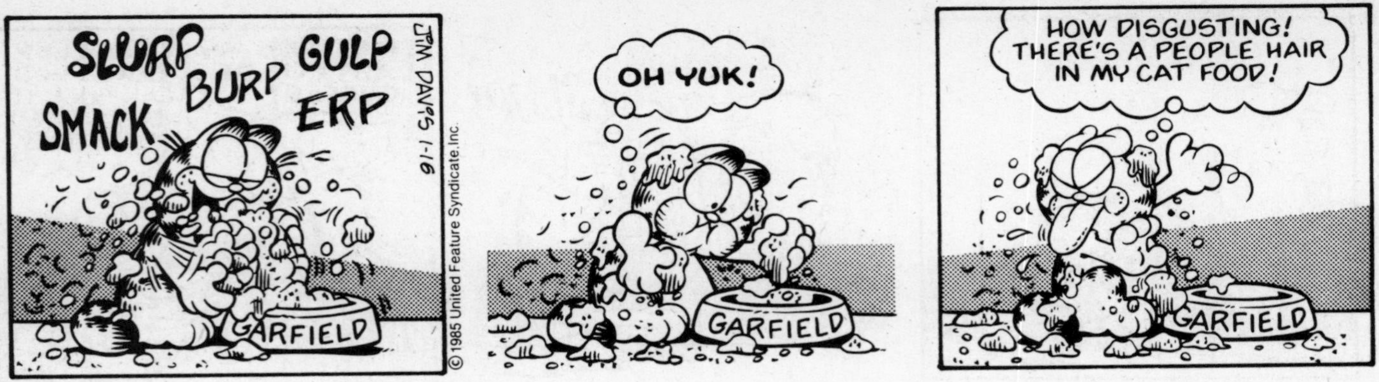
SLURP
BURP
GULP
SMACK
ERP
JIM DAVIS 1-16
© 1985 United Feature Syndicate, Inc.
GARFIELD
OH YUK!
GARFIELD
HOW DISGUSTING!
THERE'S A PEOPLE HAIR
IN MY CAT FOOD!
GARFIELD

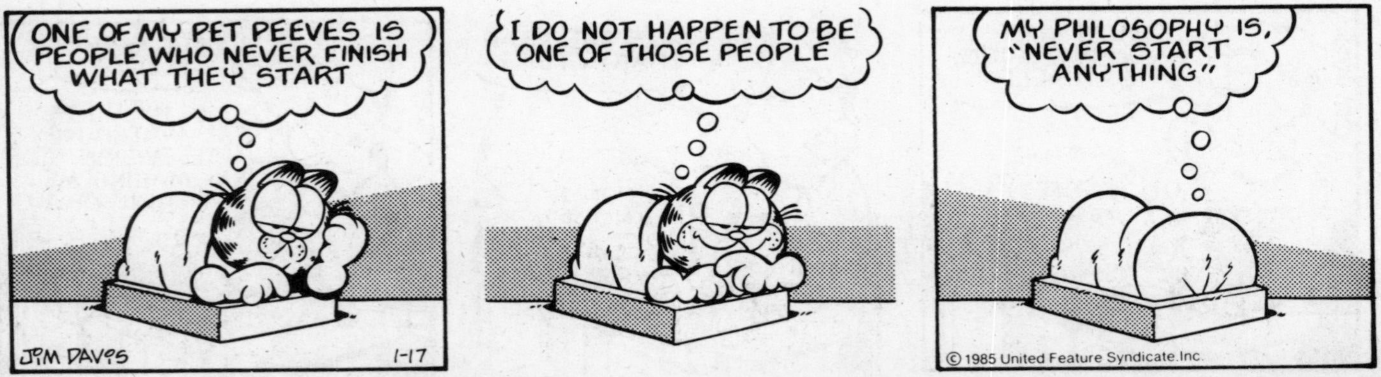
ONE OF MY PET PEEVES IS
PEOPLE WHO NEVER FINISH
WHAT THEY START
JIM DAVIS
1-17
I DO NOT HAPPEN TO BE
ONE OF THOSE PEOPLE
MY PHILOSOPHY IS,
"NEVER START
ANYTHING"
© 1985 United Feature Syndicate, Inc.

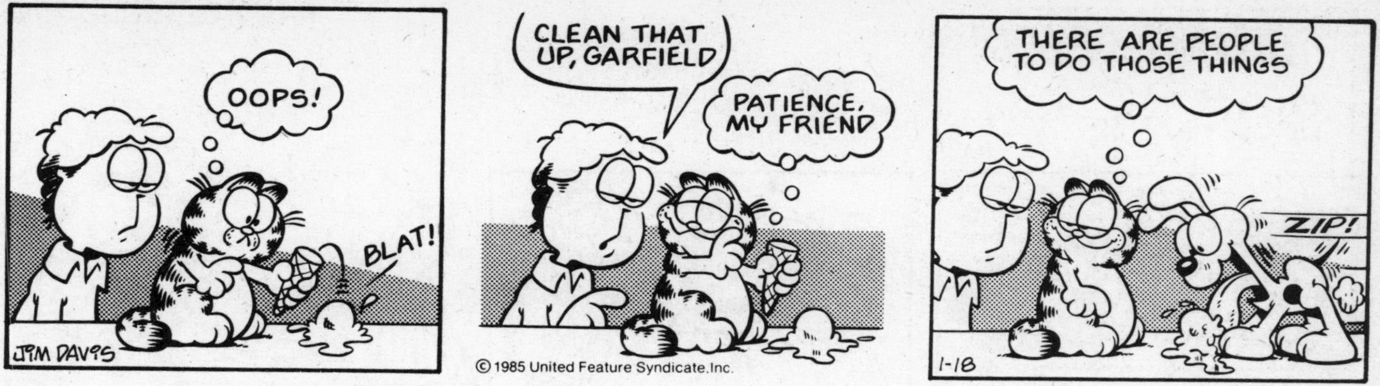
OOPS!
BLAT!
JIM DAVIS
CLEAN THAT UP, GARFIELD
PATIENCE, MY FRIEND
THERE ARE PEOPLE TO DO THOSE THINGS
ZIP!
1-18

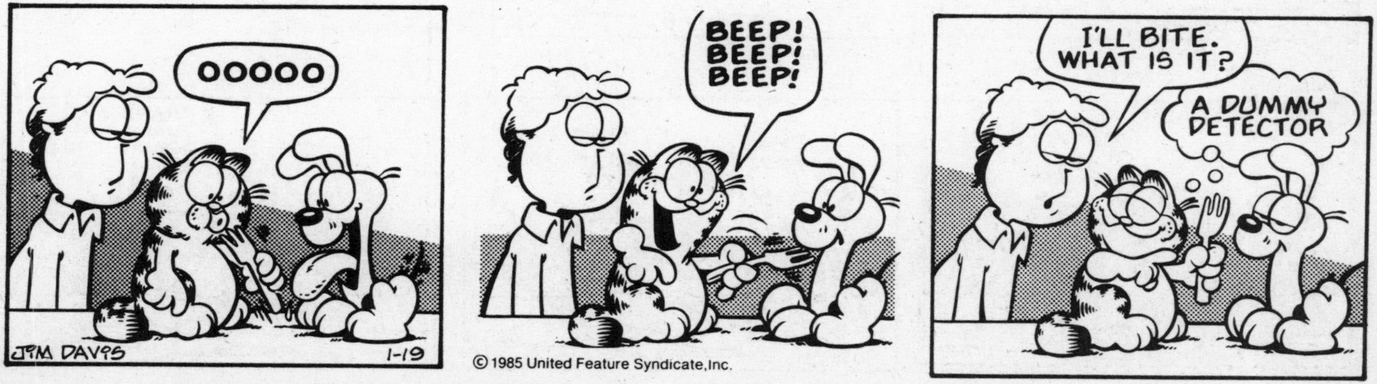
OOOOO
JIM DAVIS
1-19
BEEP! BEEP! BEEP!
I'LL BITE. WHAT IS IT?
A DUMMY DETECTOR

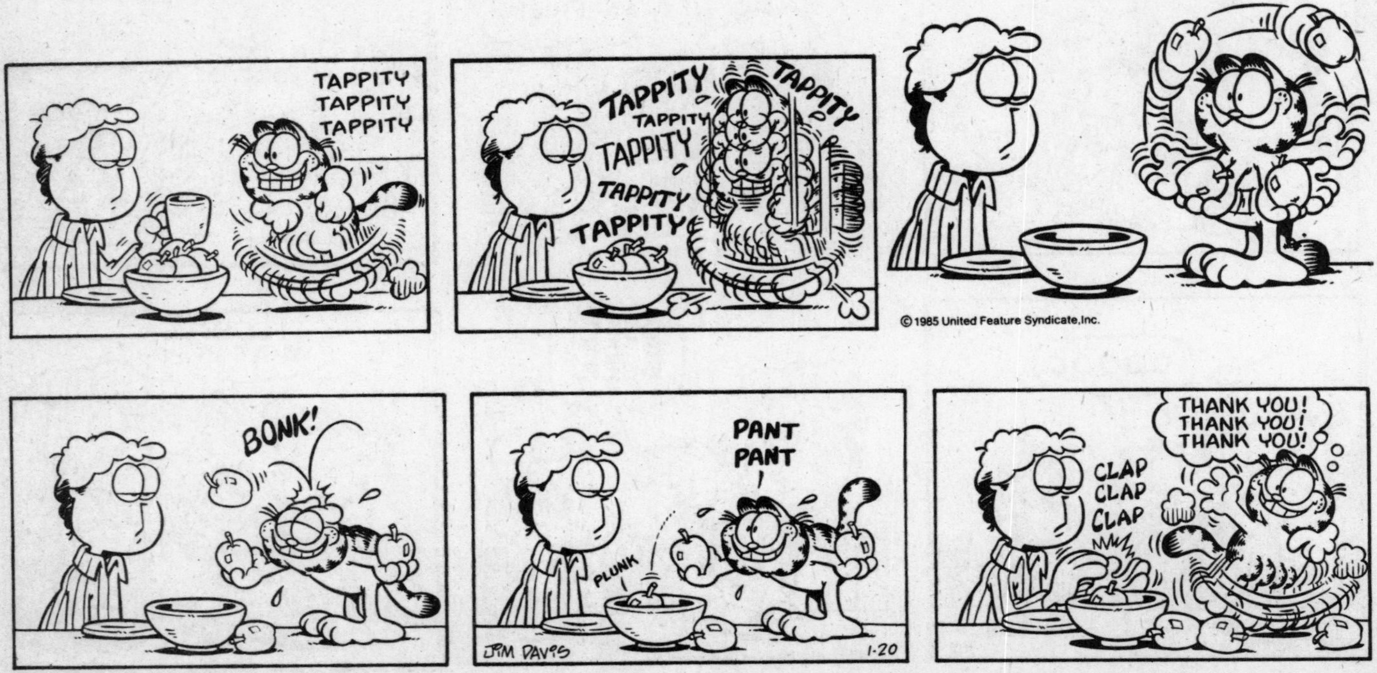
TAPPITY
TAPPITY
TAPPITY
TAPPITY
TAPPITY
TAPPITY
TAPPITY
TAPPITY
TAPPITY
TAPPITY
BONK!
PANT
PANT
PLUNK
JIM DAVIS
1-20
CLAP
CLAP
CLAP
THANK YOU!
THANK YOU!
THANK YOU!

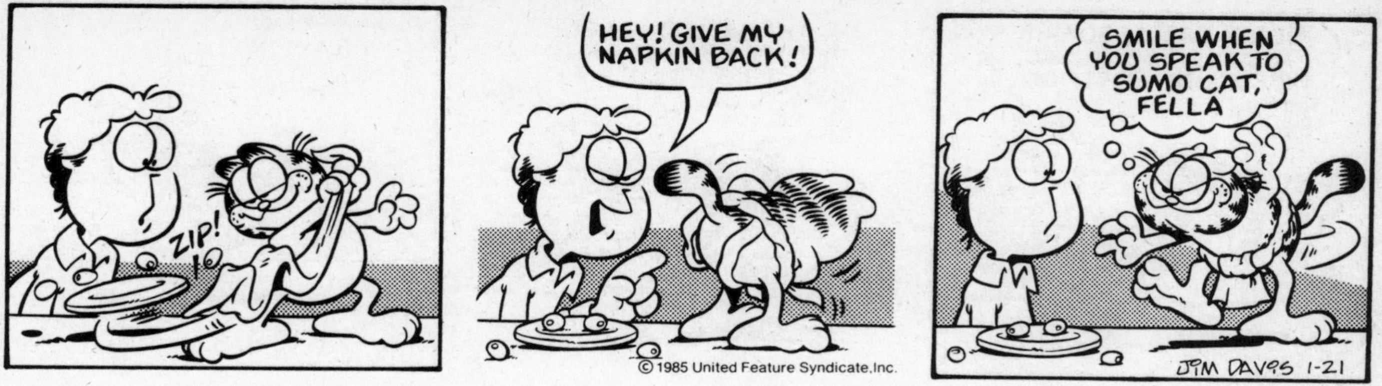
ZIP!
HEY! GIVE MY NAPKIN BACK!
SMILE WHEN YOU SPEAK TO SUMO CAT, FELLA
JIM DAVIS 1-21

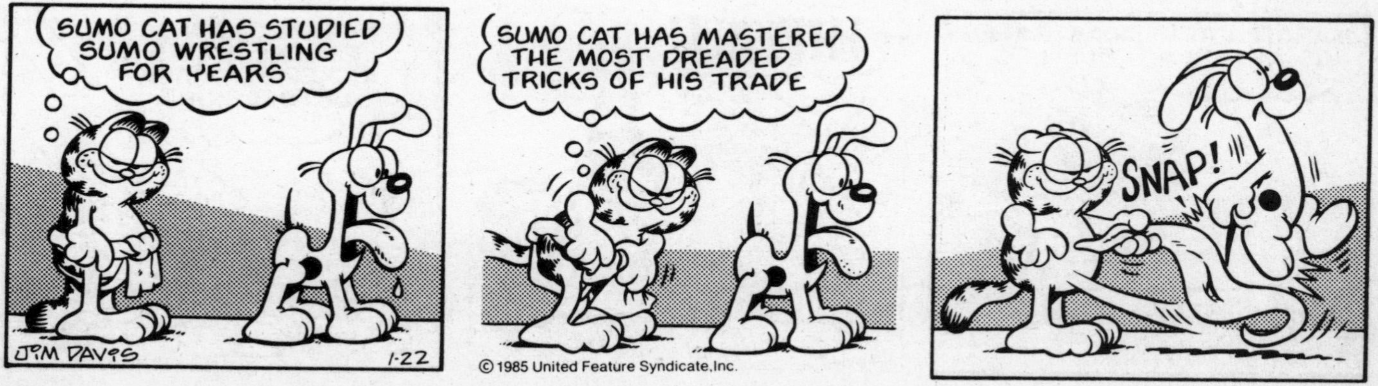
SUMO CAT HAS STUDIED SUMO WRESTLING FOR YEARS
JIM DAVIS 1-22
SUMO CAT HAS MASTERED THE MOST DREADED TRICKS OF HIS TRADE
SNAP!

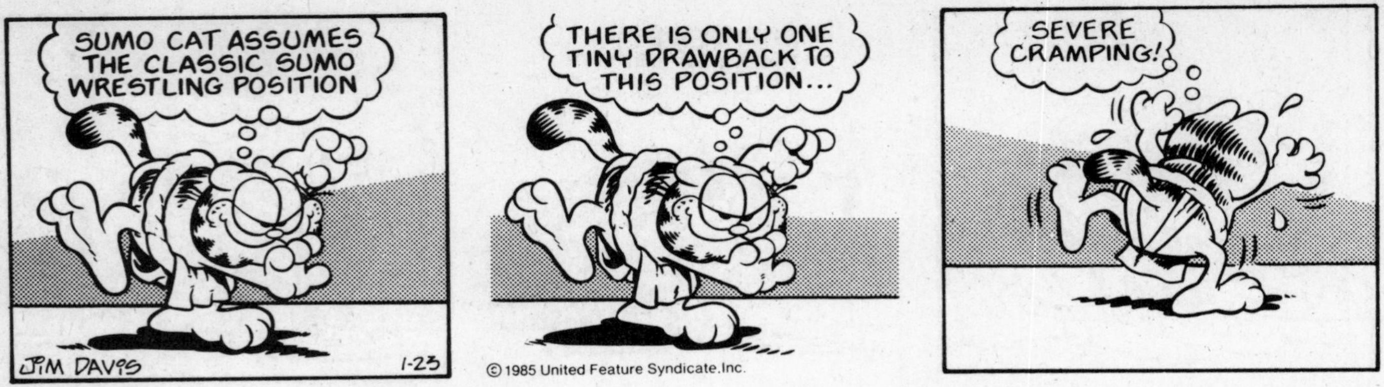
SUMO CAT ASSUMES THE CLASSIC SUMO WRESTLING POSITION
THERE IS ONLY ONE TINY DRAWBACK TO THIS POSITION...
SEVERE CRAMPING!
JIM DAVIS
1-23

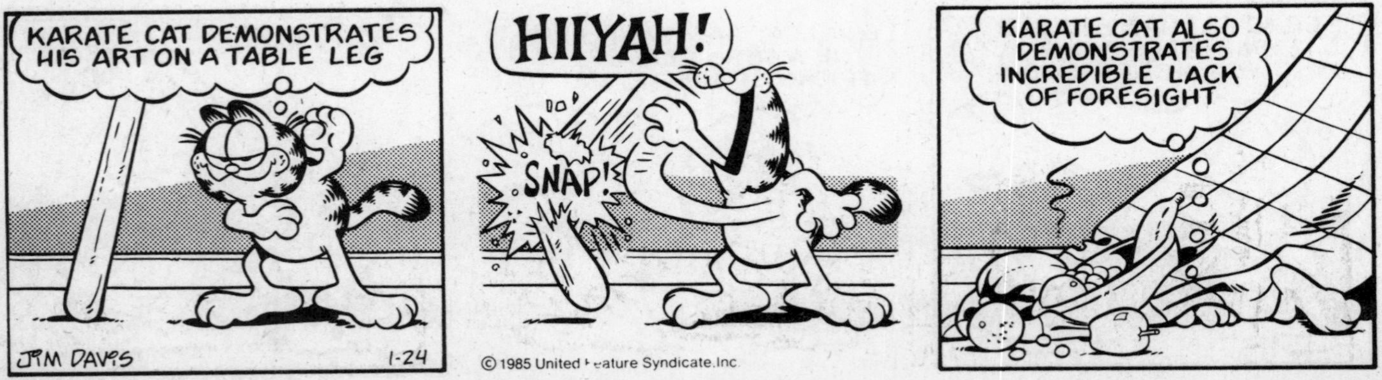
KARATE CAT DEMONSTRATES HIS ART ON A TABLE LEG
HIIYAH!
SNAP!
KARATE CAT ALSO DEMONSTRATES INCREDIBLE LACK OF FORESIGHT
JIM DAVIS
1-24

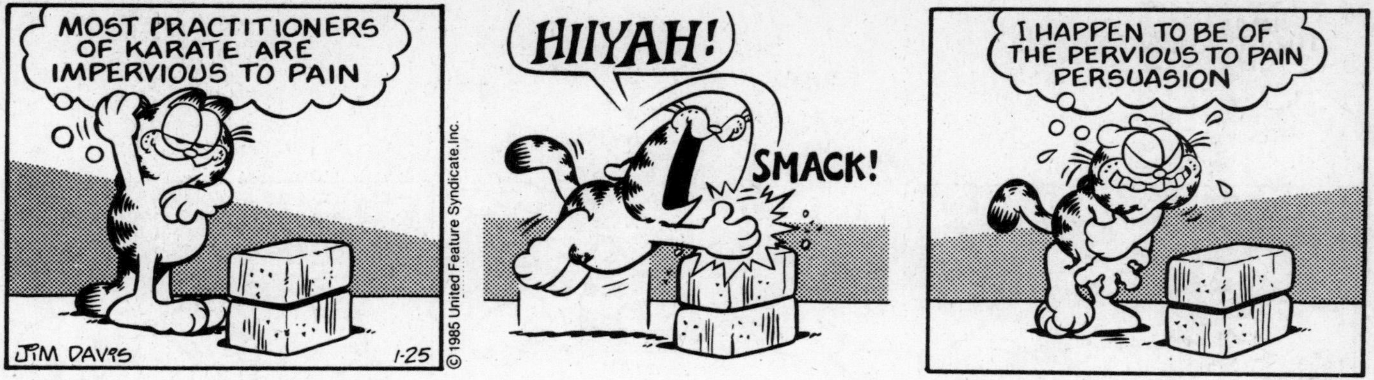
MOST PRACTITIONERS OF KARATE ARE IMPERVIOUS TO PAIN
JIM DAVIS
1-25
© 1985 United Feature Syndicate, Inc.
HIIYAH!
SMACK!
I HAPPEN TO BE OF THE PERVIOUS TO PAIN PERSUASION

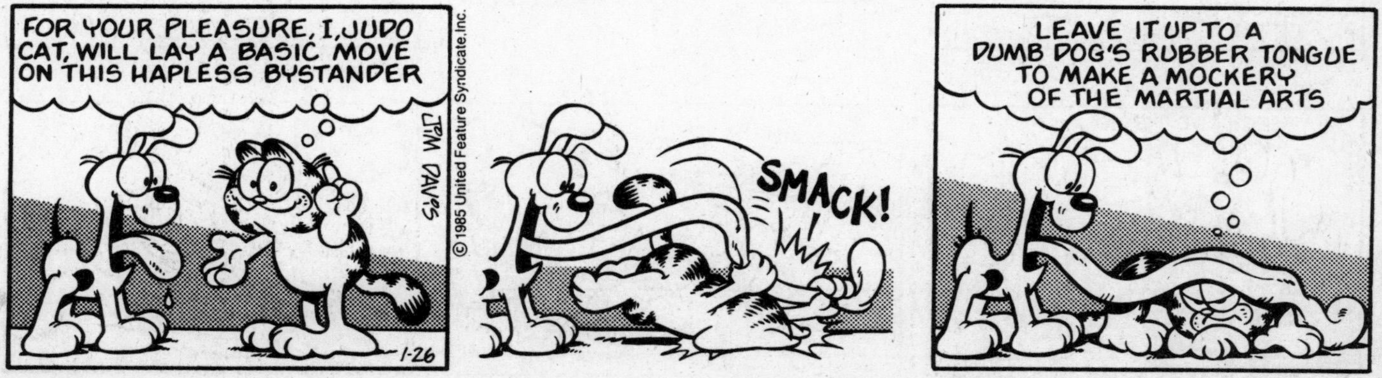
FOR YOUR PLEASURE, I, JUDO CAT, WILL LAY A BASIC MOVE ON THIS HAPLESS BYSTANDER
JIM DAVIS
1-26
© 1985 United Feature Syndicate, Inc.
SMACK!
LEAVE IT UP TO A DUMB DOG'S RUBBER TONGUE TO MAKE A MOCKERY OF THE MARTIAL ARTS

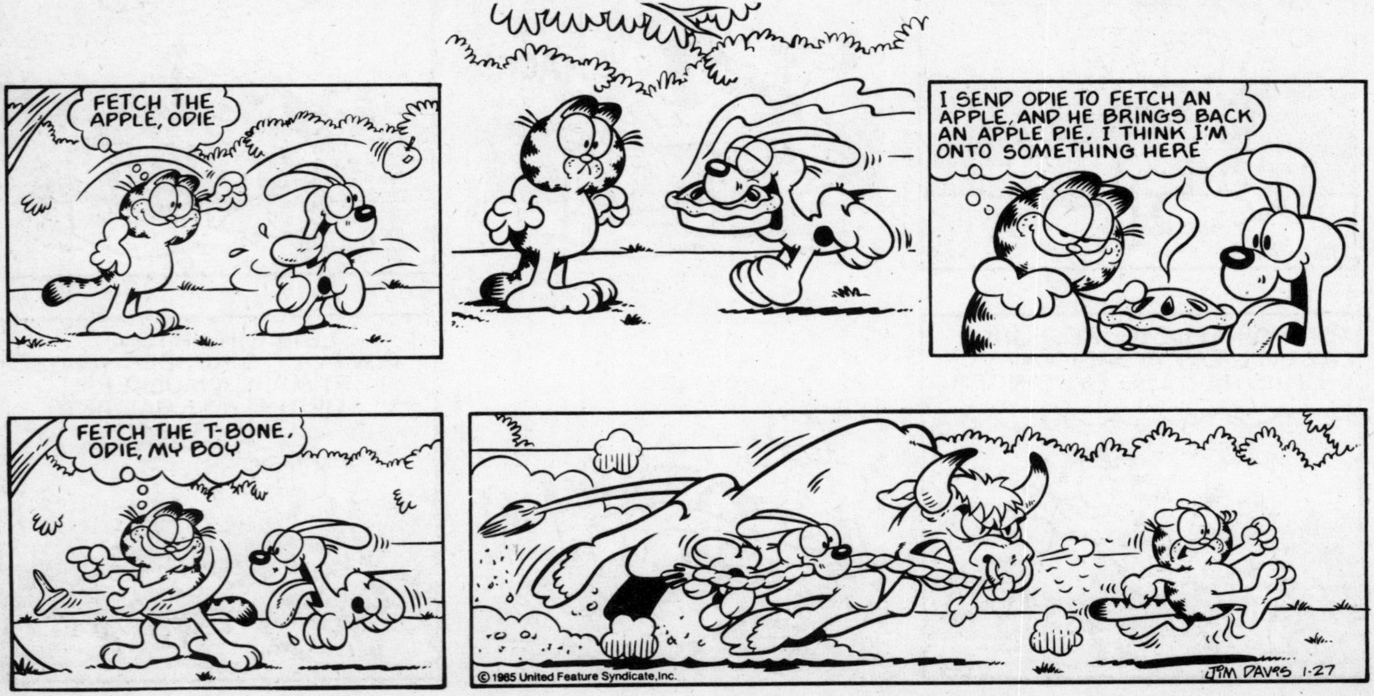
FETCH THE APPLE, ODIE
I SEND ODIE TO FETCH AN APPLE, AND HE BRINGS BACK AN APPLE PIE. I THINK I'M ONTO SOMETHING HERE
FETCH THE T-BONE, ODIE, MY BOY
© 1985 United Feature Syndicate, Inc.
JIM DAVIS 1-27

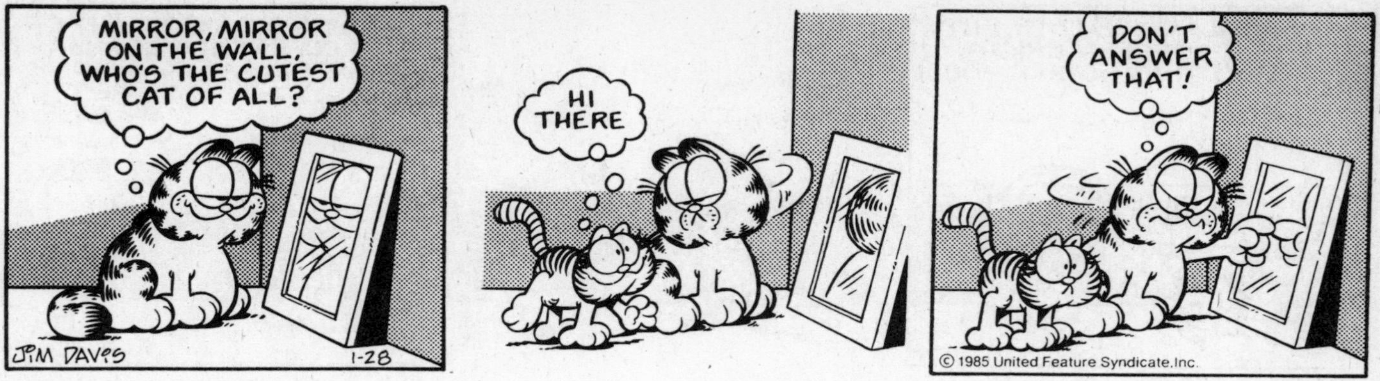
MIRROR, MIRROR ON THE WALL, WHO'S THE CUTEST CAT OF ALL?
JIM DAVIS
1-28
HI THERE
DON'T ANSWER THAT!
© 1985 United Feature Syndicate,Inc.

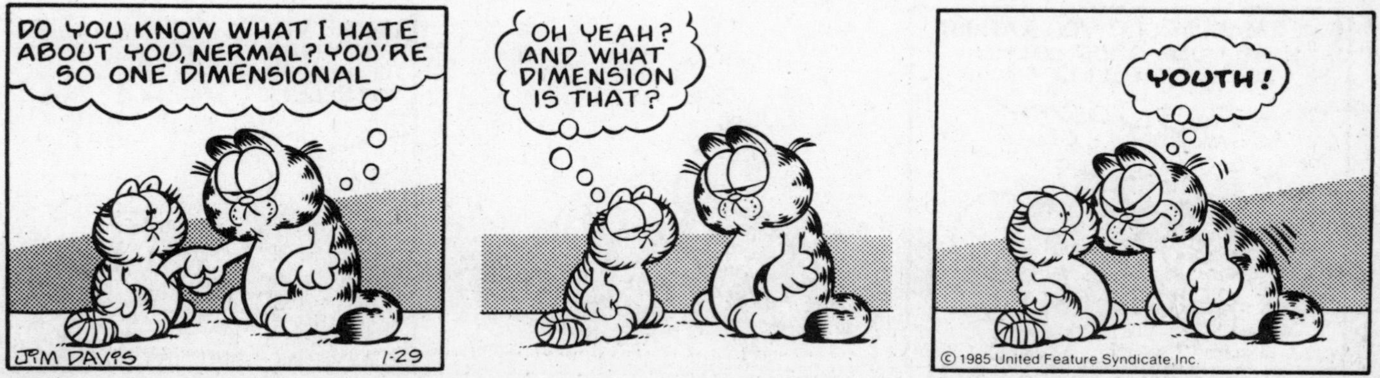
DO YOU KNOW WHAT I HATE ABOUT YOU, NERMAL? YOU'RE SO ONE DIMENSIONAL
JIM DAVIS
1-29
OH YEAH? AND WHAT DIMENSION IS THAT?
YOUTH!
© 1985 United Feature Syndicate,Inc.

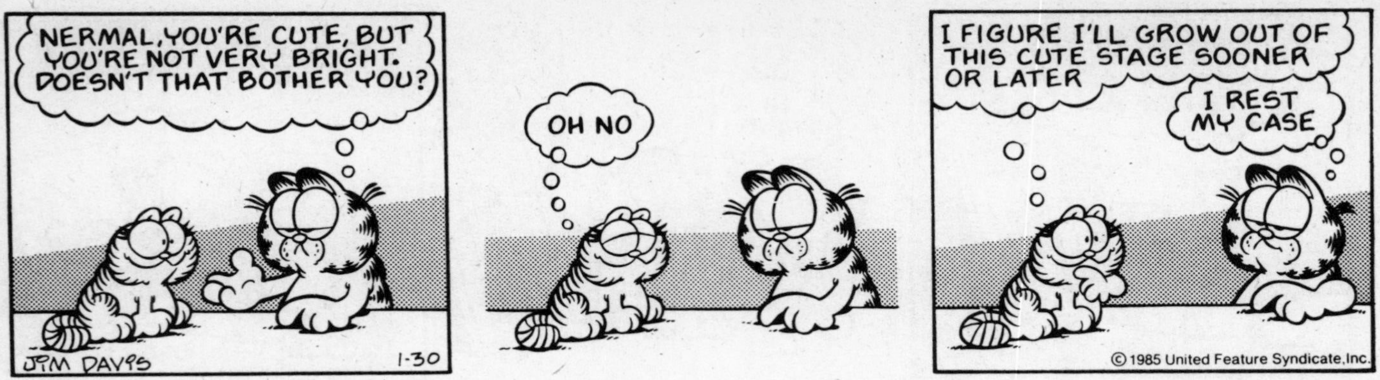
NERMAL, YOU'RE CUTE, BUT YOU'RE NOT VERY BRIGHT. DOESN'T THAT BOTHER YOU?
JIM DAVIS
1-30
OH NO
I FIGURE I'LL GROW OUT OF THIS CUTE STAGE SOONER OR LATER
I REST MY CASE
© 1985 United Feature Syndicate, Inc.

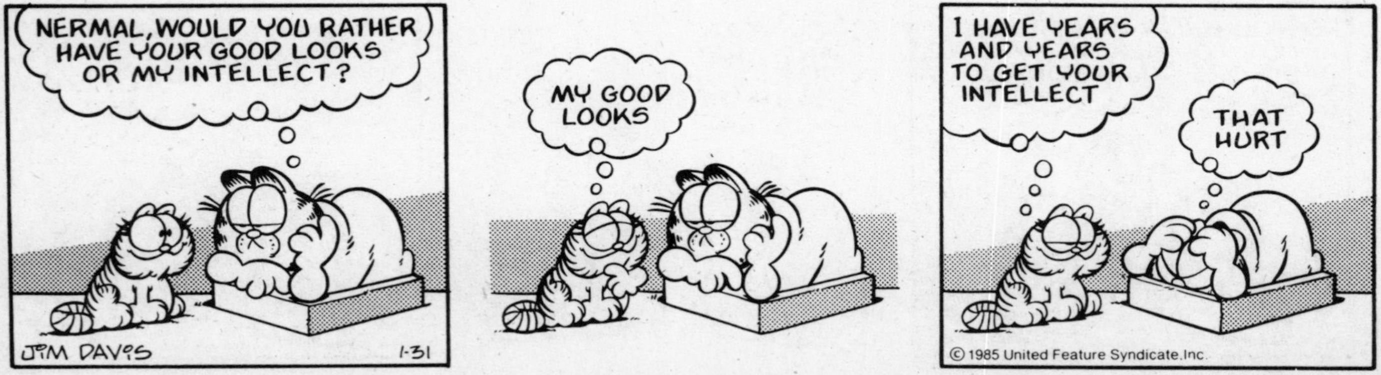
NERMAL, WOULD YOU RATHER HAVE YOUR GOOD LOOKS OR MY INTELLECT?
JIM DAVIS
1-31
MY GOOD LOOKS
I HAVE YEARS AND YEARS TO GET YOUR INTELLECT
THAT HURT
© 1985 United Feature Syndicate, Inc.

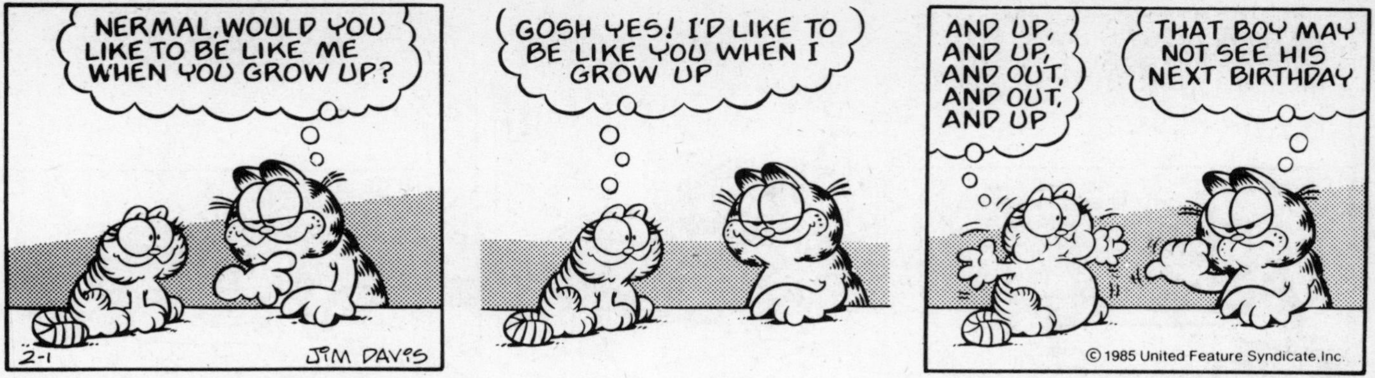
NERMAL, WOULD YOU LIKE TO BE LIKE ME WHEN YOU GROW UP?
GOSH YES! I'D LIKE TO BE LIKE YOU WHEN I GROW UP
AND UP, AND UP, AND OUT, AND OUT, AND UP
THAT BOY MAY NOT SEE HIS NEXT BIRTHDAY
2-1
JIM DAVIS
© 1985 United Feature Syndicate, Inc.

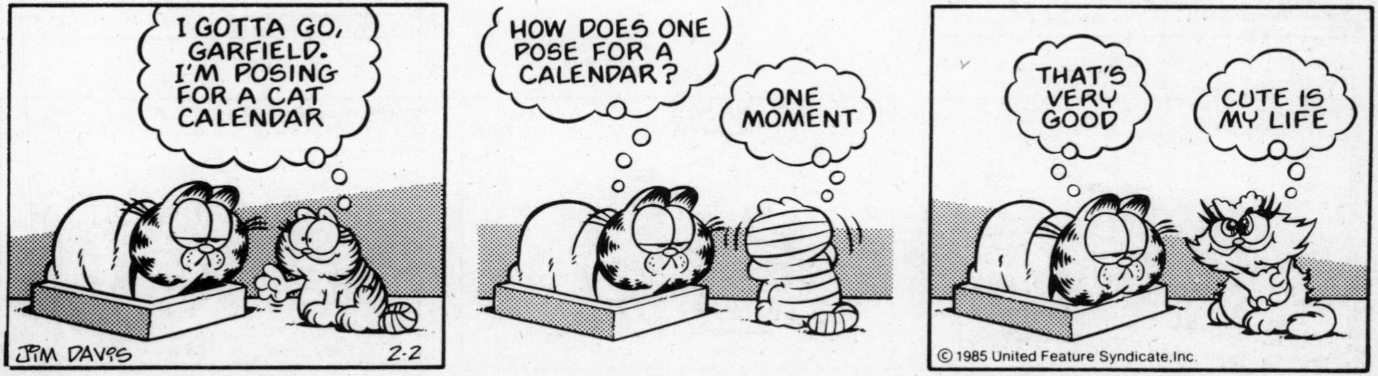
I GOTTA GO, GARFIELD. I'M POSING FOR A CAT CALENDAR
HOW DOES ONE POSE FOR A CALENDAR?
ONE MOMENT
THAT'S VERY GOOD
CUTE IS MY LIFE
JIM DAVIS
2-2
© 1985 United Feature Syndicate, Inc.

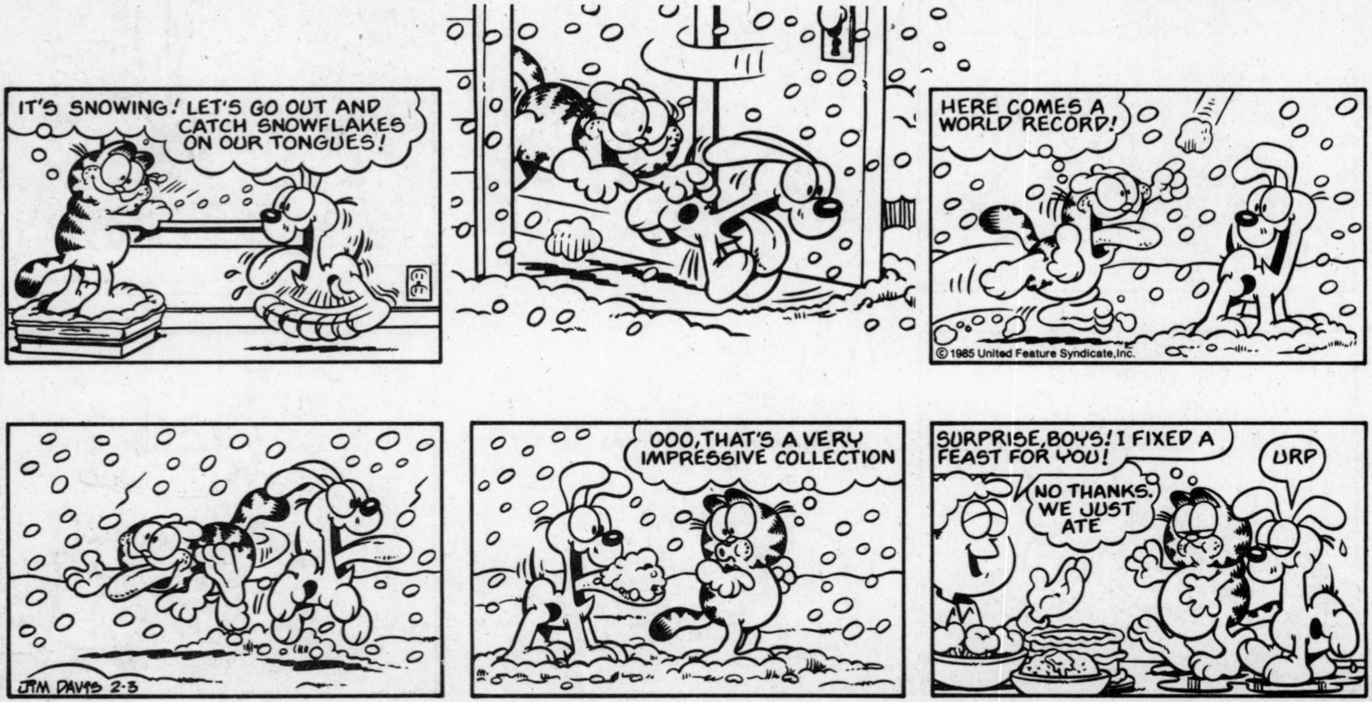
IT'S SNOWING! LET'S GO OUT AND CATCH SNOWFLAKES ON OUR TONGUES!
HERE COMES A WORLD RECORD!
© 1985 United Feature Syndicate, Inc.
JIM DAVIS 2-3
OOO, THAT'S A VERY IMPRESSIVE COLLECTION
SURPRISE, BOYS! I FIXED A FEAST FOR YOU!
NO THANKS. WE JUST ATE
URP

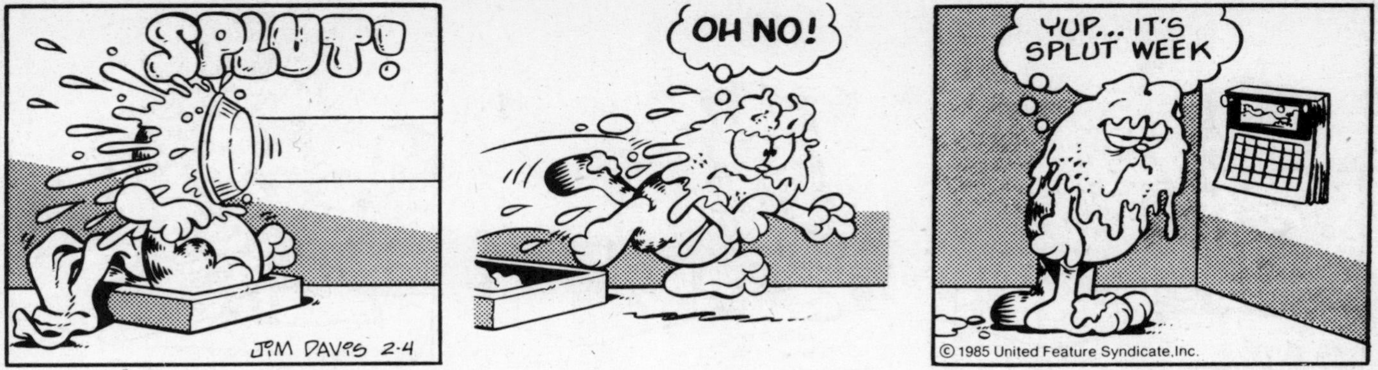
SPLUT!
JIM DAVIS 2-4
OH NO!
YUP... IT'S SPLUT WEEK
© 1985 United Feature Syndicate,Inc.

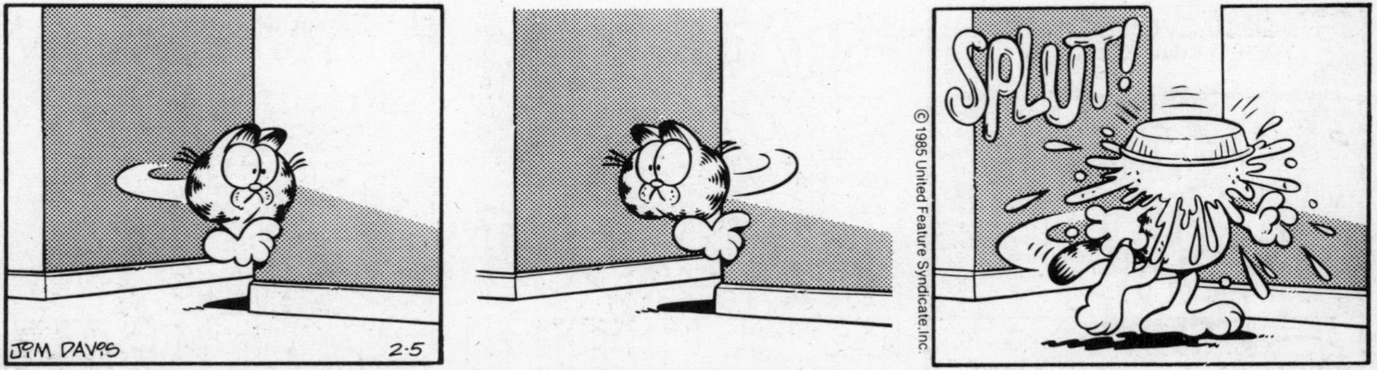
JIM DAVIS
2-5
© 1985 United Feature Syndicate,Inc.
SPLUT!

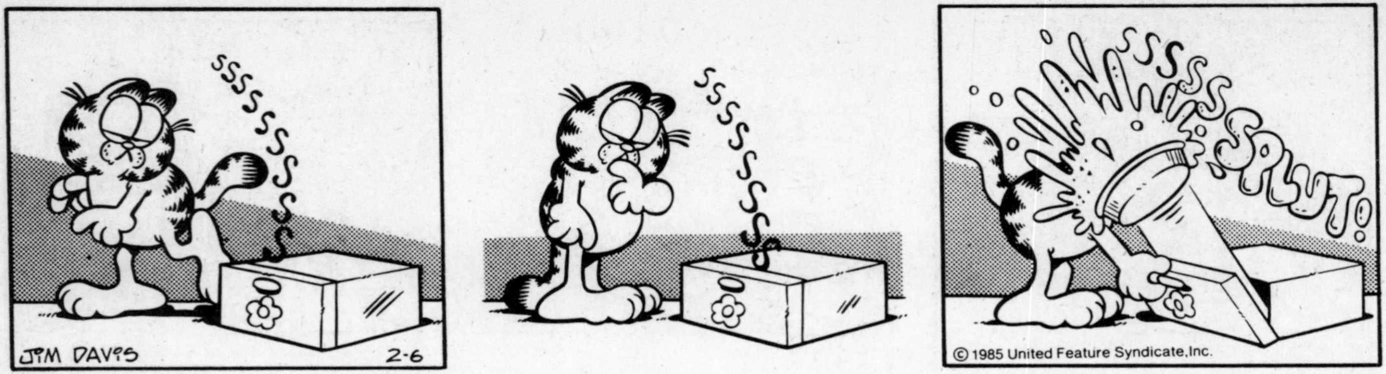
JIM DAVIS
2-6
SSSSSSSSS
SSSSSSSS
SSSSS SPLUT!
© 1985 United Feature Syndicate, Inc.

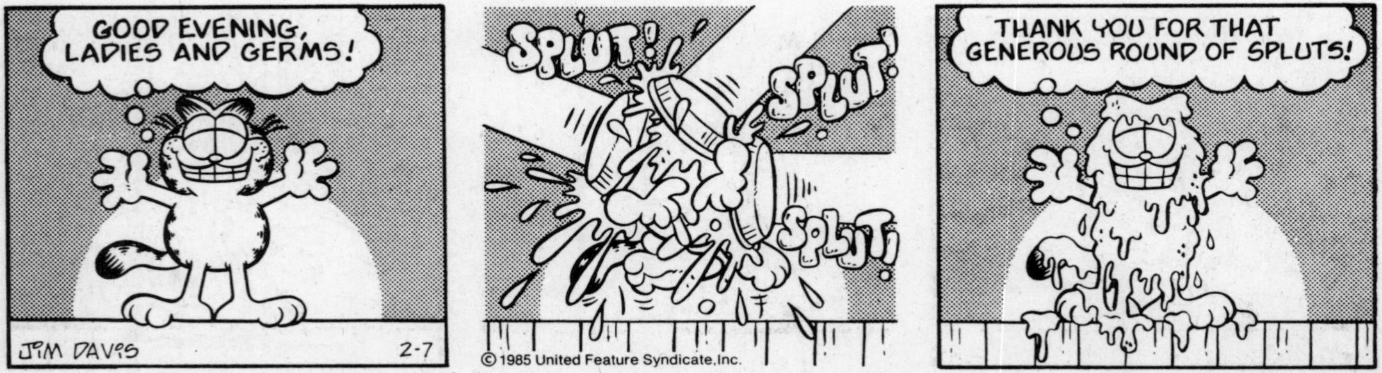
GOOD EVENING, LADIES AND GERMS!
JIM DAVIS
2-7
SPLUT!
SPLUT!
SPLUT!
© 1985 United Feature Syndicate, Inc.
THANK YOU FOR THAT GENEROUS ROUND OF SPLUTS!

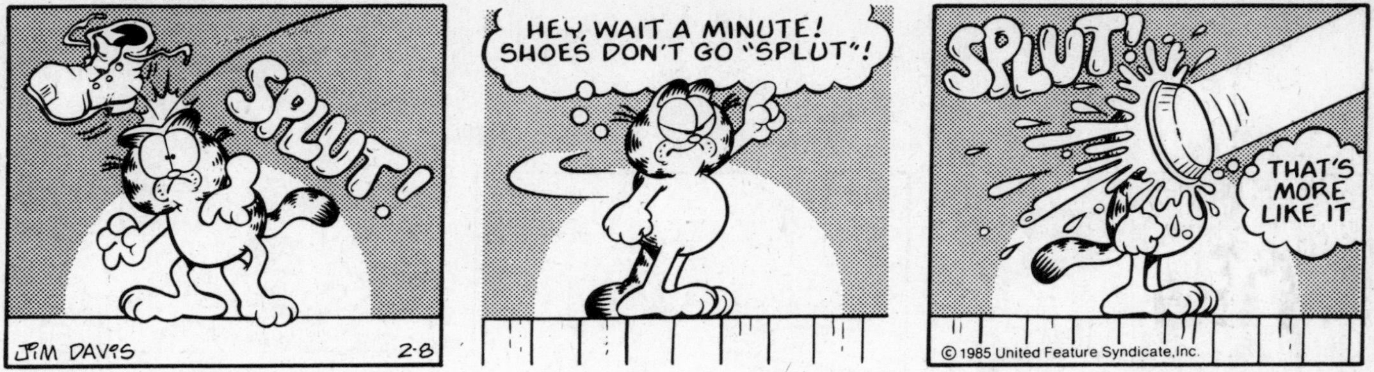
SPLUT!
HEY, WAIT A MINUTE! SHOES DON'T GO "SPLUT"!
SPLUT!
THAT'S MORE LIKE IT
JIM DAVIS 2-8
© 1985 United Feature Syndicate, Inc.

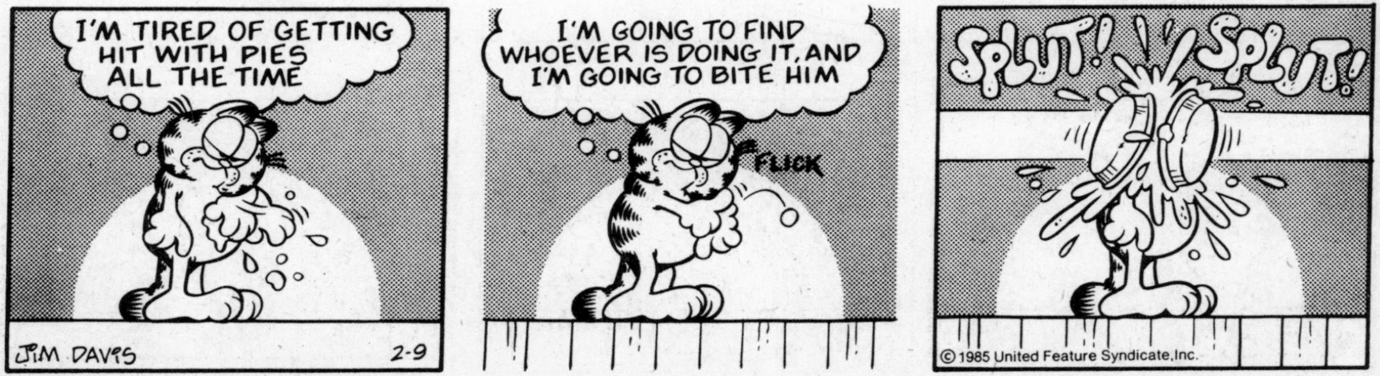
I'M TIRED OF GETTING HIT WITH PIES ALL THE TIME
I'M GOING TO FIND WHOEVER IS DOING IT, AND I'M GOING TO BITE HIM
FLICK
SPLUT!
SPLUT!
JIM DAVIS 2-9
© 1985 United Feature Syndicate, Inc.

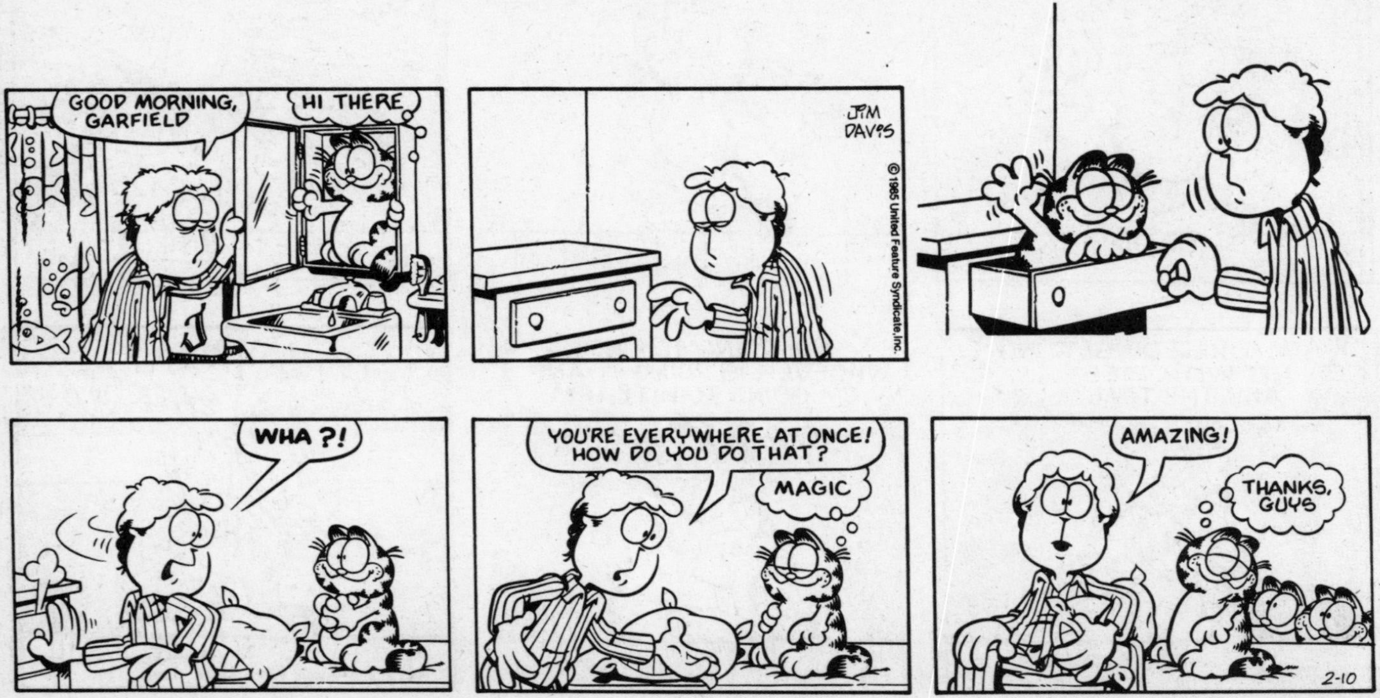
GOOD MORNING, GARFIELD
HI THERE
JIM DAVIS
© 1985 United Feature Syndicate, Inc.
WHA ?!
YOU'RE EVERYWHERE AT ONCE! HOW DO YOU DO THAT?
MAGIC
AMAZING!
THANKS, GUYS
2-10

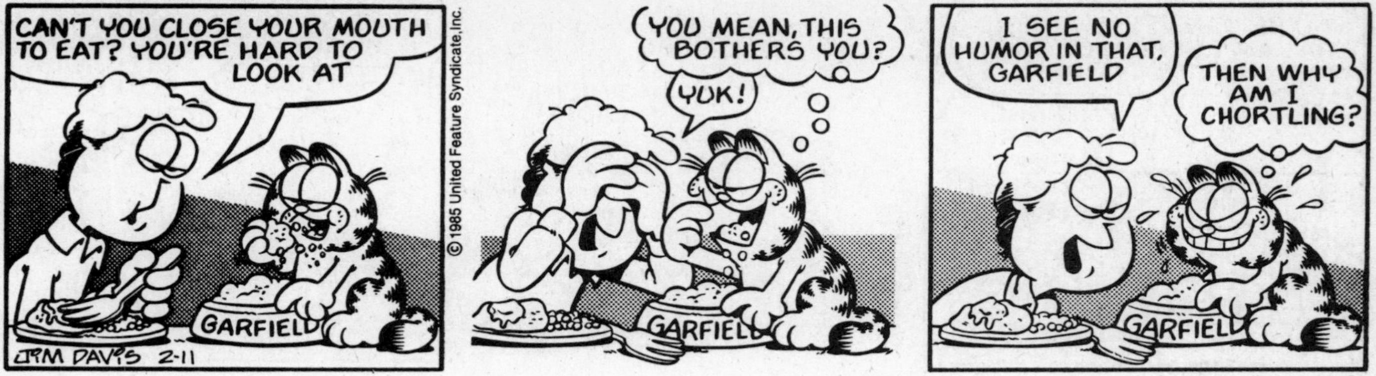
CAN'T YOU CLOSE YOUR MOUTH TO EAT? YOU'RE HARD TO LOOK AT
GARFIELD
JIM DAVIS 2-11
© 1985 United Feature Syndicate,Inc.
YOU MEAN, THIS BOTHERS YOU?
YUK!
GARFIELD
I SEE NO HUMOR IN THAT, GARFIELD
THEN WHY AM I CHORTLING?
GARFIELD

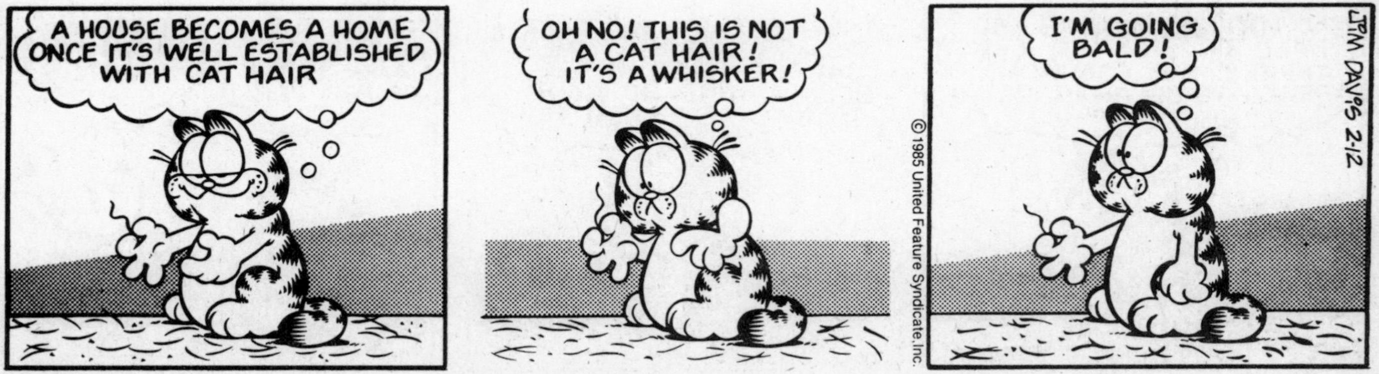
A HOUSE BECOMES A HOME ONCE IT'S WELL ESTABLISHED WITH CAT HAIR
OH NO! THIS IS NOT A CAT HAIR! IT'S A WHISKER!
© 1985 United Feature Syndicate,Inc.
I'M GOING BALD!
JIM DAVIS 2-12

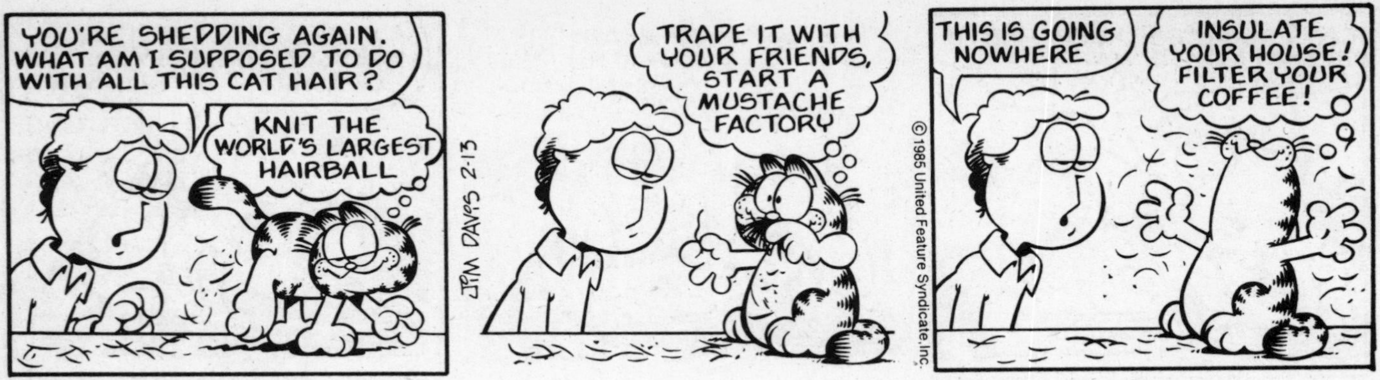
YOU'RE SHEDDING AGAIN. WHAT AM I SUPPOSED TO DO WITH ALL THIS CAT HAIR?
KNIT THE WORLD'S LARGEST HAIRBALL
JIM DAVIS 2-13
TRADE IT WITH YOUR FRIENDS, START A MUSTACHE FACTORY
THIS IS GOING NOWHERE
INSULATE YOUR HOUSE! FILTER YOUR COFFEE!
© 1985 United Feature Syndicate,Inc.

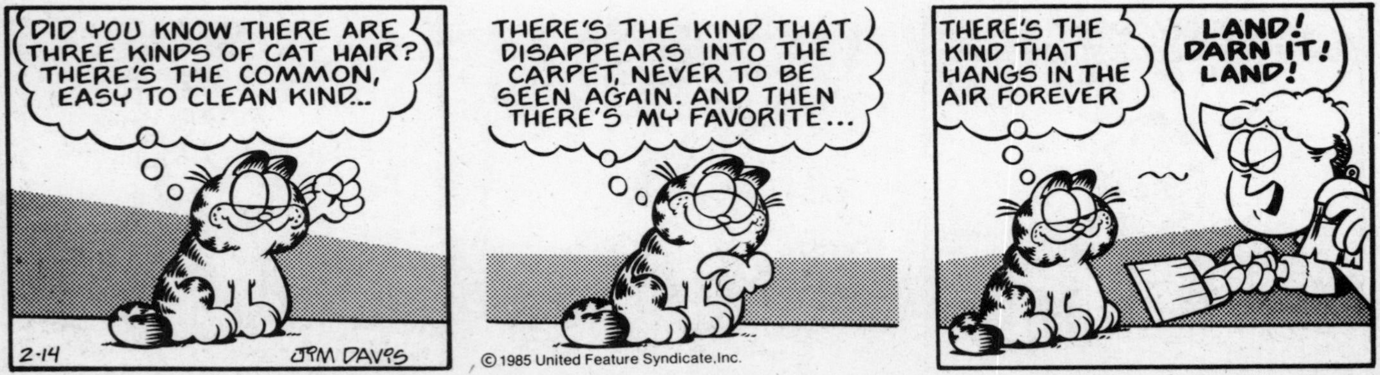
DID YOU KNOW THERE ARE THREE KINDS OF CAT HAIR? THERE'S THE COMMON, EASY TO CLEAN KIND...
2-14
JIM DAVIS
THERE'S THE KIND THAT DISAPPEARS INTO THE CARPET, NEVER TO BE SEEN AGAIN. AND THEN THERE'S MY FAVORITE...
THERE'S THE KIND THAT HANGS IN THE AIR FOREVER
LAND! DARN IT! LAND!

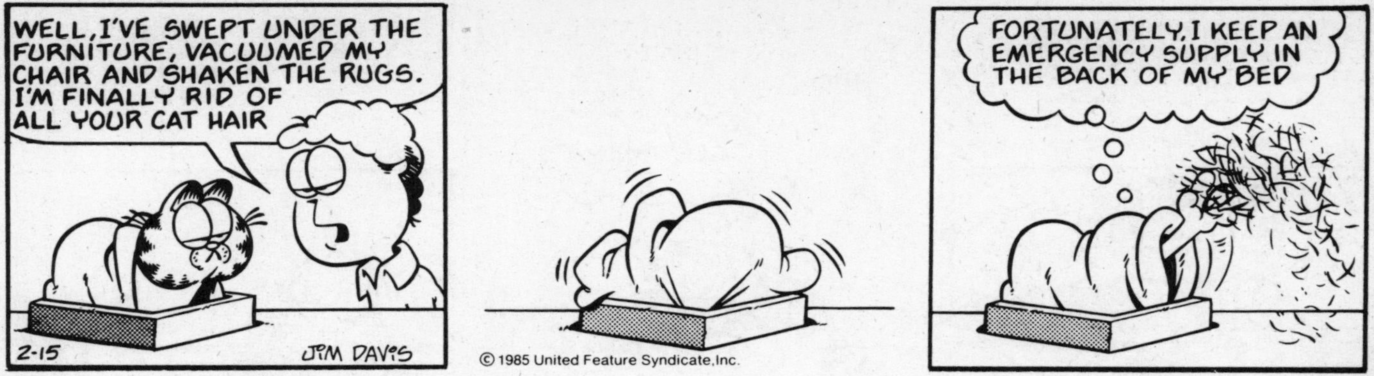
WELL, I'VE SWEPT UNDER THE FURNITURE, VACUUMED MY CHAIR AND SHAKEN THE RUGS. I'M FINALLY RID OF ALL YOUR CAT HAIR
2-15
JIM DAVIS
© 1985 United Feature Syndicate, Inc.
FORTUNATELY, I KEEP AN EMERGENCY SUPPLY IN THE BACK OF MY BED

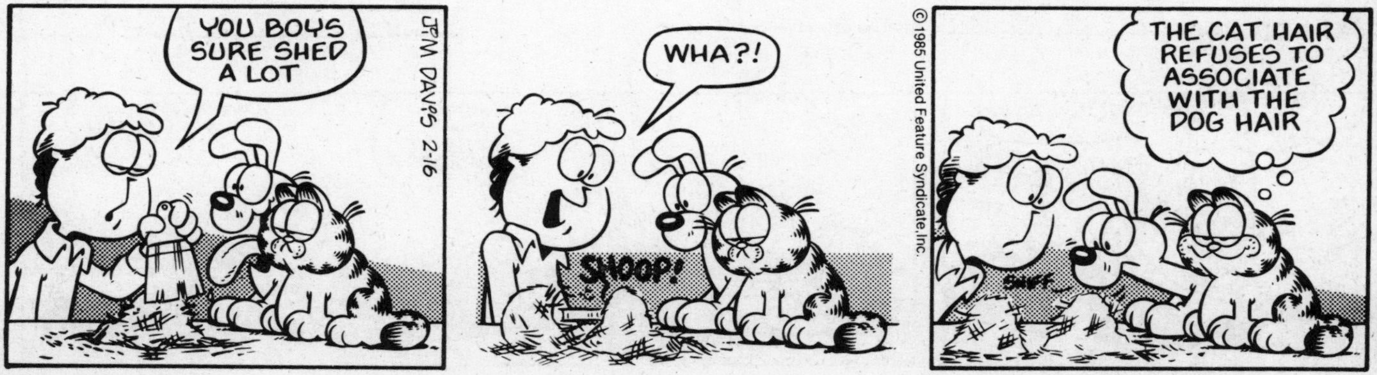
YOU BOYS SURE SHED A LOT
JIM DAVIS 2-16
WHA?!
SHOOP!
© 1985 United Feature Syndicate, Inc.
THE CAT HAIR REFUSES TO ASSOCIATE WITH THE DOG HAIR

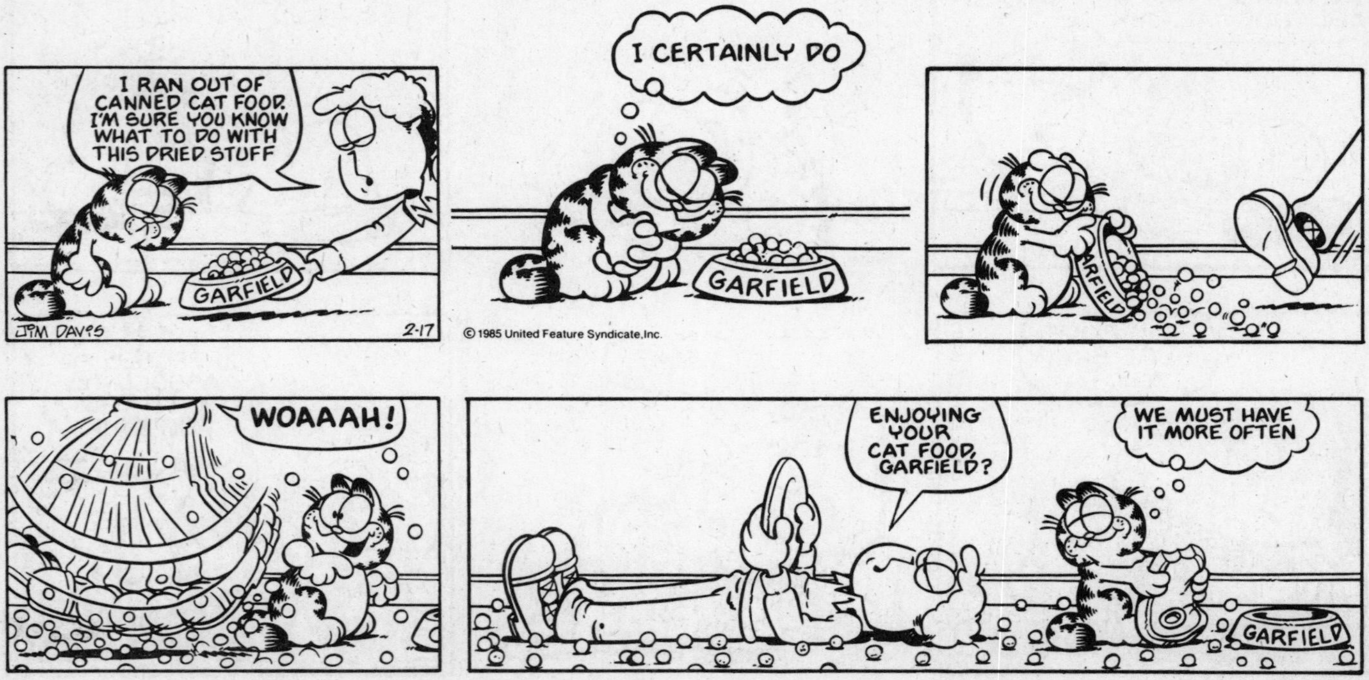
I RAN OUT OF CANNED CAT FOOD. I'M SURE YOU KNOW WHAT TO DO WITH THIS DRIED STUFF
GARFIELD
JIM DAVIS
2-17
I CERTAINLY DO
GARFIELD
© 1985 United Feature Syndicate, Inc.
GARFIELD
WOAAAH!
ENJOYING YOUR CAT FOOD, GARFIELD?
WE MUST HAVE IT MORE OFTEN
GARFIELD

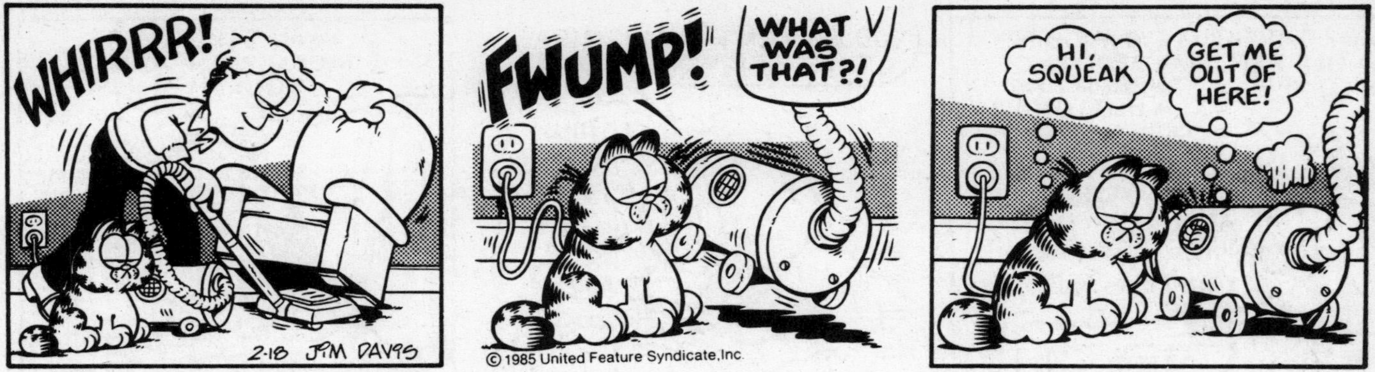
WHIRRR!
2-18 JIM DAVIS
FWUMP!
WHAT WAS THAT?!
HI, SQUEAK
GET ME OUT OF HERE!

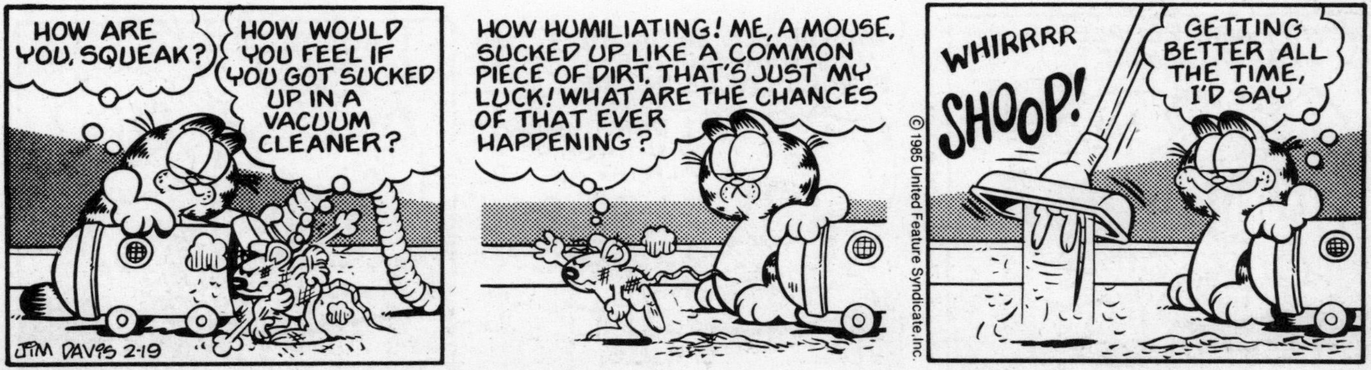
HOW ARE YOU, SQUEAK?
HOW WOULD YOU FEEL IF YOU GOT SUCKED UP IN A VACUUM CLEANER?
JIM DAVIS 2-19
HOW HUMILIATING! ME, A MOUSE, SUCKED UP LIKE A COMMON PIECE OF DIRT. THAT'S JUST MY LUCK! WHAT ARE THE CHANCES OF THAT EVER HAPPENING?
© 1985 United Feature Syndicate, Inc.
WHIRRRR
SHOOP!
GETTING BETTER ALL THE TIME, I'D SAY

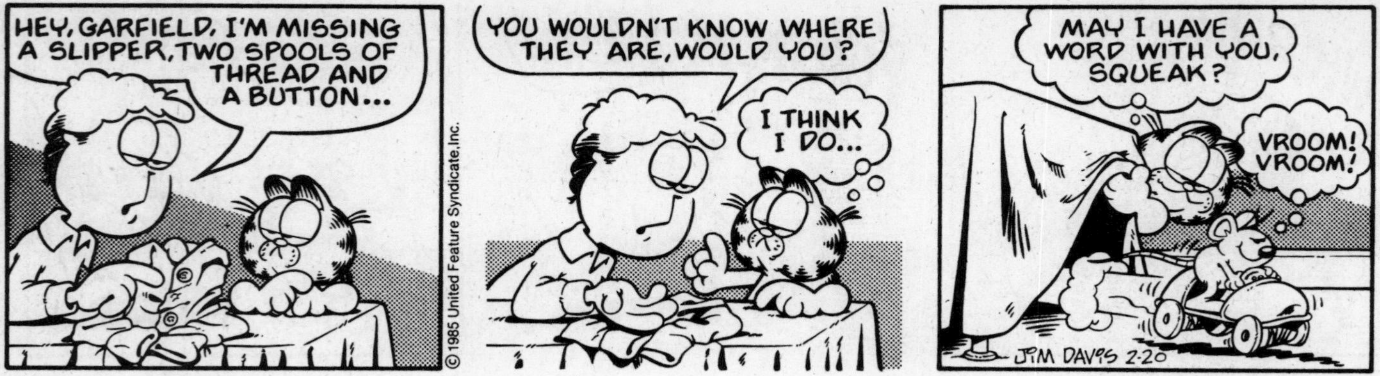
HEY, GARFIELD, I'M MISSING A SLIPPER, TWO SPOOLS OF THREAD AND A BUTTON...
© 1985 United Feature Syndicate, Inc.
YOU WOULDN'T KNOW WHERE THEY ARE, WOULD YOU?
I THINK I DO...
MAY I HAVE A WORD WITH YOU, SQUEAK?
VROOM! VROOM!
JIM DAVIS 2-20

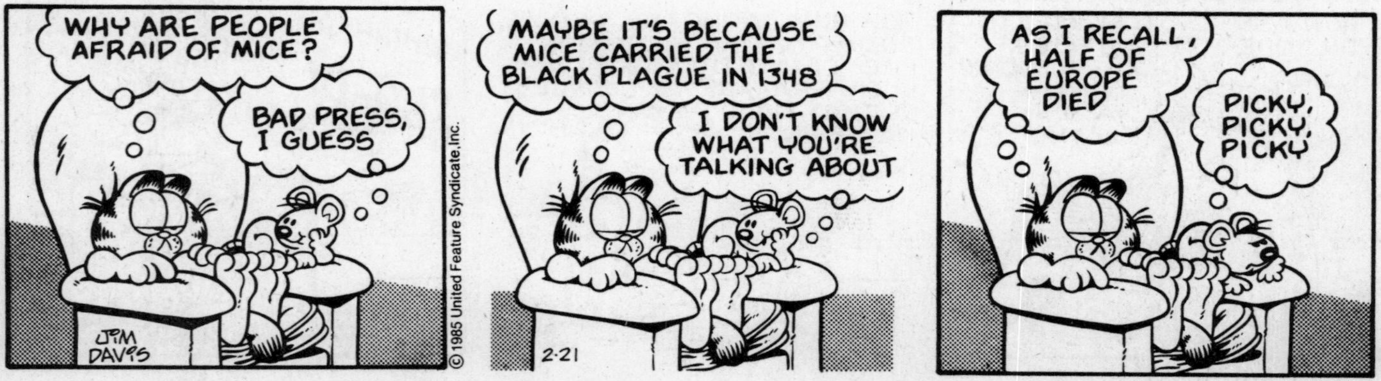
WHY ARE PEOPLE AFRAID OF MICE?
BAD PRESS, I GUESS
JIM DAVIS
© 1985 United Feature Syndicate, Inc.
MAYBE IT'S BECAUSE MICE CARRIED THE BLACK PLAGUE IN 1348
I DON'T KNOW WHAT YOU'RE TALKING ABOUT
2-21
AS I RECALL, HALF OF EUROPE DIED
PICKY, PICKY, PICKY

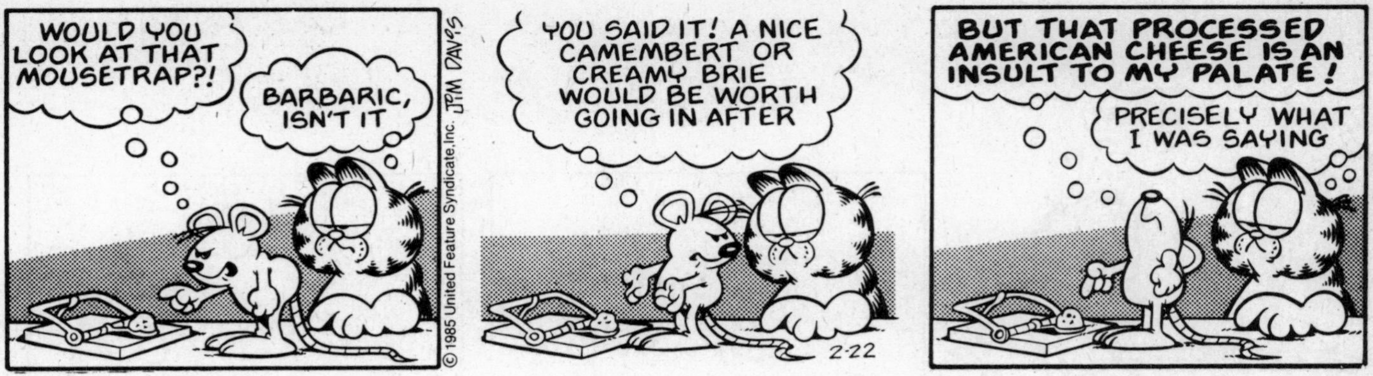
WOULD YOU LOOK AT THAT MOUSETRAP?!
BARBARIC, ISN'T IT
JIM DAVIS
© 1985 United Feature Syndicate, Inc.
YOU SAID IT! A NICE CAMEMBERT OR CREAMY BRIE WOULD BE WORTH GOING IN AFTER
2-22
BUT THAT PROCESSED AMERICAN CHEESE IS AN INSULT TO MY PALATE!
PRECISELY WHAT I WAS SAYING

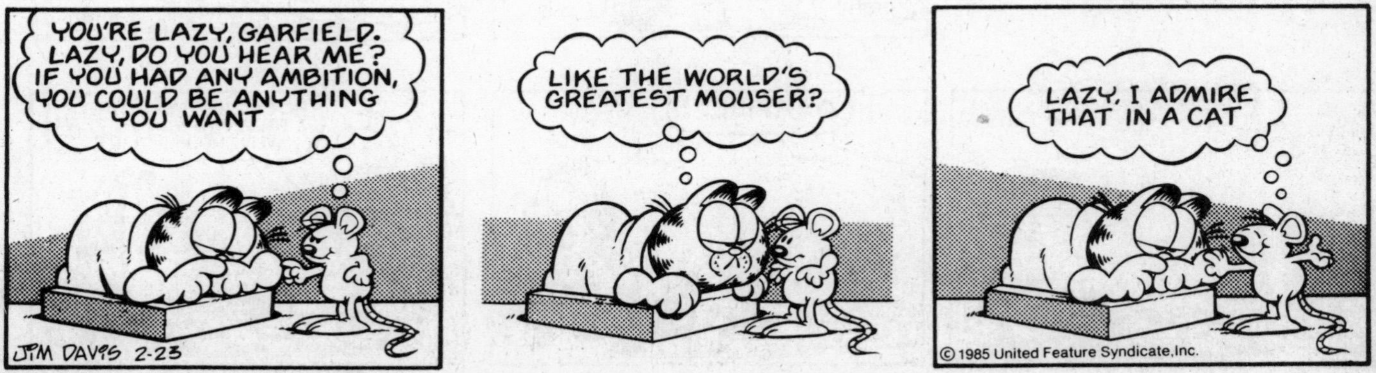
YOU'RE LAZY, GARFIELD. LAZY, DO YOU HEAR ME? IF YOU HAD ANY AMBITION, YOU COULD BE ANYTHING YOU WANT
JIM DAVIS 2-23
LIKE THE WORLD'S GREATEST MOUSER?
LAZY, I ADMIRE THAT IN A CAT
© 1985 United Feature Syndicate, Inc.

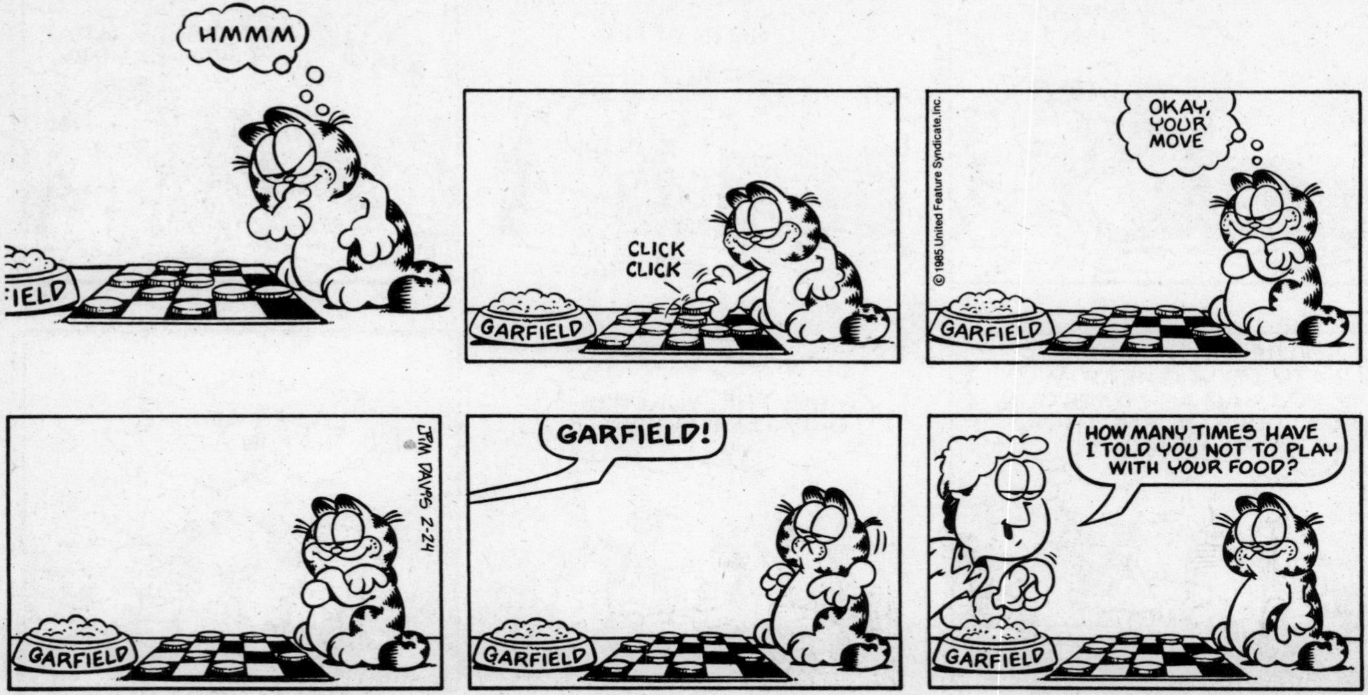
HMMM
CLICK CLICK
© 1985 United Feature Syndicate, Inc.
OKAY, YOUR MOVE
JIM DAVIS 2-24
GARFIELD!
HOW MANY TIMES HAVE I TOLD YOU NOT TO PLAY WITH YOUR FOOD?

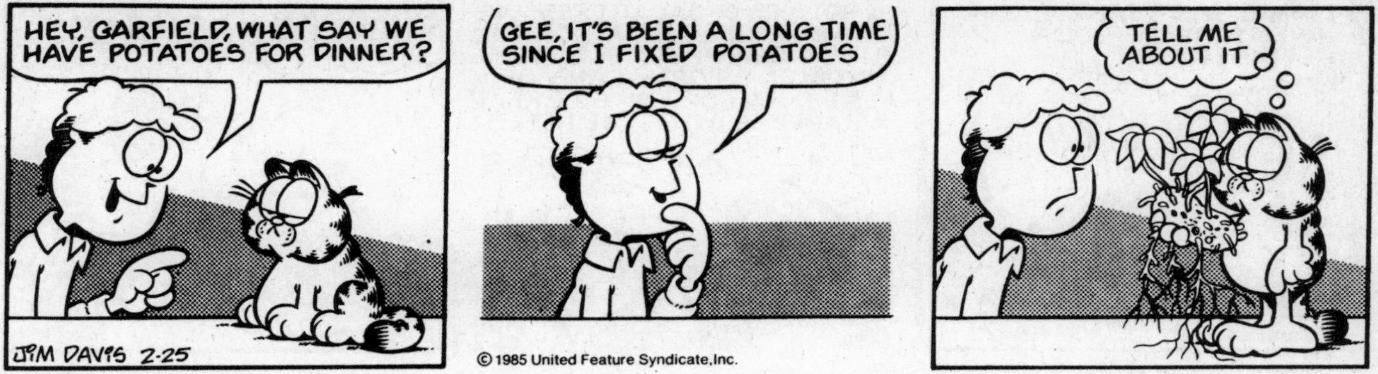
HEY, GARFIELD, WHAT SAY WE HAVE POTATOES FOR DINNER?
GEE, IT'S BEEN A LONG TIME SINCE I FIXED POTATOES
TELL ME ABOUT IT
JIM DAVIS 2-25

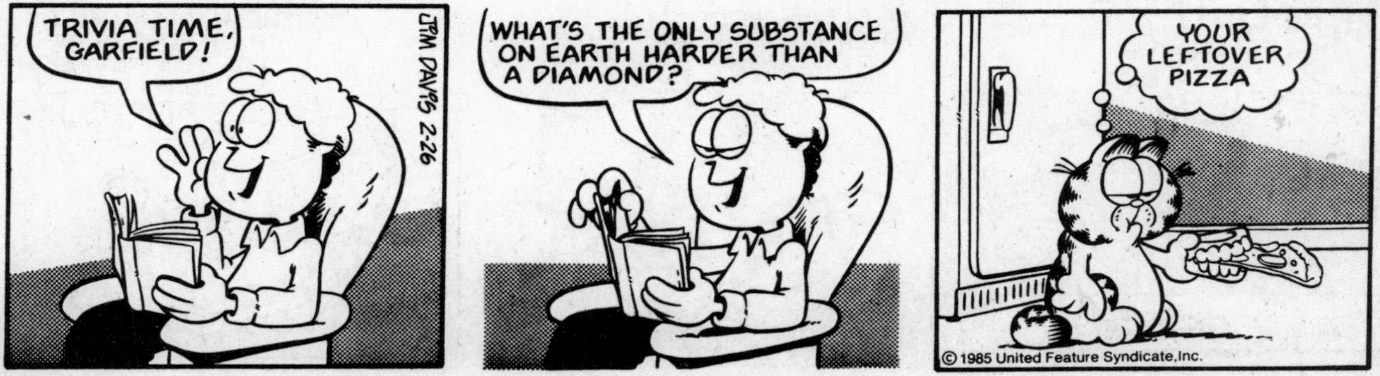
TRIVIA TIME, GARFIELD!
JIM DAVIS 2-26
WHAT'S THE ONLY SUBSTANCE ON EARTH HARDER THAN A DIAMOND?
YOUR LEFTOVER PIZZA

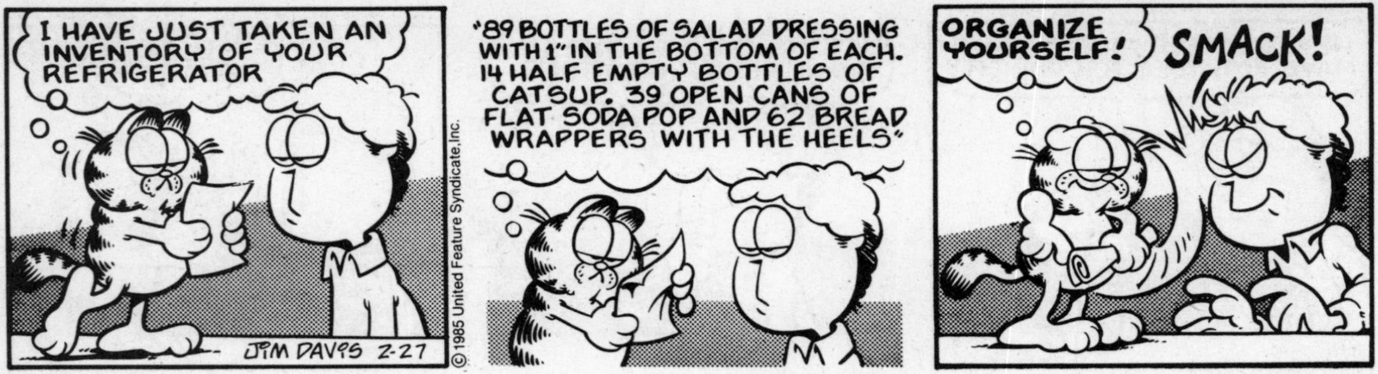
I HAVE JUST TAKEN AN INVENTORY OF YOUR REFRIGERATOR
JIM DAVIS 2-27
"89 BOTTLES OF SALAD DRESSING WITH 1" IN THE BOTTOM OF EACH. 14 HALF EMPTY BOTTLES OF CATSUP. 39 OPEN CANS OF FLAT SODA POP AND 62 BREAD WRAPPERS WITH THE HEELS"
ORGANIZE YOURSELF!
SMACK!
© 1985 United Feature Syndicate, Inc.

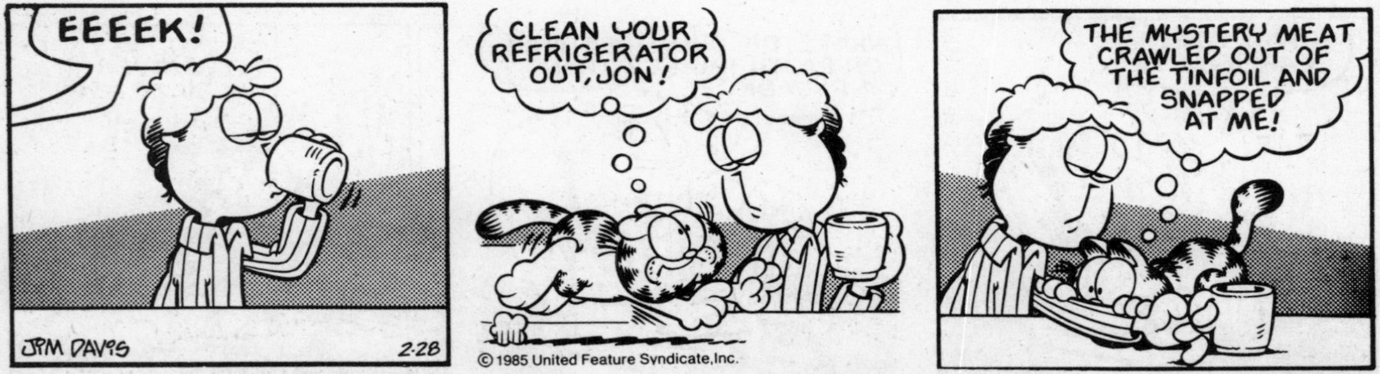
EEEEK!
JIM DAVIS
2-28
CLEAN YOUR REFRIGERATOR OUT, JON!
THE MYSTERY MEAT CRAWLED OUT OF THE TINFOIL AND SNAPPED AT ME!
© 1985 United Feature Syndicate, Inc.

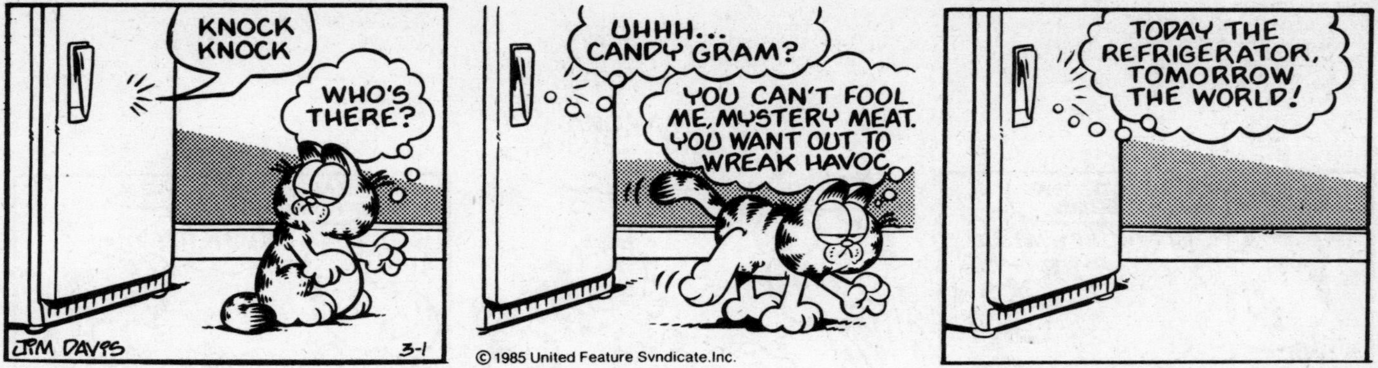
KNOCK KNOCK
WHO'S THERE?
UHHH... CANDY GRAM?
YOU CAN'T FOOL ME, MYSTERY MEAT. YOU WANT OUT TO WREAK HAVOC
TODAY THE REFRIGERATOR, TOMORROW THE WORLD!
JIM DAVIS
3-1
© 1985 United Feature Svndicate,Inc.

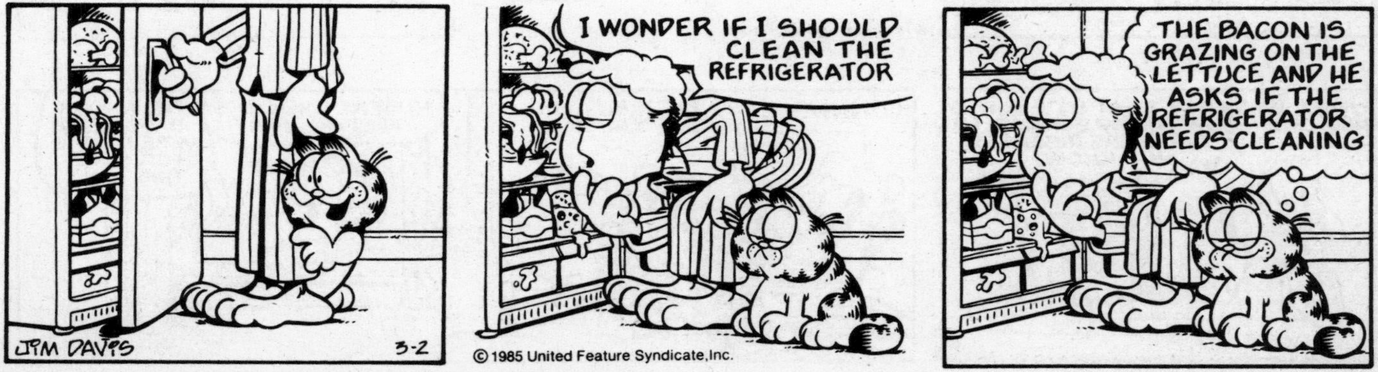
I WONDER IF I SHOULD CLEAN THE REFRIGERATOR
THE BACON IS GRAZING ON THE LETTUCE AND HE ASKS IF THE REFRIGERATOR NEEDS CLEANING
JIM DAVIS
3-2
© 1985 United Feature Syndicate,Inc.

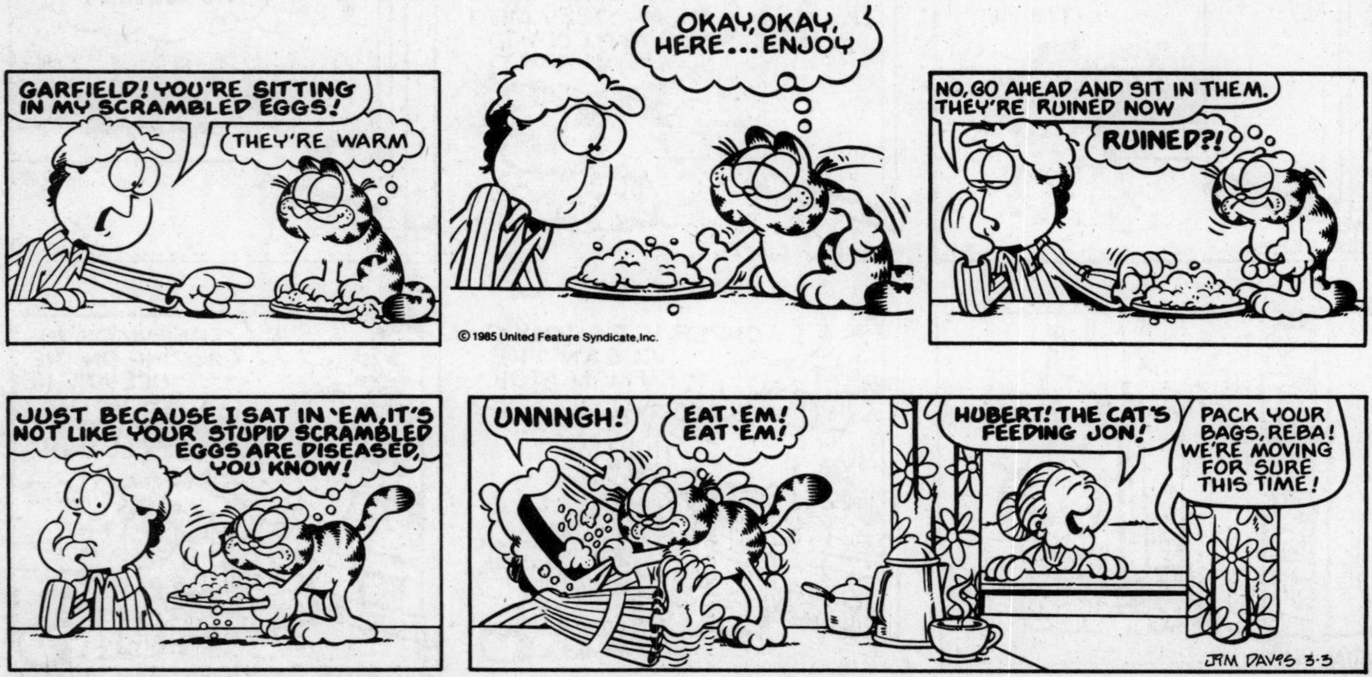
GARFIELD! YOU'RE SITTING IN MY SCRAMBLED EGGS!
THEY'RE WARM
OKAY, OKAY, HERE... ENJOY
NO, GO AHEAD AND SIT IN THEM. THEY'RE RUINED NOW
RUINED?!
JUST BECAUSE I SAT IN 'EM, IT'S NOT LIKE YOUR STUPID SCRAMBLED EGGS ARE DISEASED, YOU KNOW!
UNNNGH!
EAT 'EM! EAT 'EM!
HUBERT! THE CAT'S FEEDING JON!
PACK YOUR BAGS, REBA! WE'RE MOVING FOR SURE THIS TIME!
JIM DAVIS 3·3

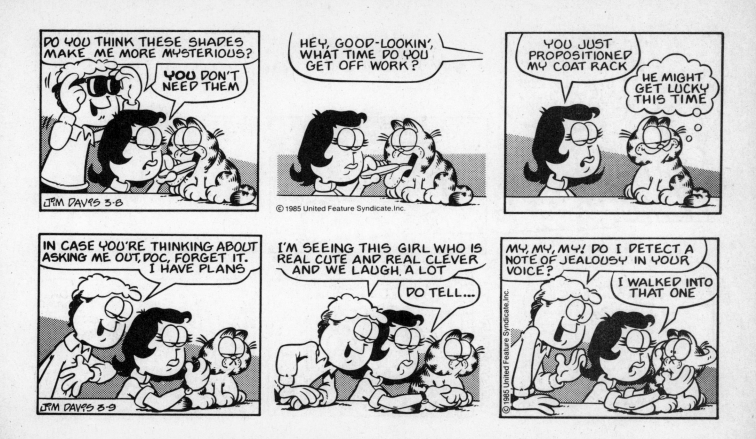

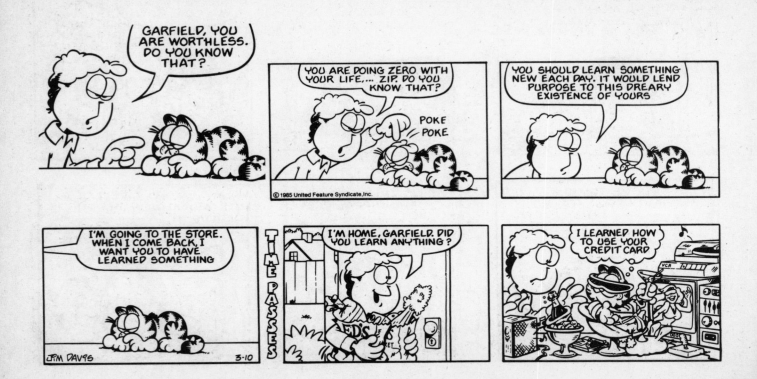

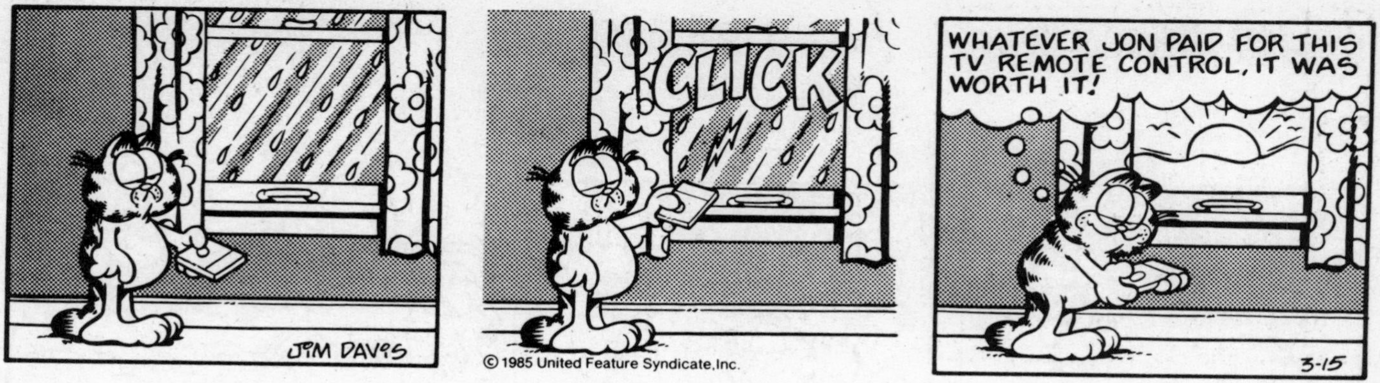
CLICK
WHATEVER JON PAID FOR THIS TV REMOTE CONTROL, IT WAS WORTH IT!
JIM DAVIS
© 1985 United Feature Syndicate, Inc.
3-15

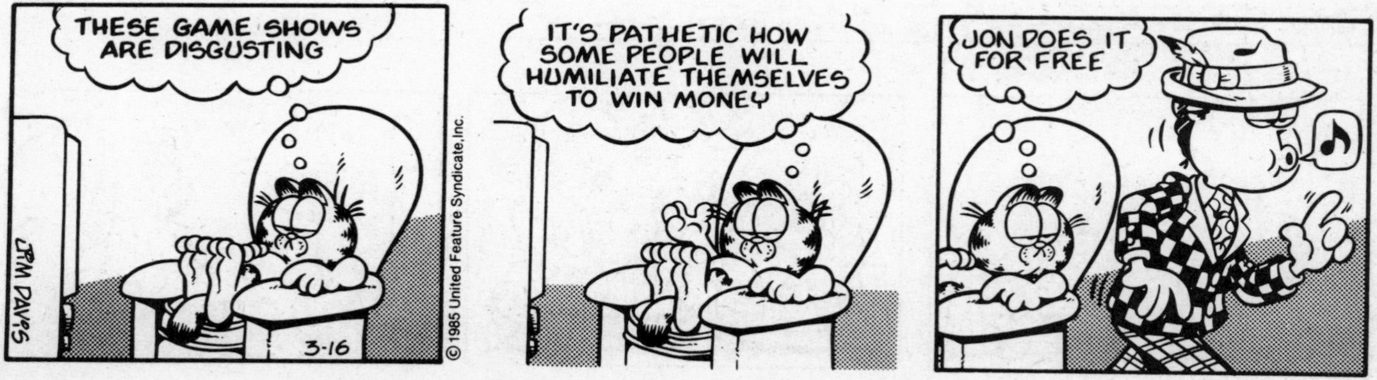
THESE GAME SHOWS ARE DISGUSTING
JIM DAVIS
3-16
© 1985 United Feature Syndicate, Inc.
IT'S PATHETIC HOW SOME PEOPLE WILL HUMILIATE THEMSELVES TO WIN MONEY
JON DOES IT FOR FREE

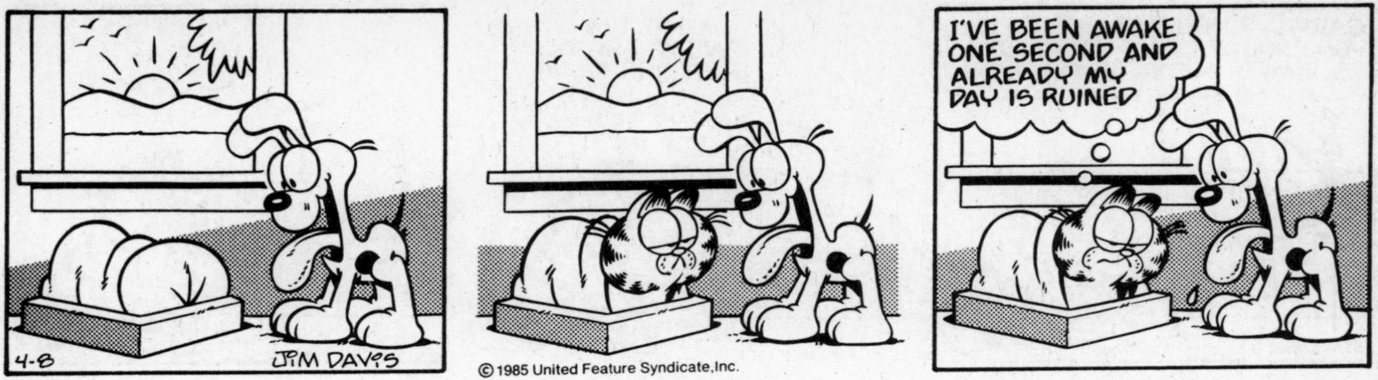
4-8
JIM DAVIS
I'VE BEEN AWAKE ONE SECOND AND ALREADY MY DAY IS RUINED

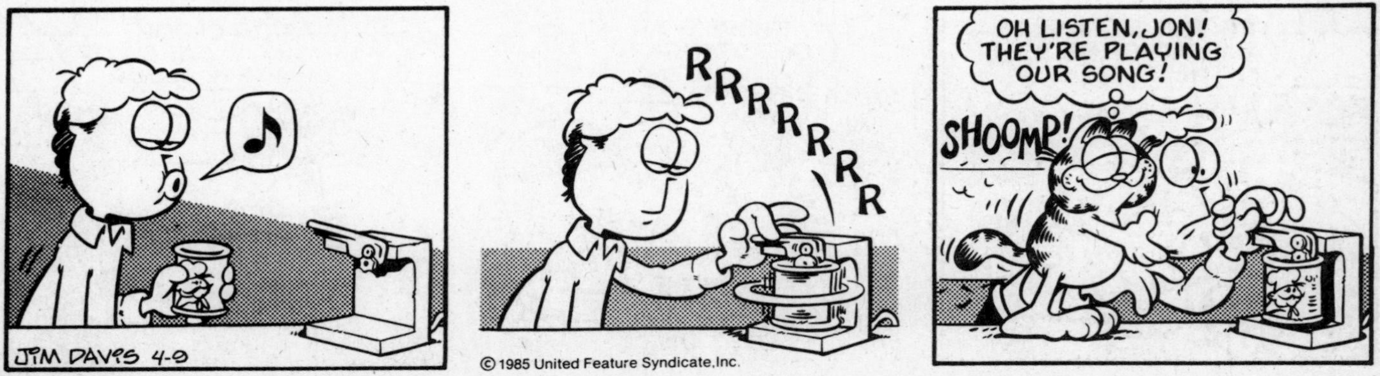
JIM DAVIS 4-9
RRRRRRRRR
SHOOMP!
OH LISTEN, JON! THEY'RE PLAYING OUR SONG!

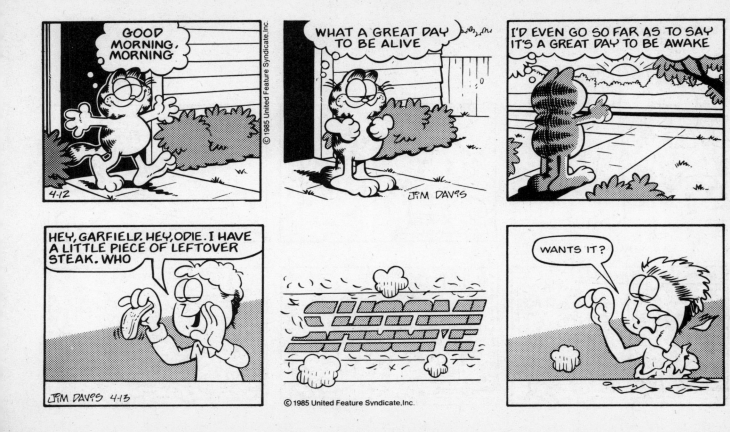

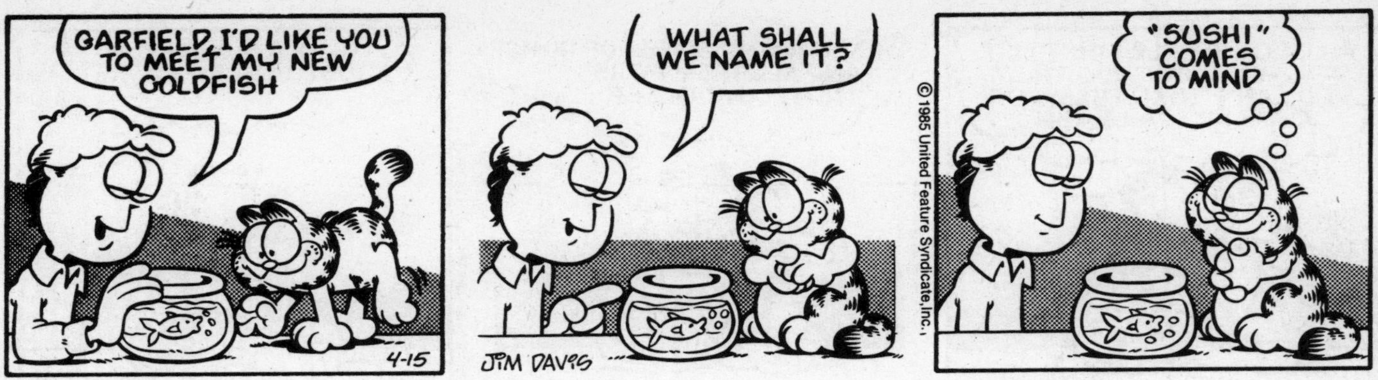
GARFIELD, I'D LIKE YOU TO MEET MY NEW GOLDFISH
4-15
WHAT SHALL WE NAME IT?
JIM DAVIS
"SUSHI" COMES TO MIND

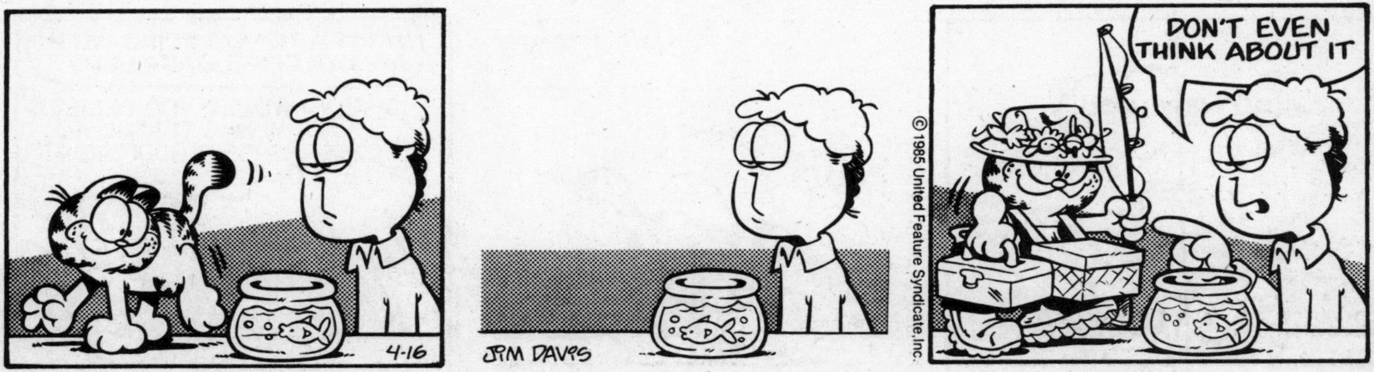
4-16
JIM DAVIS
DON'T EVEN THINK ABOUT IT

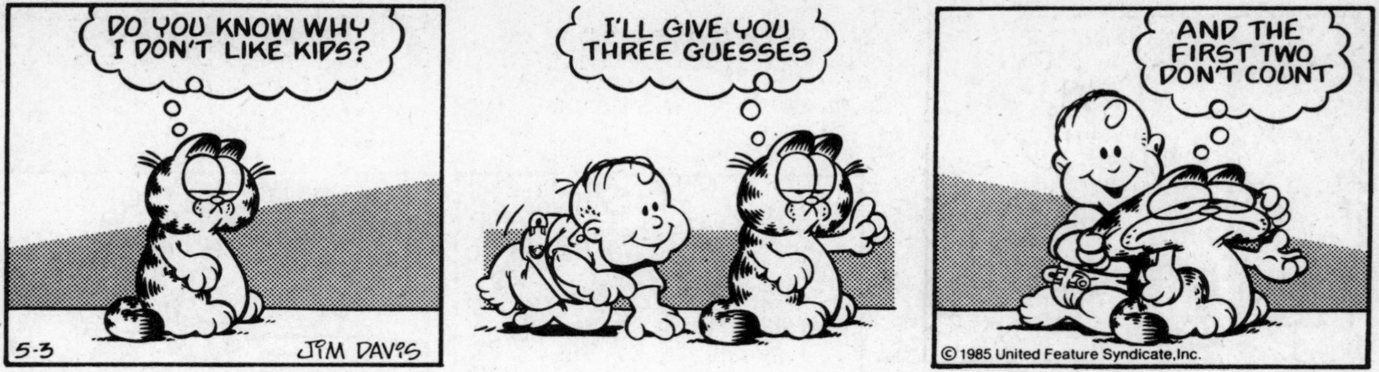
DO YOU KNOW WHY I DON'T LIKE KIDS?
5-3
JIM DAVIS
I'LL GIVE YOU THREE GUESSES
AND THE FIRST TWO DON'T COUNT
© 1985 United Feature Syndicate, Inc.

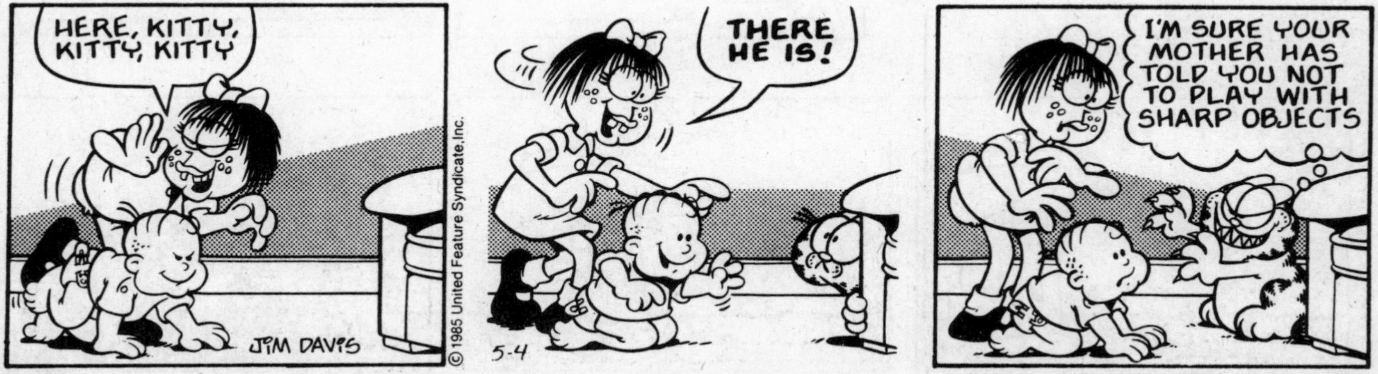
HERE, KITTY, KITTY, KITTY
JIM DAVIS
© 1985 United Feature Syndicate, Inc.
THERE HE IS!
5-4
I'M SURE YOUR MOTHER HAS TOLD YOU NOT TO PLAY WITH SHARP OBJECTS

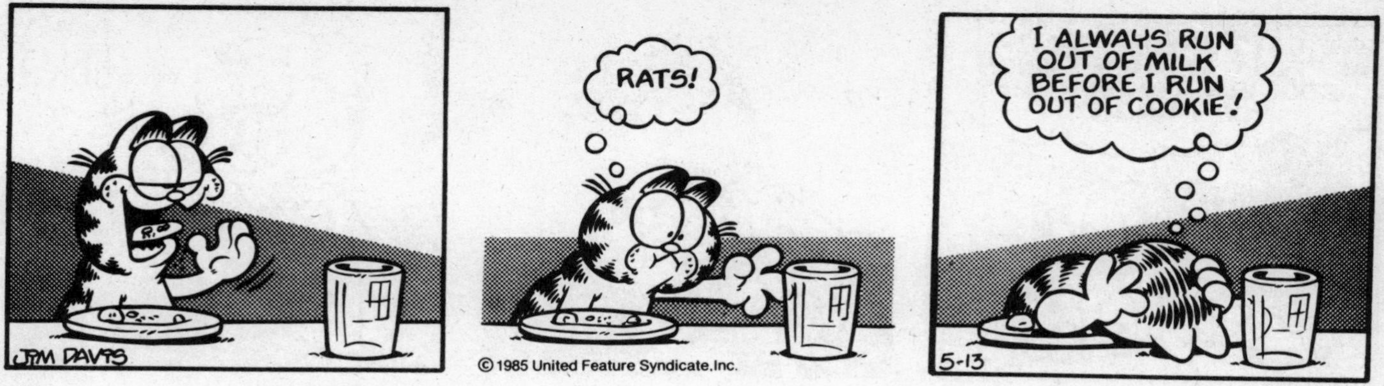
JIM DAVIS
RATS!
© 1985 United Feature Syndicate, Inc.
I ALWAYS RUN OUT OF MILK BEFORE I RUN OUT OF COOKIE!
5-13

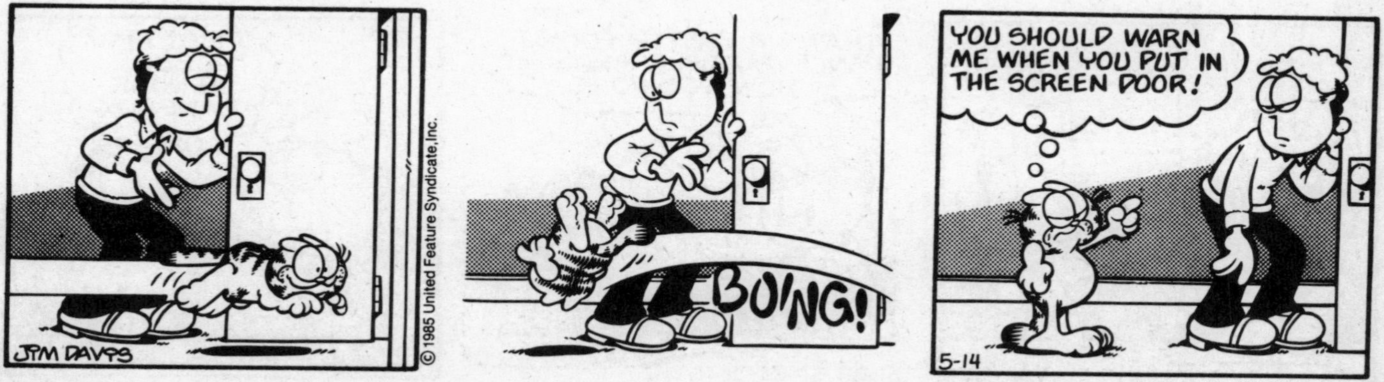
JIM DAVIS
© 1985 United Feature Syndicate, Inc.
BOING!
YOU SHOULD WARN ME WHEN YOU PUT IN THE SCREEN DOOR!
5-14

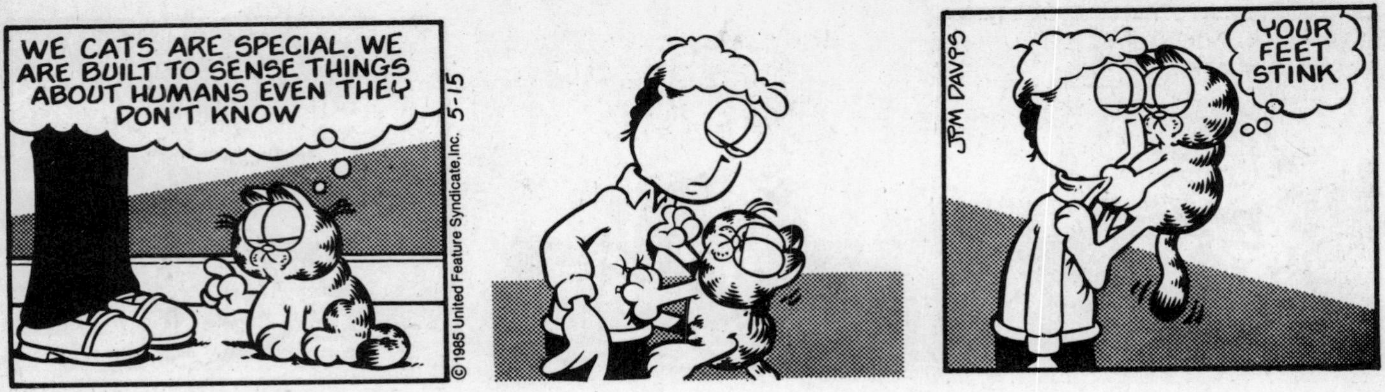
WE CATS ARE SPECIAL. WE ARE BUILT TO SENSE THINGS ABOUT HUMANS EVEN THEY DON'T KNOW
5-15
© 1985 United Feature Syndicate, Inc.
JIM DAVIS
YOUR FEET STINK

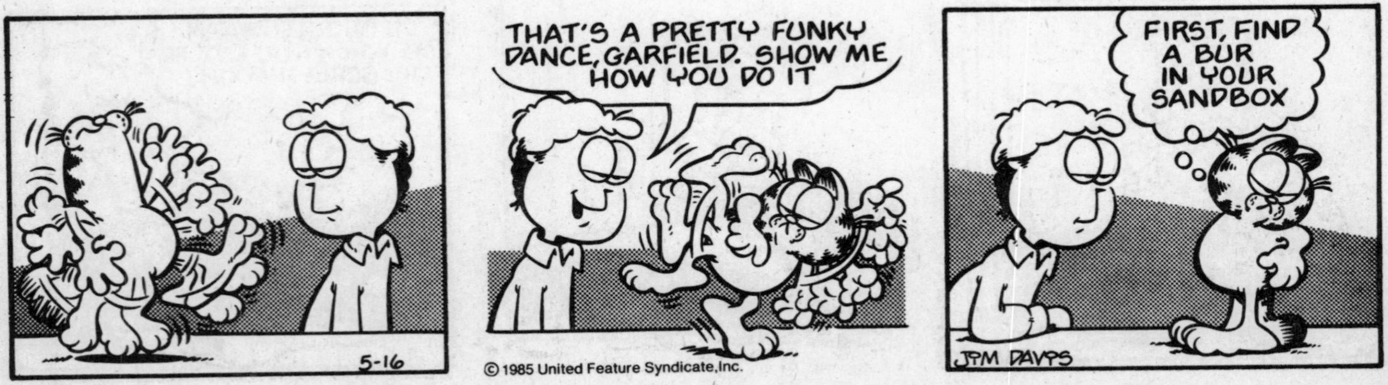
5-16
THAT'S A PRETTY FUNKY DANCE, GARFIELD. SHOW ME HOW YOU DO IT
© 1985 United Feature Syndicate, Inc.
FIRST, FIND A BUR IN YOUR SANDBOX
JIM DAVIS

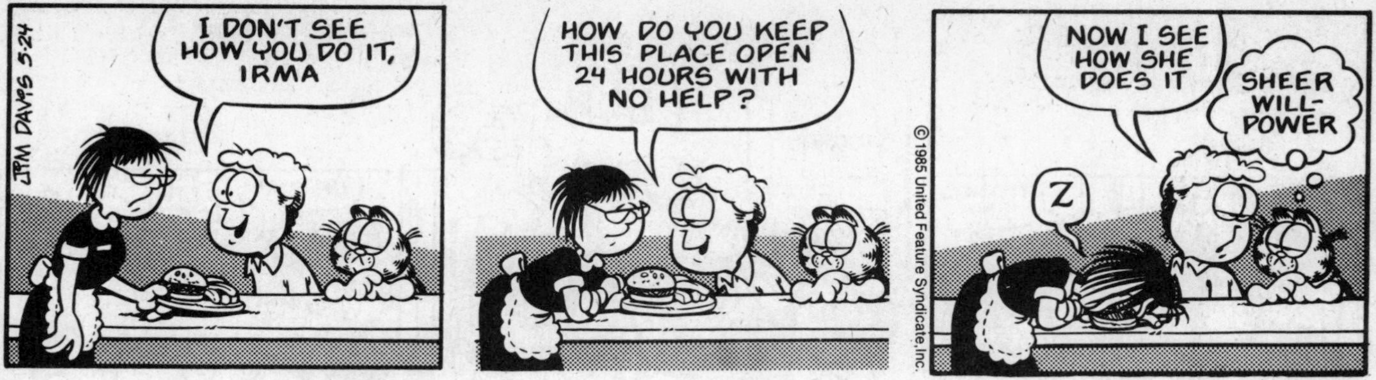
JIM DAVIS 5-24
I DON'T SEE HOW YOU DO IT, IRMA
HOW DO YOU KEEP THIS PLACE OPEN 24 HOURS WITH NO HELP?
© 1985 United Feature Syndicate, Inc.
NOW I SEE HOW SHE DOES IT
Z
SHEER WILL-POWER

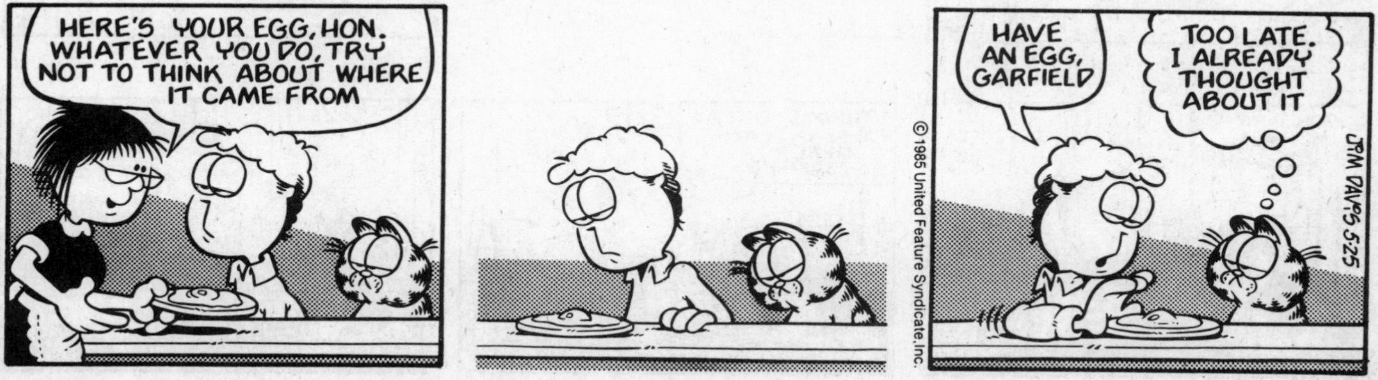
HERE'S YOUR EGG, HON. WHATEVER YOU DO, TRY NOT TO THINK ABOUT WHERE IT CAME FROM
© 1985 United Feature Syndicate, Inc.
HAVE AN EGG, GARFIELD
TOO LATE. I ALREADY THOUGHT ABOUT IT
JIM DAVIS 5-25

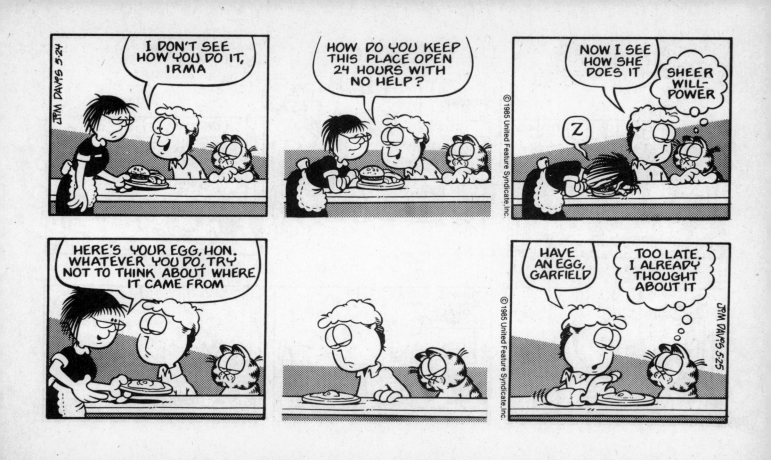

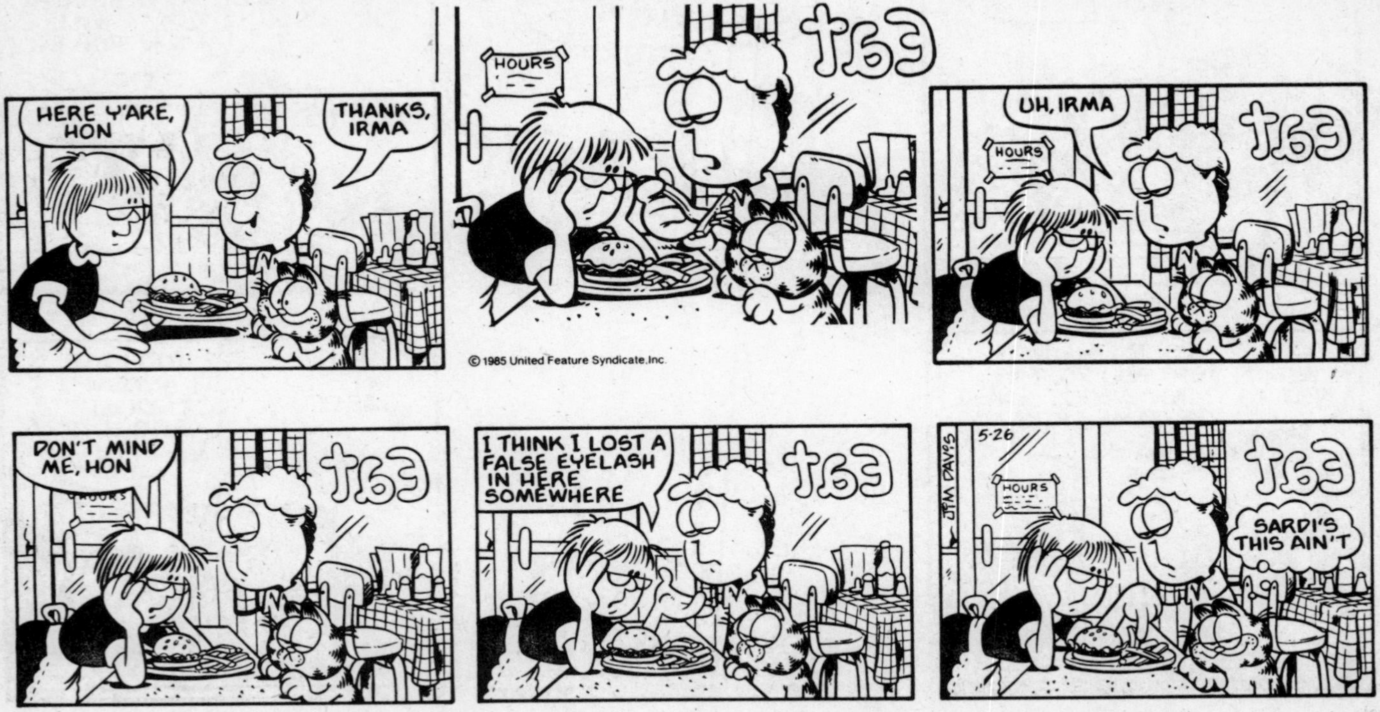
HERE Y'ARE, HON
THANKS, IRMA
HOURS
UH, IRMA
DON'T MIND ME, HON
I THINK I LOST A FALSE EYELASH IN HERE SOMEWHERE
JIM DAVIS 5·26
SARDI'S THIS AIN'T

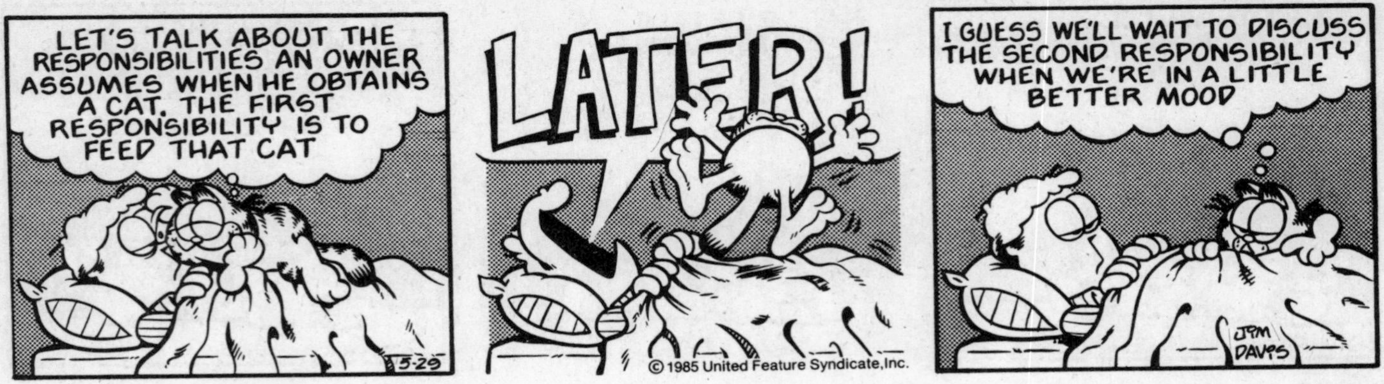
LET'S TALK ABOUT THE RESPONSIBILITIES AN OWNER ASSUMES WHEN HE OBTAINS A CAT. THE FIRST RESPONSIBILITY IS TO FEED THAT CAT
5-29
LATER!
I GUESS WE'LL WAIT TO DISCUSS THE SECOND RESPONSIBILITY WHEN WE'RE IN A LITTLE BETTER MOOD
JIM DAVIS

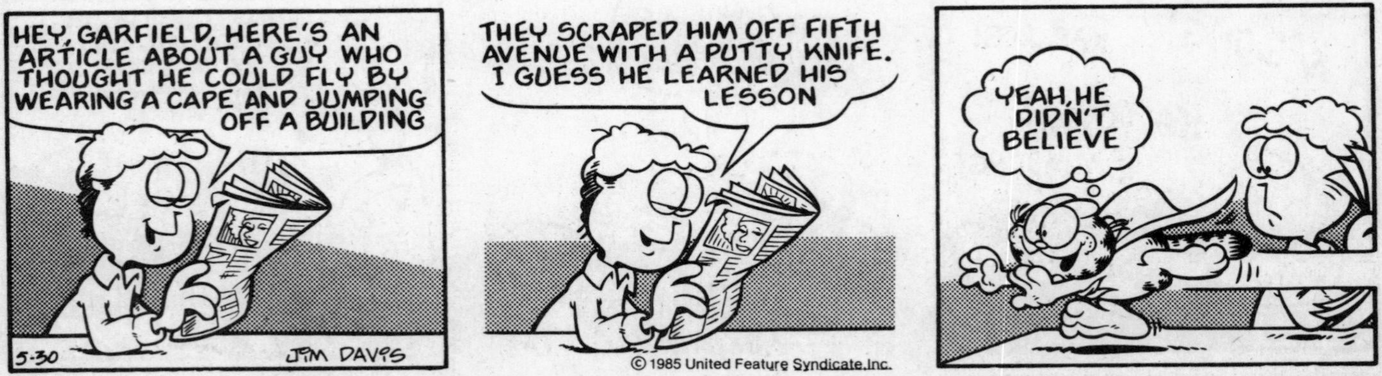
HEY, GARFIELD, HERE'S AN ARTICLE ABOUT A GUY WHO THOUGHT HE COULD FLY BY WEARING A CAPE AND JUMPING OFF A BUILDING
5-30
JIM DAVIS
THEY SCRAPED HIM OFF FIFTH AVENUE WITH A PUTTY KNIFE. I GUESS HE LEARNED HIS LESSON
YEAH, HE DIDN'T BELIEVE

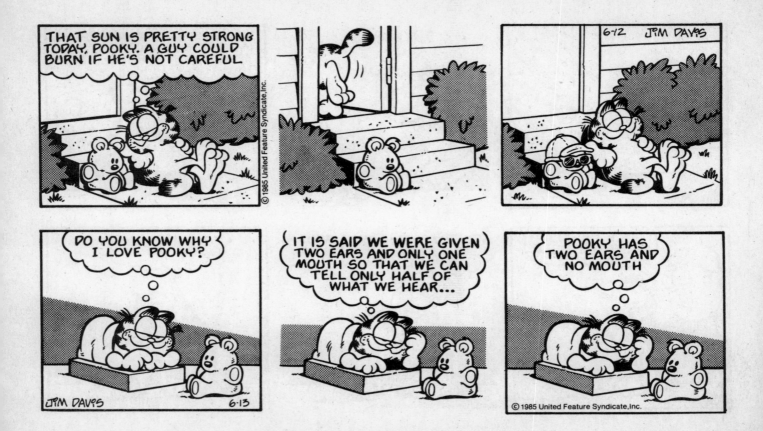

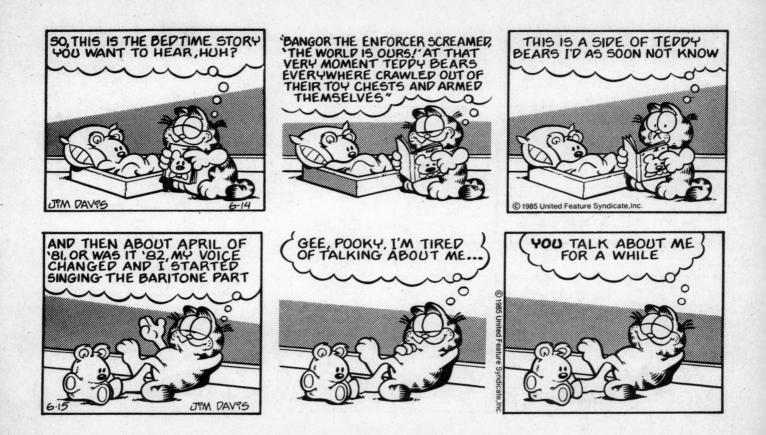

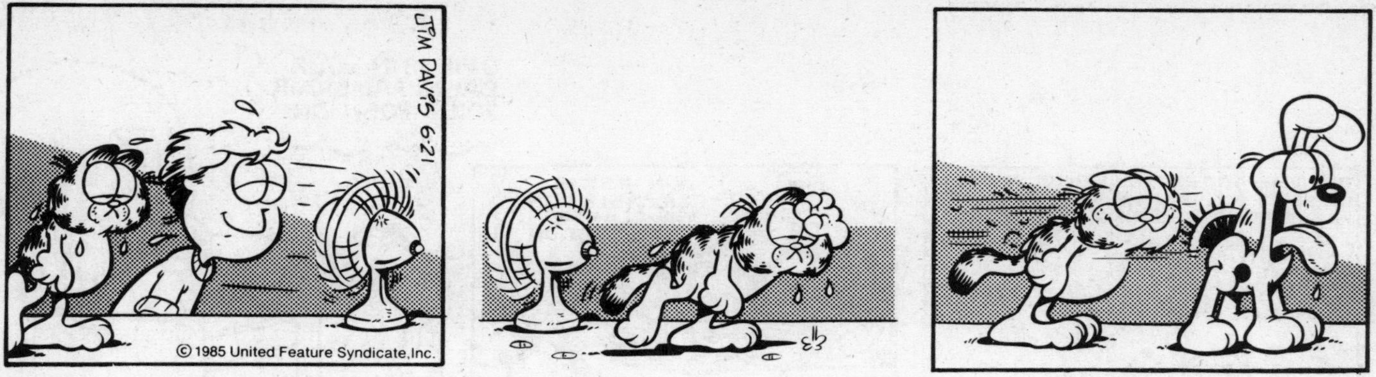
JIM DAVIS 6-21
© 1985 United Feature Syndicate, Inc.

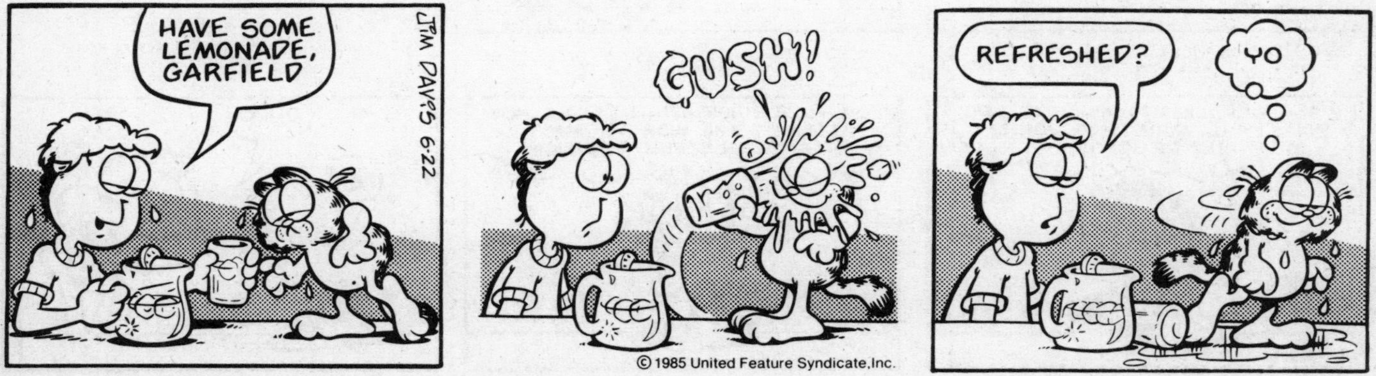
JIM DAVIS 6-22
HAVE SOME LEMONADE, GARFIELD
GUSH!
REFRESHED?
YO
© 1985 United Feature Syndicate, Inc.

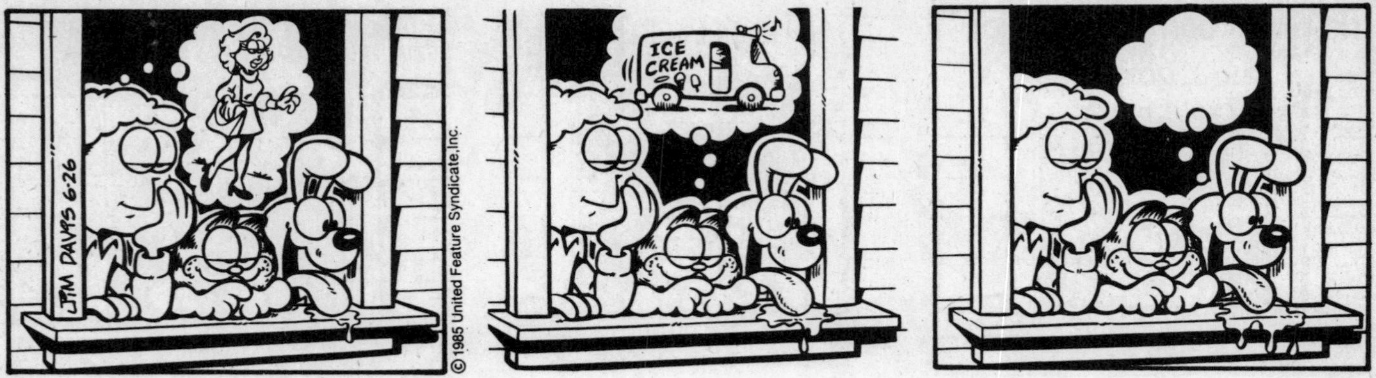
JIM DAVIS 6-26
ICE CREAM
© 1985 United Feature Syndicate, Inc.

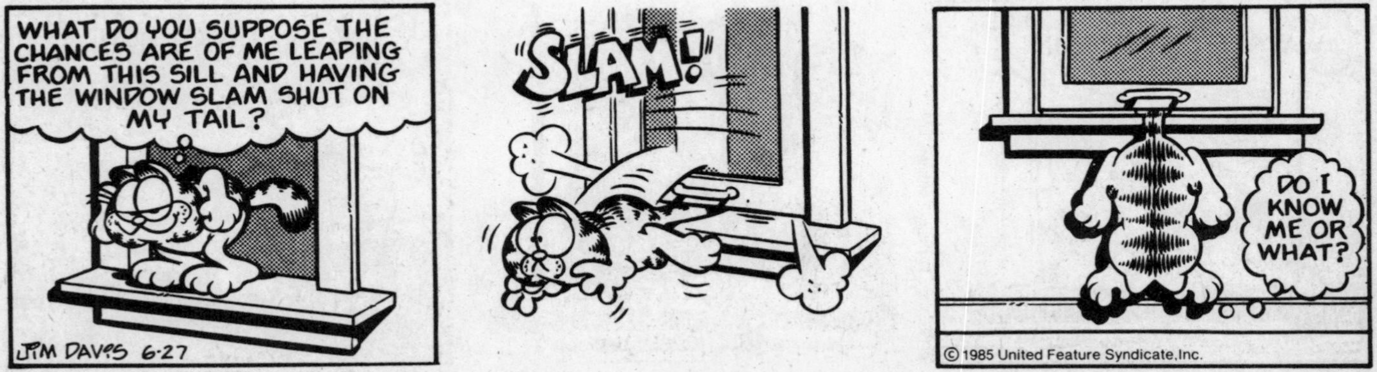
WHAT DO YOU SUPPOSE THE CHANCES ARE OF ME LEAPING FROM THIS SILL AND HAVING THE WINDOW SLAM SHUT ON MY TAIL?
JIM DAVIS 6-27
SLAM!
DO I KNOW ME OR WHAT?
© 1985 United Feature Syndicate, Inc.

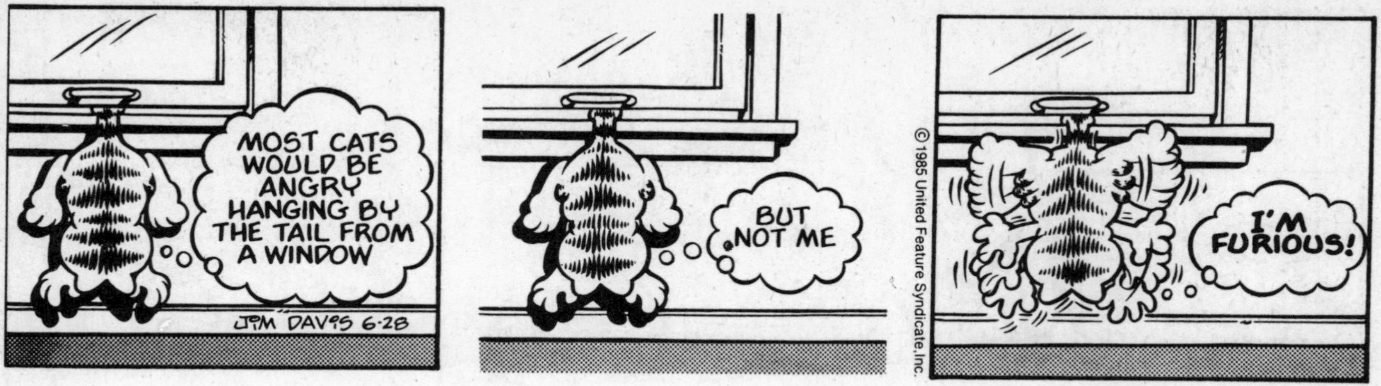
MOST CATS WOULD BE ANGRY HANGING BY THE TAIL FROM A WINDOW
JIM DAVIS 6-28
BUT NOT ME
I'M FURIOUS!
© 1985 United Feature Syndicate, Inc.

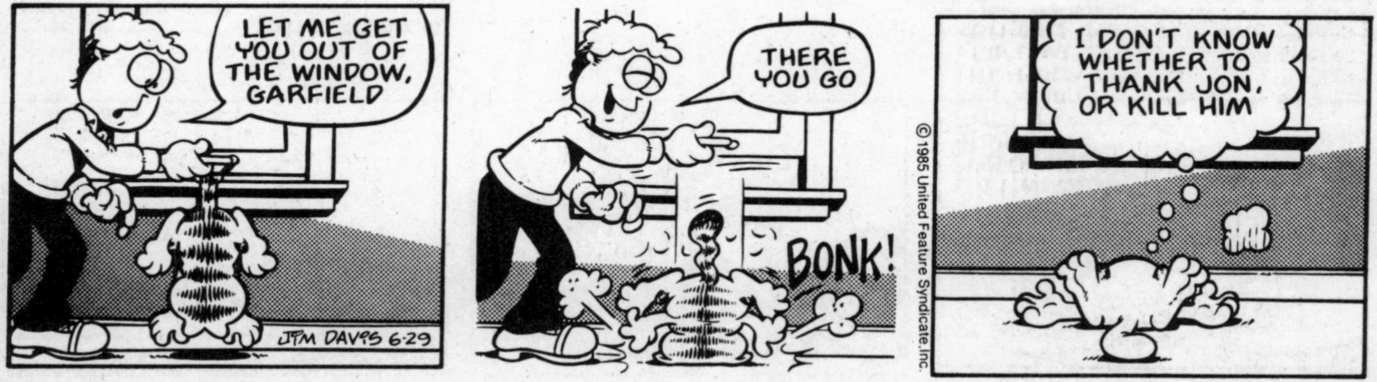
LET ME GET YOU OUT OF THE WINDOW, GARFIELD
JIM DAVIS 6-29
THERE YOU GO
BONK!
I DON'T KNOW WHETHER TO THANK JON, OR KILL HIM
© 1985 United Feature Syndicate, Inc.

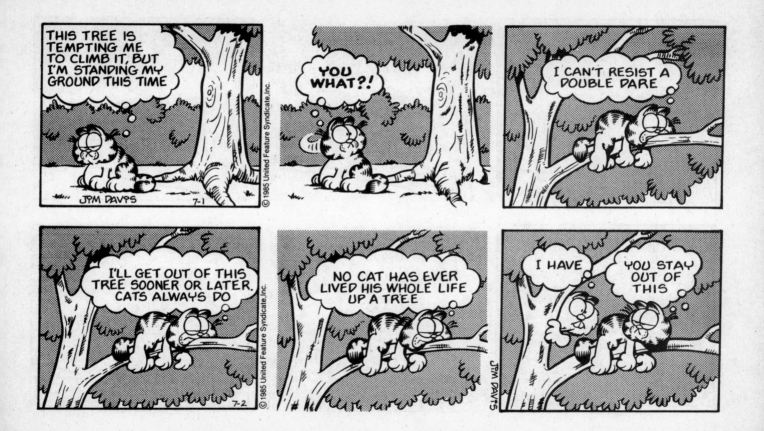

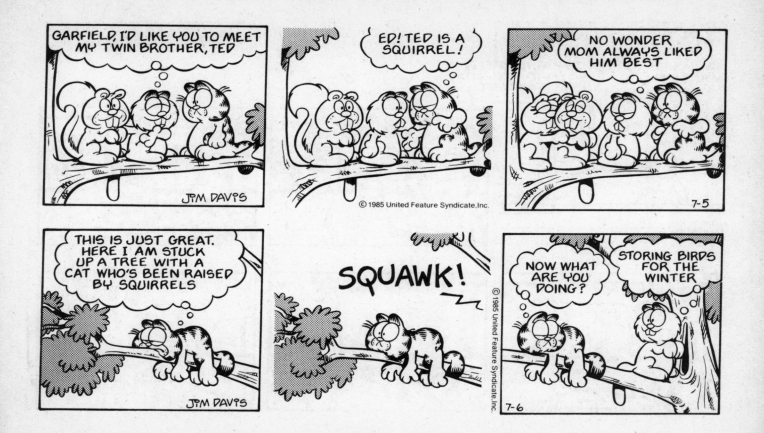

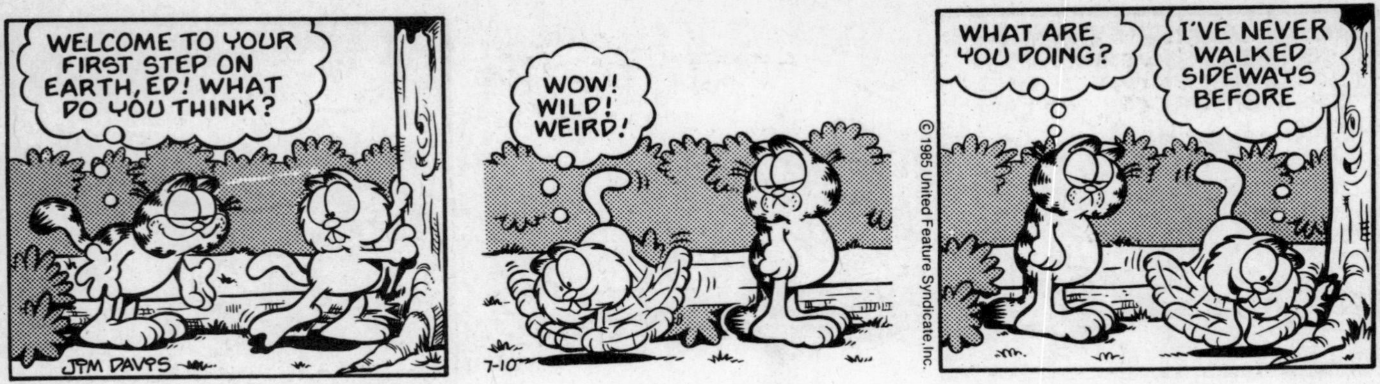
WELCOME TO YOUR FIRST STEP ON EARTH, ED! WHAT DO YOU THINK?
WOW! WILD! WEIRD!
WHAT ARE YOU DOING?
I'VE NEVER WALKED SIDEWAYS BEFORE
JIM DAVIS
7-10

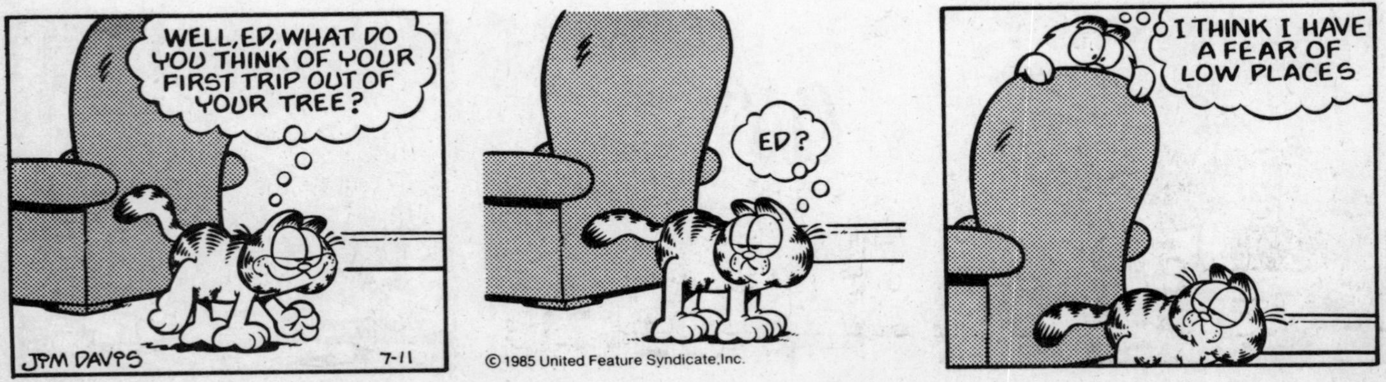
WELL, ED, WHAT DO YOU THINK OF YOUR FIRST TRIP OUT OF YOUR TREE?
ED?
I THINK I HAVE A FEAR OF LOW PLACES
JIM DAVIS
7-11

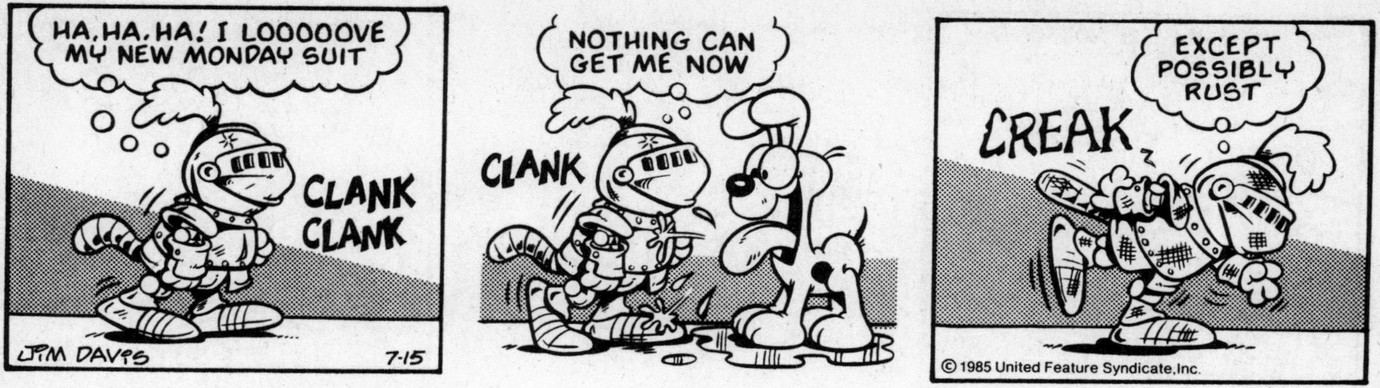
HA, HA, HA! I LOOOOOVE MY NEW MONDAY SUIT
CLANK CLANK
JIM DAVIS
7-15
NOTHING CAN GET ME NOW
CLANK
EXCEPT POSSIBLY RUST
CREAK
© 1985 United Feature Syndicate, Inc.

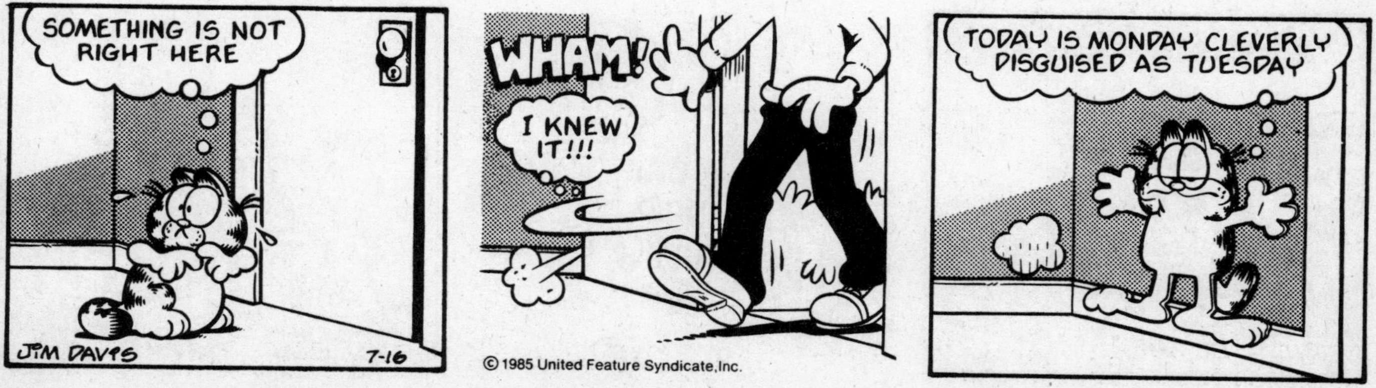
SOMETHING IS NOT RIGHT HERE
JIM DAVIS
7-16
WHAM!
I KNEW IT!!!
© 1985 United Feature Syndicate, Inc.
TODAY IS MONDAY CLEVERLY DISGUISED AS TUESDAY

HEY, GARFIELD! IT'S GOING TO BE A BEAUTIFUL DAY! LET'S SPEND IT OUTSIDE!

© 1985 United Feature Syndicate, Inc.

WHERE ARE MY SWIM TRUNKS?

THERE'S SUNTAN LOTION IN HERE SOMEWHERE

AND NOW A PICNIC LUNCH!

JIM DAVIS 7.2.1

SAND·E·WRAPS

PERFECT DAY, HERE WE COME!

RATS. MISSED IT

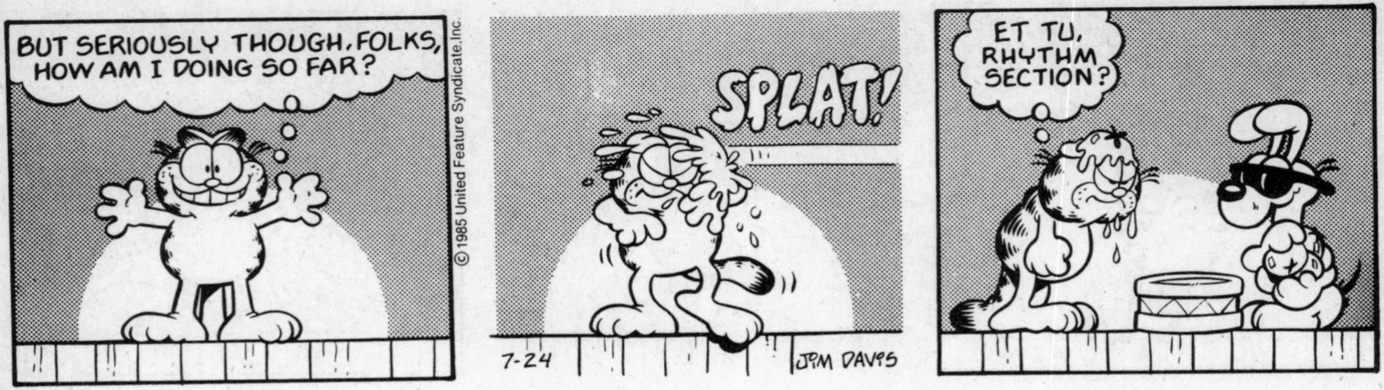

BUT SERIOUSLY THOUGH, FOLKS, HOW AM I DOING SO FAR?
© 1985 United Feature Syndicate, Inc.
SPLAT!
7-24
JIM DAVIS
ET TU, RHYTHM SECTION?

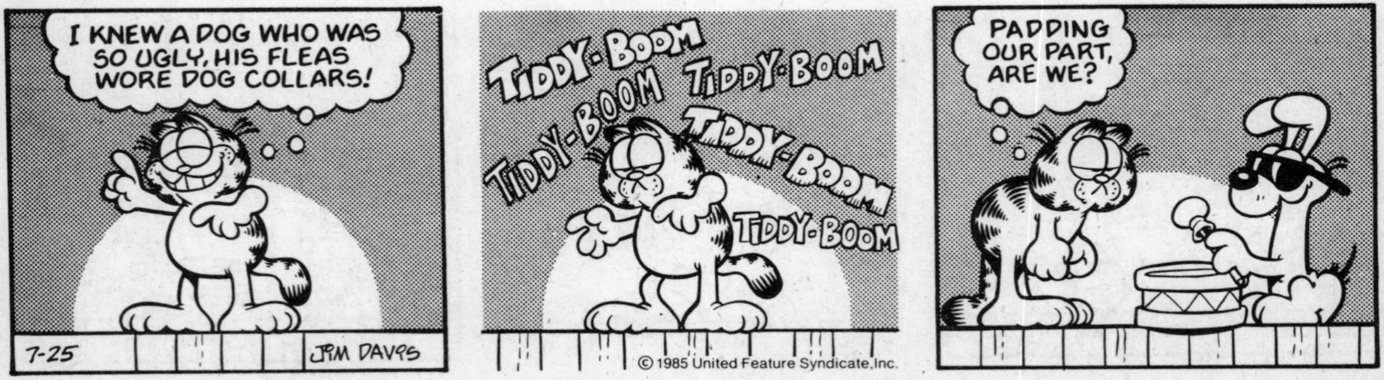

I KNEW A DOG WHO WAS SO UGLY, HIS FLEAS WORE DOG COLLARS!
7-25
JIM DAVIS
TIDDY-BOOM
TIDDY-BOOM TIDDY-BOOM
TIDDY-BOOM
TIDDY-BOOM
TIDDY-BOOM
© 1985 United Feature Syndicate, Inc.
PADDING OUR PART, ARE WE?

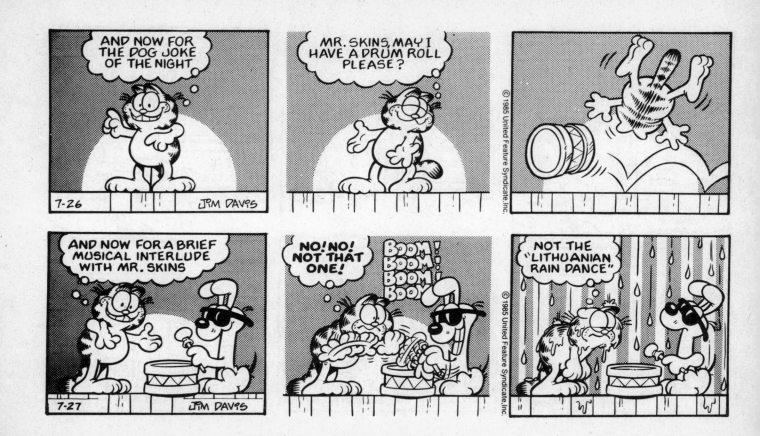

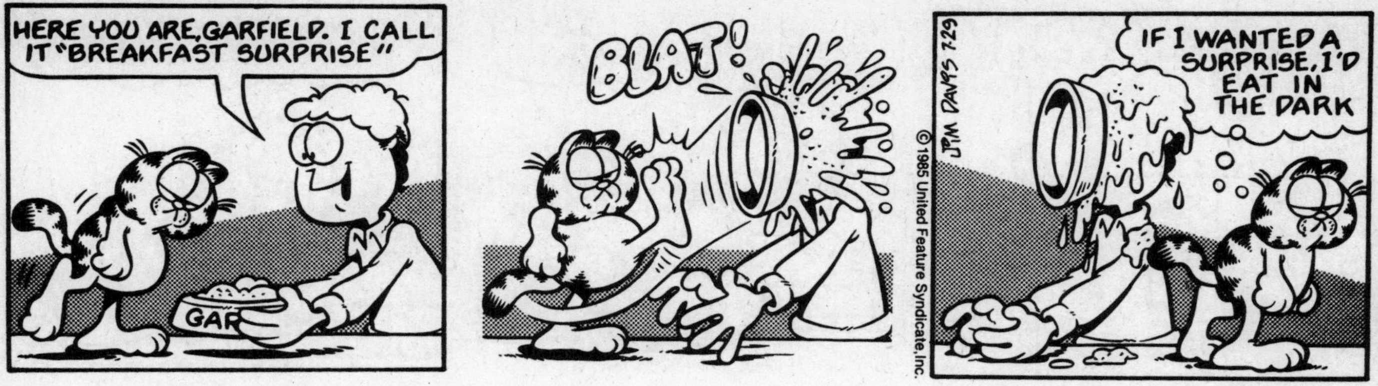
HERE YOU ARE, GARFIELD. I CALL IT "BREAKFAST SURPRISE"
BLAT!
IF I WANTED A SURPRISE, I'D EAT IN THE DARK
JIM DAVIS 7-29
© 1985 United Feature Syndicate, Inc.

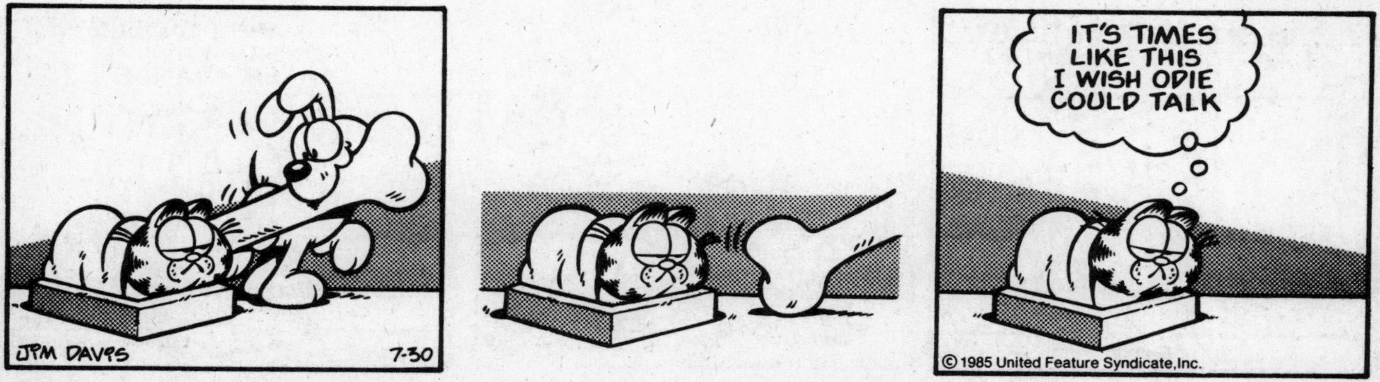
IT'S TIMES LIKE THIS I WISH ODIE COULD TALK
JIM DAVIS 7-30
© 1985 United Feature Syndicate, Inc.

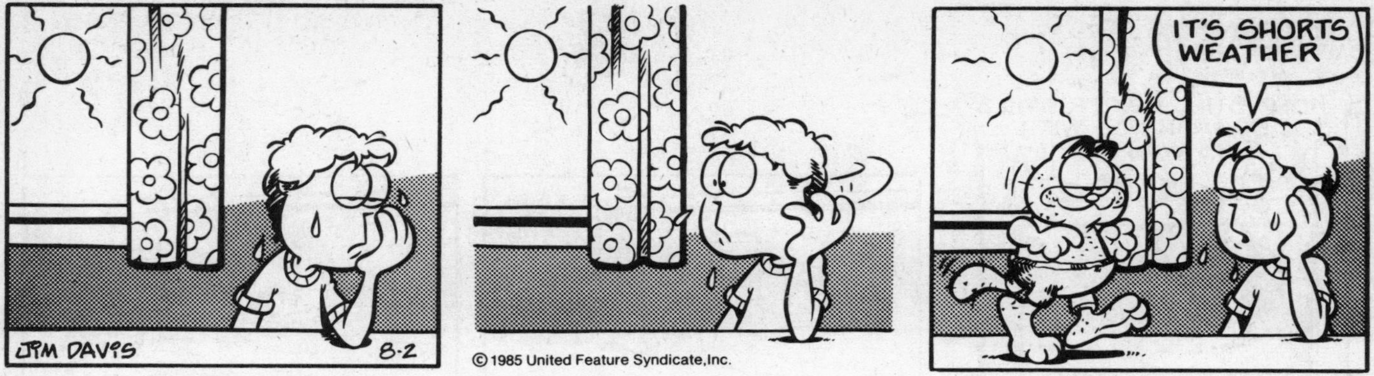
JIM DAVIS
8-2
IT'S SHORTS WEATHER

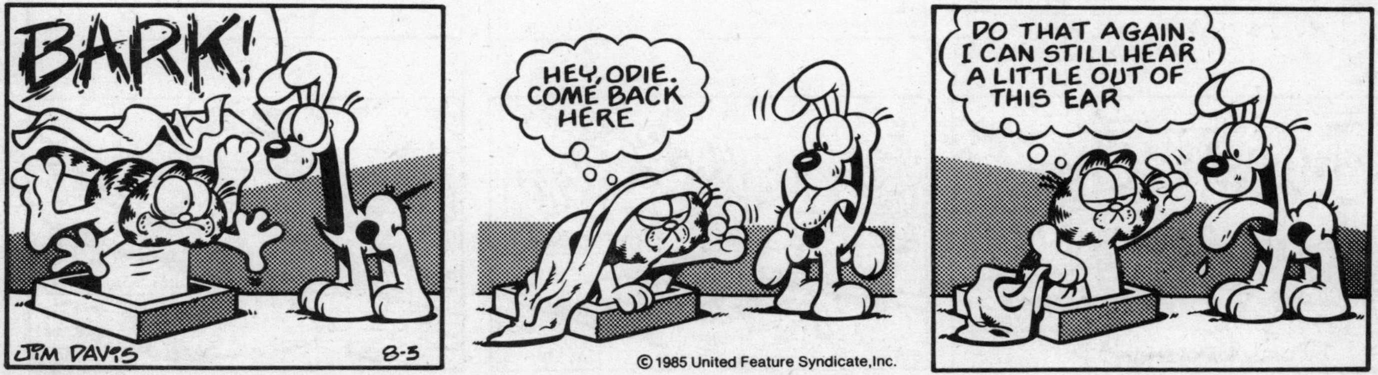
BARK!
JIM DAVIS
8-3
HEY, ODIE. COME BACK HERE
DO THAT AGAIN. I CAN STILL HEAR A LITTLE OUT OF THIS EAR

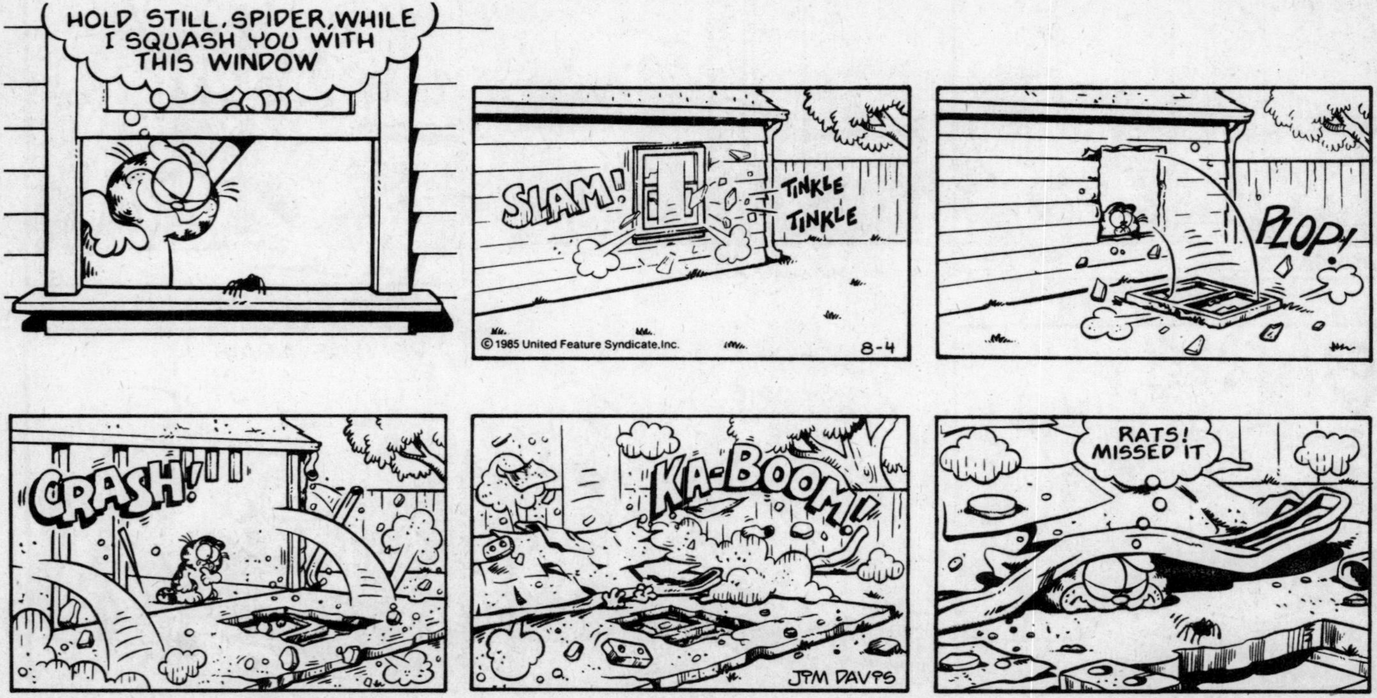
HOLD STILL, SPIDER, WHILE I SQUASH YOU WITH THIS WINDOW
SLAM!
TINKLE
TINKLE
© 1985 United Feature Syndicate, Inc.
8-4
PLOP!
CRASH!
KA-BOOM!
JIM DAVIS
RATS! MISSED IT

Garfield through the eyes of the little fans

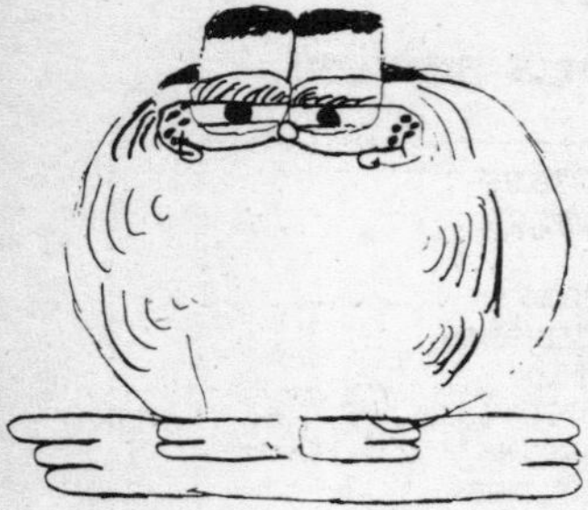

MICHAEL ALPHA
Texas

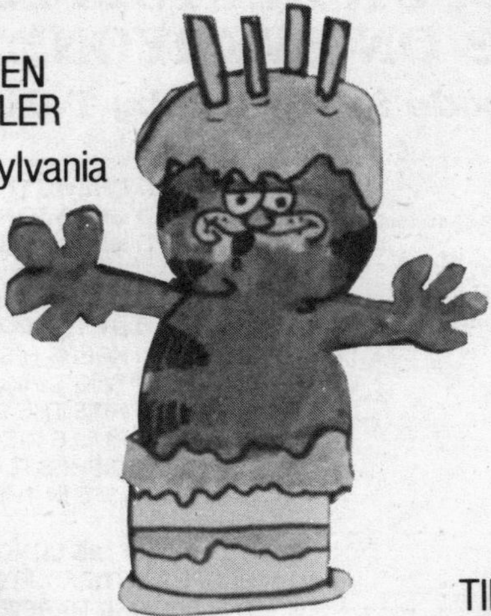

KRISTEN MUELLER
Pennsylvania

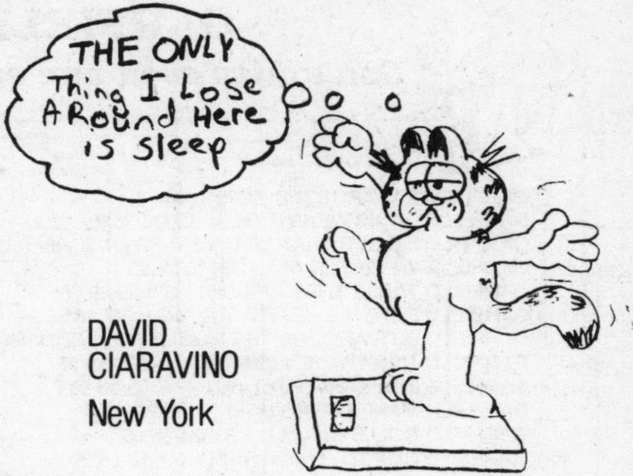
THE ONLY Thing I Lose AROUND Here is sleep

DAVID CIARAVINO
New York

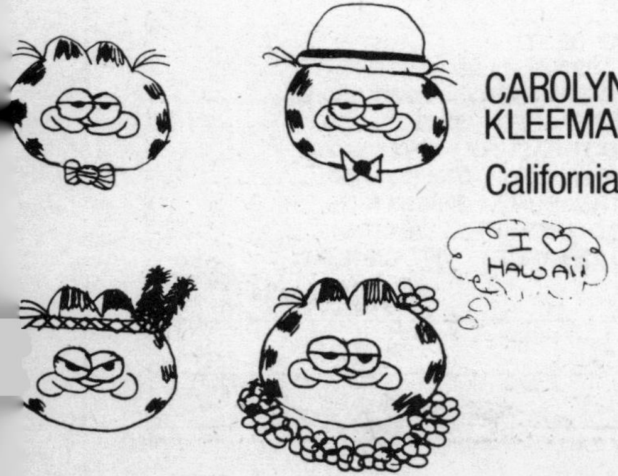
I ♡ HAWAII

CAROLYN KLEEMANN
California

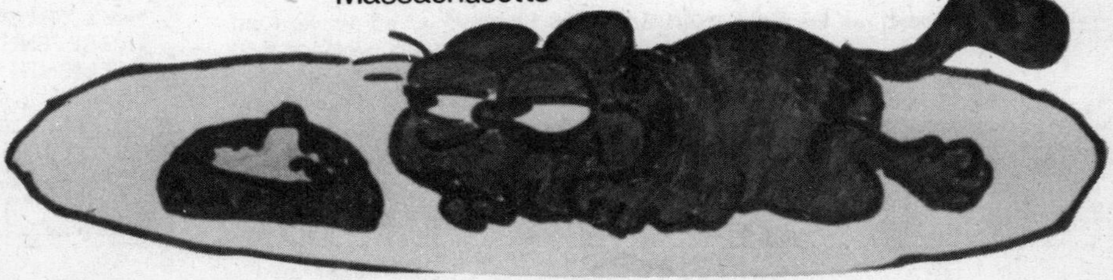

TIMMY LUCIANI
Massachusetts

STRIPS, SPECIALS, OR BESTSELLING BOOKS . . .
GARFIELD'S ON EVERYONE'S MENU
Don't miss even one episode in the Tubby Tabby's hilarious series!

__GARFIELD AT LARGE (#1)   32013/$6.95
__GARFIELD GAINS WEIGHT (#2)   32008/$6.95
__GARFIELD BIGGER THAN LIFE (#3)   32007/$6.95
__GARFIELD WEIGHS IN (#4)   32010/$6.95
__GARFIELD TAKES THE CAKE (#5)   32009/$6.95
__GARFIELD EATS HIS HEART OUT (#6)   32018/$6.95
__GARFIELD SITS AROUND THE HOUSE (#7)   32011/$6.95
__GARFIELD TIPS THE SCALES (#8)   33580/$6.95
__GARFIELD LOSES HIS FEET (#9)   31805/$6.95
__GARFIELD MAKES IT BIG (#10)   31928/$6.95
__GARFIELD ROLLS ON (#11)   32634/$6.95
__GARFIELD OUT TO LUNCH (#12)   33118/$6.95
__GARFIELD FOOD FOR THOUGHT (#13)   34129/$6.95
__GARFIELD SWALLOWS HIS PRIDE (#14)   34725/$6.95
__GARFIELD WORLDWIDE (#15)   35158/$6.95
__GARFIELD ROUNDS OUT (#16)   35388/$6.95

__GARFIELD CHEWS THE FAT (#17)   35956/$6.95
__GARFIELD GOES TO WAIST (#18)   36430/$6.95
__GARFIELD HANGS OUT (#19)   36835/$6.95
__GARFIELD TAKES UP SPACE (#20)   37029/$6.95
__GARFIELD SAYS A MOUTHFUL (#21)   37368/$6.95
__GARFIELD BY THE POUND (#22)   37579/$6.95
__GARFIELD KEEPS HIS CHINS UP (#23)   37959/$6.95
__GARFIELD TAKES HIS LICKS (#24)   38170/$6.95
__GARFIELD HITS THE BIG TIME (#25)   38332/$6.95
__GARFIELD PULLS HIS WEIGHT (#26)   38666/$6.95
__GARFIELD DISHES IT OUT (#27)   39287/$6.95
__GARFIELD LIFE IN THE FAT LANE (#28)   39776/$6.95

GARFIELD AT HIS SUNDAY BEST!
__GARFIELD TREASURY   32106/$11.95
__THE SECOND GARFIELD TREASURY   33276/$10.95
__THE THIRD GARFIELD TREASURY   32635/$11.00
__THE FOURTH GARFIELD TREASURY   34726/$10.95
__THE FIFTH GARFIELD TREASURY   36268/$12.00
__THE SIXTH GARFIELD TREASURY   37367/$10.95
__THE SEVENTH GARFIELD TREASURY   38427/$10.95
__THE EIGHTH GARFIELD TREASURY   39778/$12.00

Please send me the BALLANTINE BOOKS I have checked above. I am enclosing $_____. (Please add $2.00 for the first book and $.50 for each additional book for postage and handling and include the appropriate state sales tax.) Send check or money order (no cash or C.O.D.'s) to Ballantine Mail Sales Dept. TA, 400 Hahn Road, Westminster, MD 21157.

To order by phone, call 1-800-733-3000 and use your major credit card.

Prices and numbers are subject to change without notice. Valid in the U.S. only. All orders are subject to availability.

Name_____

Address_____

City_____ State_____ Zip_____

30   Allow at least 4 weeks for delivery   7/93